America
since 1945

Fifth Edition

America since 1945

Fifth Edition

Edited by

Robert D. Marcus

and

David Burner

St. Martin's Press
New York

Senior editor: Don Reisman
Project management: Sarah Troutt, Publication Services
Cover design: Jeheber & Peace, Inc.

For information, write:
St. Martin's Press, Inc.
175 Fifth Avenue
New York, NY 10010

ISBN 0-312-04625-1

Preface

When we put together the first edition of *America since 1945* in 1970, we had a strong sense that a special era in defining human freedom had just passed. In preparing the fifth edition of this same work in 1990, we see the beginning of yet another era in which human liberty is to be the theme.

Keeping in mind the possibilities and the dangers of this new world, we have made many changes in the selections for the fifth edition of *America since 1945*. Although we have retained many of the articles that instructors and students have found useful, half the book is new. We have retained classic articles on the cold war by Averell Harriman and Barton J. Bernstein as well as still fresh articles on American politics by Garry Wills, Alonzo Hamby, Fred Greenstein, Jonathan Schell, and Peter Carroll. We have also retained several important historic documents of the era: John F. Kennedy's inaugural address, an excerpt from Michael Harrington's *The Other America*, Howell Raines' interviews with civil rights workers; excerpts from Martin L. King, Jr.'s *Letter from Birmingham Jail*, Malcolm X's "On Revolution," the Port Huron Statement, and Betty Friedan's *The Feminine Mystique*; and Lyndon Johnson's Great Society speech. New subjects represented by primary documents include Supreme Court abortion decisions and Barry Goldwater's 1964 acceptance speech.

Many of the new selections reflect the ever-broadening range of social themes indispensable to the new history's analysis of forms of human freedom. These include a look by Kenneth T. Jackson at suburbanization and the baby boom; letters written to *Ms.* magazine; a piece by F. Chris Garcia on the politics of Latino Americans; a selection from Arlie Hochschild on work and family in the 1980s; a disturbing survey of the current economic status of African Americans; and a reflective piece by Bill McKibben on the meaning of environmental change. We have also included new readings on McCarthyism, Kennedy liberalism, Lyndon Johnson, the Great Society program, Vietnam and its domestic impact, the Reagan economic program, and the changing American role in the world economy. The updated Suggested Further Readings section offers students the opportunity to pursue these themes.

We would like to thank the following reviewers who supplied us with useful information to help guide our revisions for this fifth edition: John Barnard, Oakland University; Dorothy M. Brown, Georgetown University; Lawrence B. de Graaf, California State University, Fullerton; Bob C. Holcomb, Angelo State University; Michael E. McGerr, Indiana University; and Patrick F. Palermo, University of Dayton.

Robert D. Marcus
David Burner

Contents

America since 1945

Fifth Edition

PART ONE

1945–1952

In 1945 World War II ended and the atomic age began. It was a year of high drama that included the final defeat of the Axis powers and the establishment of the United Nations. It was the beginning of what some people hoped would be a great "American century" in which, under the guidance of the United States, the world would know a long era of peace and progress. However, the high expectations Americans had as they awaited demobilization were tempered: their great leader Franklin D. Roosevelt was dead and a modest ex-haberdasher from Missouri, Harry S Truman, uneasily wore the democratic crown. Europe was devastated; victory over Japan introduced the world to the horror of nuclear weapons; and in America the end of the war raised the question of whether the economy, deeply depressed for a decade before the war, would lapse into the same dismal state from which war production had roused it.

Many hopes and even more fears crystallized in the postwar years. The United Nations survived, the United States remained the greatest world power, and the domestic economy showed little inclination to slip back into depression. But the image of an "American century" rapidly gave way to the reality of cold war. The uneasy wartime collaboration between the Western Allies and the Soviet Union quickly reverted to the ideological conflicts of the prewar era. Within a few years, the United States and the Soviet Union, both armed with thermonuclear weapons and extensive conventional forces, squared off around the world. In 1949 the fall of China to a Communist movement led by Mao Ze-dong alarmed the American public. In 1950 the nation rearmed to fight a frustrating and inconclusive war in Korea.

Although right after World War II the domestic economy did sputter under the burdens of demobilization and inflation, in the late 1940s renewed defense spending, pent-up consumer demand after the austerity of the war, and the reopening of foreign markets through the Marshall Plan and other foreign aid pushed the economy upward. Americans forming families and raising children at a remarkable pace moved toward a social order that, in the 1950s, seemed more stable than in fact it was. Uncomfortable with both the threatening world and the shifting social values they encountered, Americans in 1952 closed ranks behind a popular and reassuring general, President-elect Dwight D. Eisenhower, who they hoped—correctly, as it turned out—would put behind them the sour era of postwar adjustment. From an economic standpoint Americans who came of age in this postwar era had perhaps the most optimistic future of any people in human history.

1. Russia and the Cold War

AVERELL HARRIMAN

From 1926, when he bargained with Leon Trotsky in Moscow over a manganese concession, until 1968, when he conferred in Paris with the North Vietnamese, Averell Harriman was probably our most experienced and influential represen- tative to the Communist world. His reminiscences are important not only for the insights he has acquired about Communist governments over the years, but also for what they reveal about developing American foreign policy.

Harriman never conceived of American-Soviet relations as a struggle to the death between hostile forces, one destined to conquer, the other to die. He strongly criticized Eisenhower's Secretary of State, John Foster Dulles, for taking "the position that Communism was evil and that countries were either for us or against us in our struggle with it." Nonetheless, Harriman was firmly of the opinion that Soviet expansionist behavior gave the United States no choice but to resist the Soviets at many points around the globe. In short, he argued that Stalin started the Cold War.

Harriman's opinions are quite typical of American policymakers in the im- mediate postwar era. He himself called it "a fairly glorious period, perhaps the most creative period in American foreign policy." The idealism he expresses—as in his account of the Marshall Plan—is undoubtedly genuine. Although some critics such as Barton J. Bernstein (in the next selection) have suggested that his liberal ideals actually defined the world in a way that made the Cold War inevitable, Harriman contends that Stalin's intransigence led to an unavoidable collapse of the wartime alliance.

There has grown a myth about Yalta that somehow or other Roosevelt and Churchill sold out Eastern Europe to Stalin. That wasn't true at all. I can't imagine why Stalin went to such extreme lengths in breaking the Yalta agreements if it had been true that they were so much to his advantage. It was agreed that the people in these countries were to decide on their own governments through free elections. But Stalin didn't permit it.

One wonders why he broke his agreement on Poland so soon. It's rather hard to guess. Personally, I think one of the reasons was that Bierut, the leading member of the Lublin Polish government—the Com- munist government—was in Moscow on Stalin's return from Yalta. He may have told Stalin that if he carried out his plan for free elections, Bierut and his comrades couldn't deliver Poland. Stalin had the idea that the Red Army would be accepted as a liberating army. In fact, he told me so. In this regard, perhaps the Communist partisans had reported too optimistically to Moscow. At any rate I think the Kremlin leaders were awfully hurt when they found that the Red Army was looked upon by the Poles, the Romanians, and others as a new invading force.

In addition, there appeared to be two schools of thought in the Kremlin hierarchy—the Politburo itself. One is apt to think of the Communist government as one single brain; it isn't. It is made up of men with sometimes differing views; this was true even under Stalin. I was conscious of the fact that members of Politburo even during the war had different views on different subjects. Let me quickly say that there was free discussion in the Politburo on *new* subjects only. On anything Stalin had decided, that was it. That couldn't be questioned. I think it is fair to say that in these discussions about new matters, Stalin listened, smoked his pipe, and walked up and down the room. Then, when he had heard enough, he said, "This is what we are going to do." If anyone left the room with a shrug of his shoulders, he might find himself on the way to Siberia the next afternoon. That may be somewhat of an exaggeration, but I think it's pretty nearly right.

In any event, I feel sure that there was a difference of opinion as to whether it would be wise for the Soviet Union in the immediate postwar period to soft-pedal Communist expansion for a time and continue to collaborate with the Western Allies to get the value of loans and trade, technical assistance, and other cooperation for the terrific job of reconstruction they faced; or whether they should push ahead and use the extraordinary opportunities in the dislocations in Europe and elsewhere to extend Communist control. Stalin once told me, "Communism breeds in the cesspools of capitalists." In this sense, Europe looked as if it were going to be in a mire.

I was so concerned about this that in early 1945, I sent messages about the need to help Western Europe, urging that the recovery of Europe would require much more than most people thought. I said that UNRRA would not be enough, food would not be enough. We would have to supply working capital and raw materials to get trade going again. Imports would be needed for raw materials for industrial production as well as for reconstruction. Without that, there would be vast unemployment and misery, in which the Communists might well take over.

I believe that Stalin hoped to get to the Atlantic, and that was perhaps the reason why he didn't carry out the Yalta agreements. The prospects for Communist takeover simply looked too good.

He said a number of things on different occasions, some of them contradictory, and it is hard to know what he had in mind. After Teheran he sent President Roosevelt a telegram in which, among other things, he said, "Now it is assured that our people will act together, jointly and in friendship, both at the present time and after the completion of the war." This is only one of the many expressions of that kind which gave some indication that he had in mind postwar cooperation. But that didn't happen. Roosevelt died, and I know that before he died he realized that his hopes had not been fully achieved; he knew Stalin had already broken some of the Yalta agreements. I know that from the telegrams I received from him to deliver to

Stalin and also from some of the people who talked to him just before his death.* ...

While I was home, I did spend several weeks in San Francisco during the United Nations Conference. At the request of Ed Stettinius, the Secretary of State, I had three off-the-record talks with editors, columnists, and reporters to give them some background on our growing problems with the Soviet government. I told them we would have real difficulties with the Soviet Union in the postwar period. This came as a great shock to many of them. At one meeting, I explained that our objectives and the Kremlin objectives were irreconcilable; they wanted to communize the world, and we wanted a free world. But I added that we would have to find ways to compose our differences if we were to live in peace on this small planet. Two men were so shocked that they got up and left. Some of the press at that time criticized me for being so unkind to what were then known as "our gallant allies," and some even suggested that I should be recalled as Ambassador. It was one of the few times in my experience that members of the press have broken the confidence of an off-the-record talk.

People ask when and why I became convinced we would have difficulties with the Soviets. This judgment developed over a period of time. ...

A talk I had with Stalin at Potsdam in July 1945 is illuminating. The first time I saw him at the conference I went up to him and said that it must be very gratifying for him to be in Berlin, after all the struggle and the tragedy. He hesitated a moment and then replied, "Czar Alexander got to Paris." It didn't need much of a clairvoyant to guess what was in his mind.

I don't think there is any doubt that, with the strong Communist Parties both in Italy and in France, he would have extended his domination to the Atlantic, if we had not acted to frustrate it. In all probability, the Communist leaders in those countries had reported to Moscow that they could take over, and I think they would have succeeded if we had not helped Western Europe to recover. Some of Western Europe would have had Communist governments under the control of Moscow. One doesn't know what the rest of Europe would have been like, but perhaps some countries would have been something less independent than Finland and allowed to be cautiously neutral at the grace of Moscow.

But that isn't what happened. I know that some young people think that everything that has been done before them wasn't just right, but we did have a fairly glorious period, perhaps the most creative period

---

* Mrs. Hoffman wrote me a letter some years later describing her conversation with Roosevelt on March 24, 1945, his last day in Washington:

The President was in his wheel chair as we left the room, and both Mrs. Roosevelt and I walked at his side. He was given a message which I learned later was a cable from you which had been decoded. He read it and became quite angry. He banged his fists on the arms of his wheel chair and said, "Averell is right; we can't do business with Stalin. He has broken every one of the promises he made at Yalta." He was very upset and continued in the same vein on the subject.

These were his exact words. I remembered them and verified them with Mrs. Roosevelt not too long before her death.

in American foreign policy, immediately after the war. It was due to the leadership of President Truman and the effective cooperation of Senator Vandenberg, the Republican Senator from Michigan, who was then Chairman of the Foreign Relations Committee. The undertakings included aid to Greece, which was under Communist attack, and Turkey, which was threatened at that time; the Marshall Plan, which was an extraordinarily ambitious and successful venture in cooperation; and that led to NATO. These things developed one from the other. Public opinion in the West was deeply disturbed by the Czech coup of March 1948 and then the Berlin blockade three months later....

I was involved in the Marshall Plan, in charge of operations in Europe for more than two years. This was a European effort, with United States help. By the way, I should recall that General Marshall's offer of aid was made to all of Europe, including Russia and Eastern Europe. In fact, Molotov came to the meeting of Foreign Ministers of the European countries called in Paris in July 1947 to consider Marshall's offer with a staff of sixty, including senior economists. However, he demanded that each country act independently. He wanted the European nations to reply to the United States along these lines, "Tell us how much money you will give us, and we will divide it on the basis of those who suffered most will get the most. Then each country will look after its own recovery." But Marshall's proposal was that the European countries should cooperate together in a mutual recovery program. Bevin and Bidault, the British and French Foreign Ministers, stood firm for the cooperative concept, and Molotov left in a huff. The Czechs and the Poles had wanted to join the Marshall Plan, but the Kremlin ordered them not to do so.

At that time the Soviets organized the Cominform and declared war on the Marshall Plan, calling it an "American imperialist plot to subjugate Western Europe." Needless to say, that was just exactly the reverse of what we wanted. We wanted a strong, united and independent Europe. Everything that we did was to minimize our role and maximize the cooperative effort of the Europeans. "Self-help and mutual aid" was the slogan. It was amazingly successful—a spirit of cooperation and unity developed within Europe which had never before existed. They abandoned some of the restrictive business and labor practices of the intra-war years and accepted the necessity of an expanding economy as the basis for a rising standard of living....

Now, Western Europe is more vital and dynamic than ever. When De Gaulle was in control, France was, perhaps, a little too nationalistic. But today the Europeans are again moving toward greater integration and closer cooperation. This was part of the objective of the Congress, and certainly of President Truman in initiating the Marshall Plan....

The Berlin blockade in June of 1948 was a startling event and led to the pressure for NATO. You have to remember that never in history has a nation destroyed its armed strength as rapidly as we did after the Second World War. The demand for bringing the boys home was irresistible. No one was to blame; it was the deep desire of the American people. We thought we had won the war and everyone in the world would want peace. We had the strongest military force in being at the end of the war, but after the Japanese surrendered, it was dissipated. The Russians didn't do that. They strengthened their forces. They developed new weapons. We in Moscow reported to Washington in late 1945 evidence which indicated that Soviet research expenditure was being doubled, that production of certain new weapons and military equipment was continuing at wartime levels, and that combat training for the Red Army was being emphasized.

Although for a time we had a monopoly in nuclear weapons, Stalin ordered the highest priority be given to developing nuclear capability. Much to the surprise of most people at the time, the Soviets exploded their first nuclear device in September 1949.

The Berlin blockade was countered not by direct force. There has been a lot of argument about that at the time and since. People can argue whether Truman's decision was right or wrong—whether to try to drive our forces through and threaten a nuclear attack, or whether to supply Berlin by airlift. In any event, the least provocative of these responses—the airlift—was chosen, and with full British cooperation it was successful. The Soviets lifted the blockade a year later.

We have had difficulty over Berlin ever since, some times more dangerous than others. Of course, one can criticize the arrangements which made Berlin the capital of occupied Germany. Frankly, Ben Cohen and I favored at the time a capital in a new location, where the three zones came together, just north of Magdeburg. I was influenced in part by the appalling way in which the Soviets had stripped Berlin of most everything they could take out, between V-E Day and the Potsdam meeting. The factories, particularly, were emptied of all machinery and machine tools. But these arrangements had been made by the European Advisory Commission in London. They had been accepted by the three Allies and would have been pretty hard to change at Potsdam.

Sometimes I have thought our presence in Berlin was of great value. Other times I have wondered if it was worthwhile. These are things that historians can argue about. But we are there in West Berlin, and the division of Germany continues along the line of the Soviet occupational zone.

Some think that General Eisenhower should have taken Berlin, but if he had done that, our Third Army wouldn't have been in Austria, and Austria, which is a free and independent country, probably would have been occupied largely by the Red Army and might have been turned into a satellite.

These are all questions which one can weigh. It is hard to say what might have been done. If one objective had been gained, something else would have been lost. I think by and large with the Soviet recalcitrance it would have made very little difference.

Some people have even argued that if General Eisenhower had liberated Prague somehow or other Czechoslovakia would be free today. That's nonsense! The Czech government under President Benes was set up under an agreement in Moscow, negotiated by Benes with Czech party leaders, including the Communists. This government returned to

Czechoslovakia from the East, as the Red Army, joined with four or five Czech divisions, advanced. Under the agreement Benes had to take Communists into the government.

I had several talks with Benes when he came to Moscow from London in March 1945 before returning to Czechoslovakia. He told me that he was not too well satisfied with the composition of the new government, but he added, "It might have been worse." Benes was confident he could control the situation in Czechoslovakia as he believed the people would support him. He told me that Stalin had assured him that the Soviets would not interfere in Czech internal affairs.

Unfortunately, Benes was ill in March 1948 when the coup took place. Of course, the Red Army had long since retired. It had withdrawn from Czechoslovakia more than two years earlier. Our troops had also withdrawn long before, so nothing we did in 1945 would have affected the outcome. Whether or not it would have been different if Benes had been well and vigorous, and whether he could have held his own, I don't know. But the Communist coup was successful without the participation of the Red Army, but undoubtedly with Moscow's collusion.

I had long talks with Jan Masaryk in San Francisco in May 1945. He was Benes' Foreign Minister. He told me I must understand that in the United Nations he would have to vote with Molotov. The Soviets were insisting that the Czech government support them in foreign policy. In return, he thought they would have a free hand at home. Unfortunately, it did not work out that way, and Masaryk himself came to a violent end in March 1948.

The Truman period was an exciting period. President Truman was a man of great determination. He was very humble at the start. He said he had not been elected; Roosevelt had been elected, and it was his responsibility to carry out Roosevelt's policies. He did the best he could. Very early he showed that he recognized the unique problems facing the United States in the world, and he had the extraordinary courage to undertake new policies and programs. And I think they were extraordinarily successful.

President Truman proposed in January 1949 the Point Four Program, announcing that since science and technology had developed to such a point that the old enemies of mankind—hunger, misery, poverty, and disease—could be overcome, it was the obligation of the United States and other more technologically advanced nations to help. That concept has moved ahead. There have been some outstanding successes in some ways and in some countries—some disappointments in others. Unfortunately, our development assistance is in rather a low state today—one of the casualties of Vietnam.

There have been lasting constructive results from the Truman period. Germany has revived and has become a strong ally; Japan has revived and is becoming a strong partner. Western Europe is more productive and united than ever. Other countries have made progress as well and are on their way to sustained economic development, for example in Asia, Korea, and Taiwan, and in Latin America, Mexico, Venezuela, and Colombia. There have been disappointments, of course. The developing countries as a whole have not been able to advance as rapidly as had been hoped, and the gap between them and the industrial nations has widened.

China was an enigma. Roosevelt first of all wanted to get the Soviet Union into the war against Japan. There was never any doubt in my mind that Stalin would attack Japan when it suited him. We could not have kept him out. The question was whether that would be soon enough to do us good. Our Chiefs of Staff estimated that it would take eighteen months after the fall of Germany to defeat the Japanese and would require an amphibious landing on the plains of Tokyo. American casualties were estimated to run up near a million with perhaps a couple of hundred thousand killed. This was a grim prospect to President Roosevelt. Yet, if the Russians attacked the Japanese Kwangtung Army in Manchuria, the Japanese strength to defend the home islands would be reduced. President Roosevelt had a deep sense of responsibility to protect American lives, and it was hoped that possibly, with Russia in the war and with American use of Soviet airfields in Siberia, we could bring Japan to surrender without invasion. Therefore, Soviet intervention seemed of vital importance.

It didn't turn out to be important because, unexpectedly, the nuclear bomb became operative and events moved so rapidly. At Yalta, when plans about Soviet entry into the war against Japan were agreed to, the nuclear bomb had not yet been completed, and nobody knew whether it would work. Even five months later at Potsdam, after the first test explosion took place, one of the most distinguished Navy officers bet an apple that it would not go off as a bomb. Of course, after things happen they seem so easy and so obvious that people say, "Why didn't you think of this at the time?"

Apart from Soviet entry into the war, Roosevelt also wanted to get Stalin to accept Chiang Kai-shek's Nationalist government as the government of China. And that, too, was part of the agreements reached at Yalta about the Far East. This was formalized in a treaty negotiated by T. V. Soong, Premier of the Nationalist government, with Stalin six months later. During these negotiations in Moscow I saw T. V. Soong almost every day. He was finally well satisfied, and in fact the world applauded the agreement....

There are certain concessions to the Russians related to the railroads and ports in Manchuria for a thirty-year period, but the important point for Chiang was that the Soviets accepted Chinese sovereignty over the area. Some of us had been concerned when the Russians got into Manchuria they would establish a "Manchurian People's Republic" just as they had the Mongolian People's Republic. The fact that the Soviets accepted Chinese sovereignty was the thing that impressed Chiang.

Curiously, Stalin did not have much respect for Mao Ze-dong. During the war he spoke about him several times, and at one time he called him a "margarine Communist." That created a great deal of puzzlement in Washington. Some didn't know what it means. It would be entirely clear to any dairy farmer what he meant—a fake, not a real product. I gained the impression from several of my talks with Stalin that he was not keen to support Mao Ze-dong in China and that, perhaps, he wanted to see a new group more amenable to Moscow, take over the Chinese Communist Party before he gave his full support.

After the war, in January 1946, he told me that he had "poor contacts with the Communists." He said that the Soviet government's "three representatives in Yenan had been recalled" and that the Soviet influence with the Chinese Communists was not great. I think there is other evidence to that effect. For example, the Red Army not only stripped Manchuria of its industrial machinery for use in the Soviet Union but also blew up facilities such as blast furnaces. However, the Mao Communists were stronger than Stalin thought, and Chiang was weaker. As events developed, Chiang's forces collapsed in 1949, and he was driven out of mainland China.

Some people have said, "We lost China." It just happens that we never owned China. Whatever we had done in China over the years had had only a limited impact. And although it is unfortunate that a government friendly to us did not survive, we could not have involved ourselves in a major war at that time in China. President Truman, in spite of all the initiatives we had taken in other parts of the world, was wise enough to exercise restraint and not become involved in a civil war in mainland China.

So not all the postwar developments were favorable. Some of them did not go as well as we had hoped they might....

President Kennedy handled the Cuban missile crisis with consummate skill and induced Khrushchev to take the offensive missiles out of Cuba. He was able to go on to an agreement with him on a limited test ban. The signing and ratification of the Limited Nuclear Test Ban Treaty marked a high water point in our relations with the Soviet Union. There were of course unsolved critical problems, particularly in regard to Germany and Southeast Asia. But the change in less than a year from the Cuban missile crisis to the test ban was so striking that I believe President Kennedy began to think seriously of a visit to the Soviet Union early in his second term should he be re-elected. But President Kennedy was assassinated three months later.

Within a year new personalities were to take over in Moscow. Khrushchev was removed from office, Brezhnev took his place as Secretary of the Party and Kosygin as Chairman of the Council of Ministers....

QUESTIONS AND ANSWERS

Q—Do you believe that there is anything America could have done to assist Chiang, particularly in the latter period when we did withdraw our support?

A—I don't think so. I went to Chunking to talk with Chiang Kai-shek in January 1946. General Marshall was there at the time. Chiang had grave doubts about coming to an agreement for a coalition with the Communists, and he may have been justified in his fears. I asked him why he did not strengthen his government at once by bringing in the

Democratic League, which included the leading Chinese intellectuals. They had recently participated in a Consultative Conference which had attempted to reconcile the contending parties. I also asked him why he didn't get rid of some of his warlords and some of the obviously corrupt people around him. He replied that they were the only ones he could count on for support if he brought the Communists into the government.

Perhaps the outcome might have been better if we had had quite a different approach. Looking at things from Moscow, my idea at the time was that we might better accept temporarily a divided China. If we could have prevented Chiang from sending his best troops into Manchuria where they were chewed up, he would have been far better off. It was hopeless for him to expect to take over the rule of Manchuria when he was having difficulty in controlling even the area where his forces were concentrated—southern China.

I also had grave doubts about the attempts to form a coalition government with the Communists. It seemed to me at the time that Chiang was too weak and the Communists too strong for him to have had much of a chance of survival.

In any event, General Marshall was sent out to attempt to mediate between the Nationalists and the Communists, and he did everything he could under his instructions. Despite General Marshall's patience and skill, the reluctance and suspicion of both sides and the inherent weakness of the Kuomintang made successful mediation impossible....

Q—Mr. Ambassador, would you comment on the motivation of Soviet foreign policy? Do you think the motivation is primarily that of power politics and national power concerns, or of Communist ideology, or are they both equally determining factors?

A—It is a combination of both. Stalin had both. He was a Russian imperialist with ambitions similar to the Czars. He was also utterly determined to promote world Communist revolution with the oracle in Moscow. Since Stalin's death the world situation has changed, but the Kremlin still has both motivations....

Q—If you could relive history, what changes would you make in the United States foreign policy during the wartime conferences and what effect that might have had on the future?

A—Well, I don't think much would have been different. You can argue about a lot of different things. People blame Eisenhower for not going to Berlin, but there had been a decision made in which the occupational zones of Germany were set. It was considered important that we should not meet and clash with the Russians, that we should decide in advance the zones each would occupy to avoid that possibility. The agreed zones were considered to be very favorable by our chiefs of staff at the time they were decided upon. They thought the Russians would be much further into Germany than they got and that we would not have gotten as far as we did. It didn't work out that way. I am not critical of them for this, as no one could have foreseen the military events.

Now if we had tried to do what Churchill proposed after V–E Day— stand on the Elbe until there was a political settlement about Eastern

Europe—I don't think it would have done any good, and we would then have been held responsible for the cold war. Furthermore, our military plans required a redeployment of our forces in Europe to the Pacific. Churchill wanted to force a political settlement about the areas occupied by the Red Army before we withdrew from the Elbe. But even if we had gotten an agreement and free elections had been held, the governments elected would, in all probability, not have lasted. There was, in fact, a free election in Hungary in 1945 in which the Smallholders party (the small peasants' party) got over 50 per cent of the votes and the Communists only about 18 per cent. The government established after this election lasted only a short time, and the Communists—supported by the Red Army—took over and squeezed out the others.

There was no way we could have prevented any of these events in Eastern Europe without going to war with the Russians. There were a few military people who considered that. This wasn't De Gaulle, but a few French and American officers talked about going in and cleaning them up while we had such superiority in air power. It is perfectly absurd to think the American people would have stood for it, even if the President wanted to do it, which he didn't.

I think it was very important that Roosevelt and Churchill made the effort to come to an agreement with Stalin. One achievement was the establishment of the United Nations. With all the disappointments, it has been effective in many activities during the twenty-five years of its life, although handicapped by the differences that exist between the great powers. The fact that Stalin broke the agreements about Eastern Europe exposed his perfidy and aggressive designs. This aroused the suspicion of the West and eventually led to steps for mutual defense.

There is a group of historians who are now attempting to rewrite the history of that time. Arthur M. Schlesinger, Jr., has pointed out that such attempts to rewrite history have happened frequently in the past. These revisionists are creating myths about what happened and what our objectives were. Some of them take facts out of context and try to build up a case for imagined objectives. Some conveniently overlook Stalin's failure to cooperate, his violation of specific agreements and aggressive actions. Of course, I am not talking about those thoughtful analysts who, with the advantage of hindsight, point out more clearly the significance of events and perhaps mistakes than was possible at the time.

The military alternatives were perhaps more obvious than the political. At the time some people wanted us to go to Vienna, up the Ljubljana Gap, and get there before the Russians, instead of landing in the south of France as we did. Yet as things have turned out, Austria is free today anyway.

Churchill was always very much worried about attempting to cross the Channel. It turned out successfully. It would have been disastrous for the British if it hadn't. Churchill wanted to go at Hitler from the south—"the soft underbelly," as he called it. He didn't want to take the risk of crossing the Channel. Stalin, after having berated and even insulted us for two years for not establishing a second front in Europe by crossing the Channel, said to me after we had successfully landed, "The history of war has never witnessed such a grandiose operation." He added neither Napoleon nor Hitler had dared attempt it. Later, after he had received detailed reports, he spoke to me again about crossing the Channel, as "an unheard of achievement in the history of warfare." The number of men and the vast amount of equipment which had been thrown into France impressed him greatly. He added "the world had never seen an individual operation of such magnitude—an unbelievable accomplishment." He was unconcerned by the fact that he had previously minimized its difficulties and had accused us of cowardice in not having undertaken it before.

Undoubtedly mistakes were made, and undoubtedly many things might have been improved. Your question is an interesting one, and I have thought a lot about it. But the facts are that, although militarily unprepared, we fought a war successfully on two fronts. With our allies in Europe, we completely defeated Hitler, and almost alone we defeated Japan in the Pacific. That was an extraordinary achievement—and particularly as it was done in less than four years. As far as our relations with the Soviet Union since the end of the war are concerned, I doubt whether any different wartime military or political decisions would have had much effect.

2. The Cold War: A Revisionist View

BARTON J. BERNSTEIN

"There is no nation which has
attitudes so pure that
they cannot be bettered
by self-examination."
—John Foster Dulles (1946)

"We are forced to act in the
world as it is, and not in the
world as we wish it were, or as
we would like it to become."
—Henry L. Stimson (1947)

Barton J. Bernstein is one of the "revisionists" whom Averell Harriman criticizes for "creating myths about what happened [in the Cold War] and what our objectives were." The revisionist position, expressed repeatedly during the 1960s, holds that Stalin was basically cautious rather than aggressive in his actions immediately after World War II; that the United States government, by aggressively pursuing American access to a world trading empire, overlooked legitimate Soviet security needs; and that, by forming the North Atlantic Treaty Organization (NATO), stamping out indigenous Communist opposition in Greece and Turkey under the Truman Doctrine of 1947, and giving Europe financial aid under the Marshall Plan, America forced the Kremlin into a hostile posture in Eastern Europe to protect itself from future military threats.

Only a small proportion of American diplomatic historians has totally accepted this analysis of American foreign policy, but the revisionist argument has influenced virtually every student in the field. The central point of revisionist thinking, that the postwar power of the United States gave it wider options than the war-weakened Soviet Union ever had, seems hard to question. Yet some theorists maintain that American and Soviet social and economic policies would eventually have converged, and abrasive conflict between the two ideologies need not have occurred at all.

We have had so little access to postwar Soviet archives, and Stalin's personality was so complex, that varied interpretations are possible. The experience of Vietnam, the breakdown of monolithic power blocs, both East and West, and the emergence of detente have all provided continuing stimuli for Cold War revisionism. And the staggering events of the late eighties in Eastern Europe and the Soviet Union, together with glasnost and the greater availability of documents about the earlier era, must provoke another rethinking in the 1990s of the now extinct Cold War.

Despite some dissents, most American scholars have reached a general consensus on the origins of the Cold War. As confirmed internationalists who believe that Russia constituted a threat to America and its European allies after Wold War II, they have endorsed their nation's acceptance of its obligations as a world power in the forties and its desire to establish a world order of peace and prosperity. Convinced that only American efforts prevented the Soviet Union from expanding past Eastern Europe, they have generally praised the containment policies of the Truman Doctrine, the Marshall Plan, and NATO as evidence of America's acceptance of world responsibility. While chiding or condemning those on the right who opposed international involvement (or had even urged preventive war), they have also been deeply critical of those on the left who have believed that the Cold War could have been avoided, or that the United States shared substantial responsibility for the Cold War.

Whether they are devotees of the new realism or open admirers of moralism and legalism in foreign policy, most scholars have agreed that the United States moved slowly and reluctantly, in response to Soviet provocation, away from President Franklin D. Roosevelt's conciliatory policy. The Truman administration, perhaps even belatedly, they suggest, abandoned its efforts to maintain the Grand Alliance and acknowledged that Russia menaced world peace. American leaders, according to this familiar interpretation, slowly cast off the shackles of innocence and moved to courageous and necessary policies.

Despite the widespread acceptance of this interpretation, there has long been substantial evidence (and more recently a body of scholarship) which suggests that American policy was neither so innocent nor so nonideological; that American leaders sought to promote their conceptions of national interest and their values even at the conscious risk of provoking Russia's fears about her security. In 1945 these leaders apparently believed that American power would be adequate for the task of reshaping much of the world according to America's needs and standards.

By overextending policy and power and refusing to accept Soviet interests, American policy-makers contributed to the Cold War. There was little understanding of any need to restrain American political efforts and desires. Though it cannot be proved that the United States could have achieved a *modus vivendi* with the Soviet Union in these years, there is evidence that Russian policies were reasonably cautious and conservative, and that there was at least a basis for accommodation. But this possibility slowly slipped away as President Harry S Truman reversed Roosevelt's tactics of accommodation. As American demands for demo-

The author wishes to express his gratitude for generous counsel to Gar Alperovitz, H. Stuart Hughes, Gabriel Kolko, Walter LaFeber, Lloyd Gardner, Allen J. Matusow, Thomas G. Paterson, Athan Theoharis, and Samuel Williamson. Research was conducted with the assistance of grants from the Rabinowitz Foundation, the American Philosophical Society, the Harry S Truman Library Institute, the Charles Warren Center of Harvard University, and the Institute of American History at Stanford University. Portions of this paper were presented at the Warren Center in November 1967, at the John F. Kennedy Institute at Harvard in 1967–1968, and at the annual meeting of the Southern Historical Association in November 1968.

cratic governments in Eastern Europe became more vigorous, as the new administration delayed in providing economic assistance to Russia and in seeking international control of atomic energy, policy-makers met with increasing Soviet suspicion and antagonism. Concluding that Soviet-American cooperation was impossible, they came to believe that the Soviet state could be halted only by force or the threat of force.

The emerging revisionist interpretation, then, does not view American actions simply as the necessary response to Soviet challenges, but instead tries to understand American ideology and interests, mutual suspicions and misunderstandings, and to investigate the failures to seek and achieve accommodation.

I

During the war Allied relations were often marred by suspicions and doubts rooted in the hostility of earlier years. It was only a profound "accident"—the German attack upon the Soviet Union in 1941—that thrust that leading anti-Bolshevik, Winston Churchill, and Marshal Josef Stalin into a common camp. This wartime alliance, its members realized, was not based upon trust but upon necessity; there was no deep sense of shared values or obvious similarity of interests, only opposition to a common enemy. "A coalition," as Herbert Feis has remarked, "is heir to the suppressed desires and maimed feelings of each of its members." Wartime needs and postwar aims often strained the uneasy alliance. In the early years when Russia was bearing the major burden of the Nazi onslaught, her allies postponed for two years a promised second front which would have diverted German armies. In December 1941, when Stalin requested recognition of 1941 Russian borders as they had been before the German attack (including the recently annexed Baltic states), the British were willing to agree, but Roosevelt rebuffed the proposals and aroused Soviet fears that her security needs would not be recognized and that her allies might later resume their anti-Bolshevik policies. So distrustful were the Allies that both camps feared the making of a separate peace with Germany, and Stalin's suspicions erupted into bitter accusations in March 1945, when he discovered (and Roosevelt denied) that British and American agents were participating in secret negotiations with the Germans. In anger Stalin decided not to send Vyacheslav Molotov, the Foreign Minister, to San Francisco for the April meeting on the founding of the United Nations Organization.

So suspicious were the Americans and British that they would not inform the Soviet Union that they were working on an atomic bomb. Some American leaders even hoped to use it in postwar negotiations with the Russians. In wartime, American opposition to communism had not disappeared, and many of Roosevelt's advisers were fearful of Soviet intentions in Eastern Europe. In turn, Soviet leaders, recalling the prewar hostility of the Western democracies, feared a renewed attempt to establish a *cordon sanitaire* and resolved to establish a security zone in Eastern Europe.

Though Roosevelt's own strategy often seems ambiguous, his general tactics are clear: they were devised to avoid conflict. He operated often as a mediator between the British and Russians, and delayed many decisions that might have disrupted the wartime alliance. He may have been resting his hopes with the United Nations or on the exercise of America's postwar strength, or he may simply have been placing his faith in the future. Whatever future tactics he might have been planning, he concluded that America's welfare rested upon international peace, expanded trade, and open markets:

...it is our hope, not only in the interest of our own prosperity, but in the interest of the prosperity of the world, that trade and commerce and access to materials and markets may be freer after this war than ever before in the history of the world.... Only through a dynamic and soundly expanding world economy can the living standards of individual nations be advanced to levels which will permit a full realization of our hopes for the future.

His efforts on behalf of the postwar world generally reflected this understanding.

During the war Roosevelt wavered uneasily between emphasizing the postwar role of the great powers and minimizing their role and seeking to extend the principles of the Atlantic Charter. Though he often spoke of the need for an open postwar world, and he was reluctant to accept spheres of influence (beyond the Western hemisphere, where American influence was pre-eminent), his policies gradually acknowledged the pre-eminence of the great powers and yielded slowly to their demands. By late 1943 Roosevelt confided to Archbishop Francis Spellman (according to Spellman's notes) that "the world will be divided into spheres of influence: China gets the Far East; the U.S. the Pacific; Britain and Russia, Europe and Africa." The United States, he thought, would have little postwar influence on the continent, and Russia would probably "predominate in Europe," making Austria, Hungary, and Croatia "a sort of Russian protectorate." He acknowledged "that the European countries will have to undergo tremendous changes in order to adapt to Russia; but he hopes that in ten or twenty years the European influence would bring the Russians to become less barbarous."

In 1944 Roosevelt recognized the establishment of zones of influence in Europe. The Italian armistice of the year before had set the pattern for other wartime agreements on the control of affairs of liberated and defeated European nations. When Stalin requested the creation of a three-power Allied commission to deal with the problems of "countries falling away from Germany," Roosevelt and Churchill first rebuffed the Russian leader and then agreed to a joint commission for Italy which would be limited to information gathering. By excluding Russia from sharing in decision-making in Italy, the United States and Great Britain, later concluded William McNeill, "prepared the way for their own exclusion from any but a marginal share in the affairs of Eastern Europe."

When Roosevelt refused to participate in an Anglo-American invasion of southeastern Europe (which seemed to be the only way of restricting Russian influence in that area), Churchill sought other ways of dealing with Russian power and of protecting British interests in Greece. In May 1944 he proposed to Stalin that they recognize Greece as a British "zone of influence" and Rumania as a Russian zone; but Stalin insisted upon seeking Roosevelt's approval and refused the offer upon learning that the United States would not warmly endorse the terms. When the Soviets liberated Rumania in September they secured temporarily the advantages that Churchill had offered. They simply followed the British-American example in Italy, retained all effective power, and announced they were "acting in the interests of all the United Nations." From the Soviet Union, W. Averell Harriman, the American ambassador, cabled, "The Russians believe, I think, that we lived up to a tacit understanding that Rumania was an area of predominant Soviet interest in which we should not interfere... The terms of the armistice give the Soviet command unlimited control of Rumania's economic life" and effective control over political organization.

With Russian armies sweeping through the Balkans and soon in a position to impose similar terms on Hungary and Bulgaria, Churchill renewed his efforts. "Winston," wrote an associate, "never talks of Hitler these days; he is always harping on the dangers of Communism. He dreams of the Red Army spreading like a cancer from one country to another. It has become an obsession, and he seems to think of little else." In October Churchill journeyed to Moscow to reach an agreement with Stalin. "Let us settle our affairs in the Balkans," Churchill told him. "Your armies are in Rumania and Bulgaria. We have interests, missions and agents there. Don't let us get at cross-purposes in small ways." Great Britain received "90 per cent influence" in Greece, and Russia "90 per cent influence" in Rumania, "80 per cent" in Bulgaria and Hungary, and "50 per cent" in Yugoslavia.

In the cases of Hungary and Bulgaria the terms were soon sanctioned by armistice agreements (approved by the United States) which left effective power with the Soviets. "The Russians took it for granted," Cordell Hull, then Secretary of State, wrote later, "that... Britain and the United States had assigned them a certain portion of the Balkans, including Rumania and Bulgaria, as their sphere of influence." In December Stalin even confirmed the agreement at a considerable price: he permitted British troops to put down a rebellion in Greece. "Stalin," wrote Churchill later, "adhered strictly and faithfully to our agreement... and during all the long weeks of fighting the communists in the streets of Athens, not one word of reproach came from *Pravda* or *Izvestia*."

At Yalta in February 1945 Roosevelt did not seem to challenge Soviet dominance in east-central Europe, which had been established by the Churchill-Stalin agreement and confirmed by the armistices and by British action in Greece. What Roosevelt did seek and gain at Yalta was a weak "Declaration on Liberated Europe"—that the powers would consult "where in their judgment conditions require" assistance to maintain peace or to establish democratic governments. By requiring unanimity the declaration allowed any one power to veto any proposal that seemed to threaten that power's interests. In effect, then, the declaration, despite its statements about democratic governments, did not alter the situation in Eastern Europe. The operative phrases simply affirmed the principle that the three powers had already established: they could consult together when all agreed, and they could act together when all agreed.

At Yalta the broadly phrased statement provoked little discussion—only a few pages in the official proceedings. Presumably the Russians did not consider it a repudiation of spheres of influence, only as rhetoric that Roosevelt wanted for home consumption. Despite later official American suggestions, the Yalta agreement was not a product of Roosevelt's misunderstanding of the Soviet meaning of "democracy" and "free elections." Rather, it ratified earlier agreements, and the State Department probably understood this.

While accepting the inevitable and acknowledging Russian influence in these areas, Roosevelt had not been tractable on the major issue confronting the three powers: the treatment of post war Germany. All three leaders realized that the decisions on Germany would shape the future relations of Europe. A dismembered or permanently weakened Germany would leave Russia without challenge on the continent and would ease her fears of future invasion. As Anthony Eden, the British Foreign Minister explained, "Russia was determined on one thing above all others, that German would not again distrub the peace of Europe.... Stalin was determined to smash Germany so that it would never again be able to make war." A strong Germany, on the other hand, could be a partial counterweight to Russia and help restore the European balance of power on which Britain had traditionally depended for protection. Otherwise, as Henry Morgenthau once explained in summarizing Churchill's fears, there would be nothing between "the white snows of Russia and the white cliffs of Dover."

The Allied policy on Germany had been in flux for almost two years. At Teheran in 1943 the Allies had agreed in principle (despite Churchill's reluctance) that Germany should be dismembered, and in 1944 Roosevelt and a reluctant Churchill, much to the distress of Foreign Minister Anthony Eden, had agreed on a loosely phrased version of the Morgenthau Plan for the dismemberment and pastoralization of Germany. Not only would the plan have eliminated German military-industrial potential and thereby allayed Russian fears, but by stripping Germany it would also have provided the resources for Russian economic reconstruction. Churchill, despite his fear of Russia and his desire for Germany as a counterweight on the continent, had temporarily agreed to the plan because it seemed to be a prerequisite for increased American economic aid and promised to eliminate German industry as a postwar rival for the trade that the debt-ridden British economy would need. Many in the State and War Departments charged that the plan was economic madness, that it would leave not only Germany but also much of war-torn Western Europe (which would need postwar German production) without the means for economic reconstruction. (Secretary of the Treasury Morgenthau concluded after discussion with many officials that they wanted a strong Germany as a "bulwark against Bolshevism.") Yielding to the pleas of the War and State Departments, Roosevelt decided upon a plan for a stronger postwar Germany, and Churchill, under pressure from advisers, also backed away from his earlier endorsement of the Morgenthau Plan and again acted upon his fears of an unopposed Russia on the continent. At Yalta, he resisted any agreement on the dismemberment of Germany. Stalin, faced with Anglo-American solidarity on this issue, acceded. The final comuniqué patched over this fundamental dispute by announcing that the three powers had pledged to "take such steps including the complete disarmament, demilitarization, and dismemberment of Germany as they deem requisite for future peace and security." The strategy of postponement had triumphed. Unable to reach a substantive agreement, the Big Three agreed to submit these problems (and the related, vital issues of reparations and boundaries) to three-power commissions.

Though Yalta has come to represent the triumph of the strategy of postponement, at the time it symbolized Allied accord. Stalin accepted a limitation of the veto power on certain quasi-judicial issues in the U.N. Security Council; Roosevelt conceded to Russia the return of the Kurile Islands, which stretched between Japan and Siberia, and special rights in Dairen and Port Arthur in Manchuria; Stalin promised to enter the Pacific war within three months of the end of the European conflict. "Stalin," as William McNeill explained, "had conceded something to the British in Yugoslavia; and Churchill had yielded a good deal in Poland."

II

Roosevelt's successor was less sympathetic to Russian aspirations and more responsive to those of Roosevelt's advisers, like Admiral William Leahy, Chief of Staff to the Commander in Chief; Harriman; James Forestall, Secretary of the Navy; and James F. Byrnes, Truman's choice for Secretary of State, who had urged that he resist Soviet efforts in Eastern Europe. As an earlier self-proclaimed foe of Russian communism, Truman mistrusted Russia. ("If we see that Germany is winning the war," advised Senator Truman after the German attack upon Russia in 1941, "we ought to help Russia, and if Russia is winning we ought to help Germany and in that way kill as many as possible.") Upon entering the White House, he did not seek to follow Roosevelt's tactics of adjustment and accommodation. Only eleven days in the presidency and virtually on the eve of the United Nations conference, Truman moved to a showdown with Russia on the issue of Poland.

Poland became the testing ground for American foreign policy, as Truman later said, "a symbol of the future development of our international relations." At Yalta the three powers had agreed that the Soviet-sponsored Lublin Committee (the temporary Polish government) should be "recognized on a broader democratic basis with the inclusion of democratic leaders from Poland itself and from Poland abroad." The general terms were broad: there was no specific formula for the distribution of power in the reorganized government, and the procedures required consultation and presumably unanimity from the representatives of the three powers. The agreement, remarked Admiral Leahy, was "so elastic that the Russians can stretch it all the way from Yalta to Washington without ever technically breaking it." ("I know, Bill—I know it. But it's the best I can do for Poland at this time," Roosevelt replied.)

For almost two months after Yalta the great powers haggled over Poland. The Lublin Committee objected to the Polish candidates proposed by the United States and Great Britain for consulation because these Poles had criticized the Yalta accord and refused to accept the Soviet annexation of Polish territory (moving the eastern boundary to the Curzon Line). In early April Stalin had offered a compromise—that about 80 per cent of the cabinet posts in the new government should be held by members of the Lublin Committee, and that he would urge the committee to accept the leading Western candidates if they would endorse the Yalta agreement (including the Curzon Line). By proposing a specific distribution of power, Stalin cut to the core of the issue that had disrupted negotiations for nearly three months, and sought to guarantee the victory he probably expected in Poland. Roosevelt died before replying, and it is not clear whether he would have accepted this 4 to 1 representation; but he had acknowledged that he was prepared to place "somewhat more emphasis on the Lublin Poles."

Now Truman was asked to acknowledge Soviet concern about countries on her borders and to assure her influence in many of these countries by granting her friendly (and probably non-democratic) governments, and even by letting her squelch anti-communist democrats in countries like Poland. To the President and his advisers the issue was (as Truman later expressed Harriman's argument) "the extension of Soviet control over neighboring states by independent action; we were faced with a barbarian invasion of Europe." The fear was not that the Soviets were about to threaten all of Europe but that they had designs on Eastern Europe, and that these designs conflicted with traditional American values of self-determination, democracy, and open markets.

Rushing back to Washington after Roosevelt's death, Harriman found most of FDR's advisers (now Truman's) sympathetic to a tougher approach. At a special White House meeting Harriman outlined what he thought were the Soviet Union's two policies—cooperation with the United States and Great Britain, and the creation of a unilateral security ring through domination of its border states. These policies, he contended, did not seem contradictory to Russian leaders, for "certain elements around Stalin" misinterpreted America's generosity and desire to cooperate as an indication of softness and concluded "that the Soviet Government could do anything that it wished without having any trouble with the United States." Before Roosevelt's death, Harriman had cabled: "It may be difficult... to believe, but it still may be true that Stalin and Molotov considered at Yalta that by our willingness to accept a general wording of the declaration on Poland and liberated Europe, by our recognition of the need of the Red Army for security behind its lines, and of the predominant interest of Russia in Poland as a friendly neighbor and as a corridor to Germany, we understood and were ready to accept Soviet policies already known to us."

Harriman wanted the American government to select a few test cases and make the Russians realize they could not continue their present policies. Such tactics, he advised, would place Russian-American relations on a more realistic basis and compel the Soviet Union to adhere to the American interpretation of the issues in dispute. Because the Soviet government "needed our [economic assistance]...in their reconstruction," and because Stalin did not wish to break with the United States, Harriman thought Truman "could stand on important issues without running serious risks." As early as January 1944 Harriman had emphasized that "the Soviet Government places the utmost importance on our cooperation" in providing economic assistance, and he had concluded: "it is a factor which should be integrated into the fabric of our overall relations." In early April Harriman had proposed that unless the United States were prepared "to live in a world dominated largely by Soviet influence, we must use our economic power to assist those countries that are naturally friendly to our concepts." In turn, he had recommended "tying our economic assistance directly into our political problems with the Soviet Union.

General George Marshall, the Army Chief of Staff, and Secretary of War Henry Stimson, however, recommended caution. Stimson observed "that the Russians perhaps were being more realistic than we were in regard to their own security," and he feared "that we would find ourselves breaking our relations with Russia on the most important and difficult question which we and Russia have gotten between us." Leahy, though supporting a firm policy, admitted that the Yalta agreement "was susceptible to two interpretations." Secretary of State Edward Stettinius read aloud the Yalta decision and concluded "that this was susceptible of only one interpretation."

Having heard his advisers' arguments, Truman resolved to force the Polish question: to impose his interpretation of the Yalta agreement even if it destroyed the United Nations. He later explained that this was the test of Russian cooperation. If Stalin would not abide by his agreements, the U.N. was doomed, and, anyway, there would not be enough enthusiasm among the American electorate to let the United States join the world body. "Our agreements with the Soviet Union so far...[have] been a one-way street." That could not continue, Truman told his advisers. "If the Russians did not wish to join us, they could go to hell." ("FDR's appeasement of Russia is over," joyously wrote Senator Arthur Vandenberg, the Republican leader on foreign policy.) Continuing in this spirit at a private conference with Molotov, the new President warned that economic aid would depend upon Russian behavior in fulfilling the Yalta agreement. Brushing aside the diplomat's contention that the Anglo-American interpretation of the Yalta agreement was wrong, the President accused the Russians of breaking agreements and scolded the Russian Foreign Minister. When Molotov replied, "I have never been talked to like that in my life," Truman warned him, "Carry out your agreement and you won't get talked to like that."

At the United Nations conference in San Francisco, when Anthony Eden, the British Foreign Minister, saw a copy of Truman's "blunt message" about Poland to Stalin, "he could scarcely believe his eyes...and cheered loudly," reported Vandenberg. But the policy of firmness was not immediately successful. American-Russian relations were further strained by the disputes at the meeting to create the U.N.—over the veto, the admission of fascist Argentina, and the persistent question of Poland. Despite Soviet objections and Roosevelt's promise at Yalta to exclude Argentina from the U.N., the United States supported the Latin American state's candidacy for membership. In committee Molotov, whom Stalin had sent to establish good will with the new President, tried to block the admission of Argentina until the Lublin Poles were also admitted, but his proposed bargain was overwhelmingly defeated. Later in the plenary session, when only three nations voted with Russia, the Soviets found additional evidence for their fears of an American bloc directed against their interests. The Truman administration's action also gave the Soviets more reason to doubt America's explanations that her interests in Poland were inspired simply by a desire to guarantee representative, democratic governments. Moreover, because of the American bloc and Soviet fears that the U.N. (like the League of Nations) might be used against her, Molotov was at first unwilling to accede to the demands of the United States and the smaller nations who wished to exclude procedural questions before the Security Council from the great power veto.

The Soviets were further embittered when the United States abruptly curtailed lend-lease six days after V-E Day. Though Truman later explained this termination as simply a "mistake," as policy-making by subordinates, his recollection was incomplete and wrong. Leo Crowley, the director of lend-lease, and Joseph Grew, the Under Secretary of State, the two subordinates most closely involved, had repeatedly warned the President of the likely impact of such action on relations with Russia, and the evidence suggests that the government, as Harriman had counseled, was seeking to use economic power to achieve diplomatic means. Termination of lend-lease, Truman later wrote, "should have been done on a gradual basis which would not have made it appear as if somebody had been deliberately snubbed." Yet, despite this later judgment, Truman had four days after signing the order in which to modify it before it was to be implemented and announced, and the lend-lease administrator (in the words of Grew) had made "sure that the President understands the situation." The administrator knew "that we would be having difficulty with the Russians and did not want them to be running all over town for help." After discussing the decision with Truman, Grew, presumably acting with the President's approval, had even contrived to guarantee that curtailment would be a dramatic shock. When the Soviet chargé d'affaires had telephoned Grew the day before the secret order was to become effective, the Under Secretary had falsely denied that lend-lease to Russia was being halted. Harriman, according to Grew's report to the Secretary of State, "said that we would be getting 'a good tough slashback' from the Russians but that we would have to face it."

Presumably to patch the alliance, Truman dispatched to Moscow Harry Hopkins, Roosevelt's former adviser and a staunch advocate of Soviet-American friendship. Hopkins denied that Truman's action was an American effort to demonstrate economic power and coerce Russia ("pressure on the Russians to soften them up," as Stalin charged). Instead he emphasized that "Poland had become a symbol of our ability to work out our problems with the Soviet Union." Stalin acknowledged "the right of the United States as a world power to participate in the Polish question," but he stressed the importance of Poland to Soviet security. Within twenty-five years the "Germans had twice invaded Russia via Poland," he emphasized. "All the Soviet Union wanted was that Poland should not be in a position to open the gates to Germany," and that required a government friendly to Russia. There was "no intention," he promised, "to interfere in Poland's internal affairs" or to Sovietize Poland.

Through the Hopkins mission, Truman and Stalin reached a compromise: 70 per cent of the new Polish government (fourteen of twenty ministers) should be drawn from the Lublin Committee. At the time there was reason to believe that such heavy communist influence would not lead to Soviet control. Stalin had reaffirmed the pledge of free elections in Poland, and Stanislaw Mikolajczyk, former Prime Minister of the exile government in London and Deputy Prime Minister in the new coalition government, was optimistic. He hoped (in Harriman's words) that "a reasonable degree of freedom and independence can be preserved now and that in time after conditions in Europe can become more stable and [as] Russian turns her attention to her internal development, controls will be relaxed and Poland will be able to gain for herself her independence of life as a nation even though he freely accepts that Poland's security and foreign policy must follow the lead of Moscow."

Truman compromised and soon recognized the new Polish government, but he did not lose his hopes of rolling back the Soviets from their spheres of influence in Eastern Europe. Basing most of his case on the Yalta "Declaration on Liberated Europe" (for which he relied on State Department interpretations), Truman hoped to force Russia to permit representative governments in its zones, and expected that free elections would diminish, perhaps even remove, Soviet authority. Refusing to extend diplomatic recognition to Rumania and Bulgaria, he emphasized that these governments were "neither representative of nor responsive to the will of the people."

"The opportunities for the democratic elements in Rumania and Bulgaria are not less than, say, in Italy, with which the Governments of the United States and the Soviet Union have already resumed diplomatic relations," replied Stalin, who was willing to exaggerate to emphasize his case. The Russians were demanding a *quid pro quo*, and they would not yield. At Potsdam, in late July, when Truman demanded "immediate reorganization" of the governments of Hungary and Bulgaria to "include representatives of all significant democratic elements" and three-power assistance in "holding...free and unfettered elections," Stalin pointed to Greece, again to remind Truman of the earlier agreements. The Russians were "not meddling in Greek affairs," he noted, adding that the Bulgarian and Rumanian governments were fulfilling the armistice agreements while in Greece "terrorism rages...against democratic elements." (One member of the American delegation later claimed that Stalin at one point made his position clear, stating that "any freely elected government [in Eastern Europe] would be anti-Soviet and that we cannot permit.") In effect, Stalin demanded that the United States abide by his construction of earlier agreements, and that Truman acknowledge what Roosevelt had accepted as the terms of the sphere-of-influence agreements–that democratic forms and anti-communist democrats of Eastern Europe be abandoned to the larger cause of Russian-American concord.

Though the Allies at Potsdam were not able to settle the dispute over influence in Eastern Europe, they did reach a limited agreement on other European issues. In a "package" deal the Soviets accepted Italy in the U.N. after a peace treaty could be arranged; the United States and Great Britain agreed to set the temporary western border of Poland at the Oder-Neisse line; and the Soviets settled for far less in reparations than they had expected. The decisions on Germany were the important settlements, and the provision on reparations, when linked with American avoidance of offering Russia economic aid, left Russia without the assistance she needed for the pressing task of economic reconstruction.

Russia had long been seeking substantial economic aid, and the American failure to offer it seemed to be part of a general strategy. Earlier Harriman had advised "that the development of friendly relations [with Russia] would depend upon a generous credit," and recommended "that the question of the credit should be tied into our overall diplomatic relations with the Soviet Union and at the appropriate time the Russians should be given to understand that our willingness to cooperate wholeheartedly with them in their vast reconstruction problem will depend upon their behavior in international matters." In January 1945 Roosevelt had decided not to discuss at Yalta the $6 billion credit to the Soviet Union, explaining privately, "I think it's very important that we hold this back and don't give them any promises until we get what we want." (Secretary Morgenthau, in vigorous disagreement, believed that both the President and Secretary of State Stettinius were wrong, and "that if they wanted to get the Russians to do something they should...do it nice.... Don't drive such a hard bargain that when you come through it does not taste good.") In future months American officials continued to delay, presumably using the prospect of a loan for political leverage. Shortly before Potsdam, the administration had secured congressional approval for a $1 billion loan fund which could have been used to assist Russia, but the issue of "credits to the Soviet Union" apparently was never even discussed.

Shunting aside the loan, the United States also retreated from Roosevelt's implied agreement at Yalta that reparations would be about $20 billion (half of which the Soviets would receive); Truman's new Secretary of State, James F. Byrnes, pointed out that the figures were simply the "basis" for discussion. (He was technically correct, but obviously Roosevelt had intended it as a general promise and Stalin had so understood it. Had it not been so intended, why had Churchill refused to endorse this section of the Yalta agreement?) Because Byrnes was unwilling to yield, the final agreement on reparations was similar to the terms that would have prevailed if there had been no agreement: the Soviet Union would fill her claims largely by removals from her own zone. That was the substance of the Potsdam agreement. The Russians also surrendered any hopes of participating in control of the heavily industrialized Ruhr, and confirmed the earlier retreat from the policy of dismemberment of Germany. They settled for an agreement that they could trade food and raw materials from their zone for 15 percent of such industrial capital equipment from the Western Zones "as is unnecessary for the German peace economy," and that the allies would transfer from the Western Zones "10 percent of such industrial capital equipment as is unnecessary for the German peace economy"—but the agreement left undefined what was necessary for the economy.

Potsdam, like Yalta, left many of the great questions unresolved. "One fact that stands out more clearly than others is that nothing is ever settled," wrote Lord Alanbrooke, Chief of the British Staff, in his diary. As he observed, neither the United States nor Russia had yielded significantly. Russia had refused to move from the areas that her armies occupied, and the United States had been vigorous in her efforts, but without offering economic assistance to gain concessions. Though the atomic bomb may not have greatly influenced Truman's actions in the months before Potsdam, the bomb certainly influenced his behavior at Potsdam. When he arrived he still wanted (and expected) Russian intervention in the Japanese war. During the conference he learned about the successful test at Alamogordo. With Russian intervention no longer necessary, Truman's position hardened noticeably. As sole possessor of the bomb, he had good reason to expect easier future dealings with Stalin. For months Stimson had been counseling that the bomb would be the "master card," and Truman, acting on Stimson's advice, even delayed the Potsdam Conference until a time when he would know about the bomb. On the eve of the conference the President had confided to an adviser, "If it explodes, as I think it will, I'll certainly have a hammer on those boys [the Russians]."

III

At Potsdam President Truman was "delighted" when Stimson brought him the news about the bomb on July 16. Upon learning more about the results of the test, Truman (according to Stimson) said "it gave him an entirely new feeling of confidence and he thanked me for having come to the conference and being present to help him in this way." The President's enthusiasm and new sense of power were soon apparent in his meetings with the other heads of state, for as Churchill notes (in Stimson's words), "Truman was evidently much fortified by something that had happened and...he stood up to the Russians in a most emphatic and decisive manner." After reading the full report on the Alamogordo explosion, Churchill said. "Now I know what happened to Truman yesterday. I couldn't understand it. When he got to the meeting after having read this report he was a changed man. He told the Russians just where they got off and generally bossed the whole meeting."

"From that moment [when we learned of the successful test] our outlook on the future was transformed," Churchill explained later. Forced earlier to concede parts of Eastern Europe to the Russians because Britain did not have the power to resist Soviet wishes and the United States had seemed to lack the desire, Churchill immediately savored the new possibilities. The Prime Minister (Lord Alanbrooke wrote in his diary about Churchill's enthusiasm) "was completely carried away ... we now had something in our hands which would redress the balance with the Russians. The secret of this explosive and the power to use it would completely alter the diplomatic equilibrium. . . . Now we had a new value which redressed our position (pushing out his chin and scowling); now we could say, "If you insist on doing this or that well . . . And then where were the Russians!"

Stimson and Byrnes had long understood that the bomb could influence future relations with Russia, and, after the successful test, they knew that Russian entry was no longer necessary to end the Japanese war. Upon Truman's direction, Stimson conferred at Potsdam with General Marshall and reported to the President that Marshall no longer saw a need for Russian intervention. "It is quite clear," cabled Churchill from Potsdam, "that the United States do not at the present time desire Russian participation in the war against Japan."

"The new explosive alone was sufficient to settle matters," Churchill reported. The bomb had displaced the Russians in the calculations of American policy-makers. The combat use of the bomb, then, was not viewed as the only way to end the Far Eastern war promptly. In July there was ample evidence that there were other possible strategies—a noncombat demonstration, a warning, a blockade. Yet, before authorizing the use of the bomb at Hiroshima, Truman did not try *any* of the possible strategies, including the three most likely: guaranteeing the position of the Japanese Emperor (and hence making surrender conditional), seeking a Russian declaration of war (or announcement of intent), or waiting for Russian entry into the war.

As an invasion of the Japanese mainland ws not scheduled until about November 1, and as Truman knew that the Japanese were sending out "peace feelers" and that the main obstacle to peace seemed to be the requirement of unconditional surrender (which threatened the position of the Emperor), he could wisely have revised the terms of surrender. At first Under Secretary of State Grew and then Stimson had urged Truman earlier to revise the terms in this way, and he had been sympathetic. But at Potsdam Stimson found that Truman and Byrnes had rejected his advice. As a result the proclamation issued from Potsdam by the United States, Great Britain, and China retained the demand for unconditional surrender when a guarantee of the Emperor's government might have removed the chief impediment to peace.

Nor was Truman willing to seek a Russian declaration of war (or even an announcement of intent). Even though American advisers had long believed that the *threat* of Russian entry might be sufficient to compel Japanese capitulation, Truman did not invite Stalin to sign the proclamation, which would have constituted a statement of Russian intent. There is even substantial evidence that Truman sought to delay Russian entry into the war.

Pledging to maintain the position of the Emperor, seeking a Russian declaration of war (or announcement of intent), awaiting Russian entry—each of these options, as well as others, had been proposed in the months before Hiroshima and Nagasaki. Each was available to Truman. Why did he not try one or more? No *definite* answer is possible. But it is clear that Truman was either incapable or unwilling to reexamine his earlier assumption (or decision) of using the bomb. Under the tutelage of Byrnes and Stimson, Truman had come to assume by July that the bomb should be used, and perhaps he was incapable of reconsidering this strategy because he found no compelling reason not to use the bomb. Or he may have consciously rejected the options because he wanted to use the bomb. Perhaps he was vindictive and wished to retaliate for Pearl Harbor and other atrocities. (In justifying the use of the bomb against the Japanese, he wrote a few days after Nagasaki, "The only language they seem to understand is the one we have been using to bombard them. When you have to deal with a beast you have to treat him as a beast.") Or, most likely, Truman agreed with Byrnes that using the bomb would advance other American policies: it would end the war before the Russians could gain a hold in Manchuria, it would permit the United States to exclude Russia from the occupation government of Japan, and it would make the Soviets more manageable in Eastern Europe. It would enable the United States to shape the peace according to its own standards.

At minimum, then, the use of the bomb reveals the moral insensitivity of the President—whether he used it because the moral implications did not compel a reexamination of assumptions, or because he sought retribution, or because he sought to keep Russia out of Manchuria and the occupation government of Japan, and to make her more manageable in Eastern Europe. In 1945 American foreign policy was not innocent, nor was it unconcerned about Russian power, nor did it assume that the United States lacked the power to impose its will on the Russian state, nor was it characterized by high moral purpose or consistent dedication to humanitarian principles.

IV

...While the Soviet Union would not generally permit in Eastern Europe conditions that conformed to Western ideals, Stalin was pursuing a cautious policy and seeking accommodation with the West. He was willing to allow capitalism but was suspicious of American efforts at economic penetration which could lead to political dominance. Though by the autumn of 1945 the governments in Russia's general area of influence were subservient in foreign policy, they varied in form and in degree of independence—democracy in Czechoslovakia (the only country in this area with a democratic tradition), free elections and the overthrow of the Communist party in Hungary, a Communist-formed coalition government in Bulgaria, a broadly based but Communist-dominated government in Poland, and a Soviet-imposed government in Rumania (the most anti-Russian of these nations). In all of these countries Communists controlled the ministries of interior (the police) and were able to suppress anti-Soviet groups, including anti-communist democrats.

Those who have attributed to Russia a policy of inexorable expansion have often neglected this immediate postwar period, or they have interpreted it simply as a necessary preliminary (a cunning strategy to allay American suspicions until the American Army demobilized and left the continent) to the consolidation and extension of power in east-central Europe. From this perspective, however, much of Stalin's behavior becomes strangely contradictory and potentially self-defeating. If he had planned to create puppets rather than an area of "friendly governments," why (as Isaac Deutscher asks) did Stalin "so stubbornly refuse to make any concessions to the Poles over their eastern frontiers?" Certainly, also, his demand for reparations from Hungary, Rumania, and Bulgaria would have been unnecessary if he had planned to take over these countries. (America's insistence upon using a loan to Russia to achieve political goals, and the nearly twenty-month delay after Russia first submitted a specific proposal for assistance, led Harriman to suggest in November that the loan policy "may have contributed to their [Russian] avaricious policies in the countries occupied or liberated by the Red Army.")

Russian sources are closed, so it is not possible to prove that Soviet intentions were conservative; nor for the same reason is it possible for those who adhere to the thesis of inexorable Soviet expansion to prove their theory. But the available evidence better supports the thesis that these years should be viewed not as a cunning preliminary to the harshness of 1947 and afterward, but as an attempt to establish a *modus vivendi* with the West and to protect "socialism in one country." This interpretation explains more adequately why the Russians delayed nearly three years before ending dissent and hardening policies in the countries behind their own military lines. It would also explain why the Communist parties in France and Italy were cooperating with the coalition governments until these parties were forced out of the coalitions in 1947. The American government had long hoped for the exclusion of these Communist parties, and in Italy, at least, American intimations of greater economic aid to a government without Communists was an effective lever. At the same time Stalin was seeking to prevent the revolution in Greece.

If the Russian policy was conservative and sought accommodation (as now seems likely), then its failure must be explained by looking beyond Russian actions. Historians must reexamine this period and reconsider American policies. Were they directed toward compromise? Can they be judged as having sought adjustment? Or did they demand acquiescence to the American world view, thus thwarting real negotiations?

There is considerable evidence that American actions clearly changed after Roosevelt's death. Slowly abandoning the tactics of accommodation, they became even more vigorous after Hiroshima. The insistence upon rolling back Soviet influence in Eastern Europe, the reluctance to grant a loan for Russian reconstruction, the inability to reach an agreement on Germany, the maintenance of the nuclear monopoly—all of these could have contributed to the sense of Russian insecurity. The point, then, is that in 1945 and 1946 there may still have been possibilities for negotiations and settlements, for accommodations and adjustments, if the United States had been willing to recognize Soviet fears, to accept Soviet power in her areas of influence, and to ease anxieties.

V

In October 1945 President Truman delivered what Washington officials called his "getting tough with the Russians" speech. Proclaiming that American policy was "based firmly on fundamental principles of righteousness and justice," he promised that the United States "shall not give our approval to any compromise with evil." In a veiled assault on Soviet actions in Eastern Europe, he declared, "We shall refuse to recognize any government imposed on any nation by the force of any foreign power." Tacitly opposing the bilateral trading practices of Russia, he asserted as a principle of American foreign policy the doctrine of the "open door"—all nations "should have access on equal terms to the trade and the raw materials of the world." At the same time, however, Truman disregarded the fact of American power in Latin America and emphasized that the Monroe Doctrine (in expanded form) remained a cherished part of American policy there: "...the sovereign states of the Western Hemisphere, without interference from outside the Western Hemisphere, must work together as good neighbors in the solution of their common economic problems."

"Soviet current policy," concluded a secret report by the Deputy Director of Naval Intelligence a few months later, "is to establish a Soviet Monroe Doctrine for the area under her shadow, primarily and urgently for security, secondarily to facilitate the eventual emergence of the USSR as a power which could not be menaced by any other world combination of powers." The report did not expect the Soviets "...to take any action during the next five years which might develop into hostilities with Anglo-Americans," but anticipated attempts to build up intelligence and potential sabotage networks, "encouragement of Communist parties in all countries potentially to weaken antagonists, and in colonial areas to pave the way for 'anti-imperialist' disorders and revolutions as a means of sapping the strength of...chief remaining European rivals, Britain and France." "Present Soviet maneuvers to control North Iran," the report explained, were conceived to "push...from their own oil...and closer to the enemy's oil." There was no need to fear military expansion beyond this security zone, suggested the report, for the Soviet Union was economically exhausted, its population undernourished and dislocated, its industry and transportation "in an advanced state of deterioration." Despite suggestions that Soviet policy was rather cautious, Truman was reaching a more militant conclusion. "Unless Russia is faced with an iron fist and strong language," asserted Truman to his Secretary of State in January, "another war is in the making. Only one language do they understand—'how many divisions have you'...I'm tired of babying the Soviets."

During the winter months Byrnes, Senator Vandenberg, and John Foster Dulles, a Republican adviser on foreign policy, publicly attacked Russian policies. Vandenberg warned "our Russian ally" that the United States could not ignore "a unilateral gnawing away at the status quo." After these attacks, Churchill, accompanied by the President, delivered at Fulton, Missouri, a speech that announced the opening of the Cold War. "From Stettin in the Baltic to Trieste in the Adriatic, an iron curtain has descended across the Continent," declared the former British war leader. Condemning the establishment of "police governments" in Eastern Europe and warning of "Communist fifth columns or ... parties elsewhere," Churchill, with Truman's approval, called for an Anglo-American alliance to create "conditions of freedom and democracy as rapidly as possible in all [these] countries." The Soviet Union, he contended, did not want war, only "the fruits of war and the indefinite expansion of their power and doctrines." Such dangers could not be removed "by closing our eyes to them ... nor will they be removed by a policy of appeasement." While he said that it was "not our duty *at this time* ... to interfere forcibly in the internal affairs" of Eastern European countries, Churchill implied that intervention was advisable when Anglo-American forces were strengthened. His message was clear:"... the old doctrine of the balance of power is unsound. We cannot afford ... to work on narrow margins, offering temptations to a trial of strength."

This was, as James Warburg later wrote, the early "idea of the containment doctrine ... [and] the first public expression of the idea of a 'policy of liberation,' " which Dulles would later promulgate. Truman's presence on the platform at Fulton implied that Churchill's statement had official American endorsement, and though the President lamely denied afterward that he had known about the contents of the speech, he had actually discussed it with Churchill for two hours. Despite official denials and brief, widespread popular opposition to Churchill's message (according to public opinion polls), American policy was becoming clearly militant. It was not responding to a threat of immediate military danger; it was operating from the position of overwhelming power, and in the self-proclaimed conviction of righteousness.

Undoubtedly Truman also agreed with the former Prime Minister when Churchill said at Fulton:

It would ... be wrong and imprudent to intrust the secret knowledge of experience of the atomic bomb, which the United States, Great Britain and Canada now share, to the world organization.... No one in any country has slept less well in their beds because this knowledge and the method and raw material to apply it are at present ... in American hands. I do not believe that we should all have slept so soundly had the positions been reversed and some Communist or neo-Fascist state monopolized, for the time being, these dread agencies. ... Ultimately, when the essential brotherhood of man is truly embodied and expressed in a world organization, these powers may be confided to it.

Here, in classic form, was a theme that would dominate the American dialogue on the Cold War—the assertion of the purity of Anglo-American intentions and the assumption that the opposing power was malevolent and had no justifiable interests, no justifiable fears, and should place its trust in a Pax Americana (or a Pax Anglo-Americana). Under Anglo-American power the world could be transformed, order maintained, and Anglo-American principles extended. Stalin characterized Churchill's message as, "Something in the nature of an ultimatum: 'Accept our rule voluntarily, and then all will be well: otherwise war is inevitable.' "

3. Harry Truman and the Fair Deal

ALONZO L. HAMBY

In 1946 President Harry S Truman enunciated a program called the Fair Deal, which was to be an extension of Franklin Roosevelt's New Deal. The rhetoric of Truman's speeches, especially his inaugural address of 1949, promised much, and Hamby argues that the Fair Deal definitely extended FDR's work. But Truman was by nature a moderate, a border-state politician whose very essence was compromise. Moreover, some centers of Democratic strength, notably the urban machines, seemed to stand still rather than to grow in social awareness. Did local leaders urge the Truman administration to "go slow" because welfare laws jeopardized their organizations? One historian even asks whether "the Democratic coalition had ceased to be a 'have-not' coalition and had become interested chiefly in maintaining earlier gains." To question the possibilities of the New Deal and Fair Deal is to ask about the possibilities of government today.

"Every segment of our population and every individual has a right to expect from our Government a fair deal," declared Harry S Truman in early 1949. In 1945 and 1946 the Truman administration had almost crumbled under the stresses of postwar reconversion; in 1947 and 1948 it had fought a frustrating, if politically rewarding, battle with the Republican Eightieth Congress. Buoyed by his remarkable victory of 1948 and given Democratic majorities in both houses of Congress, Truman hoped to achieve an impressive record of domestic reform. The president systematized his past proposals, added some new ones, and gave his program a name that would both connect his administration with the legacy of the New Deal and give it a distinct identity. The Fair Deal, while based solidly upon the New Deal tradition, differed from its predecessor in significant aspects of mood and detail. It reflected not only Truman's own aspirations but also a style of liberalism that had begun to move beyond the New Deal during World War II and had come to maturity during the early years of the cold war—"the vital center." ...

The legislative goals Truman announced for his administration, while not devised to meet the needs of an abstract theory, were well in tune with the vital-center approach: anti-inflation measures, a more progressive tax structure, repeal of the Taft-Hartley Act, a higher minimum wage, a farm program based on the concepts of abundant production and parity income, resource development and public power programs, expansion of social security, national medical insurance, federal aid to education, extensive housing legislation, and civil rights bills. The pres-

Abridged from "The Vital Center, the Fair Deal, and the Quest for a Liberal Political Economy" by Alonzo L. Hamby. *American Historical Review,* 77 (June, 1972), 653-678. Copyright © by Alonzo L. Hamby. Reprinted by permission of the author.

ident's most controversial request was for authority to increase plant facilities in such basic industries as steel, preferably through federal financing of private enterprise but through outright government construction if necessary. Roundly condemned by right-wing opponents as "socialistic" and soon dropped by the administration, the proposal was actually intended to meet the demands of a prosperous, growing capitalist economy and emerged from the Fair Deal's search for the proper degree of government intervention to preserve the established American economic structure. "Between the reactionaries of the extreme left with their talk about revolution and class warfare, and the reactionaries of the extreme right with their hysterical cries of bankruptcy and despair, lies the way of progress," Truman declared in November 1949.

The Fair Deal was a conscious effort to continue the purpose of the New Deal but not necessarily its methods. Not forced to meet the emergencies of economic depression, given a solid point of departure by their predecessors, and led by a president more prone than FDR to demand programmatic coherence, the Fair Dealers made a systematic effort to discover techniques that would be at once more equitable and more practical in alleviating the problems of unequal wealth and opportunity. Thinking in terms of abundance rather than scarcity, they attempted to adapt the New Deal tradition to postwar prosperity. Seeking to go beyond the New Deal while preserving its objectives, the Truman administration advocated a more sweeping and better-ordered reform agenda. Yet in the quest for political means, Truman and the vital-center liberals could only fall back upon one of the oldest dreams of American reform—the Jacksonian-Populist vision of a union of producing classes, an invincible farmer-labor coalition. While superficially plausible, the Fair Deal's political strategy proved too weak to handle the burden thrust upon it.

The Fair Deal seemed to oscillate between militancy and moderation. New Dealers had frequently gloried in accusations of "liberalism" or "radicalism"; Fair Dealers tended to shrink from such labels. The New Dealers had often lusted for political combat; the Fair Dealers were generally more low-keyed. Election campaigns demanded an aggressiveness that would arouse the Democratic presidential party, but the continued strength of the conservative coalition in Congress dictated accommodation in the post-election efforts to secure passage of legislative proposals. Such tactics reflected Truman's personal political experience and instincts, but they also developed naturally out of the climate of postwar America. The crisis of economic depression had produced one style of political rhetoric; the problems of prosperity and inflation brought forth another.

The Fair Deal mirrored Truman's policy preferences and approach to politics; it was no more the president's personal creation, however, than the New Deal had been Roosevelt's. Just as FDR's advisers had formulated much of the New Deal, a group of liberals developed much of the content and tactics of the Fair Deal. For the most part these were the men who had formed a liberal caucus within the administration in early 1947 shortly after the Republican triumph in the congressional elections of 1946, had worked to sway the president toward the left in his policy recommendations and campaign tactics, and had played a significant, if not an all-embracing, role in Truman's victory in 1948. Truman's special counsel, Clark M. Clifford, was perhaps the most prominent member of the group, but Clifford, although a shrewd political analyst, a persuasive advocate, and an extremely valuable administrative chief of staff, was neither the caucus's organizer nor a creative liberal thinker. Others gave the Fair Deal its substance as a program descending from the New Deal yet distinct from it.…

During 1949 and early 1950 the Truman administration managed a record of substantial legislative accomplishment, but it consisted almost entirely of additions to such New Deal programs as the minimum wage, social security, and public power. The Housing Act of 1949, with its provisions for large-scale public housing, appeared to be a breakthrough, but weak administration, local opposition, and inadequate financing subsequently vitiated hopes that it would help the poor. Acting on his executive authority, Truman took an important step by forcing the army to agree to a policy of desegregation. The heart of the Fair Deal, however—repeal of the Taft-Hartley Act, civil rights legislation, aid to education, national medical insurance, and the Brannan Plan—failed in Congress. Given the power of the well-entrenched conservative coalition and a wide-spread mood of public apathy about big new reforms, Truman could only enlarge upon the record of his predecessor.

Democratic strategists hoped for a mandate in the congressional elections of 1950. In the spring Truman made a successful whistle-stop tour of the West and Midwest, rousing party enthusiasm and apparently demonstrating a solid personal popularity. Loveland's victory provided further encouragement, and in California the aggressive Fair Dealer Helen Gahagan Douglas won the Democratic nomination for the Senate by a thumping margin. Two incumbent Fair Deal supporters—Frank Graham of North Carolina and Claude Pepper of Florida—lost their senatorial primaries, but, as Southerners who had run a foul of the race issue, they did not seem to be indicators of national trends. Nevertheless, the hope of cutting into the strength of the conservative opposition ran counter to the historical pattern of mid-term elections. The beginning of the Korean War at the end of June destroyed any chances of success.

The most immediate impact of Korea was to refuel an anti-Communist extremism that might otherwise have sputtered out. Senator Joseph R. McCarthy had begun his rise to prominence in February 1950, but he had failed to prove any of his multiple allegations and seemed definitively discredited by the investigations of a special Senate committee headed by Millard Tydings. McCarthy, it is true, was a talented demagogue who should have been taken more seriously by the liberals and the Truman administration in early 1950, but it seems probable that his appeal would have waned more quickly if the cold war with communism had not suddenly become hot. As it was, many of his Senate colleagues rushed to emulate him. In September 1950 Congress passed the McCarran Internal Security Act; only a handful of congressional liberals dared dissent from the overwhelming vote in favor. Truman's subsequent veto was intelligent and courageous, but was issued more for the history books than with any real hope of success. In the subsequent campaign, liberal Democrats, whether they had voted for the McCarran Act or not, found themselves facing charges of softness toward communism.

The war hurt the administration in other ways. It touched off a brief but serious inflation, which caused widespread consumer irritation. By stimulating demand for agricultural products it brought most farm prices up to parity levels and thereby undercut whatever attractiveness the Brannan Plan had developed in rural areas. Finally it removed the Democratic party's most effective spokesman—the president—from active participation in the campaign. Forced to play the role of war leader, Truman allowed himself only one major partisan speech, delivered in St. Louis on the eve of the balloting.

The Fair Deal might have been a winning issue in a nation oriented toward domestic concerns and recovering from an economic recession; it had much less appeal in a country obsessed with Communist aggression and experiencing an inflationary war boom. The reaction against the administration was especially strong in the Midwest. Indiana's Democratic aspirant for the Senate asked Oscar Ewing to stay out of the state. In Iowa, Loveland desperately attempted to reverse his identification with the Brannan Plan. In Missouri the managers of senatorial candidate Thomas C. Hennings, Jr. privately asked White House aides to make Truman's St. Louis speech a foreign policy address that would skip lightly over Fair Deal issues. A few days before the election the columnist Stewart Alsop returned from a Midwestern trip convinced that the region had never been more conservative. Nevertheless, Truman's political advisers, and probably Truman himself, felt that the Fair Deal still had appeal. Given the basic strength of the economy and the victories in Korea that followed the Inchon landing, the White House believed that the Democrats could easily rebut generalized charges of fumbling or softness toward communism. In mid-October the Democratic National Committee and many local leaders were so confident of success that their main concern was simply to get out the vote.

The November results, however, showed a Democratic loss of twenty-eight seats in the House of Representatives and five seats in the Senate. Truman seized every opportunity to remind all who would listen that the numbers were small by traditional mid-term standards. Liberal political analysts, including Kenneth Hechler, a White House staffer, and Gus Tyler of the International Ladies Garment Workers Union, subjected the returns to close scrutiny and all but pronounced a Democratic victory. All the same, most of the Democrats who went under had been staunch Fair Dealers. Republican candidates, including John Marshall Butler in Maryland, Richard M. Nixon in California, Everett McKinley Dirksen in Illinois, and Robert A. Taft in Ohio, scored some of the most spectacular GOP victories by blending right-wing conservatism with McCarthyism. The Midwestern losses were especially disappointing. Hechler argued that the corn-belt vote primarily reflected urban defections and that the Democrats had done comparatively well among farmers. Perhaps so, but for all practical purposes the results put an end to the Brannan strategy of constructing a farmer-labor coalition. Truman was probably more accurate than Hechler when, with characteristic overstatement, he privately expressed his disappointment: "The main trouble with the farmers is that they hate labor so badly that they will not vote for their own interests."

Thereafter, with the Chinese intervention transforming the Korean War into a more serious conflict and with the dismissal of General Douglas MacArthur in April 1951, Truman faced a tough attack from a Republican opposition determined to capitalize upon the frustrations of Korea. Finding it necessary to place party unity above all else, he quietly shelved most of his domestic legislative program and sought to bring the conservative wing of his party behind his military and defense policies. He secretly asked Richard B. Russell of Georgia, the kingpin of the Southern conservatives, to assume the Democratic leadership in the Senate. Russell, content with the substance of power, declined and gave his nod to Ernest W. McFarland of Arizona, an amiable tool of the Southern bloc; Truman made no effort to prevent McFarland's selection as Senate majority leader. The president's State of the Union message was devoted almost entirely to foreign policy and defense mobilization and mentioned social welfare programs only as an after-thought. Subsequently Truman told a press conference that while he supported the Fair Deal as much as ever, "first things come first, and our defense programs must have top priority."

Truman's success in achieving a minimum degree of party unity became apparent in the weeks of investigation and accusation that followed General MacArthur's return to America. Russell, playing the role of parliamentarian-statesman to the hilt and cashing in on his great prestige with senators of both parties, chaired the Senate committee that looked into the MacArthur incident, and he saw to it that the administration was able to deliver a thorough rebuttal to the general. The Northern liberal, Brien McMahon of Connecticut, relentlessly grilled hostile witnesses. The Western representative of oil and gas interests, Robert S. Kerr of Oklahoma, lashed out at MacArthur himself with a vehemence and effectiveness that no other Democrat could match. The tandem efforts of Russell, McMahon, and Kerr demonstrated the new party solidarity, but in terms of the Fair Deal the price was high.

In July 1951 the Federal Power Commission renounced the authority to regulate "independent" (non-pipeline-owning) natural gas producers. The ruling amounted to an administrative enactment of a bill, sponsored by Kerr, which Truman had vetoed a year earlier; Truman's close friend and most recent appointee to the Federal Power Commission, Mon Wallgren, cast the deciding vote. Although he talked like a militant liberal in a private conversation with ADA leaders, the president stalled throughout 1951 on repeated demands for the establishment of a Korean War Fair Employment Practices Committee. In December the administration established an ineffective Committee on Government Contract Compliance. Other domestic programs were soft-pedaled to near-invisibility.

Yet even the Korean War was not entirely inimical to reform. Its exigencies forced the army to transform its policy of integration into practice. Korea also provided a test for one of the basic underpinnings of the Fair Deal—Leon Keyserling's philosophy of economic expansion.

Truman did not in the end fully embrace Keyserling's policies, but in the main he followed the guidance of his chief economic adviser. The Korean War years demonstrated the extent to which Keyserling's economics diverged from conventional New Deal-World War II Keynesianism and revealed both the strengths and weaknesses of his approach.

From the outbreak of the fighting, most liberals favored either immediate strong economic controls akin to those that had held down inflation in World War II or at least the establishment of stand-by machinery that could impose them rapidly. Truman disliked such measures on the basis of both principle and politics. He and his diplomatic advisers also wanted to signal the Soviet Union that the United States regarded the North Korean attack as a limited challenge meriting a limited response. Keyserling's expansionary economics provided an attractive alternative to the liberal clamor for controls. Convinced that extensive controls would put the economy in a straitjacket and retard the expansion necessary to meet both consumer and defense needs and assuming a North Korean defeat in a few months, the administration decided to accept a short-term, war-scare inflation (probably unavoidable in any case) and concentrate on economic growth, which would be underwritten in large measure by tax incentives for business. An expanding economy would be the best long-term answer to inflation: growth policies could fit a small war into the economy, avoid the social and political strains accompanying wartime controls, and reduce inflationary pressures to a level at which fiscal and monetary policies could contain them. Liberals outside the administration watched with alarm as prices went up, but Truman and Keyserling continued to gamble on a quick end to the war and the development of an economy capable of producing both guns and butter.

Their plan might have worked fairly well had the United States not overreached itself militarily in Korea. The Chinese intervention of November 1950 wrecked hopes of a quick recovery, set off another round of scare buying, and intensified war demands upon the economy. The administration quickly threw up a price-wage control structure, but by the end of February 1951, eight months after the beginning of the Korean conflict, the consumer price index had risen eight per cent (an annual rate of twelve per cent). Keyserling agreed that the new situation necessitated controls, but he accepted them with reluctance and sought to keep them as simple as possible, even at the risk of benefiting profiteers. "We'll never be able to out-control the Russians," he told a Senate committee, "but we can out-produce them." Speaking to an ADA economic conference, he asserted that many liberals, in their opposition to tax breaks for large business and in their demands for stronger controls, were confusing the Korean War with World War II and "engaging merely in hackneyed slogans out of the past."

Most liberals disagreed with Keyserling's emphases. As production was his first imperative, an end to the wage-price spiral was theirs. "Unless we are willing seriously to endanger the basis of existence of the American middle class, we must stop prices from rising," wrote Hans Landsberg in the *Reporter*. The liberals assumed that economic expansion was possible within a framework of rigid, tightly administered controls. Chester Bowles observed that the controlled economy of World

War II had turned out a twofold increase in industrial production. John Kenneth Galbraith rejected the idea that Keyserling's expansionary policies could outrun the inflationary pressures they themselves created. The bulk of liberals regarded the administration approach as dangerous, the product of political expediency rather than sound economic analysis.

Neither Keyserling nor the more conventional liberals won a complete victory. Truman, who understood all too well the political dangers of a prolonged inflation, made substantial concessions to the controllers, led by Michael V. DiSalle, head of the Office of Price Stabilization. In the interest of fairness Truman approved a more complex system of price controls than Keyserling thought desirable, giving DiSalle considerable leeway to roll back some prices while approving advances in other areas. By March 1951 inflation was under control; during the final ten months of the year the cost-of-living index increased by less than two and one-half per cent. The waves of scare buying that followed the North Korean attack and the Chinese intervention had subsided. Higer taxes and restraints on credit were beginning to affect consumer buying. The Federal Reserve System, despite opposition from the administration, initiated a stringent monetary policy. Tax breaks for businesses expanding plant facilities presaged increased productive capacity. All these factors, along with the government stabilization program, discouraged an inflationary psychology.

At the time, however, it appeared to most economic observers that the lull was only temporary. Many of the administration's liberal critics refused even to admit the existence of a lull and called for tougher controls as if prices were still skyrocketing. More moderate analysts feared that the impact of large government defense orders would set off another inflationary spiral in the fall. Influenced by such expectations, Truman ostentatiously mounted an anti-inflation crusade, demanding that Congress not only extend his control authority, due to expire on June 30, but actually strengthen it. In fact the Defense Production Act of 1951 weakened the president's powers considerably. Truman signed it reluctantly, comparing it to "a bulldozer, crashing aimlessly through existing pricing formulas, leaving havoc in its wake." A subsequent tax bill failed to meet administration revenue requests and increased the danger of serious inflation.

Yet price stability persisted through 1952, in large measure because defense production, hampered by multiple shortages and bottlenecks, lagged far behind its timetable. In late 1951 these problems and the fear of renewed inflation led Truman to decide in favor of a "stretch-out" of defense production schedules; in doing so he overrode Keyserling's urgings for an all-out effort to break the bottlenecks and concentrate relentlessly upon expansion. Given the serious problems in defense industry, the stretch-out decision may have seemed necessary to Truman, but it also carried the dividend of economic stability.

The president had steered a course between the orthodox liberal obsession with inflation and Keyserling's easy disregard of its perils; perhaps as a result the economy failed to expand at the rate Keyserling had hoped. On balance, however, Truman's approach to the political economy of the Korean War was closer to Keyserling's, and the conflict produced a dramatic economic growth. Before the war the peak gross national product had been $285 billion in 1948; by the end of 1952 the GNP (measured in constant dollar values) had reached a rate of $350 billion. The production index of durable manufactured goods had averaged 237 in 1950; by the last quarter of 1952 it had reached 313. The expansion, even if less than Keyserling had wanted, was breathtaking. Moreover, aside from the probably unavoidable inflation that accompanied the early months of the war, this remarkable growth had occurred in a climate of economic stability. Using a somewhat more orthodox approach than Keyserling preferred, the administration had achieved one of the central goals of the Fair Deal.

In its efforts to carry on with the reforming impulse of the New Deal the Truman administration faced nearly insuperable obstacles. A loosely knit but nonetheless effective conservative coalition had controlled Congress since 1939, successfully defying Franklin Roosevelt long before it had to deal with Truman. Postwar prosperity muted economic liberalism and encouraged a mood of apathy toward new reform breakthroughs, although Truman's victory in 1948 indicated that most of the elements of the old Roosevelt coalition were determined to preserve the gains of the New Deal. The cold war probably made it more difficult to focus public attention upon reform and dealt severe blows to civil liberties. It did, however, give impetus to the movement for Negro equality.

The Fair Deal attempted to adapt liberalism to the new conditions. Under the intellectual leadership of Leon Keyserling it formulated policies that sought to transcend the conflicts of the New Deal era by encouraging an economic growth that could provide abundance for all Americans. With Charles Brannan pointing the way, the Truman administration tried to translate abundance into a political coalition that could provide the votes for its social welfare policies. The political strategy, ambitious but unrealistic, collapsed under the weight of the Korean War. Keyserling's economics, on the other hand, received a lift from Korea; in a period of adversity the Fair Deal was able to achieve at least one of its objectives.

4. Nixon Agonistes: The Checkers Speech

GARRY WILLS

Nixon-watching remains a minor national pastime. Anyone who gets to be President is usually a highly complex person, and political success at any level often requires a certain amount of evasion, or what Richard Nixon himself has called being "devious... in the best sense." However understandable evasiveness may be, it is ironic that the unflattering reputation for deviousness that has accompanied Nixon throughout his political career comes in sizable part from his own famous "Checkers" speech of 1952, a televised response to charges that the candidate had spent campaign funds on personal needs. ("Checkers" was the Nixons' cocker spaniel, an irrelevant animal Nixon dragged into the speech along with his wife's "cloth" coat.

The Checkers speech ushered in the age of television politics. Senator Estes Kefauver, investigating criminals in 1950, had made himself a household name in a series of nationally televised hearings, but he had not tailored the medium to his ends. Nixon was the first politician to realize the immense possibilities of television and to exploit almost every subtle popular response the new medium could evoke. Intellectuals have never held the Checkers speech in much esteem, seeing in it an unvarnished attempt to manipulate public emotions. Garry Wills, however, focuses on the tensions and political infighting that surged around the vice-presidential candidate during the week preceding the speech, and he argues persuasively that the Checkers speech was both Nixon's only chance to save his career and also a direct confrontation with the presidential candidate, Dwight D. Eisenhower.

One other thing I probably should tell you, because if I don't they'll probably be saying this about me too, we did get something—a gift—after the election. A man down in Texas heard Pat on the radio mention the fact that our two youngsters would like to have a dog. And, believe it or not, the day before we left on this campaign trip we got a message from Union Station in Baltimore saying that they had a package for us. We went down to get it. You know what it was? It was a little cocker spaniel dog in a crate that he sent all the way from Texas. Black and white spotted. And our little girl—Tricia, the six-year old—named it Checkers. And you know the kids love that dog and I just want to say this right now, that regardless of what they say about it, we're going to keep it.—The Checkers Speech

Riding in the staff bus during Nixon's 1968 campaign, I talked with one of his speech writers about the convention in Miami. Nixon's wooing of Strom Thurmond had been much criticized. But Nixon's man now said the acceptance speech eclipsed everything that went before: "That was so clearly the major event of the convention—a brilliant job. To talk about that convention is, simply, to talk about that speech. What did *you* think of it?" I answered that it reminded me of the Checkers speech. The comment seemed to horrify my interlocutor; and Professor Martin Anderson, traveling with Nixon as an adviser on urban matters, turned around in the seat before us to object: "People forget that the Checkers speech was a political master stroke, an act of political genius!" But I had not forgotten; that was, I assured him, my point.

Professor Anderson's defensiveness was understandable. Nixon has often been sneered at, over the years, for his television speech in the campaign of 1952. The very term "Checkers speech," reducing the whole broadcast to its saccharine doggy-passage, is a judgment in it-self. But that broadcast saved Nixon's career, and made history. By the beginning of the 1968 campaign, sixteen years later, it was a journalistic commonplace that Nixon did not appear to advantage on television. His wan first TV encounter with John Kennedy had dimmed the public's earlier impression. But Nixon only risked that debate with Kennedy be-cause he had such a record of success on the TV screen: in the history of that medium, his 1952 speech was probably a greater milestone than the presidential debate that came eight years later. Nixon first demonstrated the political uses and impact of television. In one half-hour Nixon con-verted himself from a liability, breathing his last, to one of the few peo-ple who could add to Eisenhower's preternatural appeal—who could gild the lily. For the first time, people saw a living political drama on their TV sets—a man fighting for his whole career and future—and they judged him under that strain. It was an even greater achievement than it seemed. He had only a short time to prepare for it. The show, forced on him, was meant as a form of political euthanasia. He came into the studio still reeling from distractions and new demoralizing blows.

Nixon, naturally, puts the Checkers speech, along with the whole "fund crisis," among the six crises he survived with credit. It belongs there. He probably displayed more sheer nerve in that crisis than in any of the others. As a freshman in Congress, he did not stand to lose so much by the Hiss investigation. He had, moreover, an unsuspected hoard of evidence in that encounter; and he was backed by dedicated men like Father Cronin, while backing another dedicated man, Whit-taker Chambers. In the crises he deals with after 1952, he was a Vice-President, in some way speaking for the nation, buoyed by its resources, defending it as much as himself; never totally without dignity. But at the time when he went onto the TV screen in 1952, he was hunted and alone. Nine years later he would write of that ordeal, "This speech was to be the most important of my life. I felt now that it was my battle alone. I had been deserted by so many I had thought were friends but who panicked in battle when the first shot was fired." It was, without exaggeration, "the most searing personal crisis of my life." It was also the experience that took the glitter out of politics for Mrs. Nixon....

The first news story broke on Thursday, September 18. There had been warnings in the Nixon camp all the four preceding days. A news-man in Washington asked Nixon about the fund on Sunday. Monday, three other reporters checked facts with Dana Smith, the administrator of the fund. By Wednesday, Jim Bassett, Nixon's press secretary, heard something was brewing from his old reporter friends. The candidate had just begun his first major tour—a whistlestop north through California; when the train stopped for water around midnight, a worried staff man waited with more rumors. Thursday, it broke: the New York *Post* had a story with the headline, SECRET RICH MEN'S TRUST FUND KEEPS NIXON IN STYLE FAR BEYOND HIS SALARY. The story did not justify that sensational summary, and neither did subsequent investigation. The fund was public, independently audited, earmarked for campaign expenses, and collected in small donations over two years by known Nixon campaign backers. It was neither illegal nor unethical. And the press soon discovered that the Democratic nominee, Adlai Stevenson, had similar funds, only larger in their amount and looser in their administration. Why, then, was so much made of Nixon's fund, and so little of Stevenson's?

Nixon's official explanation, at the time, was his standard charge: the commies were behind it all. By Friday morning, the day after the charge was published, there were hecklers at his train stops to shout "Tell us about the sixteen thousand!" At a town called Marysville, he did tell them. His own version of that speech, included in his book, is more moderate than some others; but even his excerpts seem gamy enough: "You folks know the work that I did investigating Communists in the United States. Ever since I have done that work the Communists and the left-wingers have been fighting me with every possible smear. When I received the nomination for the Vice-Presidency I was warned that if I continued to attack the Communists in this government they would continue to smear me. And believe me, you can expect that they will continue to do so. They started it yesterday. They have tried to say that I had taken $16,000 for my personal use." The *they* is conveniently vague throughout. The—i.e., the New York *Post* and other papers—published the charge. Go far enough back up the paragraph, through intervening "theys," and you find that the antecedent is, more immediately, "the Communists in this Government," and, in the first place, "Communists and [broad sweep here] left-wingers." The explanation is beautifully lucid and inclusive (if a little unspecific about the machinery that makes the nation's press perform the communists' bidding): since the publicizing or nonpublicizing of fund scandals is at the disposal of communists, who were (naturally) supporting Adlai Stevenson, the Stevenson fund got (naturally) no publicity like that accorded to Nixon.

Behind this funny explanation, there are scattered but clear indications, in his book, of the true story, a sad one. At one point Nixon asks why his own statement of the "basic facts" about the fund received so little attention from the press. His answer ignores the conspiratorial explanation given eight pages earlier, and supplies four reasons, two of them technical (denials never get as big a play as accusations in the press, news travels east to west and he was in California), and two more substantive: reporters are mainly Democrats (though Nixon admits that publishers are mainly Republicans, which makes for some balance), and "the big-name, influential Washington reporters cover the presidential candidates while the less-known reporters are assigned to the vice-presidential candidates." The last reason, the real one, looks like another point of newspaper mechanics—the mere logistics of press assignment; until we ask why that should matter. The answer, in Nixon's own words, is that his own press release "got lost in the welter of news and speculation over whether General Eisenhower would or would not choose to find a new running mate." *That* was the news on Eisenhower's train—because Ike's advisers were known to be searching for a way to dump Nixon, and Ike was a man who at this stage followed his advisers almost blindly. In short, the Nixon fund was a big story because Eisenhower, by his silence and hints and uneasiness, made it one. For no other reason.

It was natural for Eisenhower to acquiesce in a staff decision to drop Nixon. That staff had presented him with Nixon in the first place. (Ike's knowledge of his running mate was very slim—he thought, for instance, he was forty-two rather than thirty-nine.) The General had, in fact, learned of Nixon's choice at exactly the same time Nixon did. When Herb Brownell asked Ike what he thought of Nixon, the presidential nominee expressed surprise that the decision was his to make. He said he would leave the matter to Brownell, provided the latter consulted "the collective judgment of the leaders of the party" (the top man, in military politics, protects himself by putting a subordinate in charge of the operation, under staff scrutiny). So Brownell called a meeting of the party's leaders, and went through the form of considering Taft and others. But then Dewey got up, to speak for the winning camp. Nixon he said, and Nixon it was. That decision made, Brownell went to the phone, dialed Nixon, and had him listen in while, on another phone, he told Eisenhower that the choice had been made.

As the fund story broke, Nixon wondered where Ike stood. Thursday went by, and Friday. No word from the General—to the public, or to Nixon. But the Establishment was at work: the very thing that had made Nixon good "for balance" made him unpalatable in himself, seen through Establishment eyes. He was there to draw in the yokels. If there was any doubt about his ability to do that, no one would feel compunction at his loss: Ike was too valuable a property to be risked with anyone who might hurt him. This was the attitude on Eisenhower's train, and it spread to Nixon's as newsmen jumped over from the main tour to watch the death throes in the smaller one. The machinery of execution made itself visible Saturday morning, when the New York *Herald Tribune*—the voice of the Eastern Establishment—asked for Nixon's resignation from the ticket. It was, Nixon realized, an order. The same voice that had summoned him was now dismissing him. A waiting game had been played for three days to see if he would go without having to be ordered, and Nixon had not gone. The Saturday editorial (written Friday), following so close on the *Post*'s revelation, appearing before Nixon had conferred with Eisenhower, was the first of several "hints" that he was not wanted. Despite his studied deference toward Eisenhower, Nixon makes it clear he was not dense; "The publishers and other top officials of the *Tribune* had very close relations with Eisenhower and" (for which read, *I mean*) "with some of his most influential supporters. I assumed that the *Tribune* would not have taken this position editorially unless it also represented the thinking of the people around Eisenhower. And, as I thought more

about it, it occurred to me" (the little light bulb above a cartoon character's head—Nixon must play this role straight) "that this might well be
read as" (*obviously had to be*) "the view of Eisenhower himself, for I had
not heard from him since the trouble began two days before."

At ten o'clock Friday night a reporter told him the next day's *Herald
Tribune* would ask him to resign. Nixon, who had not heard this, was
stunned. He summoned his closest advisers, Chotiner and Bill Rogers
(who would, after more of Nixon's crises, at last be his Secretary of
State). These two had received the editorial an hour and a half earlier,
but they were not going to tell him about it till morning—afraid he
would lose sleep if he saw it (a judgment events confirmed). He asked
for the editorial and read: "The proper course of Senator Nixon in the
circumstances is to make a formal offer of withdrawal from the ticket."
So that was it. Nixon is quite candid here: "I knew now the fat was in
the fire. That sounded like the official word from Eisenhower himself."
He spent four hours discussing his options with Chotiner and Rogers.
Then, at two in the morning, he told his wife, and went through the
whole discussion again with her.

The next day, Saturday, three days after the story broke, with newsmen plaguing him for his decision, he had to brace himself for defiance of the Establishment. It was an all-day job. He asked Chotiner and
Rogers to get the ultimatum spelled out, if they could, from Ike's inner
circle—Chotiner tried to reach Dewey, Rogers called Fred Seaton. They
got no direct answer. But the indirect command was growing more insistent; sharper and sharper "hints" were thrown to the public (and,
by this roundabout path, to Nixon). Sherman Adams had summoned
a man all the way from Hawaii to join the Eisenhower train, and the
man was all too obviously a second-string Nixon: Bill Knowland, tough
anticommunist and Californian. Eisenhower had finally spoken too, off
the record. The newsmen on his train had taken a poll that came out
forty-to-two for dumping Nixon; news of this was passed along to Ike's
press secretary (Dewey's press man in the last campaign, Jim Hagerty),
along with the newsmen's opinion that Ike might be stalling to arrange
a whitewash job for Nixon. Ike did not like such talk; it questioned not
only Nixon's honesty, but his. He invited the newsmen into his compart-
ment for a talk off the record—but the main part of it was soon made
public. "I don't care if you fellows are forty-to-two against me, but I'm
taking my time on this. Nothing's decided, contrary to your idea that
this is all a setup for a whitewash of Nixon. Nixon has got to be clean
as a hound's tooth." Again, Nixon got the point: "Our little group was
somewhat[!] dismayed by reports of Eisenhower's attitude. I must admit
it made me feel like the little boy caught with jam on his face."

By Saturday night, then, the issue was clear: knuckle under, or defy
the closest thing modern America has had to a political saint. Nixon,
here as in all his crises, claims the decision was made on purely self-
less grounds; he was thinking of Ike's own welfare—switching men in
mid-campaign might make the General unpopular. (This is like worrying that the Milky Way might go out.) Not that Nixon is insincere in his
claim. Politicians are very deft at persuading themselves that the world's
best interests just happen to coincide with the advancement of their

own careers. He says he put the question to his four advisers (Chotiner, Rogers, Bassett, and Congressman Pat Hillings) this way: "Forget about me. If my staying on the ticket would lead to Eisenhower's defeat, I would never forgive myself. If my getting off the ticket is necessary to assure his victory, it would be worth it, as far as any personal embarrassment to me is concerned. Looking at it this way—should I take the initiative and resign from the ticket at this time?"

But Nixon does not feel obliged to present his friends as men crippled by nobility. Chotiner, for instance, plays straight man here, saying all the "natural" things Nixon is too lofty for: "How stupid can they be? If these damned amateurs around Eisenhower just had the sense they were born with they would recognize that this is a purely political attack ... This whole story has been blown up out of all proportion because of the delay and indecision of the amateurs around Eisenhower." Not even good old Murray, though, blunt fellow as he is, can be described in this book as attacking the Big Man himself—just the little men around him. When Nixon's friends start criticizing Eisenhower, the veil of anonymity must be lowered over them: "But now, some were beginning to blame Eisenhower, for not making a decision one way or the other." Nixon himself would never dream of questioning his leader: "What had happened during the past week had not shaken my faith in Eisenhower. If, as some of my associates thought, he appeared to be indecisive, I put the blame not on him but on his lack of experience in political warfare and on the fact that he was relying on several equally inexperienced associates. I could see his dilemma."

The decision to be made at this session was simple: obey the order relayed by the *Herald Tribune*, or risk disobedience. But, after a full day of campaigning through Oregon, he sat up with his inner circle, in Portland, debating the matter till three in the morning. Then, left alone, he went over the whole thing in his mind for two more hours. By five o'clock Sunday morning, he had set himself on a course he meant never to abandon: he would not resign. Sunday brought blow on blow meant to shake that resolution. First, there was a long telegram from Harold Stassen, still trying to clear some path for himself. He recommended, for Nixon's own good ("it will strengthen you and aid your career"), that a resignation be sent right off to Ike. Then, that afternoon, Dewey called to give Nixon the decision of "all the fellows here in New York." Dewey had a plan for breaking the stalemate caused by Nixon's refusal to resign and Eisenhower's refusal to back him: Nixon must plead his cause before the people. If the response was big enough, he could stay. And when Dewey said big enough, he meant the impossible—near-unanimity. Nixon reports the ultimatum this way: "You will probably get over a million replies, and that will give you three or four days to think it over. At the end of that time, if it is sixty percent for you and forty percent against you, say you are getting out, as that is not enough of a majority. If it is ninety to ten, stay on." It is no wonder Nixon—or, rather, "some of the members of my staff"—felt wary of this offer: "They feared a concerted campaign might be put under way to stack the replies against me." The whole plan was stacked against him. It started with the presumption that Nixon was through, and with feigned generosity gave him a chance to climb back onto the ticket. If Nixon took the offer and (as was expected) lost, then he must abide by the consequences. It was a brilliant way of forcing resignation on a man who was determined not to resign.

Nixon said he would consider it. Chotiner got in touch with Party Chairman Arthur Summerfield, to find out how the broadcast would be handled. Summerfield said they had offers from some TV sponsors to give Nixon one of their spots. Chotiner naturally protested: Nixon could hardly go on the air to defend himself against the charge of being a messenger boy for California businessmen, and explain this on time given him by some large corporation! He told Summerfield the National Committee would have to buy the time, if they expected any show at all. (Money had already been set aside for two half-hour appearances by the vice-presidential candidate. But now Summerfield was in the unfortunate position of not knowing who would be the candidate: if he gave one of the periods to Nixon, and Nixon failed, that left only one spot for his successor. At $75,000 a throw, these were not shows to be granted easily.)

Nixon had to deliver a scheduled speech that night (Sunday) at the Portland Temple Club. He was still considering the TV broadcast when he came back to his hotel. He knew this contest was not what it appeared—Nixon against the press, or the Democrats, or the people. It was Nixon against Ike—a contest that, as Stevenson would learn twice over, no one can expect to win. Candidates simply do not get 90 percent victories in America—and Nixon was being told to produce that figure or get lost. He was asked to do it in circumstances that told against him. Eisenhower had been presented by his managers as the voice of a purgative honesty meant to remedy corruption. The very fact that this arbiter of morals was silent, that Nixon was sent out to argue on his own, was an implied judgment on him. He would be guilty until proved innocent, and he could not call on the one character witness who, in this set of circumstances, mattered.

Meanwhile, the Eisenhower camp had received no answer to its "offer." Now was the time to turn the screw. No escape was to be left him. The phone rang in Portland. Ike. For the first and last time during the crisis. Giving the ultimatum all his personal weight: "I think you ought to go on a nationwide television program and tell them everything there is to tell, everything you can remember since the day you entered public life. Tell them about any money you have ever received." The public self-revelation for which Nixon would be blamed in later years was being forced on him, against all his own inclinations, personal and political. By temperament and conditioning, Nixon is reserved, with Quaker insistence on the right of privacy. Nixon's mother, a woman of tremendous self-control, later said of the Checkers speech: "At the point when he gave that itemized account of his personal expenditures, I didn't think I could take it."

Nixon asked Eisenhower if he meant to endorse him. The response was put in a particularly galling way: "If I issue a statement now backing you up, in effect people will accuse me of condoning wrongdoing." Ike knew, and Nixon knew he knew, that the results of a vast survey of Nixon's affairs would be available in a matter of hours. This study had been going on for three days; Sherman Adams, at the outset of the scandal, called Paul Hoffman, one of the architects of Eisenhower's candidacy, and ordered a thorough inquest into Nixon's finances. Hoffman went to the best. He put Price Waterhouse to work checking Nixon's accounts, and the law firm of Gibson, Dunn and Crutcher went over all legal aspects of the matter. Fifty lawyers and accountants worked on a round-the-clock basis. The results of this scrutiny were being compiled Sunday night. No wrongdoing would be found. The objective moral evidence would soon be in Eisenhower's hands. But he refused to make his own judgment based on this evidence. He wanted the people, who could not know as much as he did, to decide whether Nixon was honest, and he would follow them. The people, meanwhile, were waiting to hear Ike's decision so they could follow *him*. Nixon was caught between two juries, each of which was waiting for the other to reach a verdict before it would move.

He tried to strike a bargain: if Eisenhower was satisfied with the TV broadcast, would he *at that point* make a decision to endorse Nixon? (If he did not, then a victory scored on the TV screen would be subject to attrition, as lingering or renewed doubts worked on a situation inexplicably unresolved.) But Ike was not making bargains: he said he would need three or four days (the same period Dewey had mentioned) for the popular reaction to be accurately gauged—during which time, Nixon would presumably be stalled in Los Angeles waiting for the response, his campaign tour all too noticeably suspended. Nixon finally blew: "There comes a time when you have to piss or get off the pot!" But Seraphim piss not, neither Cherubim. The great Cherub sat blithely there, enthroned on his high pot. Nixon sculpts and prettifies the unyielding refusal: "One of Eisenhower's most notable characteristics is that he is not a man to be rushed on important decisions."

There was nothing he could do now but go ahead with the show. And if so, the sooner the better. Chotiner was back on the phone getting clearance for the $75,000. Sherman Adams and Arthur Summerfield finally yielded that point around midnight. The press corps had been alerted, an hour before, that there would be an announcement. It was one o'clock in the morning when Nixon came down; newsmen thought this must be it—his resignation. He deliberately built up suspense by saying he was breaking off—tense pause—his campaign tour. To make a statement over television. Two days from now. Tuesday night. He let them think it might still be his resignation he would announce. The more interest he could generate in the next two days, the bigger his audience on Tuesday night.

That was Monday morning. He got little sleep before he boarded a plane for Los Angeles that afternoon; during the flight, he drafted the first of a series of outlines for his talk. In Los Angeles, he got the reports from Price Waterhouse and Gibson, Dunn in time to put their findings in presentable summary. After midnight, he called his old English and history teachers at Whittier College, with a request that they find some suitable Lincoln quotes for the speech. They phoned two quotes to him by ten o'clock that morning—one witty and one maudlin (he used the latter). Nixon walked the streets with Bill Rogers, discussing approaches he might take. He was keyed up, and thought he just might bring it off.

And then the last blow fell. Tuesday, after a mere four hours of sleep, he kept at his outline resolution, as is his way. He did not go to El Capitan Theater to check the TV set or props or lighting; he wanted every minute for his preparation—it was a pattern familiar to those who have watched Nixon key himself up for a crisis by mood-setting spiritual exercises. And then, with less than an hour before he must leave for the studio, the cruel blow came, shattering his schedule, his carefully programmed psychological countdown. It was Dewey on the phone again, with a last demand: "There has been a meeting of all of Eisenhower's top advisers. They have asked me to tell you that it is their opinion that at the conclusion of the broadcast tonight you should submit your resignation to Eisenhower." The Establishment was taking no chances that its scheme might misfire. Nixon asked if that was the word from the General's own mouth. Dewey answered that the men he spoke of would not have commissioned him to make such a call at such an hour unless they were speaking for the master. (But, as usual, Ike was protected: afterward he could write, "Just before the broadcast Governor Dewey telephoned him from New York reporting the conviction of some of my supporters there"—two can play at that "some of the staff" game—"that he should resign, which the young Senator later said he had feared represented my views." Poor Senator, so fearful, so young, so avuncularly cared for in this retrospective benediction. Those who have called Nixon a master of duplicity should contrast his account of the fund crisis with the smoothed-over version in Eisenhower's book, which does not even mention the "hound's tooth" remark.)

Nixon stalled on the line to Dewey, stalled and wriggled. He said it was too late to change his prepared speech. Dewey said he could, of course, deliver his personal defense and accounting; all he had to do was tack on, at the end, a formal resignation offered to Ike. Nixon said he had to leave for the studio. Dewey: "Can I say you have accepted?" Nixon: "You will have to watch the show to see—and tell them I know something about politics too!"

Nixon had a half hour to tell his staff of this new lightning bolt, get their reaction, shower, shave, dress for the show, making meanwhile his own decision—and trying to collect his wits and memory over the notes for his talk. It had been five days full of pressure, sleeplessness, betrayal, ultimatums—climaxed with the most unsettling demand of all, made when he was at a poise of tension and could be knocked off balance so easily. A whole series of crises. Thursday: answer the charges? Friday: dodge newsmen, or face them; rely on the formal answer or return to the defense again and again; stall or throw oneself upon Ike's mercy? Saturday: heed the *Trib* and resign? Sunday: do the TV show? Monday: what to say on the show? And now, at the last minute, Tuesday: defy Dewey (and, through him, Ike)? Already the strain had shown in Nixon. Sunday in Portland, when Hillings brought a wire from Nixon's mother with the Quaker understated promise of prayers WE ARE THINKING OF YOU, Nixon broke down and cried. "I thought I had better leave the room," Hillings said, "and give him time to compose himself." Chotiner, busy calling party people to get money for the show, remembered "I was more worried about Dick's state of mind than about the Party. He was edgy and irritable."

Even the inner circle could not tell for sure whether Nixon would stand up to the pressure, or give in while he spoke. After reporting Dewey's call, he was silent, his mind working desperately at the problem. During the twenty-five-minute ride to the studio, he went over his notes (on debater-type cards). He had withdrawn to his last ditch, to make an entirely lone stand there. The one thing he demanded in studio arrangements was that even Chotiner and Rogers be kept out. Only his wife would be present, within camera range, visible to Nixon. It is as if he were dramatizing, to himself more than others, the isolation he stood in at this dying moment of defiance.

One of the criticisms made of Nixon's television speech is that the hoarse voice and hurt face, hovering on the edge of tears, were either histrionic or (if unfeigned) disproportionate and "tasteless." But no one who knows the full story can suspect Nixon of acting, or blame him for the tension he felt and conveyed—it would be like blaming a recently flayed man for "indecent exposure." Nixon was deserted, in more ways than he could tell. And he was fighting back with more nerve than anybody knew. Besides concentrating fiercely on his appeal to the audience, which had to succeed if anything else were to follow, he was reaching out across their heads to touch swords in a secret duel with Ike.

And Eisenhower understood. Stewart Alsop, in his useful little book *Nixon and Rockefeller*, quotes from an interview with one who watched Eisenhower's reactions throughout the TV show. The General had to give a speech in Cleveland as soon as Nixon went off the air; the audience for that talk was watching a large screen in the auditorium, while Eisenhower and thirty of his people clustered by the TV set in a backstage office. Even this entourage, predominantly opposed to Nixon, was touched as the show progressed; some wept openly. But Eisenhower was calm, tapping a yellow pad with his pencil, ready to jot down comments on the speech. He took no notes while the talk was in progress though the tapping stopped twice. Nixon, forced to act like a criminal who must clear himself, deftly made his actions look like those of a man with nothing to fear. And he issued a challenge: the *other* candidates must have something to fear, unless they followed his example. He devoted much of his half hour to this challenge, dictating terms to his accusers. (It is this part of the speech—moving onto the offensive—that so pleased Chotiner.)

Now I'm going to suggest some courses of conduct.

First of all, you have read in the papers about other funds. Now, Mr. Stevenson, apparently, had a couple—one of them in which a group of business people paid and helped to supplement the salaries of state employees. Here is where the money went directly into their pockets.

I think what Mr. Stevenson should do is come before the American people, as I have, and give the names of the people who have contributed to that fund, and give the names of the people who put this money into their pockets at the same time they were receiving money from their state government, and see what favors, if any, they gave out for that.

I don't condemn Mr. Stevenson for what he did. But, until the facts are in there, a doubt will be raised.

As far as Mr. Sparkman is concerned, I would suggest the same thing. He's had his wife on the payroll. I don't condemn him for that. But I think he should come before the American people and indicate what outside sources of income he has had.

I would suggest that under the circumstances both Mr. Sparkman and Mr. Stevenson should come before the American people, as I have, and make a complete statement as to their financial history. If they don't it will be an admission that they have something to hide. And I think you will agree with me.

Because, remember, a man who's to be President and a man who's to be Vice President must have the confidence of all the people. That's why I'm doing what I'm doing, and that's what I suggest that Mr. Stevenson and Mr. Sparkman, since they are under attack, should be doing.

Eisenhower stopped tapping with his pencil—jabbed it, instead, down into the yellow pad—when Nixon said any candidate who did not reveal his finances must have something to hide. Of course, Nixon did not mention Eisenhower, and his phrase about other candidates joining him "since they are under attack" left a loophole for the General. But the overall force of the passage could not be missed. All candidates, he was arguing, should act as he had. That meant *Eisenhower*, too—as Ike realized, and events were to prove. After this all the candidates did make their statements.

There were reasons why it was inconvenient for Eisenhower to make his books public—e.g., the special tax decision on earnings of his *Crusade in Europe*. Besides, as Alsop delicately puts it, "the military rarely get into the habit of making charitable contributions...." More important, Nixon was turning the tables on Ike. Eisenhower had brought him to this revelation. Nixon would force the same hard medicine down his mentor's throat.

Yet an even defter stroke followed. Dewey had been vague on how the speech should be judged. He told Nixon to have telegrams addressed to Los Angeles, and measure the talk's impact by their content. This arrangement, besides tying Nixon down for several days, still left the matter with Eisenhower. The real decision would be made by the General, assessing news reaction. Nixon would be left to play games with his switchboard and his mail, unable to vindicate himself if Eisenhower decided the show had not cleared him.

But when it came time for Nixon to mention the sending of telegrams, he said: "I am submitting to *the Republican National Committee* tonight, through this television broadcast, the decision *it is theirs to make* ...Wire and write *the Republican National Committee* whether you think I should stay or whether I should get off; and whatever *their decision is*, I will abide by it." (Italics added.) The General stabbed again, pencil into pad, a sword struck down as he fenced that image on the screen, and lost. Nixon has always been a party man; his strength lay there. Karl Mundt and Robert Humphreys, manning the Washington headquarters of the National Committee while Chairman Arthur Summerfield traveled with Ike, had routinely issued statements backing Nixon from the very first day of his troubles. Now, by a cool disarming maneuver, Nixon was taking the matter away from the Eastern Establishment and putting it in the hands of men sympathetic to the regulars, to grassroots workers—people who respond in a partisan way to partisan attacks upon one of their own, people most vulnerable to the planned schmaltz and hominess of the Checkers reference, people with small debts of their own and Republican cloth coats. If the decision was theirs to make, then—the real point of the broadcast as Nixon had reshaped it—*it was not Ike's.* It is no wonder that, while others in Cleveland wept, the man who had directed OVERLORD, the largest military operation in the world's history, the *General,* made an angry stab. He knew enough about maneuver to see he was outflanked. Alsop's informant said: "Before that, I'd always liked and admired Ike, of course, but I'd often wondered how smart he really was. After that, I knew Ike got what Dick was getting at right away."

The importance of that decision, redirecting the appeal to the National Committee, explains Nixon's breakdown when he saw he had gone off the air. Under the pressure of the performance, undertaken without rehearsal, using sketchy notes, he had done something rare for him—missed the countdown toward sign-off by a minute or two: "Time had run out. I was cut off just as I intended to say where the National Committee was located and where the telegrams and letters should be sent." He had based everything on this point; he needed every wire that would reach Washington. What if the telegrams were diffused ineffectually about the country, sent to him, to Ike, to TV channels and local campaign offices? He needed a crushing weight of response all directed to one point, and now (he thought) he would not get it. (The wires in fact did go everywhere, but in such breathtaking numbers that all doubt was swept before them.) He threw his cards to the floor in a spasm, told Pat he had failed; when Chotiner came into the studio, elated by the skilled performance, Nixon just shook his head and claimed, "I was an utter flop." Outside the theater, as his car pulled away, an Irish setter friskily rocked alongside barking: Nixon turned, Bill Rogers would remember, and twisted out a bitter, "At least I won the dog vote tonight." The end, he thought, of the Checkers speech. He was touching bottom. That night he would finally, after all his earlier resistance, resign.

But it took more kicks and blows to bring him to it. During the first hours after his broadcast, others were jubilant and support poured in; but no call came from the General (a wire had been sent off, but was stuck in the traffic-jam of them at Nixon's hotel switchboard–no one called from the Cleveland camp to give Nixon its message). The first notice he had of the telegram came over the news wires—and it brought word of still another ultimatum. Eisenhower did not often lose wars of attrition. They were his kind of battle.

The crowd waiting for Ike in Cleveland was hoarse with shouts and praise for the TV show they had witnessed. Eisenhower's own first comment was to Chairman Summerfield, about the $75,000: "Well, Arthur, you got your money's worth." Hagerty came back from the auditorium and told Eisenhower he could not deliver his prepared talk on inflation with this crowd. He would have to speak to the Nixon issue. The General knew. He had already chosen his strategy. He fashioned its main lines on the yellow pad, and tried it on his advisers. First, a sop to the crowd: "I like courage... Tonight I saw an example of courage... I have never seen anyone come through in such a fashion as Senator Nixon did tonight... When I get in a fight, I would rather have a courageous and honest man by my side than a whole boxcar full of pussyfooters."

All the praise was a cover, though. Eisenhower was a master of the basics—supply, firepower, and retention of position. After praising Nixon for courage, Ike added that he had not made his mind up on the main subject—whether Nixon would remain on the ticket: "It is obvious that I have to have something more than one single presentation, necessarily limited to thirty minutes, the time allowed Senator Nixon." But if Eisenhower, who had chosen him as his running mate, who had access to the research of the lawyers and accountants, to the advice of top politicians in the party, could not make up his mind after watching the TV show, then how could anyone in the public do so? There is only one explanation for this performance: Ike was determined not to let Nixon take the decision out of his hands. "I am not going to be swayed by my idea of what will get most votes... I am going to say: Do I myself believe this man is the kind of man America would like to have for its Vice President?" That is, at one minute he will not be swayed by what the people want and would vote for, and the next minute he is accepting the sacred pledge of finding out what the public wants and will vote for!

Then Eisenhower read them his telegram to Nixon, which shows the real thrust of his remarks: "While technically no decision rests with me, you and I know the realities of the situation require a pronouncement which the public considers decisive." (Or: Get your National Committee support, and see how far it carries you without me.) "My personal decision is going to be based on personal conclusions." (Or: I won't judge you by reaction to your talk—which is what he had promised he *would* do.) "I would most appreciate it if you can fly to see me at once." (Or: Here, Rover.) "Tomorrow evening I will be at Wheeling, W. Va." (Or. Tomorrow *you* will be at Wheeling, W. Va.) Not only was Eisenhower reasserting the personal jurisdiction Nixon had challenged; he wanted a public dramatization of the lines of authority. Having cleared himself with the public, Nixon must appear before a superior tribunal, summoned there to make his defense again, in greater detail, while judgment was pointedly suspended.

Nixon could not submit; yet, once the demand was made public, he could not go further in public defiance, either. He gave in. Rose Woods took down his dictated telegram of resignation.

But he would get in one last blow of his own. The wire was not directed toward Eisenhower, as Dewey had insisted it should be. He addressed it to the National Committee! As Rose Woods went out of the room to send the message, Chotiner followed her and tore off the top sheet of her pad. Rose said she could not have sent it anyway. Nixon is, by his own admission, subject to sharp lapses and lowering of his guard in the emotional depletion that follows on conflict. In four of his book's six crises he finds an example of that pattern: and the example for the fund crisis is his telegram to the National Committee. His loss of grip began the minute the show went off the air and he threw his cards to the floor. " 'What more can he possibly want from me?' I asked ... I didn't believe I could take any more of the suspense and tension of the past week." Chotiner went to work on him, however, and persuaded him that he could avoid both of the unpalatable things being forced on him—resignation, or compliance with Eisenhower's summons. If he just resumed his interrupted campaign-schedule (next step, Missoula, Montana), the General would have to back down. The wave of public response was already seismic. Nixon reports Chotiner's counsel this way: "Chotiner, particularly, insisted that I not allow myself to be put in the position of going to Eisenhower like a little boy to be taken to the woodshed, properly punished, and then restored to a place of dignity." At this point, there was a call from Ike's camp. Arthur Summerfield, pleased that things had turned out well, was asking for Chotiner—who soon dashed his spirits. Murray said Nixon had just dictated his resignation; he admitted, when Summerfield gasped, that the telegram was torn up—"but I'm not so sure how long it's going to stay torn." Summerfield said things could be smoothed over when Dick reached Wheeling. But Dick was not going to Wheeling: "We're flying to Missoula tonight." Summerfield wanted to know how to head off this disaster—so Chotiner set terms: Nixon will not come unless he is sure of a welcoming endorsement, without further inquisition. This was, of course, a demand that Eisenhower back down on the stated purpose of the summons, which was to go into greater detail than thirty minutes would allow.

Eisenhower, realistic about cutting his losses, saw when this news reached him that the idea of further investigation could not be sustained. He let Summerfield give Nixon's camp the proper assurances. But Nixon would still be answering a humiliating public call. Just before the plane took off for Missoula, Bert Andrews, who had worked with Nixon all through the Hiss affair, called from the Eisenhower press room in Cleveland: Ike would have no choice now but to receive Nixon warmly; Nixon would have to lose a little face in order to avoid flouting the General's summons. Nixon agreed, and let his staff arrange a flight to Wheeling after the stop at Missoula. Ike was at the airport, to throw his arm around him and call him "my boy"—looking gracious, kind, generous, as if supporting an embattled man rather than picking up strength from a victorious one. The only thing that could resolve the crisis—Ike's blue-eyed smile of benediction—had been bestowed.

But they did not forget the night when they touched swords. There would never be any trust between them. And Nixon had begun a tutelage that would gall him and breed resentment through years of friction and slights.

5. The Baby Boom and the Age of the Subdivision

KENNETH T. JACKSON

The suburban sub-division, so typical of contemporary American society and so unusual elsewhere in the world, was a product of the period immediately following World War II. Pioneered by a handful of developers, of whom William J. Levitt is the most famous, the subdivision provided relatively inexpensive housing to millions of white working-class and middle-class Americans forming new families right after World War II. This new development was fueled by an extraordinary population boom as the birthrate advanced steadily from 1946 through 1957.

In their move to the suburbs, Americans simply followed the available supply of housing. Federally sponsored mortgages and the building of new highways encouraged the construction of large "sub-divisions" built by developers who borrowed mass-production techniques from the wartime experience. The population along urban fringes increased from about twenty million at the beginning of the 1950s to more than fifty-four million at its end. And most of these families owned at least one car as well as their own house.

Then and now, arguments have flared over the significance of this uniquely American pattern of development. The separation of home and workplace had different impacts on women and men, blacks and whites, urban and rural America. The move from renter to homeowner influenced values, politics, and cultural opportunities. Much of the social history of postwar America has been written in the patterns developed immediately after the war.

At 7 P.M. (Eastern time) on August 14, 1945, radio stations across the nation interrupted normal programming for President Harry S. Truman's announcement of the surrender of Japan. It was a moment in time that those who experienced it will never forget. World War II was over. Across the nation, Americans gathered to celebrate their victory. In New York City two million people converged on Times Square as though it were New Year's Eve. In smaller cities and towns, the response was no less tumultuous, as spontaneous cheers, horns, sirens, and church bells telegraphed the news to every household and hamlet, convincing even small children that it was a very special day. To the average person, the most important consequence of victory was not the end of shortages, not the restructuring of international boundaries or reparations payments or big power politics, but the survival of husbands and sons. Some women regretted that their first decent-paying, responsible jobs would be taken away by returning veterans. Most, however, felt a collective sigh of relief. Normal family life could resume. The long vigil was over. Their men would be coming home.

In truth, the United States was no better prepared for peace than it had been for war when the German *Wehrmacht* crossed the Polish frontier in the predawn hours of September 1, 1939. For more than five years military necessity had taken priority over consumer goods, and by 1945 almost everyone had a long list of unfilled material wants.

Housing was the area of most pressing need. Through sixteen years of depression and war, the residential construction industry had been dormant, with new home starts averaging less than 100,000 per year. Almost one million people had migrated to defense areas in the early 1940s, but new housing for them was designated as "temporary," in part as an economy move and in part because the real-estate lobby did not want emergency housing converted to permanent use after the war. Meanwhile, the marriage rate, after a decade of decline, had begun a steep rise in 1940, as war became increasingly likely and the possibility of separation added a spur to decision-making. In addition, married servicemen received an additional fifty dollars per month allotment, which went directly to the wives. Soon thereafter, the birth rate began to climb, reaching 22 per 1,000 in 1943, the highest in two decades. Many of the newcomers were "good-bye babies," conceived just before the husbands shipped out, partly because of an absence of birth control, partly because the wife's allotment check would be increased with each child, and partly as a tangible reminder of a father who could not know when, or if, he would return. During the war, government and industry both played up the suburban house to the families of absent servicemen, and between 1941 and 1946 some of the nation's most promising architects published their "dream houses" in a series in the *Ladies' Home Journal*.

After the war, both the marriage and the birth rates continued at a high level. In individual terms, this rise in family formation coupled with the decline in housing starts meant that there were virtually no homes for sale or apartments for rent at war's end. Continuing a trend begun during the Great Depression, six million families were doubling up with relatives or friends by 1947, and another 500,000 were occupying quonset huts or temporary quarters. Neither figure included families living in substandard dwellings or those in desperate need of more room. In Chicago, 250 former trolley cars were sold as homes. In New York City a newly wed couple set up housekeeping for two days in a department store window in hopes that the publicity would help them find an apartment. In Omaha a newspaper advertisement proposed: "Big Ice Box, 7 × 17 feet, could be fixed up to live in." In Atlanta the city bought 100 trailers for veterans. In North Dakota surplus grain bins were turned into apartments. In brief, the demand for housing was unprecedented.

The federal government responded to an immediate need for five million new homes by underwriting a vast new construction program. In the decade after the war Congress regularly approved billions of dollars worth of additional mortgage insurance for the Federal Housing Administration. Even more important was the Servicemen's Readjustment Act of 1944, which created a Veterans Administration mortgage program similar to that of the FHA. This law gave official endorsement and support to the view that the 16 million GI's of World War II should return to civilian life with a home of their own. Also, it accepted the builders' contention that they needed an end to government controls but not to government insurance on their investments in residential construction. According to novelist John Keats, "The real estate boys read the Bill, looked at one another in happy amazement, and the dry, rasping noise they made rubbing their hands together could have been heard as far away as Tawi Tawi."

It is not recorded how far the noise carried, but anyone in the residential construction business had ample reason to rub their hands. The assurance of federal mortgage guarantees—at whatever price the builder set—stimulated an unprecedented building boom. Single-family housing starts spurted from only 114,000 in 1944, to 937,000 in 1946, to 1,183,000 in 1948, and to 1,692,000 in 1950, an all-time high. However, as Barry Checkoway has noted, what distinguished the period was an increase in the number, importance, and size of large builders. Residential construction in the United States had always been highly fragmented in comparison with other industries, and dominated by small and poorly organized house builders who had to subcontract much of the work because their low volume did not justify the hiring of all the craftsmen needed to put up a dwelling. In housing, as in other areas of the economy, World War II was beneficial to large businesses. Whereas before 1945, the typical contractor had put up fewer than five houses per year, by 1959, the median single family builder put up twenty-two structures. As early as 1949, fully 70 percent of new homes were constructed by only 10 percent of the firms (a percentage that would remain roughly stable for the next three decades), and by 1955 subdivisions accounted for more than three-quarters of all new housing in metropolitan areas.

Viewed from an international perspective, however, the building of homes in the United States remained a small-scale enterprise. In 1969, for example, the percentage of all new units built by builders of more than 500 units per year was only 8.1 percent in the United States, compared with 24 percent in Great Britain and 33 percent in France. World War II, therefore, did not transform the American housing industry as radically as it did that of Europe.

The family that had the greatest impact on postwar housing in the United States was Abraham Levitt and his sons, William and Alfred, who ultimately built more than 140,000 houses and turned a cottage industry into a major manufacturing process. They began on a small scale on Long Island in 1929 and concentrated for years on substantial houses in Rockville Center. Increasing their pace in 1934 with a 200-unit subdivision called "Strathmore" in Manhasset, the Levitts continued to focus on the upper-middle class and marketed their tudor-style houses at between $9,100 and $18,500. Private commissions and smaller subdivisions carried the firm through the remainder of the prewar period.

In 1941 Levitt and Sons received a government contract for 1,600 (later increased to 2,350) war workers' homes in Norfolk, Virginia. The effort was a nightmare, but the brothers learned how to lay dozens of concrete foundations in a single day and to preassemble uniform walls and roofs. Additional contracts for more federal housing in Portsmouth, Virginia, and for barracks for shipyard workers at Pearl Harbor provided supplemental experience, as did William's service with the Navy Seabees from 1943 to 1945. Thus, the Levitts were among the nation's largest home builders even before construction of the first Levittown.

Returning to Long Island after the war, the Levitts built 2,250 houses in Roslyn in 1946 in the $17,500 to $23,500 price range, well beyond the means of the average veteran. In that same year, however, they began the acquisition of 4,000 acres of potato farms in the Town of Hempstead, where they planned the biggest private housing project in American history.

The formula for Island Trees, soon renamed Levittown, was simple. After bulldozing the land and removing the trees, trucks carefully dropped off building materials at precise 60-foot intervals. Each house was built on a concrete slab (no cellar); the floors were of asphalt and the walls of composition rock-board. Plywood replaced 3/4-inch strip lap, 3/4-inch double lap was changed to 3/8-inch for roofing, and the horse and scoop were replaced by the bulldozer. New power hand tools like saws, routers, and nailers helped increase worker productivity. Freight cars loaded with lumber went directly into a cutting yard where one man cut parts for ten houses in one day.

The construction process itself was divided into twenty-seven distinct steps—beginning with laying the foundation and ending with a clean sweep of the new home. Crews were trained to do one job—one day the white-paint men, then the red-paint men, then the tile layers. Every possible part, and especially the most difficult ones, were pre-assembled in central shops, whereas most builders did it on site. Thus, the Levitts reduced the skilled component to 20–40 percent. The five-day work week was standard, but they were the five days during which building was possible; Saturday and Sunday were considered to be the days when it rained. In the process, the Levitts defied unions and union work rules (against spray painting, for example) and insisted that subcontractors work only for them. Vertical integration also meant that the firm made its own concrete, grew its own timber, and cut its own lumber. It also bought all appliances from wholly owned subsidiaries. More than thirty houses went up each day at the peak of production.

Initially limited to veterans, this first "Levittown" was twenty-five miles east of Manhattan and particularly attractive to new families that had been formed during and just after the war. Squashed in with their in-laws or in tiny apartments where landlords frowned on children, the GI's looked upon Levittown as the answer to their most pressing need. Months before the first three hundred Levitt houses were occupied in October 1947, customers stood in line for the four-room Cape Cod box renting at sixty dollars per month. The first eighteen hundred houses were initially available only for rental, with an option to buy after a year's residence. Because the total for mortgage, interest, principal, and taxes was *less* than the rent, almost everyone bought; after 1949 all units were for sale only. So many of the purchasers were young families that the first issue of *Island Trees*, the community newspaper, opined that "our lives are held closely together because most of us are within the same age bracket, in similar income groups, live in almost identical houses and have common problems." And so many babies were born to them that the suburb came to be known as "Fertility Valley" and "The Rabbit Hutch."

Ultimately encompassing more than 17,400 separate houses and 82,000 residents, Levittown was the largest housing development ever put up by a single builder, and it served the American dream-house market at close to the lowest prices the industry could attain. The typical Cape Cod was down-to-earth and unpretentious; the intention was not to stir the imagination, but to provide the best shelter at the least price. Each dwelling included a twelve-by-sixteen-foot living-room with a fireplace, one bath, and two bedrooms (about 750 square feet), with easy expansion possibilities upstairs in the unfinished attic or outward into the yard. Most importantly, the floor plan was practical and well-designed, with the kitchen moved to the front of the house near the entrance so that mothers could watch their children from kitchen windows and do their washing and cooking with a minimum of movement. Similarly, the living room was placed in the rear and given a picture window overlooking the back yard. This early Levitt house was as basic to post World War II suburban development as the Model T had been to the automobile. In each case, the actual design features were less important than the fact that they were mass-produced and thus priced within the reach of the middle class.

William Jaird Levitt, who assumed primary operating responsibility for the firm soon after the war, disposed of houses as quickly as other men disposed of cars. Pricing his Cape Cods at $7,990 (the earliest models went for $6,990) and his ranches at $9,500, he promised no down payment, no closing costs, and "no hidden extras." With FHA and VA "production advances," Levitt boasted the largest line of credit ever offered a private home builder. He simplified the paperwork required for purchase and reduced the entire financing and titling transaction to two half-hour steps. His full-page advertisements offered a sweetener to eliminate lingering resistance—a Bendix washer was included in the purchase price. Other inducements included an eight-inch television set (for which the family would pay for the next thirty years). So efficient was the operation that *Harper's Magazine* reported in 1948 that Levitt undersold his nearest competition by $1,500 and still made a $1,000 profit on each house. As *New York Times'* architecture critic Paul Goldberger has noted, "Levittown houses were social creations more than architectural ones—they turned the detached, single-family house from a distant dream to a real possibility for thousands of middle-class American families."

Buyers received more than shelter for their money. When the initial families arrived with their baby strollers and play pens, there were no trees, schools, churches, or private telephones. Grocery shopping was a planned adventure, and picking up the mail required sloshing through the mud to Hicksville. The Levitts planted apple, cherry, and evergreen trees on each plot, however, and the development ultimately assumed a more parklike appearance. To facilitate development as a garden community, streets were curvilinear (and invariably called "roads" or "lanes"), and through traffic was shunted to peripheral thoroughfares. Nine swimming pools, sixty playgrounds, ten baseball diamonds, and seven "village greens" provided open space and recreational opportunities. The Levitts forbade fences (a practice later ignored) and permitted outdoor clothes drying only on specially designed, collapsible racks. They even supervised lawn-cutting for the first few years—doing the jobs themselves if necessary and sending the laggard families the bill.

Architectural critics, many of whom were unaccustomed to the tastes or resources of moderate-income people, were generally unimpressed by the repetitious houses on 60-by-100-foot "cookie cutter lots" and referred to Levittown as "degraded in conception and impoverished in form." From the Wantagh Parkway, the town stretched away to the east as far as the eye could see, house after identical house, a horizon broken only by telephone poles. Paul Goldberger, who admired the individual designs, thought that the whole was "an urban planning disaster," while Lewis Mumford complained that Levittown's narrow range of house type and income range resulted in a one-class community and a backward design. He noted that the Levitts used "new-fashioned methods to compound old-fashioned mistakes."

But Levittown was a huge popular success where it counted—in the marketplace. On a single day in March 1949, fourteen hundred contracts were drawn, some with families that had been in line for four days. "I truly loved it," recalled one early resident. "When they built the Village Green, our big event was walking down there for ice cream."

In the 1950s the Levitts shifted their attention from Long Island to an equally large project near Philadelphia. Located on former broccoli and spinach farms in lower Bucks County, Pennsylvania, this new Levittown was built within a few miles of the new Fairless Works of the United States Steel Corporation, where the largest percentage of the community's residents were employed. It was composed on eight master blocks, each of about one square mile and focusing on its own recreational facilities. Totaling about 16,000 homes when completed late in the decade, the town included light industry and a big, 55-acre shopping center. According to Levitt, "We planned every foot of it—every store, filling station, school, house, apartment, church, color, tree, and shrub."

In the 1960s, the Levitt forces shifted once again, this time to Willingboro, New Jersey, where a third Levittown was constructed within distant commuting range of Philadelphia. This last town was the focus of Herbert Gans's well-known account of *The Levittowners*. The Cape Cod remained the basic style, but Levitt improved the older models to resemble more closely the psuedo-colonial design that was so popular in the Northeast.

If imitation is the sincerest form of flattery, then William Levitt has been much honored in the past forty years. His replacement of basement foundations with the radiantly heated concrete slab was being widely copied as early as 1950. Levitt did not actually pioneer many of the mass-production techniques—the use of plywood, particle board, and gypsum board, as well as power hand tools like saws, routers, and nailers, for example—but his developments were so widely publicized that in every large metropolitan area, large builders appeared who adopted similar methods—Joseph Kelly in Boston, Frank White in Portland, Louis H. Boyar and Fritz B. Burns in Los Angeles, Del Webb in Phoenix, William G. Farrington in Houston, Franklin L. Burns in Denver, Wallace E. Johnson in Memphis, Ray Ellison in San Antonio, Maurice Fishman in Cleveland, Waverly Taylor in Washington, Irving Blietz and Phillip Klutznick in Chicago, John Mowbray in Baltimore, and Carl Gellert and Ellie Stoneman in San Francisco, to name just the more well-known builders.

FHA and VA programs made possible the financing of their immense developments. Title VI of the National Housing Act of 1934 allowed a builder to insure 90 percent of the mortgage of a house costing up to nine thousand dollars. Most importantly, an ambitious entrepreneur could get an FHA "commitment" to insure the mortgage, and then use that "commitment" to sign himself up as a temporary mortgagor. The mortgage lender (a bank or savings and loan institution) would then make "production advances" to the contractor as the work progressed, so that the builder needed to invest very little of his own hard cash. Previously, even the largest builders could not bring together the capital to undertake thousand-house developments. FHA alone insured three thousand houses in Henry J. Kaiser's Panorama City, California; five thousand in Frank Sharp's Oak Forest; and eight thousand in Klutznick's Park Forest project.

However financed and by whomever built, the new subdivisions that were typical of American urban development between 1945 and 1973 tended to share five common characteristics. The first was peripheral location. A Bureau of Labor Statistics survey of home building in 1946–1947 in six metropolitan regions determined that the suburbs accounted for at least 62 percent of construction. By 1950 the national suburban growth rate was ten times that of central cities, and in 1954 the editors of *Fortune* estimated that 9 million people had moved to the suburbs in the previous decade. The inner cities did have some empty lots—serviced by sewers, electrical connections, gas lines, and streets—available for development. But the filling-in process was not amenable to mass production techniques, and it satisfied neither the economic nor the psychological temper of the times.

The few neighborhoods that were located within the boundaries of major cities tended also to be on the open land at the edges of the built-up sections. In New York City, the only area in the 1946–1947 study where city construction was greater than that of the suburbs, the big growth was on the outer edges of Queens, a borough that had been largely undeveloped in 1945. In Memphis new development moved east out Summer, Poplar, Walnut Grove, and Park Avenues, where FHA and VA subdivisions advertised "No Down Payment" or "One Dollar Down" on giant billboards. In Los Angeles the fastest-growing American city in the immediate postwar period, the area of rapid building focused on the San Fernando Valley, a vast space that had remained largely vacant since its annexation to the city in 1915. In Philadelphia thousands of new houses were put up in farming areas that had legally been part of the city since 1854, but which in fact had functioned as agricultural settlements for generations.

The second major characteristic of the postwar suburbs was their relatively low density. In all except the most isolated instances, the row house completely lost favor; between 1946 and 1956, about 97 percent of all new single-family dwellings were completely detached, surrounded on every side by their own plots. Typical lot sizes were relatively uniform around the country, averaging between 1/5 (80 by 100 feet) and 1/10 (40 by 100 feet) of an acre and varying more with distance from the center than by region. Moreover, the new subdivisions alloted a higher proportion of their land area to streets and open spaces. Levittown, Long Island, for example, was settled at a density of 10,500 per square mile, which was about average for postwar suburbs but less than half as dense as the streetcar suburbs of a half-century earlier. This design of new neighborhoods on the assumption that residents would have automobiles meant that those without cars faced severe handicaps in access to jobs and shopping facilities.

This low-density pattern was in marked contrast with Europe. In war-ravaged countries east of the Rhine River, the concentration upon apartment buildings can be explained by the overriding necessity to provide shelter quickly for masses of displaced and homeless people. But in comparatively unscathed France, Denmark, and Spain, the single-family house was also a rarity. In Sweden, Stockholm committed itself to a suburban pattern along subway lines, a decision that implied a high-density residential pattern. Nowhere in Europe was there the land, the money, or the tradition for single-family home construction.

The third major characteristic of the postwar suburbs was their architectural similarity. A few custom homes were built for the rich, and mobile homes gained popularity with the poor and the transient, but for most American families in search of a new place to live some form of tract house was the most likely option. In order to simplify their production methods and reduce design fees, most of the larger developers offered no more than a half-dozen basic house plans, and some offered half that number. The result was a monotony and repetition that was especially stark in the early years of the subdivision, before the individual owners had transformed their homes and yards according to personal taste.

But the architectural similarity extended beyond the particular tract to the nation as a whole. Historically, each region of the country had developed an indigenous residential style—the colonial-style homes of New England, the row houses of Atlantic coastal cities, the famous Charleston town houses with their ends to the street, the raised plantation homes of the damp bayou country of Louisiana, and the encircled patios and massive walls of the Southwest. This regionalism of design extended to relatively small areas; early in the twentieth century a house on the South Carolina coast looked quite different from a house in the Piedmont a few hundred miles away.

This tradition began eroding after World War I, when the American dream house became, as already noted, the Cape Cod cottage, a quaint one-and-a-half-story dwelling. This design remained popular into the post-World War II years, when Levittown featured it as a bargain for veterans. In subsequent years, one fad after another became the rage.

First, it was the split-level, then the ranch, then the modified colonial. In each case, the style tended to find support throughout the continent, so that by the 1960s the casual suburban visitor would have a difficult time deciphering whether she was in the environs of Boston or Dallas.

The ranch style, in particular, was evocative of the expansive mood of the post-World War II suburbs and of the disappearing regionality of style. It was almost as popular in Westchester County as in Los Angeles County. Remotely derived from the adobe dwellings of the Spanish colonial tradition and more directly derived from the famed prairie houses of Frank Lloyd Wright, with their low-pitched roofs, deep eaves, and pronounced horizontal lines, the typical ranch style houses of the 1950s were no larger than the average home a generation earlier. But the one-level ranch house suggested spacious living and an easy relationship with the outdoors. Mothers with small children did not have to contend with stairs. Most importantly, the postwar ranch home represented newness. In 1945 the publisher of the *Saturday Evening Post* reported that only 14 percent of the population wanted to live in an apartment or a "used" house. Whatever the style, the post-World War II house, in contrast to its turn-of-the-century predecessor, had no hall, no parlor, no stairs, and no porch. And the portion of the structure that projected farthest toward the street was the garage.

The fourth characteristic of post-World War II housing was its easy availability and thus its reduced suggestion of wealth. To be sure, upper-income suburbs and developments sprouted across the land, and some set high standards of style and design. Typically, they offered expansive lots, spacious and individualized designs, and affluent neighbors. But the most important income development of the period was the lowering of the threshold of purchase. At every previous time in American history, and indeed for the 1980s as well, the successful acquisition of a family home required savings and effort of a major order. After World War II, however, because of mass-production techniques, government financing, high wages, and low interest rates, it was quite simply cheaper to buy new housing in the suburbs than it was to reinvest in central city properties or to rent at the market price.

The fifth and perhaps most important characteristic of the postwar suburb was economic and racial homogeneity. The sorting out of families by income and color began even before the Civil War and was stimulated by the growth of the factory system. This pattern was noticeable in both the exclusive Main Line suburbs of Philadelphia and New York and in the more bourgeois streetcar developments which were part of every city. The automobile accentuated this discriminatory "Jim Crow" pattern. In Atlanta where large numbers of whites flocked to the fast-growing and wealthy suburbs north of the city in the 1920s, Howard L. Preston has reported that: "By 1930, if racism could be measured in miles and minutes, blacks and whites were more segregated in the city of Atlanta than ever before." But many pre-1930 suburbs—places like Greenwich, Connecticut; Englewood, New Jersey; Evanston, Illinois; and Chestnut Hill, Massachusetts—maintained an exclusive image despite the presence of low-income or minority groups living in slums near or within the community.

The post-1945 developments took place against a background of the decline of factory-dominated cities. What was unusual in the new circumstances was not the presence of discrimination—Jews and Catholics as well as blacks had been excluded from certain neighborhoods for generations—but the thoroughness of the physical separation which it entailed. The Levitt organization, which was no more culpable in this regard than any other urban or suburban firm, publically and officially refused to sell to blacks for two decades after the war. Nor did resellers deal with minorities. As William Levitt explained, "We can solve a housing problem, or we can try to solve a racial problem. But we cannot combine the two." Not surprisingly, in 1960 not a single one of the Long Island Levittown's 82,000 residents was black. . . .

There was a darker side to the outward movement. By making it possible for young couples to have separate households of their own, abundance further weakened the extended family in America and ordained that most children would grow up in intimate contact only with their parents and siblings. The housing arrangements of the new prosperity were evident as early as 1950. In that year there were 45,983,000 dwelling units to accommodate the 38,310,000 families in the United States and 84 percent of American households reported less than one person per room.

Critics regarded the peripheral environment as devastating particularly to women and children. The suburban world was a female world, especially during the day. Betty Friedan's 1968 *The Feminine Mystique* challenged the notion that the American dream home was emotionally fulfilling for women. As Gwendolyn Wright has observed, their isolation from work opportunities and from contact with employed adults led to stifled frustration and deep psychological problems. Similarly, Sidonie M. Gruenberg warned in the *New York Times Magazine* that "Mass-produced, standardized housing breeds standardized individuals, too—especially among youngsters." Offering neither the urbanity and sophistication of the city nor the tranquility and repose of the farm, the suburb came to be regarded less as an intelligent compromise than a cultural, economic, and emotional wasteland. No observer was more critical than Lewis Mumford, however. In his 1961 analysis of *The City in History*, which covered the entire sweep of civilization, the famed author reiterated sentiments he had first expressed more than four decades earlier and scorned the new developments which were surrounding every American city:

In the mass movement into suburban areas a new kind of community was produced, which caricatured both the historic city and the archetypal suburban refuge: a multitude of uniform, unidentifiable houses, lined up inflexibly, at uniform distances, on uniform roads, in a treeless communal waste, inhabited by people of the same class, the same income, the same age group, witnessing the same television performances, eating the same tasteless pre-fabricated foods, from the same freezers, conforming in every outward and inward respect to a common mold, manufactured in the central metropolis. Thus, the ultimate effect of the suburban escape in our own time is, ironically, a low-grade uniform environment from which escape is impossible.

Secondly, because the federally supported home-building boom was of such enormous proportions, the new houses of the suburbs were a major cause of the decline of central cities. Because FHA and VA terms for new construction were so favorable as to make the suburbs accessible to almost all white, middle-income families, the inner-city housing market was deprived of the purchasers who could perhaps have supplied an appropriate demand for the evacuated neighborhoods.

The young families who joyously moved into the new homes of the suburbs were not terribly concerned about the problems of the inner-city housing market or the snobbish views of Lewis Mumford and other social critics. They were concerned about their hopes and their dreams. They were looking for good schools, private space, and personal safety, and places like Levittown could provide those amenities on a scale and at a price that crowded city neighborhoods, both in the Old World and in the new, could not match. The single-family tract house—post–World War II style—whatever its aesthetic failings, offered growing families a private haven in a heartless world. If the dream did not include minorities or the elderly, if it was accompanied by the isolation of nuclear families, by the decline of public transportation, and by the deterioration of urban neighborhoods, the creation of good, inexpensive suburban housing on an unprecedented scale was a unique achievement in the world.

PART TWO

1952–1962

The age of Eisenhower—an era that has long been an object of nostalgia—was shorter and less serene than is often remembered. In 1953 Eisenhower became president, the Korean War ended, and Joseph Stalin died. However, the redbaiting Senator Joseph McCarthy remained a source of disruption until 1954, and the economy slumped in the immediate aftermath of Korea. And well before the 1950s had ended, Soviet achievements in space (the first Soviet satellite, Sputnik, was launched in 1957), African and Asian colonial revolutions, and the growing civil rights movement at home all pointed to a resurgence of anxiety and conflict in the coming decade of the 1960s.

If the Eisenhower years offered a respite from war, they did not bring long-term social stability. In the suburbs, Americans were adopting new life-styles that included a heavy dependence on consumer credit and the creation of an affluent adolescent subculture. And even though suburban homes and shopping centers were much the same across the continent, families were uprooted by military and corporate employers in a fashion and frequency not calculated to preserve traditional values. An era of muckraking, which began late in the decade with the writings of C. Wright Mills, John Kenneth Galbraith, Michael Harrington, and others, revealed areas of national shame and failure. The nation would soon come to noisy confrontation over the changes the 1950s had quietly wrought.

When John F. Kennedy was inaugurated in 1961, the second youngest man ever elected president replaced one who was at the time the oldest ever to serve in the office. The generation that came of age in World War I was giving way to one shaped by World War II, men such as Kennedy and his defeated Republican opponent, Richard Nixon. Kennedy's administration stirred the nation far beyond what the content of his policies would have suggested. This generation did not always have fresh perspectives, but it had a fresh style.

The new generation paced a difficult path; foreign adventures, assassinations, and domestic disorders obscured its record before its policies had a chance to bear fruit. Many of Kennedy's ideas resulted in legislation enacted after his death, when Lyndon Johnson pushed the Great Society program through Congress. And Kennedy's failed policies in Vietnam led to an undeclared, yet major, war that fractured the comity on which social stability depended.

6. Eisenhower: What Manner of Man?

FRED I. GREENSTEIN

It is a cliché that the presidency of the United States is the world's toughest job. Dwight Eisenhower was one of the last American presidents to make the job look easy. Among the most beloved of American presidents, he seemed, in Rexford Tugwell's words, "the least partisan president" since George Washington. In public pose at least, he stood where the people apparently wanted him: high above the political battle. This, in turn, rendered the battle beneath—the world of such men as Vice-President Richard Nixon and Senate Majority Leader Lyndon Johnson—that much less interesting. Depression and war had meant a generation of political excitement and conflict. After 1952, however, Americans longed for respite from turbulence; they wanted to sit back and leave things to Ike.

Eisenhower almost singlehandedly created the facade of the placid '50s: a period, critics quipped, of "the bland leading the bland." But followed by thirty years that included assassinations, resignations, failed administrations, and intensely ideological ones, Eisenhower's two terms in office, without war, economic collapse, or runaway inflation, and marred by only mild scandals, seem a great accomplishment. Though Ike made it look easy, shaping the presidency into a symbol of stability was both difficult and significant. How Eisenhower accomplished this difficult balancing act of providing both stability and legitimacy while exercising political influence with a "hidden hand" is the focus of Fred I. Greenstein's analysis of Eisenhower's leadership style.

Eisenhower's vice-president, Richard Nixon, was not the only one to remark on his complexity; many others acquainted with the nonpublic man, made similar observations. What most of them appear to have recognized was the obvious intricacy of the political psychology of a leader who in many respects displayed antithetical qualities in public and in private. The testimonies of three such observers—a journalist, a congressman, and a presidential advisor—point to an array of Eisenhower's personal qualities, each differing in its public and private manifestations, that shaped his leadership style.

Journalist Theodore White reports that in the course of covering Eisenhower at NATO in 1951 and observing him closely he was forced to reverse the impression he had formed on the basis of Eisenhower's public persona. "I made the mistake," White confessed, "so many observers did of considering Ike a simple man, a good straightforward soldier."

Yet Ike's mind was not flaccid, and gradually, reporting him as he performed, I found his mind was tough, his manner deceptive, that the rosy private smile could give way, in private, to furious outbursts of temper; that the tangled rambling rhetoric of his off-the-record remarks could, when he wished, be disciplined by his own pencil into clean hard pose.

Congressman Stuyvesant Wainwright, an Eisenhower Republican, discovered a world of difference between the impression left by the *New York Times*, which "always made him out to be a mediocre, fumbling, ignorant boob," and the informed, issue-involved president with whom he had periodic conferences. Moreover, his bond as an Eisenhower loyalist was strengthened by his awareness of the president's depth of knowledge about public affairs:

When I went in there to talk with him, I used to come away on cloud nine, I was so impressed. And not just by the man. I was impressed because he knew exactly what he was talking about. I'd read about how he had been out in the morning taking putting practice, but when we went there he knew his business. He would ask us about paragraph three of section 4B. And I used to say, "Mr. President, someone must have briefed you pretty well five minutes ago," and he would say, "No, I looked it over last night." He knew what was in the bill, and he knew what to ask. It was just the opposite from what the papers said!

It was Henry Kissinger, however, whose perception of Eisenhower changed most dramatically. He first met the former president during the last months of his life. Though physically enfeebled, Eisenhower nevertheless still exhibited a vividly forceful personality and great political sophistication and interest. Kissinger met Eisenhower in Walter Reed Hospital shortly after Nixon's election and again, with Nixon, soon after his inauguration, only seven weeks before Eisenhower's death. On the first visit Kissinger's purpose was to seek advice on how to coordinate national foreign policy-making machinery. Eisenhower's practice had been to coordinate agencies responsible for making foreign policy in the Executive Office of the President, but Kennedy had abolished this procedure and Johnson had experimented with a State Department-led interdepartmental group that promptly became the object of rivalry among agencies competing for foreign policy-making primacy. Kissinger recalls that Eisenhower

was emaciated by his illness and largely immobilized by a heart pacemaker. I had never met him before, and held about him the conventional academic opinion that he was a genial but inarticulate war hero who had been a rather ineffective President. Two of my books and several articles deplored the vacuum of leadership of his Administration—a view I have since changed. Successive heart attacks had left little doubt that he had not long to live. Despite this, his forcefulness was surprising. His syntax, which seemed so awkward in print, became much more graphic when enlivened by his cold, deep blue, extraordinarily penetrating eyes and when given emphasis by his still commanding voice.

Eisenhower promptly displayed his sensitivity to the realities of Washington politics, warning Kissinger that bureaucratic competition would doom the Johnson-initiated arrangements. The Defense Department would not "accept State Department domination of the national security process. It would either attempt end-runs or counterattack by leaking."

Kissinger's second meeting with Eisenhower was on February 2, 1969. He and Nixon told Eisenhower of a State Department proposal that the United States take a direct part in international negotiations designed to force Israeli concessions in the interest of achieving détente in the Middle East. They discussed this and other national security issues with Eisenhower, who "seemed even more emaciated" than the last time Kissinger had seen him.

He spent much of the time warning Nixon against leaks of NSC proceedings. Nixon told him about our Middle East discussion. Eisenhower argued against major American involvement in the negotiations. Probably reflecting the agony he went through over Suez in 1956, he thought the best course was to let the parties work it out themselves. If we became active we would be forced in the end to become an arbiter and then offer the parties our own guarantee of whatever final arrangement emerged. This would keep us embroiled in Middle East difficulties forever. The next day, I had not been in my office many minutes before an irate Eisenhower was on the phone. He had just read a *New York Times* story reporting that the NSC meeting had determined that the United States would not pursue a more active policy in the Middle East. With a vigor that belied my memory of his frailty—and a graphic vocabulary at variance with his sunny smile—he berated me for letting down the President by not restricting the number of participants.

These accounts reveal apparent contradictions in Eisenhower's personal qualities that I will illustrate and analyze. My illustrations of the man, however, also often illuminate his leadership style. Both White's and Kissinger's accounts capture a particularly striking dichotomy between the public man whose "tangled, rambling rhetoric" made him seem on first impression to be a vague thinker, and the private one who expressed himself with clear incisiveness, reflecting a keen analytic mind. Eisenhower channeled both the public vagueness and the private precision into his style of leadership.

Wainwright and Kissinger detected a second apparent contradiction in Eisenhower's political psychology: he professed and appeared to be nonpolitical but clearly understood and sought seriously to influence politics and policy.

Wainwright's implication that leaving meetings with Eisenhower "on cloud nine" strengthened his attachment to him points to a third aspect of the man: his extraordinary capacity to win the support of other political leaders. This "trait" paralleled the truly distinctive capacity Eisenhower had for winning support from the American public. Both in winning and sustaining this support Eisenhower *seemed* totally artless, in White's phrase "a simple man." However, underlying his capacity to win support was a dimension he did not make public, that of self-conscious artfulness. An Eisenhower whose strong temper and emotions contrasted with the beaming visage on the campaign buttons emerges in White's and Kissinger's remarks. This raises yet another consideration— that of the nature of his feelings and energies and the ways he expressed and channeled them in his leadership. Finally, there is the matter of his

specifically political feelings—his beliefs and convictions. Only an awareness of them makes possible an understanding of certain of his political
actions, which, notably in domestic policy, differed from his publicly
stated policy positions.

PUBLIC VAGUENESS AND PRIVATE PRECISION

Since Eisenhower's press conference transcripts were the single
most influential source of his reputation for vague expressions and
muddled thinking, it is well to keep in mind Kissinger's observation
that, even when Eisenhower's sentences did not parse, his meaning was
hammered home by the force and vividness of his personality. Compare
the transcript of an Eisenhower press conference with a recording of
it. In the recording, the muddled syntax recedes and his voice emphatically and persuasively conveys his message. The films of Eisenhower,
which became regular fare for the television viewers—who by the mid-
1950s included virtually the entire electorate—are even more effective.
His mobile, expressive face and dignified but comfortable comportment
emerge as the expression of a manifestly warm human being who speaks
earnestly of his and the nation's ideals. He comes across as solid and full
of common sense—a reassuring figure who lived up to his own premise
that, as the visible symbol of the nation, the president should exhibit a
"respectable image of American life before the world."

By no stretch of the imagination, however, could the bulk of his
press conference discourse be said to reveal sharply honed reasoning.
Even when he dealt with some of the complexities of an issue, he usually
did so through broad simplifications and in a colloquial manner. And
asserting that he was not informed about them, he often refused to discuss complexities. He conveyed the impression of a leader who took it
for granted that much of the detailed content of contemporary issues
was "non-presidential," frequently referring questioners to cabinet secretaries for answers to issues that he said were in their domain, not his,
or had not yet been sufficiently studied by subordinates to come to his
attention.

The intellectual thinness and syntactical flaws in press conference
texts, Eisenhower would later write, resulted from caution. With press
conferences open to quotation and broadcast, "an inadvertent misstate-
ment in public would be a calamity." But, he continued, realizing that
"it is far better to stumble or speak guardedly than to move ahead
smoothly and risk imperilling the country," by consistently focusing on
ideas rather than on phrasing, he "was able to avoid causing the nation
a serious setback through anything I said in many hours, over eight
years of intensive questioning." Then, in the understated mode he used
when he chose to draw attention to one of his strengths, he went on
to add, "I soon learned that ungrammatical sentences in the transcripts
caused many to believe I was incapable of using good English: indeed,
several people who have my private papers, many in my handwriting,
have expressed outright astonishment that in my writings syntax and
grammatical structure were at least adequate."

They were, as he well knew, more than adequate. The Eisenhower Library files contain many letters and memoranda he composed, some marked "private and confidential," others classified for security purposes, reflecting the clean, hard writing, and, by extension, thinking, to which White refers. They include dispassionate, closely reasoned assessments of contemporary issues and personalities that belie the amiable, informal, and often vague usages of his press conference discourse. Startlingly, for a man who seemed, to as acute an observer as Richard Rovere, to have an "unschematic" mind, many of his confidential writings display geometric precision in stating the basic conditions shaping a problem, deducing their implications, and weighing the costs and benefits of alternative possible responses. Eisenhower's reasoning ability and method are best revealed in one of his confidential analyses of a particularly complex, controversial issue, a six-page single-spaced letter to his one-time chief of staff, then NATO Commander Alfred Gruenther, on the "offshore islands" dispute....

THE "NONPOLITICIAN" AS A POLITICAL MAN

The letter to Gruenther reveals more than Eisenhower's rhetorical and cognitive style; it indicates that he had a capacity for practical political thought. He assessed the political motivations of others, anticipating their likely responses to alternative courses of action, and had an explicit decision-making criterion—a decision must be in the long-term public interest *and* must be acceptable domestically so that congressional support can be assured. In short, the Eisenhower who was widely thought of as nonpolitical, who himself insisted that he was not a politician, and who in private used the words "politics" and "politician" pejoratively employed reasoning processes that bespoke political skill and sensitivity.

Eisenhower's inclination and capacity to analyze the behavior of others in terms of their political motives became apparent immediately after his rise to public visibility. During his 1942 dealings with the Vichy France commander in North Africa, Admiral Jean Darlan, Eisenhower explained to Marshall what it was about the behavior of Darlan and the other Vichy leaders that led him to work with the admiral and to shape his own action in ways that would best maintain Darlan's cooperation. Acknowledging that he had "some appreciation of all the political problems created by the necessity we have met of dealing with Darlan," he noted that nevertheless "the source of all practical help here has been Darlan."

All the others... await his lead and will do nothing definitive unless he speaks. So far he has refused us nothing. If he is playing a crooked game with us locally it is so deep that he can afford to give away initial advantages of every kind, even those upon which our existence depends in our present attenuated condition.

Given this, Eisenhower felt it essential to "preserve the attitude that we are dealing with a friend rather than an enemy."

I feel it is a mistake to demand cooperation and a friendly attitude on the one hand and on the other to act here like we have a conquering Army which enforces its will by threat and views with intense suspicion every proposal of these people. This explanation is submitted to you personally so you may understand why in certain details that appear to us relatively unimportant we attempt to be magnanimous and ostentatiously trustful.

The reference to Darlan's "game" fits perfectly with an account of Eisenhower's analytic bent by a long-time aide, General Andrew J. Goodpaster, who was present at many of Eisenhower's strategy conferences at NATO and in the White House. Pointing out that Eisenhower's apprenticeship during a 1922–24 tour of duty as executive officer in Panama with the legendary military intellectual, General Fox Conner, and his work at the Command and General Staff College had instilled in him "the orderly process of reasoning and analysis that is represented in the commander's estimate of the situation," Goodpaster observed that this called for thinking of collective activities in terms of the options open to the various parties. Goodpaster perceived a parallel between Eisenhower's political (as well as military) reasoning and game theory, the formal, mathematical, decision-making mode developed in the 1940s and 1950s and extensively used in cold war nuclear deterrence calculations. "Anything that's based on the theory of games, or a doctrine or technique that conforms to that," Goodpaster commented, "fits well into... the way that General Eisenhower's mind works."

He's a great poker player, and extremely good bridge player. He plays bridge very much in poker style and he's a tremendous man for analyzing the other fellow's mind, what options are open to the other fellow, and what line he can best take to capitalize or exploit the possibilities, having figured the options open to the other man. Under Fox Conner... he became keenly interested in the command process, not just the mechanics of it so much as the analysis of what was in the commander's mind—what was in Lee's mind, for example, at Gettysburg.

In analyzing "the other fellow's mind" Eisenhower used the reasoning process he described to Gruenther: stripping a problem "down to its simplest possible form." He did not dwell on the sources or subtleties of personalities. Rather, he parsimoniously identified principal traits, focusing on those that bore directly on public performance. As he stressed in conversations with Goodpaster, he formed in his mind explicit sketches of what he called "personal equations" of his counterparts.

An example is Eisenhower's effort to unravel President Lyndon B. Johnson's motives for announcing after the Tet offensive in Vietnam that he would cease bombing the North "in the hope that this would lead to a satisfactory peace" and that he would not accept renomination. "This abrupt change in policy, without any *quid pro quo* from Hanoi, will," Eisenhower reflected, "of course, further bewilder the United States." As far as he could see, Johnson's shift lacked a cogent rationale.

It appears to be not only contrary to the President's announced determination in the matter, but a partial capitulation, at least, to the "peace at any price" people in our country.... The final and most puzzling feature of his talk was his declaration that he would not seek and would not accept the nomination of his Party for the Presidency of the United States. . . . To me it seems obvious that the President is at war with himself and while trying vigorously to defend the actions and decisions he has made in the past, and urging the nation to pursue those purposes regardless of cost, he wants to be excused from the burden of office to which he was elected. He made no mention of the leader from his own Party who should now, in his stead, carry forward the effort. Indeed, I was left with the conclusion that the President had not truly analyzed the implications of his speech. . . .

I am besieged by papers and others to "make a statement." I am . . . refusing to say anything until I can convince myself of the true motivation of this performance.

Johnson's "equation," Eisenhower felt, revolved around extreme readiness to be opportunistic about policies. He also was aware that Johnson as a congressional leader had been a pragmatic analyst of political consequences. Since even an opportunistic motive for the announcement was difficult for Eisenhower to infer, he was suspending judgment.

Eisenhower's diagnosis of Johnson, with whom he had worked closely in the party, was exceedingly negative. . . . [But he] would have considered it politically unwise to make public his distaste for Johnson. He managed, in fact, to maintain the affection of that thin-skinned man. . . .

Eisenhower's impulse to avoid personal disagreements with other political figures was established in his long years in Washington. . . . [Eisenhower] could manipulate situations to his own ends while still maintaining the personal image of a neutral spokesman for the national interest. His plan after all had been to defuse an attempt to examine a specific wartime episode by changing the topic. He proposed not to discuss the Rapido battle at all except by analogy to nineteenth-century events. It is unlikely that the lawmakers would have cared to debate with a popularly acclaimed, recently victorious supreme commander about technical problems of assault tactics and the fine points of Civil War military engagements. Moreover, his ploy probably would have succeeded, even if he were not a national hero, because he had the personal confidence and support of the bulk of Congress, who like other leaders he met face to face, found him admirable and compellingly attractive.

ARTLESSNESS AND ART
IN WINNING THE SUPPORT OF OTHER LEADERS

. . . Eisenhower's cabinet included a number of strong personalities who ranged in viewpoint from deep conservatism to middle-of-the-road Republicanism, but who nevertheless all accepted him as an appropriate spokesman for the national interest.

Speech writer Emmet Hughes provides an action portrait of how Eisenhower would rally the cabinet members during their regular meetings. His "ears never seemed to leave the discourse around him." Eisenhower's "interjections" in the discussions "were sudden, sometimes sharp or even explosive."

Again and again the President would seize on some particular matter of legislation or administration as spark for a warm homily on his personal views—

the world need for free trade, or the practical necessity (and "cheapness") of programs of mutual security, or the need to temper austere "businesslike" administration with signs of concern for "the little fellow," or the "unthinkable" dimensions of nuclear war. For almost all the persons present these fervent sermons carried an authority almost scriptural.

Eisenhower's comments impressed his colleagues not simply because they were made with intensity, but also because they reflected his extensive personal knowledge of governmental affairs. The cabinet members, Hughes sensed, were especially impressed by his personal acquaintance with other world leaders—for example, "the warmth of his friendship for Harold Macmillan or his tolerance of the idiosyncracies of Charles de Gaulle." Especially to those members of the cabinet with limited experience in national and international affairs, "such a range of acquaintanceship with things and with people seemed no less than dazzling."

Robert Bowie did not confine his explanation of Eisenhower's effectiveness to "vibrancy." Eisenhower also impressed him in settings such as National Security Council meetings because he displayed two precisely definable qualities. One, which many other observers remark on, was his ability to make decisions, "to face the issues...and resolve them." The other was his ability to cut through complex discussions and make persuasive, though unpretentious sounding, judgments.

Often the discussion would be marked by impressive analysis by various individuals who, as intellectuals, struck you as sometimes more articulate than he. But at the end, I felt that he frequently came out with a commonsense appraisal... which was wiser than the input which he'd received from the separate advisors. Somehow, almost in an intuitive way, in a way which quite clearly wasn't a one, two, three lawyer's type of analysis, nevertheless he came out with a net judgment which often struck me as wiser or more sensible than the specific positions taken by any individual.*

Eisenhower's ability to win support in group settings may have seemed artless, but it actually represented a conscious application of what he realized were proven tactics for effective leadership, although his use of such tactics no doubt became second nature to him, requiring little conscious forethought. One of the closest observers of Eisenhower's practices over an extended period of demanding leadership, his World War II Chief of Staff, Walter Bedell Smith, explained that Eisenhower consulted subordinates as much as to win them over as to canvass their views:

His personality is such that it impresses itself immediately upon senior subordinates as completely frank, completely honest, very human and very considerate.... He has great patience, and he disdains no advice regardless of source. One of his most successful methods in dealing with individuals is to assume that

---

* We have seen that Eisenhower's letter to Gruenther did in fact follow a "one, two, three" reasoning mode. This explicitly deductive reasoning style is especially evident in Eisenhower's written communications. In discussions, he presented his main points and his conclusion, giving his rationale in a comfortably conversational, less formal way.

he himself is lacking in detailed knowledge and liable to make an error and is seeking advice. This is by no means a pose, because he actually values the recommendations and suggestions he receives, although his own better information and sounder judgment might cause them to be disregarded.

Subordinates so consulted, Smith observed, tended to be highly loyal and to accept Eisenhower's policies readily, presumably because they were flattered to be taken seriously and to feel that whatever line of action Eisenhower embarked upon had been informed by consultation with them.

C. D. Jackson, the Time Inc. executive who in 1953 and early 1954 worked closely with Eisenhower as a national security consultant and speech writer, also noted Eisenhower's habitual close attentiveness to others, by observing that "the only time his features seem to sag is when he is bored." But it was clear to Jackson that Eisenhower took pains to master this appearance. Even the sag in his features, Jackson commented, "is only momentary, because his almost fantastically patient courtesy comes into play almost instantly in order to give the bore the impression that he is being listened to with interest."

Appointments Secretary Robert Gray also noted that Eisenhower's skill and ease in dealing with visitors to his office was built on experience and technique. Eisenhower's meetings with visitors were "never stiff," Gray reported, though he "could manage a near complete schedule of important appointments at quarter-hour intervals, clear his mind in the seconds it took me to escort out his old visitor and bring in the new, and be locked on the fresh subject in full concentration by the time I withdrew." If the visitor became tongue-tied in Eisenhower's presence, "the President could carry the conversation single-handedly," finding common ground through small talk until "the visitor had settled back on his chair prepared to discuss the . . . business that had brought him."

The artfulness that Eisenhower applied to what he called "leadership in conference" is revealed in his ability to advise others on how to win over groups and individuals. Evidence of what Goodpaster described as Eisenhower's keen "interest in the command process" appears in a lengthy 1948 memorandum to Defense Secretary James Forrestal discussing how the secretary should go about seeking to harmonize the centrifugal demands of the members of the Joint Chiefs of Staff. The methods suggested were those that Eisenhower was often to employ in meetings when he was president. Whenever a member shows "a tendency to become a special pleader," he wrote, "the subject should be skillfully changed and a constant effort made to achieve unanimity of conclusion, first upon broad generalities and these gradually brought closer to concrete application to particular problems."

In a wartime letter to his son, Eisenhower commented, "The one quality that can be developed by studious reflection and practice is the leadership of men." Eisenhower undoubtedly overestimated the transferability of his leadership qualities. Nevertheless as a leader of other leaders he did more than effortlessly exude charm and warmth. He worked at the job.

ARTLESSNESS AND ART IN WINNING PUBLIC SUPPORT

Eisenhower's equal success in rallying and sustaining public support also was not arrived at without effort, though it was based on a personal public attractiveness to people with which few leaders are endowed. Films of Eisenhower's public appearances reveal an animated, enthusiastic man inspiring in the public a reciprocal enthusiasm. This is evident in the wartime newsreels showing a smiling, confident, unpretentious general, easily making his way through formations of troops; in the ticker-tape parades celebrating his return to the United States in 1945; and finally in films showing the motorcades with Eisenhower, both as a candidate and president, standing in open cars, beaming, waving, and signaling the familiar V for victory as he entered the cheering communities where he was making appearances.

The sober Bradley and staid Marshall never could have elicited a comparable response. And the other World War II general to win national popularity, MacArthur, seemed to reinforce his long association with political conservatives by his austere martial air. Numerous public opinion polls at that time reveal that, although both MacArthur and Eisenhower received strong support as "most-admired American," MacArthur's support was parochial, concentrated largely among conservative Republicans, while Eisenhower's crossed partisan and ideological lines.

Striking evidence that Eisenhower took the buoyant displays that won over first troops and later electorates as still another part of his responsibility—an appearance to be cultivated if necessary—can be found in an introductory chapter he did not use in *Crusade in Europe*, but which is preserved in draft form in the Eisenhower Library. The published book deals predominantly with events, not emotions and perceptions. The omitted introduction addresses itself to suppressing and countering feelings of despondency when faced by setbacks, stalemates, or stasis.

Eisenhower recalls the tense weeks he spent in the dank tunnels of Gibraltar immediately before the North African invasion in 1942 when

following upon many months of work and planning, conducted sometimes at almost hysterical intensity, a great Allied amphibious force had sailed from its ports to attack North Africa and my staff and I were condemned to days of almost complete passivity...as we awaited the outcome. During those anxious hours I first realized, I think, how inexorably and inescapably strain and tension wear away at the leader's endurance, his judgment and his confidence. The pressure becomes more acute because of the duty of a staff constantly to present to the commander the worst side of an eventuality...and the commander inherits an additional load in preserving optimism in himself and in his command. Without confidence, enthusiasm and optimism in the command, victory is scarcely obtainable.

Realizing that "optimism and pessimism are infectious and they spread more rapidly from the head downward than in any other direction," Eisenhower "clearly saw the dual advantages to be obtained from a commander's cheerful demeanor and constant outward optimism."

One was that "the habit...tends to minimize potentialities within the individual himself" to become demoralized. The other was that it

has a most extraordinary effect upon all with whom he comes in contact. With this clear realization, I firmly determined that my mannerisms and speech in public would always reflect the cheerful certainty of victory—that any pessimism and discouragement I might ever feel would be reserved for my pillow. To translate this conviction into tangible results...I adopted a policy of circulating through the whole force to the full limit imposed by physical considerations...I did my best to meet everyone from general to private with a smile, a pat on the back and a definite interest in his problems.

Eisenhower realized that a leader must inspire confidence and support, no matter how he feels. Describing his 1952 campaign in *Mandate for Change*, Eisenhower speaks of "the candidate's stepping blithely out to face the crowd, doing his best to conceal with a big grin the ache in his bones and the exhaustion in his mind." Yet he insisted on appearing in motorcades, which was a grueling physical ordeal. And he urged politicians to follow his own practice of projecting a sense of warm enthusiasm. As one aide remembers, "I moved around with him a great deal and I've heard him tell professional politicians: 'Now here's what you do. Get out there. Don't look so serious. Smile. When the people are waving at you wave your arms and move your lips, so you look like you're talking to them. It doesn't matter what you say. Let them see you're reacting to them.' "

The smiling, confident exterior often concealed more than "pessimism and discouragement." It concealed the hard-driving side of this complex man as well as a fiery temper that he kept in check out of a deep commitment to subordinate personal feelings to the duties of leadership. The Democratic jibe that Eisenhower's was an era in which the bland led the bland is contradicted by a multitude of firsthand observations....

BELIEFS—AS HELD AND AS EXPRESSED

Political convictions—more precisely a core of convictions concerning war and peace, international community, and broad domestic policy principles—were intensely important to Eisenhower. For most people political beliefs are peripheral personality structures, a combination of habitual assumptions and short-lived responses to immediate circumstance and events. To an issue-oriented political leader like Eisenhower, however, beliefs are usually stable and can have a profound impact on feeling and action. Clear beliefs and policy positions founded on them are powerful instruments for leadership, since the leader who possesses them is better able to set priorities, communicate a public stance, and delegate specifics to associates by giving them clear guidelines for making detailed decisions.

Eisenhower's most deeply felt concern—-the preoccupation that led him to take on the presidency at an age when he was giving thought to reducing his involvement in public service—was with the state of world order. Foreign and international politics clearly were his prime focus, thought he recognized their integral link to domestic politics and policy.

The phrase "collective security" best describes his major short-run policy aim—that of welding a sturdy cold war coalition of Western and other non-Communist nations. This coalition, he was convinced, could not merely be military. It needed a solid political, economic, and ideological framework. He believed that if such a coalition could be achieved, there would be a greater likelihood of attaining the most fundamental long-run need of mankind, international harmony. Given time and Western steadfastness, "world communism" might lose its monolithic expansionistic qualities, and a strong, resourceful West could then take the lead in dissipating the cold war. And détente, he was convinced, would have to occur eventually to prevent the ultimate catastrophe—global nuclear war.

Eisenhower recurrently sought to bring home to Republican conservatives the awful significance of nuclear weaponry. Senior Republican Senator Styles Bridges of New Hampshire, for example, in 1957 rumbled publicly that the administration's foreign policy proposals were not true to cold war orthodoxy. The recording machine that from time to time was used to monitor conversations in the Oval Office captured an extended, impassioned Eisenhower exercise in setting Bridges straight. In response to Bridges's concern about "this atomic treaty"—reference to the administration's disarmament proposals—Eisenhower stressed, "this is part of a great program we have to pursue if we are going to save us from some catastrophe."

Eisenhower: Even assuming that we could emerge from a global war today as the acknowledged victor, there would be a destruction in the country [such] that there would be no possibility of our exercising a representative free government for, I would say, two decades at the minimum.... Did you ever see one of those net evaluation studies given to me every year?
    Bridges: No.
    Eisenhower: I will give you just one figure.... On a single attack...[one in which] we had enough warning for some preparation with our people and weapons...we figure something like 25 million killed, 60 million had to go to hospitals, and there were not enough hospitals. When you begin to think of things like that you know there must not be war.

As he put it to one correspondent in a 1958 letter, nuclear weapons had changed the character of war more in the twenty-one years since 1945 than any change between the beginning of the sixteenth century and Hiroshima. The usual notion of war was now obsolete; the new weaponry of extermination would leave no winner. There remained no alternative to finding means of East-West accommodation.

Eisenhower viewed his attempts as president to assure collective security in the West and bargain from strength to begin building a peaceful East-West relationship as a direct extension of his activities in the postwar years that culminated in his NATO leadership. And he thought of his efforts as a coalition builder after 1945 as a continuation of his allied leadership in the war. In his postwar prepresidential years Eisenhower harnessed his long-standing but never publicly expressed or sharply defined conservatism on domestic policy to his views on collective security. Although he felt that the American defense establishment was underfunded and precipitously demobilized in the immediate postwar years, he also was acutely sensitive to the possibility that high taxes and governmental expenditures—whether for military or domestic purposes—would weaken economic productivity through excessive federal regulation and reduction of incentives to invest. And he was preoccupied with the potential costs of an inflation that might be spurred by government spending, including "unproductive" spending on arms.*

Eisenhower was conservative enough to view the nomination of the man widely held to personify standpat Republicanism—Robert A. Taft—with equanimity in terms of domestic policy. The problem, however, was that Taft seemed prepared to lead the Republican party to abandon the Atlantic Alliance and other internationalist policies that Eisenhower deemed essential for national survival.

Just before leaving to command NATO in January 1951, Eisenhower met with Taft privately in the Pentagon. Eisenhower brought to this meeting a prepared statement in which Taft was to commit himself broadly to internationalist foreign policy principles and Eisenhower would renounce a candidacy. But when he and Taft could not agree, Eisenhower destroyed the statement and left himself in a position to accept the Republican nomination on the grounds that keeping open the option of seeking nomination was his only weapon against choice by the Republicans in 1952 of an isolationist candidate. As he put it in a 1967 interview:

I wasn't going to remove the threat of possibly becoming a candidate, although I had no idea of ever doing it, I assure you. But I just didn't want to let these people nail me down, neutralize me completely, and then still go their own happy way, one I thought was wrong.

Once Eisenhower was president and Taft was Senate Republican leader, it became clear that Eisenhower's private domestic political convictions were *more* conservative than Taft's, even though throughout the convention and campaign Eisenhower was judged further to the left on the political spectrum than either Taft or the bulk of senior Republicans.** ...

* He appears to have done much of this thinking about the need to balance adequate spending for collective security and the requirements of a sound economy when he was a chief of staff under Defense Secretary Forrestal. In his diary as early as January 1949 he notes his agreement with Forrestal on the central national security premise that "we must hold our position of strength without bankrupting ourselves." This prepresidential reflection prepared the way for his presidential "New Look" defense policy, which relied on high retaliatory power in order to restrain national security costs.

** In fact, during the six months before Taft's death when the two worked together, Eisenhower resisted such Taft proposals as an aid to education bill, which, he explained several years after Taft's death to Ohio Congressman Clarence Brown, was "far more 'liberal and radical' than anything to which I could ever agree." Shortly after Taft died, Eisenhower wrote in his diary, "In some things, I found him extraordinarily 'leftish.' This applied specifically to his attitude toward old-age pensions. He told me he believed every individual in the United States, upon reaching the age of 65, should automatically go on a minimum pension basis, paid by the Federal government."

THE EISENHOWER DICHOTOMIES

Eisenhower the man shaped the distinctive Eisenhower leadership style. His personal makeup was permeated by contrasts. Each element in his makeup has the same duality between what the public saw in him and the private man. As a thinker, the public saw a folksy, common-sense replica of the man on the street. The confidential records show a man with extraordinary capacities for detached, orderly examination of problems and personalities. In public he seemed to be removed from the political arena. But the inner Eisenhower reasoned about political contingencies with greater rigor and readiness than many political professionals and drew on a long-standing acquaintance with the labyrinths of national and international governance. His ability to win friends and influence people—both face to face and in the mass—seemed to result simply from the magnetism of his sunny personality. But he worked at his apparent artlessness, consciously choosing strategies that made people want to support him. And on occasion the sunny personality masked anger or despondency, since he viewed it as a duty of the responsible leader to exude optimism.

As president, he conveyed a warm, reassuring presence and presided over a peaceful and reasonably prosperous decade while seeming not to work at it. In fact, he pushed and disciplined himself relentlessly. Finally, his political convictions were more intense than those of many who spend their entire careers in party or elective office. But he curbed his strongly felt conservatism to profess the extent of domestic liberalism that seemed necessary to win his party middle-of-the-road support. And he moderated the harsh side of his cold war world view by taking the lead in making peace initiatives.

This was a man with a striking propensity to establish "space" between his private and public self. While this propensity also characterizes hypocrites, Eisenhower, in no letter, conversation, or diary entry reveals the mark of a hypocrite, if that term is taken to connote contradictory public and private behavior informed by cynicism. Responding to a war correspondent's description of Eisenhower's use of profanity, one letter writer suggested that a supreme commander's language ought to reflect his dependence on divine guidance. Eisenhower expostulated: "Why, dammit, I *am* a religious man!" His private political comments show a similar impatiently intense idealism, as he chafed at politicians and business and labor leaders whom he viewed as too shortsighted to act in the national interest.

Compartmentalizing public and private elements of his personal makeup required considerable effort, self-discipline, and a conception of his duties in which eschewing expression of impolitic impulses was taken for granted as an obligation of responsible leadership. Many of the Eisenhower dichotomies reflect a reassuringly benign-seeming public self and a private one with a well-developed capacity for tough-minded political realism. A personality capable of maintaining this division is perfectly suited for adapting to the contradictory public expectations that the president serve both as uncontroversial chief of state and potentially divisive prime minister. Such a person is also well suited to carry out the organizational procedures necessary to rationalize the official routines of public leadership while maintaining a capacity to develop flexible unofficial means for adapting organizational leadership to the complexities and idiosyncracies of the people he is leading.

7. Point of Order:
The Army-McCarthy Hearings
THOMAS C. REEVES

America's painful adjustment to the Cold War will be forever memorialized by the era to which Joseph R. McCarthy gave his name. In the early 1950s there was such a thing as subversion; the problem of disloyalty was real, if limited; some spies were discovered in government (although not by Senator McCarthy). But a limited security problem in the hands of a demagogue proved to have virtually unlimited political use. McCarthy became a prime agent in the Republican drive to oust the Democrats from a twenty-year hold on the federal government. Through accusation or insinuation he ruined public careers and damaged the private reputation of many innocent people.

Buoyed by these successes, McCarthy took on establishment institutions such as the church and—in the case at hand—the United States Army. He should have selected his victims with more care. Six months after his bout with the Army, a highly respected institution, his colleagues in the Senate censured him, ending his national influence.

The Army-McCarthy hearings played on television for 188 hours during their thirty-six day run from April 22 to June 16, 1954. Amid the welter of names, the confusion of charges and countercharges, the points of order and other interruptions, millions of viewers got the message. The Checkers speech had shown how television could save a political career; these hearings demonstrated how it could pitilessly destroy one. The show was unforgettable. McCarthy's sarcasm and disparaging tone of voice lost their effectiveness; he slid from fame to an alcoholic's death several years later. His flinty adversary, Joseph E. Welch, whose capacity for wit as well as for righteous indignation had thrilled 20 million viewers, was able in his retirement to play a star role as a movie lawyer. The age of television politics was indeed upon us.

To follow the account of the hearings, this cast of principal characters will be helpful:

Robert T. Stevens	*Secretary of the Army*
Senator Joseph R. McCarthy	*U.S. Senator, Wisconsin (Rep.), Chairman, Senate subcommittee*
Joseph N. Welch	*Special Counsel for the Army*
Senator Karl E. Mundt	*U.S. Senator, Kansas (Rep.), Chairman of hearings*
Ray H. Jenkins	*Chief Counsel, Senate subcommittee*

John L. McClellan	*U.S. Senator, Arkansas (Dem.),* *Subcommittee member*
Pvt. G. David Schine	*U.S. Army private and former* *McCarthy aide*
Roy M. Cohn	*Chief Counsel for Sen. McCarthy*

There was immense excitement throughout the country about the Army-McCarthy hearings. Most of the anticipation was generated, of course, by the media, which trumpeted the hearings as among the significant events of the decade. At first glance this appeared excessive, given the fact that much of the controversy focused upon the privileges of an Army private. But it was widely understood that the hearings were not actually about G. David Schine. The basic issue was Joe McCarthy. For years the senator had been condemning a wide assortment of individuals and institutions, and he appeared to be threatening the stability and integrity of one of the most popular administrations in American history. Now it was the attacker who was on trial. Millions would have the opportunity to look him squarely in the eye and judge for themselves what sort of man he was. Roy Cohn wrote later, "There was really but one name that was important, that of Joseph Raymond McCarthy. And one issue, McCarthy versus his enemies."

Subcommittee members expected the hearings to last two weeks or more. Daily sessions were scheduled from 10:30 A.M. to 12:30 P.M., and from 2:30 P.M. to 4:30 P.M. The senators, three representatives of the Army, McCarthy, Cohn, and Carr were to be seated behind a 26-foot long mahogany table at one end of the ornate caucus room on the third floor of the Senate Office Building. Each day, the Army representatives and the McCarthy group were to shift positions, equalizing their opportunities to be photographed by the three stationary television cameras covering the sessions.

The special rules adopted for the hearings permitted Ray Jenkins, the subcommittee counsel, to question witnesses first, without time limit. He was to lead witnesses through a direct examination, enabling them to present their side of the case, and then he would switch to cross examination, emphasizing the opposition's point of view. Chairman Mundt then had ten minutes to question the witness. Following that, each senator was given the same amount of time, alternating from Democratic to Republican sides of the table and from senior members down the line. At the conclusion of these questions, each side in the dispute, McCarthy and Welch or those associated with them, had ten minutes. The procedure would then be repeated, if necessary, until the interrogation of the witness was completed. Point three of the rules stipulated: "All examinations in each case shall proceed without interruption except for objections as to materiality and relevancy."

On the opening day, April 22, the caucus room was jammed to capacity with more than 400 spectators and over 100 reporters. The audience was the largest ever to view a congressional hearing. Joseph Welch later recalled, "The first sight of the hearing room was a shock to a lawyer used to the traditionally ordered interiors of courtrooms. It was utter confusion. Photographers leaped up and down to get pictures. Messengers crawled beneath chairs. The cameras turned to follow the action. Spectators came and went. People sat, stood and moved in every square inch of space and the whole crowded room was bathed in the bright lights of television." Welch took one look through the doorway and recoiled in horror. A capitol patrolman on the scene was amused by the attorney's reaction. "Don't worry," he said, "in three days there won't be twenty people here."

Senator Mundt opened the proceeding with a brief speech stressing the subcommittee's impartiality and commitment to "a maximum degree of dignity, fairness, and thoroughness." Senator McClellan, as the senior Democrat, echoed this sentiment, adding that the charges in the case were so "diametrically in conflict" that he saw no hope of reconciling them. The subcommittee's responsibility, he said, was to develop the facts and weigh the accusations. "It will be an arduous and a difficult task, one that is not pleasant to contemplate, but it is a job that must be done."

The hearing was only seventeen minutes old when Joe broke in and raised a "point of order"—a procedural subterfuge he would employ hundreds of times throughout the hearings to interject commentary. He objected to the charges raised by Adams and Stevens being labeled "Filed by the Department of the Army." "I maintain it is a disgrace and reflection upon every one of the million outstanding men in the Army to let a few civilians who are trying to hold up an investigation of Communists label themselves as the Department of the Army." Joe was rude, emotional, and angry. He was establishing a pattern of interruption and harassment that would be repeated continuously throughout the hearings.

Roy Cohn later rated McCarthy's performance "miserable." "With his easily erupting temper, his menacing monotone, his unsmiling mien, and his perpetual five-o'clock shadow, he did seem the perfect stock villain. Central casting could not have come up with a better one." At first, people were shocked by the senator's often repellent behavior. In time, as they became rather accustomed to it day after day, Joe began to seem somehow humorous and pathetic. All over the country comedians, mimics, and smart alecks could be heard droning in the senator's flat voice, "Point of order, Mr. Chairman." The line almost always got a laugh. When the attacks turned to ridicule, Joe's political power was destroyed.

The Army introduced three witnesses on the first day of the hearings. Maj. Gen. Miles Reber, a 35-year veteran and a winner of the Distinguished Service Medal, had flown from Germany to testify about the efforts of McCarthy and Cohn to obtain a speedy commission for G. David Schine. Reber did not feel that the senator was guilty of improper conduct, but he was critical of Cohn's persistent attempts to pressure him. Joe countered with an attack on the general's brother, Sam Reber, former acting United States High Commissioner for Germany. Joe claimed that the diplomat had resigned from the State Department in July 1953 "when charges that he was a bad security risk were made against him as a result of the investigations of this committee," and he alleged that this had influenced the general in his dealings with Cohn. The witness, pounding his hand in his fist, declared flatly, "I do not know and have never heard that my brother retired as a result of any action of this committee." Senator Jackson was appalled by Joe's tactic. Senator McClellan asked for a ruling on the issue, "because we may be trying members of everybody's family involved before we get through."

That afternoon, testimony by Secretary Stevens was interrupted to give Under Secretary of State Walter Bedell Smith an opportunity to appear. Smith, a secret ally of McCarthy's (Scott McLeod accompanied him to the hearing), described Cohn's contacts with him concerning a commission for Schine and said that in his judgment the young attorney's requests were neither extraordinary nor improper. Subcommittee members asked few questions. Joe thanked the retired Army general and said of him, "I think he has very many more important things to do than to discuss a private in the Army who had been promoted consistently until he is a private."

Secretary Stevens, in a lengthy statement, reviewed the Army chronology, attacked McCarthy's countercharges, and labeled the Schine case "an example of the wrongful seeking of privilege, of the perversion of power." He added several bits of new evidence to his account of events, including a threat allegedly made by Cohn when he was refused entrance to a special laboratory at Fort Monmouth. A colonel told Stevens that Cohn said "in substance": "This means war. Don't they think I am cleared for classified information? I have access to FBI files when I want them. . . . They did this on purpose to embarrass me. We will really investigate the Army now."

On the second day of the hearings it was revealed that the Army possessed 50 to 100 transcripts of telephone conversations bearing on the case. For several years the appointment secretary to the Secretary of the Army had been secretly required to monitor virtually all telephone calls handled by his superior, making verbatim stenographic records for the files. A transcript of November 7, cited by Stevens, showed Joe deprecating Cohn's efforts on behalf of Schine. "Now, in that conversation," Stevens said, "Senator McCarthy says that one of the few things that he has trouble with Mr. Cohn about was David Schine. He said that 'Roy thinks that Dave ought to be a general and operate from a penthouse on the Waldorf Astoria,' or words to that effect. Senator McCarthy then said that he thought a few weekends off for David Schine might be arranged, or words to that effect. Perhaps for the purpose of taking care of Dave's girl friends."

Joe was enraged to learn of the Army's cache of evidence, calling the practice of monitoring telephone calls "one of the most indecent and dishonest things I ever heard of." The crowd in the jampacked hearing room laughed as he protested. A lengthy and heated argument filled much of the day concerning the admissibility of the transcripts as evidence. On a motion by Senator McClellan, and with the approval of all parties, the subcommittee voted unanimously to subpoena all relevant transcripts and introduce them into evidence in their chronological order. A number of legal questions remained involving the admission of the transcripts, and Mundt soon told reporters, "About half of the lawyers in town are working on this now.... We are just trying to make doggone sure we are on solid ground."

In Milwaukee over the weekend, Joe called the hearings a "waste of time" and a "red-minnow burlesque." He said that Stevens was "inexperienced," and he hoped that someday the Secretary would wake up to "what is happening to him." Joe again complained about the existence of the transcribed telephone conversations. Bluffing, he said that he might have "possibly one or two" such transcripts in his own files.

The next day, H. Struve Hensel filed his formal reply to McCarthy with the subcommittee, accusing the senator of "malicious lies" and offering to match his financial records against McCarthy's before the subcommittee or any other body. On his return to Washington, Joe issued a blistering attack against the Assistant Secretary of Defense. "He inadvertently tipped the hand of those who have been masterminding the smear attack upon my staff and disclosed the true purpose to be what I have stated it was since its inception—namely, an attempt to roadblock all investigations of graft, corruption, and communism, and divert the committee down the side road of investigating itself."

Secretary Stevens took the stand on April 26 for the third of what would turn out to be thirteen consecutive days of testimony. Ray Jenkins examined him rigorously, probing for flaws in his account of events and demanding explanations for inconsistencies and omissions. The counsel was frequently harsh and sarcastic. Stevens faltered at times under the withering barrage of questions, and he occasionally became evasive and vague. He answered one question with "I don't think that I did, probably." When asked if he had wanted the subcommittee's probe at Fort Monmouth stopped, he replied, "Yes, sir," changed this to "No, sir," and then admitted seeking the "suspension" of the investigation (which he later denied).

The Army Secretary's testimony was filled with examples of extreme obsequiousness toward McCarthy, Cohn, and Schine. He conceded that McCarthy's investigation had accelerated the suspension of alleged security risks at Fort Monmouth. Moreover, he was unable to recall anything specific that Frank Carr had said or done that implicated him with the charges raised against McCarthy and Cohn. Mundt, Dirksen, and McCarthy made much of this failure.

Joseph Welch was too clever to permit the continuation of such pillory without resistance. He had already revealed a capacity for showmanship by parading a bevy of top Army brass into the hearing room and positioning them so that television viewers would understand that he represented the Army rather than simply three "Pentagon politicians." During one hearing, Army Chief of Staff Matthew Ridgeway made a dramatic entrance and sat down right behind Secretary Stevens. Continuously irritated by this ploy, Joe would snap at one point, "I do think that we should know just how many generals and colonels are ordered over here by the civilians in the Pentagon; why they are here and not doing their work in the Army." On April 27th, Welch seized upon the minor matter of a photograph introduced by Jenkins and magnified it into a major issue of the hearings. The resultant uproar lasted several days and produced hundreds of anti-McCarthy headlines across the country.

The photograph in question had been taken on November 17, 1953. Earlier that day, Stevens had flown to New York and invited McCarthy, Cohn, and Carr to lunch. The discussion focused upon the Fort Monmouth probe and Joe's unhappiness about comments made by the Army Secretary at a press conference. After the meeting, Stevens flew his three guests in his private plane to McGuire Air Force Base, which adjoined Fort Dix. The senator and Cohn had mentioned at lunch a desire to see Schine, and Stevens, as usual, was bending over backward to be cooperative. Eight photographs were taken at Fort Dix, including one of Stevens, Schine, base commander Col. Kenneth Bradley, and Frank Carr. Schine requested a copy of the photograph showing him next to the Army Secretary, and when it arrived he placed it on a wall in his New York office. Without Schine's knowledge, the photograph had been altered by an Air Force sergeant to include only Schine, Stevens, and Bradley.

As Cohn prepared for the hearings, he remembered seeing the photograph in Schine's office and mentioned it to Jenkins. Cohn thought it would buttress his allegation that Stevens had asked to have his picture taken with Schine at a time when the Secretary was supposedly angry with the private over improper pressure tactics. (Stevens denied the charge and the truth of the matter was never settled.) Jenkins asked to see the photograph, and Schine brought it to Washington. Staff member James Juliana had two types of copies produced for presentation at the hearings: an exact duplication of the photograph that hung on Schine's wall and another showing only Stevens and Schine. Juliana later took full responsibility for editing Colonel Bradley out of one set of copies: "It was done because I had instructions to furnish Mr. Jenkins with a picture of Secretary Stevens and Mr. Schine." Jenkins, unaware that any alterations had been made, received a copy from Juliana containing only Stevens and Schine. He used it to allege that Stevens had asked to have his picture taken *alone* with Schine.

Welch opened the hearing on April 27 with the startling charge that Jenkins had presented as evidence "a doctored or altered photograph . . . as if it were honest." He contended that Stevens was "photographed in a group," argued that the Secretary was looking at Colonel Bradley rather than Schine (Stevens's eyeglass frames made it impossible to tell), and described Stevens's slight smile as "grim."

Called as a witness, Cohn expressed surprise that the photograph was incomplete but argued that it did not matter. He had not attempted to prove, he said, that Stevens had wanted to be photographed alone with Schine. The very existence of the photograph, he claimed, with or without Colonel Bradley, revealed Stevens's friendliness toward Schine.

Wrangling and quarreling over the facts in the case of the "doctored" photograph consumed many hours, strained senators' tempers, and undoubtedly bored tens of thousands of television viewers. Jenkins frustrated witnesses with lengthy and frequently needless and repetitious questions. Welch, eloquently hinting at a dark plot by McCarthyites, seemed never to get to the point. Most of the McCarthy aides called upon to testify, such as George Anastos, were only minor participants in the case. Reporters, meanwhile, wrote lengthy stories about the "fake," "cropped," and "shamefully altered" photograph. The fact that the original Air Force photograph, used by Welch, had been altered even before it reached Schine drew virtually no attention in the media.

Actually, there was little or no reason to condemn McCarthy staff members in the matter. Cohn had undoubtedly been unaware of Juliana's personal decision to alter the photograph. Juliana's alteration did not effect Cohn's assertions about Stevens and Schine. It seems certain that Jenkins, not Cohn, decided to use the picture to illustrate Stevens's alleged desire to be photographed alone with Schine. On the stand, Juliana, Schine, and others involved in handling the photograph were frank and believable.

Throughout the clamor, Joe did his best to get the facts of the case into the record quickly and return to the central issues of the hearings. He was finally successful on the afternoon of April 30 when Stevens returned to the witness stand and resumed his often bumbling performance. By this time, however, Welch, with the assistance of the media, had succeeded in casting a cloud of suspicion on the senator and his aides that would never fully dissipate. As Joe had learned years earlier, sensational allegations made larger headlines than complex, factual explanations.

Welch's task was made easier by McCarthy's increasingly petulant behavior. By the conclusion of the seventh day of hearings, on April 30, Joe had clashed, at times bitterly, with almost every member of the subcommittee and Jenkins, as well as the Army counsel and Stevens. He had referred to the hearings as "this circus" and "this red-lined burlesque." During several of his outbursts, Joe seemed to lose his temper completely. Audience response in the hearing room seemed to be solidly anti-McCarthy.

In a row over the "doctored picture," he first directed his fire at Chairman Mundt, who was attempting to stem one of his many interruptions in the guise of a point of order.

Senator McCarthy. May I finish my point of order?

Senator Mundt. Counsel [Jenkins] advises the Chair that the senator is engaging in a statement or cross-examination rather than a point of order.

Senator McCarthy. I am getting rather sick of being interrupted in the middle of a sentence.

Senator Symington. I would like to say if this is not a point of order it is out of order. The counsel says it is not a point of order and it is not a point of order, if the counsel says it is not a point of order.

Senator McCarthy. Oh, be quiet.

Senator Symington. I haven't the slightest intention of being quiet. Counsel is running this committee, and you are not running it.

Senator McCarthy. Mr. Chairman, do I have the floor?

Senator Mundt. The Chair has the floor, and nobody is endeavoring to determine whether or not Senator McCarthy is speaking to a point of order.

Will you state your point of order and then speak to it?

Senator McCarthy. Mr. Chairman, may I suggest that when I start to say something, I not be interrupted in the middle of a sentence, and that Mr. Symington and no one else have the right to interrupt unless he addresses the Chair, and unless the Chair recognizes him. I am getting awfully sick of sitting down here at the end of the table and having whoever wants to interrupt in the middle of a sentence.

A few minutes later, he growled:

Call it a point of order or call it what you may, when counsel for Mr. Stevens, and Mr. Hensel, and Mr. Adams makes a statement and he is allowed to do it without interruption, and if that statement is false, do I have a right to correct it, or do we find halfway through my statement that Mr. Welch should not have made his statement and therefore I cannot point out that he was lying?

During a tedious interrogation of Schine by Jenkins concerning the altered photograph, Joe cried:

I want to make the very strong point of order that this is the most improper exhibition I have ever seen. You have a lawyer here who brags about being one of the greatest criminal lawyers in the country, badgering this private and he has told him ten times now that he doesn't know whether or not George Anastos was there, but to the best of his recollection Anastos was not there.

He can't gain anything further by badgering this Army private. I think it is indecent, and I think the Chair should condemn it.

Joe would become enraged when one of his staff members came under fire on the stand. Another such situation occurred on April 30 as Welch cleverly worked over James Juliana.

Mr. Welch. You did know what hung on Schine's wall when that was handed to you, sir.

Mr. Juliana. I did not know what hung on Schine's wall.

Mr. Welch. Did you think this came from a pixie? Where did you think this picture that I hold in my hand came from?

Mr. Juliana. I had no idea.

Senator Mundt. Senator McCarthy says he couldn't hear the question. It will be reread.

(Whereupon the question referred to was read by the reporter as above recorded.)

Senator McCarthy. Will counsel for my benefit define—I think he might be an expert on that—what a pixie is?

Mr. Welch. Yes. I should say, Mr. Senator, that a pixie is a close relative of a fairy.

Shall I proceed, sir? Have I enlightened you?

Senator McCarthy. As I said, I think you may be an authority on what a pixie is.

Joe said nastily to Stevens at one point, "That is a simple question, Bob, and you should be able to answer it." He quickly compounded the insult with, "Let's be a little more honest here." He later charged the Secretary with "flagrant dishonesty."

"May I have the Chair's attention," he bawled at Mundt during an exchange on rules. Later that day he again demanded Mundt's attention. "You can't listen to both at once. I know you have two ears, but you can't listen to both people at once." Two days later he suggested to the chairman that he "ask counsel for Mr. Stevens and Mr. Jenkins not to ask questions merely for the purpose of clearing their voices, but only ask them if they are looking for information."

Not even timid Senator Dworshak was exempt from Joe's wrath. On April 29 Joe objected to his line of questioning when it appeared critical of Schine. The Idaho Republican slammed a document on the table and fell silent. The next day, Joe said publicly that he regretted having selected Dworshak to serve on the subcommittee, and he threatened to reclaim his place on the body.

Millions of spectators judged the hearings primarily on the impressions they received of the major participants. They had no other choice given the complex nature of the charges exchanged by the Army and McCarthy and given the format of the hearings, which frequently prevented prolonged attention to a single line of thought. Joe's sarcasm and malice contrasted sharply with Stevens's sincerity. (The Alsops called the Secretary "one of the Administration's leading innocents-at-large.") Cohn's brusque mannerisms and rapid-fire innuendos could not begin to compete in public popularity with Welch's folksy charm and wit.

A spot check made by the Gallup organization in eight major cities after the first several days of the hearings revealed that of the 66 percent following the controversy, 41 percent favored Stevens while only 17 percent favored McCarthy. A Gallup poll published in early May showed that 43 percent of those questioned would be less likely to vote for a candidate endorsed by McCarthy—a jump of 17 percent in five months. Newspapers also noted the defeat of former Republican Congressman J. Parnell Thomas in the April 20 New Jersey primary. Thomas had pledged "1000-percent" support for McCarthy, "his objectives, and his methods." A *Fortune* magazine study revealed faltering support of McCarthy among Texas businessmen because of the clash with Stevens and the Army. Clint Murchison said that Joe had begun to "bungle." Dallas editor E. M. Dealey deplored the "brutality" of the senator's methods.

Many Republican leaders were anxious for the hearings to end, deploring the public spectacle of intraparty warfare. The President, angry and flushed, told a news conference he hoped the affair would conclude very quickly. Vice-President Nixon was quoted as saying that the hearings were getting to the "ridiculous stage." Senator Flanders told a constituent that the hearings were "a tragedy for the G.O.P. and a great field day for the Democratic Party." He added, "The responsibility for this thing lies squarely on the heads of the Republicans who have been obsessed with the value of McCarthy to the party. We are reaping what they have sown."

Others were equally embarrassed by the proceedings. The bar association of St. Louis sent a telegram to the White House urging suspension of the hearings until adoption of a code of procedure, "for the sake of preserving the dignity of governmental processes in the United States."

Joe's enemies were of a different mind, convinced that the senator was destroying himself daily before an audience of 20 million people. Senator Fulbright said that McCarthy was "using the same techniques of disruption and interruption the Communist leaders used in their conspiracy trial before Federal Judge Medina in New York." The Arkansas Democrat observed, "The hearing is a painful thing and it sickens me, but it is essential to wake up the American people to the truth about the man."

After the eighth day of hearings, on May 3, the subcommittee, at Everett Dirksen's request, met privately with the major participants in the case to explore ways to conclude the hearings rapidly. Republicans proposed that McCarthy take the stand immediately and that no further witnesses be called. Welch and the subcommittee Democrats balked at the suggestion. Welch was intent on nailing McCarthy's coffin tightly. The Democrats, of course, had partisan considerations. Senator Symington said at the hearing the next morning, "There have been statements that these hearings are disheartening to the people. There have been statements that the American people are disgusted with these hearings. Well, many times something that is disgusting or disheartening nevertheless has to be done so that we have good in the long run."

On the evening of May 3 Charles Potter secretly paid a visit to the White House at the invitation of the President. Eisenhower asked a number of questions about the hearings and passionately denounced McCarthy as "psychopathic" and "lawless." He urged an immediate end to the hearings and asked Potter to keep in touch with him. Two days later Eisenhower told a news conference that the hearings had damaged the nation's self-respect and injured its international prestige. He gave his unqualified support to Secretary Stevens.

Jenkins and all of the senators except McCarthy had exhausted their supply of questions for the Army Secretary during the morning session on April 29. Thereafter, hour after hour, session after session, Joe and Roy Cohn kept hammering away at Stevens.

Senator McCarthy. When did you first hear of the report? I am not asking you to pass on whether it is true or not. When did you first hear of the report or the allegation that Mr. Adams had made the statement that if we issued subpoenas for those who had cleared men with communistic backgrounds, that if we did that, there would be issued a report, a charge, call it what you may—

Secretary Stevens. I never heard any such statement.

Senator McCarthy. Let me finish—emanating from your department, alleging misconduct on Mr. Cohn's part?

Secretary Stevens. I never heard any such statement.

Senator McCarthy. You never did?

Secretary Stevens. No, sir.

Senator McCarthy. Did you ever come to me and complain about any alleged misconduct on Mr. Cohn's part?

Secretary Stevens. Did I ever come to you?

Senator McCarthy. Yes.

Secretary Stevens. And complain about Mr. Cohn?

Senator McCarthy. Yes.

Secretary Stevens. I think you were well aware of what our attitude was with respect to the pressure Mr. Cohn was putting on us.

Senator McCarthy. Mr. Stevens, you can answer my question; will you? Did you ever complain to me of any misconduct or any pressure on the part of Mr. Cohn?

Secretary Stevens. Mr. Adams did, repeatedly.

Senator McCarthy. You are telling on what Mr. Adams did?

Secretary Stevens. That is right.

Senator McCarthy. I am asking you. Did you, Robert T. Stevens, ever complain to me about any misconduct on the part of my chief counsel?

Secretary Stevens. I complained to you about some things when you kept trying to get Schine assigned to New York, for example, Senator.

Senator McCarthy. I think you should answer this question, Mr. Secretary. There has been considerable complaint that you have been kept on the witness stand too long. You will be kept on—

Mr. Jenkins. May I suggest, Mr. Secretary, that the answer to the question is very simple and we certainly will get along much more expeditiously if you will answer his questions. That is, did you personally ever complain to Senator McCarthy about Mr. Cohn and Mr. Cohn's alleged efforts to get preferential treatment for Schine?

Secretary Stevens. I did not personally do that.

Mr. Jenkins. That is an answer, Senator.

Secretary Stevens. And for the reason that most of the pressure was coming on to Mr. Adams from Mr. Cohn, and Adams was therefore the one that complained.

Mr. Jenkins. All right.

Senator Mundt. Senator McCarthy?

Senator McCarthy. Did you not repeatedly praise Mr. Cohn to me?

Secretary Stevens. No, sir; I don't recall that.

Senator McCarthy. Don't you recall ever praising Mr. Cohn?

Secretary Stevens. I do not.

Senator McCarthy. You never said any good about him?

Secretary Stevens. I wouldn't say I never said anything good about him, but I don't recall going out of my way to praise him.

Senator McCarthy. Didn't you repeatedly praise Mr. Cohn to me?

Secretary Stevens. I do not recall ever having done that. . . .

On May 3 Joe brought up the Peress case, and the next day he sought to debate the Fort Monmouth charges. Efforts by Jenkins and others to restrict the questions to the topics at hand were brushed aside. Joe warned of individuals in the Army "much more dangerous than the Communists themselves," and he stormed and ranted at the hapless witness for helping to plot the destruction of his investigations. The *Washington Post* commented, "The Secretary's patience and obvious honesty in the face of questions which were sometimes insulting and frequently tricky have certainly won him the sympathy and respect of the American public."

On the afternoon of May 4 Welch produced a letter from Army files that deflated a lengthy effort by McCarthy and Cohn to show that Stevens had been uncooperative during the Fort Monmouth investigation. To cover his chagrin, Joe impetuously whipped out a document from his briefcase that appeared to be a copy of a letter from J. Edgar Hoover to an Army general, dated January 26, 1951. Fifteen minutes earlier he had quietly asked Carr, "Shall I hit them with this one?" Carr had advised against it. Now Joe could no longer resist the temptation. He claimed that the document was one of a series of letters sent by the FBI Director to Army officials alerting them to security problems at the Signal Corps laboratories. Someone, he said, "was derelict when these repeated warnings from the FBI were ignored." Joe was bluffing; he did not know where the document had come from, and he did not understand what it actually was. He was to pay a high price for this hasty gamble.

Senator Jackson and Welch immediately clamored for information about the document; it was labeled "Personal and Confidential, via liaison" and had typed at the bottom "Sincerely yours, J. Edgar Hoover, Director." The Army counsel denied any knowledge of it and spoke of "this purported copy." Joe, who claimed that his document was a copy of a letter that could be found in Army files, declared "I want to make it clear that I have gotten neither this letter nor anything else from the FBI." That evening, a search in the Pentagon produced no such letter. A subcommittee staff member, Robert Collier, was sent to Hoover with McCarthy's document. (Subcommittee members continually stumbled over each other to express their unbridled admiration for the director. Symington had earlier described the bureau as "one of the greatest organizations this country has ever or ever did have.")

The next morning, during an extremely stormy session, Collier revealed that the FBI had in its files a fifteen-page memorandum sent by Hoover to the same general on the same date. McCarthy's two-and-one-quarter page document contained information relating to the same subject, and in some instances it contained the exact language found in the memorandum, but it was not a copy of anything in the bureau files. Joe fought back with the claim that his letter was an exact copy of the memorandum with security information omitted. This was flatly contradicted by Collier on the basis of his consultation with Hoover. Welch crowed, "Mr. Collier, as I understand your testimony this document that I hold in my hand is a carbon copy of precisely nothing, is that right?" Collier was compelled to agree. Joe angrily counterattacked: "I think there should be certain rules, even on your part, Mr. Welch, certain rules of honesty in cross-examination." Cohn joined in to point out that the document dealt with suspected Fort Monmouth employee Aaron Coleman. He also claimed that the senator had spoken "with complete honesty" when introducing the letter. But the damage had been done, and newspapers ran blazing headlines declaring that Hoover had challenged the accuracy of McCarthy's evidence. The director, Richard Nixon revealed years later, was secretly telling the President at this time that McCarthy was impeding the investigation of Communists. Joe was now being almost completely written off by the forces that had created him.

That afternoon, following a telephone conversation with Hoover, Collier testified in more detail about the differences between the McCarthy letter and the FBI memorandum. Joe's letter, he revealed, consisted of seven paragraphs taken verbatim from the memorandum. But evaluative comments ("Derogatory" or "No Derogatory") on individuals listed in both documents replaced bureau security information, and a parenthetical explanation had been added to account for the deletion of the material. McCarthy's document also contained a salutation, a closing, and other minor alterations. Thus it was clear that Welch was correct in claiming that the document Joe introduced into the hearings was not in fact a letter or a copy of a letter from J. Edgar Hoover.

Compounding the gravity of the situation, Hoover noted through Collier, was the fact that the FBI memorandum was highly classified. Joe had wanted to read all or part of his document into the record. At the director's suggestion, Mundt contacted the Attorney General for an opinion and refused to permit Joe to read a word of his "letter" aloud.

Hoover also emphasized, Collier said, that the designation "Espionage-R" found on both the memorandum and the McCarthy document was a routine notation and implied nothing. This bluntly contradicted Joe's claim that it proved those named in the documents were under investigation for Russian espionage.

Jenkins then called McCarthy to the stand. Joe said he had received his controversial document personally from a young officer in Army Intelligence in the spring of 1953: "I recall he stated very clearly the reason why he was giving me this information was because he was deeply disturbed because even though there were repeated reports from the FBI to the effect that there was Communist infiltration, indications of espionage in the top secret laboratories, the radar laboratories, that nothing was being done, he felt that his duty to his country was above any duty to any Truman directive to the effect that he could not disclose that information." In fact, Joe did not know where the letter had come from; it had apparently been received recently in the mail from an anonymous donor. McCarthy admitted being unaware of the fifteen-page FBI memorandum when he introduced his document as evidence and that he thought he possessed an exact copy of a letter from the Army files. While not revealing the specific contents of both documents, he noted that they contained 34 names and involved people "connected with the Sobel-Rosenberg spy ring."

When Welch took over the questioning, he dramatically contended that Joe's refusal to name his source of information violated the oath he had taken as a witness.

Mr. Welch. The oath included a promise, a solemn promise by you to tell the truth, comma, the whole truth, comma, and nothing but the truth. Is that correct, sir?

Senator McCarthy. Mr. Welch, you are not the first individual that tried to get me to betray the confidence and give out the names of my informants. You will be no more successful than those who have tried in the past, period.

Mr. Welch. I am only asking you, sir, did you realize when you took that oath that you were making a solemn promise to tell the whole truth to this committee?

Senator McCarthy. I understand the oath, Mr. Welch.

Mr. Welch. And when you took it, did you have some mental reservation, some Fifth- or Sixth-Amendment notion that you could measure what you would tell?

Senator McCarthy. I don't take the Fifth or Sixth Amendment.

Mr. Welch. Have you some private reservations when you take the oath that you will tell the whole truth that lets you be the judge of what you will testify to?

Senator McCarthy. The answer is there is no reservation about telling the whole truth.

Mr. Welch. Thank you, sir.

Then tell us who delivered the document to you.

Senator McCarthy. The answer is no. You will not get that information.

Mr. Welch. You wish, then, to put your own interpretation on your oath and tell us less than the whole truth?

Senator McCarthy. Mr. Welch. I think I made it very clear to you that neither you nor anyone else will ever get me to violate the confidence of loyal people in this government who give me information about Communist infiltration. I repeat, you will not get their names, you will not get any information which will allow you to identify them so that you or anyone else can get their jobs.

When the Army counsel became interested in the details of the alleged donation of the document by the unnamed Army Intelligence officer, Joe became extremely evasive, sounding, Roy Cohn wrote later, "like the many dozens of witnesses he himself had criticized for being unresponsive at subcommittee hearings."

Mr. Welch. How soon after you got it did you show it to anyone?
Senator McCarthy. I don't remember.
Mr. Welch. To whom did you first show it?
Senator McCarthy. I don't recall.
Mr. Welch. Can you think of the name of anyone to whom you showed it?
Senator McCarthy. I assume that it passed on to my staff, most likely.
Mr. Welch. Name the ones on your staff who had it.
Senator McCarthy. I wouldn't know.
Mr. Welch. You wouldn't know?
Senator McCarthy. No.
Mr. Welch. Well, would it include Mr. Cohn?
Senator McCarthy. It might.
Mr. Welch. It would, wouldn't it?
Senator McCarthy. I say it might.
Mr. Welch. Would it include Mr. Carr?
Senator McCarthy. It might.

Although Joe was not legally required to disclose his source of information, as Jenkins and Mundt quickly pointed out, Welch had produced great theater and again contributed significantly to the destruction of McCarthy's public image.

When Welch's turn next came around, he attempted to stress the differences between Joe's document and the FBI memorandum, but Joe seemed undaunted by the damaging revelations that had dominated the hearing. "I consider it of tremendous importance, now that the authenticity has been established, that this is a verbatim copy, a verbatim copy, from the fifteen-page report, to show the committee and the people of this country the extent to which the FBI has done their usual outstanding job, tried to get action by sending through the reports, and the usual discouraging results, no action, nothing until a congressional committee took over."

Subcommittee Democrats were determined to make the most of what journalists would soon call the "Case of the Purloined FBI Document." The next day, McClellan asked that hearing transcripts be forwarded to the Attorney General, and Symington, referring to "this obviously fraudulent letter," requested that every effort be made to identify

McCarthy's informant. Joe exploded at Symington and Jackson, claiming they were part of the effort to obstruct the search for Reds. He soon claimed in a speech at Wausau that all three Democrats were "deliberately trying to prolong these hearings" and sneered, "Now one can see what the party of twenty years of treason stands for."

Joe was becoming equally furious with the Administration. On May 6 Attorney General Brownell ruled that neither the FBI memorandum nor McCarthy's document should be made public. He said that the latter "constitutes an unauthorized use of information which is classified as Confidential." He also noted, "Mr. Hoover has examined the document and has advised me that he never wrote any such letter." Joe demanded that Brownell be called before the subcommittee in executive session for questioning about the decision, and he blasted the continued use of the Truman "blackout orders." He later told reporters that he would not be bound by Brownell's ruling unless J. Edgar Hoover also objected to the publication of the material. "I feel I have no duty, even remotely, to keep secret any information about Communists in the government and those who protect and cover them up, regardless of where I get the information." Contacted by reporters, Hoover had no comment.

Joe's daily schedule during the hearings would have ruined the health of anyone else. He and Jean met nearly every morning at their home with Cohn, Carr, and Juliana for a breakfast strategy session. At 9:00 A.M., surrounded by bodyguards provided by the police department, they walked over to the Senate Office Building for the morning hearing. Lunch was often eaten at the nearby Carroll Arms hotel. By then Joe had invariably soaked his suit with perspiration and would bolt down food and drinks in his shirt sleeves. When the afternoon hearing recessed about 4:30, Joe and his aides would huddle in the senator's office for up to three hours. Dinner would follow, either at the McCarthy home or at the Colony restaurant, and then it was back to the office for more work. Jean, Cohn, and the others would usually go home about eleven. But Joe stayed on, shuffling through documents and transcripts. Sometimes he was accompanied by his longtime friend Mark Catlin of Appleton.

Catlin, a lobbyist in Washington, thought that Joe was actually enjoying the combat and the publicity surrounding the hearings. He would often talk about whom he would "get" the following day. He would also rattle on at length about the Communists in government, leaving his friend convinced of his complete sincerity. Catlin was shocked to see the extent of Joe's alcohol problem: he drank straight vodka all night. He seemed to doze off for periods of five or six minutes, but would awake abruptly and resume his work—and drinking. That was apparently the only sleep he got. Catlin would stumble home about 6:00 A.M., leaving the senator in his office. He could not understand how Joe was able to face the cameras only a few hours later....

McCarthy's most famous attempt to divert the pattern of questioning occurred on the afternoon of June 9, with Roy Cohn still on the stand. During the morning session Welch had been causing Cohn considerable frustration with trenchant queries concerning one of the eleven memoranda. After the luncheon break, the Army attorney resumed his interrogation with a brilliant examination of the work habits of Cohn and Schine while the latter was on leave from the Army. When Cohn began to stumble, Joe excused himself, saying that he had to visit his office temporarily. When he returned several minutes later, he launched into a diatribe against Fred Fisher, Welch's young law associate who had been dropped from the case before the hearings began.

The tactic horrified Cohn, who squirmed in his seat and rolled his eyes skyward; his lips seemed to form the words "No! No!" Two days earlier he had made a private agreement with Welch: if the Army attorney would not bring up Cohn's military history (he had flunked the physical test for admission to West Point), the Fisher question would not be raised. McCarthy had agreed to the bargain. Now, however, in his desperation and anger, Joe impetuously decided to strike at Welch with everything he had. Cohn quickly scribbled a note to the senator. "This is the subject which I have committed to Welch we would not go into. Please respect our agreement as an agreement, because this is not going to do any good." Joe read the message and dismissed it. "I know Mr. Cohn would rather not have me go into this," he acknowledged a short time later. But by then he had fully committed himself to the attack.

Slowly and malevolently, Joe droned:

...in view of Mr. Welch's request that the information be given once we know of anyone who might be performing any work for the Communist party, I think we should tell him that he has in his law firm a young man named Fisher whom he recommended, incidentally, to do work on this committee, who has been for a number of years a member of an organization which was named, oh, years and years ago, as the legal bulwark of the Communist party, an organization which always swings to the defense of anyone who dares to expose Communists. I certainly assume that Mr. Welch did not know of this young man at the time he recommended him as the assistant counsel for this committee, but he has such terror and such a great desire to know where anyone is located who may be serving the Communist cause, Mr. Welch, that I thought we should just call to your attention the fact that your Mr. Fisher, who is still in your law firm today, whom you asked to have down here looking over the secret and classified material, is a member of an organization, not named by me but named by various committees, named by the Attorney General, as I recall, and I think I quote this verbatim, as "the legal bulwark of the Communist party."

The substance of the charge, of course, was fraudulent, for Welch had been fully aware of Fisher's past and had publicly announced that because of it he was not asking the attorney to participate in the case.

Joe continued, a slight grin revealing the pleasure he took in heeding Indian Charlie's advice about striking below the belt.

I am not asking you at this time to explain why you tried to foist him on this committee. Whether you knew he was a member of that Communist organization or not, I don't know. I assume you did not, Mr. Welch, because I get the impression that, while you are quite an actor, you play for a laugh, I don't think you have any conception of the danger of the Communist party.

Chairman Mundt pointed out, when McCarthy had finished, that Welch had never recommended Fisher as a subcommittee counsel. Joe sputtered a few more sentences before Welch struck back.

"Until this moment, Senator," he began, "I think I never really gauged your cruelty or your recklessness."

Fred Fisher is a young man who went to the Harvard Law School and came into my firm and is starting what looks to be a brilliant career with us.

When I decided to work for this committee I asked Jim St. Clair, who sits on my right, to be my first assistant. I said to Jim, "Pick somebody in the firm who works under you that you would like." He chose Fred Fisher and they came down on an afternoon plane. That night, when he had taken a little stab at trying to see what the case was about, Fred Fisher and Jim St. Clair and I went to dinner together. I then said to these two young men, "Boys, I don't know anything about you except I have always liked you, but if there is anything funny in the life of either one of you that would hurt anybody in this case you speak up quick."

Fred Fisher said, "Mr. Welch, when I was in law school and for a period of months after, I belonged to the Lawyers Guild," as you have suggested, Senator. He went on to say, "I am secretary of the Young Republicans League in Newton with the son of Massachusetts' governor, and I have the respect and admiration of my community and I am sure I have the respect and admiration of the 25 lawyers or so in Hale & Dorr."

I said, "Fred, I just don't think I am going to ask you to work on the case. If I do, one of these days that will come out and go over national television and it will just hurt like the dickens."

So, Senator, I asked him to go back to Boston.

Little did I dream you could be so reckless and so cruel as to do an injury to that lad. It is true he is still with Hale & Dorr. It is true that he will continue to be with Hale & Dorr. It is, I regret to say, equally true that I fear he shall always bear a scar needlessly inflicted by you. If it were in my power to forgive you for your reckless cruelty, I will do so. I like to think I am a gentleman, but your forgiveness will have to come from someone other than me.

Stung by the powerful rhetoric, Joe tried to resume his attack upon Fisher. Welch interrupted:

Mr. Welch. Senator, may we not drop this? We know he belonged to the Lawyers Guild, and Mr. Cohn nods his head at me. I did you, I think, no personal injury, Mr. Cohn.

Mr. Cohn. No, sir.

Mr. Welch. I meant to do you no personal injury, and if I did, I beg your pardon.

Let us not assassinate this lad further, Senator. You have done enough. Have you no sense of decency, sir, at long last? Have you left no sense of decency?

When Joe again attempted to smear Fisher, Welch said sternly, "Mr. McCarthy, I will not discuss this with you further. You have sat within six feet of me and could have asked me about Fred Fisher. You have brought it out. If there is a God in heaven, it will do neither you nor your cause any good. I will not discuss it further. I will not ask Mr. Cohn any more questions. You, Mr. Chairman, may, if you will, call the next witness.

The hearing room burst into applause. Mundt made no move to intervene. Joe, flushed and stunned, sat in silence.

Many of those close to McCarthy realized immediately how badly he had been hurt. Ray Kiermas, sitting in the audience, said later, "I was sick to my stomach." Ed Nellor, seated nearby, later recalled, "I got physically ill." Urban Van Susteren, who watched the confrontation on television, said years later, "It made me sick." Joe felt the pain of his humiliation keenly. Cohn wrote later, "The blow was terribly damaging to Senator McCarthy."

The media had a field day with the incident. Newspapers ran photographs of Welch in tears and later showed him engulfed in congratulatory letters and telegrams. Headlines such as HAVE YOU NO SENSE OF DECENCY? were common. Filmed accounts of the clash were featured for weeks on television and in newsreels. (The encounter would be the climax of the highly partisan documentary film "Point of Order," compiled from television kinescopes of the hearings and viewed in theaters for years.)

Joe's conduct was censured by virtually all but the most hardline ultra-conservatives. The right-wing *Wisconsin State Journal* said, "It was worse than reckless. It was worse than cruel. It was reprehensible." Columnist Doris Fleeson observed, "No one who saw that flower of evil will ever forget it." A satirical, anti-McCarthy phonograph record entitled "Point of Order" quickly proved to be a best-seller.

Joe took the stand on the late afternoon of June 9. Ray Jenkins, whose McCarthyite sympathies had long been evident, led him through a gentle examination that permitted him, with the aid of a large map (obviously designed for television viewers), to deliver a lengthy and impassioned oration on internal subversion. Throughout his more than four days as a witness, Joe returned to the theme again and again, revealing a degree of earnest fanaticism that none of the attorneys or subcommittee members publicly questioned. (Indeed, no one during the hearings challenged any of the Red-Scare assumptions Joe freely repeated. Each of the senators expressed his deepest hatred of all Communists, his belief in the presence of Red spies within the federal government, and his highest respect for J. Edgar Hoover. Not one of them criticized the activities of Red-hunting congressional committees. None of them questioned the validity of the Fort Monmouth investigation. Welch called Irving Peress "a no-good Communist" and told McCarthy at one point, "You do good work. I admire the work you do, when it succeeds.")

8. The Greatest Ride in My Life

JACK KEROUAC

The publication of Jack Kerouac's On The Road *in 1957 marked the advent of a new sensibility. Kerouac's novel describes the netherworld of the "beat" generation, which sought redemption and a sense of community in drugs and sex, exotic religion, mystical inspiration, poetry, and jazz, and rejected the materialism and mass culture of American society in the 1950s. Jack Kerouac's prose and Allen Ginsberg's poetry (Ginsberg is the "Carlo Marx" of* On The Road*) influenced a generation of restless and daring young people in the 1960s to experiment with new ways of living and of viewing the world. "Beat" and its condescending derivative "beatnik" rapidly entered the language as the mass media examined and popularized a new American avant-garde.*

The beat lifestyle was parodied and commercialized, the literary works were scorned by many professional critics, and the drug culture was attacked by moralists and the police. Americans of the 1950s greeted the new challenge to its conventions with curiosity, disdain, and ambivalence. Time *magazine described beatniks as a "pack of oddballs who celebrate booze, dope, sex and despair." In California at one time a host could rent a beatnik to add color and surprise to a party, and for a while beatnik parties seemed a necessary part of every movie.*

The beat sensibility, however, was far more durable than early critics imagined. On The Road *endured as a minor literary classic, and the poetry of Allen Ginsberg survived and flourished in the next three decades and even won over the critics. Many young people in the 1960s and a few beyond remained aware of parts of the beat message: that they could have their own music and culture, that they could experiment outside the boundaries of middle-class American life, and that their world could be more strange and more exciting than home or school had led them to imagine.*

I'd been poring over maps of the United States in Paterson for months, even reading books about the pioneers and savoring names like Platte and Cimarron and so on, and on the road-map was one long red line called Route 6 that led from the tip of Cape Cod clear to Ely, Nevada, and there dipped down to Los Angeles. I'll just stay on 6 all the way to Ely, I said to myself and confidently started. To get to 6 I had to go up to Bear Mountain. Filled with dreams of what I'd do in Chicago, in Denver, and then finally in San Fran, I took the Seventh Avenue subway to the end of the line at 242nd Street, and there took a trolley into Yonkers; in downtown Yonkers I transferred to an outgoing trolley and went to the city limits on the east bank of the Hudson River. If you drop a rose in the Hudson River at its mysterious source in the Adirondacks, think of all the places it journeys by as it goes to sea forever—think of that wonderful Hudson Valley. I started hitching up the thing. Five scattered rides took me to the desired Bear Mountain Bridge, where Route 6 arched in from New England. It began to rain in torrents when I was let off there. It was mountainous. Route 6 came over the river, wound around a traffic circle, and disappeared into the wilderness. Not only was there no traffic but the rain came down in buckets and I had no shelter. I had to run under some pines to take cover; this did no good; I began crying and swearing and socking myself on the head for being such a damn fool. I was forty miles north of New York; all the way up I'd been worried about the fact that on this, my big opening day, I was only moving north instead of the so-longed-for west. Now I was stuck on my northernmost hangup. I ran a quarter-mile to an abandoned cute English-style filling station and stood under the dripping eaves. High up over my head the great hairy Bear Mountain sent down thunderclaps that put the fear of God in me. All I could see were smoky trees and dismal wilderness rising to the skies. "What the hell am I doing up here?" I cursed, I cried for Chicago. "Even now they're all having a big time, they're doing this, I'm not there, when will I get there!"—and so on. Finally a car stopped at the empty filling station; the man and the two women in it wanted to study a map. I stepped right up and gestured in the rain; they consulted; I looked like a maniac, of course, with my hair all wet, my shoes sopping. My shoes, damn fool that I am, were Mexican huaraches, plantlike sieves not fit for the rainy night of America and the raw road night. But the people let me in and rode me *back* to Newburgh, which I accepted as a better alternative than being trapped in the Bear Mountain wilderness all night. "Besides," said the man, "there's no traffic passes through 6. If you want to go to Chicago you'd do better going across the Holland Tunnel in New York and head for Pittsburgh," and I knew he was right. It was my dream that screwed up, the stupid hearthside idea that it would be wonderful to follow one great red line across America instead of trying various roads and routes.

In Newburgh it had stopped raining. I walked down to the river, and I had to ride back to New York in a bus with a delegation of schoolteachers coming back from a weekend in the mountains—chatter-chatter blah-blah, and me swearing for all the time and the money I'd wasted, and telling myself, I wanted to go west and here I've been all day and into the night going up and down, north and south, like something that can't get started. And I swore I'd be in Chicago tomorrow, and made sure of that, taking a bus to Chicago, spending most of my money, and didn't give a damn, just as long as I'd be in Chicago tomorrow....

My first ride was a dynamite truck with a red flag, about thirty miles into great green Illinois, the truckdriver pointing out the place where Route 6, which we were on, intersects Route 66 before they both shoot west for incredible distances. Along about three in the afternoon, after an apple pie and ice cream in a roadside stand, a woman stopped for me in a little coupe. I had a twinge of hard joy as I ran after the car. But she was a middle-aged woman, actually the mother of a sons my age, and wanted somebody to help her drive to Iowa. I was all for it. Iowa! Not so far from Denver, and once I got to Denver I could relax. She drove the first few hours, at one point insisted on visiting an old church somewhere, as if we were tourists, and then I took over the wheel and, though I'm not much of a driver, drove clear through the rest of Illinois to Davenport, Iowa, via Rock Island. And here for the first time in my life I saw my beloved Mississippi River, dry in the summer haze, low water, with its big rank smell that smells like the raw body of America itself because it washes it up. Rock Island—railroad tracks, shacks, small downtown section; and over the bridge to Davenport, same kind of town, all smelling of sawdust in the warm midwest sun. Here the lady had to go on to her Iowa hometown by another route, and I got out.

The sun was going down, I walked, after a few cold beers, to the edge of town, and it was a long walk. All the men were driving home from work, wearing railroad hats, baseball hats, all kinds of hats, just like after work in any town anywhere. One of them gave me a ride up the hill and left me at a lonely crossroads on the edge of the prairie. It was beautiful there. The only cars that came by were farmer-cars; they gave me suspicious looks, they clanked along, the cows were coming home. Not a truck. A few cars zipped by. A hotrod kid came by with his scarf flying. The sun went all the way down and I was standing in the purple darkness. Now I was scared. There weren't even any lights in the Iowa countryside; in a minute nobody would be able to see me. Luckily a man going back to Davenport gave me a lift downtown. But I was right where I started from.

I went to sit in the bus station and think this over. I ate another apple pie and ice cream; that's practically all I ate all the way across the country, I knew it was nutritious and it was delicious, of course. I decided to gamble. I took a bus in downtown Davenport, after spending a half-hour watching a waitress in the bus-station café, and rode to the city limits, but this time near the gas stations. Here the big trucks roared, wham, and inside two minutes one of them cranked to a stop for me. I ran for it with my soul whoopeeing. And what a driver—a great big tough truckdriver with popping eyes and a hoarse raspy voice who just slammed and kicked at everything and got his rig under way and paid hardly any attention to me. So I could rest my tired soul a little, for one of the biggest troubles hitchhiking is having to talk to innumerable people, make them feel that they didn't make a mistake picking you up, even entertain them almost, all of which is a great strain when you're going all the way and don't plan to sleep in hotels. The guy just yelled above the road, and all I had to do was yell back, and we relaxed. And he balled that thing clear to Iowa City and yelled me the funniest stories about how he got around the law in every town that had an unfair speed limit, saying over and over again, "Them goddam cops can't put no flies on *my* ass!" Just as we rolled into Iowa City he saw another truck coming behind us, and because he had to turn off at Iowa City he blinked his tail lights at the other guy and slowed down for me to jump out, which I did with my bag, and the other truck, acknowledging this exchange, stopped for me, and once again, in the twink of nothing, I was in another big high cab, all set to go hundreds of miles across the night, and was I happy! And the new truckdriver was as crazy as the other and yelled just as much, and all I had to do was lean back and roll on. Now I could see Denver looming ahead of me like the Promised Land, way out there beneath the stars, across the prairie of Iowa and the plains of Nebraska, and I could see the greater vision of San Francisco beyond, like jewels in the night. He balled the jack and told stories for a couple of hours, then, at a town in Iowa where years later Dean and I were stopped on suspicion in what looked like a stolen Cadillac, he slept a few hours in the seat. I slept too, and took one little walk along the lonely brick walls illuminated by one lamp, with the prairie brooding at the end of each little street and the smell of the corn like dew in the night.

He woke up with a start at dawn. Off we roared, and an hour later the smoke of Des Moines appeared ahead over the green cornfields. He had to eat his breakfast now and wanted to take it easy, so I went right on into Des Moines, about four miles, hitching a ride with two boys from the University of Iowa; and it was strange sitting in their brand-new comfortable car and hearing them talk of exams as we zoomed smoothly into town. Now I wanted to sleep a whole day. So I went to the Y to get a room; they didn't have any, and by instinct I wandered down to the railroad tracks—and there're a lot of them in Des Moines—and wound up in a gloomy old Plains inn of a hotel by the locomotive roundhouse, and spent a long day sleeping on a big clean hard white bed with dirty remarks carved in the wall beside my pillow and the beat yellow window shades pulled over the smoky scene of the railyards. I woke up as the sun was reddening; and that was the one distinct time in my life, the strangest moment of all, when I didn't know who I was—I was far away from home, haunted and tired with travel, in a cheap hotel room I'd never seen, hearing the hiss of steam outside, and the creak of the old wood of the hotel, and footsteps upstairs, and all the sad sounds, and I looked at the racked high ceiling and really didn't know who I was for about fifteen strange seconds. I wasn't scared; I was just somebody else, some stranger, and my whole life was a haunted life, the life of a ghost. I was halfway across America, at the dividing line between the East of my youth and the West of my future, and maybe that's why it happened right there and then, that strange red afternoon.

But I had to get going and stop moaning, so I picked up my bag, said so long to the old hotelkeeper sitting by his spittoon, and went to eat. I ate apple pie and ice cream—it was getting better as I got deeper into Iowa, the pie bigger, the ice cream richer. There were the most beautiful bevies of girls everywhere I looked in Des Moines that afternoon—they were coming home from high school—but I had no time now for thoughts like that and promised myself a ball in Denver. Carlo Marx was already in Denver; Dean was there; Chad King and Tim Gray were there, it was their hometown; Marylou was there; and there was mention of a mighty gang including Ray Rawlins and his beautiful blond sister Babe Rawlins; two waitresses Dean knew, the Bettencourt sisters; and even Roland Major, my old college writing buddy, was there. I looked forward to all of them with joy and anticipation. So I rushed past the pretty girls, and the prettiest girls in the world live in Des Moines.

A guy with a kind of toolshack on wheels, a truck full of tools that he drove standing up like a modern milkman, gave me a ride up the long hill, where I immediately got a ride from a farmer and his son heading out for Adel in Iowa. In this town, under a big elm tree near a gas station, I made the acquaintance of another hitchhiker, a typical New Yorker, an Irishman who'd been driving a truck for the post office most of his work years and was now headed for a girl in Denver and a new life. I think he was running away from something in New York, the law most likely. He was a real rednose young drunk of thirty and would have bored me ordinarily, except that my senses were sharp for any kind of human friendship. He wore a beat sweater and baggy pants and had nothing with him in the way of a bag—just a toothbrush and handkerchiefs. He said we ought to hitch together. I should have said no, because he looked pretty awful on the road. But we stuck together and got a ride with a taciturn man to Stuart, Iowa, a town in which we were really stranded. We stood in front of the railroad-ticket shack in Stuart, waiting for the westbound traffic till the sun went down, a good five hours, dawdling away the time, at first telling about ourselves, then he told dirty stories, then we just kicked pebbles and made goofy noises of one kind and another. We got bored. I decided to spend a buck on beer; we went to an old saloon in Stuart and had a few. There he got as drunk as he ever did in his Ninth Avenue night back home, and yelled joyously in my ear all the sordid dreams of his life. I kind of liked him; not because he was a good sort, as he later proved to be, but because he was enthusiastic about things. We got back on the road in the darkness, and of course nobody stopped and nobody came by much. That went on till three o'clock in the morning. We spent some time trying to sleep on the bench at the railroad ticket office, but the telegraph clicked all night and we couldn't sleep, and big freights were slamming around outside. We didn't know how to hop a proper chain gang; we'd never done it before; we didn't know whether they were going east or west or how to find out or what boxcars and flats and de-iced reefers to pick, and so on. So when the Omaha bus came through just before dawn he hopped on it and joined the sleeping passengers—I paid for his fare as well as mine. His name was Eddie. He reminded me of my cousin-in-law from the Bronx. That was why I stuck with him. It was like having an old friend along, a smiling, good-natured sort to goof along with. . . .

. . . Eddie and I resumed on the road. We got a ride from a couple of young fellows—wranglers, teenagers, country boys in a put-together jalopy —and were left off somewhere up the line in a thin drizzle of rain. Then an old man who said nothing—and God knows why he picked us up—took us to Shelton. Here Eddie stood forlornly in the road on front of a staring bunch of short, squat Omaha Indians who had nowhere to go and nothing to do. Across the road was the railroad track and the watertank saying SHELTON. "Damn me," said Eddie with amazement, "I've been in this town before. It was years ago, during the war, at night, late at night when everybody was sleeping. I went out on the platform to smoke, and there we was in the middle of nowhere and black as hell, and I look up and see that name Shelton written on the watertank. Bound for the Pacific, everybody snoring, every damn dumb sucker, and we only stayed a few minutes, stoking up or something, and off we went. Damn me, this Shelton! I hated this place ever since!" And we were stuck in Shelton. As in Davenport, Iowa, somehow all the cars were farmer-cars, and once in a while a tourist car, which is worse, with old men driving and their wives pointing out the sights or poring over maps, and sitting back looking at everything with suspicious faces.

The drizzle increased and Eddie got cold; he had very little clothing. I fished a wool plaid shirt from my canvas bag and he put it on. He felt a little better. I had a cold. I bought cough drops in a rickety Indian store of some kind. I went to the little two-by-four post office and wrote my aunt a penny postcard. We went back to the gray road. There she was in front of us, Shelton, written on the watertank. The Rock Island balled by. We saw the faces of Pullman passengers go by in a blur. The train howled off across the plains in the direction of our desires. It started to rain harder.

A tall, lanky fellow in a gallon hat stopped his car on the wrong side of the road and came over to us; he looked like a sheriff. We prepared our stories secretly. He took his time coming over. "You boys going to get somewhere, or just going?" We didn't understand his question, and it was a damned good question.

"Why?" we said.

"Well, I own a little carnival that's pitched a few miles down the road and I'm looking for some old boys willing to work and make a buck for themselves. I've got a roulette concession and a wooden-ring concession, you know, the kind you throw around dolls and take your luck. You boys want to work for me, you can get thirty per cent of the take."

"Room and board?"

"You can get a bed but no food. You'll have to eat in town. We travel some." We thought it over. "It's a good opportunity," he said, and waited patiently for us to make up our minds. We felt silly and didn't know what to say, and I for one didn't want to get hung-up with a carnival. I was in such a bloody hurry to get to the gang in Denver.

I said, "I don't know, I'm going as fast as I can and I don't think I have the time." Eddie said the same thing, and the old man waved his hand and casually sauntered back to his car and drove off. And that was that. We laughed about it awhile and speculated about what it would have been like. I had visions of a dark and dusty night on the plains, and the faces of Nebraska families wandering by, with their rosy children looking at everything with awe, and I know I would have felt like the devil himself rooking them with all those cheap carnival tricks. And the Ferris wheel revolving in the flatlands darkness, and, Godalmighty, the sad music of the merry-go-round and me wanting to get on to my goal—and sleeping in some gilt wagon on a bed of burlap.

Eddie turned out to be a pretty absent-minded pal of the road. A funny old contraption rolled by, driven by an old man; it was made of some kind of aluminum, square as a box—a trailer, no doubt, but a weird, crazy Nebraska homemade trailer. He was going very slow and stopped. We rushed up; he said he could only take one; without a word Eddie jumped in and slowly rattled from my sight, and wearing my wool plaid shirt. Well, alackaday, I kissed the shirt good-bye; it had only sentimental value in any case. I waited in our personal godawful Shelton for a long, long time, several hours, and I kept thinking it was getting night; actually it was only early afternoon, but dark. Denver, Denver, how would I ever get to Denver? I was just about giving up and planning to sit over coffee when a fairly new car stopped, driven by a young guy. I ran like mad.

"Where you going?"

"Denver."

"Well, I can take you a hundred miles up the line."

"Grand, grand, you saved my life."

"I used to hitchhike myself, that's why I always pick up a fellow."

"I would too if I had a car." And so we talked, and he told me about his life, which wasn't very interesting, and I started to sleep some and woke up right outside the town of Gothenburg, where he let me off....

The greatest ride in my life was about to come up, a truck, with a flatboard at the back, with about six or seven boys sprawled out on it, and the drivers, two young blond farmers from Minnesota, were picking up every single soul they found on that road—the most smiling, cheerful couple of handsome bumpkins you could ever wish to see, both wearing cotton shirts and overalls, nothing else; both thick-wristed and earnest, with broad howareyou smiles for anybody and anything that came across their path. I ran up, said "Is there room?" They said, "Sure, hop on, 'sroom for everybody."

I wasn't on the flatboard before the truck roared off; I lurched, a rider grabbed me, and I sat down. Somebody passed a bottle of rotgut, the bottom ot it. I took a big swig in the wild, lyrical, drizzling air of Nebraska. "Whooee, here we go!" yelled a kid in a baseball cap, and they gunned up the truck to seventy and passed everybody on the road. "We been riding this sonofabitch since Des Moines. These guys never stop. Every now and then you have to yell for pisscall, otherwise you have to piss off the air, and hang on, brother, hang on."

I looked at the company. There were two young farmer boys from North Dakota in red baseball caps, which is the standard North Dakota farmer-boy hat, and they were headed for the harvests; their old men had given them leave to hit the road for a summer. There were two young city boys form Columbus, Ohio, high-school football players, chewing gum, winking, singing in the breeze, and they said they were hitchhiking around the United States for the summer. "We're going to LA!" they yelled.

"What are you going to do there?"

"Hell, we don't know. Who cares?"

Then there was a tall slim fellow who had a sneaky look. "Where you from?" I asked. I was lying next to him on the platform; you couldn't sit without bouncing off, it had no rails. And he turned slowly to me, opened his mouth, and said, "Mon-ta-na."

Finally there were Mississippi Gene and his charge. Mississippi Gene was a little dark guy who rode freight trains around the country, a thirty-year-old hobo but with a youthful look so you couldn't tell exactly what age he was. And he sat on the boards crosslegged, looking out over the fields without saying anything for hundreds of miles, and finally at one point he turned to me and said, "Where *you* headed?"

I said Denver.

"I got a sister there but I ain't seed her for several couple years." His language was melodious and slow. He was patient. His charge was a sixteen-year-old tall blond kid, also in hobo rags; that is to say, they wore old clothes that had been turned black by the soot of railroads and the dirt of boxcars and sleeping on the ground. The blond kid was also quiet and he seemed to be running away from something, and it figured to be the law the way he looked straight ahead and wet his lips in worried thought. Montana Slim spoke to them occasionally with a sardonic and insinuating smile. They paid no attention to him. Slim was all insinuation. I was afraid of his long goofy grin that he opened up straight in your face and held there half-moronically.

"You got any money?" he said to me.

"Hell no, maybe enough for a pint of whisky till I get to Denver. What about you?"

"I know where I can get some."

"Where?"

"Anywhere. You can always folly a man down an alley, can't you?"

"Yeah, I guess you can."

"I ain't beyond doing it when I really need some dough. Headed up to Montana to see my father. I'll have to get off this rig at Cheyenne and move up some other way. These crazy boys are going to Los Angeles."

"Straight?"

"All the way—if you want to go to LA you got a ride."

I mulled this over; the thought of zooming all night across Nebraska, Wyoming, and the Utah desert in the morning, and then most likely the Nevada desert in the afternoon, and actually arriving in Los Angeles within a foreseeable space of time almost made me change my plans. But I had to go to Denver. I'd have to get off at Cheyenne too, and hitch south ninety miles to Denver.

I was glad when the two Minnesota farmboys who owned the truck decided to stop in North Platte and eat; I wanted to have a look at them. They came out of the cab and smiled at all of us."Pisscall!" said one. "Time to eat!" said the other. But they were the only ones in the party who had money to buy food. We all shambled after them to a restaurant run by a bunch of women, and sat around over hamburgers and coffee while they wrapped away enormous meals just as if they were back in their mother's kitchen. They were brothers; they were transporting farm machinery from Los Angeles to Minnesota and making good money at it. So on their trip to the Coast empty they picked up everybody on the road. They'd done this about five times now; they were having a hell of a time. They liked everything. They never stopped smiling. I tried to talk to them—a kind of dumb attempt on my part to befriend the captains of our ship—and the only responses I got were two sunny smiles and large white cornfed teeth.

Everybody had joined them in the restaurant except the two hobo kids, Gene and his boy. When we all got back they were still sitting in the truck, forlorn and disconsolate. Now the darkness was falling. The drivers had a smoke; I jumped at the chance to go buy a bottle of whisky to keep warm in the rushing cold air of night. They smiled when I told them. "Go ahead, hurry up."

"You can have a couple shots!" I reassured them.

"Oh no, we never drink, go ahead."

Montana Slim and the two high-school boys wandered the streets of North Platte with me till I found a whisky store. They chipped in some, and Slim some, and I bought a fifth. Tall, sullen men watched us go by from false-front buildings; the main street lined with square box-houses. There were immense vistas of the plains beyond every sad street. I felt something different in the air in North Platte, I didn't know what it was. In five minutes I did. We got back on the truck and roared off. It got dark quickly. We all had a shot, and suddenly I looked, and the verdant farmfields of the Platte began to disappear and in their stead, so far you couldn't see to the end, appeared long flat wastelands of sand and sagebrush. I was astounded.

"What in the hell is this?" I cried out to Slim.

"This is the beginning of the rangelands, boy. Hand me another drink."

"Whoopee!" yelled the high-school boys. "Columbus, so long! What would Sparkie and the boys say if they was here. Yow!"

The drivers had switched up front; the fresh brother was gunning the truck to the limit. The road changed too: humpy in the middle, with soft shoulders and a ditch on both sides about four feet deep, so that the truck bounced and teetered from one side of the road to the other—miraculously only when there were no cars coming the opposite way—and I thought we'd all take a somersault. But they were tremendous drivers. How that truck disposed of the Nebraska nub—the nub that sticks out over Colorado! And soon I realized I was actually at last over Colorado, though not officially in it, but looking southwest toward Denver itself a few hundred miles away. I yelled for joy. We passed the bottle. The great blazing stars came out, the far-receding sand hills got dim. I felt like an arrow that could shoot out all the way.

And suddenly Mississippi Gene turned to me from his crosslegged, patient reverie, and opened his mouth, and leaned close, and said, "These plains put me in the mind of Texas."

"Are you from Texas?"

"No sir, I'm from Green-vell Muzz-sippy." And that was the way he said it.

"Where's that kid from?"

"He got into some kind of trouble back in Mississippi, so I offered to help him out. Boy's never been out on his own. I take care of him best as I can, he's only a child." Although Gene was white there was something of the wise and tired old Negro in him, and something very much like Elmer Hassel, the New York dope addict, in him, but a railroad Hassel, a traveling epic Hassel, crossing and recrossing the country every year, south in the winter and north in the summer, and only because he had no place he could stay in without getting tired of it and because there was nowhere to go but everywhere, keep rolling under the stars, generally the Western stars.

"I been to Og-den a couple times. If you want to ride on to Og-den I got some friends there we could hole up with."

"I'm going to Denver from Cheyenne."

"Hell, go right straight thu, you don't get a ride like this every day."

This too was a tempting offer. What was in Ogden? "What's Ogden?" I said.

"It's the place where most of the boys pass thu and always meet there; you're liable to see anybody there."

In my earlier days I'd been to sea with a tall rawboned fellow from Louisiana called Big Slim Hazard, William Holmes Hazard, who was hobo by choice. As a little boy he'd seen a hobo come up to ask his mother for a piece of pie, and she had given it to him, and when the hobo went off down the road the little boy had said, "Ma, what is that fellow?" "Why, that's a ho-bo." "Ma, I want to be a ho-bo someday." "Shet your mouth, that's not for the like of the Hazards." But he never forgot that day, and when he grew up, after a short spell playing football at LSU, he did become a hobo. Big Slim and I spent many nights telling stories and spitting tobacco juice in paper containers. There was something so indubitably reminiscent of Big Slim Hazard in Mississippi Gene's demeanor that I said, "Do you happen to have met a fellow called Big Slim Hazard somewhere?"

And he said, "You mean the tall fellow with a big laugh?"

"Well, that sounds like him. He came from Ruston, Louisiana."

"That's right. Louisiana Slim he's sometimes called. Yessir, I shore have met Big Slim."

"And he used to work in the East Texas oil fields?"

"East Texas is right. And now he's punching cows."

And that was exactly right; and still I couldn't believe Gene could have really known Slim, whom I'd been looking for, more or less, for years. "And he used to work in tugboats in New York?"

"Well now, I don't know about that."

"I guess you only knew him in the West."

"I reckon. I ain't never been to New York."

"Well, damn me, I'm amazed you know him. This is a big country. Yet I knew you must have known him."

"Yessir, I know Big Slim pretty well. Always generous with his money when he's got some. Mean, tough fellow, too; I seen him flatten a policeman in the yards at Cheyenne, one punch." That sounded like Big Slim; he was always practicing that one punch in the air; he looked like Jack Dempsey, but a young Jack Dempsey who drank.

"Damn!" I yelled into the wind, and I had another shot, and by now I was feeling pretty good. Every shot was wiped away by the rushing wind of the open truck, wiped away of its bad effects, and the good effect sank in my stomach. "Cheyenne, here I come!" I sang. "Denver, look out for your boy."

9. The John F. Kennedy Inaugural Address

John F. Kennedy set proud goals for his administration in 1961, promising that "a new generation of Americans" would march forth to battle "the common enemies of man: tyranny, poverty, disease and war itself." But the Kennedy administration was to be a brief one—two years and ten months from the "trumpet summons" of the inauguration to the muffled drums and caissons marching slowly up Pennsylvania Avenue in November 1963. This foreshortened story of beginnings and promises, then, is a hard one to interpret. Were the hopes real? Was the vitality an illusion? Was there substance behind the glittering style? Was the New Frontier a beckoning horizon or an armed border, a fresh direction or only a new rhetoric?

Kennedy's inaugural address set the tone for his administration as few such addresses have ever done. The elevation—the magnetic tone of dedication and of hope—comes across in the way of words chiseled in granite. Thousands of Americans have read these words on Kennedy's tombstone in Arlington National Cemetery. Yet a close reading of this famous speech reveals subtle counterthemes that suggest possible answers to questions subsequently raised after John F. Kennedy's death: about his place in American history, his administration's continuity with his predecessor's policies, and the substance lodged beneath the glittering language. As you read, ask yourself what the various publics listening to this speech would have understood by it. What would a civil rights worker have derived from it? A conservative congressman? A Pentagon policy planner? The Soviet foreign ministry? John F. Kennedy's presidency was never easy to evaluate, and his untimely death left him surrounded by controversy and unanswered questions that history may never quite resolve.

We observe today not a victory of party but a celebration of freedom—symbolizing an end as well as a beginning—signifying renewal as well as change. For I have sworn before you and Almighty God the same solemn oath our forebears prescribed nearly a century and three quarters ago.

The world is very different now. For man holds in his mortal hands the power to abolish all forms of human poverty and all forms of human life. And yet the same revolutionary beliefs for which our forebears fought are still at issue around the globe—the belief that the rights of man come not from the generosity of the state but from the hand of God.

We dare not forget today that we are the heirs of that first revolution. Let the word go forth from this time and place, to friend and foe alike, that the torch has been passed to a new generation of Americans—born in this century, tempered by war, disciplined by a hard and bitter peace, proud of our ancient heritage—and unwilling to witness or permit the slow undoing of those human rights to which this nation has

Reprinted from President Kennedy's Program, published in May 1961 by Congressional Quarterly Service, p. 1.

always been committed, and to which we are committed today at home and around the world.

Let every nation know, whether it wishes us well or ill, that we shall pay any price, bear any burden, meet any hardship, support any friend, oppose any foe to assure the survival and the success of liberty.

This much we pledge—and more.

To those old allies whose cultural and spiritual origins we share, we pledge the loyalty of faithful friends. United, there is little we cannot do in a host of cooperative ventures. Divided, there is little we can do—for we dare not meet a powerful challenge at odds and split asunder.

To those new states whom we welcome to the ranks of the free, we pledge our word that one form of colonial control shall not have passed away merely to be replaced by a far more iron tyranny. We shall not always expect to find them supporting our view. But we shall always hope to find them strongly supporting their own freedom—and to remember that, in the past, those who foolishly sought power by riding the back of the tiger ended up inside.

To those peoples in the huts and villages of half the globe struggling to break the bonds of mass misery, we pledge our best efforts to help them help themselves, for whatever period is required—not because the communists may be doing it, not because we seek their votes, but because it is right. If a free society cannot help the many who are poor, it cannot save the few who are rich.

To our sister republics south of our border, we offer a special pledge—to convert our good words into good deeds—in a new alliance for progress—to assist free men and free governments in casting off the chains of poverty. But this peaceful revolution of hope cannot become the prey of hostile powers. Let all our neighbors know that we shall join with them to oppose aggression or subversion anywhere in the Americas. And let every other power know that this Hemisphere intends to remain the master of its own house.

To that world assembly of sovereign states, the United Nations, our last best hope in an age where the instruments of war have far outpaced the instruments of peace, we renew our pledge of support—to prevent it from becoming merely a forum for invective—to strengthen its shield of the new and the weak—and to enlarge the area in which its writ may run.

Finally, to those nations who would make themselves our adversary, we offer not a pledge but a request: that both sides begin anew the quest for peace, before the dark powers of destruction unleashed by science engulf all humanity in planned or accidental self-destruction.

We dare not tempt them with weakness. For only when our arms are sufficient beyond doubt can we be certain beyond doubt that they will never be employed.

But neither can two great and powerful groups of nations take comfort from our present course—both sides overburdened by the cost of modern weapons, both rightly alarmed by the steady spread of the deadly atom, yet both racing to alter that uncertain balance of terror that stays the hand of mankind's final war.

So let us begin anew—remembering on both sides that civility is not a sign of weakness, and sincerity is always subject to proof. Let us never negotiate out of fear. But let us never fear to negotiate.

Let both sides explore what problems unite us instead of belaboring those problems which divide us.

Let both sides, for the first time, formulate serious and precise proposals for the inspection and control of arms—and bring the absolute power to destroy other nations under the absolute control of all nations.

Let both sides seek to invoke the wonders of science instead of its terrors. Together let us explore the stars, conquer the deserts, eradicate disease, tap the ocean depths and encourage the arts and commerce.

Let both sides unite to heed in all corners of the earth the command of Isaiah—to "undo the heavy burdens...[and] let the oppressed go free."

And if a beach-head of cooperation may push back the jungle of suspicion, let both sides join in creating a new endeavor, not a new balance of power, but a new world of law, where the strong are just and the weak secure and the peace preserved.

All this will not be finished in the first one hundred days. Nor will it be finished in the first one thousand days, nor in the life of this Administration, nor even perhaps in our lifetime on this planet. But let us begin.

In your hands, my fellow citizens, more than mine, will rest the final success or failure of our course. Since this country was founded, each generation of Americans has been summoned to give testimony to its national loyalty. The graves of young Americans who answered the call to service surround the globe.

Now the trumpet summons us again—not as a call to bear arms, though arms we need—not as a call to battle, though embattled we are—but a call to bear the burden of a long twilight struggle, year in and year out, "rejoicing in hope, patient in tribulation"—a struggle against the common enemies of man: tyranny, poverty, disease and war itself.

Can we forge against these enemies a grand global alliance, North and South, East and West, that can assure a more fruitful life for all mankind? Will you join in that historic effort?

In the long history of the world, only a few generations have been granted the role of defending freedom in its hour of maximum danger. I do not shrink from this responsibility—I welcome it. I do not believe that any of us would exchange places with any other people or any other generation. The energy, the faith, the devotion which we bring to this endeavor will light our country and all who serve it—and the glow from that fire can truly light the world.

And so, my fellow Americans: ask not what your country can do for you—ask what you can do for your country.

My fellow citizens of the world: ask not what America will do for you, but what together we can do for the freedom of man.

Finally, whether you are citizens of America or citizens of the world, ask of us here the same high standards of strength and sacrifice which we ask of you. With a good conscience our only sure reward, with history the final judge of our deeds, let us go forth to lead the land we love, asking His blessing and His help, but knowing that here on earth God's work must truly be our own.

10. The Texture of Poverty

MICHAEL HARRINGTON

The poor, Michael Harrington urges us, "need an American Dickens to record the smell and texture and quality of their lives." Yet his own brilliant mixture of reporting and social analysis did serve the essential purpose of encouraging a compassionate view of the poor, which meant first forcing people to see them. Harrington's book remains curiously stirring—an effect we might expect from a novel, not from a book that quotes the findings of empirical social science.

The Other America, *from which this excerpt is taken, was one of several muckraking social science works that forced a new perspective on poverty in modern America. John Kenneth Galbraith in* The Affluent Society *had pointed to the persistence of poverty amid affluence and questioned whether economic growth alone would eradicate it. But he noted principally "case" poverty—the sick, the old, the unbalanced—not the more structural elements that Harrington observes. Robert Lampman and Gabriel Kolko had demonstrated that the New Deal had not significantly changed the distribution of wealth. All these writers cleared the path for a new liberal program that, ironically, undermined the claims of older liberals that the New Deal had reformed the economy in the interest of poorer Americans.*

Harrington's book continues to be the most vital of the many polemics that muckraked American society in the late fifties and the sixties. It was important because it was the one book that was most read by the people in Washington. It helped launch a war on poverty that, for all its shortcomings, has made some attempt to ameliorate the living conditions of the poor and defeat the notion that the United States must always be a nation of two societies.

I

There are perennial reasons that make the other America an invisible land.

Poverty is often off the beaten track. It always has been. The ordinary tourist never left the main highway, and today he rides interstate turnpikes. He does not go into the valleys of Pennsylvania where the towns look like movie sets of Wales in the thirties. He does not see the company houses in rows, the rutted roads (the poor always have bad roads whether they live in the city, in towns, or on farms), and everything is black and dirty. And even if he were to pass through such a place by accident, the tourist would not meet the unemployed men in the bar or the women coming home from a runaway sweatshop.

Then, too, beauty and myths are perennial masks of poverty. The traveler comes to the Appalachians in the lovely season. He sees the hills, the streams, the foliage—but not the poor. Or perhaps he looks at a run-down mountain house and, remembering Rousseau rather than seeing with his eyes, decides that "those people" are truly fortunate to be living the way they are and that they are lucky to be exempt from the strains and tensions of the middle class. The only problem is that "those people," the quaint inhabitants of those hills, are undereducated, underprivileged, lack medical care, and are in the process of being forced from the land into a life in the cities, where they are misfits.

These are normal and obvious causes of the invisibility of the poor. They operated a generation ago; they will be functioning a generation hence. It is more important to understand that the very development of American society is creating a new kind of blindness about poverty. The poor are increasingly slipping out of the very experience and consciousness of the nation.

If the middle class never did like ugliness and poverty, it was at least aware of them. "Across the tracks" was not a very long way to go. There were forays into the slums at Christmas time; there were charitable organizations that brought contact with the poor. Occasionally, almost everyone passed through the Negro ghetto or the blocks of tenements, if only to get downtown to work or to entertainment.

Now the American city has been transformed. The poor still inhabit the miserable housing in the central area, but they are increasingly isolated from contact with, or sight of, anybody else. Middle-class women coming in from Suburbia on a rare trip may catch the merest glimpse of the other America on the way to an evening at the theater, but their children are segregated in suburban schools. The business or professional man may drive along the fringes of slums in a car or bus, but it is not an important experience to him. The failures, the unskilled, the disabled, the aged, and the minorities are right there, across the tracks, where they have always been. But hardly anyone else is.

In short, the very development of the American city has removed poverty from the living, emotional experience of millions upon millions of middle-class Americans. Living out in the suburbs it is easy to assume that ours is, indeed, an affluent society.

This new segregation of poverty is compounded by a well-meaning ignorance. A good many concerned and sympathetic Americans are aware that there is much discussion of urban renewal. Suddenly, driving through the city, they notice that a familiar slum has been torn down and that there are towering, modern buildings where once there had been tenements or hovels. There is a warm feeling of satisfaction, of pride in the way things are working out: the poor, it is obvious, are being taken care of.

The irony in this . . . is that the truth is nearly the exact opposite to the impression. The total impact of the various housing programs in postwar America has been to squeeze more and more people into existing slums. More often than not, the modern apartment in a towering building rents at $40 a room or more. For, during the past decade and a half, there has been more subsidization of middle- and upper-income housing than there has been of housing for the poor.

Clothes make the poor invisible too: America has the best-dressed poverty the world has ever known. For a variety of reasons, the benefits of mass production have been spread much more evenly in this area than in many others. It is much easier in the United States to be decently dressed than it is to be decently housed, fed, or doctored. Even people with terribly depressed incomes can look prosperous.

This is an extremely important factor in defining our emotional and existential ignorance of poverty. In Detroit the existence of social classes became much more difficult to discern the day the companies put lockers in the plants. From that moment on, one did not see men in work clothes on the way to the factory, but citizens in slacks and white shirts. This process has been magnified with the poor throughout the country. There are tens of thousands of Americans in the big cities who are wearing shoes, perhaps even a stylishly cut suit or dress, and yet are hungry. It is not a matter of planning, though it almost seems as if the affluent society had given out costumes to the poor so that they would not offend the rest of society with the sight of rags.

Then, many of the poor are the wrong age to be seen. A good number of them (over 8,000,000) are sixty-five years of age or better; an even larger number are under eighteen. The aged members of the other America are often sick, and they cannot move. Another group of them live out their lives in loneliness and frustration: they sit in rented rooms, or else they stay close to a house in a neighborhood that has completely changed from the old days. Indeed, one of the worst aspects of poverty among the aged is that these people are out of sight and out of mind, and alone.

The young are somewhat more visible, yet they too stay close to their neighborhoods. Sometimes they advertise their poverty through a lurid tabloid story about a gang killing. But generally they do not disturb the quiet streets of the middle class.

And finally, the poor are politically invisible. It is one of the cruelest ironies of social life in advanced countries that the dispossessed at the bottom of society are unable to speak for themselves. The people of the other America do not, by far and large, belong to unions, to fraternal organizations, or to political parties. They are without lobbies of their own; they put forward no legislative program. As a group, they are atomized. They have no face; they have no voice. . . .

II

Out of the thirties came the welfare state. Its creation had been stimulated by mass impoverishment and misery, yet it helped the poor least of all. Laws like unemployment compensation, the Wagner Act, the various farm programs, all these were designed for the middle third in the cities, for the organized workers, and for the upper third in the country, for the big market farmers. If a man works in an extremely low-paying job, he may not even be covered by social security or other welfare programs. If he receives unemployment compensation, the payment is scaled down according to his low earnings.

One of the major laws that was designed to cover everyone, rich and poor, was social security. But even here the other Americans suffered discrimination. Over the years social security payments have not even provided a subsistence level of life. The middle third have been able to supplement the Federal pension through private plans negotiated by unions, through joining medical insurance schemes like Blue Cross, and so on. The poor have not been able to do so. They lead a bitter life, and then have to pay for that fact in old age.

Indeed, the paradox that the welfare state benefits those least who need help most is but a single instance of a persistent irony in the other America. Even when the money finally trickles down, even when a school is built in a poor neighborhood, for instance, the poor are still deprived. Their entire environment, their life, their values, do not prepare them to take advantage of the new opportunity. The parents are anxious for the children to go to work; the pupils are pent up, waiting for the moment when their education has complied with the law.

Today's poor, in short, missed the political and social gains of the thirties. They are, as Galbraith rightly points out, the first minority poor in history, the first poor not to be seen, the first poor whom the politicians could leave alone.

The first step toward the new poverty was taken when millions of people proved immune to progress. When that happened, the failure was not individual and personal, but a social product. But once the historic accident takes place, it begins to become a personal fate.

The new poor of the other America saw the rest of society move ahead. They went on living in depressed areas, and often they tended to become depressed human beings. In some of the West Virginia towns, for instance, an entire community will become shabby and defeated. The young and the adventurous go to the city, leaving behind those who cannot move and those who lack the will to do so. The entire area becomes permeated with failure, and that is one more reason the big corporations shy away.

Indeed, one of the most important things about the new poverty is that it cannot be defined in simple, statistical terms. Throughout this book a crucial term is used: aspiration. If a group has internal vitality, a will—if it has aspiration—it may live in dilapidated housing, it may eat an inadequate diet, and it may suffer poverty, but it is not impoverished. So it was in those ethnic slums of the immigrants that played such a dramatic role in the unfolding of the American dream. The people found themselves in slums, but they were not slum dwellers.

But the new poverty is constructed so as to destroy aspiration; it is a system designed to be impervious to hope. The other America does not contain the adventurous seeking a new life and land. It is populated by the failures, by those driven from the land and bewildered by the city, by old people suddenly confronted with the torments of loneliness and poverty, and by minorities facing a wall of prejudice.

In the past, when poverty was general in the unskilled and semi-skilled work force, the poor were all mixed together. The bright and the dull, those who were going to escape into the great society and those who were to stay behind, all of them lived on the same street. When the middle third rose, this community was destroyed. And the entire invisible land of the other Americans became a ghetto, a modern poor farm for the rejects of society and of the economy.

It is a blow to reform and the political hopes of the poor that the middle class no longer understands that poverty exists. But, perhaps more important, the poor are losing their links with the great world. If statistics and sociology can measure a feeling as delicate as loneliness (and some of the attempts to do so will be cited later on), the other America is becoming increasingly populated by those who do not belong to anybody or anything. They are no longer participants in an ethnic culture from the old country; they are less and less religious; they do not belong to unions or clubs. They are not seen, and because of that they themselves cannot see. Their horizon has become more and more restricted; they see one another, and that means they see little reason to hope.

Galbraith was one of the first writers to begin to describe the newness of contemporary poverty, and that is to his credit. Yet because even he underestimates the problem, it is important to put his definition into perspective.

For Galbraith, there are two main components of the new poverty: case poverty and insular poverty. Case poverty is the plight of those who suffer from some physical or mental disability that is personal and individual and excludes them from the general advance. Insular poverty exists in areas like the Appalachians or the West Virginia coal fields, where an entire section of the country becomes economically obsolete.

Physical and mental disabilities are, to be sure, an important part of poverty in America. The poor are sick in body and in spirit. But this is not an isolated fact about them, an individual "case," a stroke of bad luck. Disease, alcoholism, low IQ's, these express a whole way of life. They are, in the main, the effects of an environment, not the biographies of unlucky individuals. Because of this, the new poverty is something that cannot be dealt with by first aid. If there is to be a lasting assault on the shame of the other America, it must seek to root out of this society an entire environment, and not just the relief of individuals.

But perhaps the idea of "insular" poverty is even more dangerous. To speak of "islands" of the poor (or, in the more popular term, of "pockets of poverty") is to imply that one is confronted by a serious, but relatively minor, problem. This is hardly a description of a misery that extends to 40,000,000 or 50,000,000 people in the United States. They have remained impoverished in spite of increasing productivity and the creation of a welfare state. That fact alone should suggest the dimensions of a serious and basic situation.

And yet, even given these disagreements with Galbraith, his achievement is considerable. He was one of the first to understand that there are enough poor people in the United States to constitute a subculture of misery, but not enough of them to challenge the conscience and the imagination of the nation.

Finally, one might summarize the newness of contemporary poverty by saying: These are the people who are immune to progress. But then the facts are even more cruel. The other Americans are the victims of the very inventions and machines that have provided a higher living standard for the rest of the society. They are upside-down in the economy, and for them greater productivity often means worse jobs; agricultural advance becomes hunger.

In the optimistic theory, technology is an undisguised blessing. A general increase in productivity, the argument goes, generates a higher standard of living for the whole people. And indeed, this has been true for the middle and upper thirds of American society, the people who made such striking gains in the last two decades. It tends to overstate the automatic character of the process, to omit the role of human struggle. (The CIO was organized by men in conflict, not by economic trends.) Yet it states a certain truth—for those who are lucky enough to participate in it.

But the poor, if they were given to theory, might argue the exact opposite. They might say: Progress is misery.

As the society became more technological, more skilled, those who learn to work the machines, who get the expanding education, move up. Those who miss out at the very start find themselves at a new disadvantage. A generation ago in American life, the majority of the working people did not have high-school educations. But at that time industry was organized on a lower level of skill and competence. And there was a sort of continuum in the shop: the youth who left school at sixteen could begin as a laborer, and gradually pick up skill as he went along.

Today the situation is quite different. The good jobs require much more academic preparation, much more skill from the very outset. Those who lack a high-school education tend to be condemned to the economic underworld—to low-paying service industries, to backward factories, to sweeping and janitorial duties. If the fathers and mothers of the contemporary poor were penalized a generation ago for their lack of schooling, their children will suffer all the more. The very rise in productivity that created more money and better working conditions for the rest of the society can be a menace to the poor.

But then this technological revolution might have an even more disastrous consequence: it could increase the ranks of the poor as well as intensify the disabilities of poverty. At this point it is too early to make any final judgment, yet there are obvious danger signals. There are millions of Americans who live just the other side of poverty. When a recession comes, they are pushed onto the relief rolls. (Welfare payments in New York respond almost immediately to any economic decline.) If automation continues to inflict more and more penalties on the unskilled and the semiskilled, it could have the impact of permanently increasing the population of the other America.

Even more explosive is the possibility that people who participated in the gains of the thirties and the forties will be pulled back down into poverty. Today the mass-production industries where unionization made such a difference are contracting. Jobs are being destroyed. In the process, workers who had achieved a certain level of wages, who had won working conditions in the shop, are suddenly confronted with impoverishment. This is particularly true for anyone over forty years of age and for members of minority groups. Once their job is abolished, their chances of ever getting similar work are very slim.

It is too early to say whether or not this phenomenon is temporary, or whether it represents a massive retrogression that will swell the numbers of the poor. To a large extent, the answer to this question will be determined by the political response of the United States in the sixties. If serious and massive action is not undertaken, it may be necessary for statisticians to add some old-fashioned, pre-welfare-state poverty to the misery of the other America.

Poverty in the 1960s is invisible and it is new, and both these factors make it more tenacious. It is more isolated and politically powerless than ever before. It is laced with ironies, not the least of which is that many of the poor view progress upside-down, as a menace and a threat to their lives. And if the nation does not measure up to the challenge of automation, poverty in the 1960s might be on the increase.

There are mighty historical and economic forces that keep the poor down; and there are human beings who help out in this grim business, many of them unwittingly. There are sociological and political reasons why poverty is not seen; and there are misconceptions and prejudices that literally blind the eyes. The latter must be understood if anyone is to make the necessary act of intellect and will so that the poor can be noticed.

Here is the most familiar version of social blindness: "The poor are that way because they are afraid of work. And anyway they all have big cars. If they were like me (or my father or my grandfather), they could pay their own way. But they prefer to live on the dole and cheat the taxpayers."

This theory, usually thought of as a virtuous and moral statement, is one of the means of making it impossible for the poor ever to pay their way. There are, one must assume, citizens of the other America who choose impoverishment out of fear of work (though, writing it down, I really do not believe it). But the real explanation of why the poor are where they are is that they made the mistake of being born to the wrong parents, in the wrong section of the country, in the wrong industry, or in the wrong racial or ethnic group. Once that mistake has been made, they could have been paragons of will and morality, but most of them would never even have had a chance to get out of the other America.

There are two important ways of saying this: The poor are caught in a vicious circle; or, The poor live in a culture of poverty.

In a sense, one might define the contemporary poor in the United States as those who, for reasons beyond their control, cannot help themselves. All the most decisive factors making for opportunity and advance are against them. They are born going downward, and most of them stay down. They are victims whose lives are endlessly blown round and round the other America.

Here is one of the most familiar forms of the vicious circle of poverty. The poor get sick more than anyone else in the society. That is because they live in slums, jammed together under unhygienic conditions; they have inadequate diets, and cannot get decent medical care. When they become sick, they are sick longer than any other group in the society. Because they are sick more often and longer than anyone else, they lose wages and work, and find it difficult to hold a steady job. And because of this, they cannot pay for good housing, for a nutritious diet, for doctors. At any given point in the circle, particularly when there is a major illness, their prospect is to move to an even lower level and to begin the cycle, round and round, toward even more suffering.

This is only one example of the vicious circle. Each group in the other America has its own particular version of the experience, and these will be detailed throughout this book. But the pattern, whatever its variations, is basic to the other America.

The individual cannot usually break out of this vicious circle. Neither can the group, for it lacks the social energy and political strength to turn its misery into a cause. Only the larger society, with its help and resources, can really make it possible for these people to help themselves. Yet those who could make the difference too often refuse to act because of their ignorant, smug moralisms. They view the effects of poverty—above all, the waring of the will and spirit that is a consequence of being poor—as choices. Understanding the vicious circle is an important step in breaking down this prejudice.

There is an even richer way of describing this same, general idea: Poverty in the United States is a culture, an institution, a way of life.

There is a famous anecdote about Ernest Hemingway and F. Scott Fitzgerald. Fitzgerald is reported to have remarked to Hemingway, "The rich are different." And Hemingway replied, "Yes, they have money." Fitzgerald had much the better of the exchange. He understood that being rich was not a simple fact, like a large bank account, but a way of looking at reality, a series of attitudes, a special type of life. If this is true of the rich, it is ten times truer of the poor. Everything about them, from the condition of their teeth to the way in which they love, is suffused and permeated by the fact of their poverty. And this is sometimes a hard idea for a Hemingway-like middle-class America to comprehend.

The family structure of the poor, for instance, is different from that of the rest of the society. There are more homes without a father, there are less marriage, more early pregnancy and if Kinsey's statistical findings can be used, markedly different attitudes toward sex. As a result of this, to take but one consequence of the fact, hundreds of thousands, and perhaps millions, of children in the other America never know stability and "normal" affection.

Or perhaps the policeman is an even better example. For the middle class, the police protect property, give directions, and help old ladies. For the urban poor, the police are those who arrest you. In almost any slum there is a vast conspiracy against the forces of law and order. If someone approaches asking for a person, no one there will have heard of him, even if he lives next door. The outsider is "cop," bill collector, investigator (and, in the Negro ghetto, most dramatically, he is "the Man").

While writing this book, I was arrested for participation in a civil-rights demonstration. A brief experience of a night in a cell made an abstraction personal and immediate: the city jail is one of the basic institutions of the other America. Almost everyone whom I encountered in the "tank" was poor: skid-row whites, Negroes, Puerto Ricans. Their poverty was an incitement to arrest in the first place. (A policeman will be much more careful with a well-dressed, obviously educated man who might have political connections than he will with someone who is poor.) They did not have money for bail or for lawyers. And, perhaps most important, they waited their arraignment with stolidity, in a mood of passive acceptance. They expected the worst, and they probably got it.

There is, in short, a language of the poor, a psychology of the poor, a world view of the poor. To be impoverished is to be an internal alien, to grow up in a culture that is radically different from the one that dominates the society. The poor can be described statistically; they can be analyzed as a group. But they need a novelist as well as a sociologist if we are to see them. They need an American Dickens to record the smell and texture and quality of their lives. The cycles and trends, the massive forces, must be seen as affecting persons who talk and think differently.

I am not that novelist. Yet in this book I have attempted to describe the faces behind the statistics, to tell a little of the "thickness" of personal life in the other America. Of necessity, I have begun with large groups: the dispossessed workers, the minorities, the farm poor, and the aged. Then, there are three cases of less massive types of poverty, including the only single humorous component in the other America. And finally, there are the slums, and the psychology of the poor.

Throughout, I work on an assumption that cannot be proved by Government figures or even documented by impressions of the other America. It is an ethical proposition, and it can be simply stated: In a nation with a technology that could provide every citizen with a decent life, it is an outrage and a scandal that there should be such social misery. Only if one begins with this assumption is it possible to pierce through the invisibility of 40,000,000 to 50,000,000 human beings and to see the other America. We must perceive passionately, if this blindness is to be lifted from us. . . .

III

There are few people in the United States who accept Rousseau's image of the "noble savage," of primitive, untutored man as being more natural than, and superior to, his civilized descendants. Such an idea could hardly survive in a society that has made technological progress one of its most central values. There are occasional daydreams about "getting away from it all," of going to an idyllic countryside, but these are usually passing fancies.

Yet, there is a really important remnant of Rousseau's myth. It is the conviction that, as far as emotional disturbance and mental disease go, the poor are noble savages and the rich are the prime victims of tension and conflict.

There are the literature of the harried executive, the tales of suburban neurosis, the theme of the danger of wealth and leisure. It is not so much that anyone says that the poor are healthy in spirit because they are deprived of material things. Rather, the poor are just forgotten, as usual. The novels and the popular sociology are written by the middle class about the middle class, and there is more than a little strain of self-pity. The result is an image in which personal maladjustment flourishes at the top of the society, the price the well-off pay for their power. As you go down the income scale, this theory implies, life becomes more tedious and humdrum, if less upset. (However, it should be noted that the white-collar strata have the chronicler of their quiet desperation in Paddy Chayevsky.)

The truth is almost exactly opposite to the myth. The poor are subject to more mental illness than anyone else in the society, and their disturbances tend to be more serious than those of any other class. This conclusion has emerged from a series of studies made over the past few decades. There is still considerable controversy and disagreement with regard to the reasons behind this situation. But the fact itself would seem to be beyond dispute.

Indeed, if there is any point in American society where one can see poverty as a culture, as a way of life, it is here. There is, in a sense, a personality of poverty, a type of human being produced by the grinding, wearing life of the slums. The other Americans feel differently than the rest of the nation. They tend to be hopeless and passive, yet prone to bursts of violence; they are lonely and isolated, often rigid and hostile. To be poor is not simply to be deprived of the material things of this world. It is to enter a fatal, futile universe, an America within America with a twisted spirit.

Perhaps the most classic (but still controversial) study of this subject is the book *Social Class and Mental Illness* by August B. Hollingshead and F. C. Redlich. Published in 1958, it summarizes a careful research project in New Haven, Connecticut. It is an academic, scholarly work, yet its statistics are the description of an abyss.

Hollingshead and Redlich divided New Haven into five social classes. At the top (Class I) were the rich, usually aristocrats of family as well as of money. Next came the executives and professionals more newly arrived to prestige and power. Then, the middle class, and beneath them, the workers with decent paying jobs. Class V, the bottom class, was made up of the poor. About half of its members were semi-skilled, about half unskilled. The men had less than six years of education, the women less than eight.

As it turned out, this five-level breakdown was more revealing than the usual three-class image of American society (upper, middle, and lower). For it showed a sharp break between Class V at the bottom and Class IV just above it. In a dramatic psychological sense, the skilled unionized worker lived much, much closer to the middle class than he did to the world of the poor. Between Class IV and Class V, Hollingshead and Redlich found a chasm. This represents the gulf between working America, which may be up against it from time to time but which has a certain sense of security and dignity, and the other America of the poor.

Perhaps the most shocking and decisive statistic that Hollingshead and Redlich found was the one that tabulated the rate of treated psychiatric illness per 100,000 people in New Haven. These are their results:

Classes I and II	556 per 100,000
Class III	538
Class IV	642
Class V	1,659

From the top of society down to the organized workers, there are differences, but relatively small ones. But suddenly, when one crosses the line from Class IV to Class V, there is a huge leap, with the poor showing a rate of treated psychiatric illness of almost three times the magnitude of any other class.

But the mental suffering of the poor in these figures is not simply expressed in gross numbers. It is a matter of quality as well. In Classes I and II, 65 percent of the treated psychiatric illness is for neurotic problems, and only 35 percent for the much graver disturbances of psychoses. But at the bottom, in Class V, 90 percent of the treated illness is for psychosis, and only 10 percent for neurosis. In short, not only the rate but also the intensity of mental illness is much greater for the poor.

One of the standard professional criticisms of Hollingshead and Redlich is that their figures are for treated illness (those who actually got to a doctor or clinic) and do not indicate the "true prevalence" of mental illness in the population. Whatever merits this argument has in relation to other parts of the study, it points up that these particular figures are an understatement of the problem. The higher up the class scale one is, the more likely that there will be recognition of mental illness as a problem and that help will be sought. At the bottom of society, referral to psychiatric treatment usually comes from the courts. Thus, if anything, there is even more mental illness among the poor than the figures of Hollingshead and Redlich indicate.

The one place where this criticism might have some validity is with regard to the intensity of emotional disturbance. Only 10 percent of the poor who received treatment are neurotics, yet the poor neurotic is the least likely person in the society to show up for treatment. He can function, if only in an impaired and maimed way. If there were something done about this situation, it is quite possible that one would find more neurosis in the other America at the same time as one discovered more mental illness generally.

However, it is not necessary to juggle with statistics and explanations in order to corroborate the main drift of the New Haven figures. During the fifties the Cornell University Department of Psychiatry undertook an ambitious study of "Midtown," a residential area in New York City. The research dealt with a population of 170,000 from every social class, 99 percent of them white. (By leaving out the Negroes, there probably was a tendency to underestimate the problem of poverty generally, and the particular disabilities of a discriminated minority in particular.) The goal of the study was to discover "true prevalence," and there was interviewing in depth.

The Cornell scholars developed a measure of "mental health risk." They used a model of three classes, and consequently their figures are not so dramatic as those tabulated in New Haven. Yet they bear out the essential point: the lowest class had a mental health risk almost 40 percent greater than the highest class. Once again the world of poverty was given definition as a spiritual and emotional reality.

The huge brute fact of emotional illness in the other America is fairly well substantiated. The reasons behind the fact are the subject of considerable controversy. There is no neat and simple summary that can be given at the present time, yet some of the analyses are provocative for an understanding of the culture of poverty even if they must be taken tentatively.

One of the most interesting speculations came from the Cornell study of "Midtown" in New York City. The researchers developed a series of "stress factors" that might be related to an individual's mental health risk. In childhood, these were poor mental health on the part of the parents, poor physical health for the parents, economic deprivation, broken homes, a negative attitude on the part of the child toward his parents, a quarrelsome home, and sharp disagreements with parents during adolescence. In adult life, the stress factors were poor health, work worries, money worries, a lack of neighbors and friends, marital worries, and parental worries.

The Cornell team then tested to see if there was any relationship between these factors and mental health. They discovered a marked correlation. The person who had been subjected to thirteen of these stress factors was three times more likely to be mentally disturbed than the person who had felt none of them. Indeed, the researchers were led to conclude that the sheer number of stress factors was more important than the quality of stresses. Those who had experienced any three factors were of a higher mental risk than those who had experienced two.

If the Cornell conclusions are validated in further research, they will constitute an important revision of some widely held ideas about mental health. The Freudian theory has emphasized the earliest years and the decisive trauma in the development of mental illness (for example, the death of a parent). This new theory would suggest a more cumulative conception of mental illness: as stress piles upon stress over a period of time, there is a greater tendency toward disturbance. It would be an important supplement to the Freudian ideas.

But if this theory is right, there is a fairly obvious reason for the emotional torment of the other America. The stress factors listed by the Cornell study are the very stuff of the life of the poor: physical illness, broken homes, worries about work and money, and all the rest. The slum, with its vibrant, dense life hammers away at the individual. And because of the sheer, grinding, dirty experience of being poor, the personality, the spirit, is impaired. It is as if human beings dilapidate along with the tenements in which they live.

However, some scholars have attempted to soften the grimness of this picture with a theory about "drift." The poor, they argue, have a high percentage of disturbed people, not because of the conditions of life in the urban and rural slums, but because this is the group that gets all the outcasts of society from the rest of the classes. If this thesis were true, then one would expect to find failures from the higher classes as a significant group in the culture of the poor.

Hollingshead and Redlich tested this theory in New Haven and did not find any confirmation for it. The mentally impaired poor had been, for the most part, born poor. Their sickness was a product of poverty, instead of their poverty being a product of sickness. Similarly, in the Midtown study, no evidence was turned up to indicate that the disturbed poor were the rejects from other classes. There are some exceptions to this rule: alcoholics, as noted before, often tend to fall from a high position into the bitterest poverty. Still, current research points to a direct relationship between the experience of poverty and emotional disturbance.

And yet, an ironic point turned up in the Midtown research. It was discovered that a certain kind of neurosis was useful to a minority of poor people. The obsessive-compulsive neurotic often got ahead; his very sickness was a means of advancement out of the other America and into the great world. And yet, this might only prepare for a later crisis. On the lower and middle rungs of business society, hard work, attention to detail, and the like are enough to guarantee individual progress. But if such a person moves across the line, and is placed in a position where he must make decisions, there is the very real possibility of breakdown.

IV

Someone in trouble, someone in sorrow, a fight between neighbors, a coffin carried from a house, were things that coloured their lives and shook down fiery blossoms where they walked.—Sean O'Casey

The feelings, the emotions, the attitudes of the poor are different. But different from what? In this question there is an important problem of dealing with the chaotic in the world of poverty.

The definition makers, the social scientists, and the moralists come from the middle class. Their values do not include "a fight between neighbors" as a "fiery blossom." Yet that is the fact in the other America. (O'Casey was talking about Ireland; he might as well have been describing any slum in the United States.) Before going on and exploring the emotional torment of the poor, it would be well to understand this point.

Take the gangs. They are violent, and by middle-class standards they are antisocial and disturbed. But within a slum, violence and disturbance are often norms, everyday facts of life. From the inside of the other America, joining a "bopping" gang may well not seem like deviant behavior. It could be a necessity for dealing with a hostile world. (Once, in a slum school in St. Louis, a teacher stopped a fight between two little girls. "Nice girls don't fight," she told them. "Yeah," one of them replied, "you should have seen my old lady at the tavern last night.")

Indeed, one of the most depressing pieces of research I have ever read touches on this point. H. Warren Dunham carefully studied forty catatonic schizophrenics in Chicago in the early forties. He found that none of them had belonged to gangs or had engaged in the kind of activity the middle class regards as abnormal. They had, as a matter of fact, tried to live up to the standards of the larger society, rather than conforming to the values of the slum. "The catatonic young man can be described as a good boy and one who has all the desirable traits which all the social agencies would like to inculcate in the young men of the community."

The middle class does not understand the narrowness of its judgments. And worse, it acts upon them as if they were universal and accepted by everyone. In New Haven, Hollingshead and Redlich found two girls with an almost identical problem. Both of them were extremely promiscuous, so much so that they eventually had a run-in with the police. When the girl from Class I was arrested, she was provided with bail at once, newspaper stories were quashed, and she was taken care of through private psychotherapy. The girl from Class V was sentenced to reform school. She was paroled in two years, but was soon arrested again and sent to the state reformatory.

James Baldwin made a brilliant and perceptive application of this point to the problem of the Negro in a speech I heard not long ago. The white, he said, cannot imagine what it is like to be Negro: the danger, the lack of horizon, the necessity of always being on guard and watching. For that matter, Baldwin went on, the Negro problem is really the white problem. It is not the Negro who sets dark skin and kinky hair aside as something fearful, but the white. And the resolution of the racial agony in America requires a deep introspection on the part of the whites. They must discover themselves even more than the Negro.

This is true of all the juvenile delinquents, all the disturbed people, in the other America. One can put it baldly: their sickness is often a means of relating to a diseased environment. Until this is understood, the emotionally disturbed poor person will probably go on hurting himself until he becomes a police case. When he is finally given treatment, it will be at public expense, and it will be inferior to that given the rich. (In New Haven, according to Hollingshead and Redlich, the poor are five times more likely to get organic therapy—including shock treatment—rather than protracted, individual professional care.)

For that matter, some of the researchers in the field believe that sheer ignorance is one of the main causes of the high rate of disturbance among the poor. In the slum, conduct that would shock a middle-class neighborhood and lead to treatment is often considered normal. Even if someone is constantly and violently drunk, or beats his wife brutally, people will say of such a person, "Well, he's a little odd." Higher up on the class scale an individual with such a problem would probably realize that something was wrong (or his family would). He will have the knowledge and the money to get help.

One of the researchers in the field who puts great stress on the "basic universals" of the Freudian pattern (mother figure, father figure, siblings) looks upon this factor of ignorance as crucial. He is Dr. Lawrence Kubie. For Dr. Kubie, the fundamental determinants of mental health and illness are the same in every social class. But culture and income and education account for whether the individual will handle his problem; whether he understands himself as sick; whether he seeks help, and so on. This theory leaves the basic assumptions of traditional psychoanalysis intact, but, like any attempt to deal with the poor, it recognizes that something is different.

For the rich, then, and perhaps even for the better-paid worker, breakdowns, neurosis, and psychosis appear as illness and are increasingly treated as such. But the poor do not simply suffer these disturbances; they suffer them blindly. To them it does not appear that they are mentally sick; to them it appears that they are trapped in a fate.

11. Kennedy and the Cold War

DAVID BURNER

John Fitzgerald Kennedy was one of the most attractive men ever to be President of the United States. He was, Norman Mailer once wrote, "our leading man." His confidence that he could "get the nation moving again," his handsome and stylish wife, photogenic children, and appealing and able associates touched chords in American society that his predecessor Eisenhower, for all the love and respect the General received, would not have tried to reach. Kennedy was the hero of the new men and women—in the professions, the universities, business and government—who were reaching positions of leadership, a new generation "born in this century."

The discussion here of Kennedy and liberalism recognizes this élan and its vital—if intangible—effect on American foreign policy. The account that emerges stresses Kennedy's sophisticated and balanced approach to foreign policy crises.

John Kennedy was a foreign policy President. It has been common for the presidency in this century to receive much of its definition from the global events that impinge so dramatically upon it. Kennedy, even among recent Presidents, has been distinctive in the degree of his identification with those events.

That Kennedy, an occasional reader of Ian Fleming's James Bond novels, has been associated with them in the Kennedy image is appropriate to the cold war mentality of his times. Fleming's fiction is about more than an arrogant practitioner of secret war. The violence of his stories notwithstanding, they were early efforts in a spy genre that looked beyond the simplicities of a time when militant Westerners had resolved all the details of international politics into confrontations between a free world and a solid Communist bloc. The antagonists in a Fleming story play a game in which they act for larger forces, but these are shadowy and vary from one tale to the next. James Bond, moreover, is armed with light and dazzling mechanical devices that evoke the increasingly sophisticated technological world of the cold war itself. And this understanding of power and politics found a presidential spokesman in a war hero, the skipper of a small craft, who wanted a quicker, more mobile, more expert military capable of fighting in limited wars. Major General Chester Clifton has remembered: he "made me gather up all [the weapons] we had that might be used for guerrilla warfare.... There were about twenty weapons...the most recent of them was something that had been invented in 1944. This was 1961."

The "torch has been passed to a new generation of Americans, born in this century, tempered by war, disciplined by a hard and bitter peace"—so go the famous words of the inaugural at the transfer of power from the oldest elected President in the nation's history to the youngest. The new generation, or much of it, had served under Eisenhower or MacArthur in a war. The claim is now familiar that the war had schooled the Kennedy people, made them quick to react to crisis, impatient with bureaucracy, swift to improvise. After victory in 1945 it must have seemed to the war generation that the world's ills would yield to the competent marshaling of power, and that the United States, the most powerful victor of the war, had the ability and the obligation to shape events. There was another side to the thought of this generation. Elvis Stahr, secretary of the army under Kennedy, reports that the President wished that every military officer would read *The Guns of August*, Barbara Tuchman's account of the world that stumbled into war in 1914. "It is a dangerous illusion," he said at Berkeley on March 23, 1962, "to believe that the policies of the United States, stretching as they do worldwide, under varying and different conditions, can be encompassed in one slogan or one adjective, hard or soft or otherwise." It was a "simple central theme of American foreign policy," Kennedy once said, "to support the independence of nations so that one bloc cannot gain sufficient power to finally overcome us." John Gaddis in *Strategies of Containment* calls this "the most precise public explanation by an American president of what all postwar chief executives had believed, but rarely stated: that the American interest was not to remake the world but to balance power within it." This belief has activist implications if the balancing is carried out in the Kennedy manner, by an incessant watchfulness, an infusing of military or economic aid to one region, an encouragement of progressive reform in another, a neutralization of a dangerous conflict, as in Laos, a development of a swift and versatile military, and the sending forth of a skilled force of Peace Corps volunteers. A world to be balanced and rebalanced, indeed, invites an activity more extensive and exact than a world to be remade once and for all....

Among the sectors of the public most satisfied with the new President were many liberal academicians. The inaugural address impressed them. A time would come of falling respect for the address, which has as its best-remembered lines a contrived play of opposites: "Ask not what your country can do for you—ask what you can do for your country." But it is a rare speech on a ceremonial occasion that is taken seriously enough to receive continued reviews, bad or good. The address is noteworthy for the somberness with which the new President chose to lecture his compatriots. It appeared actually to be thinking about its subject, in this respect breaking with political convention; liberals took it as promising a thinking presidency. During Kennedy's occupancy of the White House, and for a short time thereafter, too much was made of the culture that the Kennedy family was supposed to represent, manifesting itself especially in Jacqueline Kennedy, whose attractiveness and social finish lent so much to the Kennedys' public image. That the First Lady spoke French impressed even the professoriat in a nation that does not customarily learn foreign languages. All this bespoke a wistful hope that intellect allied to Democratic liberalism had entered the White House.

The administration's new appointments certainly displayed to liberals a similar polish. Robert McNamara, the cost-accounting president of Ford Motors with a mind as clean and severe as a statistical table, became secretary of defense. "He really runs, rather than walks," a cabinet colleague remembered of this man who would subdue the Pentagon brass. McNamara had been a student and teacher at the Harvard Business School, a member of the NAACP, and, at Ford, something of an outsider who lived in the university town of Ann Arbor rather than in conservative Grosse Point. For State, Kennedy first wanted Senator William J. Fulbright, the Arkansas liberal who was, however, not liberal on civil rights, and would therefore not sit well with emerging African nations. Instead, the President appointed the imperturbable Dean Rusk. A Rhodes Scholar who had been a peace advocate before World War II, an open opponent of McCarthyism, and a supporter of Adlai Stevenson even in 1960, Rusk belonged to an almost forgotten company of old-line liberals and had, when such gestures meant something, once broken a color barrier by going with Ralph Bunche of the United Nations to a Pentagon officers' mess. Rusk would try to restore even the China experts Senator Joseph McCarthy had purged from the State Department. A prime adviser who became chair of the Joint Chiefs of Staff was Maxwell Taylor. A scholar who could speak several languages and write serious books, Taylor was a liberal's general. Others on the staff—McGeorge Bundy, Walt Rostow, Chester Bowles, and Arthur Schlesinger, Jr.—constituted virtually a university faculty headed by a President whom Norman Mailer once described as resembling a detached young professor.

The Bay of Pigs, the most spectacular early act of this administration, had its origins in the Eisenhower years, when the Central Intelligence Agency had done every bit of the planning for such an invasion. But it was much in the spirit of the liberalism that attached itself to Kennedy's presidency. Fidel Castro represented the variety of leftist regimes—repressive, speaking and apparently thinking in slogans, instilling militant ideological conformity in their people—that traditional liberalism despised as a travesty of the idea of social and economic democracy. The CIA, taking the place after World War II of the wartime Office of Strategic Services, had in its first years attracted many liberal intellectuals. Such people had wished to nurture democratic progressive movements abroad as competitors to Marxist totalitarian forces.

The invasion itself, in April 1961, seemed to have been planned by amateurs. The planners, who included high administration figures, had picked a landing site inadequate for defense or advance into the interior. The invading force, using old freighters supplied by the United Fruit Company, was badly equipped and poorly coordinated. While promised air cover proved inadequate and untimely (the airplanes were operating on Eastern Standard instead of Caribbean time), the boats' hulls ripped apart on coral reefs. The only possible explanation, aside from insufficiency of technical expertise, for the backing of this careless an operation is that the invaders, the CIA, and the Kennedy administration shared in the general American notion that under Communist regimes the people suffer, long for freedom, and at the first real opportunity spontaneously rise up.

Comments subsequent to the Bay of Pigs, made within the government and not for public propaganda objectives, indicate the sincerity of that conviction. In policy committee discussions directing the American response during the Cuban missile crisis, the danger was noted of taking action that would excite the Cuban people to revolt and force the United States to intervene.

A similar logic prompted Lyndon Johnson, in the early days of this country's involvement in Vietnam, to urge in a document for governmental circulation taking measures to keep up the morale of the North Vietnamese people. Johnson's assumption that the North Vietnamese must be miserable in their captivity to the Communists and yearning for liberation is not very far from the romantic notion of "the People" that would a few years later and in the opposite cause convince the American left that the South Vietnamese were collectively willing the success of the Communist guerrillas. And in fact the American left in the late 1960s was to be composed in considerable part of radicalized former adherents of the liberalism of the Kennedy years.

In supporting the Bay of Pigs invasion, the liberals in the Kennedy administration were being faithful to the liberal Cold War heritage. In the administration's final refusal to send in air support for the beleaguered rebels, Kennedy was overcoming a major element in his upbringing: win, win, never think of losing. In doing so, he was vindicating that idea of his being self-composed that his admirers had up to then, perhaps wishfully, perceived in his deportment. His refusal in the final instance to use force conformed to the liberal idea of force exactly measured, stripped of any motives of self-gratifying chauvinism.

Yet the public, as is customary in United States history, once again supported a new administration's reckless adventure, and Washington's hostility to Castro intensified. The CIA planned to disrupt the regime, and, according to the Church committee's later Senate investigations, eight attempts were made to assassinate Castro, a more frustrating target than Rasputin. The President, though perhaps unaware of the bungled tries to kill Castro, shared in the ill will and showed no serious interest in treating the Cuban rulership as simply one more of the world's bad regimes, to be accepted and dealt with as Washington dealt with Paraguay or South Africa. In any event, Cuba was too proximate for that.

The Kennedy foreign policy sought to balance the two occasionally conflicting objectives: social reform in third-world regimes and a containment of the Marxist threat it saw them facing. In its $10 billion aid program for Latin America, the Alliance for Progress at Punta del Este, Uruguay, the administration committed itself in 1962 to land and tax reform. But the Kennedy presidency essentially continued to operate on the Cold War assumption that Marxist governments and movements constitute a separate category of evil. Under the Agency for International Development, funds went for training local police in counterinsurgency measures as well as for technical aid in sanitation and transportation. Except in his dealings with some African states, notably Kwame Nkrumah's Ghana, and his lack of sympathy for the white supremacist government of South Africa, Kennedy's foreign policy maintained along with its more directly humane objectives the government's conventional hostility to the left and willingness to befriend rightist regimes as a bulwark against revolution.

In the wake of Vietnam it has become common to argue that this nation's single-minded hatred of leftist revolutionary governments and movements is an obsession. In Central America Washington long conducted a surrogate war against the Nicaraguan Sandinistas on the grounds that they were repressive; meanwhile it gives aid to the government of El Salvador and friendship to that of Guatemala, apparently unconvinced that control by torture and death squad by non-Communist regimes means repression. The Kennedy administration's unrelenting hostility to Castro is the earlier history of this preoccupation with the sins of the left. But reconstructing the mentality of the Kennedy years requires recognizing that the instructive failure and carnage in Vietnam still lay in the future, and that Kennedy's policy faced no large and audible domestic criticism as did the Reagan policy toward Nicaragua.

The Cold War had begun in a reasonable fear of the Soviet Union, after a world war against a state in many ways remarkably similar to the Stalinist system. From its early and limited programs for protecting the western European democracies, the confrontation with Moscow spread by its own moral and strategic logic to the rest of the world, growing hazier in its definition of the enemy: now waging war on the brutal North Korean regime, now overthrowing a progressive democracy in Guatemala. Castro's Cuba was, in the most moderate and intelligent Cold War thinking, a correctly chosen target. It imprisoned, tortured, and killed far more widely than had the previous dictatorship; its connections to the Soviet Union were close; it was so located as to seem a geopolitical danger to the western hemisphere.

Washington was also angry that Cuba should dare defy its imperium over the continent and act like a fully independent nation. Nationalist pride later held American policy frozen with fear that we might suffer in Vietnam our first defeat in war. But at its simplest the Cold War, in its Cuban phases as elsewhere, has been the unfolding not of nationalism but of an idea.

In 1961 a crisis in Berlin brought the Cold War back to the continent of its origin. The Berlin airlift of 1948, when President Truman kept intact the Western presence in Berlin while Stalin attempted to choke off the city by cutting all land routes, had been the first face-off between the allies and the Soviet Union, and had won for the West its first and, until the Kennedy administration, its only clear triumph. In 1961 the Soviet Premier Nikita Khrushchev reiterated a continuing threat against the city. He announced that unless the western powers were to enter into an agreement with the USSR Moscow would sign a separate peace treaty with East Germany, the status of which had from the days of Soviet occupation been considered in suspension until the reunification of Germany under free elections. What Khrushchev was proposing would, in effect, make East Germany a sovereign republic surrounding and endangering the freedom of West Berlin. Khrushchev suggested making West Berlin a free city under United Nations guarantees, but the allies did not relish risking the city to the good intentions of East Germany or to that prospective nation's Soviet overlord. At a summit meeting in Vienna during June 1961, Kennedy and the Premier had argued inconclusively over giving permanent separate status to Communist East Germany while making West Berlin a free city under supervision of the United Nations.

In the case of Cuba the moral question had been relatively simple: if the Cuban government was sufficiently savage, sufficiently a danger, and easy enough to overthrow, then an attempt would be justifiable. In the matter of Berlin, the issue was complex, the conflicting claims plausible.

The USSR had serious concerns. Germany had won against Russia, Czarist and Bolshevik, the eastern phase of World War I; she had a favorable peace well before suffering her own defeat on the western front. That Germany in the Second World War proved an incomparable and unspeakable threat to the Soviet Union needs no argument. Unlike German reunification today, the reunification movement three decades ago represented a belligerent nationalism. A greater Germany would be an instrument of western power against the Soviet bloc. A separate eastern German nation would preclude that. A more immediate problem for the Soviet Union was the accelerating exodus to the West, through the border between East and West Berlin, of Germans whose education and skills were essential to the economy of eastern Germany and implicitly to the social stability of Moscow's other European satellite nations. As part of his scheme for Germany, Khrushchev insisted that the Communists have authority to prevent exit through the border within Berlin. Khrushchev could have had domestic considerations as well. He had achieved a slight relaxation for the police-state system in his country, and something of a shift to consumer needs. To his right were enemies who wanted more military spending than he favored. It may have been among his considerations that a tough posture toward the West could strengthen him politically at home.

But the West had its own unbudgeable concern. In the light of their use over the years by politicians, terms such as "freedom fighters," "struggling democracies," and the like are debased enough to render almost naive any claim that West Berlin was free and East Germany unfree. That happens, however, to be true: quite simply, manifestly true if freedom and its opposite are to be defined as the west speaks of them. The western allies believed that they had a commitment to defend the freedom of the West Berliners, who having lived under it would suffer its loss more than East Germans suffered its absence. Khrushchev's plan would establish East Germany permanently as a separate republic with none of the obligations that bound the Soviet Union, as one of the postwar occupiers of Germany, to act in concert with her wartime western allies in any future governance and disposition of Berlin. Whatever assurances the western powers might get on paper for the safety of West Berlin, they feared for the practical result of the Soviet demands.

Another consideration balanced against this. The western allies had their own stake in the stability of the eastern bloc. They knew that

Moscow could not afford the economic collapse of eastern Germany, and it was unpredictable what Khrushchev would do if a continued flow of refugees brought that collapse nearer. To allow the Communists to prevent passage into a freer society was ugly. But even uglier might be the reaction in Moscow to a threatened economic and social disaster in eastern Europe.

Resolution, then, had to balance against compromise, the needs of Berliners against the needs of peace. The adversary force was too powerful, and its wants too urgent, to make possible any gratifying easy use of western force; the rights of the Berliners were too important to be accorded a merely rhetorical heroism as their defense. The problem was of the kind that could not accommodate the palpitating emotions of the right.

Much of the American response was an increase in belligerence, not merely of words but of actions. The President called for an extensive civil defense program; on July 25, proposing an increase in military spending and in the armed forces, he announced a doubling of draft calls and a mobilization of some 51,000 reserve troops. But a curious incident occurred in the summer of 1961. On July 30 Democratic Senator William J. Fulbright of Arkansas, chair of the Senate Foreign Relations Committee, observed on television that the Communists might have the right to close off the border to the West. Fulbright retracted the statement. In responding in his August 10 press conference to a question that referred to Fulbright's remark, however, Kennedy was silent on the East Germans' right to free exit. Was Washington giving Moscow a hint—take if you must the course that will save the East German economy?

In August the Communists began restricting egress through the Berlin border and started construction of the infamous wall. That the act was ostensibly East German rather than Soviet in itself constituted something of a challenge to the West. Although East Germany had not yet signed a treaty with the USSR, it was acting as though sovereign—the condition that Moscow wanted to force the West to acknowledge. But such technicalities did not preoccupy Western public opinion. The clearest result was that East Germans seeking freedom or opportunity in the West were now sealed up, unless they should find a means of escape. The most feared danger was that the act might be the prelude to some attempt to swallow up West Berlin within East Germany.

Kennedy's reaction had the appearance of resoluteness: he denounced the Berlin Wall as an uninvited act, an outrage. He sent 1500 troops to West Berlin along the Autobahn through Communist Germany (former Secretary of State Dean Acheson wanted a division, but he hailed from a more primitive stage of the Cold War). Vice President Lyndon Johnson went to the city to pledge American defense. Kennedy appointed as his representative to Berlin General Lucius Clay, who had conducted the airlift of 1948, which ended in a triumph of western skill and resolve. A further crisis, over the question of who in East Berlin would regulate the movements of whatever western military had business there, gave a fresh occasion for the western allies to prove their tenacity. Under the four-power agreement among the victorious occupiers of Germany, the Soviet Union as the custodian of East Berlin had exercised that authority there. When the USSR began transferring to the East Germans the control over the movements of western personnel in the city's eastern zone, the United States saw a further attempt to nullify the postwar arrangement and to establish East Germany as a republic that would in time claim rights over West Berlin as well. In October at the border between the two Berlins, at General Clay's initiative, there was a brief but unnerving face-off of tanks, snout to snout, that ended only when the Russians pulled theirs back.

If the Kennedy administration had previously indicated to the Soviet Union that shutting off East Berlin would be understandable and acceptable, then why the militancy of the American response once the Communists had acted? Kennedy is said to have mused that because Khrushchev was losing East Germany and could not permit that, the Premier would need to halt the flow of refugees, perhaps by a wall. The President reflected that he could not prevent Khrushchev from fencing in the East Germans, but could still rally the allies to the defense of West Berlin. Perhaps, then, while later in August the administration was sincerely repelled if also relieved at the understandably self-interested Communist strangulation of the exodus from the East, its intent was to channel the West's indignation into a solidarity with the West Berliners, whose freedom, unlike that of the easterners, could be saved.

As Kennedy was piecing out his military confrontation with Khrushchev, the two men began a lengthy correspondence. Early in September the Premier told *The New York Times* of his willingness to meet with the President, suggesting the solution of a dispute then in progress between the two power blocs in Laos in return for a solution of the Berlin question. On September 25 Kennedy made a conciliatory address before the United Nations. A few days later Khrushchev began a long private correspondence with the President. To General Clay, who wanted authority to take quick unilateral action as occasion demanded, Kennedy instead recommended cautious determination and coolness. The general was brought home the following May.

The Berlin question did not end with a signed document. But there was a balance to the unplanned status at which, after months of hostility, Berlin arrived. At the expense of those eastern Germans who wanted freedom, the Communists did what they believed necessary for the rescue of the East German economy, a goal which, in the interest of geopolitical stability, would not have displeased the allies. Khrushchev, on the other hand, had not imposed his deadline for the allied recognition of a separate East Germany as a condition for retaining Western access to West Berlin.

The administration's response to the Berlin crisis was, in sum, a meticulously managed instance of the fusion of confrontation and restraint for which liberalism, in its argument with the right, had increasingly been contending. The confrontational element consisted not simply of sending military reinforcements to the city, which was a minimal action to announce the will to preserve West Berlin, but rather the decision to preserve the city. The Cold War policies crafted by liberals had committed the United States to such concerns, which took the nation far beyond the actual frontiers of its self-interest. In the fantasy world of the right, on the other hand, the United States was supposed to drive Communism back to oblivion. The Kennedy administration chose not to encourage the western alliance to undertake the destruction of the Berlin Wall and to that extent doubtless frustrated hardliners. Washington indicated its willingness to accept the wall, its determination to protect West Berlin, and its desire to do both as economically as possible; its policy was spare and well calculated to those ends. In contrast to his entrance into the Bay of Pigs invasion, which had been thrust upon him by the Eisenhower administration, Kennedy's behavior during the Berlin crisis was of the very essence of the liberal cold warrior: measured, exact, cool, and patient. His hardline adviser on Latin America, Adolf Berle, did not like the performance: "The evidence coming in now," he wrote in his diary, "suggests that a little nerve would have stopped the [Wall]."

While military confrontations were defining in part the manner of the Kennedy presidency, his administration was shaping other programs that add to the definition. The Special Forces and the Peace Corps had a number of things in common. They were intended for the war against Communism. They were to convert that war as far as possible into a project for social democracy. The Special Forces warriors and the Peace Corps volunteers had to be elites of purpose, intelligence, and technical sophistication.

The Special Forces, better known by their distinctive green berets, were in the same tradition of a mobile, autonomous elite to which the PT-boat officers of World War II had belonged. Their formation was among the schemes for the renovation of the nation's arms that Kennedy developed with Secretary of Defense Robert McNamara. The Secretary, who had headed the Ford Motor Company, had an appetite for efficiency and a reliance on modern methods of information gathering. Our need, the administration reasoned, was for a more versatile and flexible defense than the existing city-killing nuclear deterrence that would in an emergency limit our choice to doing nothing or incinerating the globe. Kennedy and McNamara wished to develop a system targeting Soviet missile sites rather than cities. Though intended to express humane as well as strategic considerations, this system appeared to the Soviet military a preparation for aggression. Troops of the Special Forces as the administration imagined them looked something like a human equivalent of this projected missile force. Designed as a cutting edge of ground operations, they were supposed to be independent, skilled in individual combat, and sensitive and knowledgeable in working with civilian populations. Special Forces personnel parachuted into Hungary, it was suggested, ought to be familiar with the major Hungarian poets.

In contrast, the idea for a Peace Corps had been around for some years before Kennedy's presidency. But the particular version of it that Kennedy took up in his campaign was in counterpoint to the unflattering image many Americans had come to have of their compatriots abroad. A novel published in 1958 by William J. Lederer and Eugene Burdick had contributed to that image.

The figure from whom *The Ugly American* takes its name is physically ugly, a sign of his plain moral character unornamented by any superficial social graces and wholly committed in a blunt, earnest way to service and good work. He is an engineer whose ideas of appropriate technology, shaped to the needs and resources of third-world communities, have no appeal for the American, French, and Asian officials he encounters. Living simply in an Asian village, he demonstrates how bicycles can be used for water pumps. His wife, observing the bent backs endemic among the elderly women of the village, shows them how long-handled brooms can free them of an affliction brought on by constant stooping. In stark contrast to the protagonist and his wife are the pleasure-seeking, the time-serving, and the merely incompetent Americans who live luxuriously in third-world cities as pampered representatives of their country and its policies. The point of the novel, of course, is that the United States needs less of their kind in the rest of the world, and more Ugly Americans bringing unvarnished honest skills and knowledge to people who need them. In conformity to their times, the authors were concerned above all about the fortunes of the war against Communism, which they believed American incompetence was losing in the third world.

The title, though not the argument, of the novel was quickly misconstrued. "Ugly American" soon came in common speech to designate Americans who were the opposite of the novel's virtuously homely figure: Americans who flaunted their money, made loud demands for American standards of comfort, disdained knowledge of the language of the country they were invading, and in general insulted their host population and embarrassed their homeland.

The point of Kennedy's Peace Corps was to field American teachers, agronomists, road surveyors, and the like who would be rewarded only by pride and commitment to the work: Ugly Americans in the original meaning of the book title. No program advanced during Kennedy's presidency so perfectly fitted his call to "ask what you can do for your country." In a speech on October 14, 1960, before a huge crowd of students at the University of Michigan, he asked extemporaneously how many of them would be willing to spend years in Asia, Africa, or Latin America. His call to sacrifice stirred the audience. He further developed the theme in an address in San Francisco on November 2 in which he observed that people "without compassion" had been sent to represent the the United States in countries suffering from poverty, disease, and illiteracy.

In office, Kennedy put his brother-in-law Sargent Shriver in charge of the Peace Corps. Installed before Vietnam and the civil rights movement had radicalized the nation's most politically articulate youth, the Corps attracted volunteers who could accept the government as a vehicle for social change. Peace Corps volunteers sometimes became the pride of their home communities. The program, of course, was to be an arm of the battle against Communist infiltration of the third world, and participants had to take a loyalty oath. But the designers of the Peace Corps sincerely sought the lessening of illiteracy and poverty as goods in themselves and perceived economic and social justice as consonant with democratic pluralism. The condensed training was rigorous; volunteers were required to learn foreign languages as they prepared to serve in the outlands, far from the exported American machineries of comfort that could minister to them. Like the political right that would later become ascendant, the liberals of Kennedy's time spoke often of such things as intrinsic to the American character and ethos; but whereas liberals called on Americans to take pride in their work, their conservative successors of the 1980s by and large encouraged Americans only to work on their pride.

The Peace Corps was designed to target specific pockets of need in impoverished regions. In this it spoke more directly to the problem of deprivation and injustice than does the most militant of ideologies, in which there is always an element of love for the internal architecture of the ideology itself. The Alliance for Progress took a similarly direct route to the alleviation of poverty. The enlistment of individuals driven by essentially private conscience was superior to revolutionary philosophies that can define no way of relating individuals to one another save by some exterior historical or social logic.

The administration was actually moving toward articulating a persuasive alternative, and counter, to Communist ideology. Previously the democratic West had offered little as an answer to Communism: either mere anticommunism, which is no more than definition by opposition and therefore devoid of substance, or capitalism, which has nothing convincing to say to the world's poor and excluded. The Peace Corps, the Alliance, even the Special Forces evince the barest tracings of the union of social democracy with democratic political pluralism, the one antithetical to Communism, the other to oligarchical rule. Kennedy, for example, seems to have intended to distribute Alliance funds so as to reward an end to structural inequality of power and wealth.

The problem lay in the anticommunist element in the mix. Anticommunism belonged there quite logically; it would have belonged there on purely philosophical terms even if it had not been an expression of this country's perceived self-interest. Even generations of socialists who have fought Communism in the name of a radical social, economic, and political egalitarianism will attest to that. But the war with third-world Communist movements—which Washington was quick to identify with any manifestation of a revolutionary left—dictated that eventually the programs initiated by Kennedy would do business, as American policy has done all along, with regimes of entrenched privilege defending themselves by repression and claiming to be a bulwark against Communist revolution. And as long as structural inequality remained—and structural inequality is exactly what such regimes are determined to protect—even the best-intentioned programs of economic relief could offer no more than relief. Anticommunism, which might have found its appropriate partner and likeness in social democracy, could not in its American form remain true to the partnership.

Unflinching in its military encounters with Communism and in its ongoing programs for the struggle, the Kennedy administration had yet to face its most dangerous moment. That moment could not have been predicted. Its origins lay not in some continuing problem like Berlin, demanding to be addressed, but in the new considerations that in 1962 led Khrushchev secretly to begin installing missiles in Cuba, to be supplied with nuclear warheads.

To the Soviet Union, the military advantages of missiles in Cuba must have been marginal. In the event of a nuclear war, missiles launched from elsewhere would be entirely sufficient to devastate the United States. It is doubtful that the slight addition the missiles could bring to Soviet strength induced Khrushchev to risk an American re-action of unpredictable magnitude, and the secrecy of the operation signifies that Khrushchev was aware of the risk. A more plausible ex-planation has to do with the fate of Cuba. The CIA's program of sab-otage, Operation MONGOOSE, was well known to both Cuba and the Soviet Union. Placing nuclear missiles in Cuba would in effect bring the island within Soviet military territory, and constitute a way of say-ing to the United States that an attack on Cuba would be an attack on the Soviet Union. Further political advantages would be an increase in Soviet prestige throughout the world, and in the domestic prestige of Khrushchev himself, who as the architect of de-Stalinization was in a precarious relation to the hardline Soviet right.

In early October 1962 aerial photographs showed the Soviet mis-sile sites. Without revealing the findings to the public, the administration quietly prepared for a response. Kennedy had learned from the disas-ter at the Bay of Pigs. He wanted advice more balanced and thoroughly debated than a single group of advisers could give him. For the purpose he drew together from the National Security Council and elsewhere an executive committee, or ExComm as it became known in crisp appropri-ateness to the cold swift decisions that the moment demanded. ExComm was an assemblage of the government's highest civilian and military offi-cials, ranging in persuasion from the dovish Ambassador to the United Nations, Adlai Stevenson, to the Joint Chiefs of Staff, who wished to take out the missile sites with an air strike. General Curtis LeMay ad-vocated a general attack on Cuban military targets. Senator Fulbright argued for an air strike as appearing less aggressive than an attack in international waters on a Soviet ship defying a naval interdiction. But McNamara and Robert Kennedy opposed the idea of an air raid, RFK comparing it to Pearl Harbor. After several days the discussants settled on a sea quarantine—the word "blockade" seemed too provocative—of ships that might be bringing in equipment for the missile system. The navy was not to be trusted with supervision of the quarantine; that job belonged to McNamara, the Pentagon's civilian chief.

The public did not learn that the world was in the midst of crisis until Monday, October 22. On television that evening the President re-vealed the presence of the missiles and the decision to impose a quaran-tine. Some have criticized him sharply for bringing the matter to public attention, which might make it more embarrassing for the Soviet Union to withdraw. To this the response has usually been that diplomacy was in process, and the purpose of the speech was to mobilize world opinion on the side of the United States. For about two days the world waited to see what its future was going to be. Then on Wednesday, after the navy had allowed a tanker to pass through, a Soviet ship containing equipment that could be used for the missiles turned back. Things seemed, for the time, a little safer.

Meanwhile, Moscow and Washington had privately been negotiating their mutual preservation. Khrushchev sent a telegram proposing a removal of the missiles in return for a promise not to invade Cuba. He then sent another asking for the removal of American missiles in Turkey. These missiles, vulnerable to a strike and therefore likely to be eliminated by the Soviet Union at the beginning of a world nuclear war before they could be launched in retaliation, were clearly no deterrent to such a war: they could be used only in a war begun by the United States. That made them provocative, as did their closeness to the Soviet Union. The United States, although indignant at the emplacement of Soviet missiles in Cuba, had not previously hesitated to locate missiles in Europe. In fact, the missiles in Turkey were obsolete, and Washington had been planning to dismantle them in any case. But Khrushchev's second telegram seemed defiant, and the idea of an air strike against the Cuban sites revived. Robert Kennedy suggested a tactful response: ignore the second telegram, publicly accept the substance of the first with an agreement not to invade Cuba, and privately let Moscow know that dismantling of the Cuban missiles would bring dismantlement of ours in Turkey. On Sunday morning, October 28, Americans awakened to learn of the Soviet announcement that the Cuban missiles were to be withdrawn.

A judgment of Kennedy's behavior that October has to begin with the prevailing American consensus, in which he shared, that nuclear arms are legitimate as deterrents, from which follows an acceptance of the continuing risks of nuclear war. Was Kennedy acting as responsibly as a willing commander of nuclear arms could act under the circumstances? He gambled the danger of starting a nuclear war against the hope that in gaining removal of the Cuban missiles he would restore and strengthen a stability that Khrushchev's bold act had threatened by its very boldness. The only convincing argument to be made for Kennedy is that, once having determined to force the removal of the missiles, he carried out that decision with care and restraint, rejecting the idea of an air strike, making no issue of Khrushchev's second telegram, and being careful during and after the crisis not to turn the affair into an angry assertion of American power.

Norman Mailer later observed that Khrushchev, by recklessly installing the missiles, had rescued the United States from the moral disadvantage the Bay of Pigs had imposed upon it. In the wake of the crisis, in fact, the two nations became more civil toward each other than they had been at any time since the beginning of the Cold War. Kennedy's June 1963 speech at American University was a warning against having "a desperate and distorted view of the other side." Teletype communication, which Khrushchev had proposed over a year earlier, was established between Moscow and Washington—the "hot line" was the popular term for it—for use in times of danger. The first reply from the Soviet Union was a perplexed inquiry into the meaning of the phrase that has a quick brown fox jump over a lazy dog. Something close to a liking for Khrushchev developed within the American public, for his

earthy exuberance—at times he seemed the classic peasant of folklore—
and for the happy resolution of the moment of high tension that he,
his country, and the American people had gone through together. The
warming of relations was both cause and effect of the negotiating of a
treaty banning the atmospheric testing of nuclear weapons.

In the days of anger over Berlin, Khrushchev had resumed nuclear testing, and the United States had followed quickly in September;
the next spring the light from an American Starfish test turned the
Hawaiian night into day and flashed the skies as far as Australia. But in
the spirit of friendship, or the discovery of the precariousness of peace,
or the simple giddy relief that followed the Cuban missile crisis, the
Soviet and the American leaders negotiated in late 1963 a treaty that
banned testing above ground.

The accusation has since been made against Kennedy that the treaty
merely halted the process of testing at a stage of weaponry favorable to
the United States. That Americans on the right opposed the agreement
does not, of course, mean that it must have been equitable, nor does it
necessarily preclude the possibility that the treaty was a power play from
an American position of strength. But if the treaty had been merely a
device for perpetuating American superiority, Khrushchev could have
taken the simple expedient of refusing to go along with it. Partly in
reaction to Herman Kahn's controversial *On Thermonuclear War* (1960),
even the notion of nuclear superiority was becoming obsolete by the
early 1960s. It was generally understood that in a nuclear exchange,
no matter which side had the slight advantage of first strike, the results
would be intolerable devastation to both sides. The simple explanation
for the treaty is the soundest: the missile crisis had rightly scared both
camps; in view of existing nuclear arsenals and knowledge, atmospheric
testing offered few if any practical advantages, while remaining a psychological irritant and an expense; and radiation spread through the
air was a proven health hazard. Critics at the time, who saw the treaty
chiefly as an act of national self-interest on the part of the Soviet Union,
and present-day American critics on the left who have discovered that
it was an act of national self-interest on the part of the United States
are both correct; otherwise there would have been no treaty.

The agreement had still to win two-thirds of the Senate. Here
Kennedy found two allies only apparently unlikely: Republican Senator Everett Dirksen of Illinois and Republican Congressman Charles
Halleck of Indiana. Halleck, as a member of the lower House, did not
take part directly in the debate or the voting, but as a leading conservative Republican politician greatly influenced opinion within his party.
The same two legislators also supported civil rights legislation. On both
issues they demonstrated not only moral sensitivity but the difference
between rightist sullenness and a conservatism aware of the distinction
between changes that threaten the health of institutions and those that
improve it.

The treaty's victory in the Senate in September 1963 by a vote of
eighty to nineteen represented in foreign policy what the victory of
civil rights legislation was to signify on the race issue. It meant that a
consensus was forming to the left of where American ultranationalists

had for a time believed and hoped that it had fixed itself: in the case of
the treaty, unremitting hostility to the Soviet Union as a transcendent
evil was giving way to a posture of armed watchfulness. Part of the story
of the rest of the decade, and of the years to follow, is the attempt on
the part of the right to rewin as much as they could of the world that
they believed had once been theirs.

During the Kennedy years, confrontation between the USSR and
the United States took on a distinctive pattern. Hostility had been acute
for longer in Truman's presidency than it was during the sporadic
clashes of Kennedy's tenure; the relationship between Gorbachev and
Ronald Reagan would be warmer, perhaps, than any that Kennedy toward the end of his days achieved with Khrushchev. But in Kennedy's
time the stretch of conflict and conciliation between the two powers sur-
passed the range during any other presidency. What more particularly
qualified the conflicts of the time, on both sides, was a character of
measure, almost of meticulousness, in the actions that attended and in
some degree resolved them. It is as though the liberal idea, expounded
against the jangled nerves of the right, of how to wage a protracted
though cold war had found an opportunity for expression in the intricate moves surrounding Berlin and the Cuban missiles, in the Peace
Corps, the Green Berets, and the test-ban treaty. And for that liberal
idea to achieve the proper staging, it needed the unlikely cooperation
of Nikita Khrushchev, who seemed to understand and lend a hand in
the motions of the dance.

The result of it all might have been an era of nervous freedom
from major international war. But meanwhile John Kennedy was almost
ignoring his own policy in a corner of Southeast Asia.

PART THREE

1962–1968

Americans, to their credit, have never been an easy people to govern. This old, near-anarchic virtue asserted itself more strongly than ever in the 1960s. They were years of extraordinary self-consciousness. The awareness of self was so encompassing—*my* people, *my* generation, *my* "thing"—that the nation became almost ungovernable in traditional ways.

The 1960s generated conflicts as well as accomplishments that would have astonished people of a generation before. Exactly as President Kennedy had said, with a decade's labor the United States landed men on the moon and brought them back safely. Much as Martin Luther

King, Jr. had prophesied, the decade saw the end of legal racial seg-regation, though much of the civil rights agenda remained unrealized. A war on poverty and a sustained economic boom provided a social safety net for millions of Americans. Government-financed medical ser-vices, through Medicare, for older Americans fundamentally altered the economic status of the aged. Federal support for education from pre-kindergarten through graduate and professional school broadened ed-ucational opportunity beyond anything the world had previously seen. After a near deadly confrontation during the 1962 Cuban Missile Crisis, the United States and the Soviet Union moved into a period of negoti-ation that reduced the risk of nuclear war.

The decade also created enormous divisiveness within American so-ciety. Allies in the civil rights movement split noisily into warring camps. The unpopular and unsuccessful Vietnam War divided opinion more sharply than had any previous foreign war. Young people developed a rich but to most Americans an enormously threatening cultural identity, with its own institutions, heroes, modes of mood alteration, and partic-ularly music. The dominant political ideology of the age, liberalism, was, as one commentator has written, "decapitated" by the assassina-tions of John F. Kennedy, Robert Kennedy, and Martin Luther King, Jr. The economy careened toward disaster, fueled by an inflation that resulted from combining wartime stimulus and a booming peacetime economy. By the end of the decade, the legitimacy of nearly every ma-jor institution—political parties, churches, universities, corporations, the government itself—had been deeply eroded.

The year 1968 was the climax of this period. The young generation seemed to fall into disarray over both goals and tactics in political and social change; the men who depended for inspiration largely on the New Deal vanished from the national political scene; and President Richard Nixon, who described himself as conservative and who promised to end the war, but offered no explicit plan, came to power.

12. Heroes of
the Civil Rights Movement

HOWELL RAINES

*On February 1, 1960, in downtown Greensboro, North Carolina, four black
students from North Carolina Agricultural and Technical College walked into a
Woolworth store, purchased a few small items, and then sat at the lunch counter
to seek equal service with white patrons. Their brave and dangerous action was
a part of a long tradition of protest in Greensboro. Parents such as Ezell Blair,
Sr., an NAACP activist, and teachers such as Nell Coley, who had inspired three
of the four protestors when they attended Dudley High School, were not surprised
by the sit-ins: "We had been teaching those kids things all along." Yet this action
threw a spark; within days the sit-in movement had spread to fifty-four cities
in nine states. Within a year, more than a hundred cities had at least partially
desegregated public facilities in response to student-led demonstrations.*

*The sit-in was simple and dramatic: human dignity was defined by the right
to be served in any restaurant, to register for a room in any motel, or to take
out a book at any public library. Yet the tactic had its limits; the stress on the
dramatic hid the long, slow, painful legal and social revolution that lay behind
these stunning moments. The strategy was local, suggesting that an issue could
be resolved by the community, whereas the civil rights movement actually required
the force of the nation and the weight of the federal government to end the system
of segregation.*

*The following interviews were conducted by a white Southern journalist,
Howell Raines, for his oral history* My Soul Is Rested: Movement Days in the
Deep South Remembered. *Both the long quiet history preceding the movement
of the 1960s in the South and the need for a strategy to promote intervention by
the federal government emerge from these interviews. The period of the sit-ins,
the "freedom rides," the marches, and the demonstrations is a focal point in one
of the most dramatic stories in American history, a story we are now learning in
moving detail from the words and memories of the participants.*

E.D. NIXON

*E.D. Nixon was a prominent black labor leader who played an important role in
beginning a boycott of segregation on buses in Montgomery, Alabama.*

I don't know how, it just came to me all at once. I said, "I'm E.D.
Nixon. I'm from Montgomery, Alabama, a city that's known as the Cradle of the Confederacy, that had stood still for more than ninety-three
years until Rosa L. Parks was arrested and thrown in jail like a common

criminal." [Breaks into a singsong.] I said, "Fifty thousand people rose up and caught hold to the Cradle of the Confederacy and began to rock it till the Jim Crow rockers began to reel and the segregated slats began to fall out." Said, "I'm from that city." And man, people just fell out. I coulda sat down then. Right then.

I've known times for years and years I was the only person in Montgomery saying anything about the mistreatment of Negroes—to the end that it got to the place that most people looked on me as a leader, even though I wasn't never designated as such, because I could call a meeting. Say it was necessary that we have a meeting, I bet you I could call forty ministers at that time, at least thirty would be present. And I could appoint a meeting at any church. See, people think because Rev. King was selected and the meetings started at his church, that he done it, but I selected the spot. I called the people together, and I told them we was going to meet at that Dexter Avenue Baptist Church ... If we'da met on the suburbs, insurance mens and doctors and things who were working downtown wouldn't leave the office to go away out. But with it right downtown in the heart there wasn't no question they could walk right around the corner to it, and that's why the meeting was set up there, but a whole lot of people don't know that. They just think Rev. King come in, organized the Montgomery Improvement Association at his church and all. That isn't true. But the question is—we're not arguing the point, I'm just giving you the facts—that the job was done and that's the important thing.

First of all, we'd talked about a bus boycott all the year. We had three other people prior to Mrs. Parks arrested who reported their incidents to us, but you couldn'ta found nobody in Montgomery would agree to have a bus boycott—and I'm not patting myself on the shoulder— unless it was approved by E.D. Nixon. The first one was a minister's daughter. Her name was Mrs. Wayne. After I talked to her I discovered that she would not make a good litigant. Now you are on the outside here. You think that anybody that got arrested would be good. Now you would think that, the average person would think that, but my training with NAACP and the Brotherhood of Sleeping Car Porters taught me different. I've handled so many cases that I know when a man would stand up and when he wouldn't. So after I talked to her, I told the group, "No use in me going to court with this case, we can't win it."

So then some of the people were getting disgusted with me, see. Some of them said they didn't know whether I was making the right approach or not. This was in October when this last case was. Then, on December one, Rosa L. Parks was arrested. When she was arrested, a friend of hers called my wife and told my wife they'd arrested Mrs. Parks and Mrs. Nixon called my office. ...

She said, "Arrested Mrs. Parks," and I said, "For what?" She said, "I don't know. Go get her," just like I could go get her. I called down there and asked them what was the charge against her, and the desk sergeant said to me, he said, "None of your so-and-so business." Of course, no use of me arguing with him, so I called a white lawyer. Our black lawyer was out of the state at the time, Fred Gray. I called a white lawyer by the name of Clifford J. Durr. I said, "Mr. Durr, they arrested Mrs. Parks."

He said, "For what?" and I said, "Something about on the bus. What I want you to do is to call up down there and find out the charges against her." So he called up down there, in a few minutes called me back and said, "The charge is violating the Alabama segregation law."

ROSA PARKS

Rosa Parks became famous for refusing to give up her bus seat to a white man, as required by local statute, in Montgomery, Alabama, in December 1955.

I had left my work at the men's alteration shop, a tailor shop in the Montgomery Fair department store, and as I left work, I crossed the street to a drugstore to pick up a few items instead of trying to go directly to the bus stop. And when I had finished this, I came across the street and looked for a Cleveland Avenue bus that apparently had some seats on it. At that time it was a little hard to get a seat on the bus. But when I did get to the entrance to the bus, I got in line with a number of other people who were getting on the same bus.

As I got up on the bus and walked to the seat I saw there was only one vacancy that was just back of where it was considered the white section. So this was the seat that I took, next to the aisle, and a man was sitting next to me. Across the aisle there were two women, and there were a few seats at this point in the very front of the bus that was called the white section. I went on to one stop and I didn't particularly notice who was getting on the bus, didn't particularly notice the other people getting on. And on the third stop there were some people getting on, and at this point all of the front seats were taken. Now in the beginning, at the very first stop I had got on the bus, the back of the bus was filled up with people standing in the aisle and I don't know why this one vacancy that I took was left, because there were quite a few people already standing toward the back of the bus. The third stop is when all the front seats were taken, and this one man was standing and when the driver looked around and saw he was standing, he asked the four of us, the man in the seat with me and the two women across the aisle, to let him have those front seats.

At his first request, didn't any of us move. Then he spoke again and said, "You'd better make it light on yourselves and let me have those seats." At this point, of course, the passenger who would have taken the seat hadn't said anything. In fact, he never did speak to my knowledge. When the three people, the man who was in the seat with me and the two women, stood up and moved into the aisle, I remained where I was. When the driver saw that I was still sitting there, he asked if I was going to stand up. I told him, no, I wasn't. He said, "Well, if you don't stand up, I'm going to have you arrested." I told him to go on and have me arrested.

He got off the bus and came back shortly. A few minutes later, two policemen got on the bus, and they approached me and asked if the driver had asked me to stand up, and I said yes, and they wanted to know why I didn't. I told them I didn't think I should have to stand up. After I had paid my fare and occupied a seat, I didn't think I should have to give it up. They placed me under arrest then and had me to get in the police car, and I was taken to jail and booked on suspicion, I believe. The questions were asked, the usual questions they ask a prisoner or somebody that's under arrest. They had to determine whether or not the driver wanted to press charges or swear out a warrant, which he did. Then they took me to jail and I was placed in a cell. In a little while I was taken from the cell, and my picture was made and fingerprints taken. I went back to the cell then, and a few minutes later I was called back again, and when this happened I found out that Mr. E.D. Nixon and Attorney and Mrs. Clifford Durr had come to make bond for me.

In the meantime before this, of course . . . I was given permission to make a telephone call after my picture was taken and fingerprints taken. I called my home and spoke to my mother on the telephone and told her what had happened, that I was in jail. She was quite upset and asked me had the police beaten me. I told her, no, I hadn't been physically injured, but I was being held in jail, and I wanted my husband to come and get me out. . . . He didn't have a car at that time, so he had to get someone to bring him down. At the time when he got down, Mr. Nixon and the Durrs had just made bond for me, so we all met at the jail and we went home. . . .

E.D. NIXON

Then we went on up to the house and I said to Mrs. Parks, "Mrs. Parks"—her mother had some coffee made—I said, "Mrs. Parks, this is the case we've been looking for. We can break this situation on the bus with your case."

She said, "Well, I haven't thought of it just like that." So we talked to her mother and her husband, and finally they came 'round, said they'd go along with it.

She said, "All right." She said, "You know, Mr. Nixon, if you say so, I'll go along with it."

I said, "Okay, we can do it."

Mrs. Parks was a married woman. She had worked for me for twelve years, and I knew her. She was morally clean, and she had a fairly good academic training. Now, she wasn't afraid and she didn't get excited about anything. If there ever was a person that we shoulda been able to break the situation that existed on the Montgomery city line, Rosa L. Parks was the woman to use. And I knew that. I probably woulda examined a dozen more before I got there if Mrs. Parks hadn't come along before I found the right 'un.—'Cause, you see, it's hard for you to see it—it's hard for the average person—it's hard for the black people here in Montgomery to see. It's hard for a whole lot of people far away from here to see it. But when you have set 'cross the table and talked with black people in investigations as long as I have over a period of years, you just know it. . . . Well, I spent years in it and I knew it . . . when I selected Mrs. Parks, that was the person.

And so after we agreed, oh, I guess we spent a couple of hours discussing this thing. Then I went home and I took a sheet of paper and

I drew right in the center of the paper. I used that for the square and then I used Hunter Station, Washington Park, Pickett Springs, all the different areas in Montgomery, and I used a slide rule to get a estimate. I discovered nowhere in Montgomery at that time a man couldn't walk to work if he wanted to. I said, "We can beat this thing."

I told my wife about it and I said, "You know what?"

She said, "What?"

I said, "We're going to boycott the buses."

She said, "Cold as it is?"

I said, "Yeah."

She said, "I doubt it."

I said, "Well, I'll tell you one thing. If you keep 'em off when it cold, you won't have no trouble keeping 'em off when it get hot."

She shook her head. She said, "My husband! If headaches were selling for a dollar a dozen, my husband would be just the man to walk in the drugstore and say, 'Give me a dozen headaches.'"[Laughs]

So anyhow, I recorded quite a few names, starting off with Rev. Abernathy, Rev. Hubbard, Rev. King, and on down the line, and I called some of the people who represent peoples so that they could get the word out. The first man I called was Reverend Ralph Abernathy. He said, "Yes, Brother Nixon, I'll go along. I think it's a good thing."

The second person I called was the late Reverend H.H. Hubbard. He said, "Yes, I'll go along with you."

And I called Rev. King, was number three, and he said, "Brother Nixon, let me think about it awhile, and call me back."

When I called him back, he was number nineteen, and of course, he agreed to go along. I said, "I'm glad you agreed because I already set the meeting up to meet at your church." 'Course, he didn't even know Mrs. Parks at that time. I couldn't attend the meeting, and I asked another man, another minister, Methodist minister, to chair the meeting with the understanding that no permanent officers be elected until I come back, and there wasn't any elected.

I wanted to be shore the right people was in office, and I felt that I was, with my work in the community, better prepared to know who the right person would be than anybody else. So nobody was elected. They set up a temporary meeting for Monday evening. So I came back Sunday morning and my wife met me at the station. I got in about nine o'clock. She give me the morning paper. They had an article...on the front page of the *Advertiser*, talking about the bus boycott, a favorable article. The kind of article I'm almost sure that that's what got him fired. But anyhow, he wrote a good article, kept his promise....

Then Mrs. Parks was tried that morning and she was found guilty. ... I'd been in court off and on for twenty years, hearing different peoples, and very seldom, if ever, there was another black man unless he was being tried. But that particular morning, the morning of December the fifth, 1955, the black man was reborn again. I couldn't believe it when they found her guilty and I had to go through the vestibule down the hall to the clerk's office to sign her appeal bond.... People came in that other door, and that door was about ten feet wide, and they was just that crowded in there, people wanting to know what happened. I said, "Well, they found her guilty. Now, I'm gon' have to make another bond for her. As soon as we can get her bond signed, we'll bring her right out." They said, "If you don't hurry and come out, we're coming in there and getchya," I couldn't *believe* it. When we got outside, police were standing outside with sawed-off shotguns, and the people all up and down the streets was from sidewalk to sidewalk out there. I looked around there, and I bet you there was over a thousand black people— black men—on the streets out there. . . .

Then we came up with a name for the organization. I said, "What about the Citizens' Committee?" Rev. Abernathy said, "No, I don't want no Citizens' Committee. Too close to the white Citizens Council." Then he came up and said, "What about the Montgomery Improvement Association?" I said, "I'll go along with it," so we agreed on it.

And Abernathy was sittin' as close as me in here to you, and he leant over. He said, "Brother Nixon, now you gon' serve as president, ain'tchya?" I said, "Naw, not unless'n you all don't accept my man." He said, "Who is your man?" I said, "Martin Luther King." He said, "I'll go along with it." French said, "I'll go along with it." So then we had not only our recommendation, our resolution, our name, we had our president.

In August of 1955 he was the guest speaker for the NAACP, and a professor over at the State Teachers College and I were sitting in the back. His name was J.E. Pierce. When King got through talking, I said, "Pierce, you know that guy made a heck of a speech."

He said, "I agree with you. He sho' did."

I said, "I don't know how I'm going to do it yet, but someday I'm gon' hang him to the stars."

JAMES FARMER

JF: I was impressed by the fact that most of the activity thus far had been of local people working on their local problems—Greensborans sitting-in in Greensboro and Atlantans sitting-in in Atlanta—and the pressure of the opposition against having outsiders come was very, very great. If any outsider came in . . . , "Get that outside agitator." . . . I thought that this was going to limit the growth of the Movement. . . . We somehow had to cut across state lines and establish the position that we were entitled to act any place in the country, no matter where we hung our hat and called home, because it was our country.

We also felt that one of the weaknesses of the student sit-in movement of the South had been that as soon as arrested, the kids bailed out. . . . This was not quite Gandhian and not the best tactic. A better tactic would be to remain in jail and to make the maintenance of segregation so expensive for the state and the city that they would hopefully come to the conclusion that they could no longer afford it. Fill up the jails, as Gandhi did in India, fill them to bursting if we had to. In other words, stay in without bail.

So those were the two things: cutting across state lines, putting the movement on wheels, so to speak, and remaining in jail, not only for its publicity value but for the financial pressure it would put upon the segregators. We decided that a good approach here would be to move away from restaurant lunch counters. That had been the Southern student sit-in movement, and anything we would do on that would be anticlimactic now. We would have to move into another area and so we decided to move into the transportation, interstate transportation....

It would be necessary, he decided, to violate custom and local law to focus attention on the federal laws barring discrimination in interstate transportation. He knew that in 1946 the Supreme Court had ruled against segregated seating on interstate buses, and in 1960, against segregated terminal facilities. The rulings were uniformly ignored throughout the South.

JF: So we, following the Gandhian technique, wrote to Washington. We wrote to the Justice Department, to the FBI, and to the President, and wrote to Greyhound Bus Company and Trailways Bus Company and told them that on May first or May fourth—whatever the date was, I forget now—we were going to have a Freedom Ride. Blacks and whites were going to leave Washington, D.C., on Greyhound and Trailways, deliberately violating the segregated seating requirements and at each rest stop would violate the segregated use of facilities. And we would be nonviolent, absolutely nonviolent, throughout the campaign, and we would accept the consequences of our actions. This was a deliberate act of civil disobedience....

Did Justice try to head you off?

JF: No, we got no reply. We got no reply from Justice. Bobby Kennedy, no reply. We got no reply from the FBI. We got no reply from the White House, from President Kennedy. We got no reply from Greyhound or Trailways. *We got no replies.* [Laughs]

He recruited an interracial group of thirteen and brought them to Washington for a week's training.

JF: We had some of the group of thirteen sit at a simulated counter asking for coffee. Somebody else refused them service, and then we'd have others come in as white hoodlums to beat 'em up and knock them off the counter and club 'em and kick 'em in the ribs and stomp 'em, and they were quite realistic, I must say. I thought they bent over backwards to be realistic. I was aching all over. [Laughs] And then we'd go into a discussion as to how the roles were played, whether there was something that the Freedom Riders did that they shouldn't have done, said that they shouldn't have said, something that they didn't say or do that they should have, and so on. Then we'd reverse roles and play it over and over again and have lengthy discussions of it.

I felt, by the way, that by the time that group left Washington, they were prepared for anything, even death, and this was a possibility, and we knew it, when we got to the Deep South.

Through Virginia we had no problem. In fact they had heard we were coming, Greyhound and Trailways, and they had taken down the

For Colored and For Whites signs, and we rode right through. Yep. The same was true in North Carolina. Signs had come down just the previous day, blacks told us. And so the letters in advance did something.

In South Carolina it was a different story.... John Lewis started into a white waiting room in some town in South Carolina...and there were several young white hoodlums, leather jackets, ducktail haircuts, standing there smoking, and they blocked the door and said, "Nigger, you can't come in here." He said, "I have every right to enter this waiting room according to the Supreme Court of the United States in the Boynton case."

They said, "Shit on that." He tried to walk past, and they clubbed him, beat him, and knocked him down. One of the white Freedom Riders...Albert Bigelow, who had been a Navy captain during World War II, big, tall, strapping fellow, very impressive, from Connecticut—then stepped right between the hoodlums and John Lewis. Lewis had been absorbing more of the punishment. They then clubbed Bigelow and finally knocked him down, and that took some knocking because he was a pretty strapping fellow, and he didn't hit back at all. [They] knocked him down, and at this point police arrived and intervened. They didn't make any arrests. Intervened.

Well, we went through the rest of South Carolina without incident and then to Atlanta, Georgia, and there we met with Dr. King. We called him and told him we were coming, and he had dinner with us and wished us well. Went to Albany first and then Atlanta. And when we were in Atlanta—my father by the way, was in Freedman's Hospital here in Washington with cancer, and I got word just about two hours before the buses left Atlanta that my father had died, and I had to go back and bury him. My mother insisted until her death five years later that my father willed his death at that time, willed the timing of it because he had my schedule. I had talked with him here in Washington during our training session, when he was in the hospital before I left, and told him what we were going to do, and he said, "Well, that's an interesting idea and I hope you survive it." He said, "I think the most dangerous part of it will be through Bama," as he put it, "and Mississippi. There, somebody will probably take a potshot at you, and I just hope they miss." And my mother says that every morning he would take out my itinerary and look at it and say, "Well, now, let's see where Junior is today." And he was relaxed about it until I got to Atlanta, and he says, "Oh, tomorrow he goes through Bama."

He died, and she says that he willed the timing of it to bring me back. It's apocryphal I'm sure. At any rate I had to return then to bury him and informed the Freedom Riders that I would rejoin them as soon as I had gotten this family obligation out of the way. I must confess that while I felt guilty at leaving, there was also a sense of relief at missing this leg of the trip, because all of us were scared. There was one reporter who was one of the Freedom Riders at this stage, and that was Simeon Booker of Johnson publications, *Jet* and *Ebony*. Simeon had come to me just before I got the telegram telling me of my father's death, or the phone call, and he said, "Jim, you know, I've decided that you are the only Freedom Rider I can outrun. So what I'm going to do is to stick with you on this trip, and I figure it's the fellow bringing up the rear who's gonna get caught." [Laughs]

HANK THOMAS

HT: The Freedom Ride didn't really get rough until we got down in the Deep South. Needless to say, Anniston, Alabama, I'm never gonna forget that, when I was on the bus that they threw some kind of incendiary device on.

He was on the first of two buses to cross into "Bama." When it pulled into the depot at Anniston, a Klan hotbed about sixty miles from Birmingham, the bus was surrounded by white men brandishing iron bars. Anniston police held them back long enough for the bus to reach the highway again, but about six miles outside town the pursuing mob caught up.

HT: I got real scared then. You know, I was thinking—I'm looking out the window there, and people are out there yelling and screaming. They just about broke every window out of the bus.... I really thought that that was going to be the end of me.

How did the bus get stopped?

HT: They shot the tires out, and the bus driver was forced to stop.... He got off, and man, he took off like a rabbit, and might well have. I couldn't very well blame him there. And we were trapped on the bus. They tried to board. Well, we did have two FBI men aboard the bus. All they were there to do were to observe and gather facts, but the crowd apparently recognized them as FBI men, and they did not try to hurt them.

It wasn't until the thing was shot on the bus and the bus caught afire that everything got out of control, and...when the bus was burning, I figured...[pauses]...panic did get ahold of me. Needless to say, I couldn't survive that burning bus. There was a possibility I could have survived the mob, but I was just so afraid of the mob that I was gonna stay on that bus. I mean, I just got that much afraid. And when we got off the bus...first they closed the doors and wouldn't let us off. But them I'm pretty sure they realized, that somebody said, "Hey, the bus is gonna explode," because it had just gassed up, and so they started scattering then, and I guess that's the way we got off the bus.* Otherwise, we probably all would have been succumbed by the smoke, and not

---

* John Patterson, then governor of Alabama, maintains that he and his public safety director, Floyd Mann, were indirectly responsible for the Freedom Riders' getting off the burning bus: "Floyd recommended that we send a state plainclothes investigator to Atlanta to catch the bus and ride with the Freedom Riders, and we did. Now this has never been reported that I know of in any paper.... We sent a man named E.L. Cowling.... He went over to Atlanta and caught the bus, and he was on the bus when they came to Anniston.... So Cowling walked up to the door of the bus and drew his pistol and backed the crowd away from the bus and told them that if anybody touched anybody he'd kill them. And he got the Freedom Riders off the burning bus. That's true."

being able to get off, probably would have been burned alive or burned on there anyway. That's the only time I was really, really afraid. I got whacked over the head with a rock or I think some kind of a stick as I was coming off the bus.

What happened in Anniston after the bus was attacked?

HT: We were taken to the hospital. The bus started exploding, and a lot of people were cut by flying glass. We were taken to the hospital, most of us, for smoke inhalation.

By whom?

HT: I don't remember. I think I was half out of it, half dazed, as a result of the smoke, and, gosh, I can still smell that stuff down in me now. You got to the point where you started having the dry heaves. Took us to the hospital, and it was incredible. The people at the hospital would not do anything for us. They would not. And I was saying, "You're *doctors*, you're medical personnel." They wouldn't. Governor Patterson got on statewide radio and said, "Any rioters in this state will not receive police protection." And then the crowd started forming outside the hospital, and the hospital told us to leave. And we said, "No, we're not going out there," and there we were. A caravan from Birmingham, about a fifteen-car caravan led by the Reverend Fred Shuttlesworth, came up from Birmingham to get us out.

Without police escort, I take it?

HT: Without police escort, but every one of those cars had a shotgun in it. And Fred Shuttlesworth had got on the radio and said—you know Fred, he's very dramatic—"I'm going to get my people." [Laughs] He said, "I'm a nonviolent man, but I'm going to get my people." And apparently a hell of a lot of people believed in him. Man, they came there and they were a welcome sight. And each one for 'em got out with their guns and everything and the state police were there, but I think they all realized that this was not a time to say anything because, I'm pretty sure, there would have been a lot of people killed.

The black drivers were openly carrying guns?

HT: Oh, yeah. They had rifles and shotguns. And that's how we got back to Birmingham.... I think I was flown to New Orleans for medical treatment, because still they were afraid to let any of us go to the hospitals in Birmingham, and by that time—it was what, two days later—I was fairly all right. I had gotten most of the smoke out of my system.

No one received any attention in the hospital in Anniston?

HT: No, no. Oh, we did have one girl, Genevieve Hughes, a white girl, who had a busted lip. I remember a nurse applying something to that, but other than that, nothing. Now that I look back on it, man, we had some vicious people down there, wouldn't even so much as *treat* you. But that's the way it was. But strangely enough, even those bad things then don't stick in my mind that much. Not that I'm full of love and goodwill for everybody in my heart, but I chalk it off to part of the things that I'm going to be able to sit on my front porch in my rocking chair and tell my young'uns about, my grandchildren about.

Postscript: That same day, Mother's Day, May 14, 1961, the second bus escaped the mob in Anniston and made it to Birmingham. At the Trailways station there, white men armed with baseball bats and chains beat the Freedom Riders at will for about fifteen minutes before the first police arrived. In 1975 a former Birmingham Klansman, who was a paid informant of the FBI at the time, told the Senate Select Committee on Intelligence that members of the Birmingham police force had promised the Klansmen that no policemen would show up to interfere with the beatings for at least fifteen minutes. In 1976 a Birmingham detective who refused to be interviewed on tape told me that account was correct—as far as it went. The detective said that word was passed in the police department that Public Safety Commissioner Eugene "Bull" Connor had watched from the window of his office in City Hall as the crowd of Klansmen, some brandishing weapons, gathered to await the Freedom Riders. Asked later about the absence of his policemen, Connor said most of them were visiting their mothers.

JOHN LEWIS

He had left the Freedom Ride in South Carolina to keep an appointment for a job interview. Returning to Nashville on May 14, he learned of the attacks in Anniston and Birmingham and that CORE, heeding Attorney General Robert Kennedy's request for a "cooling-off" period, had canceled the ride altogether. He and a group of sit-in veterans believed that if the Freedom Ride did not continue, segregationists would conclude that they could, indeed, defeat the Movement with violence and intimidation. Using money left over from the sit-in treasury and ignoring the advice of Nashville's SCLC affiliate, they bought tickets for Birmingham and announced that the Freedom Ride was on again.

At the Birmingham city limit, a policeman halted their bus and informed the driver that he was taking charge of the vehicle. When the bus pulled into the station, the "Birmingham police department put up newspapers all around the bus windows so you couldn't see out, and no one could see in." Shielded from inspection, they waited until "Bull" Connor arrived on the scene and ordered them taken into "protective custody." Thus began one of the most bizarre episodes of the Movement.

JL: So they took us all to the jail, the Birmingham city jail. Now this was on a Wednesday. We went to jail and stayed in jail Wednesday night. We didn't eat anything. We went on a hunger strike....

What sort of treatment did you get from the police?

JL: They were very, very nice. They didn't rough us up or anything like that, just very nice, as I recall. They put us in jail, segregated us

...and that Thursday we stayed in jail all day. That Thursday night around midnight, "Bull" Connor and two reporters...and maybe one or two detectives came up to the jail, and "Bull" Connor said they were going to take us back to Nashville, back to the college campus where we belonged. We said, "Well, we don't want to go back. We have a right to be on this Freedom Ride. We have a right to travel. We plan to go to Montgomery, and from Montgomery we're going to Jackson and to New Orleans." And he insisted. And people just sorta went limp, so they had people literally to pick us up and place us into these cars....

Anyway, they drove us on the highway, and "Bull" Connor was really funny. I was in the car that he was in and this young lady, Katherine Burke. He was really funny, he was really joking with us, saying that he was gonna take us back to Nashville, and we told him we would invite him to the campus, and he could have breakfast with us and that type of thing. He said he would like that. It was that type of conversation that we had going with "Bull" Connor.

We got to the Tennessee-Alabama line... They dropped us off, saying..."You can take the bus back to Nashville." They literally left us there. We didn't know anybody, didn't know any place to go. This is true.

Did it cross your mind that you might be being set up?

JL: Oh, yeah, oh, yeah. We just didn't know what had happened, and it was still dark. It was early morning-like.

The Birmingham police, including the police commissioner, had physically loaded you up in a car and carried you to the state line, a matter of 150 miles.

JL: That's right. That's right. And *left* us, just left us. What we did, we started walking down a road, and we saw a railroad track, and we crossed this railroad track and went to an old house. There was an elderly couple there, must have been in their late sixties, early seventies. We knocked on the door, and they let us in, and they was just really frightened. They'd heard about the Freedom Riders.

This was a black couple?

JL: Black couple. They were just really, really frightened. They didn't know what to do. They didn't really want to let us in, but they did, and we called Nashville and told 'em what had happened. Called Diane Nash on the telephone. She was in the local student movement office there in Nashville, and she wanted to know whether we wanted to continue the ride or whether we wanted a car to pick us up to bring us back to Nashville. We told her to send a car to take us back to Birmingham. We wanted to continue the ride.

In the meantime, we hadn't had anything to eat, and we were very hungry. 'Cause this is now Friday morning, and we hadn't had anything to eat since, I guess, early Wednesday. This man, this elderly man, got in his pickup truck and went around during the early morning to two or three stores and bought something like bologna and bread and corn-flakes. Anyway, we had a little meal there, and apparently some of the white people in the community came by, and he told 'em some of his relatives were visiting from Nashville. We waited around till the car from Nashville got there, and this was really something else. It was seven of us and the driver now, eight of us, got in that car on our way back to Birmingham, and we heard a reporter on the radio saying the students had been taken to the state line and apparently they were...back in Nashville on their college campuses....

So we drove back to Birmingham, and Rev. Shuttlesworth and several other ministers from the Alabama Christian Movement for Human Rights met us there, and we went directly back to the Greyhound bus station. And we tried to get on the bus around, I recall, three o'clock, on the Greyhound bus from Birmingham to Montgomery, and apparently Greyhound canceled the bus taking off. We were going to try to get on one at five-something, and this bus driver said something that I'll never forget. He said, "I only have one life to give and I'm not going to give it to CORE or the NAACP."

He and his group, along with about twenty fresh volunteers from Nashville, spent the night on the wooden benches of the bus station. Departing from their previous practice, the police repelled a white mob which gathered during the night. Finally a reporter who was covering the story brought a message: "Apparently you all are going to get a chance to go. Attorney General Kennedy has been in contact with Greyhound."

JL: The same bus driver came out to the bus about eight-thirty on Saturday morning, and we got on a bus from Birmingham to Montgomery. And apparently the arrangement was that every so many miles there would be a state patrol car and there would be a plane. We did see—I don't know whether it was the arrangement or not—we did see a small plane flying up above the bus for so many miles and we did have the patrol car....*

It was a nice ride between Birmingham and Montgomery. A few miles outside of Montgomery you just didn't see anything. You didn't see the plane, didn't see the state patrol car. It seemed like everything sort of disappeared, and the moment that we arrived in that station, it was the strangest feeling to me. It was something strange, that you knew something. It was really weird. It was an eerie feeling. There was a funny peace there, a quietness. You didn't see anything happening. Apparently, when you really look back, the mob there must have been so planned and was so out of sight...it just sorta appeared, just appeared on the scene.

You didn't see any sign of it as you went into the bus station?

* In fact, an airplane and sixteen highway patrol cars accompanied the bus, despite Governor Patterson's public statement that "we are not going to escort those agitators. We stand firm on that position."

JL: None. Just didn't see anything. When we drove up, we didn't see anything.... We got most of the young ladies in a cab. So they got in a cab and the black cab driver didn't want to drive, because at that time there was two white students, young ladies from Peabody or Scarritt, and in Alabama there was a law that you couldn't have an integrated cab. So the two young ladies got out, and at that very time, this mob started all over the place. So everybody, all the young ladies, got away, and the two young white girls were running down the street trying to get away. That's when John Siegenthaler got hit.*And at that time, the rest of us, mostly fellas, just literally standing there because we couldn't run—no place to go really.**

This was out in the lot?

JL: Just out in the lot. And if you've been at the bus station, there's a rail there.... Down below is the entrance to the courthouse, the Post Office building. So when the mob kept coming, several of the people, several of the fellas jumped over and were able to get in the basement of the Post Office, and the postmaster there opened it and made it possible for people to come in and escape the mob. And I said—I remember saying that we shouldn't run, we should just stand there, 'cause the mob was beating people. And the last thing that I recall, I was hit with a crate, a wooden crate what you have soda in, and was left lying in the street. And I remember the Attorney General of Alabama, MacDonald Gallion, serving this injunction that Judge Walter B. Jones had issued saying that it was unlawful for interracial groups to travel. While I was lying there on the ground, he brought this injunction.

JAMES FARMER

After his father's funeral, he flew to Montgomery, where Dr. King and Reverend Abernathy had called a mass meeting at First Baptist Church as a show of support for the Freedom Riders.

JF: Fred Shuttlesworth met me at the airport with a couple of his guys. He said, "Well, gentlemen, it's going to be a touch-and-go as to whether we get to that church. Everybody's at the church; Martin has

---

* Robert Kennedy's administrative assistant, sent to Alabama as an observer.

** Freedom Rider William Harbour: "There was nobody there. I didn't see anybody standin' around the bus station. I saw some taxicabs there. That was about it. So the bus driver opened the bus door up and just walked away from the bus. I guess in less than fifteen minutes, we had a mob of people, five or six hundred people with ax handles, chains, and everything else.... Soon as we walked off the bus, John Lewis said to me, 'Bill, it doesn't look right....'

"Everything happened so quick. There was a standstill for the first two or three minutes... They were closin' in on us, and we were standin' still tryin' to decide what should we do in order to protect the whites we had with us. But then you had a middle-aged white female hollerin', 'Git them niggers, git them niggers...,' and that urged the crowd on. From then on, they was constantly movin' in. I don't think she ever hit anybody or threw anything whatsoever. Just the idea she started, just kept pushin' and pushin' and pushin'... It started just like that."

flown in...he's there and so we are under siege. A mob has it surrounded...." And so he drove me back as close as he could, and mobs blocked the way, wouldn't let the car through, began trying to open the door. We backed up and tried another route....

Approaching the church through a nearby graveyard, he and Shuttlesworth could get no closer than three blocks to the church before running into the white toughs again.

JF: And so Fred Shuttlesworth walked into the mob. [Laughs] I must confess I was scared as hell, but Shuttlesworth—[He suddenly leaps from his chair and strides across the room, showing how the preacher shoved his way through the incredulous whites.] These goons were standing there, thousands of them with clubs. "Out of the way. Go on. Out of the way." He didn't have any trouble. They stopped and looked at him: *"That nigger's crazy."* [Laughs] And I was standing right behind him trying to be little. [Still laughing] And we got to the church and got in....

Obviously, we were going to be there all night....So we were singing, and King and I were consulting, sitting in the office of the church and talking and mapping alternative plans.

The mob kicked open the door of the church, and they just *poured* in. And people were screaming, backed up against the wall. I don't know where they came from or how they did it, but the marshalls materialized in that situation. It seemed almost fictional. *There they were* suddenly, the marshalls confronting the mob. They had arm bands on, U.S. marshalls. ...They didn't draw their guns, but they used their clubs and forced them into a park and then dispersed those who had come to the church. Martial law was declared, and we were to stay in the church under heavy guard all night and not to attempt to leave.*

Then finally, when the mob was more or less permanently dispersed, we could leave the church. [We] went to homes, ministers' homes, and we had debates as to what to do, whether we should attempt the rest of the Freedom Ride, and the conclusion was that we would go on with it. We decided that we would go on. We had to, although I am sure that everybody was scared to death at this point. Dr. King declined to go on the grounds that he was on probation and it would be a violation of probation. The SNCC people wouldn't accept that though. They said, "Look, I'm on probation too." "So am I." "Me, too." "Me, too, and I'm going."

Did you try to prevail on King to go?

JF: No, no, no, no, no. I didn't feel that I should try to urge him to go, because I was debating whether I was going. [Laughs] I tried to fink

---

* Robert Kennedy sent in the U.S. marshalls because of Governor John Patterson's reluctance to promise protection for the Freedom Riders. Even so, the white mob, estimated at several thousand, would probably have overwhelmed the marshalls during the night had not Patterson finally relented. He declared martial law and sent eight hundred national guardsmen to the church. See John Patterson's account of his battle of wills with Kennedy.

out, I must confess.... The two buses were there, and they got on the buses, and I helped them put their luggage in and get on the bus, and I said, "Well, bye." [Laughs] And one of the CORE girls, Doris Castle, a girl from New Orleans, said "Jim, you're going with us, aren't you?" I said, "Doris, I've been away from the office now for three weeks, and mail has piled up and somebody has to mind the store, so I think I've just got to get back to the office in New York to keep this thing going and raise the necessary money." She said, "Jim, *please.*" I said, "Get my luggage out of the car and put it on the goddamn bus. I'm going." How was I going to face her afterwards if something happened, and I had finked out...?"*

They rolled out of Montgomery under heavy guard, helicopters overhead, National Guard riflemen aboard the bus.

JF: I don't think any of us thought that we were going to get to Jackson, Mississippi, really. I know I didn't. I was scared and I am sure the kids were scared.... On the bus, I noticed that they were writing notes, many of them, and I walked across the aisle to see what they were writing, and they were writing names and addresses of next of kin. The girls were shoving them in their bosoms and the men putting them in pockets or wallets.... **

When the bus got to the state line, we saw this famous sign, Welcome to the Magnolia State. [Laughs] We had to chuckle at that in spite of the tenseness of the situation. The six Alabama national guardsmen left the bus, and the Mississippi national guardsmen took their place. The bus driver left the bus, and another bus driver came on. The state director of public safety came on the bus and whispered something to one of the reporters. This reporter's eyes bulged, and he passed this whispered message on to the other reporters on the bus. All except one of them left the bus and got in cars outside. So when the bus started, I asked this remaining reporter what the message had been, and he said, "The director of public safety tells us that they have it on excellent authority that this bus is going to be ambushed and destroyed inside the Mississippi border." And I said, "And you stayed on it?" He said, "What? Miss a story like that?"... [Laughs]

We had learned that Ross Barnett, who was governor at that time had been on radio and TV several times a day for several days telling people to keep calm. He said, "Those Freedom Riders, so-called Freedom Riders, are coming into Mississippi. They're coming into Jackson, but don't come into town. Stay at home. Don't come into the city. Let us handle it according to our Mississippi laws. Anybody who breaks our laws is going to jail. But let us handle it.... Don't take the law into your own hands."

---

* John Lewis recalls: "That was one of the criticisms that many of the people in SNCC and CORE had of Dr. King. There's a fantastic picture of a young guy named Paul—I can't think of his last name—and the other guy was named Matthew Walker, waving out of a bus in Montgomery to Dr. King....it was a big criticism that he came to the bus station and saw the people off and he refused to go."

** For another account of the tension on this trip, see Dave Dennis.

He was repeating that over and over and over again. And we passed one place where there were woods, heavy woods, on both sides of the road, and there was a cluster of Mississippi national guardsmen standing there on both sides of the road. I heard one of the officers of the Guard shout over a bullhorn, "Look behind every tree." So I guess that's where the ambush was expected. They had their artillery pointed at the woods on both sides. A military operation, you know.

And when we got to Jackson, "Whew, well, the outskirts of Jackson now." We drove up to the Greyhound bus terminal. A crowd of people there. I said, "Well, this is it. This is where we get it." The door opened and I led the group off the bus. It turned out that the crowd of people were not hoodlums. They were plainclothesmen and reporters. [Laughs] *They* were the crowd. As soon as we walked out of the door, they parted, and they knew precisely where I was going, to the white waiting room and not to the colored waiting room. So they parted and made a path for me leading right to the white waiting room [laughing], and I thought maybe I could have pled entrapment when we got to court, because we couldn't go anyplace else.

He and a veteran of the Nashville sit-ins named Lucretia Collins joined arms and started walking toward the white restrooms. A Captain Ray of the Jackson police was waiting for them.

JF: He blocked the way. He said "Move on." I said "Where?" He said, "Move on out." I refused on the grounds of the Supreme Court decision in the Boynton case and gave the date of it. He said, "I said, 'Move on.'" I refused again on the same grounds.

He said, "Do you understand my order?"

I said, "Perfectly."

He said, "Well, I'm going to tell you one more time, move on."

I refused the third time on the same grounds.

He said, "What's your name?"

I said, "James Farmer."

He nodded. He said, "Follow that officer and get in the patrol wagon." So Lucretia and I and the people behind us climbed in the patrol, and we started singing "We Shall Overcome" and rocking that wagon with the song. And so it went. We made a symbol out of Captain Ray's pointed finger when he said, "Follow that patrol wagon." He was like the man who was sticking his finger in the hole in the dyke, trying to hold back the flood waters, but they would overwhelm him.

Jack Young, the only black attorney in Jackson, came to see him in the jailhouse.

JF: I sent word by him to call the CORE office and tell them to keep Freedom Riders coming into Jackson as fast as possible on every bus, every train . . . and recruit madly, and train. Didn't have to do much recruiting because by this time the volunteers were barraging us. CORE was jumping with telegrams coming in, phone calls: "Send me, I'll go." "Need more Freedom Riders? Take me. I'll go."

We had 325 or 326 jailed at one time. We filled up the jails.

We had trouble with some of the Freedom Riders because the training had to be hasty, and many of the people who rushed in, including some of the SNCC people, were not prepared for this sort of thing. "We're gonna stay in 'til hell freezes over." But after two days, "You got money to bail me out?" [Laughs] "No, you're pledged to stay in for forty days." Forty days, it seems, was the maximum that you could stay in and still file an appeal.... We wanted to file appeals and get this thing adjudicated before the Supreme Court, if necessary. But we still wanted to stay in jail and make it expensive on Mississippi, and we made it expensive on them. One of the trustees in the jail brought in a newspaper that announced that there was a nuisance tax that they had in Jackson, auto-use tax, that they had planned to eliminate that year. Well, they announced they couldn't eliminate it, because the Freedom Riders were costing too much....

And we were singing the songs, the freedom songs, which they hated. "You gotta stop that singing." You know, "O-o-h, freedom, o-o-o-o-h free-*dom*, before I'd be a slave, I'd be buried in my grave and go home to my Lord and be free."..."Stop that singing!" The other prisoners upstairs began joining in on the singing.... They were in for murder, rape, theft, what have you. We developed a communications system by sending a message up a wire. They'd pull it up...an old electric wire that wasn't in use. "Stop that singing!" We refused to stop and kept on singing, and they then stopped bringing in the knick-knacks. They'd bring in candy bars and chewing gum to sell, and they wouldn't bring that to us. The kids were looking forward to that coming in each day, so we found a way to get it. We would send the money upstairs and have them buy more than they wanted with our money.

One day a black trustee who had the run on the jail came to his cell with a whispered message: " 'They're gonna send you to the prison farm. That's where they're gonna try to break you. They're gonna try to whip your ass.' They transferred us there in the dead of night...." The county prison farm proved to be but a way station on their passage to the legendary state prison at Parchman. There, black convicts in striped uniforms trailed mule-drawn plows across the endless vistas of the state's cotton fields, a tableau from another century. Yet "the singing went on, and there was still no brutality—physical brutality."

JF: They knew many of us were chain-smokers. They wouldn't allow any cigarettes in, and the guards would walk down the corridors blowing cigarette smoke into our cells. We were already climbing the walls for want of a cigarette. And they knew that most of these were college students. They wouldn't allow any books in, no books whatever. No newspapers...

And then psychological brutality—they passed out the clothing for us. We had to strip, and they then gave us shorts, just a pair of undershorts, that's all. The big guys got tiny little undershorts, and the little guys had huge undershorts. The big guys were trying to hold theirs shut, and the little guys were trying to stay in theirs and keep 'em from falling down. [Laughs] And they arranged to put two big guys in one cell and two little guys in one cell, so they couldn't swap.

The food was terrible. It was very, very bad. I went on a diet there and lost about thirty pounds.... We wanted to get out, because we were suffering in there. It was damp, and it was cold at night, too. And when they tried to get us to stop singing, we wouldn't stop singing, so they said, "If you don't stop singing, we'll take away your mattress." So they yanked those mattresses off those hard metal beds when we wouldn't stop singing. And we were sleeping on that cold, hard surface, and then they opened the window and turned on the exhaust fan, which brought cold air. I didn't know Mississippi could get that cold, but it felt cold at night. Almost everybody came down with a cold.

I finally—oh, by the way, Ross Barnett came by. Some of the other Freedom Riders recognized him from a picture. They said, "You know who that is that just walked in? That's Ross Barnett." Couldn't miss him. Not only his face, but he's a little man, small-boned man, with an enormous pot belly. [Laughs] So Ross came in, and he just walked around the cell block, just looking in, saying nothing. He stopped at my cell and says, "What's your name?" I said, "James Farmer." He said, "They treatin' you all right here?" I said, "Well, no violence, no physical brutality." He said, "So they treatin' you all right. No complaints, huh?" [Laughs] I said, "I didn't say that. We have lots of complaints. The biggest complaint is that we're in here, and we shouldn't be in here." So he nodded and walked off.

I then demanded to see the director of prisons.... Two guards came to escort me. Here I was with my tiny little shorts, trying to keep 'em up, couldn't fasten 'em, other than that, naked, walking along and going to meet the director of prisons. And he was seated there, smoking a big cigar, and there was only one chair. That was his. So I could not sit down. I had to stand. It was really quite a humiliating situation. Here he was, well-dressed, Palm Beach suit, smoking his big cigar; me standing, barefoot, too, no shoes or anything else. And I told him that we respectfully requested—the other Freedom Riders had authorized me to request that we be allowed to go outside and work, work in the farm, work in the field. "Naw, we cain't do that, 'cause the other prisoners'll kill you, and we're responsible for keeping you alive." I said, "We'll take our chances on that." He said, "No, ain't gonna do that. And furthermore," he says, "we want you to stay in there and rot. That's what we want you to do. We got to feed you, because the law says we gotta feed you, and the government will see to it we feed you. But we can make that food so damn unpalatable that you can't eat it. We can put so much salt in it that it'll turn your stomach if you swallow it, and that's just what we may do." Then he signaled that the interview was over.

At the end of forty days, CORE posted a $500 appeal bond for each of the Freedom Riders. Only after they had left the state did Mississippi spring its last surprise. Each of the three-hundred odd cases would have to be tried in the state appeals courts. The matter would not be settled through the arguing of a few selected "test cases."

JF: They agreed to that, yet one week before the arraignment, the state of Mississippi said, "Oh, no, every last one of them Freedom

Riders gotta be back here in Jackson, Mississippi, for the arraignment, and anyone who doesn't show will have to forfeit that $500 bond that CORE has put up." And the prosecuting attorney told our lawyer very frankly. "We're gonna bankrupt CORE." . . . They almost did it, too.

In an ironic final act ot the spring's high drama, CORE found itself chartering buses to haul the Freedom Riders back to Mississippi. But this time the riders were under strict orders to stay out of jail, for CORE was now saddled with legal fees, bail bond, and transportation costs of over $300,000.

JF: I called Roy Wilkins and told him of the problem, and Roy said, "Well, Jim, the NAACP will send you a check for a thousand dollars."

I said, "Fine, but a thousand dollars won't help."

Well, it helped a little bit, I guess. We put down the deposit on the buses that we were chartering. . . .

Thurgood Marshall saved us. I don't know, now that he's a Supreme Court justice, if he would want that known, but he saved us. I was at a cocktail party and Thurgood was there during this period, and he said, "Jim, how you coming along on that Freedom Ride now?"

I said, "Thurgood, Mississippi is gon' knock us out of the box. They're trying to bankrupt us and they don't know it, but they're just about succeeding 'cause we are *really* hard up now."

He said, "What's the problem, bail bond?"

I said, "Yeah. . . ."

He said, "The Inc. Fund* has got a bail bond fund. I don't know just what is in it, maybe $200,000, $250,000. It's not doing nothin'. It's just sitting there, salted away, drawing interest. You might as well use it as long as it lasts."

When he said that, I hugged him. [Laughs]

Postscript: CORE finally won in the Supreme Court and Mississippi had to refund the bond money. At the insistence of Robert Kennedy the Interstate Commerce Commission issued a directive which really did end bus segregation in parts of the South.

But the first phase of the Movement was over. So was James Farmer's moment as its leader, and so was CORE's day as the pacesetter of the Southern Movement. Now the torch would pass to SCLC and its preachers and to SNCC and its students, to these two organizations born in the South and tempered by Southern resistance for the long battle ahead in Alabama and Mississippi. And on the roadside at Anniston, at the terminal in Montgomery, in the drafty corridors of Parchman, the white folks who counted in those states had served notice that it would be a battle.

FANNIE LOU HAMER

Fannie Lou Hamer was a sharecropper who spoke out movingly in support of the black Mississippi Freedom Party delegation to the 1964 Democratic National Convention.

---

* The Inc. Fund, the NAACP Legal Defense and Education Fund, Inc., was administered by Marshall independently of the NAACP proper, the parent organization run by Wilkins.

...He brought a big old book out there, and he gave me the sixteenth section of the Constitution of Mississippi, and that was dealing with de facto laws, and I didn't know nothin' about no de facto laws, didn't know nothin' about any of 'em. I could copy it like it was in the book...but after I got through copying it, he told me to give a reasonable interpretation and tell the meaning of that section that I had copied. Well, I flunked out....

So then we started back to Ruleville and on our way back to Ruleville, this same highway patrolman that I had seen steady cruisin' around this bus stopped us. We had crossed that bridge, coming over from Indianola. They got out the cars, flagged the bus down. When they flagged the bus down, they told all of us to get off of the bus. So at this time, we just started singing "Have a Little Talk with Jesus," and we got off the bus, and all they wanted then was for us to get back on the bus. They arrested Bob [Moses] and told the bus driver he was under arrest. So we went back then to Indianola. The bus driver was fined one hundred dollars for driving a bus with too much yellow in it. Now ain't that ridiculous?

Too much yellow. Said the bus looked too much like a school bus. That's funny, but it's the truth. But you see, it was to frighten us to death. This same bus had been used year after year hauling cotton choppers and cotton pickers to Florida to try to make a livin' that winter, and he had never been arrested before. But the day he tried...to carry us to Indianola, they fined him a hundred dollars, and all of us *together*—not one, but all us together—had enough to pay the fine. So we paid the fine, and then we got back on the bus and come on to Ruleville.

So Rev. Jeff Summers, who live on Charles Street, just the next street over, he carried me out there on the Marlowe Plantation where I had worked for eighteen years. And when I got out there, my little girl—she's dead now, Dorothy—she met me and one of Pap's cousins, and said that man [who owned the plantation] had been raising a lot of Cain ever since we left, that he had been in the field more times than he usually come a day, because I had gone to the courthouse. See, the people at the courthouse would call and tell it. So they was kinda scared, and quiet natural I began to feel nervous, but I knowed I hadn't done nothin' wrong. So after my little girl told me, wasn't too long 'fore Pap got off, and he was tellin' me the same thing that the other kids had told me.

I went on in the house, and I sat down on a little old bed that belonged to the little girl, and when I sat down on the bed, this man [who owned the plantation] he come up and he asked Pap, "Did you tell Fannie Lou what I said?" and Pap said, "Yessir, I sho' did." And I got up and walked to the door, and then he asked me, "Did Pap tell you what I said?" I said, "He told me." And he said, "I mean that. You'll have to go back to Indianola and withdraw, or you have to leave this place." So I said, "Mr. Dee, I didn't go down there to register for you. I went down there to register for myself." And that made him madder, you know.

So he told me, "I want your answer now, yea or nay." And he said, "They gon' "—now, I don't know who the *they* were, whether it was the white Citizens Council or the Ku Klux Klan, 'cause I don't think one is no worse than the other—"they gon' worry me tonight. They gon' worry the hell outa me, and I'm gon' worry hell outa you. You got 'til in the mornin' to tell me. But if you don't go back there and withdraw, you got to leave the plantation."

So I knowned I wasn't goin' back to withdraw, so wasn't nothin' for me to do but leave the plantation. So Pap brought me out that same night and I come to Mrs. Tucker's, a lady live over on Byron Street. I went to her house, and I stayed, and Pap began to feel nervous when he went to the shop and saw some buckshot shells. And they don't have buckshot shells to *play* with in August and September, because you ain't huntin' or nothin' like that.

I stayed away, 'cause things then—you could see 'em at night. They would have fires in the middle of the road.... You wouldn't see no Klan signs, but just make a fire in the middle of the road. And it was *so dangerous,* I stayed in Tallahatchie County all of September and then October, and then November I come back to Ruleville. I was comin', I didn't know why I was comin', but I was just sick of runnin' and hadn't done nothin'.... I started tryin' to find a place to stay, 'cause we didn't have nothin'.

That was on a Sunday, and that Monday, the fourth of December, I went back to Indianola to the circuit clerk's office and I told him who I was and I was there to take that literacy test again.

I said, "Now, you cain't have me fired 'cause I'm already fired, and I won't have to move now, because I'm not livin' in no white man's house." I said, "I'll be here every thirty days until I become a registered voter." 'Cause that's what you would have to do: go every thirty days and see had you passed the literacy test.... I went back then the tenth of January in 1963, and I had become registered.... I passed the second one, because at the second time I went back, I had been studying sections of the Mississippi Constitution, so I would know if I got one that was simple enough that I might could pass it.

I passed that second test, but it made us become like criminals. We would have to have our lights out before dark. It was cars passing that house all times of the night, driving real slow with guns, and pickups with white mens in it, and they'd pass that house just as slow as they could pass it...three guns lined up in the back. All of that. This was the kind of stuff. Pap couldn't get nothin' to do....

So I started teachin' citizenship class, and I became the supervisor of the citizenship class in this county. So I moved around the county to do citizenship education, and later on I become a field secretary for SNCC—I guess being about one of the oldest people at that time that was a field secretary, 'cause they was real young.

They carried us on to the county jail. It wasn't the city jail. The county jail, so we could be far enough out, they didn't care how loud we hollered, wasn't nobody gon' hear us.... I was put in the cell with...I cain't think of this child's name...Evester Simpson. She's Mrs. Morris now. But anyway, I was in the cell with her, and they left Miss Ponder and somebody else out, and I started hearing screaming like I had never heard. And I could hear the sounds of the licks, but I couldn't see nobody. And I hear somebody when they say, "Cain't you say yessir, nigger? Cain't you say yessir, bitch?"

And I could understand Miss Ponder's voice. She said, "Yes, I can say yessir." He said, "Well, say it." She said, "I don't know you well enough." She never would say yessir, and I could hear when she would hit the flo', and then I could hear them licks just soundin'. [Softly] That was somethin'. That's a experience—that's a experience that I wouldn't want to go through again. But anyway, she kept screamin', and they kept beatin' on her, and finally she started prayin' for 'em, and she asked God to have mercy on 'em, because they didn't know what they was doin'.

And after then . . . I heard some real *keen* screams, and that's when they passed my cell with a girl, she was fifteen years old, Miss Johnson. June Johnson. They passed my cell, and the blood was runnin' down in her face, and they put her in another cell.

And then finally they come to my room, and one of them men told me, "Get up from there, fatso," and he carried me outa that cell. They first asked me, when they first come to the cell, they asked me where I was from, and I told 'em. And they said, "We gon' check that out," and I reckon they was callin' the white folks here. Well, the white folks here knowed I had tried to register, so they was gon' give me as much trouble as possible, 'cause when they come back, the man say, "You from Ruleville, all right." Said, "You, bitch, you, we gon' make you wish you was dead." And let me tell you, before they stopped beatin' me, I wish they would have hit me one lick that could have ended the misery that they had me in. They had me to lay down on this bunk bed with my face down, and they had two black prisoners. You know, a lot of folks would say, "Well, I woulda died before I'd done that." But nobody know the condition that those prisoners was in, before they were s'posed to beat me. And I heard that highway patrolman tell that black man, said, "If you don't beat her, you *know* what we'll do to you." And he didn't have no other choice.

So they had me lay down on my face, and they beat with a thick leather thing that was wide. And it had sumpin' in it *heavy*. I don't know what that was, rocks or lead. But everytime they hit me, I got just as hard, and I put my hands behind my back, and they beat me in my hands 'til my hands . . . my hands was as navy blue as anything you ever seen . . . that blood, I guess, and then beatin' it 'til it just turned black.

And then after the first one beat, they ordered the second one to beat me, and when the second one started beatin', it was just—it was just too much. I started wiggling . . . you know, kickin' my feet back there. The highway patrolman walked over there and had the first one had beat, told him to sit on my feet . . . while the second one beat. . . . But anyway, they finally told me to get up, and I just couldn't hardly get up, and they kept on tellin' me to get up. I finally could get up, but when I got back to my cell bed, I couldn't set down. I would *scream*. It hurted me to set down.

JULIAN BOND

Julian Bond, an ardent opponent of the Vietnam War, was refused admission to the Georgia State Senate after his election to that body in the mid–1960s.

I don't know if you remember a famous photograph—it was in *Life* magazine and then the New York *Times*—taken at the Selma March. It was a series of pictures in *Life*. The first one shows this crowd of marchers with John Lewis at the head. The second one shows them going toward the police. The next one shows the police beginning to charge, John standing his ground. The third one shows the police among them. They've hit John on the head and he's going down. It shows Hosea just like this, heading for the rear. [He rises from his chair, and demonstrates the pose of retreat caught in the photograph.] That picture appeared in the New York *Times* the day *after* the beating occurred in a full-page [fund-raising] advertisement for SCLC, and that just burned us up [in SNCC], you know. If we had had the ability to do it, the technical ability to quickly have a picture taken, fly it to New York, get it in the *Times*, have the copy all ready, or if we'd even thought in that way, we would have done it ourselves. We had more right to do it. It was *our* chairman who was leading the march.

It wasn't Dr. King. See, we began, most of the times, to separate Dr. King from SCLC, and our anger was directed at the bureaucrats who were there who were sucking money and our publicity, 'cause publicity was money. If you got your name in the New York *Times*, your organizational name in the New York *Times*, you could reprint that, send it out to your mailing list and they'd send you some dough.

But SCLC was hoggin' all the publicity and all the money and doing very little to deserve it. During the period when we had people working all over Mississippi, throughout most of the Black Belt in Alabama and southwest Georgia, SCLC had Martin Luther King and two or three other staff people and that was it. But they'd piggyback on everything we did—and sometimes at our invitation, you know. We would sometimes ask King to go someplace, because we knew the attention he drew would be helpful to the local scene, even if it wasn't helpful to us. But it was irritation, nonetheless. When King went into Selma...we had had five people there for a year beforehand, really softening the community up. And the first big police clash there didn't come across that bridge, but came a year earlier when Forman spoke at a mass meeting in Selma in Brown's Chapel A.M.E. Church, and the police, Jim Clark and his posse, gathered outside the church and wouldn't let anybody leave all night—people had to spend the whole night in the church—and were beating people up as they did sneak away. So we just resented SCLC's ability to capitalize on things we thought we were doing....

13. Breaking with the Past

ANNE MOODY

"Strong women," writes Andrew J. Young, "were the backbone of the [civil rights] movement." The list is long: Fannie Lou Hamer, Ella Baker, Casey Hayden, Mary King, Septima Clark, Dorothy Cotton, Jane Stembridge, Rosa Parks, Virginia Foster Durr, Ruby Doris Smith, Jo Ann Robinson, and many more. Their role has been obscured in part because the Southern Christian Leadership Conference was dominated by male ministers, because women played their roles more quietly, and because many more men than women died in the violent confrontations the movement provoked. In Andrew Young's words again: "Men and women struggling for freedom, but gradually becoming aware that freedom might mean different things for men and women, is an untold story of the civil rights movement."

In the last few years, as memoirs of participants in the movement have begun to appear, historians are beginning to piece out this untold story. A glimpse of that history has long been available in Anne Moody's stunning autobiography, published in 1968, Coming of Age in Mississippi. *Her account makes clear how many kinds of courage it took for a woman to join the movement, even for a student at a college like Tougaloo in the early 1960s with numerous indications of support. What enabled poor, unknown Mississippians in the back country, like Fannie Lou Hamer, to respond to SNCC workers and walk to the courthouse to register is a mystery we still strive to understand.*

In mid-September [1962] I was back on campus [Tougaloo]. But didn't very much happen until February when the NAACP held its annual convention in Jackson. They were having a whole lot of interesting speakers: Jackie Robinson, Floyd Patterson, Curt Flood, Margaretta Belafonte, and many others. I wouldn't have missed it for anything. I was so excited that I sent one of the leaflets home to Mama and asked her to come.

Three days later I got a letter from Mama with dried-up tears on it, forbidding me to go to the convention. It went on for more than six pages. She said if I didn't stop that shit she would come to Tougaloo and kill me herself. She told me about the time I last visited her, on Thanksgiving, and she had picked me up at the bus station. She said she picked me up because she was scared some white in my hometown would try to do something to me. She said the sheriff had been by, telling her I was messing around with that NAACP group. She said he told her if I didn't stop it, I could not come back there any more. He said that they didn't need any of those NAACP people messing around in Centreville. She ended the letter by saying that she had burned the leaflet I sent her. "Please don't send any more of that stuff here. I don't want nothing to happen to us here," she said. "If you keep that up, you will never be able to come home again."

I was so damn mad after her letter, I felt like taking the NAACP convention to Centreville. I think I would have, if it had been in my power to do so. The remainder of the week I thought of nothing except going to the convention. I didn't know exactly what to do about it. I didn't want Mama or anyone at home to get hurt because of me.

I had felt something was wrong when I was home. During the four days I was there, Mama had tried to do everything she could to keep me in the house. When I said I was going to see some of my old classmates, she pretended she was sick and said I would have to cook. I knew she was acting strangely, but I hadn't known why. I thought Mama just wanted me to spend most of my time with her, since this was only the second time I had been home since I entered college as a freshman.

Things kept running through my mind after that letter from Mama. My mind was so active, I couldn't sleep at night. I remembered the one time I did leave the house to go to the post office. I had walked past a bunch of white men on the street on my way through town and one said, "Is that the gal goin' to Tougaloo?" He acted kind of mad or something, and I didn't know what was going on. I got a creepy feeling, so I hurried home. When I told Mama about it, she just said, "A lotta people don't like that school." I knew what she meant. Just before I went to Tougaloo, they had housed the Freedom Riders there. The school was being criticized by whites throughout the state.

The night before the convention started, I made up my mind to go, no matter what Mama said. I just wouldn't tell Mama or anyone from home. Then it occurred to me—how did the sheriff or anyone at home know I was working with the NAACP chapter on campus? Somehow they had found out. Now I knew I could never go to Centreville safely again. I kept telling myself that I didn't really care too much about going home, that it was more important to me to go to the convention.

I was there from the very beginning. Jackie Robinson was asked to serve as moderator. This was the first time I had seen him in person. I remembered how when Jackie became the first Negro to play Major League baseball, my uncles and most of the Negro boys in my hometown started organizing baseball leagues. It did something for them to see a Negro out there playing with all those white players. Jackie was a good moderator, I thought. He kept smiling and joking. People felt relaxed and proud. They appreciated knowing and meeting people of their own race who had done something worth talking about.

When Jackie introduced Floyd Patterson, heavyweight champion of the world, the people applauded for a long, long time. Floyd was kind of shy. He didn't say very much. He didn't have to, just his being there was enough to satisfy most of the Negroes who had only seen him on TV. Archie Moore was there too. He wasn't as smooth as Jackie, but he had his way with a crowd. He started telling how he was run out of Mississippi, and the people just cracked up.

I was enjoying the convention so much that I went back for the night session. Before the night was over, I had gotten autographs from every one of the Negro celebrities.

I had counted on graduating in the spring of 1963, but as it turned out, I couldn't because some of my credits still had to be cleared with Natchez College. A year before, this would have seemed like a terrible disaster, but now I hardly even felt disappointed. I had a good excuse to stay on campus for the summer and work with the Movement, and this was what I really wanted to do. I couldn't go home again anyway, and I couldn't go to New Orleans—I didn't have money enough for bus fare.

During my senior year at Tougaloo, my family hadn't sent me one penny. I had only the small amount of money I had earned at Maple Hill. I couldn't afford to eat at school or live in the dorms, so I had gotten permission to move off campus. I had to prove that I could finish school, even if I had to go hungry every day. I knew Raymond and Miss Pearl were just waiting to see me drop out. But something happened to me as I got more and more involved in the Movement. It no longer seemed important to prove anything. I had found something outside myself that gave meaning to my life.

I had become very friendly with my social science professor, John Salter, who was in charge of NAACP activities on campus. All during the year, while the NAACP conducted a boycott of the downtown stores in Jackson, I had been one of Salter's most faithful canvassers and church speakers. During the last week of school, he told me that sit-in demonstrations were about to start in Jackson and that he wanted me to be the spokesman for a team that would sit-in at Woolworth's lunch counter. The two other demonstrators would be classmates of mine, Memphis and Pearlena. Pearlena was a dedicated NAACP worker, but Memphis had not been very involved in the Movement on campus. It seemed that the organization had had a rough time finding students who were in a position to go to jail. I had nothing to lose one way or the other. Around ten o'clock the morning of the demonstrations, NAACP headquarters alerted the news services. As a result, the police department was also informed, but neither the policemen nor the newsmen knew exactly where or when the demonstrations would start. They stationed themselves along Capitol Street and waited.

To divert attention from the sit-in at Woolworth's, the picketing started at J. C. Penney's a good fifteen minutes before. The pickets were allowed to walk up and down in front of the store three or four times before they were arrested. At exactly 11 A.M., Pearlena, Memphis, and I entered Woolworth's from the rear entrance. We separated as soon as we stepped into the store, and made small purchases from various counters. Pearlena had given Memphis her watch. He was to let us know when it was 11:14. At 11:14 we were to join him near the lunch counter and at exactly 11:15 we were to take seats at it.

Seconds before 11:15 we were occupying three seats at the previously segregated Woolworth's lunch counter. In the beginning the waitresses seemed to ignore us, as if they really didn't know what was going on. Our waitress walked past us a couple of times before she noticed we had started to write our orders down and realized we wanted service. She asked us what we wanted. We began to read to her from our order slips. She told us that we would be served at the back counter, which was for Negroes.

"We would like to be served here," I said.

The waitress started to repeat what she had said, then stopped in the middle of the sentence. She turned the lights out behind the counter, and she and the other waitresses almost ran to the back of the store, deserting all their white customers. I guess they thought that violence would start immediately after the whites at the counter realized what was going on. There were five or six other people at the counter. A couple of them just got up and walked away. A girl sitting next to me finished her banana split before leaving. A middle-aged white woman who had not yet been served rose from her seat and came over to us. "I'd like to stay here with you," she said, "but my husband is waiting."

The newsmen came in just as she was leaving. They must have discovered what was going on shortly after some of the people began to leave the store. One of the newsmen ran behind the woman who spoke to us and asked her to identify herself. She refused to give her name, but said she was a native of Vicksburg and a former resident of California. When asked why she had said what she had said to us, she replied, "I am in sympathy with the Negro movement." By this time a crowd of cameramen and reporters had gathered around us taking pictures and asking questions, such as Where were we from? Why did we sit-in? What organization sponsored it? Were we students? From what school? How were we classified?

I told them that we were all students at Tougaloo College, that we were represented by no particular organization, and that we planned to stay there even after the store closed. "All we want is service," was my reply to one of them. After they had finished probing for about twenty minutes, they were almost ready to leave.

At noon, students from a nearby white high school started pouring in to Woolworth's. When they first saw us they were sort of surprised. They didn't know how to react. A few started to heckle and the newsmen became interested again. Then the white students started chanting all kinds of anti-Negro slogans. We were called a little bit of everything. The rest of the seats except the three we were occupying had been roped off to prevent others from sitting down. A couple of the boys took one end of the rope and made it into a hangman's noose. Several attempts were made to put it around our necks. The crowds grew as more students and adults came in for lunch.

We kept our eyes straight forward and did not look at the crowd except for occasional glances to see what was going on. All of a sudden I saw a face I remembered—the drunkard from the bus station sit-in. My eyes lingered on him just long enough for us to recognize each other. Today he was drunk too, so I don't think he remembered where he had seen me before. He took out a knife, opened it, put it in his pocket, and then began to pace the floor. At this point, I told Memphis and Pearlena what was going on. Memphis suggested that we pray. We bowed our heads, and all hell broke loose. A man rushed forward, threw Memphis from his seat, and slapped my face. Then another man who worked in the store threw me against an adjoining counter.

Down on my knees on the floor, I saw Memphis lying near the lunch counter with blood running out of the corners of his mouth.

As he tried to protect his face, the man who'd thrown him down kept kicking him against the head. If he had worn hard-soled shoes instead of sneakers, the first kick probably would have killed Memphis. Finally a man dressed in plain clothes identified himself as a police officer and arrested Memphis and his attacker.

Pearlena had been thrown to the floor. She and I got back on our stools after Memphis was arrested. There were some white Tougaloo teachers in the crowd. They asked Pearlena and me if we wanted to leave. They said that things were getting too rough. We didn't know what to do. While we were trying to make up our minds, we were joined by Joan Trumpauer. Now there were three of us and we were integrated. The crowd began to chant, "Communists, Communists, Communists." Some old man in the crowd ordered the students to take us off the stools.

"Which one should I get first?" a big husky boy said.

"That white nigger," the old man said.

The boy lifted Joan from the counter by her waist and carried her out of the store. Simultaneously, I was snatched from my stool by two high school students. I was dragged about thirty feet toward the door by my hair when someone made them turn me loose. As I was getting up off the floor, I saw Joan coming back inside. We started back to the center of the counter to join Pearlena. Lois Chaffee, a white Tougaloo faculty member, was now sitting next to her. So Joan and I just climbed across the rope at the front end of the counter and sat down. There were now four of us, two whites and two Negroes, all women. The mob started smearing us with ketchup, mustard, sugar, pies, and everything on the counter. Soon Joan and I were joined by John Salter, but the moment he sat down he was hit on the jaw with what appeared to be brass knuckles. Blood gushed from his face and someone threw salt into the open wound. Ed King, Tougaloo's chaplain, rushed to him.

At the other end of the counter, Lois and Pearlena were joined by George Raymond, a CORE field worker and a student from Jackson State College. Then a Negro high school boy sat down next to me. The mob took spray paint from the counter and sprayed it on the new demonstrators. The high school student had on a white shirt; the word "nigger" was written on his back with red spray paint.

We sat there for three hours taking a beating when the manager decided to close the store because the mob had begun to go wild with stuff from other counters. He begged and begged everyone to leave. But even after fifteen minutes of begging, no one budged. They would not leave until we did. Then Dr. Beittel, the president of Tougaloo College, came running in. He said he had just heard what was happening.

About ninety policemen were standing outside the store; they had been watching the whole thing through the windows, but had not come in to stop the mob or do anything. President Beittel went outside and asked Captain Ray to come and escort us out. The captain refused, stating the manager had to invite him in before he could enter the premises, so Dr. Beittel himself brought us out. He had told the police that they had better protect us after we were outside the store. When we got outside, the policemen formed a single line that blocked the mob from us. However, they were allowed to throw at us everything they had collected. Within ten minutes, we were picked up by Reverend King in his station wagon and taken to the NAACP headquarters on Lynch Street.

After the sit-in, all I could think of was how sick Mississippi whites were. They believed so much in the segregated Southern way of life, they would kill to preserve it. I sat there in the NAACP office and thought of how many times they had killed when this way of life was threatened. I knew that the killing had just begun. "Many more will die before it is over with," I thought. Before the sit-in, I had always hated the whites in Mississippi. Now I knew it was impossible for me to hate sickness. The whites had a disease, an incurable disease in its final stage. What were our chances against such a disease? I thought of the students, the young Negroes who had just begun to protest, as young interns. When these young interns got older, I thought, they would be the best doctors in the world for social problems.

Before we were taken back to campus, I wanted to get my hair washed. It was stiff with dried mustard, ketchup and sugar. I stopped in at a beauty shop across the street from the NAACP office. I didn't have on any shoes because I had lost them when I was dragged across the floor at Woolworth's. My stockings were sticking to my legs from the mustard that had dried on them. The hairdresser took one look at me and said, "My land, you were in the sit-in, huh?"

"Yes," I answered. "Do you have time to wash my hair and style it?"

"Right away," she said, and she meant right away. There were three other ladies already waiting, but they seemed glad to let me go ahead of them. The hairdresser was real nice. She even took my stockings off and washed my legs while my hair was drying.

There was a mass rally that night at the Pearl Street Church in Jackson, and the place was packed. People were standing two abreast in the aisles. Before the speakers began, all the sit-inners walked out on the stage and were introduced by Medgar Evers. People stood and applauded for what seemed like thirty minutes or more. Medgar told the audience that this was just the beginning of such demonstrations. He asked them to pledge themselves to unite in a massive offensive against segregation in Jackson, and throughout the state. The rally ended with "We Shall Overcome" and sent home hundreds of determined people. It seemed as though Mississippi Negroes were about to get together at last.

Before I demonstrated, I had written Mama. She wrote me back a letter, begging me not to take part in the sit-in. She even sent ten dollars for bus fare to New Orleans. I didn't have one penny, so I kept the money. Mama's letter made me mad. I had to live my life as I saw fit. I had made that decision when I left home. But it hurt to have my family prove to me how scared they were. It hurt me more than anything else— I knew the whites had already started the threats and intimidations. I was the first Negro from my hometown who had openly demonstrated, worked with the NAACP, or anything. When Negroes threatened to do anything in Centreville, they were either shot like Samuel O'Quinn or run out of town, like Reverend Dupree.

I didn't answer Mama's letter. Even if I had written one, she wouldn't have received it before she saw the news on TV or heard it on the radio. I waited to hear from her again. And I waited to hear in the news that someone in Centreville had been murdered. If so, I knew it would be a member of my family.

14. Letter from Birmingham Jail

MARTIN LUTHER KING, JR.

Martin Luther King began writing his "Letter from Birmingham Jail" on the margins of the Birmingham News *issue that contained a letter from eight Christian and Jewish clergymen condemning the black demonstrations in Alabama. He continued writing on scraps of toilet paper and completed the letter on a legal pad provided by his lawyers, who had also smuggled in the pen with which he finished this great document of the civil rights movement.*

Birmingham was King's thirteenth experience of jail. Only months before, he had been imprisoned in Albany, Georgia. At that time he had worried about his children's reaction to seeing him in jail. The children's mother had explained to their daughter Yolanda that "Daddy was in jail so that all people could go where they liked." This had satisfied the child, who commented, "Good, tell him to stay in jail until I can go to Funtown [a local segregated amusement park]." This reply was so important to King that he alluded to it in this famous letter. The reference was significant because King's most controversial tactic in Birmingham, barely mentioned in the letter, was the inclusion of children, even small grade-school children, among his marchers. Shortly after writing the letter and leaving jail, King had watched a confrontation between an angry policeman and an eight-year-old girl walking with her mother: "What do you want?" asked the policeman; "Freedom," replied the child, looking straight at him. During this scene, King remembered an old woman who had said about her involvement in the Montgomery bus boycott: "I'm doing it for my children and for my grandchildren." In 1963, seven years later, King commented, "The children and grandchildren are doing it for themselves."

The vision of policemen clubbing men, women, and children, of police dogs attacking crowds, of women and children bruised, bloodied, and smashed against walls and pavement by high pressure fire hoses shocked the world and transformed American public opinion. In February 1963 a civil rights bill had died in Congress: "Nobody paid any attention," said Robert Kennedy. After the Birmingham demonstration in the spring of 1963 and its glorious symbolic coda, the March on Washington that August, everyone paid attention. The eight Christian and Jewish clergymen from Alabama never answered King's letter, which was, in fact, unanswerable, but the churches of the nation did quickly move into the forefront of the coalition of concern that produced the great civil rights legislation of the mid-1960s. These enactments remain the great legacy of the movement and a substantial, although partial, realization of the dream King presented in the letter from Birmingham Jail and the "I Have a Dream" speech at the Lincoln Memorial later that same year.

My Dear Fellow Clergymen:

  While confined here in the Birmingham city jail, I came across your recent statement calling my present activities "unwise and untimely." Seldom do I pause to answer criticism of my work and ideas. If I sought to answer all the criticisms that cross my desk, my secretaries would have little time for anything other than such correspondence in the course of the day, and I would have no time for constructive work. But since I feel that you are men of genuine good will and that your criticisms are sincerely set forth, I want to try to answer your statement in what I hope will be patient and reasonable terms.

I think I should indicate why I am here in Birmingham, since you have been influenced by the view which argues against "outsiders coming in." I have the honor of serving as president of the Southern Christian Leadership Conference, an organization operating in every southern state, with headquarters in Atlanta, Georgia. We have some eighty-five affiliated organizations across the South, and one of them is the Alabama Christian Movement for Human Rights. Frequently we share staff, educational and financial resources with our affiliates. Several months ago the affiliate here in Birmingham asked us to be on call to engage in a nonviolent direct-action program if such were deemed necessary. We readily consented, and when the hour came we lived up to our promise. So I, along with several members of my staff, am here because I was invited here. I am here because I have organizational ties here.

But more basically, I am in Birmingham because injustice is here. Just as the prophets of the eighth century B.C. left their villages and carried their "thus saith the Lord" far beyond the boundaries of their home towns, and just as the Apostle Paul left his village of Tarsus and carried the gospel of Jesus Christ to the far corners of the Greco-Roman world, so am I compelled to carry the gospel of freedom beyond my own home town. Like Paul, I must constantly respond to the Macedonian call for aid.

Moreover, I am cognizant of the interrelatedness of all communities and states. I cannot sit idly by in Atlanta and not be concerned about what happens in Birmingham. Injustice anywhere is a threat to justice everywhere. We are caught in an inescapable network of mutuality, tied in a single garment of destiny. Whatever affects one directly, affects all indirectly. Never again can we afford to live with the narrow, provincial "outside agitator" idea. Anyone who lives inside the United States can never be considered an outsider anywhere within its bounds.

You deplore the demonstrations taking place in Birmingham. But your statement, I am sorry to say, fails to express a similar concern for the conditions that brought about the demonstrations. I am sure that none of you would want to rest content with the superficial kind of social analysis that deals merely with effects and does not grapple with underlying causes. It is unfortunate that demonstrations are taking place in Birmingham, but it is even more unfortunate that the city's white power structure left the Negro community with no alternative.

In any nonviolent campaign there are four basic steps: collection of the facts to determine whether injustices exist; negotiation; self-purification; and direct action. We have gone through all these steps in Birmingham. There can be no gainsaying the fact that racial injustice engulfs this community. Birmingham is probably the most thoroughly segregated city in the United States. Its ugly record of brutality is widely known. Negroes have experienced grossly unjust treatment in the courts. There have been more unsolved bombings of Negro homes and churches in Birmingham than in any other city in the nation. These are the hard, brutal facts of the case. On the basis of these conditions, Negro leaders sought to negotiate with the city fathers. But the latter consistently refused to engage in good-faith negotiation.

Then, last September, came the opportunity to talk with leaders of Birmingham's economic community. In the course of the negotiations, certain promises were made by the merchants—for example, to remove the stores' humiliating racial signs. On the basis of these promises, the Reverend Fred Shuttlesworth and the leaders of the Alabama Christian Movement for Human Rights agreed to a moratorium on all demonstrations. As the weeks and months went by, we realized that we were the victims of a broken promise. A few signs, briefly removed, returned; the others remained.

As in so many past experiences, our hopes had been blasted, and the shadow of deep disappointment settled upon us. We had no alternative except to prepare for direct action, whereby we would present our very bodies as a means of laying our case before the conscience of the local and the national community. Mindful of the difficulties involved, we decided to undertake a process of self-purification. We began a series of workshops on nonviolence, and we repeatedly asked ourselves: "Are you able to accept blows without retaliating?" "Are you able to endure the ordeal of jail?" We decided to schedule our direct-action program for the Easter season, realizing that except for Christmas, this is the main shopping period of the year. Knowing that a strong economic-withdrawal program would be the by-product of direct action, we felt that this would be the best time to bring pressure to bear on the merchants for the needed change.

Then it occurred to us that Birmingham's mayoralty election was coming up in March, and we speedily decided to postpone action until after election day. When we discovered that the Commissioner of Public Safety, Eugene "Bull" Connor, had piled up enough votes to be in the run-off, we decided again to postpone action until the day after the run-off so that the demonstrations could not be used to cloud the issues. Like many others, we waited to see Mr. Connor defeated, and to this end we endured postponement after postponement. Having aided in this community need, we felt that our direct-action program could be delayed no longer.

You may well ask: "Why direct action? Why sit-ins, marches and so forth? Isn't negotiation a better path?" You are quite right in calling for negotiation. Indeed, this is the very purpose of direct action. Nonviolent direct action seeks to create such a crisis and foster such a tension that a community which has constantly refused to negotiate is forced to confront the issue. It seeks so to dramatize the issue that it can no longer be ignored. My citing the creation of tension as part of the work of the nonviolent-resister may sound rather shocking. But I must confess that I am not afraid of the word "tension." I have earnestly opposed violent tension, but there is a type of constructive, nonviolent tension which is necessary for growth. Just as Socrates felt that it was necessary to create a tension in the mind so that individuals could rise from the bondage of myths and half-truths to the unfettered realm of creative analysis and objective appraisal, so must we see the need for nonviolent gadflies to create the kind of tension in society that will help men rise from the dark depths of prejudice and racism to the majestic heights of understanding and brotherhood.

The purpose of our direct-action program is to create a situation so crisis-packed that it will inevitably open the door to negotiation. I therefore concur with you in your call for negotiation. Too long has our beloved Southland been bogged down in a tragic effort to live in monologue rather than dialogue.

One of the basic points in your statement is that the action that I and my associates have taken in Birmingham is untimely. Some have asked: "Why didn't you give the new city administration time to act?" The only answer that I can give to this query is that the new Birmingham administration must be prodded about as much as the outgoing one, before it will act. We are sadly mistaken if we feel that the election of Albert Boutwell as mayor will bring the millennium to Birmingham. While Mr. Boutwell is a much more gentle person than Mr. Connor, they are both segregationists, dedicated to maintenance of the status quo. I have hope that Mr. Boutwell will be reasonable enough to see the futility of massive resistance to desegregation. But he will not see this without pressure from devotees of civil rights. My friends, I must say to you that we have not made a single gain in civil rights without determined legal and nonviolent pressure. Lamentably, it is an historical fact that privileged groups seldom give up their privileges voluntarily. Individuals may see the moral light and voluntarily give up their unjust posture; but, as Reinhold Niebuhr has reminded us, groups tend to be more immoral than individuals.

We know through painful experience that freedom is never voluntarily given by the oppressor; it must be demanded by the oppressed. Frankly, I have yet to engage in a direct-action campaign that was "well timed" in the view of those who have not suffered unduly from the disease of segregation. For years now I have heard the word "Wait!" It rings in the ear of every Negro with piercing familiarity. This "Wait" has almost always meant "Never." We must come to see, with one of our distinguished jurists, that "justice too long delayed is justice denied."

We have waited for more than 340 years for our constitutional and God-given rights. The nations of Asia and Africa are moving with jet-like speed toward gaining political independence, but we still creep at horse-and-buggy pace toward gaining a cup of coffee at a lunch counter. Perhaps it is easy for those who have never felt the stinging darts of segregation to say, "Wait." But when you have seen vicious mobs lynch your mothers and fathers at will and drown your sisters and brothers at whim; when you have seen hate-filled policemen curse, kick and even kill your black brothers and sisters; when you see the vast majority of your twenty million Negro brothers smothering in an airtight cage of poverty in the midst of an affluent society; when you suddenly find your tongue twisted and your speech stammering as you seek to explain to your six-year-old daughter why she can't go to the public amusement park that has just been advertised on television, and see tears welling up in her eyes when she is told that Funtown is closed to colored children, and see ominous clouds of inferiority beginning to form in her little mental sky, and see her beginning to distort her personality by developing an unconscious bitterness toward white people; when you have to concoct an answer for a five-year-old son who is asking: "Daddy, why do white people treat colored people so mean?"; when you take a cross-country drive and find it necessary to sleep night after night in the uncomfortable corners of your automobile because no motel will accept you; when you are humiliated day in and day out by nagging signs reading "white" and "colored"; when your first name becomes "nigger," your middle name becomes "boy" (however old you are) and your last name becomes "John," and your wife and mother are never given the respected title "Mrs."; when you are harried by day and haunted by night by the fact that you are a Negro, living constantly at tiptoe stance, never quite knowing what to expect next, and are plagued with inner fears and outer resentments; when you are forever fighting a degenerating sense of "nobodiness"—then you will understand why we find it difficult to wait. There comes a time when the cup of endurance runs over, and men are no longer willing to be plunged into the abyss of despair. I hope, sirs, you can understand our legitimate and unavoidable impatience.

You express a great deal of anxiety over our willingness to break laws. This is certainly a legitimate concern. Since we so diligently urge people to obey the Supreme Court's decision of 1954 outlawing segregation in the public schools, at first glance it may seem rather paradoxical for us consciously to break laws. One may well ask: "How can you advocate breaking some laws and obeying others?" The answer lies in the fact that there are two types of laws: just and unjust. I would be the first to advocate obeying just laws. One has not only a legal but a moral responsibility to obey just laws. Conversely, one has a moral responsibility to disobey unjust laws. I would agree with St. Augustine that "an unjust law is no law at all."

Now, what is the difference between the two? How does one determine whether a law is just or unjust? A just law is a man-made code that squares with the moral law or the law of God. An unjust law is a code that is out of harmony with the moral law. To put it in the terms of St. Thomas Aquinas: An unjust law is a human law that is not rooted in eternal law and natural law. Any law that uplifts human personality is just. Any law that degrades human personality is unjust. All segregation statutes are unjust because segregation distorts the soul and damages the personality. It gives the segregator a false sense of superiority and the segregated a false sense of inferiority. Segregation, to use the terminology of the Jewish philosopher Martin Buber, substitutes an "I-it" relationship for an "I-thou" relationship and ends up relegating persons to the status of things. Hence segregation is not only politically, economically and sociologically unsound, it is morally wrong and sinful. Paul Tillich has said that sin is separation. Is not segregation an existential expression of man's tragic separation, his awful estrangement, his terrible sinfulness? Thus it is that I can urge men to obey the 1954 decision of the Supreme Court, for it is morally right; and I can urge them to disobey segregation ordinances, for they are morally wrong.

Let us consider a more concrete example of just and unjust laws. An unjust law is a code that a numerical or power majority group compels a minority group to obey but does not make binding on itself. This is *difference* made legal. By the same token, a just law is a code that a majority compels a minority to follow and that it is willing to follow itself. This is *sameness* made legal.

Let me give another explanation. A law is unjust if it is inflicted on a minority that, as a result of being denied the right to vote, had no part in enacting or devising the law. Who can say that the legislature of Alabama which set up that state's segregation laws was democratically elected? Throughout Alabama all sorts of devious methods are used to prevent Negroes from becoming registered voters, and there are some counties in which, even though Negroes constitute a majority of the population, not a single Negro is registered. Can any law enacted under such circumstances be considered democratically structured?

Sometimes a law is just on its face and unjust in its application. For instance, I have been arrested on a charge of parading without a permit. Now, there is nothing wrong in having an ordinance which requires a permit for a parade. But such an ordinance becomes unjust when it is used to maintain segregation and to deny citizens the First-Amendment privilege of peaceful assembly and protest.

I hope you are able to see the distinction I am trying to point out. In no sense do I advocate evading or defying the law, as would the rabid segregationist. That would lead to anarchy. One who breaks an unjust law must do so openly, lovingly, and with a willingness to accept the penalty. I submit that an individual who breaks a law that conscience tells him is unjust, and who willingly accepts the penalty of imprisonment in order to arouse the conscience of the community over its injustice, is in reality expressing the highest respect for law.

Of course, there is nothing new about this kind of civil disobedience. It was evidenced sublimely in the refusal of Shadrach, Meshach and Abednego to obey the laws of Nebuchadnezzar, on the ground that a higher moral law was at stake. It was practiced superbly by the early Christians, who were willing to face hungry lions and the excruciating pain of chopping blocks rather than submit to certain unjust laws of the Roman Empire. To a degree, academic freedom is a reality today because Socrates practiced civil disobedience. In our own nation, the Boston Tea Party represented a massive act of civil disobedience.

We should never forget that everything Adolf Hitler did in Germany was "legal" and everything the Hungarian freedom fighters did in Hungary was "illegal." It was "illegal" to aid and comfort a Jew in Hitler's Germany. Even so, I am sure that, had I lived in Germany at the time, I would have aided and comforted my Jewish brothers. If today I lived in a Communist country where certain principles dear to the Christian faith are suppressed, I would openly advocate disobeying that country's antireligious laws.

I must make two honest confessions to you, my Christian and Jewish brothers. First, I must confess that over the past few years I have been gravely disappointed with the white moderate. I have almost reached the regrettable conclusion that the Negro's great stumbling block in his stride toward freedom is not the White Citizen's Counciler or the Ku Klux Klanner, but the white moderate, who is more devoted to "order" than to justice; who prefers a negative peace which is the absence of tension to a positive peace which is the presence of justice; who constantly says: "I agree with you in the goal you seek, but I cannot agree with your methods of direct action"; who paternalistically believes he can set the timetable for another man's freedom; who lives by a mythical concept of time and who constantly advises the Negro to wait for a "more convenient season." Shallow understanding from people of good will is more frustrating than absolute misunderstanding from people of ill will. Lukewarm acceptance is much more bewildering than outright rejection.

I had hoped that the white moderate would understand that law and order exist for the purpose of establishing justice and that when they fail in this purpose they become the dangerously structured dams that block the flow of social progress. I had hoped that the white moderate would understand that the present tension in the South is a necessary phase of the transition from an obnoxious negative peace, in which the Negro passively accepted his unjust plight, to a substantive and positive peace, in which all men will respect the dignity and worth of human personality. Actually, we who engage in nonviolent direct action are not the creators of tension. We merely bring to the surface the hidden tension that is already alive. We bring it out in the open, where it can be seen and dealt with. Like a boil that can never be cured so long as it is covered up but must be opened with all its ugliness to the natural medicines of air and light, injustice must be exposed, with all the tension its exposure creates, to the light of human conscience and the air of national opinion before it can be cured.

In your statement you assert that our actions, even though peaceful, must be condemned because they precipitate violence. But is this a logical assertion? Isn't this like condemning a robbed man because his possession of money precipitated the evil act of robbery? Isn't this like condemning Socrates because his unswerving commitment to truth and his philosophical inquiries precipitated the act by the misguided populace in which they made him drink hemlock? Isn't this like condemning Jesus because his unique God-consciousness and never-ceasing devotion to God's will precipitated the evil act of crucifixion? We must come to see that, as the federal courts have consistently affirmed, it is wrong to urge an individual to cease his efforts to gain his basic constitutional rights because the quest may precipitate violence. Society must protect the robbed and punish the robber.

I had also hoped that the white moderate would reject the myth concerning time in relation to the struggle for freedom. I have just received a letter from a white brother in Texas. He writes: "All Christians know that the colored people will receive equal rights eventually, but it is possible that you are in too great a religious hurry. It has taken

Christianity almost two thousand years to accomplish what it has. The teachings of Christ take time to come to earth." Such an attitude stems from a tragic misconception of time, from the strangely irrational notion that there is something in the very flow of time that will inevitably cure all ills. Actually, time itself is neutral; it can be used either destructively or constructively. More and more I feel that the people of ill will have used time much more effectively than have the people of good will. We will have to repent in this generation not merely for the hateful words and actions of the bad people but for the appalling silence of the good people. Human progress never rolls in on wheels of inevitability; it comes through the tireless efforts of men willing to be co-workers with God, and without this hard work, time itself becomes an ally of the forces of social stagnation. We must use time creatively, in the knowledge that the time is always ripe to do right. Now is the time to make real the promise of democracy and transform our pending national elegy into a creative psalm of brotherhood. Now is the time to lift our national policy from the quicksand of racial injustice to the solid rock of human dignity.

You speak of our activity in Birmingham as extreme. At first I was rather disappointed that fellow clergymen would see my nonviolent efforts as those of an extremist. I began thinking about the fact that I stand in the middle of two opposing forces in the Negro Community. One is a force of complacency, made up in part of Negroes who, as a result of long years of oppression, are so drained of self-respect and a sense of "somebodiness" that they have adjusted to segregation; and in part of a few middle-class Negroes who, because of a degree of academic and economic security and because in some ways they profit by segregation, have become insensitive to the problems of the masses. The other force is one of bitterness and hatred, and it comes perilously close to advocating violence. It is expressed in the various black nationalist groups that are springing up across the nation, the largest and best known being Elijah Muhammad's Muslim movement. Nourished by the Negro's frustration over the continued existence of racial discrimination, this movement is made up of people who have lost faith in America, who have absolutely repudiated Christianity, and who have concluded that the white man is an incorrigible "devil."

I have tried to stand between these two forces, saying that we need emulate neither the "do-nothingism" of the complacent nor the hatred and despair of the black nationalist. For there is the more excellent way of love and nonviolent protest. I am grateful to God that, through the influence of the Negro church, the way of nonviolence became an integral part of our struggle.

If this philosophy had not emerged, by now many streets of the South would, I am convinced, be flowing with blood. And I am further convinced that if our white brothers dismiss as "rabble-rousers" and "outside agitators" those of us who employ nonviolent direct action, and if they refuse to support our nonviolent efforts, millions of Negroes will, out of frustration and despair, seek solace and security in black-nationalist ideologies—a development that would inevitably lead to a frightening racial nightmare.

Oppressed people cannot remain oppressed forever. The yearning for freedom eventually manifests itself, and that is what has happened to the American Negro. Something within has reminded him of his birthright of freedom, and something without has reminded him that it can be gained. Consciously or unconsciously, he has been caught up by the *Zeitgeist*, and with his black brothers of Africa and his brown and yellow brothers of Asia, South America and the Caribbean, the United States Negro is moving with a sense of great urgency toward the promised land of racial justice. If one recognizes this vital urge that has engulfed the Negro community, one should readily understand why public demonstrations are taking place. The Negro has many pent-up resentments and latent frustrations, and he must release them. So let him march; let him make prayer pilgrimages to the city hall; let him go on freedom rides—and try to understand why he must do so. If his repressed emotions are not released in nonviolent ways, they will seek expression through violence; this is not a threat but a fact of history. So I have not said to my people: "Get rid of your discontent." Rather, I have tried to say that this normal and healthy discontent can be channeled into the creative outlet of nonviolent direct action. And now this approach is being termed extremist.

But though I was initially disappointed at being categorized as an extremist, as I continued to think about the matter I gradually gained a measure of satisfaction from the label. Was not Jesus an extremist for love: "Love your enemies, bless them that curse you, do good to them that hate you, and pray for them which despitefully use you, and persecute you." Was not Amos an extremist for justice: "Let justice roll down like waters and righteousness like an ever-flowing stream." Was not Paul an extremist for the Christian gospel: "I bear in my body the marks of the Lord Jesus." Was not Martin Luther an extremist: "Here I stand; I cannot do otherwise, so help me God." And John Bunyan: "I will stay in jail to the end of my days before I make a butchery of my conscience." And Abraham Lincoln: "This nation cannot survive half slave and half free." And Thomas Jefferson: "We hold these truths to be self-evident, that all men are created equal..." So the question is not whether we will be extremists, but what kind of extremists we will be. Will we be extremists for hate or for love? Will we be extremists for the preservation of injustice or for the extension of justice? In that dramatic scene on Calvary's hill three men were crucified. We must never forget that all three were crucified for the same crime—the crime of extremism. Two were extremists for immorality, and thus fell below their environment. The other, Jesus Christ, was an extremist for love, truth and goodness, and thereby rose above his environment. Perhaps the South, the nation and the world are in dire need of creative extremists....

If I have said anything in this letter that overstates the truth and indicates an unreasonable impatience, I beg you to forgive me. If I have said anything that understates the truth and indicates my having a patience that allows me to settle for anything less than brotherhood, I beg God to forgive me.

I hope this letter finds you strong in the faith. I also hope that circumstances will soon make it possible for me to meet each of you, not as an integrationist or a civil-rights leader but as a fellow clergyman and a Christian brother. Let us all hope that the dark clouds of racial prejudice will soon pass away and the deep fog of misunderstanding will be lifted from our fear-drenched communities, and in some not too distant tomorrow the radiant stars of love and brotherhood will shine over our great nation with all their scintillating beauty.

Yours for the cause of Peace and Brotherhood,

Martin Luther King, Jr.

15. On Revolution

MALCOLM X

Malcom X emerged as one of the first to attack the civil rights movement from the left. As a member of the Black Muslims (Nation of Islam), a black nationalist group, Malcom X rejected the Christian millennialism of Martin Luther King, Jr., the belief in nonviolence, and the notion that whites could be converted to racial integration. This speech delivered in November 1963, three months after King's "I Have a Dream" speech, strikes the themes that dominated black power movements in the ensuing years: solidarity with African nationalism, emphasis on revolution with the attendant threat of violence, and insistence on black separatism rather than integration with whites.

During the years after Malcolm X left the Muslims, he moderated some of his rhetoric. But overall he remains important as one of the first major black voices in the 1960s to speak from the city streets rather than from the rural southern base that King represented. Of course, the principal successes in the drive against segregation and discrimination did come in the South; the issues Malcolm X raised—what economic and political future for African Americans lies beyond the achievement of civil rights—remain to be resolved.

We want to have just an off-the-cuff chat between you and me, us. We want to talk right down to earth in a language that everybody here can easily understand. We all agree tonight, all of the speakers have agreed, that America has a very serious problem. Not only does America have a very serious problem, but our people have a very serious problem. America's problem is us. We're her problem. The only reason she has a problem is she doesn't want us here. And every time you look at yourself, be you black, brown, red or yellow, a so-called Negro, you represent a person who poses such a serious problem for America because you're not wanted. Once you face this as a fact, then you can start plotting a course that will make you appear intelligent, instead of unintelligent.

What you and I need to do is learn to forget our differences. When we come together, we don't come together as Baptists or Methodists. You don't catch hell because you're a Baptist, and you don't catch hell because you're a Methodist. You don't catch hell because you're a Methodist or Baptist, you don't catch hell because you're a Democrat or a Republican, you don't catch hell because you're a Mason or an Elk, and you sure don't catch hell because you're an American; because if you were an American, you wouldn't catch hell. You catch hell because you're a black man. You catch hell, all of us catch hell, for the same reason.

So we're all black people, so-called Negroes, second-class citizens, ex-slaves. You're nothing but an ex-slave. You don't like to be told that. But what else are you? You are ex-slaves. You didn't come here on the

"Mayflower." You came here on a slave ship. In chains, like a horse, or a cow, or a chicken. And you were brought here by the people who came here on the "Mayflower," you were brought here by the so-called Pilgrims, or Founding Fathers. They were the ones who brought you here.

We have a common enemy. We have this in common: We have a common oppressor, a common exploiter, and a common discriminator. But once we all realize that we have a common enemy, then we unite— on the basis of what we have in common. And what we have foremost in common is that enemy—the white man. He's an enemy to all of us. I know some of you all think that some of them aren't enemies. Time will tell....

As long as the white man sent you to Korea, you bled. He sent you to Germany, you bled. He sent you to the South Pacific to fight the Japanese, you bled. You bleed for white people, but when it comes to seeing your own churches being bombed and little black girls murdered, you haven't got any blood. You bleed when the white man says bleed; you bite when the white man says bite; and you bark when the white man says bark. I hate to say this about us, but it's true. How are you going to be nonviolent in Mississippi, as violent as you were in Korea? How can you justify being nonviolent in Mississippi and Alabama, when your churches are being bombed, and your little girls are being murdered, and at the same time you are going to get violent with Hitler, and Tojo, and somebody else you don't even know?

If violence is wrong in America, violence is wrong abroad. If it is wrong to be violent defending black women and black children and black babies and black men, then it is wrong for America to draft us and make us violent abroad in defense of her. And if it is right for America to draft us, and teach us how to be violent in defense of her, then it is right for you and me to do whatever is necessary to defend our own people right here in this country....

There's no such thing as a nonviolent revolution. The only kind of revolution that is nonviolent is the Negro revolution. The only revolution in which the goal is loving your enemy is the Negro revolution. It's the only revolution in which the goal is a desegregated lunch counter, a desegregated theater, a desegregated park, and a desegregated public toilet; you can sit down next to white folks—on the toilet. That's no revolution. Revolution is based on land. Land is the basis of all independence. Land is the basis of freedom, justice, and equality.

The white man knows what a revolution is. He knows that the black revolution is world-wide in scope and in nature. The black revolution is sweeping Asia, is sweeping Africa, is rearing its head in Latin America. The Cuban Revolution—that's a revolution. They overturned the system. Revolution is in Asia, revolution is in Africa, and the white man is screaming because he sees revolution in Latin America. How do you think he'll react to you when you learn what a real revolution is? You don't know what a revolution is. If you did, you wouldn't use that word.

Revolution is bloody, revolution is hostile, revolution knows no compromise, revolution overturns and destroys everything that gets in its way. And you, sitting around here like a knot on the wall, saying, "I'm going to love these folks no matter how much they hate me." No, you need a revolution. Whoever heard of a revolution where they lock arms, as Rev. Cleage was pointing out beautifully, singing "We Shall Overcome"? You don't do that in a revolution. You don't do any singing, you're too busy swinging. It's based on land. A revolutionary wants land so he can set up his own nation, an independent nation....

When you want a nation, that's called nationalism. When the white man became involved in a revolution in this country against England, what was it for? He wanted this land so he could set up another white nation. That's white nationalism. The American Revolution was white nationalism. The French Revolution was white nationalism. The Russian Revolution too—yes, it was—white nationalism. You don't think so? Why do you think Khrushchev and Mao can't get their heads together? White nationalism. All the revolutions that are going on in Asia and Africa today are based on what?—black nationalism. A revolutionary is a black nationalist. He wants a nation. I was reading some beautiful words by Rev. Cleage, pointing out why he couldn't get together with someone else in the city because all of them were afraid of being identified with black nationalism. If you're afraid of black nationalism, you're afraid of revolution. And if you love revolution, you love black nationalism.

To understand this, you have to go back to what the young brother here referred to as the house Negro and the field Negro back during slavery. There were two kinds of slaves, the house Negro and the field Negro. The house Negroes—they lived in the house with master, they dressed pretty good, they ate good because they ate his food—what he left. They lived in the attic or the basement, but still they lived near the master; and they loved the master more than the master loved himself. They would give their life to save the master's house—quicker than the master would. If the master said, "We got a good house here," the house Negro would say, "Yeah, we got a good house here." Whenever the master said "we," he said "we." That's how you can tell a house Negro.

If the master's house caught on fire, the house Negro would fight harder to put the blaze out than the master would. If the master got sick, the house Negro would say, "What's the matter, boss, *we* sick?" *We* sick! He identified himself with his master, more than his master identified with himself. And if you came to the house Negro and said, "Let's run away, let's escape, let's separate," the house Negro would look at you and say, "Man, you crazy. What you mean, separate? Where is there a better house than this? Where can I wear better clothes than this? Where can I eat better food than this?" That was that house Negro. In those days he was called a "house nigger." And that's what we call them today, because we've still got some house niggers running around here.

This modern house Negro loves his master. He wants to live near him. He'll pay three times as much as the house is worth just to live near his master, and then brag about "I'm the only Negro out here." "I'm the only one on my job." "I'm the only one in this school." You're nothing but a house Negro. And if someone comes to you right now and says, "Let's separate," you say the same thing that the house Negro said on the plantation. "What you mean, separate? From America, this good white man? Where you going to get a better job than you get here?" I mean, this is what you say. "I ain't left nothing in Africa," that's what you say. Why, you left your mind in Africa.

On that same plantation, there was the field Negro. The field Negroes—those were the masses. There were always more Negroes in the field than there were Negroes in the house. The Negro in the field caught hell. He ate leftovers. In the house they ate high up on the hog. The Negro in the field didn't get anything but what was left of the in-sides of the hog. They call it "chitt'lings" nowadays. In those days they called them what they were—guts. That's what you were—gut-eaters. And some of you are still gut-eaters.

The field Negro was beaten from morning to night; he lived in a shack, in a hut; he wore old, castoff clothes. He hated his master. I say he hated his master. He was intelligent. That house Negro loved his master, but that field Negro—remember, they were in the majority, and they hated the master. When the house caught on fire, he didn't try to put it out; that field Negro prayed for a wind, for a breeze. When the master got sick, the field Negro prayed that he'd die. If someone came to the field Negro and said, "Let's separate, let's run," he didn't say "Where we going?" He'd say, "Any place is better than here." You've got field Negroes in America today. I'm a field Negro. The masses are the field Negroes. When they see this man's house on fire, you don't hear the little Negroes talking about "*our* government is in trouble." They say, "*The* government is in trouble." Imagine a Negro: "*Our* government"! I even heard one say "*our* astronauts". They won't even let him near the plant—and "*our* astronauts"! "*Our* Navy"—that's a Negro that is out of his mind, a Negro that is out of his mind.

Just as the slavemaster of that day used Tom, the house Negro, to keep the field Negroes in check, the same old slavemaster today has Negroes who are nothing but modern Uncle Toms, twentieth-century Uncle Toms, to keep you and me in check, to keep us under control, keep us passive and peaceful and nonviolent. That's Tom making you nonviolent. It's like when you go to the dentist, and the man's going to take your tooth. You're going to fight him when he starts pulling. So he squirts some stuff in your jaw called novocaine, to make you think they're not doing anything to you. So you sit there and because you've got all of that novocaine in your jaw, you suffer—peacefully. Blood running all down your jaw, and you don't know what's happening. Because someone has taught you to suffer—peacefully.

The white man does the same thing to you in the street, when he wants to put knots on your head and take advantage of you and not have to be afraid of your fighting back. To keep you from fighting back, he gets these old religious Uncle Toms to teach you and me, just like novocaine, to suffer peacefully. Don't stop suffering—just suffer peacefully. As Rev. Cleage pointed out, they say you should let your blood flow in the streets. This is a shame. You know he's a Christian preacher. If it's a shame to him, you know what it is to me.

There is nothing in our book, the Koran, that teaches us to suf-fer peacefully. Our religion teaches us to be intelligent. Be peaceful, be courteous, obey the law, respect everyone; but if someone puts his hand on you, send him to the cemetery. That's a good religion. In fact, that's that old-time religion. That's the one that Ma and Pa used to talk about: an eye for an eye, and a tooth for a tooth, and a head for a head, and a life for a life. That's a good religion. And nobody resents that kind of religion being taught but a wolf, who intends to make you his meal.

This is the way it is with the white man in America. He's a wolf—and you're sheep. Any time a shepherd, a pastor, teaches you and me not to run from the white man and, at the same time, teaches us not to fight the white man, he's a traitor to you and me. Don't lay down a life all by itself. No, preserve your life, it's the best thing you've got. And if you've got to give it up, let it be even-steven.

The slavemaster took Tom and dressed him well, fed him well and even gave him a little education—a *little* education; gave him a long coat and a top hat and made all the other slaves look up to him. Then he used Tom to control them. The same strategy that was used in those days is used today, by the same white man. He takes a Negro, a so-called Negro, and makes him prominent, builds him up, publicizes him, makes him a celebrity. And then he becomes a spokesman for Negroes—and a Negro leader.

I would like to mention just one other thing quickly, and that is the method that the white man uses, how the white man uses the "big guns," or Negro leaders, against the Negro revolution. They are not a part of the Negro revolution. They are used against the Negro revolution.

16. The Port Huron Statement

STUDENTS FOR A DEMOCRATIC SOCIETY

The radical tradition in America is a series of episodes, not a continuous story. Where conservatives and liberals never cease reaching back for real or imaginary forebears, radicals have generally insisted on forgetting the history of radicalism as the first act in any new beginning. In the early 1960s, when the Students for a Democratic Society spread from campus to campus, drawing together activists in the civil rights and peace movements, the group received compliments for precisely this tendency to forget the radical past. It was "pragmatic," "non-ideological," and "non-programmatic." The Port Huron Statement, drawn up at the first SDS convention in 1962, achieved wide circulation on the campuses as an "agenda for a generation."

The document, written principally by Tom Hayden, is impressive in surprising ways. Its tentative assertions, social science language, and generally nationalist and cooperative stance contrast sharply with the image of campus militancy of the later 1960s. In its quiet way, however, it states the main themes of the youth political movement: its rejection of social alienation, lack of community bureaucracy, and 50s style anti-communism. It is the beginning of a quest, not a set of final answers. Where that quest led is one of the fascinating topics of the decade.

INTRODUCTION: AGENDA FOR A GENERATION

We are people of this generation, bred in at least modest comfort, housed now in universities, looking uncomfortably to the world we inherit.

When we were kids the United States was the wealthiest and strongest country in the world; the only one with the atom bomb, the least scarred by modern war, and initiator of the United Nations that we thought would distribute Western influence throughout the world. Freedom and equality for each individual, government of, by, and for the people—these American values we found good, principles by which we could live as men. Many of us began maturing in complacency.

As we grew, however, our comfort was penetrated by events too troubling to dismiss. First, the permeating and victimizing fact of human degradation, symbolized by the Southern struggle against racial bigotry, compelled most of us from silence to activism. Second, the enclosing fact of the Cold War, symbolized by the presence of the Bomb, brought awareness that we ourselves, and our friends, and millions of abstract "others" we knew more directly because of our common peril, might die at any time. We might deliberately ignore, or avoid, or fail to feel all other human problems, but not these two, for these were too immediate and crushing in their impact, too challenging in the demand that we as individuals take the responsibility for encounter and resolution.

While these and other problems either directly oppressed us or rankled our consciences and became our own subjective concerns, we began to see complicated and disturbing paradoxes in our surrounding America. The declaration "all men are created equal..." rang hollow before the facts of Negro life in the South and the big cities of the North. The proclaimed peaceful intentions of the United States contradicted its economic and military investments in the Cold War status quo.

We witnessed, and continue to witness, other paradoxes. With nuclear energy whole cities can easily be powered, yet the dominant nation-states seem more likely to unleash destruction greater than that incurred in all wars of human history. Although our own technology is destroying old and creating new forms of social organization, men still tolerate meaningless work and idleness. While two-thirds of mankind suffers undernourishment, our own upper classes revel amidst superfluous abundance. Although world population is expected to double in forty years, the nations still tolerate anarchy as a major principle of international conduct and uncontrolled exploitation governs the sapping of the earth's physical resources. Although mankind desperately needs revolutionary leadership, America rests in national stalemate, its goals ambiguous and tradition-bound instead of informed and clear, its democratic system apathetic and manipulated rather than "of, by, and for the people."

Not only did tarnish appear on our image of American virtue, not only did disillusion occur when the hypocrisy of American ideals was discovered, but we began to sense that what we had originally seen as the American Golden Age was actually the decline of an era. The world-wide outbreak of revolution against colonialism and imperialism, the entrenchment of totalitarian states, the menace of war, overpopulation, international disorder, supertechnology—these trends were testing the tenacity of our own commitment to democracy and freedom and our abilities to visualize their application to a world in upheaval.

Our work is guided by the sense that we may be the last generation in the experiment with living. But we are a minority—the vast majority of our people regard the temporary equilibriums of our society and world as eternally-functional parts. In this is perhaps the outstanding paradox: we ourselves are imbued with urgency, yet the message of our society is that there is no viable alternative to the present. Beneath the reassuring tones of the politicians, beneath the common opinion that America will "muddle through," beneath the stagnation of those who have closed their minds to the future, is the pervading feeling that there simply are no alternatives, that our times have witnessed the exhaustion not only of Utopias, but of any new departures as well. Feeling the press of complexity upon the emptiness of life, people are fearful of the thought that at any moment things might be thrust out of control. They fear change itself, since change might smash whatever invisible framework seems to hold back chaos for them now. For most Americans, all crusades are suspect, threatening. The fact that each individual sees apathy in his fellows perpetuates the common reluctance to organize for change. The dominant institutions are complex enough to blunt the minds of their potential critics, and entrenched enough to swiftly dissipate or entirely repel the energies of protest and reform, thus limiting human expectancies. Then, too, we are a materially improved society, and by our own improvements we seem to have weakened the case for further change.

Some would have us believe that Americans feel contentment amidst prosperity—but might it not be better be called a glaze above deeply felt anxieties about their role in the new world? And if these anxieties produce a developed indifference to human affairs, do they not as well produce a yearning to believe there *is* an alternative to the present, that something *can* be done to change circumstances in the school, the workplaces, the bureaucracies, the government? It is to this latter yearning, at once the spark and engine of change, that we direct our present appeal. The search for truly democratic alternatives to the present, and a commitment to social experimentation with them, is a worthy and fulfilling human enterprise, one which moves us and, we hope, others today. On such a basis do we offer this document of our convictions and analysis: as an effort in understanding and changing the conditions of humanity in the late twentieth century, an effort rooted in the ancient, still unfulfilled conception of man attaining determining influence over his circumstances of life....

THE STUDENTS

In the last few years, thousands of American students demonstrated that they at least felt the urgency of the times. They moved actively and directly against racial injustices, the threat of war, violations of individual rights of conscience and, less frequently, against economic manipulation. They succeeded in restoring a small measure of controversy to the campuses after the stillness of the McCarthy period. They succeeded, too, in gaining some concessions from the people and institutions they opposed, especially in the fight against racial bigotry.

The significance of these scattered movements lies not in their success or failure in gaining objectives—at least not yet. Nor does the significance lie in the intellectual "competence" or "maturity" of the students involved—as some pedantic elders allege. The significance is in the fact the students are breaking the crust of apathy and overcoming the inner alienation that remain the defining characteristics of American college life.

If student movements for change are still rarities on the campus scene, what is commonplace there? The real campus, the familiar campus, is a place of private people, engaged in their notorious "inner emigration." It is a place of commitment to business-as-usual, getting ahead, playing it cool. It is a place of mass affirmation of the Twist, but mass reluctance toward the controversial public stance. Rules are accepted as "inevitable," bureaucracy as "just circumstances," irrelevance as "scholarship," selflessness as "martyrdom," politics as "just another way to make people, and an unprofitable one, too."

Almost no students value activity as citizens. Passive in public, they are hardly more idealistic in arranging their private lives: Gallup concludes they will settle for "low success, and won't risk high failure." There is not much willingness to take risks (not even in business), no settling of dangerous goals, no real conception of personal identity except one manufactured in the image of others, no real urge for personal fulfillment except to be almost as successful as the very successful people. Attention is being paid to social status (the quality of shirt collars, meeting people, getting wives or husbands, making solid contacts for later on); much, too, is paid to academic status (grades, honors, the med school rat race). But neglected generally is real intellectual status, the personal cultivation of the mind.

"Students don't even give a damn about the apathy," one has said. Apathy toward apathy begets a privately-constructed universe, a place of systematic study schedules, two nights each week for beer, a girl or two, and early marriage; a framework infused with personality, warmth, and under control, no matter how unsatisfying otherwise.

Under these conditions university life loses all relevance to some. Four hundred thousand of our classmates leave college every year.

But apathy is not simply an attitude; it is a product of social institutions, and of the structure and organization of higher education itself. The extracurricular life is ordered according to *in loco parentis* theory, which ratifies the Administration as the moral guardian of the young.

The accompanying "let's pretend" theory of student extracurricular affairs validates student government as a training center for those who want to spend their lives in political pretense, and discourages initiative from the more articulate, honest, and sensitive students. The bounds and style of controversy are delimited before controversy begins. The university "prepares" the student for "citizenship" through perpetual rehearsals and, usually, through emasculation of what creative spirit there is in the individual.

The academic life contains reinforcing counterparts to the way in which extracurricular life is organized. The academic world is founded on a teacher-student relation analogous to the parent-child relation which characterizes *in loco parentis*. Further, academia includes a radical separation of the student from the material of study. That which is studied, the social reality, is "objectified" to sterility, dividing the student from life—just as he is restrained in active involvement by the deans controlling student government. The specialization of function and knowledge, admittedly necessary to our complex technological and social structure, has produced an exaggerated compartmentalization of study and understanding. This has contributed to an overly parochial view, by faculty, of the role of its research and scholarship, to a discontinuous and truncated understanding, by students, of the surrounding social order; and to a loss of personal attachment, by nearly all, to the worth of study as a humanistic enterprise.

There is, finally, the cumbersome academic bureaucracy extending throughout the academic as well as the extracurricular structures, contributing to the sense of outer complexity and inner powerlessness that transforms the honest searching of many students to a ratification of convention and, worse, to a numbness to present and future catastrophes. The size and financing systems of the university enhance the permanent trusteeship of the administrative bureaucracy, their power leading to a shift within the university toward the value standards of business and the administrative mentality. Huge foundations and other private financial interests shape the under-financed colleges and universities, not only making them more commercial, but less disposed to diagnose society critically, less open to dissent. Many social and physical scientists, neglecting the liberating heritage of higher learning, develop "human relations" or "morale-producing" techniques for the corporate economy, while others exercise their intellectual skills to accelerate the arms race.

Tragically, the university could serve as a significant source of social criticism and an initiator of new modes and molders of attitudes. But the actual intellectual effect of the college experience is hardly distinguishable from that of any other communications channel—say, a television set—passing on the stock truths of the day. Students leave college somewhat more "tolerant" than when they arrived, but basically unchallenged in their values and political orientations. With administrators ordering the institution, and faculty the curriculum, the student learns by his isolation to accept elite rule within the university, which prepares him to accept later forms of minority control. The real function of the educational system—as opposed to its more rhetorical function of "searching for truth"—is to impart the key information and styles that will help the student get by, modestly but comfortably, in the big society beyond.

THE SOCIETY BEYOND

Look beyond the campus, to America itself. That student life is more intellectual, and perhaps more comfortable, does not obscure the fact that the fundamental qualities of life on the campus reflect the habits of society at large. The fraternity president is seen at the junior manager levels; the sorority queen has gone to Grosse Pointe; the serious poet burns for a place, any place, to work; the once-serious and never serious poets work at the advertising agencies. The desperation of people threatened by forces about which they know little and of which they can say less; the cheerful emptiness of people "giving up" all hope of changing things; the faceless ones polled by Gallup who listed "international affairs" fourteenth on their list of "problems" but who also expected thermonuclear war in the next few years; in these and other forms, Americans are in withdrawal from public life, from any collective effort at directing their own affairs.

Some regard these national doldrums as a sign of healthy approval of the established order—but is it approval by consent or manipulated acquiescence? Others declare that the people are withdrawn because compelling issues are fast disappearing—perhaps there are fewer breadlines in America, but is Jim Crow gone, is there enough work and work more fulfilling, is world war a diminishing threat, and what of the revolutionary new peoples? Still others think the national quietude is a necessary consequence of the need for elites to resolve complex and specialized problems of modern industrial society—but, then, why should *business* elites help decide foreign policy, and who controls the elites anyway, and are they solving mankind's problems? Others, finally, shrug knowingly and announce that full democracy never worked anywhere in the past—but why lump qualitatively different civilizations together, and how can a social order work well if its best thinkers are skeptics, and is man really doomed forever to the domination of today?

There are no convincing apologies for the contemporary malaise. While the world tumbles toward final war, while men in other nations are trying desperately to alter events, while the very future qua future is uncertain—America is without community, impulse, without the inner momentum necessary for an age when societies cannot successfully perpetuate themselves by their military weapons, when democracy must be viable because of the quality of life, not its quantity of rockets.

The apathy here is, first *subjective*—the felt powerlessness of ordinary people, the resignation before the enormity of events. But subjective apathy is encouraged by the *objective* American situation—the actual structural separation of people from power, from relevant knowledge, from pinnacles of decision-making. Just as the university influences the student way of life, so do major social institutions create the circumstances in which the isolated citizen will try hopelessly to understand his world and himself.

The very isolation of the individual—from power and community and ability to aspire—means the rise of a democracy without publics. With the great mass of people structurally remote and psychologically hesitant with respect to democratic institutions, those institutions themselves attenuate and become, in the fashion of the vicious circle, progressively less accessible to those few who aspire to serious participation in social affairs. The vital democratic connection between community and leadership, between the mass and the several elites, has been so wrenched and perverted that disastrous policies go unchallenged time and again.

POLITICS WITHOUT PUBLICS

The American political system is not the democratic model of which its glorifiers speak. In actuality it frustrates democracy by confusing the individual citizen, paralyzing policy discussion, and consolidating the irresponsible power of military and business interests.

A crucial feature of the political apparatus in America is that greater differences are harbored within each major party than the differences existing between them. Instead of two parties presenting distinctive and significant differences of approach, what dominates the system is a natural interlocking of Democrats from Southern states with the more conservative elements of the Republican party. This arrangement of forces is blessed by the seniority system of Congress which guarantees congressional committee domination by conservatives—ten of 17 committees in the Senate and 13 of 21 in the House of Representatives are chaired currently by Dixiecrats.

The part overlap, however, is not the only structural antagonist of democracy in politics. First, the localized nature of the party system does not encourage discussion of national and international issues: thus problems are not raised by and for people, and political representatives usually are unfettered from any responsibilities to the general public except those regarding parochial matters. Second, whole constituencies are divested of the full political power they might have: many Negroes in the South are prevented from voting, migrant workers are disenfranchised by various residence requirements, some urban and suburban dwellers are victimized by gerrymandering, and poor people are too often without the power to obtain political representation. Third, the focus of political attention is significantly distorted by the enormous lobby force, composed predominantly of business interests, spending hundreds of millions each year in an attempt to conform facts about productivity, agriculture, defense, and social services, to the wants of private economic groupings.

What emerges from the party contradiction and insulation of privately-held power is the organized political stalemate: calcification dominates flexibility as the principle of parliamentary organization, frustration is the expectancy of legislators intending liberal reform, and Congress becomes less and less central to national decision-making especially in the area of foreign policy. In this context, confusion and blurring is built into the formulation of issues, long-range priorities are not discussed in the rational manner needed for policy-making, the politics of personality and "image" become a more important mechanism than the construction of issues in a way that affords each voter a challenging and real option. The American voter is buffeted from all directions by pseudo-problems, by the structurally-initiated sense that nothing political is subject to human mastery. Worried by his mundane problems which never get solved, but constrained by the common belief that politics is an agonizingly slow accommodation of views, he quits all pretense of bothering.

A most alarming fact is that few, if any, politicians are calling for changes in these conditions. Only a handful even are calling on the President to "live up to" platform pledges; no one is demanding structural changes, such as the shuttling of Southern Democrats out of the Democratic Party. Rather than protesting the state of politics, most politicians are reinforcing and aggravating that state. While in practice they rig public opinion to suit their own interests, in word and ritual they enshrine "the sovereign public" and call for more and more letters. Their speeches and campaign actions are banal, based on a degrading conception of what people want to hear. They respond not to dialogue, but to pressure: and knowing this, the ordinary citizen sees even greater inclination to shun the political sphere. The politician is usually a trumpeter to "citizenship" and "service to the nation," but since he is unwilling to seriously rearrange power relationships, his trumpetings only increase apathy by creating no outlets. Much of the time the call to "service" is justified not in idealistic terms, but in the crasser terms of "defending the free world from communism"—thus making future idealistic impulses harder to justify in anything but Cold War terms.

In such a setting of status quo politics, where most if not all government activity is rationalized in Cold War anti-communist terms, it is somewhat natural that discontented, super-patriotic groups would emerge through political channels and explain their ultra-conservatism as the best means of Victory over Communism. They have become a politically influential force within the Republican Party, at a national level through Senator Goldwater, and at a local level through their important social and economic roles. Their political views are defined generally as the opposite of the supposed views of communists: complete individual freedom in the economic sphere, non-participation by the government in the machinery of production. But actually "anti-communism" becomes an umbrella by which to protest liberalism, internationalism, welfareism, the active civil rights and labor movements. It is to the disgrace of the United States that such a movement should become a prominent kind of public participation in the modern world—but, ironically, it is somewhat to the interests of the United States that such a movement should be a public constituency pointed toward realignment of the political parties, demanding a conservative Republican Party in the South and an exclusion of the "leftist" elements of the national GOP.

THE ECONOMY

American capitalism today advertises itself as the Welfare State. Many of us comfortably expect pensions, medical care, unemployment compensation, and other social services in our lifetimes. Even with one-fourth of our productive capacity unused, the majority of Americans are living in relative comfort—although their nagging incentive to "keep up" makes them continually dissatisfied with their possessions. In many places, unrestrained bosses, uncontrolled machines, and sweatshop conditions have been reformed or abolished and suffering tremendously relieved. But in spite of the benign yet obscuring effects of the New Deal reforms and the reassuring phrases of government economists and politicians, the paradoxes and myths of the economy are sufficient to irritate our complacency and reveal to us some essential causes of the American malaise.

We live amidst a national celebration of economic prosperity while poverty and deprivation remain an unbreakable way of life for millions in the "affluent society," including many of our own generation. We hear glib references to the "welfare state," "free enterprise," and "shareholder's democracy" while military defense is the main item of "public" spending and obvious oligopoly and other forms of minority rule defy real individual initiative or popular control. Work, too, is often unfulfilling and victimizing, accepted as a channel to status or plenty, if not a way to pay the bills, rarely as a means of understanding and controlling self and events. In work and leisure the individual is regulated as part of the system, a consuming unit, bombarded by hard-sell, soft-sell, lies and semi-true appeals to his basest drives. He is always told that he is a "free" man because of "free enterprise."...

THE MILITARY-INDUSTRIAL COMPLEX

The most spectacular and important creation of the authoritarian and oligopolistic structure of economic decision-making in America is the institution called "the military-industrial complex" by former President Eisenhower—the powerful congruence of interest and structure among military and business elites which affects so much of our development and destiny. Not only is ours the first generation to live with the possibility of world-wide cataclysm—it is the first to experience the actual social preparation for cataclysm, the general militarization of American society. In 1948 Congress established Universal Military Training, the first peacetime conscription. The military became a permanent institution. Four years earlier, General Motors' Charles E. Wilson had heralded the creation of what he called the "permanent war economy," the continuous use of military spending as a solution to economic problems unsolved before the post-war boom, most notably the problem of the seventeen million jobless after eight years of the New Deal. This has left a "hidden crisis" in the allocation of resources by the American economy.

Since our childhood these two trends—the rise of the military and the installation of a defense-based economy—have grown fantastically. The Department of Defense, ironically the world's largest single organization, is worth $160 billion, owns 32 million acres of America and employs half the 7.5 million persons directly dependent on the military for subsistence, has an $11 billion payroll which is larger than the net annual income of all American corporations. Defense spending in the Eisenhower era totaled $350 billions and President Kennedy entered office pledged to go even beyond the present defense allocation of 60 cents from every public dollar spent. Except for a war-induced boom immediately after "our side" bombed Hiroshima, American economic prosperity has coincided with a growing dependence on military outlay—from 1941 to 1959 America's Gross National Product of $5.25 trillion included $700 billion in goods and services purchased for the defense effort, about one-seventh of the accumulated GNP. This pattern has included the steady concentration of military spending among a few corporations. In 1961, 86 percent of Defense Department contracts were awarded without competition. The ordnance industry of 100,000 people is completely engaged in military work; in the aircraft industry, 94 percent of 750,000 workers are linked to the war economy; shipbuilding, radio and communications equipment industries commit 40 percent of their work to defense; iron and steel, petroleum, metal-stamping and machine shop products, motors and generators, tools and hardware, copper, aluminum and machine tools industries all devote at least 10 percent of their work to the same cause.

The intermingling of Big Military and Big Industry is evidenced in the 1,400 former officers working for the 100 corporations who received nearly all the $21 billion spent in procurement by the Defense Department in 1961. The overlap is most poignantly clear in the case of General Dynamics, the company which received the best 1961 contracts, employed the most retired officers (187), and is directed by a former Secretary of the Army. A *Fortune* magazine profile of General Dynamics said: "The unique group of men who run Dynamics are only incidentally in rivalry with other U.S. manufacturers, with many of whom they actually act in concert. Their chief competitor is the USSR. The core of General Dynamics' corporate philosophy is the conviction that national defense is a more or less permanent business." Little has changed since

Wilson's proud declaration of the Permanent War Economy back in the 1944 days when the top 200 corporations possessed 80 percent of all active prime war-supply contracts...

TOWARDS AMERICAN DEMOCRACY

Every effort to end the Cold War and expand the process of world industrialization is an effort hostile to people and institutions whose interests lie in perpetuation of the East-West military threat and the postponement of change in the "have not" nations of the world. Every such effort, too, is bound to establish greater democracy in America. The major goals of a domestic effort would be:

1 *America must abolish its political party stalemate.*

Two genuine parties, centered around issues and essential values, demanding allegiance to party principles shall supplant the current system of organized stalemate which is seriously inadequate to a world in flux... What is desirable is sufficient party disagreement to dramatize major issues, yet sufficient party overlap to guarantee stable transitions from administration to administration.

Every time the President criticizes a recalcitrant Congress, we must ask that he no longer tolerate the Southern conservatives in the Democratic Party. Every time a liberal representative complains that "we can't expect everything at once" we must ask if we received much of anything from Congress in the last generation. Every time he refers to "circumstances beyond control" we must ask why he fraternizes with racist scoundrels. Every time he speaks of the "unpleasantness of personal and party fighting" we should insist that pleasantry with Dixiecrats is inexcusable when the dark peoples of the world call for American support.

2 *Mechanisms of voluntary association must be created through which political information can be imparted and political participation encouraged.*

Political parties, even if realigned, would not provide adequate outlets for popular involvement. Institutions should be created that engage people with issues and express political preference, not as now with huge business lobbies which exercise undemocratic *power* but which carry political *influence* (appropriate to private, rather than public, groupings) in national decision-making enterprise. Private in nature, these should be organized around single issues (medical care, transportation systems reform, etc.), concrete interest (labor and minority group organizations); multiple issues or general issues. These do not exist in America in quantity today. If they did exist, they would be a significant politicizing and educative force bringing people into touch with public life and affording them means of expression and action. Today, giant lobby representatives of business interests are dominant, but not educative. The Federal government itself should counter the latter forces whose intent is often public deceit for private gain, by subsidizing the preparation and decentralized distribution of objective materials on all public issues facing government.

3 *Institutions and practices which stifle dissent should be abolished, and the promotion of peaceful dissent should be actively promoted.*

The First Amendment freedoms of speech, assembly, thought, religion and press should be seen as guarantees, not threats, to national security. While society has the right to prevent active subversion of its laws and institutions, it has the duty as well to promote open discussion of all issues—otherwise it will be in fact promoting real subversion as the only means of implementing ideas. To eliminate the fears and apathy from national life it is necessary that the institutions bred by fear and apathy be rooted out: the House Un-American Activities Committee, the Senate Internal Security Committee, the loyalty oaths on Federal loans, the Attorney General's list of subversive organizations, the Smith and McCarran Acts. The process of eliminating the blighting institutions is the process of restoring democratic participation. Their existence is a sign of the decomposition and atrophy of participation.

4 *Corporations must be made publicly responsible.*

It is not possible to believe that true democracy can exist where a minority utterly controls enormous wealth and power. The influence of corporate elites on foreign policy is neither reliable nor democratic; a way must be found to subordinate private American foreign investment to a democratically-constructed foreign policy...

Labor and government as presently constituted are not sufficient to "regulate" corporations. A new re-ordering, a new calling of responsibility is necessary: more than changing "work rules" we must consider changes in the rules of society by challenging the unchallenged politics of American corporations. Before the government can really begin to control business in a "public interest," the public must gain more substantial control of government: this demands a movement for political as well as economic realignments. We are aware that simple government "regulation," if achieved, would be inadequate without increased worker participation in management decision-making, strengthened and independent regulatory power, balances of partial and/or complete public ownership, various means of humanizing the conditions and types of work itself, sweeping welfare programs and regional *public* development authorities. These are examples of measures to re-balance the economy toward public—and individual—control.

5 *The allocation of resources must be based on social needs. A truly "public sector" must be established, and its nature debated and planned.*

At present the majority of America's "public sector," the largest part of our public spending, is for the military. When great social needs are so pressing, our concept of "government spending" is wrapped up in the "permanent war economy."...

The main *private* forces of economic expansion cannot guarantee a steady rate of growth, nor acceptable recovery from recession—especially in a demilitarizing world. Government participation will inevitably expand enormously, because the stable growth of the economy demands increasing "public" investments yearly. Our present outpour of more than $500 billion might double in a generation, irreversibly involving government solutions. And in future recessions, the compensatory fiscal action by the government will be the only means of avoiding the twin disasters of greater unemployment and a slackening rate of growth. Furthermore, a close relationship with the European Common Market will involve competition with numerous planned economies and may aggravate American unemployment unless the economy here is expanding swiftly enough to create new jobs.

All these tendencies suggest that not only solutions to our present social needs but our future expansion rests upon our willingness to enlarge the "public sector" greatly. Unless we choose war as an economic solvent, future public spending will be of non-military nature—a major intervention into civilian production by the government...

6 *America should concentrate on its genuine social priorities: abolish squalor, terminate neglect, and establish an environment for people to live in with dignity and creativeness.*

A. A program against *poverty* must be just as sweeping as the nature of poverty itself. It must not be just palliative, but directed to the abolition of the structural circumstances of poverty. At a bare minimum it should include a *housing* act far larger than the one supported by the Kennedy Administration, but one that is geared more to low- and middle-income needs than to the windfall aspirations of small and large private entrepreneurs, one that is more sympathetic to the quality of communal life than to the efficiency of city-split highways. Second, *medical care* must become recognized as a lifetime human right just as vital as food, shelter and clothing—the Federal government should guarantee health insurance as a basic social service turning medical treatment into a social habit, not just an occasion of crisis, fighting sickness among the aged, not just by making medical care financially feasible but by reducing sickness among children and younger people. Third, existing institutions should be expanded so the Welfare State cares for *everyone's* welfare according to need. *Social Security* payments should be extended to everyone and should be proportionately greater for the poorest. A *minimum wage* of at least $1.50 should be extended to all workers (including the 16 million currently not covered at all). Programs for equal *educational opportunity* are as important a part of the battle against poverty.

B. A full-scale public initiative for civil rights should be undertaken despite the clamor among conservatives (and liberals) about gradualism, property rights, and law and order. The executive and legislative branches of the Federal government should work by enforcement *and* enactment against any form of exploitation of minority groups. No Federal cooperation with racism is tolerable—from financing of schools, to the development of Federally-supported industry, to the social gatherings of the President. Laws hastening school desegregation, voting rights, and economic protection for Negroes are needed right now. The moral force of the Executive Office should be exerted against the Dixiecrats specifically, and the national complacency about the race question generally. Especially in the North, where one-half of the country's Negro people now live, civil rights is not a problem to be solved in isolation from other problems. The fight against poverty, against slums, against the stalemated Congress, against McCarthyism, are all fights against the discrimination that is nearly endemic to all areas of American life.

C. The promise and problems of long-range *Federal economic development* should be studied more constructively...

D. We must meet the growing complex of "city" problems; over 90 percent of Americans will live in urban areas within two decades. Juvenile delinquency, untended mental illness, crime increase, slums, urban tenantry and non-rent controlled housing, the isolation of the individual in the city—all are problems of the city and are major symptoms of the present system of economic priorities and lack of public planning. Private property control (the real estate lobby and a few selfish landowners and businesses) is as devastating in the cities as corporations are on the national level. But there is no comprehensive way to deal with these problems now amidst competing units of government, dwindling tax resources, suburban escapism (saprophitic to the sick central cities), high infrastructure costs and no one to pay them...

E. *Mental health institutions* are in dire need; there were fewer mental hospital beds in relation to the numbers of mentally-ill in 1959 than there were in 1948. Public hospitals, too, are seriously wanting; existing structures alone need an estimated $1 billion for rehabilitation. Tremendous staff and faculty needs exist as well, and there are not enough medical students enrolled today to meet the anticipated needs of the future.

F. Our *prisons* are too often the enforcers of misery. They must be either re-oriented to rehabilitative work through public supervision or be abolished for their dehumanizing social effects. Funds are needed, too, to make possible a decent prison environment.

G. *Education* is too vital a public problem to be completely entrusted to the province of the various states and local units. In fact, there is no good reason why America should not progress now toward internationalizing rather than localizing, its education system—children and young adults studying everywhere in the world, through a United Nations program, would go far to create mutual understanding. In the meantime, the need for teachers and classrooms in America is fantastic. This is an area where "minimal" requirements should hardly be considered as a goal—there always are improvements to be made in the education system, e.g., smaller classes and many more teachers for them, programs to subsidize the education for the poor but bright, etc.

H. America should eliminate *agricultural policies* based on scarcity and pent-up surplus. In America and foreign countries there exist tremendous needs for more food and balanced diets. The Federal government should finance small farmers' cooperatives, strengthen programs of rural electrification, and expand policies for the distribution of agricultural surpluses throughout the world (by Food-for-Peace and related UN programming). Marginal farmers must be helped to either become productive enough to survive "industrialized agriculture" or given help in making the transition out of agriculture—the current Rural Area Development program must be better coordinated with a massive national "area redevelopment" program.

I. *Science* should be employed to constructively transform the conditions of life throughout the United States and the world. Yet at the present time the Department of Health, Education, and Welfare and the National Science Foundation together spend only $300 million annually for scientific purposes in contrast to the $6 billion spent by the Defense Department and the Atomic Energy Commission. One-half of all research and development in America is directly devoted to military purposes. Two imbalances must be corrected—that of military over non-military investigation, and that of biological-natural-physical science over the sciences of human behavior. Our political system must then include planning for the human use of science: by anticipating the political consequences of scientific innovation, by directing the discovery and exploration of space, by adapting science to improved production of food, to international communications systems, to technical problems of disarmament, and so on. For the newly-developing nations, American science should focus on the study of cheap sources of power, housing and building materials, mass education techniques, etc. Further, science and scholarship should be seen less as an apparatus of conflicting power blocs, but as a bridge toward supra-national community: the International Geophysical Year is a model for continuous further cooperation between the science communities of all nations.

17. The Feminine Mystique

BETTY FRIEDAN

Women have always been a majority treated as a minority: suffering from discrimination in politics, in schools, on the job, and in social relationships. In the industrialized countries, however, women have been fighting back, winning a place for themselves in the economic, cultural, and political worlds.

But something went wrong in the United States in the twentieth century; while women in other countries increasingly found satisfying careers outside the home, American women seemed to be retreating. More of them worked, but at less demanding or rewarding jobs. And they had more children than their peers in other countries. Safely ensconced in the growing suburbs after World War II, apparently uninterested in politics or a career, they seemed calm and safe—the envy, one assumed, of the world. But they had one problem. "The Problem," Betty Friedan called it, "that has no name": more and more of them were miserable. The bored housewife syndrome became a national parlor game, broadcast through the mass media, discussed in countless living rooms and doubtless in as many bedrooms. Betty Friedan brought the problem into the open in her influential The Feminine Mystique (1963), a book that heralded the sort of assertiveness on the part of American women that had not been seen since the women's suffrage movement.

In part, this new militancy reflects the general climate of political activism in the 1960s; in part it grows from new opportunities open to women. But clearly much of it is a direct response to the peculiar circumstances of postwar society, whose attitude toward woman's role Betty Friedan has captured in vigorous polemic.

In the early 1960's *McCall's* has been the fastest growing of the women's magazines. Its contents are a fairly accurate representation of the image of the American woman presented, and in part created, by the large-circulation magazines. Here are the complete editorial contents of a typical issue of *McCall's* (July, 1960):

1. A lead article on "increasing baldness in women," caused by too much brushing and dyeing.
2. A long poem in primer-size type about a child, called "A Boy Is A Boy."
3. A short story about how a teenager who doesn't go to college gets a man away from a bright college girl.
4. A short story about the minute sensations of a baby throwing his bottle out of the crib.
5. The first of a two-part intimate "up-to-date" account by the Duke of Windsor on "How the Duchess and I now live and spend our time. The influence of clothes on me and vice versa."

6. A short story about a nineteen-year-old girl sent to a charm school to learn how to bat her eyelashes and lose at tennis. ("You're nineteen, and by normal American standards, I now am entitled to have you taken off my hands, legally and financially, by some beardless youth who will spirit you away to a one-and-a-half-room apartment in the Village while he learns the chicanery of selling bonds. And no beardless youth is going to do that as long as you volley his backhand.")

7. The story of a honeymoon couple commuting between separate bedrooms after an argument over gambling at Las Vegas.

8. An article on "how to overcome an inferiority complex."

9. A story called "Wedding Day."

10. The story of a teenager's mother who learns how to dance rock-and-roll.

11. Six pages of glamorous pictures of models in maternity clothes.

12. Four glamorous pages on "reduce the way models do."

13. An article on airline delays.

14. Patterns for home sewing.

15. Patterns with which to make "Folding Screens—Bewitching—Magic."

16. An article called "An Encyclopedic Approach to Finding a Second Husband."

17. A "barbecue bonanza," dedicated "to the Great American Mister who stands, chef's cap on head, fork in hand, on terrace or back porch, in patio or backyard anywhere in the land, watching his roast turning on the spit. And to his wife without whom (sometimes) the barbecue could never be the smashing summer success it undoubtedly is . . . "

There were also the regular front-of-the-book "service" columns on new drug and medicine developments, child-care facts, columns by Clare Luce and by Eleanor Roosevelt, and "Pots and Pans," a column of readers' letters.

The image of woman that emerges from this big, pretty magazine is young and frivolous, almost childlike; fluffy and feminine; passive; gaily content in a world of bedroom and kitchen, sex, babies, and home. The magazine surely does not leave out sex; the only passion, the only pursuit, the only goal a woman is permitted is the pursuit of a man. It is crammed full of food, clothing, cosmetics, furniture, and the physical bodies of young women, but where is the world of thought and ideas, the life of the mind and spirit? In the magazine image, women do no work except housework and work to keep their bodies beautiful and to get and keep a man.

This was the image of the American woman in the year Castro led a revolution in Cuba and men were trained to travel into outer space; the year that the African continent brought forth new nations, and a plane whose speed is greater than the speed of sound broke up a Summit Conference; the year artists picketed a great museum in protest against the hegemony of abstract art; physicists explored the concept of antimatter; astronomers, because of new radio telescopes, had to alter their concepts of the expanding universe; biologists made a breakthrough in the fundamental chemistry of life; and Negro youth in Southern schools forced the United States, for the first time since the Civil War, to face a moment of democratic truth. But this magazine, published for over 5,000,000 American women, almost all of whom have been through high school and nearly half to college, contained almost no mention of the world beyond the home. In the second half of the twentieth century in America, woman's world was confined to her own body and beauty, the charming of man, the bearing of babies, and the physical care and serving of husband, children, and home. And this was no anomaly of a single issue of a single women's magazine.

I sat one night at a meeting of magazine writers, mostly men, who work for all kinds of magazines, including women's magazines. The main speaker was a leader of the desegregation battle. Before he spoke, another man outlined the needs of the large women's magazine he edited:

Our readers are housewives, full time. They're not interested in the broad public issues of the day. They are not interested in national or international affairs. They are only interested in the family and the home. They aren't interested in politics, unless it's related to an immediate need in the home, like the price of coffee. Humor? Has to be gentle, they don't get satire. Travel? We have almost completely dropped it. Education? That's a problem. Their own education level is going up. They've generally all had a high-school education and many, college. They're tremendously interested in education for their children—fourth-grade arithmetic. You just can't write about ideas or broad issues of the day for women. That's why we're publishing 90 per cent service now and 10 per cent general interest.

Another editor agreed, adding plaintively: "Can't you give us something else besides 'there's death in your medicine cabinet'? Can't any of you dream up a new crisis for women? We're always interested in sex, of course."

At this point, the writers and editors spent an hour listening to Thurgood Marshall on the inside story of the desegregation battle, and its possible effect on the presidential election. "Too bad I can't run that story," one editor said. "But you just can't link it to woman's world."

As I listened to them, a German phrase echoed in my mind— "*Kinder, Kuche, Kirche*," the slogan by which the Nazis decreed that women must once again be confined to their biological role. But this was not Nazi Germany. This was America. The whole world lies open to American women. Why, then, does the image deny the world? Why does it limit women to "one position, one role, one occupation"? Not long ago, women dreamed and fought for equality, their own place in the world. What happened to their dreams; when did women decide to give up the world and go back home?

A geologist brings up a core of mud from the bottom of the ocean and sees layers of sediment as sharp as a razor blade deposited over the years—clues to changes in the geological evolution of the earth so vast that they would go unnoticed during the lifespan of a single man. I sat for many days in the New York Public Library, going back through bound volumes of American women's magazines for the last twenty years. I found a change in the image of the American woman, and in the boundaries of the woman's world, as sharp and puzzling as the changes revealed in cores of ocean sediment.

In 1939, the heroines of women's magazine stories were not always young, but in a certain sense they were younger than their fictional counterparts today. They were young in the same way that the American hero has always been young: they were New Women, creating with a gay determined spirit a new identity for women—a life of their own. There was an aura about them of becoming, of moving into a future that was going to be different from the past. The majority of heroines in the four major women's magazines (then *Ladies' Home Journal, McCall's, Good Housekeeping, Woman's Home Companion*) were career women—happily, proudly, adventurously, attractively career women—who loved and were loved by men. And the spirit, courage, independence, determination— the strength of character they showed in their work as nurses, teachers, artists, actresses, copywriters, saleswomen—were part of their charm. There was a definite aura that their individuality was something to be admired, not unattractive to men, that men were drawn to them as much for their spirit and character as for their looks.

These were the mass women's magazines—in their heyday. The stories were conventional: girl-meets-boy or girl-gets-boy. But very often this was not the major theme of the story. These heroines were usually marching toward some goal or vision of their own, struggling with some problem of work or the world, when they found their man. And this New Woman, less fluffily feminine, so independent and determined to find a new life of her own, was the heroine of a different kind of love story. She was less aggressive in pursuit of a man. Her passionate involvement with the world, her own sense of herself as an individual, her self-reliance, gave a different flavor to her relationship with the man. The heroine and hero of one of these stories meet and fall in love at an ad agency where they both work. "I don't want to put you in a garden behind a wall," the hero says. "I want you to walk with me hand in hand, and together we could accomplish whatever we wanted to" ("A Dream to Share," *Redbook*, January, 1939).

These New Women were almost never housewives; in fact, the stories usually ended before they had children. They were young because the future was open. But they seemed, in another sense, much older, more mature than childlike, kittenish young housewife heroines today. One, for example, is a nurse ("Mother-in-Law," *Ladies' Home Journal*, June, 1939). "She was, he thought, very lovely. She hadn't an ounce of picture book prettiness, but there was strength in her hands, pride in her carriage and nobility in the lift of her chin, in her blue eyes. She had been on her own ever since she left training, nine years ago. She had earned her way, she need consider nothing but her heart."

One heroine runs away from home when her mother insists she must make her debut instead of going on an expedition as a geologist. Her passionate determination to live her own life does not keep this New Woman from loving a man, but it makes her rebel from her parents; just as the young hero often must leave home to grow up. "You've got more courage than any girl I ever saw. You have what it takes," says the boy who helps her get away ("Have a Good Time, Dear," *Ladies' Home Journal*, May 1939)...

I found the last clear note of the passionate search for individual identity that a career seems to have symbolized in the pre–1950 decades in a story called "Sarah and the Seaplane," (*Ladies' Home Journal*, February, 1949). Sarah, who for nineteen years has played the part of docile daughter, is secretly learning to fly. She misses her flying lesson to accompany her mother on a round of social calls. An elderly doctor houseguest says: "My dear Sarah, every day, all the time, you are committing suicide. It's a greater crime than not pleasing others, not doing justice to yourself." Sensing some secret, he asks if she is in love. "She found it difficult to answer. In love? In love with the good-natured, the beautiful Henry [the flying teacher]? In love with the flashing water and the lift of wings at the instant of freedom, and the vision of the smiling, limitless world? 'Yes,' she answered, 'I think I am.'"

The next morning, Sarah solos. Henry "stepped away, slamming the cabin door shut, and swung the ship about for her. She was alone. There was a heady moment when everything she had learned left her, when she had to adjust herself to be alone, entirely alone in the familiar cabin. Then she drew a deep breath and suddenly a wonderful sense of competence made her sit erect and smiling. She was along! She was answerable to herself alone, and she was sufficient.

"'I can do it!' she told herself aloud... The wind blew back from the floats in glittering streaks, and then effortlessly the ship lifted itself free and soared." Even her mother can't stop her now from getting her flying license. She is not "afraid of discovering my own way of life." In bed that night she smiles sleepily, remembering how Henry had said, "You're my girl."

"Henry's girl! She smiled. No, she was not Henry's girl. She was Sarah. And that was sufficient. And with such a late start it would be some time before she got to know herself. Half in a dream now, she wondered if at the end of that time she would need someone else and who it would be."

And then suddenly the image blurs. The New Woman, soaring free, hesitates in midflight, shivers in all that blue sunlight and rushes back to the cozy walls of home. In the same year that Sarah soloed, the *Ladies' Home Journal* printed the prototype of the innumerable paeans to "Occupation: Housewife" that started to appear in the women's magazines, paeans that resounded throughout the fifties. They usually begin with a woman complaining that when she has to write "housewife" on the census blank, she gets an inferiority complex. ("When I write it I realize that here I am, a middle-aged woman, with a university education, and I've never made anything out of my life. I'm just a housewife.") Then the author of the paean, who somehow never is a housewife (in this case, Dorothy Thompson, newspaper woman, foreign correspondent, famous columnist, in *Ladies' Home Journal*, March, 1949), roars with laughter. The trouble with you, she scolds, is you don't realize you are expert in a dozen careers, simultaneously. "You might write: business manager, cook, nurse, chauffeur, dressmaker, interior decorator, accountant, caterer, teacher, private secretary—or just put down philanthropist...All your life you have been giving away your energies, your skills, your talents, your services, for love." But still, the housewife complains, I'm nearly fifty and I've never done what I hoped to do in my youth—music—I've wasted my college education.

Ho-ho, laughs Miss Thompson, aren't your children musical because of you, and all those struggling years while your husband was finishing his great work, didn't you keep a charming home on $3,000, a year, and make all your children's clothes and your own, and paper the living room yourself, and watch the markets like a hawk for bargains? And in time off, didn't you type and proofread your husband's manuscripts, plan festivals to make up the church deficit, play piano duets with the children to make practicing more fun, read their books in highschool to follow their study? "But all this vicarious living—through others," the housewife sighs. "As vicarious as Napoleon Bonaparte," Miss Thompson scoffs, "or a Queen. I simply refuse to share your self-pity. You are one of the most successful women I know."

As for not earning any money, the argument goes, let the housewife compute the cost of her services. Women can save more money by their managerial talents inside the home than they can bring into it by outside work. As for woman's spirit being broken by the boredom of household tasks, maybe the genius of some women has been thwarted, but "a world full of feminine genius, but poor in children, would come rapidly to an end...Great men have great mothers."

And the American housewife is reminded that Catholic countries in the Middle Ages "elevated the gentle and inconspicuous Mary into the Queen of Heaven, and built their loveliest cathedrals to 'Notre Dame—Our Lady'...The homemaker, the nurturer, the creator of children's environment is the constant recreator of culture, civilization, and virtue. Assuming that she is doing well that great managerial task and creative activity, let her write her occupation proudly: 'housewife.'"

In 1949, the *Ladies' Home Journal* also ran Margaret Mead's *Male and Female*. All the magazines were echoing Farnham and Lundberg's *Modern Woman: The Lost Sex*, which came out in 1942, with its warning that careers and higher education were leading to the "masculinization of women with enormously dangerous consequences to the home, the children dependent on it and to the ability of the woman, as well as her husband, to obtain sexual gratification."

And so the feminine mystique began to spread through the land, grafted onto old prejudices and comfortable conventions which so easily give the past a stranglehold on the future. Behind the new mystique were concepts and theories deceptive in their sophistication and their assumption of accepted truth. These theories were supposedly so complex that they were inaccessible to all but a few initiates, and therefore irrefutable. It will be necessary to break through this wall of mystery and look more closely at these complex concepts, these accepted truths, to understand fully what has happened to American women.

The feminine mystique says that the highest value and the only commitment for women is the fulfillment of their own femininity. It says that the great mistake of Western culture, through most of its history, has been the undervaluation of this femininity. It says this femininity is so mysterious and intuitive and close to the creation and origin of life that man-made science may never be able to understand it. But however special and different, it is in no way inferior to the nature of man; it may even in certain respects be superior. The mistake, says the mystique, the root of women's troubles in the past is that women envied men, women tried to be like men, instead of accepting their own nature, which can find fulfillment only in sexual passivity, male domination, and nurturing maternal love.

But the new image this mystique gives to American women is the old image: "Occupation: housewife." The new mystique makes the housewife-mothers, who never had a chance to be anything else, the model for all women; it presupposes that history has reached a final and glorious end in the here and now, as far as women are concerned. Beneath the sophisticated trappings, it simply makes certain concrete, finite, domestic aspects of feminine existence—as it was lived by women whose lives were confined, by necessity, to cooking, cleaning, washing, bearing children—into a religion, a pattern by which all women must now live or deny their femininity.

Fulfillment as a woman had only one definition for American women after 1949—the housewife-mother. As swiftly as in a dream, the image of the American woman as a changing, growing individual in a changing world was shattered. Her solo flight to find her own identity was forgotten in the rush for the security of togetherness. Her limitless world shrunk to the cozy walls of home.

The transformation, reflected in the pages of the women's magazines, was sharply visible in 1949 and progressive through the fifties. "Femininity Begins at Home," "It's a Man's World Maybe," "Have Babies While You're Young," "How to Snare a Male," "Should I Stop Work When We Marry?" "Are You Training Your Daughter to be a Wife?" "Careers at Home," "Do Women Have to Talk So Much?" "Why GI's Prefer Those German Girls," "What Women Can Learn from Mother Eve," "Really a Man's World, Politics," "How to Hold On to a Happy Marriage," "Don't Be Afraid to Marry Young," "The Doctor Talks about Breast-Feeding," "Our Baby Was Born at Home," "Cooking to Me is Poetry," "The Business of Running a Home."

By the end of 1949, only one out of three heroines in the women's magazines was a career woman—and she was shown in the act of renouncing her career and discovering that what she really wanted to be was a housewife. In 1958, and again in 1959, I went through issue after issue of the three major women's magazines (the fourth, *Woman's Home Companion*, had died) without finding a single heroine who had a career, a commitment to any work, art, profession, or mission in the world, other than "Occupation: housewife." Only one in a hundred heroines had a job; even the young unmarried heroines no longer worked except at snaring a husband.

These new happy housewife heroines seem strangely younger than the spirited career girls of the thirties and forties. They seem to get younger all the time—in looks, and a childlike kind of dependence. They have no vision of the future, except to have a baby. The only active growing figure in their world is the child. The housewife heroines are

forever young, because their own image *ends* in childbirth. Like Peter
Pan, they must remain young, while their children grow up with the
world. They must keep on having babies, because the feminine mystique
says there is no other way for a woman to be a heroine...

With the career woman out of the way, the housewife with interests in the community becomes the devil to be exorcised. Even PTA
takes on a suspect connotation, not to mention interest in some international cause (see "Almost a Love Affair," *McCall's*, November, 1955).
The housewife who simply has a mind of her own is the next to go.
The heroine of "I Didn't Want to Tell You" (*McCall's*, January, 1958) is
shown balancing the checkbook by herself and arguing with her husband about a small domestic detail. It develops that she is losing her
husband to a "helpless little widow" whose main appeal is that she can't
"think straight" about an insurance policy or mortgage. The betrayed
wife says: "She must have sex appeal and what weapon has a wife against
that?" But her best friend tells her: "You're making this too simple.
You're forgetting how helpless Tania can be, and how grateful to the
man who helps her..."

"I couldn't be a clinging vine if I tried," the wife says. "I had a
better than average job after I left college and I was always a pretty
independent person. I'm not a helpless little woman and I can't pretend
to be." But she learns, that night. She hears a noise that might be a
burglar; even though she knows it's only a mouse, she calls helplessly
to her husband, and wins him back. As he comforts her pretended
panic, she murmurs that, of course, he was right in their argument that
morning. "She lay still in the soft bed, smiling sweet, secret satisfaction,
scarcely touched with guilt."

The end of the road, in an almost literal sense, is the disappearance
of the heroine altogether, as a separate self and the subject of her own
story. The end of the road is togetherness, where the woman has no
independent self to hide even in guilt; she exists only for and through
her husband and children.

Coined by the publishers of *McCall's* in 1954, the concept "togetherness" was seized upon avidly as a movement of spiritual significance
by advertisers, ministers, newspaper editors. For a time, it was elevated
into virtually a national purpose. But very quickly there was sharp social
criticism, and bitter jokes about "togetherness" as a substitute for larger
human goals—for men. Women were taken to task for making their husbands do housework, instead of letting them pioneer in the nation and
the world. Why, it was asked, should men with the capacities of statesmen, anthropologists, physicists, poets, have to wash dishes and diaper
babies on weekday evenings or Saturday mornings when they might use
those extra hours to fulfill larger commitments to their society?

Significantly, critics resented only that men were being asked to
share "woman's world." Few questioned the boundaries of this world for
women. No one seemed to remember that women were once thought
to have the capacity and vision of statesmen, poets, and physicists. Few
saw the big lie of togetherness for women.

Consider the Easter 1954 issue of *McCall's* which announced the
new era of togetherness, sounding the requiem for the days when

women fought for and won political equality, and the women's magazines "helped you to carve out large areas of living formerly forbidden to your sex." The new way of life in which "men and women in ever-increasing numbers are marrying at an earlier age, having children at an earlier age, rearing larger families and gaining their deepest satisfaction" from their own homes, is one which "men, women, and children are achieving together . . . not as women alone, or men alone, isolated from one another, but as a family, sharing a common experience."

The picture essay detailing that way of life is called "a man's place is in the home." It describes, as the new image and ideal, a New Jersey couple with three children in a gray-single split-level house. Ed and Carol have "centered their lives almost completely around their children and their home." They are shown shopping at the supermarket, carpentering, dressing the children, making breakfast together. "Then Ed joins the members of his car pool and heads for the office."

Ed, the husband, chooses the color scheme for the house and makes the major decorating decisions. The chores Ed likes are listed: putter around the house, make things, paint, select furniture, rugs, and draperies, dry dishes, read to the children and put them to bed, work in the garden, feed and dress and bathe the children, attend PTA meetings, cook, buy clothes for his wife, buy groceries.

Ed doesn't like these chores: dusting, vacuuming, finishing jobs he's started, hanging draperies, washing pots and pans and dishes, picking up after the children, shoveling snow or mowing the lawn, changing diapers, taking the baby-sitter home, doing the laundry, ironing. Ed, of course, does not do these chores.

For the sake of every member of the family, the family needs a head. This means Father, not Mother . . . Children of both sexes need to learn, recognize and respect the abilities and functions of each sex . . . He is not just a substitute mother, even though he's ready and willing to do his share of bathing, feeding, comforting, playing. He is a link with the outside world he works in. If in that world he is interested, courageous, tolerant, constructive, he will pass on these values to his children.

There were many agonized editorial sessions, in those days at *McCall's*. "Suddenly, everybody was looking for this spiritual significance in togetherness, expecting us to make some mysterious religious movement out of the life everyone had been leading for the last five years—crawling into the home, turning their backs on the world—but we never could find a way of showing it that wasn't a monstrosity of dullness," a former *McCall's* editor reminisces. "It always boiled down to, goody, goody, goody, Daddy is out there in the garden barbecuing. We put men in the fashion pictures and the food pictures, and even the perfume pictures. But we were stifled by it editorially.

"We had articles by psychiatrists that we couldn't use because they would have blown it wide open: all those couples propping their whole weight on their kids but what else could you do with togetherness but child care? We were pathetically grateful to find anything else where we could show father photographed with mother. Sometimes, we used to wonder what would happen to women, with men taking over the decorating, child care, cooking, all the things that used to be hers alone. But we couldn't show women getting out of the home and having a career. The irony is, what we meant to do was to stop editing for women as women, and edit for men and women together. We wanted to edit for people, not women."

But forbidden to join man in the world, can women be people? Forbidden independence, they finally are swallowed in an image of such passive dependence that they want men to make the decisions, even in the home. The frantic illusion that togetherness can impart a spiritual content to the dullness of domestic routine, the need for a religious movement to make up for the lack of identity, betrays the measure of women's loss and the emptiness of the image. Could making men share the housework compensate women for their loss of the world? Could vacuuming the living-room floor together give the housewife some mysterious new purpose in life?

In 1956, at the peak of togetherness, the bored editors of *McCall's* ran a little article called "The Mother Who Ran Away." To their amazement, it brought the highest readership of any article they had ever run. "It was our moment of truth," said a former editor. "We suddenly realized that all those women at home with their three and a half children were miserably unhappy."

But by then the new image of American woman, "Occupation: housewife," had hardened into a mystique, unquestioned and permitting no questions, shaping the very reality is distorted.

By the time I started writing for women's magazines, in the fifties, it was simply taken for granted by editors, and accepted as an immutable fact of life by writers, that women were not interested in politics, life outside the United States, national issues, art, science, ideas, adventure, education, or even their own communities, except where they could be sold through their emotions as wives and mothers.

Politics, for women, became Mamie's clothes and the Nixons' home life. Out of conscience, a sense of duty, the *Ladies' Home Journal* might run a series like "Political Pilgrim's Progress," showing women trying to improve their children's schools and playgrounds. But even approaching politics through mother love did not really interest women, it was thought in the trade. Everyone knew those readership percentages. An editor of *Redbook* ingeniously tried to bring the bomb down to the feminine level by showing the emotions of a wife whose husband sailed into a contaminated area.

"Women can't take an idea, an issue, pure," men who edited the mass women's magazines agreed. "It had to be translated in terms they can understand as women." This was so well understood by those who wrote for women's magazines that a natural childbirth expert submitted an article to a leading woman's magazine called "How to Have a Baby in a Atom Bomb Shelter." "The article was not well written," an editor told me, "or we might have bought it." According to the mystique, women, in their mysterious femininity, might be interested in the concrete biological details of having a baby in a bomb shelter, but never in the abstract idea of the bomb's power to destroy the human race.

Such a belief, of course, becomes a self-fulfilling prophecy. In 1960, a perceptive social psychologist showed me some sad statistics which seemed to prove unmistakably that American women under thirty-five are not interested in politics. "They may have the vote, but they don't dream about running for office," he told me. "If you write a political piece, they won't read it. You have to translate it into issues they can understand—romance, pregnancy, nursing, home furnishings, clothes. Run an article on the economy, or the race question, civil rights, and you'd think that women had never heard of them."

Maybe they hadn't heard of them. Ideas are not like instincts of the blood that spring into the mind intact. They are communicated by education, by the printed word. The new young housewives, who leave high school or college to marry, do not read books, the psychological surveys say. They only read magazines. Magazines today assume women are not interested in ideas. But going back to the bound volumes in the library, I found in the thirties and forties that the mass-circulation magazines like *Ladies' Home Journal* carried hundreds of articles about the world outside the home. "The first inside story of American diplomatic relations preceding declared war"; "Can the U.S. Have Peace After This War?" by Walter Lippmann; "Stalin at Midnight," by Harold Stassen; "General Stilwell Reports on China"; articles about the last days of Czechoslovakia by Vincent Sheean; the persecution of Jews in Germany; the New Deal; Carl Sandburg's account of Lincoln's assassination; Faulkner's stories of Mississippi, Margaret Sanger's battle for birth control.

In the 1950s they printed virtually no articles except those that serviced women as housewives, or described women as housewives, or permitted a purely feminine identification like the Duchess of Windsor or Princess Margaret. "If we get an article about a woman who does anything adventurous, out of the way, something by herself, you know, we figure she must be terribly aggressive, neurotic," a *Ladies' Home Journal* editor told me. Margaret Sanger would never get in today.

In 1960, I saw statistics that showed that women under thirty-five could not identify with a spirited heroine of a story who worked in an ad agency and persuaded the boy to stay and fight for his principles in the big city instead of running home to the security of a family business. Nor could these new young housewives identify with a young minister, acting on his belief in defiance of convention. But they had no trouble at all identifying with a young man paralyzed at eighteen. ("I regained consciousness to discover that I could not move or even speak. I could wiggle only one finger of one hand." With help from faith and a psychiatrist, "I am now finding reasons to live as fully as possible.")

Does it say something about the new housewife readers that, as any editor can testify, they can identify completely with the victims of blindness, deafness, physical maiming, cerebral palsy, paralysis, cancer, or approaching death? Such articles about people who cannot see or speak or move have been an enduring staple of the women's magazines in the era of "Occupation: housewife." They are told with infinitely realistic detail over and over again, replacing the articles about the nation, the world, ideas, issues, art and science; replacing the stories about adventurous spirited women. And whether the victim is man, woman or child, whether the living death is incurable cancer or creeping paralysis, the housewife reader can identify...

A baked potato is not as big as the world, and vacuuming the living room floor—with or without makeup—is not work that takes enough thought or energy to challenge any woman's full capacity. Women are human beings, not stuffed dolls, not animals. Down through the ages man has known that he was set apart from other animals by his mind's power to have an idea, a vision, and shape the future to it. He shares a need for food and sex with other animals, but when he loves, he loves a man, and when he discovers and creates and shapes a future different from his past, he is a man, a human being.

This is the real mystery: why did so many American women, with the ability and education to discover and create, go back home again, to look for "something more" in housework and rearing children? For, paradoxically, in the same fifteen years in which the spirited New Woman was replaced by the Happy Housewife, the boundaries of the human world have widened, the pace of world change has quickened, and the very nature of human reality has become increasingly free from biological and material necessity. Does the mystique keep American woman from growing with the world? Does it force her to deny reality, as a woman in a mental hospital must deny reality to believe she is a queen? Does it doom women to be displaced persons, if not virtual schizophrenics, in our complex, changing world?

It is more than a strange paradox that as all professions are finally open to women in America, "career woman" has become a dirty word; that as higher education becomes available to any woman with the capacity for it, education for women has become so suspect that more and more drop out of high school and college to marry and have babies; that as so many roles in modern society become theirs for the taking, women so insistently confine themselves to one role. Why, with the removal of all the legal, political, economic, and educational barriers that once kept woman from being man's equal, a person in her own right, an individual free to develop her own potential, should she accept this new image which insists she is not a person but a "woman," by definition barred from the freedom of human existence and a voice in human destiny?

The feminine mystique is so powerful that women grow up no longer knowing that they have the desires and capacities the mystique forbids. But such a mystique does not fasten itself on a whole nation in a few short years, reversing the trends of a century, without cause. What gives the mystique its power? Why did women go home again?

18. Acceptance Speech 1964

BARRY GOLDWATER

Barry Goldwater's acceptance speech at the Republican National Convention in 1964 makes an interesting contrast to John F. Kennedy's inaugural address in 1961. In the Kennedy inaugural we can feel the elevation, the magnetism of his rhetoric. Yet we wonder what it is all about. To what is the trumpet summoning us? What is the "maximum danger" in the world in 1961? So many years later, we are still moved even when we do not exactly know why.

Interpreting Goldwater's acceptance speech presents the opposite problem. Today it seems competent but ordinary. The interpretive struggle is to understand why at the time it was delivered it seemed exciting, even sinister. When Goldwater talks about freedom, equality, diversity, and the preference for action by governmental units "closest to the people involved," we must examine the full context of 1964 to read this address as a civil rights worker or a conservative congressman would have understood it. Similarly, we must look closely at why Goldwater's pronouncements in foreign policy would have carried a different meaning from Kennedy's equally bellicose language. Why did so many Americans hear in this speech virulent opposition to civil rights legislation, threats to the New Deal welfare legislation including Social Security, and adventurism in American foreign policy?

As it turned out, Goldwater was a prophet of the political language of the next quarter century and beyond. The speeches of Ronald Reagan in the 1980s and, to a lesser extent, George Bush in the 1990s contain much of the rhetoric that so many Americans rejected in 1964. Perhaps Goldwater's address was simply historically premature.

MY GOOD FRIEND and Great Republican, Dick Nixon and your charming wife, Pat; my running mate—that wonderful Republican who has served us so well for so long—Bill Miller and his wife, Stephanie; to Thruston Morton, who's done such a commendable job in chairmaning this convention; to Mr. Herbert Hoover who I hope is watching, and to the great American and his wife, General and Mrs. Eisenhower. To my own wife, my family, and to all of my fellow Republicans here assembled, and Americans across this great nation:

From this moment, united and determined, we will go forward together dedicated to the ultimate and undeniable greatness of the whole man.

Together we will win.

I accept your nomination with a deep sense of humility. I accept, too, the responsibility that goes with it, and I seek your continued help and your continued guidance. My fellow Republicans, our cause is too great for any man to feel worthy of it. Our task would be too great for any man did he not have with him the heart and the hands of this great Republican party.

And I promise you tonight that every fibre of my being is consecrated to our cause, that nothing shall be lacking from the struggle that can be brought to it by enthusiasm, by devotion and plain hard work.

In this world no person, no party can guarantee anything, but what we can do and what we shall do is to deserve victory and victory will be ours. The Good Lord raised this mighty Republican, Republic to be a home for the brave and to flourish as the land of the free—not to stagnate in the swampland to collectivism, not to cringe before the bully of Communism.

Now my fellow Americans, the tide has been running against freedom. Our people have followed false prophets. We must, and we shall return to proven ways—not because they are old, but because they are true.

We must, and we shall, set the tide running again in the cause of freedom. And this party, with its every action, every word, every breath and every heart beat, has but a single resolve, and that is freedom.

Freedom made orderly for this nation by our constitutional government. Freedom under a government limited by laws of nature and of nature's God. Freedom balanced so that order lacking liberty will not become the slavery of the prison cell; balanced so that liberty lacking order will not become the license of the mob and of the jungle.

Now, we Americans understand freedom, we have earned it; we have lived for it, and we have died for it. This nation and its people are freedom's models in a searching world. We can be freedom's missionaries in a doubting world.

But, ladies and gentlemen, first we must renew freedom's mission in our own hearts and in our own homes.

During four futile years the Administration which we shall replace has distorted and lost the faith. It has talked and talked and talked and talked the words of freedom but it has failed and failed and failed in the works of freedom.

Now failure cements the wall of shame in Berlin; failures blot the sands of shame at the Bay of Pigs; failures marked the slow death of freedom in Laos; failures infest the jungles of Vietnam, and failures haunt the houses of our once great alliances and undermines the greatest bulwark ever erected by free nations, the NATO community.

Failures proclaim lost leadership, obscure purpose, weakening wills and the risk of inciting our sworn enemies to new aggressions and to new excesses.

And because of this Administration we are tonight a world divided. We are a nation becalmed. We have lost the brisk pace of diversity and the genius of individual creativity. We are plodding along at a pace set by centralized planning, red tape, rules without responsibility and regimentation without recourse.

Rather than useful jobs in our country, people have been offered bureaucratic make-work; rather than moral leadership, they have been given bread and circuses; they have been given spectacles, and yes, they've been given scandals.

Tonight there is violence in our streets, corruption in our highest offices, aimlessness among our youth, anxiety among our elderly, and there's a virtual despair among the many who look beyond material success toward the inner meaning of their lives. And where examples of morality should be set, the opposite is seen. Small men seeking great wealth or power have too often and too long turned even the highest levels of public service into mere personal opportunity.

Now certainly simple honesty is not too much to demand of men in government. We find it in most. Republicans demand it from everyone.

They demand it from everyone no matter how exalted or protected his position might be.

The growing menace in our country tonight, to personal safety, to life, to limb and property, in homes, in churches, on the playgrounds and places of business, particularly in our great cities, is the mounting concern or should be of every thoughtful citizen in the United States. Security from domestic violence, no less than from foreign aggression, is the most elementary and fundamental purpose of any government, and a government that cannot fulfill this purpose is one that cannot long command the loyalty of its citizens.

History shows us, demonstrates that nothing, nothing prepares the way for tyranny more than the failure of public officials to keep the streets safe from bullies and marauders.

Now we Republicans see all this as more—much more—than the result of mere political differences, or mere political mistakes. We see this as the result of a fundamentally and absolutely wrong view of man, his nature and his destiny.

Those who seek to live your lives for you, to take your liberty in return for relieving you of yours; those who elevate the state and downgrade the citizen, must see ultimately a world in which earthly power can be substituted for Divine Will. And this nation was founded upon the rejection of that notion and upon the acceptance of God as the author of freedom.

Now those who seek absolute power, even though they seek it to do what they regard as good, are simply demanding the right to enforce their own version of heaven on earth, and let me remind you they are the very ones who always create the most hellish tyranny.

Absolute power does corrupt, and those who seek it must be suspect and must be opposed. Their mistaken course stems from false notions, ladies and gentlemen, of equality. Equality, rightly understood as our founding fathers understood it, leads to liberty and to the emancipation of creative differences; wrongly understood, as it has been so tragically in our time, it leads first to conformity and then to despotism.

Fellow Republicans, it is the cause of Republicanism to resist concentrations of power, private or public, which enforce such conformity and inflict such despotism.

It is the cause of Republicanism to insure that power remains in the hands of the people—and, so help us God, that is exactly what a Republican President will do with the help of a Republican Congress.

It is further the cause of Republicanism to restore a clear understanding of the tyranny of man over man in the world at large. It is our cause to dispel the foggy thinking which avoids hard decisions in the delusion that a world of conflict will somehow resolve itself into a world of harmony, if we just don't rock the boat or irritate the forces of aggression—and this is hogwash.

It is, further, the cause of Republicanism to remind ourselves, and the world, that only the strong can remain free; that only the strong can keep the peace.

Now I needn't remind you, or my fellow Americans regardless of party, that Republicans have shouldered this hard responsibility and marched in this cause before. It was Republican leadership under Dwight Eisenhower that kept the peace, and passed along to this Administration the mightiest arsenal for defense the world has ever known.

And I needn't remind you that it was the strength and the believable will of the Eisenhower years that kept the peace by using our strength, by using it in the Formosa Strait, and in Lebanon, and by showing it courageously at all times.

It was during those Republican years that the thrust of Communist imperialism was blunted. It was during those years of Republican leadership that this world moved closer not to war but closer to peace than at any other time in the last three decades.

And I needn't remind you, but I will, that it's been during Democratic years that our strength to deter war has been stilled and even gone into a planned decline. It has been during Democratic years that we have weakly stumbled into conflicts, timidly refusing to draw our own lines against aggression, deceitfully refusing to tell even our own people of our full participation and tragically letting our finest men die on battlefields unmarked by purpose, unmarked by pride or the prospect of victory.

Yesterday it was Korea; tonight it is Vietnam. Make no bones of this. Don't try to sweep this under the rug. We are at war in Vietnam. And yet the President, who is the Commander in Chief of our forces, refuses to say, refuses to say mind you, whether or not the objective over there is victory, and his Secretary of Defense continues to mislead and misinform the American people and enough of it has gone by.

And I needn't remind you, but I will, it has been during Democratic years that a billion persons were cast into communist captivity and their fate cynically sealed.

Today—today in our beloved country we have an Administration which seems eager to deal with Communism in every coin known— from gold to wheat; from consulates to confidence, and even human freedom itself.

Now the Republican cause demands that we brand Communism as the principal disturber of peace in the world today. Indeed, we should brand it as the only significant disturber of the peace. And we must make clear that until its goals of conquest are absolutely renounced, and its relations with all nations tempered, Communism and the governments it now controls are enemies of every man on earth who is or wants to be free.

Now, we here in America can keep the peace only if we remain vigilant, and only if we remain strong. Only if we keep our eyes open and keep our guard up can we prevent war.

And I want to make this abundantly clear—I don't intend to let peace or freedom be torn from our grasp because of lack of strength, or lack of will—and that I promise you Americans.

I believe that we must look beyond the defense of freedom today to its extension tomorrow. I believe that the Communism which boasts it will bury us will instead give way to the forces of freedom. And I can see in the distant and yet recognizable future the outlines of a world worthy of our dedication, our every risk, our every effort, our every sacrifice along the way. Yes, a world that will redeem the suffering of those who will be liberated from tyranny.

I can see, and I suggest that all thoughtful men must contemplate, the flowering of an Atlantic civilization, the whole world of Europe reunified and free, trading openly across its borders, communicating openly across the world.

This is a goal far, far more meaningful than a moon shot.

It's a truly inspiring goal for all free men to set for themselves during the latter half of the twentieth century. I can see and all free men must thrill to the events of this Atlantic civilization joined by a straight ocean highway to the United States. What a destiny! What a destiny can be ours to stand as a great central pillar linking Europe, the Americans and the venerable and vital peoples and cultures of the Pacific.

I can see a day when all the Americas—North and South—will be linked in a mighty system—a system in which the errors and misunderstandings of the past will be submerged one by one in a rising tide of prosperity and interdependence.

We know that the misunderstandings of centuries are not to be wiped away in a day or wiped away in an hour. But we pledge, we pledge, the human sympathy—what our neighbors to the South call an attitude of sympatico—no less than enlightened self-interest will be our guide.

And I can see this Atlantic civilization galvanizing and guiding emergent nations everywhere. Now I know this freedom is not the fruit of every soil. I know that our own freedom was achieved through centuries by unremitting efforts by brave and wise men. And I know that the road to freedom is a long and a challenging road, and I know also that some men may walk away from it, that some men resist challenge, accepting the false security of governmental paternalism.

And I pledge that the America I envision in the years ahead will extend its hand in help in teaching and in cultivation so that all new nations will be at least encouraged to go our way; so that they will not wander down the dark alleys of tyranny or to the deadend streets of collectivism.

My fellow Republicans, we do no man a service by hiding freedom's light under a bushel of mistaken humility.

I seek an America proud of its past, proud of its ways, proud of its dreams and determined actively to proclaim them. But our examples to the world must, like charity, begin at home.

In our vision of a good and decent future, free and peaceful, there must be room, room for the liberation of the energy and the talent of the individual, otherwise our vision is blind at the outset.

We must assure a society here which while never abandoning the needy, or forsaking the helpless, nurtures incentives and opportunity for the creative and the productive.

We must know the whole good is the product of many single contributions. And I cherish the day when our children once again will restore as heroes the sort of men and women who, unafraid and undaunted, pursue the truth, strive to cure disease, subdue and make fruitful our natural environment, and produce the inventive engines of production, science and technology.

This nation, whose creative people have enhanced this entire span of history, should again thrive upon the greatness of all those things which we—we as individual citizens—can and should do.

During Republican years, this again will be a nation of men and women, of families proud of their role, jealous of their responsibilities, unlimited in their aspirations—a nation where all who can will be self-reliant.

We Republicans see in our constitutional form of government the great framework which assures the orderly but dynamic fulfillment of the whole man, and we see the whole man as the great reason for instituting orderly government in the first place.

We can see in private property and in economy based upon and fostering private property the one way to make government a durable ally of the whole man rather than his determined enemy.

We see in the sanctity of private property the only durable foundation for constitutional government in a free society.

And beyond that we see and cherish diversity of ways, diversity of thoughts, of motives, and accomplishments. We don't seek to live anyone's life for him. We only seek to secure his rights, guarantee him opportunity, guarantee him opportunity to strive with government performing only those needed and constitutionally sanctioned tasks which cannot otherwise be performed.

We, Republicans, seek a government that attends to its inherent responsibilities of maintaining a stable monetary and fiscal climate, encouraging a free and a competitive economy and enforcing law and order.

Thus do we seek inventiveness, diversity and creative difference within a stable order, for we Republicans define governments role where needed at many, many levels, preferably though the one closest to the people involved: our towns and our cities, then our counties, then our states then our regional contacts and only then the national government.

That, let me remind you, is the land of liberty built by decentralized power. On it also we must have balance between the branches of government at every level.

Balance, diversity, creative difference—these are the elements of Republican equation. Republicans agree, Republicans agree heartily, to disagree on many, many of their applications. But we have never disagreed on the basic fundamental issues of why you and I are Republicans.

This is a party—this Republican party is a party for free men. Not for blind followers and not for conformists.

Back in 1858 Abraham Lincoln said this of the Republican party, and I quote him because he probably could have said it during the last week or so: "It was composed of strained, discordant, and even hostile elements." End of quote.

Yet all of these elements agreed on one paramount objective: to arrest the progress of slavery, and place it in the course of ultimate extinction.

Today, as then, but more urgently and more broadly than then, the task of preserving and enlarging freedom at home and of safeguarding it from the forces of tyranny abroad is great enough to challenge all our resources and to require all our strength.

Anyone who joins us in all sincerity we welcome. Those, those who do not care for our cause, we don't expect to enter our ranks in any case. And let our Republicanism so focused and so dedicated not be made fuzzy and futile by unthinking and stupid labels.

I would remind you that extremism in the defense of liberty is no vice.

And let me remind you also that moderation in the pursuit of justice is no virtue!

By the beauty of the very system we Republicans are pledged to restore and revitalize, the beauty of this Federal system of ours is in its reconciliation of diversity with unity. We must not see malice in honest differences of opinion, and no matter how great, so long as they are not inconsistent with the pledges we have given to each other in and through our Constitution.

Our Republican cause is not to level out the world or make its people conform in computer-regimented sameness. Our Republican cause is to free our people and light the way for liberty throughout the world. Ours is a very human cause for very humane goals. This party, its good people, and its unquestionable devotion to freedom will not fulfill the purposes of this campaign which we launch here now until our cause has won the day, inspired the world, and shown the way to a tomorrow worthy of all our yesteryears.

I repeat, I accept your nomination with humbleness, with pride and you and I are going to fight for the goodness of our land. Thank you.

19. The Great Society

LYNDON B. JOHNSON

Lyndon Johnson announced his Great Society program in a speech delivered at the University of Michigan in 1964. A man of large dreams and grandiose vision, Johnson promised to tackle the full range of social problems that American society faced in the mid-1960s: racial injustice, poverty, a decaying environment, and the need to improve the quality of life.

Here Johnson spoke of leading the nation's intelligentsia toward the formulation of social policies in the Great Society legislation of the mid and late 1960s. But the implementation of this far-reaching social program became tangled with the pursuit of victory in Vietnam. The outcome of these dreams has had a mixed reception. The Great Society was the major effort in the recent history of American reform; much of our opinion of the reform tradition in American politics will be based on our assessment of the programs that Lyndon Johnson created in a few frenetic years.

I have come today from the turmoil of your capital to the tranquility of your campus to speak about the future of your country.

The purpose of protecting the life of our nation and preserving the liberty of our citizens is to pursue the happiness of our people. Our success in that pursuit is the test of our success as a nation.

For a century we labored to settle and to subdue a continent. For half a century we called upon unbounded invention and untiring industry to create an order of plenty for all of our people.

The challenge of the next half century is whether we have the wisdom to use that wealth to enrich and elevate our national life, and to advance the quality of our American civilization.

Your imagination, your initiative, and your indignation will determine whether we build a society where progress is the servant of our needs, or a society where old values and new visions are buried under unbridled growth. For in your time we have the opportunity to move not only toward the rich society and the powerful society, but upward to the Great Society.

The Great Society rests on abundance and liberty for all. It demands an end to poverty and racial injustice, to which we are totally committed in our time. But that is just the beginning.

The Great Society is a place where every child can find knowledge to enrich his mind and to enlarge his talents. It is a place where leisure is a welcome chance to build and reflect, not a feared cause of boredom and restlessness. It is a place where the city of man serves not only the needs of the body and the demands of commerce but the desire for beauty and the hunger for community.

It is a place where man can renew contact with nature. It is a place which honors creation for its own sake and for what it adds to the understanding of the race. It is a place where men are more concerned with the quality of their goals than the quantity of their goods.

But most of all, the Great Society is not a safe harbor, a resting place, a final objective, a finished work. It is a challenge constantly renewed, beckoning us toward a destiny where the meaning of our lives matches the marvelous products of our labor.

So I want to talk to you today about three places where we begin to build the Great Society—in our cities, in our countryside, and in our classrooms.

Many of you will live to see the day perhaps fifty years from now, when there will be 400 million Americans—four-fifths of them in urban areas. In the remainder of this century urban population will double, city land will double, and we will have to build homes, highways, and facilities equal to all those built since this country was first settled. So in the next forty years we must rebuild the entire urban United States.

Aristotle said: "Men come together in cities in order to live, but they remain together in order to live the good life." It is harder and harder to live the good life in American cities today.

The catalogue of ills is long: there is the decay of the centers and the despoiling of the suburbs. There is not enough housing for our people or transportation for our traffic. Open land is vanishing and old landmarks are violated.

Worst of all expansion is eroding the precious and time-honored values of community with neighbors and communion with nature. The loss of these values breeds loneliness and boredom and indifference.

Our society will never be great until our cities are great. Today the frontier of imagination and innovation is inside those cities and not beyond their borders. . . .

A second place where we begin to build the Great Society is in our countryside. We have always prided ourselves on being not only America the strong and America the free, but America the beautiful. Today that beauty is in danger. The water we drink, the food we eat, the very air that we breathe, are threatened with pollution. Our parks are overcrowded, our seashores overburdened. Green fields and dense forests are disappearing.

A few years ago we were greatly concerned about the "Ugly American." Today we must act to prevent an ugly America.

For once the battle is lost, once our natural splendor is destroyed, it can never be recaptured. And once man can no longer walk with beauty or wonder at nature his spirit will wither and his sustenance be wasted.

A third place to build the Great Society is in the classrooms of America. There your children's lives will be shaped. Our society will not be great until every young mind is set free to scan the farthest reaches of thought and imagination. We are still far from that goal. . . .

Each year more than 100,000 high school graduates, with proved ability, do not enter college because they cannot afford it. And if we cannot educate today's youth, what will we do in 1970 when elementary school enrollment will be 5 million greater than 1960? And high school enrollment will rise by 5 million. College enrollment will increase by more than 3 million.

In many places, classrooms are overcrowded and curricula are out-dated. Most of our qualified teachers are underpaid, and many of our paid teachers are unqualified. So we must give every child a place to sit and a teacher to learn from. Poverty must not be a bar to learning, and learning must offer an escape from poverty.

But more classrooms and more teachers are not enough. We must seek an educational system which grows in excellence as it grows in size. This means better training for our teachers. It means preparing youth to enjoy their hours of leisure as well as their hours of labor. It means exploring new techniques of teaching, to find new ways to stimulate the love of learning and the capacity for creation.

These are three of the central issues of the Great Society. While our government has many programs directed at those issues, I do not pretend that we have the full answer to those problems....

But I do promise this: We are going to assemble the best thought and the broadest knowledge from all over the world to find those an-swers for America. I intend to establish working groups to prepare a series of White House conferences and meetings—on the cities, on natural beauty, on the quality of education, and on other emerging challenges. And from these meetings and from this inspiration and from these studies we will begin to set our course toward the Great Society.

The solution to these problems does not rest on a massive program in Washington, nor can it rely solely on the strained resources of local authority. They require us to create new concepts of cooperation, a creative federalism, between the national capital and the leaders of local communities.

Within your lifetime powerful forces, already loosed, will take us toward a way of life beyond the realm of our experience, almost beyond the bounds of our imagination.

For better or for worse, your generation has been appointed by history to deal with those problems and to lead America toward a new age. You have the chance never before afforded to any people in any age. You can help build a society where the demands of morality, and the needs of the spirit, can be realized in the life of the nation.

So, will you join in the battle to give every citizen the full equality which God enjoins and the law requires, whatever his belief, or race, or the color of his skin?

Will you join in the battle to give every citizen an escape from the crushing weight of poverty?

Will you join in the battle to make it possible for all nations to live in enduring peace—as neighbors and not as mortal enemies?

Will you join in the battle to build the Great Society, to prove that our material progress is only the foundation on which we will build a richer life of mind and spirit?

There are those timid souls who say this battle cannot be won; that we are condemned to a soulless wealth. I do not agree. We have the power to shape the civilization that we want. But we need your will, your labor, your hearts, if we are to build that kind of society.

Those who came to this land sought to build more than just a new country. They sought a new world. So I have come here today to your campus to say that you can make their vision our reality. So let us from this moment begin our work so that in the future men will look back and say: It was then, after a long and weary way, that man turned the exploits of his genius to the full enrichment of his life.

20. Lyndon Johnson Steps Aside

DORIS KEARNS

Lyndon Baines Johnson possessed a remarkable faith that America could accomplish almost anything. In his first three years as President, Johnson's domestic achievements seemed to justify that faith. Whipped and prodded by Johnson's pride, daring, and political skill, Congress passed more laws for civil rights, health, education, the arts, science, the eradication of poverty, and aid for the cities than in any other era in American history. Never popular among intellectuals, rejected by radicals and many liberals for his foreign policy and by conservatives for his domestic successes, he nevertheless deserved the tribute from the novelist Ralph Ellison that he would "have to settle for being recognized as the greatest American president for the poor and for the Negroes."

Yet by late 1967, Johnson's administration was a shambles and his credibility destroyed. The war in Vietnam had become immensely unpopular and the civil rights revolution had stirred demands beyond what society was willing to meet. Cities had been exploding in riots since 1964, and now college students and opponents of the war were joining in the disruption. Johnson became a virtual prisoner in the White House, fearing hostile crowds wherever he went. With the Tet Offensive in late January and February 1968, the progress of the war seemed more bleak than ever.

At the center of all these pressures was President Johnson. How could his pride, his daring, and his political skill serve him now? How could he escape humiliation and maintain what he considered a necessary course for his administration and the nation? Doris Kearns, Johnson's confidant during the last five years of his life, probes these questions in her look at his decision in March 1968 to withdraw from the presidential race.

All his life Johnson had believed that power was something you obtained if you had the energy and drive to work harder than everyone else. Power, in turn, made good works possible, and good works brought love and gratitude, which then provided the inspiration and vitality for further work. This formula informed Johnson's personal experience: time and again he had been able to parlay his limited resources into substantial political holdings, rising from Congressman to Senator to Majority Leader to Vice President and finally to President. But now, three years after his landslide victory, the American people had, Johnson believed, broken the cycle of power, energy, and good works by denying him the appreciation he deserved for all that he had produced. Indeed, by Johnson's assessment, his administration had produced more than any administration in history, and he could document his claim: he had given more laws, more houses, more medical services, more jobs to more people, than any other President. Surely, he had earned the love

love and gratitude of the American people. Yet as he looked around him in 1967 Johnson found only paralyzing bitterness. He could not comprehend the nature of the unrest or the cause of his unpopularity.

"How is it possible," Johnson repeatedly asked, "that all these people could be so ungrateful to me after I had given them so much? Take the Negroes. I fought for them from the first day I came into office. I spilled my guts out in getting the Civil Rights Act of 1964 through Congress. I put everything I had into that speech before the joint session in 1965. I tried to make it possible for every child of every color to grow up in a nice house, to eat a solid breakfast, to attend a decent school, and to get a good and lasting job. I asked so little in return. Just a little thanks. Just a little appreciation. That's all. But look at what I got instead. Riots in 175 cities. Looting. Burning. Shooting. It ruined everything. Then take the students. I wanted to help them, too. I fought on their behalf for scholarships and loans and grants. I fought for better teachers and better schools. And look what I got back. Young people by the thousands leaving their universities, marching in the streets, chanting that horrible song about how many kids I had killed that day. And the poor, they, too, turned against me. When Congress cut the funds for the Great Society, they made me Mr. Villain. I remember once going to visit a poor family in Appalachia. They had seven children, all skinny and sick. I promised the mother and father I would make things better for them. I told them all my hopes for their future. They seemed real happy to talk with me, and I felt good about that. But then as I walked toward the door, I noticed two pictures on the shabby wall. One was Jesus Christ on the cross; the other was John Kennedy. I felt as if I'd been slapped in the face."

So strong was Johnson's need for affection, and so vital his need for public gratitude, that he experienced this rejection of his "good works" as an absolute rejection of himself. Denied the appreciation which not only empowered but sustained his self, the love which validated his identity, the anatomy which gave Lyndon Johnson's ego its shape was dissolved. His energy and capacity to direct that energy outward abandoned him. Every presidential responsibility (speeches, conducting meetings, greeting visitors) took inordinate effort. The man who had battened on the goodwill of crowds, accelerating his pace in proportion to the crowd's number and affection, now could not leave the White House without being harassed by demonstrators and pickets. He had once liked to unwind with reporters, Congressmen, and staff, holding forth upon his strategy for the Great Society. But now Vietnam dominated his every word and a savage rain of vituperation fell upon his staff, the Congress, and reporters.

Now he began to marshal all his resources to fashion a defense, and the energies absorbed in this task of defending the self were no longer available for the everyday demands of leadership. Even at small group meetings Johnson now seemed unaware of what those present were thinking or even talking about. He gave the impression of not seeing his audience at all, having lost his sensitivity to the subtleties of tone and emphasis. This was not simply the passive inattention of a tired mind; it was the active inattention of a preoccupied mind, a mind whose focus was increasingly limited in mobility and scope.

Johnson had traversed 1965, 1966, and most of 1967 retreating into a dreamlike world in which the tide on both the war and the Great Society was just about to turn. By early 1968 this dream had died. Daily contact with the real world—with the evidence of a deepening inflation, with the results of the Tet offensive, and with the challenge of the primaries—was forcing Johnson back to reality. If the days of accomplishment were truly finished, as Johnson suspected, what then was the point? No good works, no love, no self-esteem. Only the endless repetition of sordid, unhappy days. Johnson's enthusiasm and vitality steadily receded. He was really tired, and he knew it.

Hating the days, Johnson hated the nights even more. He began dreaming again the dream of paralysis that had haunted him since early childhood. Only this time he was lying in a bed in the Red Room of the White House, instead of sitting in a chair in the middle of the open plains. His head was still his, but from the neck down his body was the thin, paralyzed body that had been the affliction of both Woodrow Wilson and his own grandmother in their final years. All his presidential assistants were in the next room. He could hear them actively fighting with one another to divide up his power: Joe Califano wanted the legislative program; Walt Rostow wanted the decisions on foreign policy; Arthur Okun wanted to formulate the budget; and George Christian wanted to handle relations with the public. He could hear them, but he could not command them, for he could neither talk nor walk. He was sick and stilled, but not a single aide tried to protect him.

The dream terrified Johnson, waking from his sleep. Lying in the dark, he could find no peace until he got out of bed, and, by the light of a small flashlight, walked the halls of the White House to the place where Woodrow Wilson's portrait hung. He found something soothing in the act of touching Wilson's picture; he could sleep again. He was still Lyndon Johnson, and he was still alive and moving; it was Woodrow Wilson who was dead. This ritual, however, brought little lasting peace; when morning came, Johnson's mind was again filled with fears. Only gradually did he recognize the resemblance between this dream and the stampede dream of his boyhood. Making the connection, his fears intensified; he was certain now that paralysis was his inevitable fate. Remembering his family's history of early strokes, he convinced himself that he, too, would suffer a stroke in his next term. Immobilized, still in office nominally, yet not actually in control: this seemed to Johnson the worst situation imaginable. He could not rid himself of the suspicion that a mean God had set out to torture him in the cruelest manner possible. His suffering now no longer consisted of his usual melancholy; it was an acute throbbing pain, and he craved relief. More than anything he wanted peace and quiet. An end to the pain.

Through the fall and winter of 1967, Johnson later reported, the decision to withdraw from politics took hold. He discussed it, he wrote in a section of his memoirs that reads as if it were a defense attorney's brief, with a number of people, among them John Connally, George Christian, General Westmoreland, William S. White, Horace Busby, and, of course, Lady Bird. He claimed he had considered announcing it at the end of the State of the Union message in early January, 1968; he had asked Horace Busby to write a draft statement. But when he got to the Capitol that night—and his explanation is not entirely convincing from this man of meticulous detail—he reached into his pocket and discovered that he had forgotten to bring it with him. The announcement was not made. Then between the end of January and the middle of March came the Tet offensive, McCarthy's victory, the collapse of the gold market, the publication of the Riot Commission Report, and, most importantly, Robert Kennedy's entrance into the presidential race.

"I felt," Johnson said, "that I was being chased on all sides by a giant stampede coming at me from all directions. On one side, the American people were stampeding me to do something about Vietnam. On another side, the inflationary economy was booming out of control. Up ahead were dozens of danger signs pointing to another summer of riots in the cities. I was being forced over the edge by rioting blacks, demonstrating students, marching welfare mothers, squawking professors, and hysterical reporters. And then the final straw. The thing I feared from the first day of my Presidency was actually coming true. Robert Kennedy had openly announced his intention to reclaim the throne in the memory of his brother. And the American people, swayed by the magic of the name, were dancing in the streets. The whole situation was unbearable for me. After thirty-seven years of public service, I deserved something more than being left alone in the middle of the plain, chased by stampedes on every side."

All his life Johnson had held before himself the image of the daring cowboy, the man with the capacity to outrun the wild herd, riding at a dead run in the dark of the night, knowing there were prairie dog holes all around. It was this definition of manly courage, opposed to what he saw as a feminine tendency to run away from responsibility, that had deterred Johnson in August, 1964, from abandoning the Presidency— and at that point the only stampede he faced was his own fear that the memorial film of John F. Kennedy would provoke a rush of delegates to Robert F. Kennedy. How much more difficult it would be for him now—when the stampede had already started—to justify his running away!

So Johnson found himself in an untenable position in early 1968. It was impossible to quit and impossible to stay. If he left office and went back to Texas, he would be acting like a coward; if he stayed for another four years, he would be paralyzed before his term was out. For months his position was all the more untenable because he did not know that it was untenable. He was in the grip of that supreme despair which, as Kierkegaard says, is not to know one is in despair. No matter how hard he tried to think it out, he got nowhere. One line of action was as bad as the other. No matter how hectic his activity, he could not drive the demons away. But then, Johnson explained, one day—exactly what day is not clear—he realized the total impossibility of his situation. The realization came to him in a dream. In the dream he saw himself swimming in a river. He was swimming from the center toward one shore. He swam and swam, but he never seemed to get any closer. He turned around to swim to the other shore, but again he got nowhere. He was simply going round and round in circles. The dream reminded

Johnson of his grandfather's story about driving the cattle across the river, where they, too, got caught in a whirl, circling round and round in the same spot.

Aware now of the bind he was in, Johnson finally found a way to extricate himself. He ingeniously reasoned that he could withdraw from politics without being seen as a coward. To follow his reasoning, we must understand the intensity of his concern for the verdict of history. The desire to leave something permanent behind as evidence of the work of a lifetime had been with him from the days of his youth, but never had it been so preoccupying a force as it was in the spring of 1968. At a time when the present was filled with unhappiness, Johnson turned to the future for uplift. Widen the constituency, flee once again from the pain of intimacy, multiply your resources. Looking ahead to posterity, Johnson began thinking that his current difficulties might prove to be a blessing in disguise. There was still the opportunity to restore his reputation if he acted nobly at this critical moment. "If the American people don't love me, their descendants will."

Eyes fixed on the future, Johnson believed he would be judged by history for his success or failure in fulfilling three presidential functions: providing domestic peace and tranquility, providing for the national security, and providing for the general welfare. In each area, he saw a conflict between his role as President of all the people and his role as candidate of the Democratic Party. In each area, he reasoned, he would be more likely to reach his goals if he was not a candidate, but a chief of state above the partisan battle.

First, on questions of national security: Critics argued that Johnson's decision to halt the bombing north of the 20th parallel reflected a substantial change in policy shaped by the combination of the Tet offensive, the New Hampshire primary, his meeting with the "Wise Old Men"—George Ball, General Omar Bradley, Mac Bundy, Arthur Dean, Douglas Dillon, Abe Fortas, Robert Murphy, General Matthew Ridgway, and Cy Vance—and the appointment of Clark Clifford as Secretary of Defense. The critics were right in suggesting that Johnson was affected by these events, but they had not quite put their finger on the reason why. Johnson himself admitted that *Tet* had been a psychological victory for the North Vietnamese. He also admitted that his talks with Clifford and his meeting with his outside advisers reinforced his belief that many of his own people, not to speak of the public at large, did not understand the "real" situation in Vietnam. Clifford's growing doubts undoubtedly posed a special problem for Johnson. When McNamara changed his mind on the war, his shift could be written off for many different reasons—his "idealism," his distaste for blood, his friendship with Robert Kennedy. But none of these motives could explain Clifford's shift. He was neither a dissenter nor a turncoat, but an emissary from the corporate world, a world of men apart from the personal and political motives which Johnson believed characterized most of the dissent, where the only standards of judgment were interest, utility, and power. "Now, I make it a practice to keep in touch with friends in business and the law across the land," Clifford explained at a meeting in late March, 1968. "I ask them their views about various matters. Until a few months ago, they were generally supportive of the war.... Now all that has changed. There has been a tremendous erosion of support among these men...these men now feel that we are in a hopeless bog. The idea of going deeper into the bog strikes them as mad. They want to see us get out of it. These are leaders of opinion in their communities. What they believe is sooner or later believed by many other people. It would be very difficult—I believe it would be impossible—for the President to maintain public support for the war without the support of these men.

Then Johnson knew. The herald had finally arrived to report that the walls were crumbling. Johnson was losing the support of the barons, and with it, his ability to lead. So he would change his tactics, but not his objectives and never his convictions. For this man, a master of compromising other men's views, could not compromise his own, his record before his only remaining constituency, the judgment of history. The bombing halt would defuse the internal debate in the administration and particularly with his circle of officials and advisers. The compromise at the 20th parallel would—and did—have the effect of buying further time in the pursuit of military victory. It would—and did—afford Johnson the opportunity to initiate a policy of Vietnamization.

One might ask, then, what about all the military arguments that had repeatedly been made against curtailing or halting the bombing? Several new factors served to relieve Johnson of much of the pressure previously exerted by the military, as well as to neutralize the doubts in his own mind. First, Johnson had by 1968 let the military bomb almost everything they had previously complained they were not allowed to; the list of restricted targets had become very small indeed. By 1968 the only remaining options—closing Haiphong, bombing the agricultural dikes—carried in Johnson's mind much too high a risk of Chinese intervention. Not only had most other targets been bombed—over and over—but doing so had not reduced the size of the war in the South nor improved our bargaining position with the North Vietnamese. Second, if the United States was in fact doing as well as Westmoreland claimed, then the curtailment of the bombing could proceed as it had always been meant someday to proceed—from a position of strength, not weakness. Finally, the alleged military risk of a bombing halt could be lessened further by the judicious employment of bombing missions below the 20th parallel.

So it was that, in finally offering an end to the air war against the North, Johnson was not forced to see himself as a coward, running away from Vietnam. To the contrary, he convinced himself that he was the same man of courage, determined to save South Vietnam, daring a new initiative in a continuing course. Moreover, by coupling this initiative with withdrawal from the presidential race, he made sure that it would not be read as a political trick. If, on the other hand, it failed to produce negotiations, then at least Johnson had laid the groundwork for further escalation. If the situation in South Vietnam was as good as the military claimed, then it was just possible that Hanoi would finally come to the peace table. And if that happened, then Johnson believed that he would be honored by history for having mapped out a policy in Southeast Asia that had ensured America's national security for years to come.

If concern for the future affected Johnson's decisions about "national security," it also affected his thinking about "the general welfare." By the spring of 1968 the tax surcharge had become the most pressing domestic issue. Without the surtax the American economy was in danger and Johnson knew it. And the situation at home was substantially exacerbated by deepening financial problems abroad. British devaluation of the pound in late 1967 had triggered a general deterioration in the gold market and a crisis of confidence in the dollar. By the middle of March the gold market was in a state of panic. Speculation was rampant that the United States, too, might be forced to devalue.

Johnson saw the deepest fears of his generation reflected in this situation. He believed that the stalemate on taxes was being interpreted abroad as a failure of the democratic process and a clear indication that America had neither the will nor the ability to control its economic affairs. The specter of 1929 haunted him daily; he worried that if the economy collapsed, history would subject Lyndon Johnson to endless abuse. Yet as long as he was a candidate, Johnson was convinced, the Republicans in Congress would stall the surtax, so they could campaign in the fall against "Johnson's inflation" as well as "Johnson's war." Therefore, in this case, too, withdrawing from the race was the only answer. Here, too, posterity would see his abdication as an act of courage, not cowardice.

Withdrawing would also strengthen the President in his search for domestic peace. Johnson looked back to the previous summer and recalled the accusation that he had chosen a partisan course during the Detroit riots. If he reacted strongly to civil disorders, he would be accused of currying favor on the right; if he reacted temperately, he would be vulnerable to the opposite charge. Either charge might reduce his reputation in the annals of history. Johnson wanted to be remembered as the preserver of domestic peace, a man who had enforced the law with equity and fairness to all. But here, too, as with Vietnam and the tax bill, the favorable judgment of history could be better secured only by withdrawing from politics.

Abdication was thus the last remaining way to restore control, to turn rout into dignity, collapse into order. It served to advance Johnson's immediate purposes and his long-term goals. As the situation stood, Johnson was about to lose the Wisconsin primary and the forecasts looked equally dim for the primaries in Oregon, Indiana, and California. To win the nomination under these circumstances would have been—though possible—a Pyrrhic victory. It would have torn the nation apart. Johnson recognized this. His concerns for the present and the future, for national unity and posterity, for the war and the economy, joined together. He decided to retreat with honor.

Having made his decision in private, Johnson now made plans to share it with his countrymen on March 31, 1968. He addressed a nationwide TV audience that night from the White House. He began unceremoniously by reviewing his administration's efforts to find a basis for constructive peace talks. He then moved directly to his proposal for a bombing halt: "I am taking the first step to de-escalate the conflict. Tonight I have ordered our aircraft and our naval vessels to make no attacks on North Vietnam, except in the area of the Demilitarized Zone." This meant, he said, stopping the bombing in areas inhabited by "almost 90%" of North Vietnam's population. "I call upon President Ho Chi Minh to respond positively and favorably to this new step of peace."

He spoke gravely, gently; gone was the undertone of sarcasm, and the appearance of piety. He finished the section on Vietnam in thirty minutes. Then the moment came which would startle the nation. Even those who had read the phrases of abdication could not be certain he would read them, nor could Johnson himself—he had, after all, written out other withdrawals only to pull them back—until the irretrievable words rolled up on the Teleprompter: he glanced at Lady Bird and he hesitated for an inexpressible moment, which must have compressed the stormy inward clashes of a lifetime, then continued because the words were there, right in front of him, and the only way he could master his contradictions—the only way he ever knew—was to move ahead:

"This country's ultimate strength lies in the unity of our people. There is division in the American house now. There is divisiveness among us all tonight. And holding the trust that is mine, as President of all the people, I cannot disregard the peril to the progress of the American people and the hope and prospect of peace for all people.... With America's sons in the fields far away, with America's future under challenge right here at home ... I do not believe that I should devote an hour or a day of my time to any personal partisan causes.... Accordingly, I shall not seek, and will not accept, the nomination of my party for another term as your President."

There was a mood of euphoria in the capital the next day. Even Johnson seemed pleased. What huge tensions must have been released. A few days later, Hanoi agreed to negotiate in Paris. To many, it seemed that the road to peace might now be open. The polls showed a sharp increase in Johnson's popularity. And the President, who, a short time before, could speak publicly only at military installations, was once again cheered in the streets of Chicago.

Johnson began to speak excitedly of his plans for the Lyndon B. Johnson Library and the Lyndon B. Johnson School of Public Affairs, and the writing of his memoirs. He set up a schedule of seminars and lectures for the following years and took pleasure in the large numbers of schools which were asking him to speak: Yale, and even Harvard.

In May, he returned, solaced and refreshed, from a visit with Harry Truman, one of the two living members of that exclusive group to which he would soon belong. "You know the great thing about Truman," he told me, "is that once he makes up his mind about something—anything, including the A bomb—he never looks back and asks, 'Should I have done it? Oh! Should I have done it?' No, he just knows he made up his mind as best he could and that's that. There's no going back. I wish I had some of that quality, for there's nothing worse than going back over a decision made, retracing the steps that led to it, and imagining what it'd be like if you took another turn. It can drive you crazy.

"Truman was one of the few comforts I had all during the war," Johnson continued. "Reminded me of all the hell he'd been through, but somehow he managed to ride it out. Ike was helpful, too. Once I complained to him about the trouble Fulbright and friends were making for me. He told me, 'Why, I'd just go ahead and smack them, just pay no attention to these overeducated Senators, that's all there is to it.' Another time, when Fulbright was busy talking things over with his Russian friends, I said to Truman, 'Imagine him not wanting the Russians to stop and wanting us to stop." Truman interrupted me: 'But you are the President. You make the policy, not him.'"

In June, Robert Kennedy was shot. Afterward, Johnson said little; but some time later, reflectively, and with some bitterness: "It would have been hard on me to watch Bobby march to 'Hail to the Chief,' but I almost wish he had become President so the country could finally see a flesh-and-blood Kennedy grappling with the daily work of the Presidency and all the inevitable disappointments, instead of their storybook image of great heroes who, because they were dead, could make anything anyone wanted happen." Later in June, he signed the Omnibus Crime Act. "I don't want to do it, but I have no choice. Nixon has forced me into it by all the election bullshit blaming the Democrats for crime in the streets. That label will be disastrous in November."

After Kennedy was killed, as the summer wore on his mood changed; he became withdrawn, canceled previous plans for new, bold domestic proposals—including a plan for income maintenance that he had already approved. "Better not propose anything radical now because the Republicans will defeat it with an election coming up, and it will have less chance of passing later." So he would simply put the idea into a speech. Then he decided to wait for his last State of the Union, only to strike even the mention of such a program because "it will hurt its chances of ever being passed if it's connected to me." In Vietnam, there was no change: a continuing stalemate on the battlefield and at the peace table. His feared rival, Robert Kennedy, was dead, while his chosen successor, Hubert Humphrey, was doing badly in appearances around the country and in polls, which showed him running well behind McCarthy—whose nomination would be unacceptable to the convention—and even Nixon.

"Senator Eastland was in to see me the other day," he said one evening in late July, "and he wants me to run. In fact, a lot of them have been in. Eastland says Hubert hasn't caught on. I'm the only one who can hold the South. I don't agree, but he is organizing something for me. And he says he is happy with Medicare. Can you imagine that? He also told me that Fortas will come out of committee in mid-November though Dirksen will leave us. He says that one thousand delegates can be delivered to Humphrey, but he's losing them. And he's afraid the convention will be a holocaust, with McCarthy walking out."

Perhaps Eastland had said all this, but James Eastland of Mississippi had never before shown much knowledge or interest in national politics; and even at the time I suspected that I was hearing, attributed to Eastland, Johnson's own, not completely inaccurate, but wholly wishful, analysis. Humphrey did appear to be a weak candidate, and McCarthy was an impossibility. Much of Humphrey's strength had been assembled and delivered by Johnson in the drive to halt Kennedy. Under such circumstances, it was natural to think that anything might happen, or might be made to happen. It was all illusion, of course. Johnson's candidacy would have caused an explosion, fragmenting, perhaps irrevocably, the Democratic Party. It might have been possible had he never withdrawn, but now Convention Hall would be crowded with delegates originally selected to support Kennedy and McCarthy, along with many Humphrey delegates who opposed Johnson and the war.

His increasing irritation was accompanied by a sharp renewal of interest in the military situation in Vietnam. He stepped up his consultations with the military. I thought from what he said—just hints, but ominous hints—that he might be planning a major escalation, hoping for a military victory that would transform the political scene. Secretary of Defense Clark Clifford, and others in the administration, shared this apprehension.

There is little doubt that, as the convention neared, Johnson began to feel that his withdrawal might not be irrevocable, that he might find vindication more real and immediate than the verdict of history—in the vote of the Democratic Party and American people. "Nixon can be beaten," he said over and over again. "He's like a Spanish horse who runs faster than anyone for the first nine lengths and then turns around and runs backward. You'll see," he predicted, "he'll do something wrong in the end. He always does." Indeed, Nixon lost several million votes in the closing weeks of the 1968 campaign, transforming a landslide into a squeaker. But not until he had become President was he to confirm that even a diminished Johnson was unequaled in his capacity to sense the weaknesses and potentialities of other men.

Johnson's increasingly irascible and frenetic manner cannot be attributed solely to resurgent hope; it was also a return of anguishing internal pressures, momentarily released by his withdrawal, and masked by the consequent public acclamation. He was beginning to go through it all, all over again. And, finally, with the same paralyzing result. There was no mobilization of support for the nomination, no stirring new proposals to memorialize his dedication to the Great Society. And what was to have been his final memorable act, a summit meeting with Kosygin to lay the groundwork for a new détente, was canceled when Soviet forces invaded Czechoslovakia. Nor was he able to bring peace in Vietnam; despite the bombing halt announced on October 31, the stalemate on the war continued.

21. The War on Poverty

CHARLES MURRAY

The social policies of Lyndon B. Johnson's Great Society program, particularly the programs identified with the war on poverty, have been the subject of vast intellectual and political controversy. On the one hand, critics like Charles Murray can demonstrate with clear evidence that a large number of programs that have not been helpful. On the other hand, supporters of social intervention like Lisbeth B. Schorr, in her 1988 volume Within Our Reach, *can interpret this history of policy and evaluation differently. Murray argues that the reforms neither helped nor were cost-effective. Schorr argues that social policy is an arena of experimentation and that evaluation over a period of years has enabled practitioners to discover which programs succeed in improving the health and welfare of children, reducing teenage pregnancy and dropout rates, and a host of other social problems.*

Who is correct? Essentially the question cannot be answered because observers measure social costs and benefits differently. The issue becomes a question of what we want, of political will.

The planners of the Great Society thought that the eradication of poverty could come quickly and even relatively cheaply. As Murray demonstrates, they were wrong. But a quarter-century of careful evaluation of social programs, as well as comparisons with the experience of other countries, makes equally clear that if American society decides to pay the price, it can make considerable improvements in addressing the poverty, failure, bad health, and "rotten outcomes" that are the experiences of tens of millions. These issues have never been absent from twentieth-century American political debate; nor will they vanish as the nation moves into the twenty-first century.

...We return to the fall of 1964, when the first antipoverty bill had just been passed and the Office of Economic Opportunity (OEO) was being organized. Our focus shifts from the academicians, the journalists, the cabinet officers and congressional leaders to the people who did the work—the middle- and lower-echelon officials who designed and implemented the programs that constituted the War on Poverty.

They were an assortment of New Frontiersmen (Sargent Shriver at OEO being the most conspicuous example) and people who came into the bureaucracy especially to play a role in the great social reform that Johnson had launched. Few were bureaucrats, few were from the social-work tradition. They tended to see themselves as pragmatic idealists. "Hardnosed" was a favorite self-description in the Kennedy years, and it carried over. The first poverty warriors did not intend to get bogged down in interminable debates about doctrine. They had a job to do and, from the accounts of people who participated in those early years of the Great Society, it was an exciting job. The recountings have the flavor of war stories—of all-night sessions preparing for crucial Senate hearings; of small, sweaty working groups designing new programs on impossibly short schedules; of meetings in Newark or Chicago or Biloxi where the people across the table were not mayors and city planners, but the heads of tenants' associations and ghetto churches and street gangs. Speaking of his staff, the director of one of the early programs wrote:

All were the antithesis of the stereotyped bureaucrat cautiously protecting his career. Their approach right down the line was: "What needs to be done? How can we do it best, and faster?" When the answers were clear, they were all willing to risk their careers and their health and sacrifice their personal lives, to get the job done well and quickly. Something happened to us all...that created a rare combination of shared dedication, excitement, and satisfaction.

Such people characterized the early years both in Washington and in the field offices. They had no serious doubts that they would have an impact on the poverty problem. It seemed obvious to them (as it did to many observers at the time) that the only reason we continued to have poverty at a time of such manifest national affluence was that nobody had really been trying to get rid of it. Once the effort was made, so their assumption went, progress would surely follow.

Their optimism had two bases. One was that the programs depended on human responses that seemed natural and indeed nearly automatic to them. The gloomy implications of the "culture of poverty" argument did not carry much weight at OEO in 1964 and 1965. A sensible, hard-working poor person would find much to work with in the opportunities offered by the initial antipoverty programs. Or to put it another way, if the people who ran the programs had suddenly found themselves poor, they probably would have been quite successful in using the antipoverty programs to rescue themselves. The early programs put chips on the table; as their advocates had promised, they did indeed give some of the poor a chance at a piece of the action, with the operative word being "chance." The staff at OEO and its companion agencies scattered around Washington did not think that the loan programs or the community development programs would transform the ghetto instantaneously, but they had no doubt that such programs would be individually successful—steps in the right direction.

In the case of the training programs such as the Job Corps, success seemed to be still more natural. The logistics of providing training were straightforward. The educational technology was adequate and in place. There were plenty of welfare recipients who said they wanted jobs and who acted as though they wanted jobs. During the 1960s, and especially after the Vietnam War heated up, jobs were available for people with the kinds of skills that could be acquired in the training programs. The training programs would work, without question. What was to stop them?

It would be important to document the successes that were about to emerge. In the spirit of cost-effectiveness that McNamara had taken to the Pentagon, the early poverty warriors were prepared to be judged on the hardest of hardnosed measures of success. The programs would be removing enough people from the welfare rolls, from drug addiction, and from crime to provide an economically attractive return on the investment.

But how was this information to be obtained? Social scientists who had been at the periphery of the policy process—sociologists, psychologists, political scientists—had the answer: scientific evaluation. The merits of doing good would no longer have to rest on faith. We would be able to *prove* that we had done good, as objectively as a scientist proves an hypothesis.

In the space of a few years, applied social science and especially program evaluation became big business. In Eisenhower's last year in office, 1960, the Department of Health, Education, and Welfare (HEW) spent $46 million on research and development other than health research. It took three more years for the budget to reach $90 million, followed by sizable jumps in 1964 and 1965. Then, in a single year, 1966, the budget doubled from $154 million to $313 million. Similar patterns prevailed at the other departments, agencies, institutes, and bureaus engaged in the antipoverty struggle.

The product of all this activity and money was a literature describing what was being accomplished by the antipoverty programs. It is what scholars call a "fugitive" literature, with most reports being printed in editions of a few dozen photocopies submitted to the government sponsor. The release of a major evaluation might get a column or two on a back page of a few of the largest newspapers. But otherwise, the work of the evaluators went unread by the outside world.

Within those governmental circles where the reports *were* read, they led to a rapid loss of innocence about what could be expected from the efforts to help people escape from welfare dependency. Starting with the first evaluation reports in the mid-sixties and continuing to the present day, the results of these programs have been disappointing to their advocates and evidence of failure to their critics.

The War on Poverty had originally struck on two fronts: For depressed neighborhoods and entire communities, "community action" programs were funded in profusion, to further all sorts of objectives; for individuals, manpower programs provided training or job opportunities. We shall be discussing the substance of what the evaluators found, not only in 1964–67 but subsequently, when we examine explanations for the breakdown in progress. For now, a few examples will convey the tenor of the findings.

THE COMMUNITY ACTION PROGRAMS

The community action programs fared worst. A number of histories and case studies are available to the public at large, Moynihan's *Maximum Feasible Misunderstanding* being the best known. With the advantage of hindsight, it is not surprising that the community development programs so seldom got off the ground. Faith in spontaneity and in *ad hoc*

administrative arrangements were traits of the sixties that met disillusionment in many fields besides the antipoverty programs. Surprising
or not, the record they compiled was dismal. For every evaluation report that could document a success, there was a stack that told of local
groups that were propped up by federal money for the duration of the
grant, then disappeared, with nothing left behind.

Each project had its own tale to tell about why it failed—an ambitious city councilman who tried to horn in, a balky banker who reneged
on a tentative agreement, and so on. There were always villains and
heroes, dragons and maidens. But failure was very nearly universal.

The course of the projects followed a pattern. To see how this
worked in practice, we have the example of the Economic Development Administration's major employment and urban development program in Oakland, the subject of a scholarly case study. This was the
sequence:

The story broke with considerable fanfare. *The Wall Street Journal* of 25 April 1966 had it on page one, under the headline "UR-
BAN AID KICKOFF: ADMINISTRATION SELECTS OAKLAND AS
FIRST CITY IN REBUILDING PROGRAM." The governor of California and the assistant secretary of commerce for economic development
held a press conference announcing a program of $23 million in federal
grants and loans. The program was an assortment of community-run
economic development projects bankrolled by the government. Various
incentives were designed to prompt private business to invest in the
ghetto. In the short term, 2,200 jobs were to be provided, and more
were to follow from "spinoffs." These jobs would go to the unemployed
residents of the inner city.

As far as its national publicity told the story, the program was a
great success. A book (*Oakland's Not for Burning*) was in the bookstores
by 1968, claiming that the program "may have made the difference"
in preventing a riot in Oakland. *The New Yorker* told its readers that
the program had "managed to break a longtime deadlock between the
Oakland ghetto and the local business and government Establishment."
Oakland was a showcase of the War on Poverty.

It was not until a year after these stories had appeared that the *Los
Angeles Times* printed a follow-up story revealing that the activities described in the book and in *The New Yorker* had in actuality never gotten
beyond the planning stage. All told, only twenty jobs had been created.
The program was bogged down in bureaucratic infighting. The authors
of the case study, writing from the perspective of four years later, concluded that the effect of the project on "despair and disillusionment"
among blacks was probably to have made matters worse.

The Oakland project was not chosen for study as an example of
failure; the study began while hopes were still high. The Oakland experience was representative, not exceptional, and the gradual realization
of this by those connected with the poverty programs was one source
of their dampened hopes for the "hand, not a handout" approach. Few
of them reacted by giving up; through the rest of the 1960s and well
into the 1970s, it was argued that the community action programs were

slowly learning from their failures and would do better next time. But if their proponents did not give up, neither did they speak so boldly about the imminent end of the dole.

THE TRAINING PROGRAMS

The failure of the training programs was a greater surprise still. These of all programs were expected to be a sure bet. They dealt with individuals, not institutions, and teaching a person who wants to learn is something we know how to do. But starting with the first evaluation reports in the mid-sixties and continuing to the present day, the results failed to show the hoped-for results, or anything close to them. The programs were seldom disasters; they simply failed to help many people get and hold jobs that they would not have gotten and held anyway.

As with the community development programs, the findings varied in detail but not in pattern. In one of the most recent and technically precise studies of the Manpower Development and Training Act (MDTA), the linchpin of Kennedy's original program and one that eventually grew to a multibillion dollar effort, the final conclusion is that male trainees increased their earnings between $150 and $500 *per year* immediately after training, "declining to perhaps half this figure after five years." For the females, the study found a continuing effect of $300 to $600 per year. A panel study of the effects of vocational training found a wage increase of 1.5 percent that could be attributed to the training. The early studies of Job Corps trainees found effects of under $200 per year, and these early findings have been repeated in subsequent work. Effects of this magnitude were far from the results that had been anticipated when the programs began.

Even as the program designers and evaluators debated what to do next and how to do it better, they could not avoid recognizing some discomfiting realities. It was quickly learned that people on welfare do not necessarily enroll in job training programs once they become available. Those who enroll do not necessarily stick it through to the end of the program. Those who stick it through do not necessarily get jobs. And, of those who find jobs, many quickly lose them. Sometimes they lose them because of their lack of seniority when layoffs occur. Sometimes they lose them because of discrimination. Sometimes they lose them because they fail to show up for work or don't work very hard when they do show up. And—more often than anyone wanted to admit—people just quit, disappearing from the evaluator's scorecard.

Unable to point to large numbers of trainees who were escaping from welfare dependency, the sponsors of the training programs turned to other grounds for their justification. They found two. First, a cost-effectiveness case could be wrenched even from small increments in income. If the average trainee's earnings increase even by a few hundred dollars, sooner or later the increase will add up to more than the cost of the training, and it was this type of calculation to which the sponsors were reduced. "The average effect [on earnings] for all enrollees is quite large," we find in one evaluation of Job Corps, then read on to the next sentence, where it is revealed that the "quite large" effect amounted to $3.30 per week. It was a statistically significant gain.

Second, the training programs lent themselves to upbeat anecdotes about individual success stories: John Jones, an ex-con who had never held a job in his life, became employed because of program X and is saving money to send his child to college. Such anecdotes, filmed for the evening news, were much more interesting than economic analyses. They also were useful in hearings before congressional appropriations committees. Tacit or explicit, a generalization went with the anecdote: John Jones's story is typical of what this project is accomplishing or will accomplish for a large number of people. That such success stories were extremely rare, and that depressingly often John Jones would be out of his job and back in jail a few months after his moment in the spotlight—these facts were not commonly publicized. The anecdotes made good copy. Thus the training programs continued to get a good press throughout the 1970s. They were the archetypal "hand, not a handout" programs, and they retained much of the intellectual and emotional appeal that had made them popular in the early 1960s. To some extent, whether they worked or not was irrelevant.

We have been scanning a record that has accumulated over the years since the first antipoverty projects in the early 1960s. But the loss of innocence came early. It soon became clear that large numbers of the American poor were not going to be moved off the welfare rolls by urban development schemes or by training programs.

At another time, that might have been the end of the attempt. Or, at another time, perhaps we would have done a better job of learning from our mistakes and have developed less ambitious, more effective programs. But the demands for urban renewal programs and jobs programs and training programs were growing, not diminishing, as the disappointing results began to come in. We were not in a position to back off, and, in fact, funding for such programs continued to grow for years. Neither, however, could we depend on such programs to solve the poverty problem.

The forces converged—not neatly, not at any one point that we can identify as the crucial shift. But the intellectual analysis of the nature of structural poverty had given a respectable rationale for accepting that it was not the fault of the poor that they were poor. It was a very small step from that premise to the conclusion that it is not the fault of the poor that they fail to pull themselves up when we offer them a helping hand. White moral confusion about the course of the civil rights movement in general and the riots in particular created powerful reasons to look for excuses. It was the system's fault. It was history's fault. Tom Wicker summed up the implications for policy toward the poor:

Really compassionate and effective reforms to do something about poverty in America would have to recognize, first, that large numbers of the poor are always going to have to be helped. Whether for physical or mental reasons, because of environmental factors, or whatever, they cannot keep pace.... Thus the aim of getting everyone off welfare and into "participation in our affluent society" is unreal and a pipe dream.... [A] decent standard of living ought to be made available not just to an eligible few but to everyone, and without degrading restrictions and policelike investigations.

The column ran on the day before Christmas, 1967. It followed by only a few months an announcement from the White House. Joseph Califano, principal aide to Lyndon Johnson, had called reporters into his office to tell them that a government analysis had shown that only 50,000 persons, or *1 percent* of the 7,300,000 people on welfare, were capable of being given skills and training to make self-sufficient. The repudiation of the dream—to end the dole once and for all—was complete.

PART FOUR

1968–1980

The new Nixon bureaucrats were another group of hard young men—now growing old—who had been touched by the experience of World War II and the political realignment of Europe that followed it. The nation was now ruled by a man long familiar to the electorate as an anti-communist crusader in Congress during the late 1940s, and as Eisenhower's Vice-President in the 1950s. When Nixon became President in 1969, the war in Vietnam, already the longest in the history of the United States, was still dragging on. As Eisenhower had done in the 1950s, Nixon eventually settled a war he had not started.

247

But the subdued mood that came with the winding down of the war after 1970 did not last long. The story that set the political tone of the second Nixon administration was hardly front page news when it first appeared. The report on June 18, 1972, that five men had been arrested in the headquarters of the Democratic National Committee in the Watergate complex, appeared on page 30 of the *New York Times*. Readers that day, unaware of the future significance of this apparently trivial item, would have had reason for optimism about much of national life. The Vietnam War seemed to be winding down, relations with the Soviet Union were improving, and the Nixon administration seemed headed for another four years, promising economic and diplomatic progress an a further healing of the political wounds of the sixties.

Instead, a new period of political excitement and constitutional crisis developed. Even before the end of the war, the economy, buffeted by major shifts in world economic relations, entered severe recession. The crisis of confidence and legitimacy continued to scar the entire decade of the 1970s.

By August 1974, Nixon had resigned in disgrace. He was replaced by Gerald Ford, whom Nixon had appointed Vice-President to fill the unexpired term of Spiro Agnew, who had resigned in response to scandals reaching back to his days as governor of Maryland. The nation's economy was in disarray, and South Vietnam was on the verge of falling to the Communists. The nation was also glimpsing the dark side of its technological prowess: ecological time bombs in our chemical dumps and nuclear plants as well as in our streams, lakes, and oceans. Many of the bright hopes of the 1960s appeared to have died. The civil rights movement was in eclipse, the young were quiet, and the welfare state had come under renewed attack. Only the women's movement, which had arisen in the sixties, demonstrated some expanding vitality.

In 1977 the new Democratic administration led by Jimmy Carter seemed set to lead the nation into a post-Watergate era. Carter was a Southerner, a former governor of Georgia, a successful businessman, an outsider to the Washington establishment, and a born-again Christian. He tempered the goals of the New Deal with an innate conservatism that seemed to reflect the mood of the decade. But his promise was never fulfilled. Foreign crises and domestic economic problems doomed the Carter administration. In 1980 the American people overwhelmingly rejected Carter and replaced him with Ronald Reagan, a mellow reactionary who seemed to harken back to old virtues and a more ebullient view of American destiny.

22. The Tet Offensive and a Double Reality

JAMES WILLIAM GIBSON

President Lyndon Johnson believed that a calculated, steady increase in force would convince his opponents in Vietnam that they could not win the war. Sustained bombing of North Vietnam began in March 1965. Johnson also sent hundreds of thousands of combat troops into South Vietnam to aid Vietnamese units threatened by Communist Vietcong attack. Finally, Johnson authorized independent action by American soldiers; the first "search and destroy mission" involving large numbers of American troops took place several miles northwest of the capital of Saigon in late June 1965. After that time, whenever Washington deployed more soldiers, so too did Saigon's opponent.

In his book published in 1986, The Perfect War: Technowar in Vietnam, *James William Gibson discusses the application of technology and management to the war. We could calculate what technology, what degree of force, and what resources would be sufficient to defeat an enemy of identifiable size and technological limits. With our superior capacities we could inflict punishment beyond the level that our adversaries could tolerate. We could devise computer programs to measure how well we were doing, a complex and sophisticated quantitative scorecard of destruction.*

With the Tet offensive in 1968, in which the North Vietnamese and the Vietcong launched an attack in major cities of South Vietnam, the assumptions of technowar were broadly called into question in the United States, mainly by press coverage of the enemy's dramatic strategy. The war was now being lost in the hearts and minds of the American people.

The following glossary will help readers follow the story.

VC	Vietcong—South Vietnamese guerrillas allied with North Vietnam
DRV	North Vietnam
PAVN or NVA	North Vietnamese army
SVN	South Vietnam
GVN	South Vietnamese government
ARVN	South Vietnamese Army
MACV	U.S. military command
CIA	Central Intelligence Agency (U.S.A.)
DIA	Defense Intelligence Agency (U.S.A.)
ISA	International Security Agency (U.S.A.)

Each year General Westmoreland submitted troop requests and budget estimates to his superiors—the Joint chiefs of Staff, the secretary of defense, the senior White House staff, and the President. Fiscal years began in July; the debate on troop increases for 1968 began in March 1967. In 1966 Westmoreland had wanted 124 maneuver battalions and their logistical support units for 1967, a grand total of 555,741 authorized troop spaces. Senior officials reduced this figure to 470,366 troop spaces for 1967. He submitted basically the same request for fiscal year 1968, but with the important modification that these 555,741 spaces be structured to add two and one-third combat divisions. If he secured this significant increase in combat troops, then additional logistical units could be added later—it would be difficult to deny requests for supporting combat troops already in the field. Ideally, though, Westmoreland wanted a Technowar factory of even greater dimensions. According to memos in the *Pentagon Papers*, "The optimum force required to implement the concept of operations and to exploit success is considered $4\frac{2}{3}$ divisions or the equivalent; 10 tactical fighter squadrons with one additional base; and the full mobile riverine force. The order of magnitude estimate is 201,250 spaces in addition to the 1967 ceiling of 470,366 for a total of *671,616*."

In April 1967, Westmoreland presented his case to President Johnson. First he noted that with 470,000 troops "we will not be in danger of being defeated but it will be nip and tuck to oppose the reinforcements the enemy is capable of providing. In the final analysis we are fighting a war of attrition in Southeast Asia." Production had to increase if the war was to be brought to a victorious conclusion: "Unless the will of the enemy is broken or unless there was an unraveling of the VC infrastructure the war could go on for five years." Force increases of two and one-third divisions would reduce that time to three years, while the optimum war factory would require only two years to produce victory. Westmoreland thought the Vietcong and NVA might reinforce their troops if the Americans increased theirs, but he was confident U.S. forces could maintain a production rate beyond the "cross-over" point. Military intelligence had determined that "The VC and DRV strength in SVN now totals 285,000 men. It appears that last month we reached the cross-over point in areas excluding the two northern provinces. *Attrition will be greater than additions to this force*."

Note how this report presents Technowar as a production system that can be rationally managed and warfare as a kind of activity that can be scientifically determined by constructing computer models. Increase their resources and the war-managers claim to know what will happen. What constitutes their knowledge is an array of numbers—numbers of U.S. and allied forces, numbers of VC and NVA forces, body counts, kill ratios—numbers that appear scientific. Yet these numbers, the official representations of Technowar, had no referent in reality. During 1967 and 1968, the contradictions created by systematic falsifications of official reports exploded. In February 1968, at the very moment when war-managers saw American victory as inevitable, the Vietcong emerged in full power. The ensuing debacle momentarily exposed the vast gulf between warfare at ground level and Technowar's representations of it.

... Enemy losses are projected from body counts. ... The *Pentagon Papers* contains a chart of losses from 1966.

Not only was the body count accepted as accurate, but it was further *multiplied by 1.5, meaning a 50 percent increase!* In this way an entire apparatus of lies was constructed. Numbers become the base for generating more numbers and differences between numbers become the debit or credit of defeat versus progress. Numbers as the definitive signs of truth outlive verbal commentary that expresses doubts as to their validity. The VC/NVA loss chart for 1966 was included in McNamara's 17 November Draft Memorandum for the President. The secretary of defense wondered about the figures: "Moreover, it is possible that our attrition estimates substantially overstates actual VC/NVA losses. For example, the VC/NVA apparently lose about one-sixth as many weapons as people, suggesting the possibility that many of the killed are unarmed porters or bystanders."

But once stated, the implications are not expounded; instead, the question is dropped and discussion shifts to another subject. This same phenomenon of institutionalizing and compounding false numbers occurs with the enemy order of battle figures, reported by Westmoreland at 285,000 troops. In December 1966, CIA analyst Samuel Adams began examining information used to compile the OB. Much to his surprise, he found little documentation in support of the established numbers. Instead, information entered into official files years earlier was recirculated as the years went by. South Vietnamese sources gave 103,573 men and women as members of part-time guerrilla forces in 1964; the figure remained constant through 1966. A CIA study conducted in 1965 said that political cadre numbered 39,175. Service troops numbered 18,553 according to the Joint Chiefs of Staff, while main-force combat troops totaled around 110,000. Added together, the total came to just over 271,000.

Adams did not like this figure. Not only was it based on old intelligence, but it was such a low figure that according to official body counts, the Vietcong should already be decimated. Obviously, someone was still alive to contest American forces severely. After examining more recent captured enemy documents, Adams concluded that the order of battle for Vietcong and NVA forces should be doubled to around 600,000 men and women. Adams's superior, George Carver, sent him to an order of battle conference in Honolulu convened by General Earle Wheeler, chairman of the Joint Chiefs of Staff. Military intelligence officers working for General Westmoreland had also come up with a new estimate. Colonel Gains B. Hawkins said, "You know, there's a lot more of these little bastards out there than we thought there were." Hawkins served as chief of General Westmoreland's order of battle intelligence section. His new figure was 500,000. Adams at first thought the new figures would be recorded and that the dispute was over. However, nothing was released to the public afterward.

On March 9, 1967, General Wheeler cabled General Westmoreland to warn him of the dangers this new estimate posed to Technowar: "If these figures should reach the public domain they would, literally, blow the lid off Washington. Please do whatever is necessary to insure that these figures are not repeat not released to news media or otherwise exposed to public knowledge." Westmoreland complied. In April he told President Johnson that the cross-over point had been reached. In May his intelligence chief, General McChristian, showed him new estimates for Vietcong guerrilla forces and political cadre that were significantly greater than the old figures. According to McChristian, "After reading the cable, General Westmoreland said to me that if he sent it to Washington it would be a 'political bombshell.' " The cable was not sent.

During May the central consortium of U.S. intelligence agencies met to write an official National Intelligence Estimate on "The Capabilities of the Vietnamese Communists for Fighting in South Vietnam." Adams and Carver wanted a figure "in the half-million range." The military's representative, George Fowler of the Defense Intelligence Agency, a joint service military intelligence agency, protested: "Gentlemen, we cannot agree to this estimate as currently written. What we object to are the numbers. We feel we should continue with the official order of battle." Debate between military and CIA analysts went on for weeks. At one point, a military officer told Adams, "You know, our basic problem is that we've been told to keep the numbers under 300,000."

In an attempt to reach a consensus, George Carver went to Saigon in September 1967 to confer with military and civilian officials. In particular, Carver approached Robert W. Komer, at the time President Johnson's personal representative in Vietnam, a man with ambassadorial status formally in charge of pacification programs. Komer thought the order of battle should eliminate as *categories* for consideration all Vietcong local guerrilla and militia forces. He described such forces as "low-grade, part-time hamlet self-defense groups, mostly weaponless." His choice of abolishing Vietcong guerrilla forces and the subsequent endorsement of this theoretical abolition by other important commanders warrant explication. Recall that in the deep logic of mechanistic anti-communism and Technowar, the foreign Other's military forces are like those of the United States, except with less technology. The United States military did not have part-time guerrillas as an integral part of its forces. Theoretically abolishing them followed this constant pattern of projection. Second, by U.S. reasoning the local guerrillas were the logical category to abolish, since their low level of war technology made them less of a threat than main-force Vietcong and North Vietnamese units. Because the social world is abolished in Technowar, abolishing those military forces closest to the people—indeed, local militias were literally the local people—makes complete sense.

Carver soon received a cable from Richard Helms, director of the Central Intelligence Agency, ordering him to reach agreement with the military—to accept their figures. Later General Creighton Abrams (Westmoreland's deputy) cabled General Wheeler also to suggest that local guerrillas be eliminated as a category from the order of battle. The Board of National Estimates followed this policy and so approved a new official figure of 299,000 foreign Others. No dissent was allowed in the National Intelligence Estimate. When the conference had opened in May, Helms informed participants that no dissenting footnotes with different figures would be included. The war-managers thus went on record with the 299,000 figure and theoretically abolished all local guerrilla forces from consideration as part of "The Capabilities of the Vietnamese Communists for Fighting in South Vietnam."

Other leading officials similarly contributed to eliminating Vietcong by edict. When General McChristian's tour as chief of intelligence for MACV expired in September 1967, he was replaced by Brigadier General Phillip B. Davidson, Jr. Davidson told Westmoreland that the cross-over point had been reached and told his intelligence analysts that henceforth all order of battle estimates would be cleared by him: "The figure of combat strength and particularly of guerrillas must take a steady and significant downward trend as I am convinced this reflects true enemy status. Due to the sensitivity of this project, weekly strength figures will hereafter be cleared personally by me." After the military had won its struggle with the CIA, Davidson continued to exercise tight control of all estimates. He sent out a form for intelligence analysts under his supervision controlling all changes in the order of battle: "This addition of [blank] in enemy strength does not increase total enemy strength in excess of that agreed upon at the September 1967 CIA/DIA/MACV Enemy Strength Conference." Thus Davidson declared by managerial command that there could be no more than 299,000 Vietcong troops. Even for additions that did not threaten the ceiling, Davidson required four officers to sign the report before forwarding it to him—that is, to risk their careers by offending him with additions.

By October, MACV was in the final stages of preparing a press release containing the new order of battle figures and reports of Technowar's impending victory. Ambassador Ellsworth Bunker thought the draft still contained a minor reference to guerrillas that might "mislead" people. He sent Walt Rostow a secret cable calling for eliminating any mention of these 120,000 guerrillas to "forestall many confusing and undesirable questions." At the time Rostow was commanding a "psychological strategy committee" in the White House to present the Vietnam War to the public as favorably as possible. Rostow agreed to eliminating all references to local guerrillas. He even asked a researcher in the White House to create a report showing progress in pacification programs. The researcher refused, prompting Rostow to say, "I'm sorry you won't support your President."

In November President Johnson asked General Westmoreland to return to the United States to speak on war progress. On the fifteenth, Westmoreland arrived at Andrews Air Force Base near Washington, D.C., and announced: "I am very, very encouraged. I have never been more encouraged in the four years that I have been in Vietnam. We are making real progress. Everyone is encouraged." The next day he addressed a closed session of the House Armed Services Committee and offered victory within two years.

On the twenty-first, General Westmoreland addressed the National Press Club. He said that Phase II (American buildup and counterattack) was nearly completed, and that elimination of enemy main-force units was now in progress and success the inevitable conclusion: "With 1968, the new phase is now starting. We have reached an important point when the end comes into view." Westmoreland implied that the time between the present production rate and when combat would become a matter of "mopping up" was not long. "Mopping up," cleansing Vietnam of the enemy, would take only two years for a small, residual force. Scholars and journalists agree that Westmoreland's campaign was effective. According to journalist Don Oberdorfer: "The success of November 1967 convinced many Americans that their fears and doubts had been erroneous and that the end was indeed in sight. For the moment, the revival of public confidence stemmed the erosion of support for the war."

Thus by the fall of 1967, war-managers lived with multiple systematic falsifications, some created by subordinates at ground level, others by superior commanders at battalion, brigade, division, and corps levels, and still more systematic falsifications imposed by senior officials at MACV, the Pentagon, and the White House. False body counts made Technowar appear highly productive. The new order of battle both reinforced this illusion and presented a smaller enemy whose decimation was predictable.

One other factor contributed to U.S. delusions about war progress in the fall of 1967. That spring, North Vietnamese and Vietcong forces slowly began disengaging from combat with U.S. forces. As this trend continued throughout summer and fall, U.S. commanders saw enemy withdrawal as proof of their forthcoming victory. Since Technowar ran at full production, then the enemy must run at full production, too.

The disengagement of the Vietcong marked preparation for a massive, nationwide attack scheduled to begin January 31, 1968, the first day of Tet (the lunar new year), the principal Vietnamese holiday season. On that day, according to Vietnamese custom, the first person who came "calling" in your home was an omen for your forthcoming year. Historians differ in what Vietnamese Communists hoped to achieve with this attack. The "minimal gains" interpretation suggests that the Vietcong hoped that by attacking the cities—hitherto exempt from combat except for commando attacks and occasional rocket bombardments— ARVN forces would withdraw from the countryside to defend cities. Rural areas would then be open for Vietcong political and military operations. City dwellers would be shown U.S. and GVN impotence. A massive attack would force the United States to recognize its limits, and negotiations toward American withdrawal would begin. One major resolution passed by leading VC and NVA commanders supports this interpretation; it says in part: "At a certain time we can apply the strategy of fighting and negotiating at the same time, in order to support the armed struggle, and thus accelerate the disintegration of the puppet army and regime, and create more conditions favorable for our people to win a decisive victory." A Tet offensive would thus shift the direction of the war toward long-term victory, but would not mean the end of the war.

Scholars closely associated with the U.S. military or civilian war-managers view these Tet ambitions differently. Former Army General Dave Richard Palmer contends that the North Vietnamese recognized that the United States had reached the cross-over point and thus "sensed that time was on the side of the enemy, that a continuation of the protracted war of attrition would inevitably lead to defeat." To avoid this, Communist leaders theorized that a massive nationwide attack would trigger a general uprising by the people. Palmer says this Vietnamese concept of a general uprising was "the orgasm of revolution." Vietcong troops would control large sections of cities and large towns. Some ARVN units would defect and others would disintegrate. The GVN would collapse and a coalition government would be formed. United States forces would have to retreat to coastal enclaves before leaving Vietnam for good. In this view, the foreign Other hoped to bring an immediate end to the war. A poem Ho Chi Minh sent to diplomats across the world and read on radio in late December and early January is said to indicate their true intent:

> This spring will be far better than any spring past,
> As truth of triumph spreads with trumpet blast.
> North and South, rushing heroically together, shall smite
>   the American invaders.
> Go forward!
> Certain victory is ours at last!

On January 31, 1968, Vietcong troops attacked five of the six major cities, thirty-six of forty-four provincial capitals, sixty-four of 242 district capitals, and numerous airfields, munitions dumps, and other military and economic facilities. A Vietcong commando team destroyed part of the American embassy in Saigon. Both ARVN and U.S. military forces retreated to the cities. Vietcong forces held parts of towns and cities for weeks. Much to their surprise, the United States immediately began shelling and bombing urban areas. One U.S. Army major surveyed the former city of Ben Tre after bombers had leveled it and said, "We had to destroy the town to save it." In Saigon, 9,580 dwellings were destroyed, with thousands of civilian casualties. MACV's inspector general subsequently attributed most damage to U.S. forces. Much of Hue, the ancient capital of Vietnam, was also destroyed. Vietcong forces rounded up and executed several hundred GVN leaders during the weeks they held the city, while U.S. airpower killed several thousand civilians. Tet was a major battle from the beginning of February until early March, after which fighting slowly eased and cities returned to U.S.-GVN control. Few U.S. or ARVN soldiers returned to the countryside until late spring and summer.

Tet came as a surprise. American leaders really believed they had beaten the Vietcong by the autumn of 1967; they had become trapped in their own web of systematic falsifications. Captured documents indicating that a national attack was forthcoming were dismissed as *unbelievable*. As one U.S. Army intelligence officer said, "If we'd gotten the whole battle plan, it wouldn't have been credible to us." A major booklet issued to Vietcong political and military cadre was entitled "For an Understanding of the New Situation and the New Tasks." It outlined a threefold mission of hitting important U.S. military facilities, trying to cause ARVN to collapse, and generating popular support for the general uprising. United States intelligence received this pamphlet on November 25, 1967. On

January 5, MACV distributed a press release based on captured documents. The headline read: "Captured Document Indicates Final Phases of the Revolution at Hand." A partial translation said:

Use very strong military attacks in coordination with the uprisings of the local population to take over towns and cities. Troops should flood the lowlands. They should move toward liberating the capital city, take power and try to rally enemy brigades and regiments to our side one by one. Propaganda should be broadly disseminated among the population in general, and leaflets should be used to reach enemy officers and enlisted personnel.

The very same Vietcong forces that leading war-managers theoretically abolished in the order of battle debate took part in Tet. CIA analyst George Carver attended a meeting with McNamara on February 4, 1968. McNamara noticed that approximately half of the enemy units participating were not listed on the official order of battle. Few People's Army of Vietnam (PAVN or NVA) took part in the attack. Missing units were nearly all Vietcong guerillas who had been previously abolished!

Westmoreland and his associates proclaimed enemy defeat during the Tet Offensive. MACV estimated that from 67,000 to 84,000 enemy troops attacked and 45,000 had been killed. Even though many deaths were from units that MACV had previously eliminated from the enemy's credit account, all new bodies were *subtracted* from the official order of battle. By this reasoning, MACV issued a new OB on March, 15 declaring only 204,000 enemy troops remained! Showing victory while American and ARVN forces retreated took much work. One high-ranking intelligence officer attached to MACV's order of battle section describes it in letters to his wife. Naval Commander James Meacham, chief of OB studies, thought their efforts were doomed:

March 2, 1968: Tomorrow will be a sort of day of truth. We shall then see if I can make the computer sort out the losses since the Tet Offensive began in such a manner as to prove that we are winning the war. If I can't we shall of course jack the figures around until we do show progress. Every month we make progress here.... The MACV bunch is definitely on the defensive (mentally as well as militarily).

March 13: You should have seen the antics my people and I had to go through...to make the February enemy strength calculations come out the way the general wanted them. We started with the answer and plugged in all sorts of figures until we found a combination the machine could digest, and then we wrote all sorts of estimates showing why the figures were right which we had to use. And we continue to win the war.

March 21: We had a crash project to prepare a briefing for the press on enemy strength as of 29 February—complete with viewgraphs.... I have never in my life assembled such a peak of truly gargantuan falsehoods. The reporters will think we are putting on a horse and dog show when we try to sell them this crap.

His foreboding was warranted. Important leaders saw problems with the numbers. Arthur Goldberg, the United States ambassador to the United Nations, was not impressed when he heard that the Vietcong had suffered 45,000 killed during February and early March. He asked his military briefers what the estimated ratio of enemy wounded-to-killed was. Officers replied that they normally counted 3.5 Vietnamese wounded for every digit in the body count; by this reasoning the enemy suffered 157,500 wounded. Goldberg noticed that this arithmetic signified the enemy's bankruptcy—only one-third of its forces remained if the official order of battle was accepted. Yet in his communications with the Joint Chiefs of Staff, Westmoreland presented requests for troops that far exceeded his 1968 budget of 525,000 soldiers. Four objectives for 1968 were presented in this request:

—First, to counter the enemy offensive and to destroy or eject the NVA
    invasion force in the north;
—Second, to restore security in the cities and towns;
—Third, to restore security in the heavily populated areas of the coun-
    tryside;
—Fourth, to regain the initiative through offensive operations.

General Earle Wheeler went to Saigon on February 23. On the twenty-seventh he delivered a report to President Johnson stressing how demanding winning the war would be. United States forces needed to guard cities: "It is clear that this task will absorb a substantial portion of U.S. forces." United States forces also needed to help ARVN leave the cities and go fight the VC: "MACV estimates that U.S. forces will be required in a number of places to assist and encourage the Vietnamese Army to leave the cities and towns and reenter the country. This is especially true in the Delta [the most populous area]." Most important, there were not enough American troops to sustain production past the crossover. According to Wheeler, "...MACV does not have adequate forces at this time to resume the offensive in the remainder of the country, nor does it have adequate reserves against the contingency of simultaneous large-scale enemy offensive action throughout the countryside."

Pentagon war-managers recommended 206,756 additional troop "spaces" on top of the 1968 ceiling of 525,000. These extra forces would include three combat divisions, another 300 to 400 tactical fighter-bombers (fifteen squadrons), and increased navy ships. In response, President Johnson initiated an "A to Z" review, presided over by men who either previously or currently held powerful positions determining United States foreign policy. Robert McNamara had resigned late in 1967. His heir, Clark Clifford, directed the Senior Informal Advisory Group, or the "Wise Old Men." At lower levels of the military and State Department apparatus, a new series of studies examining past practice and recommendations for the future was commissioned.

According to an intelligence organization in the Department of Defense, the International Security Agency, prospects for increased production were limited:

Even with the 200,000 additional troops requested by MACV, we will not be in a position to drive the enemy from SVN or destroy his forces....

The more likely enemy response [to U.S. escalation], however, is that with which he has responded to previous increases in force levels, viz., a matching increase on his part. Hanoi has maintained a constant ratio of one maneuver battalion to 1.5 U.S. maneuver battalions from his reserve in NVN of from 45–70 maneuver battalions (comprising 40,000–60,000 men in 5–8 divisions).

Even if the enemy stands and fights as he did before Tet, the results can only be disappointing in terms of attriting his capability.

Over the past year the United States has been killing between 70 and 100 VC/NVA per month per U.S. combat battalion in theater. *The return per combat battalion deployed has been falling off,* but even assuming that additional deployments will double the number of combat battalions, and assuming that the kill-ratios will remain constant, we could expect enemy deaths, at best, on the order of 20,000 per month, but the infiltration system from North Vietnam alone could supply 13,000–16,000 per month, regardless of our bombing pattern, leaving the remainder—4,000—to be recruited in South Vietnam—a demonstrably manageable undertaking for the VC.

If the enemy could afford such production, ISA staff doubted that the United States could: "We will have to mobilize reserves, increase our budget by billions, and see U.S. casualties climb to 1,300–1,400 per month. Our balance of payments will be worsened, considerably, and we will need a larger tax increase—justified as a war tax, or wage and price controls...." On March 25, the Senior Informal Advisory Group received an order of battle briefing by CIA analyst George Carver. He presented the case for doubling the OB to 600,000 and noted that since most U.S. and GVN forces had retreated to towns and cities, GVN rural pacification no longer existed. ISA had also made this point emphatically. President Johnson noticed an abrupt change in the group after this briefing. He tracked down Carver and had him repeat his performance on March 28. That same day Johnson rejected Westmoreland's request for an additional 206,000 troops, instead establishing a 1968 ceiling of 549,500 spaces, roughly 24,500 more than originally planned. Three days later he made his decision public and announced he would not seek a second presidential term.

Note, though, that Westmoreland was *only* limited to 550,000 troops. Establishing such a high level is not the same as ending the war and withdrawing U.S. forces. To the contrary, the war and the bureaucratic struggle over enemy order of battle and the cross-over point both continued. In April the CIA and MACV held another OB conference. The CIA wanted a 600,000 figure, including local guerrillas. Military war-managers insisted on low figures. Westmoreland said: "There is a much larger issue involved here than intelligence methodology. The acceptance of this inflated strength ... is contrary to our national interest. The effect that its inevitable public announcement would have on the American public ... is obvious." Westmoreland won this struggle. Estimates of Vietcong forces remained low in military documents and press releases. Mechanistic anticommunism with its concept of the foreign Other invading the sovereign state of South Vietnam prevailed. Questions concerning how the Vietnamese class structure and history of resistance toward invaders could generate a strong guerrilla force and mass political organizations for farmers, women, youth, and other social groupings were dismissed.

However, even within this conceptual universe, reports on productivity demonstrated systemic flaws. Thomas Thayer, of the Office of

Systems Analysis, drew attention to several important studies conducted in the latter half of 1968. First, if North Vietnam increased the percentage of its population in the military to a figure equal to South Vietnam, it could double its forces. Even by accepting the incredibly high body count projected by MACV during the first six months of 1968—the Tet Offensive and its spring second wave—then the DRV cold fight for up to *thirty years* before its manpower account went bankrupt. Vietcong forces could only fight for another three and a half years, a figure reflecting the order of battle, but three and a half years of fighting at Tet levels meant tremendous American casualties. Even these projections failed to note that the enemy also controlled the pace of battle, and could thus control their casualty rate....

In November 1968, Richard Nixon was elected President; a new team of senior civilian war-managers assumed command. What happened to all these studies when the uppermost levels of the bureaucracy changed? Journalist Seymour Hersh touched upon this question in his investigation of Henry Kissinger, *The Price of Power*. After Nixon appointed him as national security adviser, Kissinger asked the Rand Corporation to prepare a list of policy options for Vietnam. Daniel Ellsberg, who then worked at Rand and had written part of the *Pentagon Papers*, prepared a list of policy options which did not include any U.S. action leading to victory. Kissinger and his colleague Thomas C. Schelling noted this absence. Ellsberg replied to their inquiry, "I don't believe there is a win option in Vietnam." Ellsberg did include a complete withdrawal option. Later on, Kissinger and his staff dropped the withdrawal option from copies presented to other government officials. Defeat remained unthinkable....

Many crucial studies demonstrating Technowar failure thus came to the attention of leading war-managers in the year following the 1968 Tet Offensive through March of 1969. President Johnson, Defense Secretaries Robert McNamara and his Democratic successor, Clark Clifford, and General Westmoreland all left their respective positions in this period. President Nixon, Defense Secretary Melvin Laird, and General Creighton Abrams (formerly Westmoreland's deputy) replaced them. National Security Study Memorandum No. 1 indicates that these men and their second echelon knew that a significant section of the government bureaucracy thought Technowar bankrupt and had considerable empirical evidence and traditional debit-credit production logic to demonstrate their case.

Yet, *defeat was unthinkable:* debit could always be changed to credit by increasing war production. MACV's reports of massive productivity either beyond the cross-over point or close to it and projections of pacifying 90 percent of the Vietnamese within the year were "empirical" findings that resonated with a whole way of conceptualizing and acting upon the world.

Full ground operations continued—search-and-destroy as an assembly line—until U.S. forces began major reductions in late 1971. Note the distribution of U.S. casualties. From 1965 through 1967 the United States suffered 15,895 killed and 52,200 wounded. Nineteen sixty-eight brought 14,615 killed and 46,800 wounded. Remaining years of U.S. search-and-destroy (1969–1971) produced 14,998 killed and 52,900 wounded. These figures are not restricted to ground operations alone, but instead include all U.S. combat casualties from different sub-assemblies of Technowar. Much of the national news media, particularly network television news, and many historians saw the Tet Offensive, the Senior Informal Advisory Group's denial of Westmoreland's request for a troop increase, and the subsequent beginning of peace talks as definitive evidence that ground war had ended. This erroneous assessment was aided by President Nixon's 1969 announcements calling for "Vietnamization" of the war, providing more weapons to ARVN. More weapons went to ARVN to give them indisputable technological superiority, but ground war did not end in 1968. United States troops continued to fight and die....

23. Report from Vietnam

MICHAEL HERR

The United States war in Vietnam, as Jean-Paul Sartre described it in his essay "On Genocide," was a "war of example," primarily an assertion of American willingness to resist "wars of national liberation" sponsored by major Communist powers. Sartre pointed out that such a war could have no specific outcome. The limitlessness of the United States' goal of demonstrating the great price a country would have to pay to pursue a war of national liberation, Sartre claimed, made genocide a part of strategy. The United States would bomb the small nation "back to the Stone Age," "defoliate" its forest and farmlands, "zippo" its villages, and "pattern bomb" its towns and countrysides. With mindless destruction raised to a strategic objective, a certain type of rogue warrior would be the only possible hero; the rest were "grunts" mired in the slaughter, having to kill, hoping to survive, breathing in and breathing out, as Michael Herr says, but doomed to live with a horror of purposelessness that they could never share with the everyday world to which they prayed to return. This was not the John Wayne kind of war the generation after World War II grew up with, where purpose and heroism weighed in against the horrors. This was the world shown in the film Apocalypse Now, *an unfocused anger that is the only legacy of Vietnam.*

Michael Herr's book Dispatches *has been widely acclaimed as one of the most successful depictions of the American war in Vietnam. It was in part a media war: reporters showed in their own actions and in their reporting the desire—and choice—to live dangerously that we Americans have identified with war since the days of Ernest Hemingway. But it was also a battle of technology against the silent, black-pajama-clad Viet Cong. (And of the modern globalism of the United States set against obscurely understood struggles that drifted back through three thousand years of history and may continue for three thousand more.) And it was a defense of Saigon, where, for a century or so, the West had comfortably exploited the East. Michael Herr's staccato prose captures the images of the war for us in the present, when its larger meanings for the United States still remain beyond our grasp.*

I THE REPORTER

Going out at night the medics gave you pills, Dexedrine breath like dead snakes kept too long in a jar. I never saw the need for them myself, a little contact or anything that even sounded like contact would give me more speed than I could bear. Whenever I heard something outside of our clenched little circle I'd practically flip, hoping to God that I wasn't the only one who'd noticed it. A couple of rounds fired off in the dark a kilometer away and the Elephant would be there kneeling on my chest, sending me down into my boots for a breath. Once I thought I saw a light moving in the jungle and I caught myself just under a whisper saying, "I'm not ready for this, I'm not ready for this." That's when I decided to drop it and do something else with my nights. And I wasn't going out like the night ambushers did, or the Lurps, long-range recon patrollers who did it night after night for weeks and months, creeping up on VC base camps or around moving columns of North Vietnamese. I was living too close to my bones as it was, all I had to do was accept it. Anyway, I'd save the pills for later, for Saigon and the awful depressions I always had there.

I knew one 4th Division Lurp who took his pills by the fistful, downs from the left pocket of his tiger suit and ups from the right, one to cut the trail for him and the other to send him down it. He told me that they cooled things out just right for him, that he could see that old jungle at night like he was looking at it through a starlight scope. "They sure give you the range," he said.

This was his third tour. In 1965 he'd been the only survivor in a platoon of the Cav wiped out going into the Ia Drang Valley. In '66 he'd come back with the Special Forces and one morning after an ambush he'd hidden under the bodies of his team while the VC walked all around them with knives, making sure. They stripped the bodies of their gear, the berets too, and finally went away, laughing. After that, there was nothing left for him in the war except the Lurps.

"I just can't hack it back in the World," he said. He told me that after he'd come back home the last time he would sit in his room all day, and sometimes he'd stick a hunting rifle out the window, leading people and cars as they passed his house until the only feeling he was aware of was all up in the tip of that one finger. "It used to put my folks real uptight," he said. But he put people uptight here too, even here.

"No man, I'm sorry, he's just too crazy for me," one of the men in his team said. "All's you got to do is look in his eyes, that's the whole fucking story right there."

"Yeah, but you better do it quick," someone else said. "I mean, you don't want to let him catch you at it."

But he always seemed to be watching for it, I think he slept with his eyes open, and I was afraid of him anyway. All I ever managed was one quick look in, and that was like looking at the floor of an ocean. He wore a gold earring and a headband torn from a piece of camouflage parachute material, and since nobody was about to tell him to get his hair cut it fell below his shoulders, covering a thick purple scar. Even at division he never went anywhere without at least a .45 and a knife, and he thought I was a freak because I wouldn't carry a weapon.

"Didn't you ever meet a reporter before?" I asked him.

"Tits on a bull," he said. "Nothing personal."

But what a story he told me, as one-pointed and resonant as any war story I ever heard, it took me a year to understand it:

"Patrol went up the mountain. One man came back. He died before he could tell us what happened."

I waited for the rest, but it seemed not to be that kind of story; when I asked him what had happened he just looked like he felt sorry for me, fucked if he'd waste time telling stories to anyone dumb as I was.

His face was all painted up for night walking now like a bad hallucination, not like the painted faces I'd seen in San Francisco only a few weeks before, the other extreme of the same theater. In the coming hours he'd stand as faceless and quiet in the jungle as a fallen tree, and God help his opposite numbers unless they had at least half a squad along, he was a good killer, one of our best. The rest of his team were gathered outside the tent, set a little apart from the other division units, with its own Lurp-designated latrine and its own exclusive freeze-dry rations, three-star war food, the same chop they sold at Abercrombie & Fitch. The regular division troops would almost shy off the path when they passed the area on their way to and from the mess tent. No matter how toughened up they became in the war, they still looked innocent compared to the Lurps. When the team had grouped they walked in a file down the hill to the lz across the strip to the perimeter and into the treeline.

I never spoke to him again, but I saw him. When they came back in the next morning he had a prisoner with him, blindfolded and with his elbows bound sharply behind him. The Lurp area would definitely be off limits during the interrogation, and anyway, I was already down at the strip waiting for a helicopter to come and take me out of there....

II AIRMOBILITY

In the months after I got back the hundreds of helicopters I'd flown in began to draw together until they'd formed a collective meta-chopper, and in my mind it was the sexiest thing going; saver-destroyer, provider-waster, right hand–left hand, nimble, fluent, canny and human; hot steel, grease, jungle-saturated canvas webbing, sweat cooling and warming up again, cassette rock and roll in one ear and door-gun fire in the other, fuel, heat, vitality and death, death itself, hardly an intruder. Men on the crews would say that once you'd carried a dead person he would always be there, riding with you. Like all combat people they were incredibly superstitious and invariably self-dramatic, but it was (I knew) unbearably true that close exposure to the dead sensitized you to the force of their presence and made for long reverberations; long. Some people were so delicate that one look was enough to wipe them away, but even bone-dumb grunts seemed to feel that something weird and extra was happening to them.

Helicopters and people jumping out of helicopters, people so in love they'd run to get on even when there wasn't any pressure. Choppers rising straight out of small cleared jungle spaces, wobbling down onto city rooftops, cartons of rations and ammunition thrown off, dead and wounded loaded on. Sometimes they were so plentiful and loose that you could touch down at five or six places in a day, look around, hear the talk, catch the next one out. There were installations as big as cities with 30,000 citizens, once we dropped in to feed supply to one man. God knows what kind of Lord Jim phoenix numbers he was doing in there, all he said to me was, "You didn't see a thing, right Chief? You weren't even here." There were posh fat air-conditioned camps like comfortable middle-class scenes with the violence tacit, "far away"; camps named for commanders' wives, LZ Thelma, LZ Betty Lou; number-named hilltops in trouble where I didn't want to stay; trail, paddy, swamp, deep hairy bush, scrub, swale, village, even city, where the ground couldn't drink up what the action spilled, it made you careful where you walked.

Sometimes the chopper you were riding in would top a hill and all the ground in front of you as far as the next hill would be charred and pitted and still smoking, and something between your chest and your stomach would turn over. Frail gray smoke where they'd burned off the rice fields around a free-strike zone, brilliant white smoke from phosphorus ("Willy Peter/Make you a buh liever"), deep black smoke from 'palm, they said that if you stood at the base of a column of napalm smoke it would suck the air right out of your lungs. Once we fanned over a little ville that had just been airstruck and the words of a song by Wingy Manone that I'd heard when I was a few years old snapped into my head, "Stop the War, These Cats Is Killing Themselves." Then we dropped, hovered, settled down into purple lz smoke, dozens of children broke from their hootches to run in toward the focus of our landing, the pilot laughing and saying, "Vietnam, man. Bomb 'em and feed 'em, bomb 'em and feed 'em."

Flying over jungle was almost pure pleasure, doing it on foot was nearly all pain. I never belonged in there. Maybe it really was what its people had always called it, Beyond; at the very least it was serious, I gave up things to it I probably never got back. ("Aw, jungle's okay. If you know her you can live in her real good, if you don't she'll take you down in an hour. Under.") Once in some thick jungle corner with some grunts standing around, a correspondent said, "Gee, you must really see some beautiful sunsets in here," and they almost pissed themselves laughing. But you could fly up and into hot tropic sunsets that would change the way you thought about light forever. you could also fly out of places that were so grim they turned to black and white in your head five minute after you'd gone.

That could be the coldest one in the world, standing at the edge of a clearing watching the chopper you'd just come in on taking off again, leaving you there to think about what it was going to be for you now: if this was a bad place, the wrong place, maybe even the last place, and whether you'd made a terrible mistake this time.

There was a camp at Soc Trang where a man at the lz said, "If you come looking for a story this is your lucky day, we got Condition Red here," and before the sound of the chopper had faded out, I knew I had it too....

Airmobility, dig it, you weren't going anywhere. It made you feel safe, it made you feel Omni, but it was only a stunt, technology. Mobility was just mobility, it saved lives or took them all the time (saved mine I don't know how many times, maybe dozens, maybe none), what you really needed was a flexibility far greater than anything the technology could provide, some generous, spontaneous gift for accepting surprises, and I didn't have it. I got to hate surprises, control freak at the crossroads, if you were one of those people who always thought they had to know what was coming next, the war could cream you. It was the same with your ongoing attempts at getting used to the jungle or the blow-you-out climate or the saturating strangeness of the place which didn't lessen with exposure so often as it fattened and darkened in accumulating alienation. It was great if you could adapt, you had to try, but it wasn't the same as making a discipline, going into your own reserves and developing a real war metabolism, slow yourself down when your heart tried to punch its way through your chest, get swift when everything went to stop and all you could feel of your whole life was the entropy whipping through it. Unlovable terms.

The ground was always in play, always being swept. Under the ground was his, above it was ours. We had the air, we could get up in it but not disappear in *to* it, we could run but we couldn't hide, and he could do each so well that sometimes it looked like he was doing them both at once, while our finder just went limp. All the same, one place or another it was always going on, rock around the clock, we had the days and he had the nights. you could be in the most protected space in Vietnam and still know that your safety was provisional, that early death, blindness, loss of legs, arms or balls, major and lasting disfigurement— the whole rotten deal—could come in on the freakyfluky as easily as in the so-called expected ways, you heard so many of those stories it was a wonder anyone was left alive to die in firefights and mortar-rocket attacks. After a few weeks, when the nickel had jarred loose and dropped and I saw that everyone around me was carrying a gun, I also saw that any one of them could go off at any time, putting you where it wouldn't matter whether it had been an accident or not. The roads were mined, the trails booby-trapped, satchel charges and grenades blew up jeeps and movie theaters, the VC got work inside all the camps as shoeshine boys and laundresses and honey-dippers, they'd starch your fatigues and burn your shit and then go home and mortar your area. Saigon and Cholon and Danang held such hostile vibes that you felt you were being dry-sniped every time someone looked at you, and choppers fell out of the sky like fat poisoned birds a hundred times a day. After a while I couldn't get on one without thinking that I must be out of my fucking mind. . . .

"Boy, you sure get offered some shitty choices," a Marine once said to me, and I couldn't help but feel that what he really meant was that you didn't get offered any at all. Specifically, he was just talking about a couple of C-ration cans, "dinner," but considering his young life you couldn't blame him for thinking that if he knew one thing for sure, it was that there was no one anywhere who cared less about what *he* wanted. There wasn't anybody he wanted to thank for his food, but he was grateful that he was still alive to eat it, that the motherfucker hadn't scarfed him up first. He hadn't been anything but tired and scared for six months and he'd lost a lot, mostly people, and seen far too much, but he was breathing in and breathing out, some kind of choice all by itself.

He had one of those faces, I saw that face at least a thousand times at a hundred bases and camps, and the youth sucked out of the eyes, the color drawn from the skin, cold white lips, you knew he wouldn't wait for any of it to come back. Life had made him old, he'd live it out old. All those faces, sometimes it was like looking into faces at a rock concert, locked in, the event had them; or like students who were very heavily advanced, serious beyond what you'd call their years if you didn't know for yourself what the minutes and hours of those years were made up of. Not just like all the ones you saw who looked like they couldn't drag their asses through another day of it. (How do you feel when a nineteen-year-old kid tells you from the bottom of his heart that he's gotten too old for this kind of shit?) Not like the faces of the dead or wounded either, they could look more released than overtaken. These were the faces of boys whose whole lives seemed to have backed up on them, they'd be a few feet away but they'd be looking back at you over a distance you knew you'd never really cross. We'd talk, sometimes fly together, guys going out on R&R, guys escorting bodies, guys who'd flipped over into extremes of peace or violence. Once I flew with a kid who was going home, he looked back down once at the ground where he'd spent the year and spilled his whole load of tears. Sometimes you even flew with the dead.

Once I jumped on a chopper that was full of them. The kid in the op shack had said that there would be a body on board, but he'd been given some wrong information. "How bad do you want to get to Danang?" he'd asked me, and I'd said, "Bad."

When I saw what was happening I didn't want to get on, but they'd made a divert and a special landing for me, I had to go with the chopper I'd drawn, I was afraid of looking squeamish. (I remember, too, thinking that a chopper full of dead men was far less likely to get shot down than one full of living.) They weren't even in bags. They'd been on a truck near one of the firebases in the DMZ that was firing support for Khe Sanh, and the truck had hit a Command-detonated mine, then they'd been rocketed. The Marines were always running out of things, even food, ammo and medicine, it wasn't so strange that they'd run out of bags too. The men had been wrapped around in ponchos, some of them carelessly fastened with plastic straps, and loaded on board. There was a small space cleared for me between one of them and the door gunner, who looked pale and so tremendously furious that I thought he was angry with me and I couldn't look at him for a while. When we went up the wind blew through the ship and made the ponchos shake and tremble until the one next to me blew back in a fast brutal flap, uncovering the face. They hadn't even closed his eyes for him.

The gunner started hollering as loud as he could, "Fix it! Fix it!," maybe he thought the eyes were looking at him, but there wasn't anything I could do. My hand went there a couple of times and I couldn't, and then I did. I pulled the poncho tight, lifted his head carefully and tucked the poncho under it, and then I couldn't believe that I'd done it. All during the ride the gunner kept trying to smile, and when we landed at Dong Ha he thanked me and ran off to get a detail. The pilots jumped down and walked away without looking back once, like they'd never seen that chopper before in their lives....

III SAIGON

In Saigon I always went to sleep stoned so I almost always lost my dreams, probably just as well, sock in deep and dim under that information and get whatever rest you could, wake up tapped of all images but the ones remembered from the day or the week before, with only the taste of a bad dream in your mouth like you'd been chewing on a roll of dirty old pennies in your sleep. I'd watched grunts asleep putting out the REM's like a firefight in the dark, I'm sure it was the same with me. They'd say (I'd ask) that they didn't remember their dreams either when they were in the zone, but on R&R or in the hospital their dreaming would be constant, open, violent and clear, like a man in the Pleiku hospital on the night I was there. It was three in the morning, scary and upsetting like hearing a language for the first time and somehow understanding every word, the voice loud and small at the same time, insistent, calling, "*Who? Who?* Who's in the next room?" There was a single shaded light over the desk at the end of the ward where I sat with the orderly. I could only see the first few beds, it felt like there were a thousand of them running out into the darkness, but actually there were only twenty in each row. After the man had repeated it a few times there was a change like the break in a fever, he sounded like a pleading little boy. I could see cigarettes being lighted at the far end of the ward, mumbles and groans, wounded men returning to consciousness, pain, but the man who'd been dreaming slept through it....As for my own dreams, the ones I lost there would make it through later, I should have known, some things will just naturally follow until they take. The night would come when they'd be vivid and unremitting, that night the beginning of a long string, I'd remember then and wake up half believing that I'd never really been in any of those places.

Saigon *cafarde*, a bitch, nothing for it but some smoke and a little lie-down, waking in the late afternoon on damp pillows, feeling the emptiness of the bed behind you as you walked to the windows looking down at Tu Do. Or just lying there tracking the rotations of the ceiling fan, reaching for the fat roach that sat on my Zippo in a yellow disk of grass tar. There were mornings when I'd do it before my feet even hit the floor. Dear Mom, stoned again.

In the Highlands, where the Montagnards would trade you a pound of legendary grass for a carton of Salems, I got stoned with some infantry from the 4th. One of them had worked for months on his pipe, beautifully carved and painted with flowers and peace symbols. There was a reedy little man in the circle who grinned all the time but hardly spoke. He pulled a thick plastic bag out of his pack and handed it over to me. It was full of what looked like large pieces of dried fruit. I was stoned and hungry, I almost put my hand in there, but it had a bad weight to it. The other men were giving each other looks, some amused, some embarrassed and even angry. Someone had told me once, there were a lot more ears than heads in Vietnam; just information. When I handed it back he was still grinning, but he looked sadder than a monkey.

In Saigon and Danang we'd get stoned together and keep the common pool stocked and tended. It was bottomless and alive with lurps, seals, recondos, Green-Beret bushmasters, redundant mutilators, heavy rapers, eye-shooters, widow-makers, nametakers, classic essential American types; point men, *isolatos* and outriders like they were programmed in their genes to do it, the first taste made them crazy for it, just like they knew it would. You thought you were separate and protected, you could travel the war for a hundred years, a swim in that pool could still be worth a piece of your balance.

We'd all heard about the man in the Highlands who was "building his own gook," parts were the least of his troubles. In Chu Lai some Marines pointed a man out to me and swore to God they'd seen him bayonet a wounded NVA and then lick the bayonet clean. There was a famous story, some reporters asked a door gunner, "How can you shoot women and children?" and he'd answered, "It's easy, you just don't lead 'em so much." Well, they said you needed a sense of humor, there you go, even the VC had one. Once after an ambush that killed a lot of Americans, they covered the field with copies of a photograph that showed one more young, dead American, with the punch line mimeographed on the back, "Your X-rays have just come back from the lab and we think we know what your problem is."

Beautiful for once and only once, just past dawn flying toward the center of the city in a Loach, view from a bubble floating at 800 feet. In that space, at that hour, you could see what people had seen forty years before, Paris of the East, Pearl of the Orient, long open avenues lined and bowered over by trees running into spacious parks, precisioned scale, all under the soft shell from a million breakfast fires, camphor smoke rising and diffusing, covering Saigon and the shining veins of the river with a warmth like the return of better times. Just a projection, that was the thing about choppers, you had to come down sometimes, down to the moment, the street, if you found a pearl down there you got to keep it.

By 7:30 it was beyond berserk with bikes, the air was like L.A. on short plumbing, the subtle city war inside the war had renewed itself for another day, relatively light on actual violence but intense with bad feeling: despair, impacted rage, impotent gnawing resentment; thousands of Vietnamese in the service of a pyramid that wouldn't stand for five years, plugging the feed tube into their own hearts, grasping and gorging; young Americans in from the boonies on TDY, charged with hatred and grounded in fear of the Vietnamese; thousands of Americans sitting in their offices crying in bored chorus, "You can't get these people to do a fucking thing, you can't get these people to do a fucking thing." And all the others, theirs and ours, who just didn't want to play, it sickened them. That December the GVN Department of Labor had announced that the refugee problem had been solved, that "all refugees [had] been assimilated into the economy," but mostly they seemed to have assimilated themselves into the city's roughest corners, alleyways, mud slides, under parked cars. Cardboard boxes that had carried air-conditioners and refrigerators housed up to ten children, most Americans and plenty of Vietnamese would cross the street to avoid trash heaps that fed whole families. And this was still months before Tet, "refugees up the gazops," a flood. I'd heard that the GVN Department of Labor had nine American advisors for every Vietnamese.

In Broddards and La Pagode and the pizzeria around the corner, the Cowboys and Vietnamese "students" would hang out all day, screaming obscure arguments at each other, cadging off Americans, stealing tips from the tables, reading Pléiade editions of Proust, Malraux, Camus. One of them talked to me a few times but we couldn't really communicate, all I understood was his obsessive comparison between Rome and Washington, and that he seemed to believe that Poe had been a French writer. In the late afternoon the Cowboys would leave the cafés and milk bars and ride down hard on Lam Son Square to pick the Allies. They could snap a Rolex off your wrist like a hawk hitting a field mouse; wallets, pens, cameras, eyeglasses, anything; if the war had gone on any longer they'd have found a way to whip the boots off your feet. They'd hardly leave their saddles and they never looked back. There was a soldier down from the 1st Division who was taking snapshots of his friends with some bar girls in front of the Vietnamese National Assembly. He'd gotten his shot focused and centered but before he pushed the button his camera was a block away, leaving him in the bike's backwash with a fresh pink welt on his throat where the cord had been torn and helpless amazement on his face, "Well I'll be dipped in shit!"; as a little boy raced across the square, zipped a piece of cardboard up the soldier's shirtfront and took off around the corner with his Paper Mate. The White Mice stood around giggling, but there were a lot of us watching from the Continental terrace, a kind of gasp went up from the tables, and later when he came up for a beer he said, "I'm goin' back to the war, man, this fucking Saigon is too much for me." There was a large group of civilian engineers there, the same men you'd see in the restaurants throwing food at each other, and one of them, a fat old boy, said, "You ever catch one of them li'l nigs just pinch 'em. Pinch 'em hard. Boy, they hate that."

Five to seven were bleary low hours in Saigon, the city's energy ebbing at dusk, until it got dark and movement was replaced with apprehension. Saigon at night was still Vietnam at night, night was the war's truest medium, night was when it got really interesting in the villages, the TV crews couldn't film at night, the Phoenix was a night bird, it flew in and out of Saigon all the time.

Maybe you had to be pathological to find glamour in Saigon, maybe you just had to settle for very little, but Saigon had it for me, and danger activated it. The days of big, persistent terror in Saigon were over, but everyone felt that they could come back again any time, heavy like 1963–5, when they hit the old Brinks BOQ on Christmas Eve, when they blew up the My Canh floating restaurant, waited for it to be rebuilt and moved to another spot on the river, and then blew up again, when they bombed the first U.S. embassy and changed the war forever from the intimate inside out. There were four known VC sapper battalions in the Saigon-Cholon area, dread sappers, guerrilla superstars, they didn't even have to do anything to put the fear out. Empty ambulances sat parked at all hours in front of the new embassy. Guards ran mirrors and "devices" under all vehicles entering all installations, BOQ's were fronted with sandbags, checkpoints and wire, high-gauge grilles filled our windows, but they still got through once in a while, random terror but real, even the supposedly terror-free safe spots worked out between the Corsican mob and the VC offered plenty of anxiety. Saigon just before Tet; guess, guess again.

Those nights there was a serious tiger lady going around on a Honda shooting American officers on the street with a .45. I think she'd killed over a dozen in three months; the Saigon papers described her as "beautiful," but I don't know how anybody knew that. The commander of one of the Saigon MP battalions said he thought it was a man dressed in an *ao dai* because a .45 was "an awful lot of gun for a itty bitty Vietnamese woman."

Saigon, the center, where every action in the bushes hundreds of miles away fed back into town on a karmic wire strung so tight that if you touched it in the early morning it would sing all day and all night. Nothing so horrible ever happened upcountry that it was beyond language fix and press relations, a squeeze fit into the computers would make the heaviest numbers jump up and dance. You'd either meet an optimism that no violence could unconvince or a cynicism that would eat itself empty every day and then turn, hungry and malignant, on whatever it could for a bite, friendly or hostile, it didn't matter. Those men called dead Vietnamese "believers," a lost American platoon was "a black eye," they talked as though killing a man was nothing more than depriving him of his vigor.

It seemed the least of the war's contradictions that to lose your worst sense of American shame you had to leave the Dial Soapers in Saigon and a hundred headquarters who spoke goodworks and killed nobody themselves, and go out to the grungy men in the jungle who talked bloody murder and killed people all the time. It was true that the grunts stripped belts and packs and weapons from their enemies; Saigon wasn't a flat market, these goods filtered down and in with the other spoils: Rolexes, cameras, snakeskin shoes from Taiwan, air-brush portraits of nude Vietnamese women with breasts like varnished beach balls, huge wooden carvings that they set on their desks to give you the finger when you walked into their offices. In Saigon it never mattered what they told you, even less when they actually seemed to believe it. Maps, charts, figures, projections, fly fantasies, names of places, of operations, of commanders, of weapons; memories, guesses, second guesses, experiences (new, old, real, imagined, stolen); histories, attitudes—you could let it go, let it all go. If you wanted some war news in Saigon you had to hear it in stories brought from the field by friends, see it in the lost watchful eyes of the Saigonese, or do it like Trashman, reading the cracks in the sidewalk.

Sitting in Saigon was like sitting inside the folded petals of a poisonous flower, the poison history, fucked in its root no matter how far back you wanted to run your trace. Saigon was the only place left with a continuity that someone as far outside as I was could recognize. Hue and Danang were like remote closed societies, mute and intractable. Villages, even large ones, were fragile, a village could disappear in an afternoon, and the countryside was either blasted over cold and dead or already back in Charles' hands. Saigon remained, the repository and the arena, it breathed history, expelled it like toxin, Shit Piss and Corruption. Paved swamp, hot mushy winds that never cleaned anything away, heavy thermal seal over diesel fuel, mildew, garbage, excrement, atmosphere. A five-block walk in that could take it out of you, you'd get back to the hotel with your head feeling like one of those chocolate apples, tap it sharply in the right spot and it falls apart in sections. Saigon, November 1967: "The animals are sick with love." Not much chance anymore for history to go on unselfconsciously.

You'd stand nailed there in your tracks sometimes, no bearings and none in sight, thinking, *Where the fuck am I?*, fallen into some unnatural East-West interface, a California corridor cut and bought and burned deep into Asia, and once we'd done it we couldn't remember what for. It was axiomatic that it was about ideological space, we were there to bring them the choice, bringing it to them like Sherman bringing the Jubilee through Georgia, clean through it, wall to wall with pacified indigenous and scorched earth. (In the Vietnamese sawmills they had to change the blades every five minutes, some of our lumber had gotten into some of theirs.)

There was such a dense concentration of American energy there, American and essentially adolescent, if that energy could have been channeled into anything more than noise, waste and pain it would have lighted up Indochina for a thousand years. . . .

24. Hawk vs. Dove

MYRA MACPHERSON

The generation that grew up in the 1960s and for whom the American war in Vietnam was a formative experience has begun its move into the command positions of American society. Vietnam is "their" war just as rock is "their" music. Myra MacPherson's Long Time Passing: Vietnam and the Haunted Generation *reminds us of the truth of the slogan that although the war is over, the battle is not. In fact, American society has been remarkably slow in absorbing the experience of this war comfortably into its consciousness. There is no agreed-upon mythology, no set of "lessons" accepted by policymakers, and few common cultural symbols of the war except for the very moving Vietnam Memorial in Washington, D.C., dedicated in 1982. And even that memorial gives no clue about the war. MacPherson quotes the father of a wounded Vietnam veteran: "It doesn't say whether the war is right or wrong. That's for everyone to decide on his own. It just says, 'Here is the price we paid.'"*

In her discussion of "Hawk vs. Dove," MacPherson interviews two men of that generation who did not serve in Vietnam but who were profoundly affected by the war. Steven Cohen went from anti-war activism to a lifetime of peacemaking and liberal causes. Serving in the State Department under Jimmy Carter, he worked for arms control and human rights.

Elliott Abrams was a conservative Democrat through most of the 70s. But he became a Reagan Republican and served in the State Department during the 1980s. He remains true to the perspective he gained as a pro-war undergraduate at Harvard in 1969.

They both were among the Ivy League's brightest; they both were exempt from service for medical reasons; they both ended up in government in the State Department. There the similarity ends. One was a hawk, the other a dove.

As foreign policy experts—one for Carter, the other for Reagan—they took diametrically opposite views of how we should deal with repressive governments and their human rights—or lack of human rights—policies.

Vietnam was remembered more and more in the eighties as our escalation in Central America passed from the headlines into the consciousness of America. Poll after poll showed that the vast majority of the citizens had no stomach for another war like the last. The controversy and concern mounted as Reagan proposed millions more in aid, sent troops for "exercise" maneuvers in Honduras, ran a "covert" operation in Nicaragua, put marines in Lebanon, invaded Grenada, and continued to alarm with his hard-line rhetoric.

Both the hawk and the dove formed their present foreign policy positions during Vietnam. Elliott Abrams was the rarest of species—an outspoken hawk at Harvard, class of 1969. The year of the takeover of University Hall, the police, the strike.

"I always felt that refusing to go to classes was an extraordinarily odd way of making a political protest," says Abrams sardonically.

Amherst graduate Steve Cohen, on the other hand, is representative of those men who were deeply committed to the peace movement. His antiwar activism took on paramount importance in his life, more so than for most. Still, he embodies the kind of students who believed strongly in trying to end the war and felt that dedication to antiwar work absolved them of guilts or conflicts that came with their student deferment.

Abrams remained fevently faithful to our involvement in Vietnam and uses the outcome there to dot his many arguments for our continued "containing communism" presence in Central America. Carter populated his administration with antiwar advocates from the sixties. Reagan has found, instead, doctrinaire conservatives like Abrams. A devoted neoconservative and fervent anti-Communist, Abrams is Assistant Secretary of State for Human Rights and Humanitarian Affairs.

His view of today's foreign policy was shaped vastly by Vietnam. "It always seemed to me that the so-called NLF forces, the Buddhists, were in fact not going to take over, but rather that the Communists were going to take over. The notion that if the United States would just leave, the killing would stop was unbelievably foolish. That's why I like to make Vietnam analogies when discussing El Salvador. If the opposition wins in El Salvador, the Castroite forces will take over."

But what of the view that Vietnam was not our cause to be involved in? That our presence there created such death and devastation? That the outcome was inevitable, that a "win" "was too costly politically"?

Abrams vehemently puts forth all the revisionist arguments: "One need not believe wholeheartedly in the domino theory to say, in fact, that 'If the United States pulls out and abandons South Vietnam, there will be a Communist government in the South and Laos and Cambodia will fall as well.' That's exactly what happened. What *nobody* quite predicted was the extent of the bloodbath that took place Cambodia. We never claimed then that *all* the opposition in the South was Communist. What we *did* claim was that the Communists had the guns and that they would take over if the opposition won. And that is what happened and all the Buddhists and all the Catholics and all the labor leaders and the intellectuals—the ones we used to hear about being in the opposition— are *dead* or they are in jail or they are in exile."

Abrams launches into a lesser-of-two-evils worldview of support for authoritarian countries. The larger evil is always communism.

"Anybody who does not think South Vietnam was 'freer' under President Diem or Thieu than it is now is crazy." He argues that Nicaragua was "freer under Somoza than it is today." He sees "a steady march toward totalitarianism" in Central America. "If there is one thing that unites them, it is that they're getting Soviet support and Cuban support. At what point do we stop this nonsense and realize that they do not *want* a free society? We're not *pushing* them into the hands of the Soviets? They're leaping into it because that is the kind of society they *want*."

"There is no problem in pointing out enormous failures in American policy. For example, Somoza. Not only is it indefensible morally, it is foolish politically to support a government that doesn't have the support of its people. *But*, that said, I think the fallacy of the left argument is that people end up in the Soviet camp only if and when we push them into it. Did we push Mao into it? Castro or Ho Chi Minh? There *is* such a thing as a Communist. The average government in the world is pretty rotten and repressive—right and left. There is just no evidence with respect, for example, to the Sandinistas, who *proclaim* themselves Marxist-Leninists, to think, Well, really, they're Democrats or nationalists who turned sour on America. Any more than this is true about the North Vietnamese. Carter *welcomed* the Sandinistas. His administration gave them $125 million in aid and tried to work with them and they *jumped* into the hands of the Russians.

"I find it a very odd notion of human rights or morality to be *indifferent* to the victory of Communists. As in Vietnam. Real-live, genuine, Communist party-type Communists who will absolutely destroy liberty in that country! How it can be in the cause of human rights for *that* to be the end result is the question the left has never been able to answer for *me*."

Abrams brushes aside widespread church-based attacks on our policy of supporting the repressive El Salvadoran government.

"It seems the churches are making absolutist moral judgments and closing their eyes to some very difficult moral questions about 'Who is the other side?' and 'What fate do we have in mind for these people if the opposition wins?'"

The sixties' peace movement had a large impact—in Abrams's view, a negative one—on the conduct of current foreign policy. "Opposition to Vietnam was infused with a sense of morality. They were the 'good guys.' That business of the opposition being more moral and progressive than the people the United States Government is supporting remains with us and is one of the central problems of American foreign policy still."

Abrams belongs to a conservative chorus that has never ended: that we could have won in Vietnam if we had mined Haiphong Harbor earlier and bombed the dikes. All that bombardment—three times the tonnage dropped on Germany and Japan in World War II—was not "strategic" enough. "I believe the Christmas bombing is what ultimately forced them to negotiate. It was not inevitable that they win, any more than it was inevitable that North Korea beat South Korea. And if it would have required a few thousand American troops stationed there for years in order to prevent this *unbelievably damaging* American defeat, then I think most Americans would have been willing to do it. We had *business* being there, just as we have business being in Central America to resist the expansion of communism."

Abrams said much of the same at Harvard in the mid-sixties. He purses his lips into a satisfied smile. "We were the ones who were the counterculture in a place like Harvard. I was at Adams House and every night somebody would get up with some antiwar speech. Of course some of us would get up to make a reply. I remember the night I got up to speak—and everybody hissed *before* I spoke. I thought, Now you've really made it."

Abrams has a flat, almost prissy, automaton-precision manner. It is softened in person by a less intense demeanor, but he remains ready to pounce, like a champion debater. He seems never swayed by doubts, governed by unrelenting absolutes.

Abrams feels that his Harvard colleagues remain hopelessly misguided and "unwilling to reach the logical conclusions" of the evils of communism. "I do think, for the most normal reasons, that most people didn't want to go to Vietnam or into the Army. It was a *huge* interference, if you had graduate school or a career or marriage planned. In addition, nobody wanted to get killed. I think, for the students who did not want to go for all those *personal* reasons, there was a psychological reaction: 'Either I am a coward or I'm unpatriotic—*or* the war is indefensible.' So which is it? Nobody wishes to conclude that 'The real reason I don't want to go to Vietnam is that I'm afraid to get shot.' It *must* be that Thieu is a corrupt dictator."

Abrams himself did not go to Vietnam or into the service. He applied for OCS (Officer Candidate School) but was turned down because of a bad back. Abrams has "often asked myself" why he has never wavered on an absolute approach taken so young.

"It was never possible for me to believe in the 'Hate America' campaign that was popular in the sixties. Spell America with a 'k' and all that. Also, I went to a very progressive, very left-wing high school in Greenwich Village from 1961 to 1965 [Elizabeth Irwin High School]. Everybody was already into marijuana, SNCC, SDS, antiwar, sandals. When I got to college and everybody from Scarsdale was discovering this 'new great lifestyle,' it put me off. I had been through it. It was not an expression of individuality or dissent, but rather just another form of conformity."

Through marriage Abrams joined a coterie of neoconservatives—former liberals who abandoned their past allegiances with a vengeance equalled only by the drunk-turned-teetotaler. His mother-in-law is Midge Decter, who recoiled from her own intellectual-liberal-Jewish parenting. She extrapolated from the experience of those around her to blister the sixties generation and their parents in *Radical Children, Liberal Parents*. She is married to Norman Podhoretz, the once-liberal editor of *Commentary*, now steeped in conservatism, who has added another tome to the Vietnam revisionism, *Why We Were in Vietnam*.

Decter's book "did not spring up from an ideology. It came from raising four children and seeing how it works," says her son-in-law. "She became a stricter mother with each successive child.

"The parents of most in my generation had essentially given them the view that they could do what they want. That is, I think, part of the reason the poor old deans in the sixties got chopped up. They were the first people who had ever said to a lot of middle- and upper-middle-class kids, 'No, you can't do that.' Some of them retain the old rhetoric and some don't, but nobody believes in that crap anymore—'no limits, no orders, no discipline.' Everybody has learned the hard way that you cannot live that way," says Abrams.

"When it comes to the *real* test—how to live your life and raise your kids—everybody has either openly or tacitly acknowledged that all that sixties propaganda was mostly garbage."

Another voice who remembers that time presents a more moderate view. "They weren't all spoiled brats *then* and they aren't all IBM salesmen now. Some were incredibly bright, moved a lot of people, were dedicated then, and remain so today."

David Halberstam, author of *The Best and the Brightest*, was talking about those in the youth brigade who impressed him in the sixties. One of them was Stephen Cohen, who Halberstam met as an intense twenty-two-year-old working on Eugene McCarthy's 1968 Presidential campaign.

Cohen is in his late thirties but looks older. He is balding; there is gray in his curly beard. There is a reflective, professorial quality about him. Deeply touched by his youthful involvement in the peace movement, Cohen remains faithful to causes. He is involved in antinuclear work and in trying to fend off some of the damage that many Americans feel Reagan's policies are inflicting upon the poor, elderly, and disadvantaged. A major successful battle was the 1982 fight to defeat the Administration's proposed tax exemption for segregated schools.

Cohen was at Amherst, graduating two years ahead of Abrams at Harvard. From 1966 to 1972, he was a part-time student and full-time antiwar activist and peace candidate organizer. After Amherst, he was "technically enrolled" in Harvard Graduate School and then Yale Law School. He was one of those brainy students who could show up on campus three weeks before exams, cram on high-potency vitamins and black coffee, take the tests, pass—and go back out organizing. He now teaches at Georgetown University Law School. In the Carter administration, Cohen was on the State Department policy planning staff on arms control and was Deputy Assistant Secretary for Human Rights.

His message is in marked contrast to fellow Ivy Leaguer Abrams who followed him into the State Department.

We talk of the hawkish quick-fix, early-on selective bombing argument for winning in Vietnam. "Look, you know you can say the moon is made of cheese, but it's not. There were only two things that would have made them cave. One was a *massive* land invasion of American troops, one to two million at a time—and thousands more dead. Or two—nuclear weapons.

"The things that happened—Cambodia—all these things are horrible. But what could we have done to prevent it? To have had a Korean situation; that would have caused so much suffering and killing, it would have been impossible."

As for El Salvador, "There is no 'centrist,' there is no *middle* in that country, even if there *was* substantial land reform. Reagan compares the guerrillas of El Salvador all the time with the Sandinistas. They are not democratic, but they are not monolithic either. Opponents of Reagan would do a lot of good to admit that the opposition leadership *is* Marxist. The choice is either a horribly repressive government, the way it is now, or a Marxist-totalitarian solution," Cohen contends. "The major questions are: What is the cost of changing things? Can we make it better? At what cost?"

One of the many sobering aspects of Vietnam is that the "either-or," "right-or-wrong" concept didn't work. There were strong social and moral claims to be made against the government we created and maintained, but we also learned that those claiming to be a populist alternative were hardly flower children. Still, clearly reacting to the Vietnam debacle, Cohen opposes U.S. intervention against Marxist-oriented guerrillas and particularly favors keeping our hands off Central America.

"Insist on no Soviet military aid, no Soviet advisers, but indicate tolerance for a Marxist form of government. The idea that there is a new set of dominoes necessarily going to topple is incorrect," he says. "They probably *will* have a Marxist-totalitarian government in El Salvador and we should say, 'No Soviet troops or aid, but *we* will extend to you what aid you need.'"

Cohen buys an appeal to economics, rather than a military approach, in Central America. "If we can get along with Yugoslavia, Rumania, People's Republic of China, for God's sake why not Central America? Whether they are Marxist or not, they are desperate for economic ties with the West. The Soviet's economy is terrible. We should encourage the French, Germans, and other Western countries to get involved in development there also.

"But Reagan has created this mythology that Cuban support is critical. What we're likely to see is not troops but American planes or ships used to blockade Nicaragua." He sighs. "And that could escalate into larger conflicts."

Cohen's reasons for opposing Vietnam had their origin in world events that occurred before he was born. "I cared so deeply about Vietnam because I am Jewish and I cannot forget the Holocaust. I couldn't understand the lack of protest. The lesson I derived was; 'If your country is doing something wrong, you've got to try to change it.' I remember a quotation: 'To be silent is to lie.' I tried to live my life by that. Vietnam, *of course*, was not the equivalent of the Holocaust, but we were killing a helluva lot of people."

Cohen grimaces about those who hoisted the NLF banner. "Och! They [the other side] were as bad or worse, certainly no better. You don't glorify these people. That prolonged the war, I think."

In his senior year at Amherst, Cohen worked tirelessly for Allard Lowenstein in what became the "Dump Johnson" movement, then worked for McCarthy. His life was chaotic, intense, driven. For months he went three or four days at a time without sleep.

He spoke out on campuses wherever he could, not in moral terms but pragmatic ones. The war was a civil war; there was a nationalist element to it; the cost was out of proportion to winning it; there was government duplicity.

By that time, Cohen had an ulcer and was 1-Y. "If I had wanted to, I think I could have gone, despite the ulcer. I took advantage of it and have some guilt. I rationalize in two ways. One, I did work all that time committed to ending the war. Second, I would have refused induction, I believe. I would *not* have gone into the reserves. But I thought if I had taken the stand and gone to jail I was not going to be doing any good politically."

Ironically, he later says, "Had there been *no* student deferments or loopholes, the war would have ended a lot sooner. Those deferments and loopholes neutralized the opposition of the middle- and upper-class parents."

Cohen feels that there are two major facets about Vietnam that Americans have not faced.

"The people who were for the war have not faced up to the moral issue of what we were doing there. To say that the 'other side was doing it too' does not make it right for America."

The second is a harsh indictment of what he considers the self-defeating actions of many in the peace movement. He feels these actions prolonged the war.

"I fought hard against associating lifestyle issues—drugs, rock music, sex—with the peace movement because they so alienated and turned off people who would have been genuinely against the war. Students generally made a fundamental strategic error by not continuing the 'Clean for Gene' appeal to the middle class."

Cohen looks pained even now as he remembers the factionalism and infighting before the October 1969 Moratorium. He was with the pragmatics who wanted to broaden the base and were pushing for housewives, concerned businessmen, and laborers to join. "Sam Brown and I had a vicious brawl on what direction we should take. Another group— remember the Mobe [New Mobilization]? The more radical? Well, they had this list of nine demands on a whole area of things. God, I can't remember—'Free the New Jersey Eight,' 'Equal Rights for Gay Senior Transvestites,' what have you," he says wryly. He adds, "Some of the demands were quite reasonable—but they weren't to another class of people."

Cohen and others, such as labor activist Carl Wagner, had succeeded in doing what the peace movement had not. They had gotten Walter Reuther and the UAW leadership on their side. Reuther and his group offered to march—which would have had dramatic appeal and an effect on the rank and file whose sons were going to war—if the Moratorium expressed only one demand: withdrawal from Vietnam.

The fights in the Mobe and Moratorium headquaters raged, according to Cohen. Mobe leaders were insistent. They were not going to drop their other demands. Cohen and company argued that Reuther and the UAW were taking a political risk as it was. The Mobe argued that they were not taking a risk. "Besides, what did they matter?" they asked. Union leaders were out of touch with the rank and file anyway. In the end, Sam Brown and his larger-based Moratorium sided with the Mobe.

"Six months later, Sam Brown came to me and said, 'You were right. We should have taken your course.'" Cohen saw a pivotal chance ruined. "I was traumatized. The *one* thing we had been working for was to get the blue-collor on our side.

"Laying aside the tactic of *massive* draft resistance—which no one could persuade enough kids to do—the war would have ended a year or two earlier had the movement *not* adopted radical tactics," Cohen believes. Just at the time when polls showed many in the public were opposing the war, "That realization collided with one violent disruption after another on campus. The Nixon administration was able to present itself as reasonable and moderate in contrast to the students. That prevented a crest we had reached earlier from recurring."

"The movement was many things. There were the New Left, the Rennie Davises and that junk, but there were many moderates who were effective, who unfortunately didn't get the media attention."

Cohen sees complex psychological reasons for what he terms the "acting out" participants in the peace movement. "A strong motivating force for many in college was political guilt. People in better universities felt guilty about coming from affluence and guilty about people starving in this country. They felt guilty about their stereos and nice life—which they *didn't* want to give up. But, believe me, there was a tremendous amount of guilt that people were poor—and that they also were the ones going to Vietnam. That guilt led to looking for an easy, quick catharsis. They got it by yelling 'pig' at a bunch of cops, trashing windows. When you look at it now, what did anyone hope to achieve by breaking windows? There was catharsis in adopting a lifestyle opposite to the establishment."

Impressions are the warp and woof of much of the conversation, views, and theories about the sixties; no ordered, controlled study will ever tie those threads together in some scientific sampling. I ask Cohen why he feels so certain of his guilt-catharsis theory.

"It's my instinct," he says with a smile, "I've worked an awful long time in politics and I have an instinct about what motivates people. There were so few people going to jail at that time that it seemed such a politically futile act," he argues. "There was no point in going to Canada. And the way to assuage my guilt was *not* to go fight in a war that was so morally wrong. Sure, self-interest motivated a lot in the movement, but my answer to that is 'So what?' The real question is would they have gone if America or America's interest had been threatened? I believe they would."

His friends from the past remain active today—working for ratification of SALT II and the nuclear freeze and are involved with local social issues.

"For some, Vietnam did create a political conscience. They're still at it. They're just not all that visible. They've got mortgages and families, but they're still doing things."

The legacy for a generation?

"That's hard. The people I know are in a privileged position. I can't tell how it affected the lives of those who fought and were maimed by it. For those in my socioeconomic class, it was easy to avoid service and we were really no more than inconvenienced. By 1969 there was no way anyone with a good lawyer would be inducted."

There remains one vast division in the generation. No one, not even the most dedicated—although they now decry the way the veteran was treated—shows any inclination to push for veterans' causes. "They should get whatever benefits veterans usually get," says Cohen, "and that Agent Orange stuff is outrageous." What about helping with delayed stress or Agent Orange? "You decide what you want to work for on the basis of what interests you, what you can relate to." Unfortunately for veterans who need help, the war experience is just not in most activists' frame of reference.

Cohen's personal legacy? "I benefited from it because I got involved in political experiences I wouldn't have had for ten to fifteen years. It's a perverse outcome. The war was so horrible in terms of what it did to this country and to Vietnam.

"But I don't think I paid any real price for it."

25. Letters to *Ms.*

EDITED BY MARY THOM

In the period since World War II, and particularly since the 1960s, the United States has experienced a major economic transformation that has forced a vastly greater change in the role of women than of men. We have evolved from a nation immensely richer than all others, in which a middle-class man's wages generally could support a family, to one that, although still wealthy, no longer dominates the global economy; the nearly universal expectation now is that families require two wage earners.

The modern women's movement, which rose in the late 1960s and continues in our time, is in large measure a response to this major cultural and economic shift. Women once supported men's roles in the market economy; who now supports women as they themselves participate directly in that economy? How should men and women relate to one another in this new world? Ms. magazine, in the years after 1972, offered a forum to discuss these and other questions.

Published in the standard glossy magazine format, Ms. was first edited by writer Gloria Steinem with initial financial support from the Ford Foundation. It not only propagandized for feminist reforms, but also tried to make women aware of sexism in American society. Its very title was a challenge: women were no longer to be addressed in a way that indicated their marital status, as if that status defined them.

The "Letters to Ms." column offers a fascinating glimpse into some of the social history of the 1970s and beyond. In the selection offered here from Mary Thom's collection, readers debate paid work, housework, sexuality, child rearing, friendship: all of the issues that the changes in women's lives made urgent. With much questioning and few conclusions they chart the course of a continuing revolution.

1

Much enjoyed "The Liberated Orgasm," but where, may I ask, are men supposed to acquire all this knowledge (it may surprise some sexually frustrated women that we are not born with a Casanova's know-how)? From women who don't openly discuss sexual problems, don't tell their men where things feel best on their bodies, don't use their mouths and hands freely, and don't generally initiate new techniques—yet still expect full sexual satisfaction? Any good male lover—no matter how much he thinks he may have contributed to his present level of sex-

From *Letters to Ms. 1972–1987* edited by Mary Thom. Copyright ©1987 by the Ms. Foundation for Education and Communication, Inc. and The Miller Press, Inc. Reprinted by permission of Henry Holt and Company, Inc.

pertise—will remember at least one especially good woman who taught him "a thing or two."

Lawrence Schenker
Fort Leonard Wood, Missouri
November 1972 Issue

2

I am now twenty-five. From the age of seventeen until rather recently, I lived as a sexually impotent male, in college, in the army, and in law school. Were it not for the women's movement, I would still be such today.

The problem was that I believed the locker-room theories of sex: that women are "scores"; a sexual encounter is a "conquest" by the male; and a man's part is "to perform." When I encountered a woman who had a fully developed sense of herself as a person with needs, desire, and imagination, in a situation in which making love was for each of us a means of pleasing and expressing appreciation for the other, the word *impotence* became just a word for me, and not a central fact of my life. I suggest that as long as we keep telling young men that women are not really people, a lot of them are going to face the same frustrations I did for so long, without ever knowing why.

Name Withheld
May 1974 Issue

3

I have been actively dating men for two years since the end of my five-year marriage. During this time, I have been involved with men twenty-seven years my senior and ten years my junior. I'm twenty-eight.

I have found older men are *consistently* hung up about the following things: their masculinity, their superiority and dominance, and their intellect.

Older men are very easily threatened by the most incredible things! Paying my own way, for example, gives them anxiety attacks. When I convince an older man that my time is important to me, that I will only see him at prearranged times, and that I resent his "dropping by" when I have other things to do, he comes unglued. Many older men still hold on to that old stereotype of the single girl waiting breathlessly by the phone.

Of course, sex is invariably a problem. Older men view women as potential notches in their belts. They equate liberation with promiscuity and find it completely incomprehensible that you don't want to go to bed with them. Sexual freedom to me means not only the freedom to say yes but the freedom to say no!

And the games older men play! All that nonsense is so far behind me now that I don't even remember how to come back with the "helpless little me" response.

If we agree, however, that the basis for a good relationship is open communication, then younger men are the only way to go! They know how to talk, how to get in touch with their feelings. For one thing, their more recent education has included the latest discoveries in psychology and human interaction. They're not afraid of who they are. They're freer of sex-role stereotyping; they're able to express emotion; they're not afraid of feeling. They're more able to consider women as equals. The whole macho tradition has been so little a part of their experience that in short there are fewer years of social conditioning to have to combat. And these are just some of the reasons why the answer to your question is *yes*, it *is* better with a younger man!

Sue Clarry
Sunnyvale, California
October 1976 Issue

4

Speaking as a woman who was divorced after twenty-five years of marriage and who is now well into her fifties, I have made it a point to make sure that my lovers are free from disease before contact. When I have discussed this with women younger than myself, the reaction has been astonishment—"I wouldn't dare"; "How unromantic!"

My experience over the past seven years has been most enlightening. First of all, no man has expressed anger at my suggestion that he be examined for VD (blood test *and* smears), though most have been surprised. I, of course, also go for the necessary tests when I decide to accept a new lover. The attitude of the men, after thinking it over, has generally been that it was a good idea and well worth doing.

Name Withheld
May 1978 Issue

5

I had just put the kids to bed, the house was a wreck, and I still had the dinner dishes to do. But this month's *Ms.* had just arrived, and I couldn't resist sitting down with it for a minute.

Well, one article led to another before I realized that any minute the door would open on the shambles around me. What would I say?

The door opened. It was time to practice what I'd been reading. "I left the dishes for you for a change," I said, cool as a revolutionary. Click!

My wife, home from her graduate-school class, was flabbergasted! I hope she doesn't cancel our subscription.

Mike Tighe
Davis, California
July 1973 Issue

6

While trying to complete the endless errands necessary to get married, my fiancé and I dutifully arrived at the county clerk's office with the items needed to obtain a marriage license. The woman behind the desk filled out several forms and then handed a large legal sheet to us for our signatures. My fiancé got to sign on the line marked Principal, and I got to sign on the blank line underneath.

Next the woman handed me a suspicious-looking plastic bag marked New Homemaker's Kit. It contained the following items: (1) a can of Spray 'n Wash; (2) some Bon Ami polishing cleaner; (3) a bottle of Fantastik; (4) a bottle of Bufferin; (5) coupons for *TV Guide* (so I know when the soap operas are on?), panty hose, and a long list of recommended magazines (*Ms.* was not on the list).

Saving the best for last, the kit included a paperback Harlequin Romance! Inside the front cover were comments from satisfied readers. One summed up the attitude of the New Homemaker's Kit beautifully: "Harlequins help me to escape from housework into a world of romance, adventure, and travel."

Phebe Duff Kelly
Little Rock, Arkansas
September 1978 Issue

7

Your article about children in the office reminded me of stories in old women's magazines about mothers of six children, great home-cooked meals and immaculate houses, who turn out three best sellers a year on the side. It ain't always that easy.

My baby was born in July, and in September I started taking him to my office a few days a week. (I'm a teaching fellow in linguistics at the University of Michigan.) Everybody—my office mates, employers, and students—was cooperative—except the baby. Unlike Alix, Tony did not "mostly sleep and eat for months." Even at the age of one month, he slept very little during the day. Being in the office, with all that activity, disrupted what little schedule he had, so he didn't sleep at all, and I got no work done.

In addition, the office turned out to be an unhealthy place for babies. It was drafty, dirty, and full of people with infections, all of which he caught. Perhaps the worst effect was the anxiety I felt when he was noisy, which was often. People assured me that they didn't mind, but I certainly did, and they soon would have as well. Certain kinds of babies and offices just don't go well together.

Gail Raimi Dreyfuss
Ann Arbor, Michigan
July 1975 Issue

8

I'm afraid Sandra Thompson isn't going to get any sympathy from me regarding her dilemma as a mother.

Evidently, motherhood was not a well-thought-out choice, since she seems to have ignored its realities.

Of course children have to be watched every minute. *Of course* people will look none too kindly upon a child throwing a tantrum in public, especially in a restaurant (where some people are trying to escape from their *own* screaming kids).

It appears that Thompson wants the rest of us to support her choice of life style, not to mention her offspring.

Pam Palmer
Los Angeles, California
March 1980 Issue

9

Sandra Thompson makes an excellent point with her question on child-care facilities at places of employment, and I agree that private companies could provide them. But to ask the government to pick up the tab is unfair. Why should part of my taxes go to caring for someone else's child, or worse, why should I have to pay more tax to accomplish this? I am childless by choice, and part of this decision is based on my financial situation. She is a parent by choice, and should have based her decision partially on her finances. Anyone who has a child should be capable of providing the proper care for that child.

Children are children and should be allowed to be, as Thompson states in her "restaurant" section. But has she never been to a restaurant and had to sit through a meal made unbearable by a screaming or crying child? Children in restaurants are comparable to campaign loudspeakers cruising the streets—an invasion of privacy!

Laura Lynn Nelson
Killington, Vermont
March 1980 Issue

10

Dr. Loos is putting her advice in the wrong place. Instead of telling low-income women that they "must stop having children until they have the ability to support them *on their own*," which means a low-income woman may *never* be able to have a child, Dr. Loos *could* instead advise the government to raise the minimum wage (perhaps with subsidies to small businesses and farms that cannot compensate for the difference). And Dr. Loos *could* have advised the public schools to change their ways, to concentrate on the students' self-confidence *first*, skills *second*. She is, much like blaming the victim, advising the victim. With advice given to the appropriate party, living conditions and the ability to support one's own family could improve for both sexes.

Otherwise, what I hear Dr. Loos saying is only one step away from sterilization of the poor.

Carolyn Chute
Gorham, Maine
October 28, 1982

11

I am becoming resentful of the tyrannical notion that there is only one "correct" way to give birth, i.e., "natural" childbirth. When I become pregnant, I will eat right, sleep well, exercise, and abstain from alcohol, drugs, and even my beloved coffee. But, by God, when the delivery time comes, I will take anesthesia, and gratefully, too. I do not need to feel myself being ripped open by an eight-pound baby to stir my "motherly instincts" or to "stimulate bonding." So what if the baby is groggy for a few minutes? It won't undo the previous nine months of good prenatal care, and the risk is low enough to make it worth it for me. My mother had me under anesthesia, and somehow I managed to become a National Merit scholar in spite of it, thank you. So what's wrong with "Wake me when it's over"?

Martha Barry
Gorham, Maine
December 1984 Issue

12

After a generation of protest and question about the role of women in the modern world, the archetype of motherhood is on the rise again. Every time I pick up a newspaper or magazine, I see articles on having children after thirty-five or on single motherhood.

In one of the September "birth stories," a woman states that going through labor and giving birth to a child is an act of complete courage. I say that it takes an act of complete courage for a woman to choose *not* to give birth to a child. It takes an act of complete courage for a woman to explore other ways of being in the world besides motherhood. It takes an act of courage for a woman to give birth to a book, a painting, a business, an idea, a dance. Giving birth to *oneself* is an act of complete courage.

Nancy Wakeman
San Francisco, California
December 1984 Issue

13

Last week I sat through a nasty twelve-hour custody hearing. My fourteen-year-old brother wishes to live with my father, where he is loved, valued as a person, and where his opinions are considered. Unfortunately, my father is homosexual and lives with his lover of eight years. My brother will be awarded to my mother simply because she is his mother and heterosexual.

My brother has been beaten by his stepfather, but it seems, according to the courts, that it is better to live in a home where you are physically, verbally, and emotionally abused than to live with your gay father, where you are loved.

Name Withheld
June 1983 Issue

14

As a follow-up to "Toys for Free Children," I'd like to tell you the good news: my two-year-old daughter is playing with her Playskool Tool Bench today. . . . The bad news: she's using it as a stove.

Lavonne Peck Bergman
Berkeley, California
April 1974 Issue

15

Why do some men bother women they don't know, and what can women do about it? By *bother*, I mean all those things a man can do to a woman without violating the law: staring, whistling, smacking the lips, making comments—from almost complimentary to downright crude— approaching her and trying to start a conversation against her will, feeling a woman in a crowd while walking swiftly in the other direction, and following her to her home, car, or place of business.

My methods of coping with these situations are unsatisfactory, but they are the best I've come up with. I ignore the starers, whistlers, smackers, feelers, and rude comment makers. At first (and isn't this typical?), I thought maybe all this was my fault—something *I* was doing was causing these men to annoy me. But I've found that many other women share my experience, including my mother.

I enjoy the company of men—but not the variety that tries to pick up a woman on the street. I come home after one of these experiences and sit down and list all the nice men I've known in my life to prove to myself that not all men are bad. This may seem a small problem at first, but it is basic to men's attitudes toward women and effects the quality of a woman's life.

Joyce Williams
Chicago, Illinois
April 1975 Issue

16

Women *do* make men violent. The hatred (fear?) that many men feel toward women comes out in the form of violence: insults, rape, or allowing another man to beat up a woman.

I used to live in a town full of churches, of bars, and of trucks too big for the streets. Spring tried to come even there, so I went to the town's one green spot—an industrial park divided by a polluted creek. I sat down to read a copy of *Ms.* while my dog sniffed at the garbage.

Within ten minutes, three boys appeared across the creek. The *instant* they spotted me, they started in, shouting obscenities at me. The more I ignored them, the more enraged they became.

Suddenly, *I* was too angry to ignore them anymore. What gave them the right to harass me, a person reading in a public park? I lost my temper and screamed at them to quit bugging me; *they started to throw rocks at me!* I was amazed to see the violence I had inspired by just being there. I still can't understand hatred like this in people so young. But violence only begets violence, and if I had a gun...

Ildi Holdstock
Burnaby, British Columbia
March 1975 Issue

17

I met Janet during my freshman year in college, and after much looking each other over, we became friends. Despite our diverse backgrounds—me, middle-class black raised in Harlem; she, an upper-middle-class Jew raised in Shaker Heights—we had a lot of common ground. I recall a roast-beef dinner when I was in a financial depression, seafood crepes on my birthday, and terse advice but a safe place to stay when I was emotionally torn apart after my first real relationship ended. I always knew I could get an objective opinion if I asked for one and only an "Oh, Kathy" when I did something she thought dumb. Janet showed me a different world through books she gave me (which came complete with her critique of each), through her friends, and glimpses of her life in her conversations.

Janet decided to go home and attend law school. I visited her there once, met her parents, and visited her friends. She commented on how at ease I made her parents feel, as I was the first black person they had ever entertained at home, and how proud she was of all of us. Then I never heard from Janet again—no card, no call, no letters, and mine to her were never returned.

After reading the article, I think I understand why it all ended. I was literally the only black person in her whole social circle, and maybe there was no place for me in her new life. I just wished we could have discussed it openly. It wouldn't have made the hurt any less, only bearable.

Name Withheld
November 1983 Issue

18

I have been working for six years in a suburban law office in New Jersey, where the staff consists of seven secretaries (female) and four lawyers (male). It has always been the custom in this office for each "girl" to have her turn at "kitchen duty." She is expected to set the table in the library with dainty place mats, napkins, spoons, and eatables (such as crackers, which the firm finances) and to make coffee. At twelve o'clock everyone in the office, including the lawyers (if they are so inclined), comes into the library, and we all have lunch. Afterward, the woman who has kitchen duty for the day wipes up the table and washes the dishes, including the lunch containers that each person brings in.

I participated unwillingly in this program for six years. Three weeks ago I decided that I had had it and announced that I was no longer to be given kitchen duty; that I would go out for lunch some of the time and when I had lunch in, I'd do my own dishes.

To say that my announcement caused a sensation is to put it mildly. At present, none of the women are speaking to me except when absolutely necessary in the course of work. I have been told by one of the lawyers that no one can understand my attitude and that the women (and, I assume, he) have completely lost respect for me.

I have taken a stand. How it will turn out, I have no idea.

Name Withheld
March 1978 Issue

19

Any woman who has worked both outside and in the home will tell you who it is who doesn't have the time to be sick: there is scarcely a job in the world that won't wait just one day while you get over the flu—except that of being a mother.

For ten hours a week, I teach college English at a state jail; this affords me lots of prestige, because people (correctly) assume that college teaching is a job that demands a high level of ingenuity, commitment, education, and love. For five or six hours a week, whenever I can find the time, I write; this affords me lots of prestige, because people (correctly) assume that writing is a job that demands a high level of ingenuity, commitment, education, and love. For 168 hours a week, I am the mother of a two-and-a-half-year-old child; for this I receive virtually no prestige, despite the fact that parenting is a job that demands a high level of ingenuity, commitment, education, and love.

Come *on*, you guys.

H. Nancy Spector
Juneau, Alaska
September 1979 Issue

20

I thought that most of my clicks were behind me, but tonight, as I cleared the table, I had a new one. I was complimenting myself (since no one else had) on a meal I'd gone to some trouble to prepare. I began to wonder why so many of us wait trembling for "the verdict" at every meal; why my mother and so many others risk antagonizing their families by having the gall to ask outright if everything is okay.

I decided it's not just neurosis. We really know they're judging even when they don't say so. Housewifing is an occupation in which every single waking act is judged by the person who means the most to you in the world. Is the house clean? Is the food good? Was it too expensive? Are the children well behaved?

A thousand times a day our contracts come up for renewal. No wonder our nerves are shot.

Kathleen Phillips Satz
El Cerrito, California
November 1982 Issue

21

The words *congressperson* and *chairperson* are awkward words, typical of the ugly words created by scholars and scientists. Working people traditionally simplify language. God bless the English peasants who gave us a handy, if irregular slanguage, by combining Anglo-Saxon and Norman French and discarding the formalities of both.

Why not use a vowel like *o: congresso* or *chairo?* And for those who don't want to use the syllable *man*, likewise change *foreman, boilerman, anchorman, newspaperman*, et cetera.

The language, agreed, needs more neutral words. Now's the time to make the changes more creatively. Incidentally, we might as well face it: we've got to invent some neutral pronouns. Saying "his or her" all the time is awkward unless we want to slur it into "hizar."

As a man, perhaps I have no right to make such suggestions, but as a user of words, I think I do. Building a new and livable world will necessitate thousands of little changes.

P.S. I've been the chairo of *many* committees, and I like the word.

Pete Seeger
Beacon, New York
February 5, 1974

22

Last week we had lunch in a restaurant. Our waiter said, "Well, girls, have you decided what you would like to eat?" We then explained to him that we were no longer girls. We were women. He laughed and pointed to two older women at another table and said that he had even called them "girls." Later, still infuriated, we called him "boy." He went off in a rage. We tried to explain to him that he was as much a boy as we were girls. He didn't understand.

Lynn Ubell
April Dworetz
Great Neck, New York
April 1973 Issue

23

I am writing about the column in January entitled "In a Class by Herself" by Paula Span. Ms. Span refers to the subject of the article as a "fifteen-year-old woman." I fully agree that to call an adult female a *girl* is insulting and demeaning. There is, however, a time when males are boys and females are girls. If this keeps up we are going to have "ten-year-old women" and "five-year-old women," and heaven knows where it will stop.

Lisa Smith
Garden City, New York
December 27, 1975

24

Will "ring around the collar" commercials go on year after year *forever*? Am I the only one who feels insulted when the camera zooms in on the face of the *wife* looking guilty and ashamed? For heaven's sake, it's *his* shirt! I'm ashamed that American women continue to buy the product.

Name Withheld
December 3, 1980

25

You have given me the supreme insult of my life by offering to let me subscribe to *Ms.* I hate the sound of it. It sounds like the hiss of a snake.

Are you proud of what you have helped do to our world? The family is almost destroyed; children by the millions have no parents or homes; divorces, crimes, dehumanization, are the norm now. Has it been worth all this just to get some women in the military academies?

Mrs. H. Sims
Mount Olivet, Kentucky
January 1977 Issue

26

Out of curiosity I purchased the April issue of *Ms.* It appears to have one dominant message—the goal of castrating all males.

I originally believed that the women's movement was only interested in equal rights, wages, and job opportunities. Now I fully understand your philosophy. Your articles are filled with incest and sick attitudes, and they express a general hatred of most males. I have one feeling for your group: pity.

William D. Nueske
Phoenix, Arizona
August 1977 Issue

26. Watergate

JONATHAN SCHELL

The Watergate crisis was a bizarre, abrupt series of mysterious events, each out of harmony with the one before—trivial burglaries, odd dealings with reclusive billionaires, Saturday night bloodless massacres, a statement by the President of the United States that he was not a "crook," unseemly hassles with reporters, the near impeachment and the resignation of a president. The theatrical story dominated not just the news but the national imagination for many months. Since its dramatic conclusion, theories about its meaning and cause flourish like weeds in a horticulturist's nightmare. Impeachment is such a drastic measure that a president under its threat would have to experience almost every kind of failure. He would find his political support hopelessly collapsed, his morality highly suspect, his associates seriously tainted, his policies in disarray. And even then he would have to be unlucky as well. It is almost impossible for a president to be forced to resign. But all this happened to Richard M. Nixon.

Jonathan Schell offers one of the more persuasive and even-tempered views of the spectacle. Schell emphasizes both the problems of conducting foreign policy in secret and Nixon's personality as contributing influences leading to the Watergate scandals. Other writers, however, have emphasized other explanations: new Nixon men, for instance, undermining old party arrangements, new Texas and California money threatening the East. We must understand the whole history of the Cold War, the intelligence apparatus it spawned, and the domestic political and economic arrangements that it influenced before a full assessment of this catastrophe will become apparent.

In mid-1972, as President Nixon returned to the United States from his trip to Russia—where he had signed the first Soviet-American agreements on the limitation of nuclear arms—and as his reëlection campaign got under way, the systemic crisis that had been threatening the survival of Constitutional government in the United States ever since he took office was deepening. The crisis had apparently had its beginnings in the war in Vietnam. Certainly the lines connecting the crisis to the war were numerous and direct. The war had been the principal issue in the struggle between the President and his political opposition—a struggle that had provoked what he called the Presidential Offensive, which was aimed at destroying independent centers of authority in the nation. In more specific ways, too, the evolution of the Administration's usurpations of authority had been bound up with the war. Almost as soon as the President took office, he had ordered a secret bombing campaign against Cambodia (theretofore neutral). When details of the campaign leaked out, he had placed warrantless wiretaps on the phones of newsmen and White House aides. And when J. Edgar Hoover, the Director of the Federal Bureau of Investigation, seemed to be on the verge of getting hold of summaries of those tapped conversations, the President, in his efforts to prevent this, had entered into a venomous hidden struggle with the Director, and the Nixon White House had tried to damage the Director's reputation in the press. In another incident growing out of the war, the White House had hired undercover operatives to "nail" Daniel Ellsberg (as their employers expressed it) after Ellsberg gave the Pentagon Papers to the press; and then some of these operatives had been transferred to the Committee for the Re-Election of the President, where they went on to plan and execute criminal acts against the Democrats.

The evolution of the warrantless-wiretap incident and of the Pentagon Papers incident illustrated one of the ways in which the crisis of the Constitutional system was deepening. Large quantities of secret information were building up in the White House, first in connection with the war policy and then in connection with the President's plans in insure his reëlection. Every day, as the White House operatives went on committing their crimes, the reservoir of secrets grew. And the very presence of so many secrets compelled still more improper maneuverings, and thus the creation of still more secrets, for to prevent any hint of all that information from reaching the public was an arduous business. There had to be ever-spreading programs of surveillance and increasing efforts to control government agencies. Only agencies that unquestioningly obeyed White House orders could be relied upon to protect the White House secrets, and since in normal times it was the specific obligation of some of the agencies to uncover wrongdoing, wherever it might occur, and bring the wrongdoers to justice, some agencies had to be disabled completely. In effect, investigative agencies such as the F.B.I. and Central Intelligence Agency had to be enlisted in the obstruction of justice.

At some point back at the beginning of the Vietnam war, long before Richard Nixon became President, American history had split into two streams. One flowed aboveground, the other underground. At first, the underground stream was only a trickle of events. But during the nineteen-sixties—the period mainly described in the Pentagon Papers— the trickle grew to a torrent, and a significant part of the record of foreign affairs disappeared from public view. In the Nixon years, the torrent flowing underground began to include events in the domestic sphere, and soon a large part of the domestic record, too, had plunged out of sight. By 1972, an elaborate preëlection strategy—the Administration strategy of dividing the Democrats—was unfolding in deep secrecy. And this strategy of dividing the Democrats governed not only a program of secret sabotage and espionage but the formation of Administration policy on the most important issues facing the nation. Indeed, hidden strategies for consolidating Presidential authority had been governing expanding areas of Administration policy since 1969, when it first occurred to the President to frame policy not to solve what one aide called "real problems" but to satisfy the needs of public relations. As more and more events occurred out of sight, the aboveground, public record of the period became impoverished and misleading. It became a carefully smoothed surface beneath which many of the most significant events of the period were being concealed. In fact, the split between the Administration's real actions and policies was largely responsible for the new form of government that had arisen in the Nixon White House—a form in which images consistently took precedence over substance, and affairs of state were ruled by what the occupants of the White House called scenarios. The methods of secrecy and the techniques of public relations were necessary to one another, for the people, lacking access to the truth, had to be told something, and it was the public-relations experts who decided what that something would be.

When the President made his trip to Russia, some students of government who had been worried about the crisis of the American Constitutional system allowed themselves to hope that the relaxation of tensions in the international sphere would spread to the domestic sphere. Since the tensions at home had grown out of events in the international sphere in the first place, it seemed reasonable to assume that an improvement in the mood abroad would give some relief in the United States, too. These hopes were soon disappointed. In fact, the President's drive to expand his authority at home was accelerated; although the nation didn't know it, this was the period in which White House operatives advanced from crimes whose purpose was the discovery of national-security leaks to crimes against the domestic political opposition. The Presidential Offensive had not been called off; it had merely been routed underground. The President spoke incessantly of peace, and had arranged for his public-relations men to portray him as a man of peace, but there was to be no peace—not in Indo-China, and not with a constantly growing list of people he saw as his domestic "enemies." Détente, far from relaxing tensions at home, was seen in the White House as one more justification for its campaign to crush the opposition and seize absolute power.

On Sunday, June 18, 1972, readers of the front page of the *Times* learned, among other things, that heavy American air strikes were continuing over North Vietnam, that the chairman of President Nixon's Council of Economic Advisers, Herbert Stein, had attacked the economic proposals of Senator George McGovern, who in less than a month was to become the Presidential nominee of the Democratic Party, and that the musical "Fiddler on the Roof" had just had its three-thousand-two-hundred-and-twenty-fifth performance on Broadway. Readers of page 30 learned, in a story not listed in the "News Summary and Index," that five men had been arrested in the headquarters of the Democratic National Committee, in the Watergate office building, with burglary tools, cameras, and equipment for electronic surveillance in their possession. In rooms that the men had rented, under aliases, in the adjacent Watergate Hotel, thirty-two hundred-dollar bills were found, along with a notebook containing the notation "E. Hunt" (for E. Howard Hunt, as it turned out) and, next to that, the notation "W. H." (for the White House). The men were members of the Gemstone team, a White House undercover group, which had been attempting to install bugging devices in the telephones of Democrats.

Most of the high command of the Nixon Administration and the Nixon reëlection committee were out of town when the arrests were made. The President and his chief of staff, H. R. Halderman, were on the President's estate in Key Biscayne, Florida. The President's counsel, John Dean, was in Manila, giving a lecture on drug abuse. John Mitchell, the former Attorney General, who was then director of the Committee for the Re-Election of the President, and Jeb Magruder, a former White House aide, who had become the committee's assistant director, were in California. In the hours and days immediately following the arrests, there was a flurry of activity at the headquarters of the committee, in a Washington office building; in California; and at the White House. Magruder called his assistant in Washington and had him remove certain papers—what later came to be publicly known as Gemstone materials—from his files. Gordon Liddy, by then the chief counsel of the Finance Committee to Re-Elect the President, went into the headquarters himself, removed from his files other materials having to do with the break-in, including other hundred-dollar bills, and shredded them. At the White House, Gordon Strachan, an aide to Haldeman, shredded a number of papers having to do with the setting up of the reëlection committee's undercover operation, of which the break-in at the headquarters of the Democratic National Committee was an important part. Liddy, having destroyed all the evidence in his possession, offered up another piece of potential evidence for destruction: himself. He informed Dean that if the White House wished to have him assassinated he would stand at a given street corner at an appointed time to make things easy. E. Howard Hunt went to his office in the Executive Office Building, took from a safe ten thousand dollars in cash he had there for emergencies, and used it to hire an attorney for the burglars. In the days following, Hunt's name was expunged from the White House telephone directory. On orders from John Ehrlichman, the President's chief domestic-affairs adviser, his safe was opened and his papers were removed. At one point, Dean—also said to have been acting under instructions from Ehrlichman—gave an order for Hunt to leave the country, but then the order was rescinded. Hunt's payment to an attorney for the burglars was the first of many. The President's personal attorney, Herbert Kalmbach, was instructed by Dean and, later, by Ehrlichman, Haldeman, and Mitchell to keep on making payments, and he, in turn, delegated the task to Anthony Ulasewicz, a retired New York City policeman who had been hired to conduct covert political investigations for the White House. Theirs was a hastily improvised operation. Kalmbach and Ulasewicz spoke to each other from phone booths. (Phone booths apparently had a strong attraction for Ulasewicz. He attached a change-maker to his belt to be sure to have enough coins for his calls, and he chose to make several of his "drops" of the payoff money in them.) He and Kalmbach used aliases and code language in their conversations. Kalmbach became Mr. Novak and Ulasewicz became Mr. Rivers—names that seem to have been chosen for no specific reason. Hunt, who had some forty mystery stories published, was referred to as "the writer," and Haldeman, who wore a crewcut, as "the brush." The payoff money became "the laundry," because when Ulasewicz arrived at Kalmbach's hotel room to pick up the first installment he put it in a laundry bag. The burglars were "the players," and the payoff scheme was "the script." Apparently, the reason the White House conspirators spoke to one another from phone booths was that they thought the Democrats might be wiretapping them, just as they had wiretapped the Democrats. In late June, the President himself said to Haldeman, of the Democrats, "When they start bugging us, which they have, our little boys will not know how to handle it. I hope they will, though." Considerations like these led Kalmbach, Ulasewicz, and others working for the White House to spend many unnecessary hours in phone booths that summer.

All these actions were of the sort that any powerful group of conspirators might take upon the arrest of some of their number. Soon, however, the White House was taking actions that were possibly only because the conspirator occupied high positions in the government, including the highest position of all—the Presidency. For almost four years, the President had been "reorganizing" the executive branch of the government with a view to getting the Cabinet departments and the agencies under his personal control, and now he undertook to use several of these agencies to cover up crimes committed by his subordinates. In the early stages of the coverup, his efforts were directed toward removing a single evidentiary link: the fact that the Watergate burglars had been paid with funds from his campaign committee. There was a vast amount of other information that needed to be concealed—information concerning not just the Watergate break-in but the whole four-year record of the improper and illegal activities of the White House undercover operators, which stretched from mid-1969, when the warrantless wiretaps were placed, to the months in 1972 when the secret program for dividing the Democrats was being carried out—but if this one fact could somehow be suppressed, then the chain of evidence would be broken, and the rest of it might go undetected. On June 23rd, the President met with Haldeman and ordered him to have the C.I.A. request that the F.B.I. halt its investigation into the origin of the Watergate burglars' funds, on the pretext that C.I.A. secrets might come to light if the investigation went forward. The problem, Haldeman told the President, was that "the F.B.I. is not under control, because Gray doesn't exactly know how to control it." Patrick Gray was Acting Director of the F.B.I. "The way to handle this now," he went on, "is for us to have Walters call Pat Gray and just say, 'Stay to hell out of this.'" The reference was to Vernon Walters, Deputy Director of the C.I.A. A moment later, Haldeman asked the President, concerning the F.B.I., "And you seem to think the thing to do is get them to stop?" "Right, fine," the President answered. But he wanted Haldeman to issue the instructions. "I'm not going to get that involved," he said. About two hours later, Haldeman and Ehrlichman met with C.I.A. Director Richard Helms and Deputy Director Walters, and issued the order.

The maneuver gave the White House only a temporary advantage. Six days later, on June 29th, Gray did cancel interviews with two people who could shed light on the origin of the burglars' funds. (On the twenty-eighth, Ehrlichman and Dean had handed him all the materials taken from Hunt's safe, and Dean had told him that they were never to "see the light of day." Gray had taken them home, and later he burned them.) But soon a small rebellion broke out among officials of the F.B.I. and the C.I.A. Meetings were held, and at one point Gray and Walters told each other they would rather resign than submit to the White House pressure and compromise their agencies. Several weeks after the request was made, the F.B.I. held the interviews after all. The rebellion in the ranks of the federal bureaucracy was not the first to break out against the Nixon White House. As early as 1969, some members of the Justice Department had fought Administration attempts to thwart the civil-rights laws. In 1970, members of the State Department and members of the Office of Education, in the Department of Health, Education, and Welfare, had protested the invasion of Cambodia. In 1970, too, J. Edgar Hoover had refused to go along with a White House scheme devised by a young lawyer named Tom Huston for illegal intelligence-gathering. The executive bureaucracy was one source of the President's great power, but it was also acting as a check on his power. In some ways, it served this function more effectively than the checks provided by the Constitution, for, unlike the other institutions of government, it at least had some idea of what was going on. But ultimately it was no replacement for the Constitutional checks. A President who hired and fired enough people could in time bring the bureaucracy to heel. And although a Bray, a Walters, or a Helms might offer some resistance to becoming deeply involved in White House crimes, they would do nothing to expose the crimes. Moreover, the bureaucracy had no public voice, and was therefore powerless to sway public opinion. Politicians of all persuasions could—and did—heap abuse on "faceless," "briefcase-toting" bureaucrats and their "red tape," and the bureaucracy had no way to reply to this abuse. It had only its silent rebellions, waged with the passive weapons of obfuscation, concealment, and general foot-dragging. Decisive opposition, if there was to be any, had to come from without.

With respect to the prosecutorial arm of the Justice Department, the White House had aims that were less ambitious than its aims with respect to the F.B.I. and the C.I.A., but it was more successful in achieving them. Here, on the whole, the White House men wished merely to keep abreast of developments in the grand-jury room of the U.S. District Court, where officials of the Committee for the Re-Election of the President were testifying on Watergate, and this they accomplished through the obliging coöperation of Henry Petersen, the chief of the Criminal Division, who reported regularly to John Dean and later to the President himself. Dean subsequently described the coöperation to the President by saying, "Petersen is a soldier. He played—he kept me informed. He told me when we had problems, where we had problems, and the like. Uh, he believes in, in, in you. He believes in this Administration. This Administration had made him." What happened in the grand-jury room was further controlled by the coordinating of perjured testimony from White House aides and men working for the campaign committee. As for the prosecutors, a sort of dim-wittedness—a failure to draw obvious conclusions, a failure to follow up leads, a seeming willingness to construe the Watergate case narrowly—appeared to be enough to keep them from running afoul of the White House.

While all these moves were being made, the public was treated to a steady stream of categorical denials that the White House or the President's campaign committee had had anything to do with the break-in or with efforts to cover up the origins of the crime. The day after the break-in, Mitchell, in California, described James McCord, one of the burglars, as "the proprietor of a private security agency who was employed by our Committee months ago to assist with the installation of our security system." Actually, McCord was the committee's chief of security at the moment when he was arrested. Mitchell added, "We want to emphasize that this man and the other people involved were not operating either in our behalf or with our consent.... There is no place in our campaign or in the electoral process for this type of activity, and we will not permit nor condone it." On June 19th, two days after the break-in, Ronald Ziegler, the President's press secretary, contemptuously dismissed press reports of White House involvement. "I'm not going to comment from the White House on a third-rate burglary attempt," he said. On June 20th, when Lawrence O'Brien, the chairman of the Democratic Party, revealed that the Party had brought a one-million-dollar civil-damages suit against the Committee for the Re-Election of the President and the five burglary suspects, charging invasion of privacy and violation of the civil rights of the Democrats, Mitchell stated that the action represented "another example of sheer demagoguery on the part of Mr. O'Brien." Mitchell said, "I reiterate that this committee did not authorize and does not condone the alleged actions of the five men apprehended there."

Among the nation's major newspapers, only one, *The Washington Post*, consistently gave the Watergate story prominent headlines on the front page. Most papers, when they dealt with the story at all, tended to treat it as something of a joke. All in all, the tone of the coverage was not unlike the coverage of the Clifford Irving affair the previous winter, and the volume of the coverage was, if anything, less. "Caper" was the word that most of the press settled upon to describe the incident. A week after the break-in, for instance, the *Times* headlined its Watergate story "WATERGATE CAPER." When another week had passed, and Howard Hunt's connection with the break-in had been made known, *Time* stated that the story was "fast stretching into the most provocative caper of 1972, an extraordinary bit of bungling of great potential advantage to the Democrats and damage to the Republicans in this election year." In early August, the *Times* was still running headlines like "THE PLOT THICKENS IN WATERGATE WHODUNIT" over accounts of the repercussions of the burglary. "Above all, the purpose of the break-in seemed obscure," the *Times* said. "But these details are never explained until the last chapter." The President held a news conference six weeks after the break-in, and by then the story was of such small interest to newsmen that not one question was asked concerning it.

Disavowals such as those made by Mitchell and Ziegler carried great weight in the absence of incontrovertible evidence refuting them. The public had grown accustomed to deception and evasion in high places, but not yet to repeated, consistent, barefaced lying at all levels. The very boldness of the lies raised the cost of contradicting them, for to do so would be to call high officials outright liars. Another effective White House technique was to induce semi-informed or wholly un-informed spokesmen to deny charges. One of these spokesmen was Clark Mac-Gregor, a former member of Congress from Minnesota, who became reëlection-campaign director early in July, when John Mitchell resigned, pleading family difficulties. A few weeks later, when Senator McGovern described the break-ins as "the kind of thing you expect under a person like Hitler," MacGregor called McGovern's remark "character assassination." The practice of using as spokesmen officials who were more or less innocent of the facts was one more refinement of the technique of dissociating "what we say" from "what we do." In this manner, honest men could be made to lend the weight of their integrity to untruths. They spoke words without knowing whether the words were true or false. Such spokesmen lent their vocal cords to the campaign but left their brains behind, and confused the public with words spoken by nobody.

On September 15th, the five men who had been caught in the Democratic National Committee headquarters were indicted—together with E. Howard Hunt and G. Gordon Liddy, who were elsewhere in the Watergate complex at the time of the break-in—for the felonies of burglary, conspiracy, and wiretapping. A few days later, the seven defendants pleaded not guilty. As the case stood at the moment, their crimes were officially motiveless. The prosecutors had not been able to suggest who might have asked employees of the Committee for the Re-Election of the President to wiretap the Democratic headquarters, or why a check belonging to that committee should have found its way into the bank account of Bernard Barker. That afternoon, the President met with Haldeman and Dean, and congratulated Dean on his work, "Well," he said, "the whole thing is a can of worms. . . . But the, but the way you, you've handled it, it seems to me, has been very skillful, because you—putting your fingers in the dikes every time that leaks have sprung here and sprung there." Representative Wright Patman, the Chairman of the House Banking and Currency Committee, was planning to hold hearings on the Watergate break-in, and the President, Dean, and Haldeman went on to discuss ways of "turning that off," as Dean put it. Dean reported to the two others that he was studying the possibility of blackmailing members of the Patman committee with damaging information about their own campaigns, and then the President suggested that Gerald Ford, the minority leader of the House, would be the man to pressure Patman into dropping the hearings. Ford should be told that "he's got to get at this and screw this thing up while he can," the President said. Two and a half weeks later, a majority of the members of the committee voted to deny Patman the power to subpoena witnesses. But Patman made the gesture of carrying on anyway for a while, and asked questions of an empty chair.

At the end of September—more than a month before the election—*The Washington Post* reported that John Mitchell had had control of a secret fund for spying on the Democrats. Throughout October, denials continued to pour out from the Administration. As before, some were outright lies by men who knew the facts, and others were untruths spoken by men who were simply repeating what they had been told. On October 2nd, Acting Director Gray of the F.B.I. said that it was unreasonable to believe that the President had deceived the nation about Watergate. "Even if some of us [in federal law enforcement agencies] are crooked, there aren't that many that are. I don't believe everyone is a Sir Galahad, but there's not been one single bit of pressure put on me or any of my special agents." In reality, of course, Gray had once considered resigning because the pressure from the White House to help with the coverup had been so intense, and even as he spoke he was keeping the contents of E. Howard Hunt's safe in a drawer of a dresser at his home in Connecticut. Gray went on to say, "It strains the credulity that the President of the United States—if he had a mind to— could have done a con job on the whole American people." Gray added, "He would have to control the United States."

In the months since the election, the issue of Watergate had faded, and the papers had devoted their front pages to other news. Shortly after the trial began, however, the front-page news was that all the defendants but two had pleaded guilty. In the courtroom, Judge John Sirica, who presided, found himself dissatisfied with the questioning of witnesses by the government prosecutors. The prosecutors now had a suggestion as to the burglars' motive. They suggested that it might be blackmail. They did not say of whom or over what. At the trial, the key prosecution witness, the former F.B.I. agent Alfred Baldwin, related that on one occasion he had taken the logs of the Watergate wiretaps to the headquarters of the Committee for the Re-Election of the President. But this suggested nothing to the Justice Department, one of whose spokesmen had maintained when the indictment was handed up in September that there was "no evidence" showing that anyone except the defendants was involved. Sirica demurred. "I want to know where the money comes from," he said to the defendant Bernard Barker. "There were hundred-dollar bills floating around like coupons." When Barker replied that he had simply received the money in the mail in a blank envelope and had no idea who might have sent it, Sirica commented, "I'm sorry, but I don't believe you." When the defense lawyers protested Sirica's questioning, he said, "I don't think we should sit up here like nincompoops. The function of a trial is to search for the truth."

All the Watergate defendants but one were following the White House scenario to the letter. The exception was James McCord. He was seething with scenarios of his own. He hoped to have the charges against him dismissed, and, besides, he had been angered by what he understood as a suggestion from one of his lawyers that the blame for the Watergate break-in be assigned to the C.I.A., his old outfit, to which he retained an intense loyalty. There was some irony in the fact that McCord's anger had been aroused by an Administration plan to involve the C.I.A. in its crimes. McCord believed that Nixon's removal of C.I.A. director Richard Helms, in December of 1972—at the very time that McCord himself was being urged to lay the blame for Watergate at the door of the C.I.A.—was designed to pave the way for an attempt by the Administration itself to blame the break-in on the agency and for a takeover of the agency by the White House. He had worked for the White House, but he did not see the reorganizational wars from the White House point of view. He saw them from the bureaucrats' point of view; in his opinion, President Nixon was attempting to take over the C.I.A. in a manner reminiscent of attempts by Hitler to take control of German intelligence agencies before the Second World War. The White House, that is, belatedly discovered that it had a disgruntled "holdover" on its hands. And this particular holdover really was prepared to perform sabotage; he was prepared, indeed, to sabotage not just the President's policies but the President himself, and, what was more, he had the means to do it. McCord was putting together a scenario that could destroy the Nixon Administration. In a letter delivered to his White House contact, the undercover operative John Caulfield, McCord pronounced a dread warning: If the White House continued to try to have the C.I.A. take responsibility for the Watergate burglary, "every tree in the forest will fall," and "it will be a scorched desert." Piling on yet another metaphor of catastrophe, he wrote, "Pass the message that if they want it to blow, they are on exactly the right course. I am sorry that you will get hurt in the fallout." McCord was the first person in the Watergate conspiracy to put in writing exactly what the magnitude of the Watergate scandal was. Many observers had been amazed at the extreme hard line that the President had taken since his landslide reëlection—the firings in the bureaucracies, the incomprehensible continuation of the attack on Senator McGovern, the renewed attacks on the press, the attacks on Congress's power of the purse, the bombing of Hanoi. They could not know that at the exact moment when President Nixon was wreaking devastation on North Vietnam, James McCord was threatening to wreak devastation on him.

On February 7th, the Senate, by a vote of seventy-seven to none, established a select Committee on Presidential Campaign Activities, to look into abuses in the Presidential campaign of 1972, including the Watergate break-in; and the Democratic leadership appointed Senator Sam Ervin, of North Carolina, the author of the resolution to establish the Select Committee, to be its chairman. Three days later, the Administration secretly convened a Watergate committee of its own, in California—at the La Costa Resort Hotel and Spa, not far from the President's estate in San Clemente, with John Dean, H. R. Haldeman, John Ehrlichman, and Richard Moore, a White House aide, in attendance. The meeting lasted for two days. Its work was to devise ways of hampering, discrediting, and ultimately blocking the Ervin committee's investigation.

The President's drive to take over the federal government was going well. By the end of March those legislators who were worried about the possibility of a collapse of the Constitutional system were in a state of near-hopelessness. It seemed that the President would have his will, and Congress could not stop him; as for the public, it was uninterested in Constitutional matters. Senator Muskie had now joined Senator McGovern in warning against the dangers of "one-man rule," and he said that the Administration's proposal for preventing the release of "classified" information, no matter how arbitrarily the "classified" designation had been applied, could impose "the silence of democracy's graveyard."

Senator William Fulbright, of Arkansas, had expressed fear that the United States might "pass on, as most of the world has passed on, to a totalitarian system." In the press, a new feeling seemed to be crystallizing that Congress had had its day as an institution of American life. Commentators of all political persuasions were talking about Congress as though it were moribund. Kevin Phillips, a political writer who had played an important role in formulating "the Southern strategy," and who had once worked in John Mitchell's Justice Department, wrote, in an article in *Newsweek* called "Our Obsolete System," that "Congress's separate power is an obstacle to modern policy-making." He proposed a "fusion of powers" to replace the Constitution's separation of powers. "In sum," he wrote, "we may have reached a point where separation of powers is doing more harm than good by distorting the logical evolution of technology-era government." In *The New Republic,* the columnist TRB, who, like Senator McGovern and Senator Muskie, was worried that "one-man rule" was in prospect, wrote, "President Nixon treats Congress with contempt which, it has to be admitted, is richly deserved. We have a lot of problems—the economy, inflation, the unfinished war, Watergate—but in the long run the biggest problem is whether Congress can be salvaged, because if it can't, our peculiar 18th-century form of government, with separation of powers, can't be salvaged," And he wrote, "A vacuum has to be filled. The authority of Congress has decayed till it is overripe and rotten. Mr. Nixon has merely proclaimed it." At the Justice Department, Donald Santarelli, who was shortly to become head of the Law Enforcement Assistance Administration, told a reporter, "Today, the whole Constitution is up for grabs." These observers took the undeniable fact that the Congress was impotent as a sign that the Congress was obsolete. And the executive branch, having helped reduce the Congress to helplessness, could now point to that helplessness as proof that the Congress was of no value.

The coverup and the takeover had merged into a single project. For four years, the President's anger at his "enemies" had been growing. As his anger had grown, so had the clandestine repressive apparatus in the White House whose purpose was to punish and destroy his enemies. And as this apparatus had grown, so had the need to control the Cabinet departments and the agencies; and the other branches of government, because they might find out about it—until, finally, the coverup had come to exceed in importance every other matter facing the Administration. For almost a year now, the coverup had been the motor of American politics. It had safeguarded the President's reëlection, and it had determined the substance and the mood of the Administration's second term so far. In 1969, when President Nixon launched his Presidential Offensive, he had probably not foreseen that the tools he was developing then would one day serve him in a mortal struggle between his Administration and the other powers of the Republic; but now his assault on the press, the television networks, the Congress, the federal bureaucracy, and the courts had coalesced into a single, coordinated assault on the American Constitutional democracy. Either the Nixon Administration would survive in power and the democracy would die or the Administration would be driven from power and the democracy would have another chance to live. If the newly reëlected President should be able to thwart investigations by the news media, the agencies of federal law enforcement, the courts, and Congress, he would be clear of all accountability, and would be above the law; on the other hand, if the rival institutions of the Republic should succeed in laying bare the crimes of his Administration and in bringing the criminals to justice, the Administration would be destroyed.

In the latter part of March, the pace of events in this area of the coverup quickened. Under the pressure of the pending sentences, two of the conspirators were breaking ranks: James McCord and Howard Hunt. McCord, who had been threatening the White House with exposure since December, now wrote a letter to Judge Sirica telling what he knew of the coverup. Hunt, for his part, was angry because he and the other defendants and their lawyers had not been paid as much money as they wanted in return for their silence. In November, 1972, he called Charles Colson to remind him that the continuation of the coverup was a "two-way street," and shortly after the middle of March he told Paul O'Brien, an attorney for the reëlection committee, that if more funds weren't forthcoming immediately he might reveal some of the "many things" he had done for John Haldeman—an apparent reference to the break-in at the office of Daniel Ellsberg's psychiatrist. Shortly thereafter, O'Brien informed Dean of Hunt's demand. These events on one edge of the coverup had an immediate influence on the chemistry of the whole enterprise. On March 21st, John Dean, convinced now that the coverup could not be maintained, met with the President and told him the story of it as he knew it from beginning to end. The President's response was to recommend that the blackmail money be paid to Hunt. "I think you should handle that one pretty fast," he said. And later he said, "But at the moment don't you agree that you'd better get the Hunt thing? I mean, that's worth it, at the moment." And he said, "That's why, John, for your immediate thing you've got no choice with Hunt but the hundred and twenty or whatever it is. Right?" The President was willing to consider plans for limited disclosure, and the meeting ended with a suggestion form Haldeman, who had joined the two other men: "We've got to figure out where to turn it off at the lowest cost we can, but at whatever cost it takes."

The defection of Hunt and McCord had upset the delicate balance of roles demanded by the coverup. Information that had to be kept secret began to flow in a wide loop through the coverup's various departments. Not only Hunt and McCord but Dean and Magruder began to tell their stories to the prosecutors. The prosecutors, in turn, relayed the information to Attorney General Kleindienst and Assistant Attorney General Petersen, who then relayed it to the President, who then relayed it to Haldeman and Ehrlichman, who in this period were desperately attempting to avoid prosecution, and were therefore eager to know what was happening in the Grand Jury room. Any defections placed the remaining conspirators in an awkward position. In order to get clear of the collapsing coverup, they had to become public inquisitors of their former subordinates and collaborators. Such a transformation, however, was not likely to sit well with the defectors, who were far from eager to shoulder the blame for the crimes of others, and who, furthermore, were in possession of damaging information with which to retaliate.

Notwithstanding these new tensions, the President sought to continue the coverup. In the weeks following his meeting with Dean on March 21st, his consistent strategy was what might be called the hors d'oeuvre strategy. The President described the strategy to Haldeman and Ehrlichman after a conversation with Dean on April 14th by saying, "Give 'em an hors d'oeuvre and maybe they won't come back for the main course." His hope was that by making certain public revelations and by offering a certain number of victims to the prosecutors he could satisfy the public's appetite, so that it would seek no more revelations and no more victims. (This technique, which Ehrlichman, on another occasion, called a "modified limited hang-out," was also what Haldeman had had in mind when he suggested that they should "turn it off at the lowest cost" they could.) Hors d'oeuvres of many kinds came under consideration. Some were in the form of scapegoats to be turned over to the prosecutors, and others were in the form of incomplete or false reports to be issued to the public. By now, the country's appetite for revelations was well developed, and in the White House it was decided that no less a man than Mitchell was needed to satisfy it.

As Ehrlichman explained the new plan to the President, Mitchell would be induced to make a statement saying "I am both morally and legally responsible."

"How does it redound to our advantage?" the President asked.

"That you have a report from me based on three weeks' work," Ehrlichman replied, "that when you got it, you immediately acted to call Mitchell in as the provable wrongdoer, and you say, 'My God, I've got a report here. And it's clear from this report that you are guilty as hell. Now John . . . go on in there and do what you should.'"

That way, the President could pose as the man who had cracked the conspiracy.

Shortly thereafter, Mitchell was called down to the White House, and Ehrlichman proposed the plan. Mitchell did not care for it. He not only maintained his innocence but suggested that the guilt lay elsewhere; namely, in the White House. Ehrlichman told the President when Mitchell had left that Mitchell had "lobbed, uh, mud balls at the White House at every opportunity." Faced with Mitchell's refusal to play the scapegoat, the President, Haldeman, and Ehrlichman next invited Dean to step into the role. Soon after Ehrlichman's unsatisfactory experience with Mitchell, the President met with Dean and attempted to induce him to sign a letter of resignation because of his implication in the scandal.

The President approached the subject in an offhand manner. "You know, I was thinking we ought to get the odds and ends, uh . . . we talked, and, uh, it was confirmed that—you remember we talked about resignations and so forth," he said.

"Uh huh," Dean replied

"But I should have in hand something, or otherwise they'll say, 'What the hell did you—after Mr. Dean told you all of this, what did you do?'" The President went on.

Again Dean answered "Uh huh."

The President then related that even Henry Petersen had been concerned about "this situation on Dean," and Dean once more answered with an "uh huh."

"See what I mean?" the President asked the uncommunicative Dean.

"Are we talking Dean, or are we talking Dean, Ehrlichman, and Haldeman?" Dean finally asked.

"Well, I'm talking Dean," the President answered.

But Dean, like Mitchell before him, was talking Ehrlichman and Haldeman, too, and would not resign unless they also resigned. He did not want to be an hors d'oeuvre any more than Mitchell did. And since Dean was in possession of highly detailed information that implicated not only Haldeman and Ehrlichman but the President as well, the President was unable to "bite the Dean bullet," as he put it, until he also was willing to let Haldeman and Ehrlichman go. Their turn came quickly. By now the President was under intense pressure to act soon. If he did not, he could hardly pose as the man who had cracked the case. On April 17th, the day after the unproductive conversation with Dean, the President said to Haldeman and Ehrlichman, "Let me say this . . . It's a hell of a lot different [from] John Dean. I know that as far as you're concerned, you'll go out and throw yourselves on a damned sword. I'm aware of that. . . . The problem we got here is this. I do not want to be in a position where the damned public clamor makes, as it did with Eisenhower, with Adams, makes it necessary or calls—to have Bob come in one day and say, 'Well, Mr. President, the public—blah, blah, blah— I'm going to leave.'" But Ehrlichman was not willing to throw himself on a sword. The person he was willing to throw on a sword was Dean. "Let me make a suggestion," he responded. It was that the President give Dean a leave of absence and then defer any decision on Ehrlichman and Haldeman until the case had developed further. However, the President pursued the point, seeming at times to favor Haldeman's and Ehrlichman's resignation, and finally Ehrlichman did what McCord, Hunt, Mitchell, and Dean had done before him. He lobbed mud balls at the White House—which in this case meant the President.

If he and Haldeman should resign, Ehrlichman observed, "we are put in a position of defending ourselves." And he went on, "The things that I am going to have to say about Dean are: basically that Dean was the sole proprietor of this project, that he reported to the President, he reported to me only incidentally."

"'Reported to the President'?" the President inquired.

A moment later, speaking in his own defense, the President said, "You see the problem you've got there is that Dean does have a point there which you've got to realize. He didn't see me when he came out to California. He didn't see me until the day you said, 'I think you ought to talk to John Dean.'"

At this point, Ehrlichman retreated into ambiguity, and said, "But you see I get into a very funny defensive position then vis-à-vis you and vis-à-vis him, and it's very damned awkward. And I haven't thought it clear through. I don't know where we come out."

On April 17th, the President made a short statement saying simply that there had been "major developments in the case concerning which it would be improper to be more specific now." He was unable to offer any diversionary reports or propitiatory victims to deflect the public's wrath at the forthcoming disclosures. He and his aides had talked over countless schemes, but all of them had foundered on the unwillingness of any of the aides to sacrifice themselves for him—or for "the Presidency," as he had asked them to do. The coverup was all one piece, and it cohered in exposure just as it had cohered in concealment.

The President had become adept at recollecting whatever was needed at a particular moment. By April of 1973, he and his aides were spending most of their time making up history out of whole cloth to suit the needs of each moment. Unfortunately for them, the history they were making up was self-serving history, and by April their individual interests had grown apart. Each of them had begun to "recollect" things to his own advantage and to the detriment of the others. As their community of interests dissolved under the pressure of the investigation, each of them was retreating into his own private, self-interested reality. The capacity for deception which had once divided them from the country but united them with one another now divided them from one another as well.

In the White House, the fabric of reality had disintegrated altogether. What had got the President into trouble from the start had been his remarkable capacity for fantasy. He had begun by imagining a host of domestic foes. In retaliating against them he had broken the law. Then he had compounded his lawbreaking by concealing it. And, finally, in the same way that he had broken the law although breaking it was against his best interests, he was bringing himself to justice even as he thought he was evading justice. For, as though in anticipation of the deterioration of his memory, he had installed another memory in the Oval Office, which was more nearly perfect than his own, or anyone else's merely human equipment: he had installed the taping system. The Watergate coverup had cast him in the double role of conspirator and investigator. Though the conspirator in him worked hard to escape the law, it was the investigator in him that gained the upper hand in the end. While he was attempting to evade the truth, his machines were preserving it forever.

At the moment when the President announced "major developments" in the Watergate case, the national process that was the investigation overwhelmed the national process that was the coverup. The events that followed were all the more astounding to the nation because, at just the moment when the coverup began to explode, the President, in the view of many observers, had been on the point of strangling the "obsolete" Constitutional system and replacing it with a Presidential dictatorship. One moment, he was triumphant and his power was apparently irresistible; the next moment, he was at bay. For in the instant the President made his announcement, the coverup cracked—not just the Watergate coverup but the broader coverup, which concealed the underground history of the last five years—and the nation suffered an inundation of news. The newspaper headlines now came faster and thicker than ever before in American history. The stories ran backward in time, and each day's newspaper told of some event a little further in the past as reporters traced the underground history to the early days of the Administration, and even into the terms of former Administrations. With the history of half a decade pouring out all at once, the papers were stuffed with more news than even the most diligent reader could absorb. Moreover, along with the facts, non-facts proliferated as the desperate men in the White House put out one false or distorted statement after another, so that each true fragment of the story was all but lost in a maze of deceptions, and each event, true or false, came up dozens of times, in dozens of versions, until the reader's mind was swamped. And, as if what was in the newspapers were not already too much, television soon started up, and, in coverage that was itself a full-time job to watch, presented first the proceedings of the Ervin committee and then the proceedings of the House Judiciary Committee, when it began to weigh the impeachment of the President. And, finally, in a burst of disclosure without anything close to a precedent in history, the tapes were revealed—and not just once but twice. The first set of transcripts was released by the White House and was doctored, and only the second set, which was released by the Judiciary Committee, gave an accurate account of the President's conversations.

As the flood of information flowed into the public realm, overturning the accepted history of recent years, the present scene was also transformed. The Vice-President was swept from office when his bribetaking became known, but so rapid was the pace of events that his departure was hardly noticed. Each of the institutions of the democracy that had been menaced by the President—and all had been menaced—was galvanized into action in its turn: the press, the television networks, the Senate, the House of Representatives, and, finally, in a dispute over release of the tapes, the Supreme Court. The public, too, was at last awakened, when the President fired the Special Prosecutor whom he had appointed to look into the White House crimes. In an outpouring of public sentiment that, like so much else that happened at the time, had no precedent in the nation's history, millions of letters and telegrams poured in to Congress protesting the President's action. The time of letters sent by the President to himself was over, and the time of real letters from real people had come. No one of the democracy's institutions was powerful enough by itself to remove the President; the efforts of all were required—and only when those efforts were combined was he forced from office.

27. Jimmy Carter:
A Crisis of Confidence

PETER CARROLL

Jimmy Carter, sharply aware of the public's lack of confidence in its political institutions, was elected president by running against politics, against Washington, and against "insiders." Once elected, he found himself the victim of all that he had campaigned against: the Washington establishment, the media, the exaggerated and unrealistic expectations of the American people, and the demand for a political smoothness that the public mistrusts in candidates but admires in presidents. Being fuzzy on the issues as a candidate proved profitable, but as president his shifts in belief were harmful. On issues on which he expressed a clear policy, such as energy, he ran into insurmountable opposition. Peter Carroll's book on the 1970s remains the best account of the decade. In this excerpt Carroll discusses some of Carter's attempts to deal with problems he encountered in office.

Carter never succeeded in overcoming the crisis of legitimacy that gripped American institutions throughout the 1970s. In 1975 a national poll indicated that 69 percent of the public thought that "over the last ten years, this country's leaders have consistently lied to the people." In 1976 another poll indicated that public confidence had dropped in the past decade from 73 to 42 percent for the medical profession and from 55 to 16 percent for major companies. Similar declines were reported for other institutions. A nation adjusting from the abundance and sense of control of the 1960s to the scarcities and sense of closing frontiers of the 1970s was extraordinarily critical of its leaders. Historians may have been less harsh with the leaders of the 1970s than the public, and more willing to see the era as a period of painful transition that neither policy nor rhetoric could greatly soften or legitimize.

"Our people were sick at heart," said Jimmy Carter, explaining his election victory, "and wanted new leadership that could heal us, and give us once again a government of which we could feel proud." Carter's inauguration symbolized this affirmation of traditional values. Instead of formal attire, the two chief executives, Carter and Ford, wore ordinary business suits, and the new President took the oath of office with the nickname "Jimmy." Then, he stirred the Washington crowds by leading the parade from Capitol Hill to the White House on foot. ("He's walking!" people shrieked. "He's walking!") "I have no new dream to set forth today," he admitted, "but rather urge a fresh faith in the old dream.... We must once again have full faith in our country—and in one another." Evoking "a new spirit"—the phrase appeared five times in his inaugural speech—Carter called for the restoration of political morality, a government "at the same time...competent and compassionate."

Carter's appeal for moral leadership, effective as campaign oratory, raised new problems once the mantle of authority passed to his own shoulders. "This is not the time to tax Mr. Carter again for his fuzziness on the issues," acknowledged *The New York Times* on his first day in office. "But he should recognize that he lacks the eloquence to hide it." With a paper-thin electoral victory and a rising proportion of citizens who refused to vote, the new administration took power in an atmosphere of persistent distrust. "One result was certain," observed veteran reporter Haynes Johnson. "The [new] president would be watched more critically than ever before."

Recognizing these suspicions, Carter attempted to demystify the operations of government and create an impression of rule by ordinary people. He reduced the size of the White House staff by one-third, ordered cabinet officers to drive their own cars, and required that government regulations be written "in plain English for a change." His administration instituted new ethical guidelines for executive employees, mandating public disclosure of financial holdings, divestiture of potential conflicts of interest, and closing what Carter called "the revolving door" between government service and corporate appointment. "Government officials can't be sensitive to your problems," the President remarked in a televised "fireside chat" two weeks after taking office, "if we are living like royalty here in Washington."

Carter's disavowal of professional politicians, partly a function of his own inexperience, partly the result of a self-conscious style, determined the structure of power within the White House. As his closest advisers, he retained the people who had shaped his campaign strategy—all Washington outsiders from Georgia: Hamilton Jordan, Jody Powell, and Charles Kirbo. More problematic was his nomination to head the Office of Management and Budget, Georgia banker Bert Lance, state highway commissioner under Carter and an early, generous contributor to the presidential campaign. "What has been Mr. Lance's experience in the federal government?" asked Senator William Proxmire scornfully. "He has none—zero, zip, zilch, not one year, not one week, not one day." Even more controversial was the choice for attorney general, former federal judge Griffin Bell, also from Georgia. Bell's political views— membership in clubs that excluded Jews and blacks, enthusiastic support for Nixon's nomination of Judge Carswell, and a legal ruling that upheld the removal from office of Georgia legislator Julian Bond for opposing the Vietnam war—aroused liberal suspicions about the administration's political sympathies. But despite unexpected angry rhetoric, the democratic Senate indulged the President's preferences.

While public attention focused on questions of inexperience and cronyism, however, the bulk of Carter's high-level nominations revealed the administration's close ties to another, even more powerful interlocking establishment, the corporate elite that supported the Trilateral Commission. "If after the inauguration you find a Cy Vance as secretary of state and Zbigniew Brzezinski as head of national security," Hamilton Jordan told an interviewer during the recent campaign, "then I would say we failed." Yet Carter appointed Vance and Brzezinski to those very posts! And besides these two administrators and Vice President

Mondale, Carter also turned to the Trilateral Commission for Secretary of the Treasury W. Michael Blumenthal, Secretary of Defense Harold Brown, United Nations ambassador Andrew Young, and a dozen other slightly lower appointees. "Conservatives with high integrity," consumer advocate Ralph Nader described them, who would "follow the wrong policies straight instead of crooked."

It was perhaps no coincidence, then, that the only Carter selection rejected by the Senate was an apparent insider who inadvertently had become associated with genuine outsiders, Theodore Sorensen, a former Kennedy adviser, nominated by Carter to head the CIA. Six years earlier, Sorensen had filed an affidavit in the *Pentagon Papers* case, in which he acknowledged leaving government service in 1964 with sixty-seven boxes of documents, including papers marked "classified." Such confessions confirmed Senate fears about Sorensen's antipathy to extralegal activities by the intelligence organization. "It is now clear," maintained Sorensen in withdrawing his name, "that a substantial portion of the United States Senate and the intelligence community is not yet ready to accept...an outsider who believes as I believe."

The orthodoxy of Carter's appointments, however, could not compensate for their lack of political experience. Within one month of the inauguration, the administration needlessly aroused the fury of the Democratic leadership of Congress, surely its most valuable political ally, by announcing the cancellation of nineteen water projects in the interests of fiscal austerity. Challenged by this attack on traditional "pork-barrel" legislation—the division of public spoils among the politicians in power—congressional leaders roared defiance, threatened to crush the remainder of the President's programs, and authorized the disputed appropriations anyway. In the face of such opposition, Carter prudently retreated, neither vetoing nor even denouncing the unwanted measure. He had lost not only the immediate issue, but considerable goodwill on Capitol Hill as well. Yet after one hundred days in office, Carter enjoyed rising popularity, garnering a 75 percent approval rating in the Harris poll. There was, observed the venerable presidential adviser Clark Clifford, "a return of the confidence of the people in our government."

Carter's ability to revitalize public spirit nevertheless depended on the cooperation of Congress. Since the fall of Richard Nixon, congressional leaders had become especially jealous of legislative power, reluctant to compromise with any administration and, often, even with each other. Moreover, the elections of 1974, 1976, and 1978 brought to office a spate of new politicians—half the House Democrats had not served under Nixon—who remained uncommitted to the traditional committee system and hostile to the control of party leaders. A survey conducted at the University of Pittsburgh showed party loyalty and party voting within Congress at the lowest level in thirty-six years. "If this were France," grieved Speaker Thomas "Tip" O'Neill, "the Democratic Party would be five parties."

The administration's attempt to restore public confidence in the federal government also collided with a more sinister dimension of congressional independence: the penchant of numerous representatives for graft. On the eve of Carter's election, *The Washington Post*, chief sleuth in the Watergate scandals, accused over one hundred congressmen of taking bribes from South Korea lobbyist Tongsun Park in exchange for enacting favorable legislation. The resulting "Koreagate" investigation, headed by former Watergate prosecutor Leon Jaworski, found "substantial" support for the charges. But because of intelligence restraints on the evidence, only three sitting congressmen were reprimanded for their conduct, and one former representative, Richard Hanna of California, went to prison. In a separate case, thirteen-term Michigan Democrat Charles Diggs was convicted of taking illegal kickbacks from staff employees, but managed to win reelection in 1978. The next year, he became the first congressman since 1921 to be censured by the House of Representatives for padding his payroll and taking public funds for personal use.

The discovery of widespread congressional corruption also smeared the White House. When United States attorney David Marston, a former aide of Republican Senator Schweiker, probed too closely into a kickback scheme involving two Pennsylvania Democrats, one of the suspects, Representative Joshua Eilberg, telephoned the President to recommend cashiering Marston, a proposal Carter endorsed. "This was a routine matter for me," said the President in self-defense, "and I did not consider my taking the telephone call...nor relaying his request to the attorney general to be ill advised at all." But the Marston affair evoked memories of Watergate and kept the case alive. Indicted on conflict-of-interest charges and defeated at the polls, Eilberg pleaded guilty in 1979. Representative Daniel Flood, charged with similar violations, won a mistrial, then pleaded ill-health to avoid a retrial; he retired in 1980. Meanwhile, FBI investigators were gathering some remarkable evidence, including videotaped motion pictures of congressmen taking bribes from mysterious Arab millionaires. The cases, coded Abscam, broke the headlines in 1980.

For two prestigious senators—liberal Republican Edward Brooke of Massachusetts, the only black in the upper house, and Herman Talmadge, scion of southern conservatism—messy divorce trials led to revelations of the illegal accumulation of funds. The charges contributed to Brooke's electoral defeat in 1978. Talmadge, having recovered from alcoholism, staged a strong personal defense. But in 1979, the Senate denounced his "reprehensible" conduct for bringing "dishonor and disrepute" on that body, and he lost a bid for reelection in 1980.

The reluctance of Congress to discipline its members intensified public distrust of the political process. "For some citizens," warned Carter in his first state of the union message, "the government has almost become like a foreign country." Responding to the decline of voter participation, the President proposed a liberalization of voter registration, urging the removal of "antiquated and unnecessary obstacles." But a Congress content with its own rule felt no need for reform. In the 1978 elections, voter participation dropped under 38 percent, the lowest turnout since 1942. Though most congressional incumbents won reelection, party loyalty virtually disappeared. In the state elections, voters readily split tickets in response to single issues and candidate personality, and while Republicans made only modest gains in Congress, they captured 298 new seats in the state legislatures. "This is the most profound change for us," said a gloating Republican National Chairman Bill Brock. The mood of the citizenry emerged clearly in the low television ratings obtained by election-night news shows, which in New York City ran third behind a rerun of Peter Seller's *The Pink Panther*. It was no surprise, then, that by the summer of 1979, a Gallup poll found public approval of Congress at an abysmal 19 percent.

The intractability of Congress severely diminished the political power of Jimmy Carter, leaving the nominal head of the Democratic party with a shrinking constituency in the country which, in turn, further weakened his influence on Capitol Hill. "Nixon had his enemies list," quipped Senator James Abourezk. "Carter has his friends list." As White House proposals vanished in Congress, the President's popularity steadily declined, raising what *Newsweek* magazine called "the Eptitude Question—the suspicion abroad in Washington's power factories that Carter and his Georgia irregulars have not yet fully mastered their jobs." After one year in office, Carter's approval rating slid below 50 percent. "He is soothing flatterer and a sensible president," noted *The New York Times*, "but not yet a leader, or teacher, even for a quiet time." This disenchantment fed upon itself, the erosion of support causing presidential failure, which eroded still more support until the ominous summer weekend in 1979 when Carter's popularity statistics dropped even below those of Richard Nixon on the eve of resignation.

Carter's declining fortunes surely reflected his political incompetence. But he suffered as much for his personal style as he did for the policies he pursued. The very traits that had made the Georgian such an attractive candidate in 1976—images of compassion, homeyness, innocence—contradicted popular expectations of presidential authority, the decisive manipulation of power. Where Nixon personified a callous imperiousness and Ford simple bumbling, Carter, by contrast, epitomized neither boldness nor dullness, instead communicated images of hesitancy, obfuscation, ultimately of impotence. Carter's attempt to exercise compassionate power, almost by definition, could satisfy no one.

The difficulty of balancing moral justice with raw power emerged during Carter's first full day in office when, to fulfill one of his most controversial campaign pledges, the President offered "full, complete, and unconditional pardon" to the draft resisters of the Vietnam war, provided only that they had not engaged in violent crimes. (With considerably less fanfare, Carter later commuted the prison sentence of the unrepentant Watergate burglar G. Gordon Liddy.) Such gestures attempted to separate the administration from the troubles of the past. But Carter underestimated the force of memory. "It's the saddest day in American history," complained the director of the Veterans of Foreign Wars upon learning of the presidential pardon, "sadder than Watergate and Vietnam itself." "The most disgraceful thing a President has ever done," protested Barry Goldwater. "If I had known this would happen," snapped one bitter veteran, "I would have gone to Canada, too, and hung out." A Harris survey found that public opinion opposed the reprieve, and the Senate nearly passed a resolution criticizing the

President's action. "I don't intend to pardon any more people from the Vietnam era," Carter soon assured a radio audience.

Nor did the Vietnam pardon win the gratitude of the peace movement. By excluding military offenders—deserters and veterans with less-than-honorable discharges—the President ignored a far larger group of war resisters which was also, according to the American Civil Liberties Union, "more likely to be poor, from minority groups and less educated." Though Carter instructed the Defense Department to re-examine the status of antiwar veterans, the Pentagon established strict criteria for upgrading discharges, and Congress specifically prohibited the expenditure of funds to advertise the project. When the program terminated in October 1977, only 9 percent of the eligible veterans had applied for review. By then, the President had also signed the Cranston-Thurmond bill which denied veterans' benefits to participants in the upgrading program. Carter's much publicized moralism, in perpetuating the distinction between civilian and military opposition to the Vietnam war, thus surrendered to political expediency.

The President demonstrated considerably greater compassion for intimate associates accused of crimes—but also bore unfortunate consequences for this loyalty. In 1977, budget director Lance drew congressional criticism for his loose financial practices—taking large personal overdrafts from his bank—prior to assuming federal office. Carter remained staunchly supportive of his friend, dodging reporters' questions and denying any improprieties. But public pressure forced Lance's resignation anyway and the President suffered for his unswerving faith. Lance did not win acquittal until 1980. The President showed similar tolerance for the harmful commentary of his brother, Billy, who insulted Jews and blacks with impunity. But Billy Carter's financial transactions as a lobbyist for Libya smacked of corruption and the "Billygate" scandal tarnished the administration. Carter also defended his close adviser, Hamilton Jordan, against charges of personal misconduct, snorting cocaine at New York's Club 54. Such allegations called into question the President's own standards.

The blurring of morality and power politics also affected Carter's foreign policy—and returned to plague the administration when it encountered moral values different from its own. "Our commitment to human rights must be absolute," said Carter in his inaugural speech, "but let no one confuse our idealism with weakness." While pursuing détente with the Soviet Union and negotiating SALT II, the President determined to promote "human rights" within Soviet borders. Such a program contradicted the assumptions of recent diplomacy, the acceptance of big-power spheres of influence in which other powers exerted no leverage. "We must replace balance-of-power politics with world order politics," the Trilateralist had suggested in the recent campaign. Soon after taking office, Carter personally wrote to Soviet dissident Andrei Sakharov, assuring that "the American people ... will continue our firm commitment to promote respect for human rights not only in our country but also abroad." By unexpectedly altering American policy, the administration challenged the Soviet leadership, which responded by hardening its position on SALT. "Washington's claims to teach others how to live cannot be accepted by any sovereign state," retorted President Brezhnev.

Besides delaying SALT, the human rights issue exposed obvious contradictions in United States policy. The State Department used Carter's stand to justify the cessation of military aid to repressive regimes such as Argentina and Uruguay, but for reasons of national security rationalized continuing aid to South Korea. Even worse, administration policy raised an ugly specter of revenge. Challenged by Carter's attack, the Soviet Union could not afford to retreat from its traditional suppression of dissent. "Carter painted himself into a corner," observed Harvard's Adam Ulam. Nor would the White House halt SALT negotiations in protest. "It's not worth going into another cold war," explained a Carter aide. To protest Soviet domestic conduct, the President ordered minor retaliations—the cancellation of a computer sale to Tass for use at the 1980 Olympics, the delay of a shipment of drill bits—and allowed such symbols to serve as a substitute for policy. Utterly ineffective in influencing the Soviet leadership, Carter's denunciations also made the idea of rapprochement unpalatable to the American public.

The defense of human rights soon embroiled the United States in a new type of diplomacy, the manipulation of individual lives as a way of rendering impotent the most powerful government on earth. Seeking to demonstrate his consistency of policy, Carter referred in his second press conference to atrocities committed by Uganda's Idi Amin which, said the President, "disgusted the entire civilized world." The African dictator promptly clamped travel restrictions on the two hundred Americans living in Uganda and ordered them to attend a personal meeting. Fearing reprisals, the White House briefly considered landing troops to defend American citizens. But the futility of such action persuaded the President to settle for a protest letter that denounced the taking of hostages. Scorning American hypocrisy, Amin kept the world in suspense over a long weekend, before conceding he had no evil intent.

Two weeks later, the seizure of hostages came closer to home when a small group of Hanafi Muslims occupied three buildings in Washington, D.C., holding 134 people at gunpoint to protest their persecution by Black Muslims. Sensitive to what *Newsweek* magazine called "the ghosts of Attica," the administration ordered negotiations with the invaders, finally ending the siege peacefully after three days. The result, said the President, "was a vivid proof that a slow and careful approach was the effective way."

Such takeovers, spawned in a terrorist politics, reached epidemic proportions in the late seventies. In New York, an American Nazi held an entire factory at bay; in Indianapolis, an angry debtor wired a shotgun to the head of his mortgage holder for sixty-two hours. One gunman in Cleveland refused to surrender until he had talked to President Carter. "Taking hostages is a very creative act," explained an experienced police psychiatrist. "It gives you real power." In such situations, federal authorities recommended continued negotiations. "Society should aim to outwit the terrorist," advised a government manual, "rather than to outfight him." But indulging terrorism lent credibility to the tactic. Commenting on Carter's "dealing *viva voce* with hostage-holders," the recently paroled Watergate conspirator E. Howard Hunt expressed an ominous thought: "I'll bet he hasn't answered the telephone for the last time."

Carter's confidence in the power of moral persuasion miscalculated the strength of entrenched interests to resist presidential appeals, an error that soon devastated the administration's attempt to settle what it considered the most pressing domestic issue of the age: the energy crisis. The terrible winter of 1977 underscored the problem. As record snowfalls and subzero temperatures forced the closing of schools and factories, causing layoffs for an estimated 1.6 million workers, a grim President told the nation to "face the fact that the energy shortage is permanent." "Live thriftily," he advised, "and remember the importance of helping our neighbors."

These moral homilies served as the centerpiece of the President's much-awaited energy program, unveiled in a series of televised speeches in April 1977. Comparing the crisis to moral warfare, Carter reiterated the importance of old-fashioned frugality: energy conservation. "It is the cheapest, most practical way to meet our energy needs," he told a joint session of Congress, "and to reduce our dependence on foreign oil." To stimulate conservation, the President proposed a tax package to penalize energy waste and to encourage greater efficiency. The program offered few alternatives to the continued reliance on imported oil (which by 1977 amounted to half the nation's energy supply), suggesting small tax credits for the installation of solar devices and describing nuclear power "as a last resort." Opposing the development of breeder reactors, Carter insisted that "effective conservation efforts can minimize the shift toward nuclear power."

The President's emphasis on reduced energy consumption immediately challenged entrenched corporate interests. "This country did not conserve its way to greatness," protested a defender of the Texas gas industry. "It produced itself to greatness." Carter's plan to raise consumer prices through taxation rather than deregulation threatened corporate profits; "a windfall loss," complained an economist at Standard Oil. "Our problem isn't a shortage of oil," stated Ronald Reagan, "it's a surplus of government." The wrath of the business community descended quickly on Congress, which rallied to protect its diverse constituents. "It's like it was the day after Pearl Harbor," suggested Representative Morris Udall, "and you interviewed the Congressman from Detroit and he said, 'The Japanese attack was outrageous, but before we rush into war, let's see how it would affect the [auto] industry,' and then somebody else said, 'It was dastardly, but consider the effect on oil,' and another Congressman said, 'War could be very serious for recreation and tourism.'" Such pressures rapidly transformed Carter's clarion call for the "moral equivalent of war" into its acronym, MEOW, a pussycat proposal that could not slide through the legislature.

Though the President obtained approval for a Department of Energy to coordinate government policy, the remainder of his program collapsed in shambles. Unable to rally public opinion ("I don't feel much like talking about energy and foreign policy," an unemployed steelworker told him at an "Energy Round Table." "I am concerned about how I am going to live."), the President watched helplessly while the Senate dismantled the energy tax program and even overcame a two-week filibuster to endorse the deregulation of natural gas. "The moral equivalent of the Vietnam war," exclaimed a White House aide. When the President took his crusade for conservation to yet another television audience, *The Boston Globe* extended that metaphor further, calling the speech "the moral equivalent of Sominex."

Having failed in 1977, the President renewed his battle for an energy program the next year. "Further delay will only lead to more harsh and painful solutions," he warned. But the absence of fuel shortages—indeed, the existence of surpluses on the West Coast—encouraged consumers to burn ever larger quantities of imported oil. "I don't see the inevitability of a crunch," assured a petroleum industry spokesman. "The possibility is there but it's not a crisis." On the anniversary of his first energy speech, Carter conceded the importance of stimulating new oil production and recommended the decontrol of prices paired with a windfall profits tax to allow rebates for the poor. But Congress rebuffed the proposal. Nor did alternative technologies attract political support. "To think of alternative energy sources," observed economist Lester Thurow, "is to think of vigorous well-organized opponents." On May 3, 1978, advocates of solar power sponsored a Sun Day, reminiscent of the environmentalists' Earth Day of 1970, but won no inroads in government policy. Nuclear power remained economically suspect. "It's time for it to compete," said a Carter official in rejecting additional government subsidies. "It's been too much a pampered child of the federal government."

The National Energy Act, finally passed in November 1978, bore scant resemblance to Carter's initial program, leaving the nation ill-prepared for an impending crisis of resources. "I have not given up on my original proposal that there should be some constraint on consumption," said Carter in signing the bill, "and thus on oil imports," Within two months, news from the Middle East reinforced that advice. The eruption of civil war in Iran against the rule of the Shah sharply curtailed oil production, and the OPEC nations took the opportunity to announce a 14.5 percent increase in oil prices. "Market conditions do not warrant a price increase of this magnitude," protested the White House. But the administration did little more than plead for reconsideration. To the American people, the President urged that they "honor the 55-m.p.h. speed limit, set thermostats no higher than 65 degrees and limit discretionary driving."

While the public calmly accommodated these inconveniences, the problem of energy resources suddenly escalated beyond the bounds of ordinary imagination. "The world has never known a day quite like today," announced Walter Cronkite on March 30, 1979. "It faced the considerable uncertainties and dangers of the worst nuclear power plant accident of the atomic age. And the horror tonight is that it could get much worse." Two days earlier, a stuck valve at the nuclear power facility at Three Mile Island, Pennsylvania, had overheated the reactor core, threatening to wash the countryside in a shower of deadly radiation. While technicians worked feverishly to avert a cataclysmic meltdown, one hundred thousand civilians fled their homes for safety. It took nearly two weeks to bring the errant reactor under control. "We were damn lucky," admitted a member of a special presidential commission established to investigate the calamity. "No one understood what was going on at the time, and it scares the hell out of me." The then popular film, *China Syndrome*, the story of a similar reactor failure, dramatized a growing public suspicion about nuclear power—an anxiety not just about the dangers of radioactivity, but about the failure of the industry and the regulatory agencies to tell the truth about the omnipresent risk.

Such fears sent a chill through the troubled industry. Even before the Three Mile Island calamity, the rising cost of nuclear reactors had caused cancellation of twenty planned projects. Soon afterward, eleven more were dropped and no new orders were made in 1979. The seventy-one plants remaining in operation provided about 11 percent of the nation's electrical energy, far below earlier estimates. But despite sharp criticism of the nuclear industry as well as condemnation of the safety procedures established by the Nuclear Regulatory Commission, the President's advisers recommended the continuation of nuclear power. "We cannot simply shut down our nuclear power plants," insisted Carter; they "must play an important role in our energy future."

The near disaster at Three Mile Island, by exposing the limitations of technological performance, shocked the nation into a reconsideration of the energy crisis. Taking advantage of the unsettled mood, Carter again appealed for support of his energy program. "The fundamental cause of our nation's energy crisis," he told a prime-time television audience in April 1979, "is petroleum," and he warned about overdependence on "a thin line of oil tankers stretching halfway around the earth . . . [to] one of the most unstable regions in the world." To encourage domestic production, Carter announced the gradual decontrol of oil prices beginning immediately and pleaded with Congress for a windfall profits tax to equalize the sacrifice. He also requested "standby authority" to impose a national rationing plan. At a time when gasoline cost seventy cents a gallon, pessimistic observers predicted that the President's scheme would produce an increase of twenty cents per gallon.

Despite the recent peril, however, Congress remained unimpressed. While praising the decontrol decision, most congressional leaders criticized the tax proposal. In May, the legislature handed the President a major defeat by rejecting the plan for standby rationing. "The members don't pay any attention to him," said Speaker O'Neill. "They put their heads in the sand," Carter complained. "The average motorist is going to be faced with more shortages of gasoline in the future. We ought to be ready for it, and we're not."

The crisis came sooner than expected. By May, gasoline lines in California ran as long as five hundred cars, and prices at the pump already touched one dollar per gallon. "It's sort of like sex," assured an official of Gulf Oil. " Everybody's going to get all the gasoline they need, but they're damn sure not going to get all they want." Then, in June, OPEC announced a gigantic 50 percent hike in oil prices. The news created panic conditions. Despite odd-even rationing schemes, tempers steamed easily, causing fistfights, stabbings, and shootings, and in Levittown, Pennsylvania, the cradle of suburbia, gasoline shortages provoked a full-scale riot. To make matters worse, the nation's independent truckers staged a wildcat strike to protest rising diesel costs, idling 60 percent of the long-haul interstate traffic. "When the President and all them senators can't get no steak," said a striker, "then they'll do something."

"The future of the Democratic Party is tied to energy," Carter had recently advised congressional leaders. "It could cost us control of the Senate and White House. It could be the issue that puts the democrats out of power for a very long time." Cutting short a vacation, the President retreated to his Camp David hideaway to prepare another address on the energy crisis. But the speech never came. As his popularity ratings cascaded to all-time lows, Carter recognized the futility of moral appeal. "If I give this speech," he told an aide, "they'll kill me." Canceling the broadcast, the President summoned teams of consultants to Camp David to discuss the sorry state of the nation. Mayors, governors, congressmen, academics, and private citizens—135 in all—spoke candidly, while the President and his wife Rosalynn took notes. After a week of suspense, Carter returned from the mountain.

"All the legislation in the world can't fix what's wrong with America," a solemn President addressed the nation. "It is a crisis of confidence. It is a crisis that strikes at the very heart and soul and spirit of our nation...and [it] is threatening to destroy the social and political fabric of America." Stressing the decline of traditional values—"hard work, strong families, close-knit communities and our faith in God"—Carter lamented the growing loss of assurance about the American future. "Looking for a way out of this crisis, our people have turned to the federal government and found it isolated from the mainstream of our nation's life; Washington, D.C., has become an island....This is not a message of happiness or reassurance," he concluded. "But it is the truth. And it is a warning."

The struggle for renewal, Carter suggested, should begin "on the battlefield of energy." For the third time in his administration, the President revealed a major energy package, promising to "win for our nation a new confidence—and...seize control of our common destiny." First, he ordered a freeze on the amount of oil imported from abroad and recommended additional cutbacks during the next decade. Second, he proposed the formation of an $88 billion government-funded corporation to produce synthetic fuel from coal and shale. Third, he suggested the creation of an "energy mobilization" committee to cut through bureaucratic red tape. "We will protect our environment," he pledged. "But when this nation critically needs a refinery or pipeline, we will build it."

Carter's dramatic appeal struck close to the national conscience, rapidly improving his political prospects. But just as quickly, the President destroyed his advantage. Two days after promising to restore a sense of national unity, the White House announced that the entire cabinet had offered to resign and that Carter had accepted the departure of five top administrators, producing a major reorganization of the executive branch. The upheaval shocked public opinion and renewed fears that the government had drifted out of control. By the end of July, surveys showed Carter's approval ratings at a dismal 25 percent—exactly the nadir on the eve of the Camp David meetings.

Emboldened by the administration's self-defeating maneuvers, Congress delayed enactment of the President's plan, carefully cultivating exemptions to the windfall profits tax. Not until the spring of 1980, after nearly a year of oil decontrol, did the legislature approve a modified profits tax, which brought substantially lower funds for the government. Congress also authorized stricter safety rules for nuclear power, ordering reactors kept away from population centers and establishing stringent penalties for violations. To encourage production, Congress established the U.S. Synthetic Fuels Corporation, provided a solar-energy bank, and authorized funding for an alcohol fuel program and for a Strategic Petroleum Reserve. "If OPEC tries to blackmail us," explained Majority Leader Wright, "we'll have a spare tire."

By the time Congress enacted an energy program, however, the issue of resources had been subsumed by its larger consequences—an economy on the brink of collapse. The deterioration of the American economy under Cater reflected as much the failures of presidential policy as it did persistent and fundamental structural problems that no administration could meet. Basic to these difficulties was the question of faith—the impact of future expectations as a driving force for inflation and as a drag on corporate investment. Having inherited an inflation rate below 5 percent, Carter saw the figure increase to 6 percent in 1977, 9 percent in 1978, and 13.3 percent in 1979, while official unemployment statistics fell slightly from 7.4 percent to about 6 percent. Worse, the rate of productivity of United States business steadily declined, running at—0.9 percent in 1979.

Upon taking office, Carter expected to speed recovery from the recession of 1974-75 by cutting taxes and increasing government spending. But his refusal to fund public works projects antagonized organized labor, and conservatives criticized the growing deficit: "The increase in the federal budget is stirring up new fears," warned Arthur Burns, "new expectations of inflation that to some degree may be a self-fulfilling prophecy." As unemployment continued to drop, however, and the severe cold boosted prices, the administration decided to scrap a promised tax rebate. Opting for fiscal restraint, Lance predicted "no new programs if we are going to . . . get a balanced budget by 1981." Retorted Senator Hubert Humphrey, "There is *no* way to balance the budget by 1981."

Even if Carter had managed, as he promised in April 1977, "to discipline the growth of government spending," the rate of inflation would have continued to increase. Cost-of-living escalators, built into labor and business contracts as a hedge against inflation, had developed a self-generating momentum, one increase automatically stimulating the next. A lag of investment in the modernization of facilities—partly because of preferred opportunities abroad and partly because of fear of inflation—contributed to a decline of productivity. "We already have so much capacity," explained Stanford economist Ezra Solomon, "it's much easier to buy a company ready-made than to add capacity." Such trends weakened American competition with foreign manufacturers, causing a decline of such basic industries as steel and automobiles. These losses, combined with a growing reliance on imported oil, produced unprecedented deficits in the balance of trade, reaching $28 billion in 1979. The result was a rapid depreciation of the dollar overseas, which returned in the form of further inflated prices for imported goods such as OPEC oil. Finally, the rising cost of energy added across-the-board increases throughout the economy.

By the late seventies, these economic trends were threatening the survival of the nation's tenth largest business, the Chrysler Corporation. After losing $205 million in 1978 and over $700 million in the first three quarters of 1979, the third largest automobile manufacturer appealed to the federal government for a billion-dollar tax credit to remain solvent. The misfortunes of Chrysler closely mirrored the general predicament of American capitalism. Slow to convert to small-car manufacturing, Chrysler chose not to build its own factory and instead contracted with Volkswagen to import four-cylinder engines. These arrangements severely limited Chrysler's productivity, especially when the small cars Dodge Omni and Plymouth Horizon became the corporation's best-sellers. Yet even these vehicles suffered from basic deficiencies—the only American cars ever rated "Not Acceptable" by Consumers Union. With a shrinking share of the automobile market, Chrysler sold its European holdings to foreign manufacturers and reduced its facilities at home.

Chrysler's appeal for public assistance ignited an angry debate about the limits of government responsibility for the economy. "You just can't have a free-enterprise system without failures," asserted Senator Proxmire. "Are we going to guarantee businessmen against their own incompetence by eliminating any incentive for avoiding the specter of bankruptcy?" But the collapse of Chrysler, warned its president Lee Iacocca, "would have a falling-dominoes effect" in the economy. "The people who made the bad decisions at Chrysler are no longer there," argued Michigan Representative James Blanchard. "No one should hold half a million workers responsible for the decisions of a few officials long since gone." After forcing Chrysler to make significant economic concessions, including renegotiation of its contract with the United Auto Workers, Congress finally approved a $1.5 billion loan guarantee in 1979.

The structural problems of the American economy were intensified by new government legislation—agricultural price supports, increases in the minimum wages, benefits for the steel industry, and higher social security payroll taxes. Together with rising food and fuel costs and a depreciated dollar, such expenditures sparked a new inflationary spiral in 1978. "You can't figure your real return, so you postpone investments," Treasury Secretary Blumenthal explained. "Your costs rise, your real profits shrink, your stock values go down; it costs more to borrow. It goes on and on." A May 1978 Gallup poll showed that a majority of Americans saw inflation as the nation's most serious problem. Yet the administration hesitated to act, pleading simply for voluntary restraint.

The relentless inflation, however, together with the trade deficit, imperiled the stability of the dollar in international markets, moving the economy closer to a crisis situation. At an economic summit conference in Bonn and in a subsequent meeting of the World Bank in Washington, the President pledged "my own word of honor" to fight inflation. "I do not have all the answers," Carter told a television audience in October. "Nobody does." But he proposed a program of voluntary guidelines, calling for 7 percent limits on wage gains and 6.5 percent rises in prices. "We must face a time of national austerity," he urged. "Hard choices are necessary if we want to avoid consequences that are even worse." But, commented *The Wall Street Journal*, "few believed that the Carter plan would win the battle."

The lack of confidence in the Carter remedy precipitated another run on the dollar, further toppling its value. To halt this erosion, the administration intervened boldly, raising the discount rate a full percentage point, tightening credit, purchasing dollars abroad, and accelerating the sale of gold. But the policy aroused new fears of a recession. "Using high interest rates to psychologically support the dollar and try to fight inflation is part of the old-time conservative religion," protested consumer advocate Roger Hickey. "Millions of Americans will be sacrificial lambs in the anti-inflation war."

The sudden announcement of a major boost in OPEC prices — they would soar sixty percent in 1979—quickly undermined the credibility of carter's economic program. "Sometimes a party must sail against the wind," declared Senator Kennedy in protesting the administration's commitment to balance the budget. "The party that tore itself apart over Vietnam in the 1960s cannot afford to tear itself apart today over budget cuts in basic social programs." As the inflation rate soared to 13 percent in January 1979, labor leader George Meany called for "equality of sacrifice, not the sacrifice of equality." Ignoring the President's plea for wage restraints, the Teamsters and United Airlines workers went on strike while an AFL-CIO local in Washington won a lawsuit that denied the legality of the administration's voluntary guidelines. Lacking effective controls, the White House encouraged the Federal Reserve system to raise interest rates to a record-breaking 15 percent in 1979, virtually assuring a recession in the coming election year. "There are no economic miracles waiting to be performed," conceded Carter in his 1980 economic report to Congress. . . .

The frustrations of American policy in the Middle East reflected an inability to understand, much less encourage, the forces of revolutionary nationalism outside the context of the cold war, a myopia that soon undermined United States interests in the Persian Gulf. Despite the rhetoric of human rights, the Carter administration preferred to overlook State Department reports of violations committed by the government of the Shah against so-called "terrorists." "Because of the great leadership of the Shah," the President toasted his ally on New Year's Eve 1977, Iran was "an island of stability in one of the more troubled areas of the world." Following the policies of Nixon and Ford, Carter allowed Iran to receive the largest quantities of American arms with sales amounting to $15 billion between 1974 and 1978. So supportive was Carter of the Shah that the administration forbade American intelligence agents to establish contact with Iranian dissidents, lest their presence imply a weakening of the regime.

The eruption of revolutionary violence in Iran in 1978 caused no shift in Carter's policies. In public statements, he reiterated support for the Shah and authorized the continuation of the sale of arms and crowd-control equipment. As a show of strength, the President ordered a task force to sail in the Persian Gulf. But three days later, he countermanded the order. "We've learned our lessons the hard way," he said, "in Vietnam." Meanwhile, the State Department tried to instigate a military coup to ensure emergence of a friendly regime, but seriously underestimated the strength of the revolution. Nor could the United States protect American citizens from the harassment of crowds. Bell Helicopter employees in Teheran began wearing T-shirts emblazoned with bullet holes; KEEP A LOW PROFILE they read. Not until January 1979 did the administration accept the inevitability of change, persuading the Shah to surrender his peacock throne.

Carter's prolonged support of the Shah undermined the possibility of accommodation with the new regime. Quickly the United States lost access to Iranian oil and saw the cancellation of $7 billion of uncompleted arms contracts, a serious blow to the balance of payments. The United States also surrendered sensitive listening posts used to monitor Soviet missiles, raising questions about the ability to verify the new SALT treaty. Within Iran, anti-American tempers continued to erupt. On Valentine's Day 1979, revolutionary forces in Teheran overran the United States embassy, seizing seventy employees. But other soldiers, loyal to the Ayatollah Khomeini, ended the siege after two hours. "There is no way we could get those people out by using force," admitted a White House official. "We just have to wheedle them out the best we can." Unable to protect American lives, the State Department prepared to evacuate the seven thousand Americans remaining in Iran. "This is a volatile world," concluded Senator Church, chairman of the Foreign Relations Committee. "The thing we must learn is that the U.S. can live with a great deal of change and upheaval. But the one thing we can't do is stabilize it. There's no way to put a lid on it."

While relations between the United States and Iran deteriorated, the Shah basked in exile in the Bahamas, visited frequently by associates of David Rockefeller and Henry Kissinger, who urged the administration to give the former ally refuge. "The 10,000 Iranian students in the U.S. make this a rather less safe place than other countries," explained one government official. "How would you like it," replied another in May 1979, "if the U.S. mission in Teheran were taken hostage and held in return for the Shah? It might make good copy, but it would also make for a hell of a tough decision."

Five months later, the fantasy turned to nightmare. When the President, responding to Rockefeller pressure, finally agreed to allow the Shah to enter the United States for a gall bladder operation, militants in Iran seized the American embassy, captured sixty hostages, and demanded the repatriation of the Shah and his fortune. Showing contempt for international laws that had protected diplomats even in major conflagrations, the militants threatened their captives with death, paraded them blindfolded in scenes that would reappear on American television screens for a year. "Death to Carter," chanted the angry crowds.

"My initial reaction," said Carter, "is to do something." But "none of us would want to do anything that would worsen the danger in which our fellow Americans have been placed." Frustrated by the impotence of government, citizens vented their rage by attacking Iranian students, burning Iranian flags, and boycotting Iranian products. NO MORE IRANIAN STUDENTS WILL BE PERMITTED ON THESE PREMISES, read a sign posted on the Mustang Ranch, a bordello near Reno, UNTIL THE HOSTAGES ARE RELEASED. The crisis instilled a new sense of patriotism as Americans closed ranks behind the President. According to a Gallup poll, Carter's approval ratings jumped from 30 percent to 61 percent in the four weeks after the capture of the embassy.

While the nation poised for action, the administration worked to soothe public passion. "It is a time not for rhetoric," advised Secretary Vance, "but for quiet, careful and firm diplomacy." But appeals to the United Nations, to the World Court, to American allies throughout the world, brought no relief. To eliminate economic pressure, the administration clamped an embargo on imported Iranian oil and to prevent the removal of Iranian assets from Rockefeller's Chase Manhattan Bank, it froze Iranian deposits. There the matter rested. "It would not be possible, or even advisable," Carter told a press conference one week before he announced his candidacy for reelection, "for me to set a deadline about when, or if, I would take certain action in the future."

Carter's credibility now hinged on the patience of the American people, their willingness to accept the limits of American power. "If one works for years at becoming a pitiful, helpless giant," observed former Energy Secretary James Schlesinger in a paraphrase of Nixon's plea on the eve of the Cambodia invasion, "one might just succeed. It all goes back to the retreat and rout of American foreign policy in recent years. Wild as he is, the Ayatollah Khomeini would not have touched the Soviet Embassy." Harkening to Carter's cold war metaphors, Americans recoiled from this vision of global impotence—and wondered, too, how it all had happened.

PART FIVE

1980 to the Present

Ronald Reagan succeeded precisely where Jimmy Carter had failed: in making the American people feel better. A master at communicating by television, his message that America's "best days" lay ahead, not behind, was just what the public wanted to hear. Outwardly one of the most ideological of presidents, he argued the conservative case in a folksy, nonthreatening way. His administration doubled the defense budget, cut taxes, continued the Carter administration's movement toward deregulation of the economy, and made an unsuccessful effort to cut back domestic spending. The renewed confidence showed in a strong economic performance through most of the decade.

The 1980s, however, was also the age of mismanagement. As usual, the United States was the luckiest of nations, surviving and even thriving on the greater mismanagement of its communist adversaries. Still, the record of its problems was extraordinary. A mismanaged environment left many lakes and streams emptied of plants and fish, toxic waste sites untended, and public resources despoiled. A popular but mismanaged tax policy produced the most massive budget deficit in American history. Deregulation turned out to mean increasing inequality between rich and poor, a giant collapse in bank financing, and a dizzying spiral of mergers that made American industry more debt-ridden rather than more productive. The defense build-up seemed not to add to security (by the end of the decade the Navy wondered why its outmoded and dangerous battleships did not function), the contract process in the Department of Defense was rife with scandal, and billions had been spent on a Strategic Defense Initiative that many scientists considered farcical.

The greatest failure of the Reagan Administration came in social policy. The decade ended with many more Americans hungry and homeless than when it began, with the educational system in crisis, with the social and economic status of minorities in steady decline, and with an increasing proportion of children and women making up the nation's poor.

Other American institutions fared little better. The declining competitiveness of American industry became a standard lament. The nation began to adjust to its status as a debtor nation after decades of being the world's creditor. American agriculture declined through most of the decade, suffering like industry from foreign competition. In city after city the phenomenon was seen of empty factories transformed into shopping malls (where imported products largely replaced those "made in USA").

Confidence in American cultural and educational institutions faded as well. Widely circulated reports indicated that the nation was "at risk" because of the low quality of its education. Religion suffered a blow from the scandalous behavior of television evangelists. The arts came under attack for not catering to the conservative mood. Americans, commentators noted at the end of decade, felt better, but not really good.

28. Ronald Reagan: New Dealer?

DAVID A. STOCKMAN

David Stockman, director of the Office of Management and Budget in the first years of the Reagan administration, had the responsibility of implementing "supply-side economics." This ideology called for cutting government spending, lowering taxes, and stabilizing the money supply to fuel private investment and economic growth. The theory was that increased economic prosperity would "trickle down" to provide greater social welfare for the American public than had the various programs inherited from the New Deal and the Great Society. As director of the budget, Stockman had to cut federal programs to allow such tax cutting and economic growth. But as quickly as he found areas to cut, both Congress and the President, responding to interest group pressures, found reasons to reduce Stockman's "whacks" to mere "nicks" or to no cut at all. Instead of budget cuts, Stockman watched in dismay as federal budget deficits soared into the hundreds of billions annually, far beyond anything that had ever occurred in a peacetime economy.

Stockman says of President Reagan:

Ordinarily, Ronald Reagan was an incorrigible optimist. One of his favorite stories was the one about the two boys getting their Christmas presents. The first boy was a pessimist, the second an optimist. The pessimist gets a roomful of toys. He's miserable, because he's sure there's some catch involved. The optimist gets a roomful of horse manure. He's delighted. He digs around in the room for hours on end. With all that horse manure, he figured there just <u>had</u> to be a pony in there somewhere!

Stockman argues that Reagan practiced supply-side economics in taxation and New Deal politics in federal spending. In effect, Reagan was "waiting for the pony": unwilling to raise taxes for social welfare, providing government support for inefficient sectors of the economy, and increasing national security investments. Is it Stockman's peculiar perspective that makes Ronald Reagan look like a New Dealer? Or is what we now call political conservatism merely a reflex reaction? Conservatism criticizes the liberal domestic political consensus with which we have lived for the past half-century, but does it offer any alternative?

'You ain't seen nothing yet.' The White House made that its official campaign slogan for 1984. When it did, I knew that my own days were numbered, and that even the reluctant loyalty I had maintained during the long battle to reverse the President's tax policy was no longer defensible. Now I had to resort to out-and-out subversion—scheming with the congressional leaders during the first half of 1985 to force a tax hike. But that failed too, leaving me with no choice but to resign in the knowledge that my original ideological excesses had given rise to a fiscal and political disorder that was probably beyond correction.

Politics had triumphed: first by blocking spending cuts and then by stopping revenue increases. There was nothing left to do...

That the politics of American democracy made a shambles of my anti-welfare state theory I can now understand. Whatever its substantive merit, it rested on the illusion that the will of the people was at drastic variance with the actions of the politicians.

But the political history of the past five years mostly invalidates that proposition. We have had a tumultuous national referendum on everything in our half-trillion-dollar welfare state budget. By virtue of experiencing the battle day after day in the legislative and bureaucratic trenches, I am as qualified as anyone to discern the verdict. Lavish Social Security benefits, wasteful dairy subsidies, futile UDAG grants, and all the remainder of the federal subventions do not persist solely due to weak-kneed politicians or the nefarious graspings of special-interest groups.

Despite their often fuzzy rhetoric and twisted rationalizations, congressmen and senators ultimately deliver what their constituencies demand. The notion that Washington amounts to a puzzle palace on the Potomac, divorced from the genuine desires of the voters, thus constitutes more myth than truth. So does the related proposition eloquently expressed in the editorial pages of *The Wall Street Journal*. Somehow it manages to divine a great unwashed mass of the citizenry demanding the opposite of the spending agendas presented by the Claude Peppers, the homebuilders' lobby, and the other hired guns of K street.

But those who suggest the existence of an anti-statist electorate are in fact demanding that national policy be harnessed to their own particular doctrine of the public good. The actual electorate, however, is not interested in this doctrine; when it is interested at all, it is interested in getting help from the government to compensate for a perceived disadvantage. Consequently, the spending politics of Washington do reflect the heterogeneous and parochial demands that arise from the diverse, activated fragments of the electorate scattered across the land. What you see done in the halls of the politicians may not be wise, but it is the only real and viable definition of what the electorate wants.

I cannot be so patient with the White House. By 1984, it had become a dreamland. It was holding the American economy hostage to a reckless, unstable fiscal policy based on the politics of high spending and the doctrine of low taxes. Yet rather than acknowledge that the resulting massive buildup of public debt would eventually generate serious economic troubles, the White House proclaimed a roaring economic success. It bragged that its policies had worked as never before when, in fact, they had produced fiscal excesses that had never before been imagined.

The brash phrasemakers of the White House had given George Orwell a new resonance—and right on schedule. In 1984 we were plainly drifting into unprecedented economic peril. But they had the audacity to proclaim a golden age of prosperity.

What economic success there was had almost nothing to do with our original supply-side doctrine. Instead, Paul Volcker [of the Federal Reserve Board] and the business cycle had brought inflation down and economic activity surging back. But there was nothing new, revolutionary, or sustainable about this favorable turn of events. The cycle of economic boom and bust had been going on for decades, and by election day its oscillations had reached the high end of the charts. That was all.

To be sure, credit is due where it is deserved. Paul Volcker will surely go down as the greatest Federal Reserve Chairman in history for the masterful and courageous manner in which he purged the American and world economy of runaway inflation. This success turned out to require the traditional, painful, costly cure of a deep recession, but it took all that Volcker brought to the task—a strong will, an incisive mind, and a towering personal credibility—to see it through.

There is also little doubt that Volcker's feat would not have been possible without Ronald Reagan's unwavering support during the dark days of 1982. The President stands almost alone among Washington's current politicians in his instinctive comprehension that inflation is a profoundly destructive phenomenon. He has often been misled by the mumbo-jumbo of his advisers. But when it counted, the President gave Volcker the political latitude to do what had to be done. It was a genuine achievement.

Unfortunately, Volcker's hard-won victory was not what the White House media men had in mind when they proclaimed that 'America is back'. They were boasting of something far more grand: that the business cycle itself had been vanquished and that the nation had entered an era of unprecedented economic growth and wealth creation. As they had it, profound new possibilities for economic performance and social progress over the long haul had now been guaranteed by the policies in place. It sounded too good to be true and it was.

'You ain't seen nothing yet' was to have unintended, ironic meaning. It pointed to a frightful day of reckoning, a day that will reveal just how arrogant, superficial, and willfully ignorant the White House phrasemakers really were.

By the end of 1985 the economic expansion was three years old and the numbers demonstrated no miracle. Real GNP growth had averaged 4.1 percent—an utterly unexceptional, prosaic business cycle recovery by historical standards, and especially so in light of the extraordinary depth of the 1981–82 recession. The glowing pre-election GNP and employment numbers, therefore, had manifested only the truism that when the business cycle turns down, it will inevitably bounce back for a while.

Still, the White House breastbeating had to do with the future, and that depends upon the fundamental health of the economy and the soundness of policy. Yet how can economic growth remain high and inflation low for the long run when the administration's de facto policy is to consume two thirds of the nation's net private savings to fund the federal deficit?

The fundamental reality of 1984 was not the advent of a new day, but a lapse into fiscal indiscipline on a scale never before experienced in peacetime. There is no basis in economic history or theory for believing that from this wobbly foundation a lasting era of prosperity can actually emerge.

Indeed, just beneath the surface the American economy was already being twisted and weakened by Washington's free lunch joy ride. Thanks to the half-revolution adopted in July 1981, more than a trillion dollars has already been needlessly added to our national debt—a burden that will plague us indefinitely. Our national savings has been squandered to pay for a tax cut we could not afford. We have consequently borrowed enormous amounts of foreign capital to make up for the shortfall between our national production and our national spending. Now, the US economy will almost surely grow much more slowly than its potential in the decade ahead. By turning ourselves into a debtor nation for the first time since World War I, we have sacrificed future living standards in order to service the debts we have already incurred.

Borrowing these hundreds of billions of dollars has also distorted the whole warp and woof of the US economy. The high dollar exchange rate that has been required to attract so much foreign capital has devastated our industries of agriculture, mining, and manufacturing. Jobs, capital, and production have been permanently lost.

All of this was evident in 1984, and so was its implication for the future. We had prosperity of a sort—but it rested on easy money and borrowed time. To lift the economy out of recession against the weight of massive deficits and unprecedented real interest rates, the Fed has had to throw open the money spigots as never before. This in turn has stimulated an orgy of debt creation on the balance sheets of American consumers and corporations that is still gathering momentum today. Its magnitude is numbing. When the government sector's own massive debt is included, the nation will shortly owe $10 trillion—three times more than just a dozen years ago.

One thing is certain. At some point global investors will lose confidence in our easy dollars and debt-financed prosperity, and then the chickens will come home to roost. In the short run, we will be absolutely dependent upon a $100 billion per year inflow of foreign capital to finance our twin deficits—trade and the federal budget. Faced with a sinking dollar, the Fed will have no choice but to suddenly and dramatically tighten monetary policy, forcing up interest rates to attract the foreign savings needed to underwrite our lavish current spending.

This action will cause a recession, but this time neither Paul Volcker nor Ronald Reagan will have the wherewithal to stay the course. American politics will resound with the pleas of debtors demanding relief in the form of out-and-out reflation. Since out balance sheets already reflect the highest ratios of debt in peacetime history, there will be no margin at all to weather an interruption of cash flow: not at the federal level, where we are borrowing three times more relative to GNP than at the comparable stage of any previous cycle; nor at the corporate and household level, where debt service relative to income has soared off the charts.

The clock is thus ticking away inexorably toward another bout of inflationary excess. If we stay the course we are now on, the decade will end with a worse hyperinflation than the one with which it began. Indeed, the increased fragility and instability of the global economy, along with still fresh memories of the debauched financial assets of the 1970s, will make this inflationary cycle even more violent and destructive.

One reason I plotted to raise taxes in 1985, then, was to help correct an economic policy course that was leading to long-run disaster.

But there was also another, more compelling reason. As the original architect of the fiscal policy error now threatening so much grief, I was appalled by the false promises of the 1984 campaign. Ronald Reagan had been induced by his advisers and his own illusions to embrace one of the more irresponsible platforms of modern times. He had promised, as it were, to alter the laws of arithmetic. No program that had a name or line in the budget would be cut; no taxes would be raised. Yet the deficit was pronounced intolerable and it was pledged to be eliminated.

This was the essence of the unreality. The President and his retainers promised to eliminate the monster deficit with spending cuts when for all practical purposes they had already embraced or endorsed ninety-five percent of all the spending there was to cut.

The White House itself had surrendered to the political necessities of the welfare state early on. By 1985, only the White House speechwriters carried on a lonely war of words, hurling a stream of presidential rhetoric at a ghostly abstraction called Big Government.

The White House's claim to be serious about cutting the budget had, in fact, become an institutionalized fantasy. I had tried diplomatically and delicately to convey the facts that made this so, but the only response I got was a new whispering campaign led by Ed Meese: Stockman is too pessimistic; he's been on the Hill too long; he's one of *them*!

Maybe so. Ever since September 1981 I'd been reduced to making one-sided spending deals. The politicians mostly got what their constituents wanted, but here and there we trimmed the edges. But my relentless dealmaking inherently yielded savings that amounted to rounding errors in a trillion-dollar budget because it was based on bluff and searching out for obscure tidbits of spending that could be excised without arousing massive political resistance. Thus, for example, we did get the second-tier COLA in the railroad retirement program capped below the inflation rate. This reduced overall spending by 0.0001 percent!

But nothing meaningful could be done about federal spending because even the President no longer had a plausible program to do anything about it. The White House had thrown in the towel on all the big spending components that could make a difference on the deficit. And it had abandoned nearly every policy principle that could have been the basis for organizing a renewed anti-spending coalition.

The domestic budget is huge, but nearly ninety percent of it is accounted for by a handful of big programs: Social Security and other social insurance; Medicare; the safety net, veterans, agriculture, and transportation.

By 1984, the White House had explicitly decided not to challenge these big components of the welfare state budget in any significant way.

Jim Baker had been proven correct about the political consequences of attacking the basic entitlement and COLA of the 36 million citizens receiving Social Security and Medicare. I had eventually been reduced to trying to get the Congress to modestly trim the Medicare entitlement. But in the election/budget year of 1984 even the President rejected proposals for increased patient cost sharing, and then went on to plant his feet in concrete against any cuts in Social Security at all.

These two programs accounted for half of the welfare state budget, yet by 1985 the only option we had left was to squeeze a few percent of their massive $270 billion cost from the doctors and hospitals that delivered the services the old folks were now guaranteed to receive. Right then and there the fiscal arithmetic of coping with a $200 billion deficit through spending cuts alone had become prohibitive.

The President had also inadvertently safeguarded the smaller civil service retirement system from cuts, too. The administration budget carried a proposal to cap civil service COLAs and penalize early retirement (before age sixty-two), but its legislative prospects depended crucially on applying the same concept to the even more generous military retirement program. Both proposals were put in the President's budget, but the Joint Chiefs of Staff soon complained loudly. The President then cancelled the military reforms, buttressing the $25 billion civil service retirement program as he did so.

Likewise, the $27 billion complex of veterans' programs was also given immunity in a curious way. The White House appointed a VA administrator, by the name of Harry Walters, who spent a large part of his time denouncing the President's budget director at American Legion conventions. Whatever tiny veterans' cuts I managed to stuff into the budget were made instantly non-operative by Mr. Walters's ability to claim with impunity that he spoke for the President. No one at the White House ever said he didn't.

After the first round of cuts in the $75 billion complex of welfare, food stamp, and safety net programs, the White House raised the white flag there, too. The President promised the governors not to tamper seriously with Medicaid—the largest program—and appointed a task force which recommended that we repeal some of the nutrition program reforms we had already made. While we continued to send up to the Hill small, technical proposals to nick a billion or two, the clear White House message was that the safety net was now inviolate.

That position reflected the overwhelming sentiment of the public, and in that sense was justifiable. But it also constituted another big block of evidence that the President's anti-spending rhetoric amounted to an illusion.

By the mid-1980s the Reagan transportation budget in constant dollars topped Jimmy Carter's best year by fifteen percent, Johnson's by about forty percent, and Kennedy's by about fifty percent. Big Government? That was something for the speechwriters to fight as long as they didn't mention any names. The problem with all these local roads and buses was that other politicians had an equally strong case for aiding local projects—classrooms, public libraries, day care centers, alcoholism clinics and jailhouses. Spending continued largely unabated in all cases.

Indeed, the White House record was nearly bereft of any consistent anti-spending policy principles by 1984, and that fact had not escaped the notice of all the other politicians on Capitol hill. Early on we had demonstrated that even in the politically easiest cases there was no consistent standard for what constituted appropriate federal spending.

That's why we ended up giving several billion dollars to Exxon, Union Oil and some gas pipelines to build synthetic fuel plants. When Meese chimed in with the point that these corporations had already invested a small fraction of one percent of their own equity in these projects, the President had an answer.

'We can't cause an honest business to lose money,' he said. All these projects turned out to be total white elephants, but the lesson was clear. If Exxon couldn't be permitted to drill a dry hole right in the Roosevelt Room where the decision was made, what other business subsidy had a chance of being eliminated.

Nor was this an aberration. Right before the 1984 election, the giant timber companies sought an economic bailout that would cost $1.5 billion over several years. We had fought this proposal since 1982, but now it was alleged to make the crucial difference that would put Oregon in the President's electoral column, possibly along with the other forty-nine states. I protested that the bill would hand over $15 to $30 million each to seven Fortune 500 companies, including poverty cases like Boise Cascade. 'No,' replied the President, 'we can't veto. The companies wouldn't really pay us that money anyway. They would just pass it on to consumers.'

If there was any thin sliver of the welfare state where the Reagan Administration might have raised the free enterprise and anti-spending banner, it was against the socialistic enterprises of US Agriculture. But by 1984 we had accommodated to the political facts of life here, too....

As I prepared to make one last run at the deficit monster in late 1984, I soon found myself impaled upon an awful dilemma. Given the fiscal facts of life, I somehow believed that the White House would be prepared to wriggle out of its militant no-tax-increase campaign pledges. With everyone for the welfare state and no one against it, the only thing left to do was to pay for it. But I was mistaken once again. Ed Meese made that crystal clear at the first post-election meeting of the cabinet.

'We have three great goals for the second term,' he said, 'but the first and highest is to keep our pledge not to raise taxes.'

So now our goal was *'Don't pay for a red cent of Big Government, just blame "them" for all the red ink of it.'* After four years in office the Reaganites had no more sense that governance involved making unpalatable choices than they had in the Wexford garage way back at the beginning.

So I attempted to stimulate one more round of Ping-Pong. The final play *had* to yield a tax increase. It was vital.

The first step was easy and involved the establishment of a $50 billion target for deficit reduction in the President's 1986 budget—the minimum credible goal under the circumstances.

I next got out my supply-side catechism book and scrounged for spending cuts that would not poison the political environment or violate iron-clad presidential commitments. This eliminated most of the budget—Social Security, the safety net, veterans' benefits—but there was still one small corner to work in.

Dozens of small economic subsidies and state and local grants could be attacked on principle, even if there was little hope of prevailing on Capitol Hill. I thus targeted Amtrak, EDA, the Ex-Im Bank, federally owned power marketing authorities, student aid, the Small Business Administration, mass transit subsidies, REA, and many more. These savings barely added up to $35 billion, but with a small defense trim, the usual quota of smoke and mirrors, and debt service savings, the President's 1986 spending-cut total was gussied up to match the $50 billion target.

But not without a struggle, because the relevant cabinet officers fought to the last drop of blood against even these minor cuts. Jim Sanders, the SBA administrator, was soon even visibly campaigning on the Hill to defeat my proposal to eliminate subsidized loans for used-car dealers.

The next step was to get the Senate GOP leadership on board. The College of Cardinals was more than willing to get the disagreeable business of raising taxes over with. Dole, Domenici, Hatfield, Laxalt, Packwood, Simpson, Danforth, Heinz, Chafee, Boschwitz, Gorton, even Armstrong and McClure, were ready. To a man, they knew you weren't going to meaningfully reduce the deficit without additional revenue.

But the responsible leaders of the Senate were now in a quandary. If they came right out for higher taxes, they would soon be on a collision course with the White House, inviting renewed stalemate.

Finally we came up with a long shot: We would try to cobble together the largest spending-cut package possible in the Senate. All those who knew we also needed to raise taxes agreed to bite their tongues for a while. The Senate spending-cut-only package would be the final house-cleaning of the welfare state. Anything we could persuade fifty-one senators to cut or throw overboard would be included in it.

Then we would bounce it over to the House side. Since the Democratic majority wanted to cut no spending at all, they would bounce back a budget package with taxes in it. The politicians of Capitol Hill would next compromise between the two and then bounce a decent-sized deficit reduction package which included both tax increases and spending cuts down Pennsylvania Avenue. Then we would find out if it was Clint Eastwood—'make my day'—or a modicum of reason that would determine the nation's economic and fiscal future.

Dole and Domenici worked the strategy all spring. Day after day we round-tabled in Dole's office, and this time it was the real thing. We marched through one program at a time, one Republican faction at a time, until we had got through the whole trillion-dollar budget. Never before had the game of fiscal governance been played so seriously, so completely, or so broadly as it was in Bob Dole's office in the spring of 1985. Rarely before have two political leaders displayed such patience, determination, and ability as did Bob Dole and Pete Domenici.

By May it was time for the Senate to start voting on its package designed to reduce the deficit by $55 billion in 1986, and by rising amounts in the out-years. One by one the Republican politicians came with their final demands as to what *couldn't* be cut if we were to have their vote. And we needed nearly every single vote among the fifty-three Republicans because no Democrats would play this lousy game of having to tiptoe around the President in public.

As the long, final day of the Republican budget round-tabling passed into the middle of the night in Bob Dole's office, I finally saw, as the politicians circled the budget one last time, the awesome staying power of the Second Republic.

We had killed impact aid in February 1981 in the Cutting Room, but it had been resurrected repeatedly in the interim until the Dole-Domenici budget abolished it again. Now along came Senator Jim Abdnor of South Dakota, who stood to lose $300,000 at a single Air Force base school district out yonder in the badlands. In the end his vote went in the yes column and $100 million in impact aid went back into the budget.

The Johnson War on Poverty was long dead, and what remained was only a $300 million echo in the federal budget. The Dole-Domenici budget silenced this echo, but only until ultra-conservative senator Charles Grassley of Iowa came along and traded his vote for LBJ's tattered legacy.

Senator Bob Kasten was a Kempite anti-taxer, so he visited Dole's Cutting Room too. He wanted to make sure that we were not planning to raise a tax in a recovery year. He also wanted to make sure that we were not planning to cut any spending for farm subsidies and UDAG in an election year. He left satisfied on all counts, for, like all the others, his was the last vote that added up to fifty.

Bill Cohen from Maine was justifiably mad because the northwestern senators had prevailed in overriding my plan to make the Bonneville Power Administration pay back its debt to Uncle Sam. I had pleaded until I was blue in the face with Senators Gorton, Evans, and Hatfield for even a token $100 million per year in repayment on its $8 billion debt. But they had three votes, I had none, and so we had saved no money.

Bill Cohen said rural housing was just as important to his state, but unlike them he would compromise rather than insist on rule or ruin. After $4 billion in spending had been haggled back into the budget, he pronounced the remaining cut reasonable.

We had come up with a $5,000 annual cap on college student aid that saved billions, but Bob Stafford, chairman of the Higher Education Subcommittee, regretted that he couldn't go along. Someone might need $8,000 or $10,000 from Uncle Sam to go to Harvard or Middlebury College in Vermont. We gratefully took his vote and a token cut in lieu of real reform and moved on.

We ended up adding money back for the Ex-Im Bank, soil conservation, Medicare, mass transit, Amtrak, child nutrition, education for the handicapped, National Institutes of Health, vocational rehabilitation, and the Small Business Administration, too.

The latter four programs had got about $1 billion in added funding when Senator Lowell Weicker had glared my way and bellowed, 'How long are we going to allow this little pissant to dictate around here? He's had his head up his ass from day one.'

If it hadn't been for the difficulty of speaking from that position, I might have called him a name too. But I had some quick figuring to do because the vote was coming shortly.

We had cut about $54 billion from the 1986 budget. That consisted of $24 billion in defense and about $10 billion in debt service and smoke and mirrors. So after all the round-tabling in Bob Dole's Cutting Room, we had picked through the half-trillion-dollar welfare state budget and come up with $20 billion that Republican senators wre willing to cut.

Ninety-six percent stays, four percent goes. That's what we had come to in Bob Dole's Cutting Room after the most thorough, inspired, and detailed attempt ever made by the collectivity of the nation's Republican politicians to decide what it was they wanted from Big Government and what they could do without.

Just the same, the Senate Republicans were heroes that night when they walked the plank and passed the Dole-Domenici budget. They had put a cap on the COLAs of 40 million voters. They had cut, nicked, and squeezed wherever their collective politics permitted. It was utterly the best that could be done.

But it was all for naught. In rapid order the remainder of the Republican politicians weighed in, blowing the Dole budget and the Ping-Pong game to smithereens.

Jack Kemp joined Claude Pepper in leading the charge to save the COLAs of the old folks. The Merrill Lynch bull charged in again and agreed with Kemp and the House Republicans. Nobody was going to walk the plank on Social Security.

Dole and Domenici then came up with an oil tax to fill up the hole left by the COLAs demise. The President said absolutely not. He would wait for the pony.

There was not a rational possibility left to deal with the irrationality that had descended upon the nation.

I gathered up my black books, knowing that what I started four years before had come to a dismal end.

I could not help recalling what my father had said about that mess out in the tomato field twenty-seven years before.

'What counts around here is what you do, not what you intend.'

What I had done was helped make another mess.

'One of these days you will learn,' he had said.

Maybe at last I had.

29. The Chicano Community

F. CHRIS GARCIA

*Demographers have already begun to speak of the "Hispanization" of the popu-
lation of the United States. Of the many Spanish-speaking Americans, Chicanos,
or Mexican-Americans, are the largest single group. Their population has grown
particularly since World War II, as millions have migrated to the United States.
In many school districts throughout the Southwest and in California Mexican-
Americans form a majority. In New York City, Dominican-Americans make up
the largest of recent immigrant groups.*

*Among the many challenges Americans face, one of the largest is the achieve-
ment of a genuinely multicultural society capable of using the talents of all its
citizens. The terms of international competition make this increasingly essential.
The largest single battleground is in education. It was not long ago that we were
comfortable with schools whose primary function was to "sort" young people into
those who would advance and those who would not. If many of those who did
not complete school were from minority groups, that was unfortunate, but it was
not seen as a problem affecting the national interest. Those who left school early
could still find semi-skilled or unskilled work, could contribute to the economy,
and might even prosper. As lower-skilled factory and industrial jobs are disappearing, today's schools are struggling to overcome this long laissez-faire heritage
and find better ways to educate young people from all cultural backgrounds. But
the process is slow, and when leaders of the Chicano community look at current
statistics, they are understandably impatient.*

*The downturn in real wages since 1973 has injured the prospects of Chicanos
as it has those of other minorities and blue-collar Americans. The Mexican-
American community is coming of age politically at a difficult time in American
history, which explains some of the pessimism in Garcia's account of its role in
American society. Still, the support of what he calls "external forces," largely the
social and economic need for a well-trained labor force in the coming years, could
have a transforming effect on national priorities that would be beneficial to many
of the groups who have not shared in the bounty of American life.*

World War II brought many changes [to the Chicano Community]. In
the economic upturn that followed, there was a new demand for both
industrial and agricultural labor. The movement to the cities accelerated. Regional economic needs and interests reasserted themselves; they
were again instrumental in shaping national legislation in the agricultural arena. The bracero program, reestablished in 1942 and patterned
after a similar program in effect from 1917 to 1920, was based on a
bilateral agreement between Mexico and the United States and was intended to supply labor for agriculture. The United States underwrote
Mexicans' travel costs, insured a minimum wage, and guaranteed their

From F. Chris Garcia's *Latinos In the Political System* © 1988 by the University of Notre
Dame Press.

just and equitable treatment. Agricultural interests were required to post a bond for every bracero and to abide by the agreements negotiated by the two governments. The program, in effect, was a federal subsidy of agriculture's labor needs.

Although intended only as a limited-term war measure to meet specific labor shortages in the agricultural sector, the advantages of the bracero program to both countries suggested its continuance. For Mexico, it was a temporary solution for high levels of unemployment and made for a significant flow of capital to Mexico in wages earned and sent home. For U.S. agriculture, it gave promise of a steady supply of labor that was readily controlled and minimally paid, and for whom no long-term responsibilities were assumed.

The program extended annually after the war, was formalized in 1951 as Public Law 78. The reasons given for the extension were labor shortages stemming from U.S. involvement in the Korean War; it is better understood as a continuation of the traditional U. S. manipulation and control of the flow of Mexican labor. The program was terminated in 1964, when annual immigration quotas of 120,000 were established for all the nations of the Western Hemisphere.

Large-scale abuses were common in the program. Mexico protested these abuses and each time the agreement was renegotiated sought to protect its citizens from inequitable wages and overt discrimination in working conditions, housing, and general treatment. The U.S. government relinquished the determination of wage rates to the agricultural employers, but continued to take responsibility for contracting and transporting Mexican laborers across the border. Nearly 5 million Mexicans came to the United States as a result of the program. The peak years were from 1954 to 1962, when 70 percent of all Mexicans involved in the program were working in the United States. We have no figures to tell us how many of these laborers returned to Mexico.

A steady flow of undocumented workers paralleled this importation of braceros. The undocumented proved to be a mixed blessing for agricultural interest. On the one hand, they were generally hired for wages substantially below the modest levels that agribusiness established for braceros, and bonds were not required to be posted for them. They were widely used as strikebreakers to thwart unionizing activities in agriculture. But there were obvious drawbacks. A labor pool made up of largely undocumented workers was very unstable. Since such workers were under no binding agreement to any employer, they were free to seek the highest wage, within the restrictions imposed by specific jobs and particular industries and under the continuous threat that the employer would terminate the job by calling the Immigration and Naturalization Service just before he was to meet the payroll. To the extent that agribusiness failed to establish a uniform wage, there was a constant temptation for undocumented workers to move on in search of better employment. Moreover, since the undocumented worker was not covered by an agreement restricting him to agricultural tasks, he would always be attracted by industrial jobs in cities, where wages and working conditions were generally better. During World War II, the informal agreements between industry and agribusiness that prohibited the hiring of Mexican labor for factory work were in abeyance.

We understand today how an initial bilateral agreement between Mexico and the United States to supply braceros became in time a unilateral program dictated by U.S. agricultural interests, supported by the federal government. Once agricultural employers took control of the bracero program, they sought to expand their control also over the undocumented worker. Agricultural entrepreneurs ended up by transporting undocumented workers to the border, where they were immediately rehired as braceros, thereby transforming what was once an unregulated labor supply into a legal and semicontrolled work force bound to the agricultural sector.

After a regulated labor pool was firmly reestablished for agribusiness, in 1954 the Immigration and Naturalization Service vigorously launched "Operation Wetback." Undocumented workers, unstable and intractable as a labor source, were now to be removed. An astonishing 3.8 million Mexican aliens (and citizens) were apprehended and expelled in the next five years. Of the total number deported during that time, fewer than 2 percent left as a result of formal proceedings. The vast majority were removed simply by the *threat* of deportation. "Looking Mexican" was often sufficient reason for official scrutiny. The search focused initially on California and then Texas; it soon extended as far as Spokane, Chicago, St. Louis, and Kansas City.

For urban Chicanos and Mexicans World War II had effects similar to those for their rural cousins. On the positive side, war industries provided the semblance of occupational opportunity for many, though often in unskilled, semiskilled, and low-level service capacities. Still, the rigid tie between class and ethnicity seemed somewhat weakened.

World Was II posed a major dilemma for the United States. In its official pronouncements and acts, the country strongly condemned the racism explicit in Nazism. Yet at the same time, the United States had a segregated military force. This was also a time when President Roosevelt issued Executive Order No. 9066, which authorized the internment of Japanese who were U.S. citizens and whose sole "crime" was living and working on the West Coast.

This contradiction also manifested itself in ugly confrontations between Mexicans and Anglos. The press, for its part, helped to raise feelings against Mexicans. The violent confrontations between servicemen and local police against Mexican residents began late in 1942 and continued until mid-1943. The overt racial bias of the press with regard to Mexicans has been thoroughly documented. It suggests the power of the press in shaping public opinion and in justifying major abuses by law enforcement and military personnel. The so-called zoot suit riots illustrate the power of the press in mobilizing prejudice:

The zoot-suiters of Los Angeles...were predominantly Mexican youth with some Negro disciples, between the ages of sixteen and twenty. They wore absurdly long coats with padded shoulders, porkpie hats completed by a feather in the back, watch chains so long they almost touched the ground, and peg-top trousers tapering to narrow cuffs ... at best, as one pundit observed, they were "not characterized primarily by intellect." They formed themselves into bands with flamboyant names; the "Mateo Bombers," "Main Street Zooters," "The Califa," "Sleepy Lagooners," "The Black Legion," and many more. Their targets for physical harm were members of the armed forces, with a special predilection for sailors. The latter fought back with devastating effect. The situation quickly deteriorated to the point that the Navy declared Los Angeles out of bounds. The city council outlawed wearing of zoot suits for the duration and the city simmered down.

Some investigators, more objective than the press, have reversed the roles, with the navy on the offensive and the Mexican young obliged to defend themselves. The firsthand accounts show that the police actually encouraged and supported the servicemen's aggression. And not only did the police refuse to halt the violence, they often contributed to it. . . .

A landmark court decision in 1945 (*Méndez v. Westminister School District*) barred *de jure* segregation of Chicano students. A similar legal action in Texas in 1948 was also successfully pressed. The results of both court actions, as well as others during the 1950s, helped set the stage for the Supreme Court's *Brown v. Board of Education* decision in 1954, and clearly established the illegality of the deliberate segregation of Chicano and Mexican schoolchildren on the basis of race, and of bilingual education as a partial remedy for segregation. The success of these efforts served to encourage civil rights suits in other areas, notably against job discrimination in New Mexico. . . .

In the 1960s and early 1970s, activist, sometimes radical, organizations appeared. These organizations came to be known collectively as the Chicano movement. Often very critical of certain of the basis assumptions of U.S. society, they sought fundamental transformations in the distribution of power in the United States. Many promoted radical alternatives, preferring socialism, for example, to the prevailing economic and political system. Others hoped to create various kinds of alternative or separatist institutions, with alternative schools, community control of law enforcement, health, educational, and political institutions, and the like. They were looking, in short, for a radical and equitable transformation of a racist society. Almost all such groups emphasized the distinctiveness of Mexican culture. They actively promoted Chicano cultural norms and values. Chicano culture represented the common ground that bound together all the members of the group. Political terms such as "Chicano" and *La Raza Nueva* were used to symbolize unity, and were intended to increase the cohesiveness of otherwise diverse elements.

Charismatic leaders appeared. Reies López Tijerina hoped to restore lost Spanish and Mexican land grants in New Mexico through the widely publicized and often dramatic activities of the *Alianza Federal de Pueblos Libres*. Rodolfo "Corky" Gonzales, former prizefighter and disaffected Democratic party official, organized the Crusade for Justice and established several alternative community institutions in the Denver area. The miserable working conditions of Mexican agricultural laborers became the special concern of the United Farm Workers Organizing Committee, led by César Chávez.

Throughout the Southwest and Midwest, political and educational issues sparked new organizing activity. In Texas, José Angel Gutiérrez and others overthrew the minority Anglo-dominated governments of several South Texas cities and counties, primarily through a third party, *El Partido de La Raza Unida*. To secure educational change, students in secondary schools and colleges formed Chicano organizations to stage massive school walkouts. These organizations served as foci for various kinds of diffused activities; they brought a variety of grievances under a single banner, and made a collective approach to these grievances possible.

Anglo decision-makers, reacting to the politics of direct action and confrontation, were sometimes repressive, sometimes progressive; many of the gains made could be attributed to the "threatening" activities of such militant organizations. The protest groups, however, were often short-lived. They called for a great expenditure of time and effort and involved considerable risk.

The student groups were ideologically very diverse: some were moderate-liberal; others were radical. The Mexican-American Youth Organization, a precursor in Texas to the *Raza Unida* party, gave José Angel Gutiérrez, Mario Compeán, and others apprenticeship training in community-based and campus-based politics. *El Movimiento Estudiantíl Chicano de Aztlán*, a campus-based organization, was fairly radical and had many chapters throughout the Southwest; it was very active in support of the farm workers' movement and many other nonschool issues. The United Mexican American Students and the Chicano Youth Organization were other prominent student organizations during the period. Although such organizations often worked off-campus, they pushed also for increased recruitment of Chicano students and faculty, for opening new educational opportunities to Chicanos, and for curricula more relevant to Chicano concerns. Many of these demands were embodied in the new Chicano Studies programs developed in many colleges and universities.

The importance of these campus-based organizations cannot be over-emphasized. They provided invaluable resources for both on-campus and off-campus activities. Many interacted with both staff and faculty. Student groups were effective agents of political mobilization; they had the idealism, ideological commitment, and the relatively supportive environment necessary for sustained organizational activities. Many of these campus organizations, however, were unable to contend with the rapid turnover of student populations, with increasing administrative intransigence, and internal division created by law enforcement *provocateurs* and ultraleftist organizations.

Prior to the 1970s there were few Chicano professional associations, which is not surprising, given the small number of Chicano professionals. As the system yielded to pressure, however, and greater numbers of Chicanos became teachers, lawyers, physicians, and business managers, organization became viable. Many started with less than a dozen members; in many of the academic disciplines, the formation of Chicano/Latino caucuses in major Anglo professional organizations was a necessary first step. Public and private foundations, responding to demands for increased numbers of Chicano professionals, provided support to foster organizational activity. Among these were the *Southwest*

Council de la Raza, the Mexican-American Legal Defense and Educational Fund (MALDEF), and the *National Task Force de la Raza*.

Until 1970 Mexicans were traditionally concentrated in the nonunion ranks of the U.S. economy. Starting in the early 1920s they attempted to form their own unions or to affiliate with unions in Mexico and the United States. The leadership of established industrial unions in this country was never Chicano, although some change is now taking place. Latino workers —Mexicans, Puerto Ricans, and others—are beginning to coalesce in organizations such as the Labor Council for Latin American Advancement.

With the establishment of "national" offices based in Washington, several Chicano organizations began to grow in the mid-1970s. Interorganizational cooperation between Chicanos and Latinos in general has become more common. There have been several attempts to weld "Hispanic" organizations together in some sort of federation, notably the newly created Forum of National Hispanic Organizations and the Hispanic Higher Education Coalition. In the late 1970s such Washington-based groups as the *National Council de la Raza*, MALDEF, and the Mexican-American Women's National Association could coordinate to express the common concerns of Chicano organizations.

Chicanos have gravitated toward public employment, having found opportunities there, particularly in lower-status positions, somewhat more open than in the private sector. Organizations within the public sector, such as IMAGE, a nationwide group of employees that seeks to enhance the working conditions and positions of Chicanos and other Latinos within the government, have emerged. Although there are few high-level government officials of Mexican origin, organizations of Latino officials have come into being. The National Association of Latino Elected and Appointed Officials tries to increase communication between Chicano and Latino decision-makers, particularly on the local level. The Congressional Hispanic Caucus, consisting of the six Latino members of Congress, is the group with the highest governmental status at the federal level.

Two broad coalitions of interests make up the major political parties in the United States, and in general, Chicanos have been exploited by both. Many of the successes of the Democratic party can be attributed to the 70 to 90 percent electoral support regularly given by Chicano voters. Minimal rewards, in the form of minor patronage and policy concessions, have been returned to the Chicano community by the Democratic party, which for the most part has taken the Chicano vote for granted. In very close elections, Democrats have made extravagant promises to Chicanos, but once the election is over, the Anglo Democratic leadership has generally failed to follow through. The Republican party has only limited appeal for Chicanos; Republican leaders have not made a very serious effort to broaden their base by attracting Chicano participation.

Minor parties, including socialist and Marxist-oriented parties, have not been very successful in recruiting Chicanos to their cause. The most successful third party movement for Chicanos, *El Partido de la Raza Unida* (LRUP), at the height of its influence in the early 1970s played a pivotal role in determining the outcome of several local elections, primarily in South Central Texas. In small localities with large Chicano populations, it succeeded in school, town, and county government elections, often stressing the unresponsiveness of the major parties, and arguing for cultural nationalism. The *Partido* provided an alternative that threatened the customary hegemonic position of the major parties. Both the Democratic and the Republican parties reacted by supporting minor institutional reform: they set up "Hispanic" offices within their party organizations, and the Democratic party went so far as to guarantee Chicano representation in its party structure. Conflicts within its own ranks over strategic issues led *La Raza Unida* to fragment into smaller locally based units. Punitive measures sponsored by the State of Texas and specifically aimed at breaking up the *Partido* contributed to its decline. Modifications in electoral laws proved problematic to third parties that attempted to place their candidates on the ballot. By raising the number of required petition-signers or votes received to qualify for inclusion on the ballot, third parties could be excluded.

By the late 1970s the organizational base of the Chicano community had been largely transformed. Many of the more radical and ideological organizations had either disappeared or were mere shadows of their former selves. Leaders who cut their political teeth in such organizations have become part of older, more broadly based organizations or have joined the new professional organizations that continue to advocate, with renewed spirit, specific political reforms. The organizational structure changes as collective and individual political sophistication continues to grow.

The structural characteristics of the Chicano population suggest why Chicanos have gained national visibility. All demographic description starts by emphasizing the youthfulness of the Chicano population, the median age for Chicanos being seven years younger than the national population. A youthful population is one that will be active for a longer period, with the bulk of its members in an early phase of labor force participation, or only just beginning to prepare for that phase. A youthful population has its future before it; schooling, family formation, and child-rearing are crucial issues. And given their rapid numerical growth, Chicanos must play an increasingly important role in the United States in the next decades.

With journalistic phrases like "people on the move," "awakening giant," "emerging minority," and "sleeping giant," writers have drawn attention to the "sudden" visibility of Chicanos. Some are surprised by this visibility. Even the most casual traveler through the southwestern United States has observed the centuries-old Spanish and Mexican influence on architecture, cuisine, language, art, music, and the very layout of towns and cities. Chicano presence in the Southwest has never been hidden. It is the sudden awareness that Chicanos also reside outside these traditional southwestern enclaves and that Chicano issues are not simply regional in nature that has drawn the continuing attention of the mass media. Indeed, the rapid *growth* and continuing *dispersion* of the Chicano population is producing the new national awareness.

The Chicano population has grown substantially over the last decade. Although this growth is attributed in part to improved methods of survey and enumeration by gathering agencies such as the Census Bureau, the greater part of the increase comes from the real growth of the Chicano population. This growth rate has been conservatively estimated at 2.2 percent per year; a more liberal estimate is 3.5 percent per year. The first figure indicates a doubling of the Chicano population every twenty-five to twenty-seven years; the second, a doubling in less than twenty years.

This phenomenal rate of growth is in stark contrast with decreasing growth rates for the U.S. population as a whole. While U.S. birth rates are stabilizing at just above the replacement level, the Chicano population is maintaining the highest rate of growth of all major racial and ethnic groups in the country. Early marriage and the emphasis placed on family accounts for these high fertility rates. Chicano families are generally about 25 percent larger than the average American family, and one in every five Chicano families consists of six or more persons.

There is, however, a trend toward lower birth rates. Younger Chicanas are having fewer children and spacing them out longer over the childbearing years. Still, even among younger and better-educated women, the emphasis on childbearing appears to remain strong; voluntary childlessness among married Chicanas, or those who were married, is virtually unknown.

The high fertility rates of Chicanos suggest major structural differences between them and the Anglo population. Although the Anglo birth rate has decreased owing to later marriages, birth spacing, and the use of contraceptives to synchronize childbearing with the demands of increased female employment, this has not always been the case. From the late 1930s to the early 1940s the United States had high rates of immigration and fertility; the two together produced a period of high population growth. The Chicano population explosion today is in many ways reminiscent of that earlier era, with high rates of immigration (both legal and undocumented) and birth rates. All signs point to a significant growth of the Chicano population in the 1980s.

There is now considerable discussion regarding total Hispanic population growth in the United States and whether this collective group will overtake blacks as the largest national minority group. Precise projections are impossible since they depend on how long current high rates of growth in the Hispanic population are sustained. Still, it is now expected that the Hispanic population will become the largest majority in the United States in the foreseeable future. Further, since Chicanos make up the majority—60 percent—of this population group, they will be among the more visible elements in what is increasingly referred to as the "Hispanization" of the United States.

If high birth rates are important, so also is immigration. The century-old relationship between the United States and Mexico continues to affect both nations. Immigrants, natural resources, and profits continue to flow north. Legal immigration from Mexico to the United States at present allows between forty and fifty thousand visas each year for permanent residence. Those looking for "commuter status," which allows them to work in the United States while living in Mexico, have to endure, barring political connections, a three-year waiting period.

Mexican workers caught in Mexico's economic sluggishness are aware that wages in the United States for identical work are sometimes seven times higher than at home, and many are thus led to risk illegal entry. Such illegal entry is only increased by the active recruitment by "coyotes," who transport Mexicans across the border for a fee. Undocumented workers are a significant part of the U.S. labor force, particularly for work that most American citizens regard as demeaning, low paying, dirty and unstable. Undocumented workers have always come to the United States in circumstances of multiple jeopardy, as minorities unprotected from employer exploitation and abuse. Such conditions continue unabated today.

A majority of the undocumented workers in the United States come as sojourners in search of economic opportunity; few have any desire to remain here as permanent residents. Despite the widespread impression that Mexican undocumented workers come across the border in search of the promised land, *corridos*, or ballads, by and about them celebrate the less hostile, more familiar ambience they plan to return to.

The flow of immigration, both legal and undocumented, is extensive: more than a million persons annually are apprehended by the Border Patrol for seeking entry without inspection. Annual deportations, both voluntary and involuntary, continue to increase steadily. These statistics suggest improved enforcement capabilities; they also measure, however crudely, the growth in the number of Mexicans wanting to cross the permeable U.S.–Mexico border. That flow increases in part because of labor force needs. Jobs are available to Mexican migrants largely in the secondary labor market, where the lack of fringe benefits makes these low-paying, seasonal jobs unattractive to domestic workers. The Mexican worker historically has been desirable. Mexicans— particularly without legal rights and privileges—are especially desirable for agribusiness, marginal industries, seasonal work, or in businesses quickly affected by economic downturns.

Although only a small fraction of the undocumented workers come to the United States with any intention of staying, there is no reason to believe that Mexican immigration will cease, at least in the foreseeable future. The flow of nearly a century and a half, responding to the need for labor by U.S. employers, seems to argue against the possibility of immigration being terminated. The growth of the Chicano population, because of higher fertility and continued immigration, is increasingly visible. The continued dispersion of the Chicano population out of the Southwest into the industrial Midwest, particularly into cities like Chicago, Gary, Hammond, Kansas City, Detroit, Flint, and Saginaw, will go on. It is not difficult to understand the attraction of the Midwest: a Chicano worker with a high-school education will earn approximately $4,000 more per year there than his cousin can expect to earn in the Southwest.

Such differentials in income are significant. The Midwest, highly unionized and with a long-established industrial base, is very different from the Southwest, which is only now beginning to unionize, and where light manufacturing is still the rule. In the Southwest, also, labor-intensive industries in agriculture and mining are giving way to highlevel service industries in aerospace, electronics, and petrochemicals that require a labor force that is technically trained. This new labor force tends to be made up largely of transplanted Easterners.

Chicanos in the Midwest, Pacific Northwest, Florida, and other parts of the United States need to be seen as a vanguard. Although farther removed from their origins, they still maintain and perpetuate their Mexican heritage. Their entry into an area is almost always followed by the rapid opening of small Chicano businesses that specifically cater to their needs. Spanish-language mass at the Catholic Church typically follows, along with Spanish-language radio programs and bilingual programs in the schools. The taking root of Chicano businesses, services, and traditions produces a Midwestern version of the Southwestern or Mexican environment. The ability of Chicanos to transfer their ethnic preferences from one location to another tells something of the strength and durability of their cultural ties.

Midwestern Chicanos, finding themselves among non-Chicano Latinos, necessarily interact, but not always easily or without hostility and suspicion. New patterns, however, are becoming evident as efforts at cooperative ventures are made. Chicanos in Milwaukee, Chicago, and Detroit, for example, discovering that they face problems very similar to those of other Latinos, seek to create coalitions that form the basis for a national Latino thrust. These contacts have understandably progressed further among Cuban, Puerto Rican, and Chicano leaders at the national level than at the local level, particularly as the strategy of nationally organized coalition-building has spread.

The dispersal of Chicanos has had positive and negative effects, making it obvious that Chicano issues cannot be dealt with simply as a regional (Southwestern) matter. Chicanos now reside in every state in the Union; the 1980s will undoubtedly see almost half the Chicano population residing outside the five southwestern states. Had the dispersal of Chicanos not occurred, most of the southwestern states would be overwhelmingly Chicano. Although the size of population does not automatically translate into political power, political negotiation and coalition-building would have taken very different forms if the Southwest had become a single and greater Chicano enclave....

30. Joey's Problem:
Nancy and Evan Holt

ARLIE HOCHSCHILD

The women's movement in the 1980s, argues Arlie Hochschild, is a "stalled revolution." Despite twenty-five years of federal laws against discrimination in the workplace, women remain in a far from equal situation with men. Part of that inequality, Hochschild argues, comes from the inequities of the "second shift," at home. Work is structured so that in order to rise, one needs "backstage support" for the management of family, household, all the chores once done by housewives and servants. This reality conditions the expectations of both men and women in today's marriages, making the management of the household a battleground rather than a bond in most marriages. The structure of the workplace and various social sanctions still encourage men to resist assuming responsibility for child care and housekeeping while they often encourage women to compromise their professional aspirations. These pressures produce a variety of marital scenarios depending on the cultural values, nature, and economic situation of the family.

Hochschild, a sociologist at the University of California at Berkeley, has studied a number of families with two wage earners—either by choice or by necessity—and how they cope with "the second shift." She has also looked at the career and family aspirations of her students. Although she finds many patterns of adjustment, she generalizes that her women students are "poised to step into the biography of Nancy Holt," whose mode (and whose husband's mode) of coping with the issues of work and family turned into "Joey's Problem." Such conflicts are at the core of the history of the women's movement in the last decades.

Nancy Holt arrives home from work, her son, Joey, in one hand and a bag of groceries in the other. As she puts down the groceries and opens the front door, she sees a spill of mail on the hall floor, Joey's half-eaten piece of cinnamon toast on the hall table, and the phone machine's winking red light: a still-life reminder of the morning's frantic rush to distribute the family to the world outside. Nancy, for seven years a social worker, is a short, lithe blond woman of thirty who talks and moves rapidly. She scoops the mail onto the hall table and heads for the kitchen, unbuttoning her coat as she goes. Joey sticks close behind her, intently explaining to her how dump trucks dump things. Joey is a fat-cheeked, lively four-year-old who chuckles easily at things that please him.

Having parked their red station wagon, Evan, her husband, comes in and hangs up his coat. He has picked her up at work and they've arrived home together. Apparently unready to face the kitchen commotion but not quite entitled to relax with the newspaper in the living room, he slowly studies the mail. Also thirty, Evan, a warehouse furniture salesman, has thinning pale blond hair, a stocky build, and a tendency to lean on one foot. In his manner there is something both affable and hesitant.

From the beginning, Nancy describes herself as an "ardent feminist," an egalitarian (she wants a similar balance of spheres and equal power). Nancy began her marriage hoping that she and Evan would base their identities in both their parenthood and their careers, but clearly tilted toward parenthood. Evan felt it was fine for Nancy to have a career, if she could handle the family too.

As I observe in their home on this evening, I notice a small ripple on the surface of family waters. From the commotion of the kitchen, Nancy calls, "Eva-an, will you *please* set the table?" The word *please* is thick with irritation. Scurrying between refrigerator, sink, and oven, with Joey at her feet, Nancy wants Evan to help; she has asked him, but reluctantly. She seems to resent having to ask. (Later she tells me, "I *hate* to ask; why should I ask? It's begging.") Evan looks up from the mail and flashes an irritated glance toward the kitchen, stung, perhaps, to be asked in a way so barren of appreciation and respect. He begins setting out knives and forks, asks if she will need spoons, then answers the doorbell. A neighbor's child. No, Joey can't play right now. The moment of irritation has passed.

Later as I interview Nancy and Evan separately, they describe their family life as unusually happy—except for Joey's "problem." Joey has great difficulty getting to sleep. They start trying to put him to bed at 8:00. Evan tries but Joey rebuffs him; Nancy has better luck. By 8:30 they have him *on* the bed but not *in* it; he crawls and bounds playfully. After 9:00 he still calls out for water or toys, and sneaks out of bed to switch on the light. This continues past 9:30, then 10:00 and 10:30. At about 11:00 Joey complains that his bed is "scary," that he can only go to sleep in his parents' bedroom. Worn down, Nancy accepts this proposition. And it is part of their current arrangement that putting Joey to bed is "Nancy's job." Nancy and Evan can't get into bed until midnight or later, when Evan is tired and Nancy exhausted. She used to enjoy their love-making, Nancy tells me, but now sex seems like "more work." The Holts consider their fatigue and impoverished sex life as results of Joey's Problem.

The official history of Joey's Problem—the interpretation Nancy and Evan give me—begins with Joey's fierce attachment to Nancy, and Nancy's strong attachment to him. On an afternoon walk through Golden Gate Park, Nancy devotes herself to Joey's every move. Now Joey sees a squirrel; Nancy tells me she must remember to bring nuts next time. Now Joey is going up the slide; she notices that his pants are too short—she must take them down tonight. The two enjoy each other. (Off the official record, neighbors and Joey's baby-sitter say that Nancy is a wonderful mother, but privately they add how much she is "also like a single mother.")

For his part, Evan sees little of Joey. He has his evening routine, working with his tools in the basement, and Joey always seems happy to be with Nancy. In fact, Joey shows little interest in Evan, and Evan hesitates to see that as a problem. "Little kids need their moms more than they need their dads," he explains philosophically; "All boys go through an oedipal phase."

Perfectly normal things happen. After a long day, mother, father, and son sit down to dinner. Evan and Nancy get the first chance all day to talk to each other, but both turn anxiously to Joey, expecting his mood to deteriorate. Nancy asks him if he wants celery with peanut butter on it. Joey says yes. "Are you sure that's how you want it?" "Yes." Then the fidgeting begins. "I don't like the strings on my celery." "Celery is made up of strings." "The celery is too big." Nancy grimly slices the celery. A certain tension mounts. Every time one parent begins a conversation with the other, Joey interrupts. "I don't have anything to drink." Nancy gets him juice. And finally, "Feed me." By the end of the meal, no one has obstructed Joey's victory. He has his mother's reluctant attention and his father is reaching for a beer. But talking about it later, they say, "This is normal when you have kids."

Sometimes when Evan knocks on the baby-sitter's door to pick up Joey, the boy looks past his father, searching for a face behind him: "Where's Mommy?" Sometimes he outright refuses to go home with his father. Eventually Joey even swats at his father, once quite hard, on the face for "no reason at all." This makes it hard to keep imagining Joey's relation to Evan as "perfectly normal." Evan and Nancy begin to talk seriously about a "swatting problem."

Evan decides to seek ways to compensate for his emotional distance from Joey. He brings Joey a surprise every week or so—a Tonka truck, a Tootsie Roll. He turns weekends into father-and-son times. One Saturday, Evan proposes the zoo, and hesitantly, Joey agrees. Father and son have their coats on and are nearing the front door. Suddenly Nancy decides she wants to join them, and as she walks down the steps with Joey in her arms, she explains to Evan, "I want to help things out."

Evan gets few signs of love from Joey and feels helpless to do much about it. "I just don't feel good about me and Joey," he tells me one evening, "that's all I can say." Evan loves Joey. He feels proud of him, this bright, good-looking, happy child. But Evan also seems to feel that being a father is vaguely hurtful and hard to talk about.

The official history of Joey's problem was that Joey felt the "normal" oedipal attachment of a male child to his mother. Joey was having the emotional problems of growing up that any parent can expect. But Evan and Nancy add the point that Joey's problems are exacerbated by Evan's difficulties being an active father, which stem, they feel, from the way Evan's own father, an emotionally remote self-made businessman, had treated him. Evan tells me, "When Joey gets older, we're going to play baseball together and go fishing."

As I recorded this official version of Joey's Problem through interviews and observation, I began to feel doubts about it. For one thing, clues to another interpretation appeared in the simple pattern of footsteps on a typical evening. There was the steady pacing of Nancy, preparing dinner in the kitchen, moving in zigzags from counter to refrigerator to counter to stove. There were the lighter, faster steps of Joey, running in large figure eights through the house, dashing from his Tonka truck to his motorcycle man, reclaiming his sense of belonging in this house, among his things. After dinner, Nancy and Evan mingled footsteps in the kitchen, as they cleaned up. Then Nancy's steps began again: click, click, click, down to the basement for laundry, then thuck, thuck, thuck up the carpeted stairs to the first floor. Then to the bathroom where she runs Joey's bath, then into Joey's room, then back to the bath with Joey. Evan moved less—from the living room chair to Nancy in the kitchen, then back to the living room. He moved to the dining room to eat dinner and to the kitchen to help clean up. After dinner he went down to his hobby shop in the basement to sort out his tools; later he came up for a beer, then went back down. The footsteps suggest what is going on: Nancy was at work on her second shift.

BEHIND THE FOOTSTEPS

Between 8:05 A.M. and 6:05 P.M., both Nancy and Evan are away from home, working a "first shift" at full-time jobs. The rest of the time they deal with the varied tasks of the second shift: shopping, cooking, paying bills; taking care of the car, the garden, and yard; keeping harmony with Evan's mother who drops over quite a bit, "concerned" about Joey, with neighbors, their voluble baby-sitter, and each other. And Nancy's talk reflects a series of second-shift thoughts: "We're out of barbecue sauce . . . Joey needs a Halloween costume . . . The car needs a wash . . ." and so on. She reflects a certain "second-shift sensibility," a continual attunement to the task of striking and restriking the right emotional balance between child, spouse, home, and outside job.

When I first met the Holts, Nancy was absorbing far more of the second shift than Evan. She said she was doing 80 percent of the housework and 90 percent of the childcare. Evan said she did 60 percent of the housework, 70 percent of the childcare. Joey said, "I vacuum the rug, and fold the dinner napkins," finally concluding, "Mom and I do it all." A neighbor agreed with Joey. Clearly, between Nancy and Evan, there was a "leisure gap": Evan had more than Nancy. I asked both of them, in separate interviews, to explain to me how they had dealt with housework and childcare since their marriage began.

One evening in the fifth year of their marriage, Nancy told me, when Joey was two months old and almost four years before I met the Holts, she first seriously raised the issue with Evan. "I told him: 'Look, Evan, it's not working. I do the housework, I take the major care of Joey, *and* I work a full-time job. I get pissed. This is *your* house too. Joey is *your* child too. It's not all *my* job to care for them.' When I cooled down I put to him, 'Look, how about this: I'll cook Mondays, Wednesdays, and Fridays. You cook Tuesdays, Thursdays, and Saturdays. And we'll share or go out Sundays.' "

According to Nancy, Evan said he didn't like "rigid schedules." He said he didn't necessarily agree with her standards of housekeeping, and didn't like that standard "imposed" on him, especially if she was "sluffing off" tasks on him, which from time to time he felt she was. But he went along with the idea in principle. Nancy said the first week of the new plan went as follows. On Monday, she cooked. For Tuesday, Evan planned a meal that required shopping for a few ingredients, but on his way home he forgot to shop for them. He came home, saw nothing he could use in the refrigerator or in the cupboard, and suggested to Nancy that they go out for Chinese food. On Wednesday, Nancy cooked. On Thursday morning, Nancy reminded Evan, "Tonight it's your turn." That night Evan fixed hamburgers and french fries and Nancy was quick to praise him. On Friday, Nancy cooked. On Saturday, Evan forgot again.

As this pattern continued, Nancy's reminders became sharper. The sharper they became, the more actively Evan forgot—perhaps anticipating even sharper reprimands if he resisted more directly. This cycle of passive refusal followed by disappointment and anger gradually tightened, and before long the struggle had spread to the task of doing the laundry. Nancy said it was only fair that Evan share the laundry. He agreed in principle, but anxious that Evan would not share, Nancy wanted a clear, explicit agreement. "You ought to wash and fold every other load," she had told him. Evan experienced this "plan" as a yoke around his neck. On many weekdays, at this point, a huge pile of laundry sat like a disheveled guest on the living-room couch.

In her frustration, Nancy began to make subtle emotional jabs at Evan. "I don't know *what's* for dinner," she would say with a sigh. Or "I can't cook now, I've got to deal with this pile of laundry." She tensed at the slightest criticism about household disorder; if Evan wouldn't do the housework, he had absolutely *no* right to criticize how she did it. She would burst out angrily at Evan. She recalled telling him: "After work *my* feet are just as tired as *your* feet. I'm just as wound up as you are. I come home. I cook dinner. I wash and I clean. Here we are, planning a second child, and I can't cope with the one we have."

About two years after I first began visiting the Holts, I began to see their problem in a certain light: as a conflict between their two gender ideologies. Nancy wanted to be the sort of woman who was needed and appreciated both at home and at work—like Lacey, she told me, on the television show "Cagney and Lacey." She wanted Evan to appreciate her for being a caring social worker, a committed wife, and a wonderful mother. But she cared just as much that she be able to appreciate *Evan* for what *he* contributed at home, not just for how he supported the family. She would feel proud to explain to women friends that she was married to one of these rare "new men."

A gender ideology is often rooted in early experience, and fueled by motives formed early on and such motives can often be traced to some cautionary tale in early life. So it was for Nancy. Nancy described her mother:

My mom was wonderful, a real aristocrat, but she was also terribly depressed being a housewife. My dad treated her like a doormat. She didn't have any self-confidence. And growing up, I can remember her being really depressed. I grew up bound and determined not to be like her and not to marry a man like my father. As long as Evan doesn't do the housework, I feel it means he's going to be like my father—coming home, putting his feet up, and hollering at my mom to serve him. That's my biggest fear. I've had *bad* dreams about that.

Nancy thought that women friends her age, also in traditional marriages, had come to similarly bad ends. She described a high school

friend: "Martha barely made it through City College. She had no interest in learning anything. She spent nine years trailing around behind
her husband [a salesman]. It's a miserable marriage. She hand washes all
his shirts. The high point of her life was when she was eighteen and the
two of us were running around Miami Beach in a Mustang convertible.
She's gained seventy pounds and she hates her life. " To Nancy, Martha
was a younger version of her mother, depressed, lacking in self-esteem,
a cautionary tale whose moral was "if you want to be happy, develop a
career and get your husband to share at home." Asking Evan to help
again and again felt like "hard work" but it was essential to establishing
her role as a career woman.

For his own reasons, Evan imagined things very differently. He
loved Nancy and if Nancy loved being a social worker, he was happy and
proud to support her in it. He knew that because she took her caseload
so seriously, it was draining work. But at the same time, he did not see
why, just because she chose this demanding career, *he* had to change *his
own* life. Why should her personal decision to work outside the home
require him to do more inside it? Nancy earned about two-thirds as
much as Evan, and her salary was a big help, but as Nancy confided,
"If push came to shove, we could do without it." Nancy was a social
worker because she loved it. Doing daily chores at home was thankless
work, and certainly not something Evan needed her to appreciate about
him. Equality in the second shift meant a loss in his standard of living,
and despite all the high-flown talk, he felt he hadn't *really* bargained for
it. He was happy to help Nancy at home if she needed help; that was
fine. That was only decent. But it was too sticky a matter "committing"
himself to sharing.

Two other beliefs probably fueled his resistance as well. The first
was his suspicion that if he shared the second shift with Nancy, she
would "dominate him." Nancy would ask him to do this, ask him to do
that. It felt to Evan as if Nancy had won so many small victories that he
had to draw the line somewhere. Nancy had a declarative personality;
and as Nancy said, "Evan's mother sat me down and told me once that
I was too forceful, that Evan needed to take more authority." Both
Nancy and Evan agreed that Evan's sense of career and self was in
fact shakier than Nancy's. He had been unemployed. She never had.
He had had some bouts of drinking in the past. Drinking was foreign
to her. Evan thought that sharing housework would upset a certain
balance of power that felt culturally "right." He held the purse strings
and made the major decisions about large purchases (like their house)
because he "knew more about finances" and because he'd chipped in
more inheritance than she when they married. His job difficulties had
lowered his self-respect, and now as a couple they had achieved some
ineffable "balance"—tilted in his favor, she thought—which, if corrected
to equalize the burden of chores, would result in his giving in "too
much." A certain driving anxiety behind Nancy's strategy of actively
renegotiating roles had made Evan see agreement as "giving in." When
he wasn't feeling good about work, he dreaded the idea of being under
his wife's thumb at home.

Underneath these feelings, Evan perhaps also feared that Nancy was avoiding taking care of *him*. His own mother, a mild-mannered alcoholic, had by imperceptible steps phased herself out of a mother's role, leaving him very much on his own. Perhaps a personal motive to prevent that happening in his marriage—a guess on my part, and unarticulated on his—underlay his strategy of passive resistance. And he wasn't altogether wrong to fear this. Meanwhile, he felt he was "offering" Nancy the chance to stay home, or cut back her hours, and that she was refusing his "gift," while Nancy felt that, given her feelings about work, this offer was hardly a gift.

In the sixth year of her marriage, when Nancy again intensified her pressure on Evan to commit himself to equal sharing, Evan recalled saying, "Nancy, why don't you cut back to half time, that way you can fit everything in." At first Nancy was baffled: "We've been married all this time, and you *still* don't get it. Work is important to me. I worked *hard* to get my MSW. Why *should* I give it up?" Nancy also explained to Evan and later to me, "I think my degree and my job has been my way of reassuring myself that I won't end up like my mother." Yet she'd received little emotional support in getting her degree from either her parents or in-laws. (Her mother had avoided asking about her thesis, and her in-laws, though invited, did not attend her graduation, later claiming they'd never been invited.)

In addition, Nancy was more excited about seeing her elderly clients in tenderloin hotels than Evan was about selling couches to furniture salesmen with greased-back hair. Why shouldn't Evan make as many compromises with his career ambitions and his leisure as she'd made with hers? She couldn't see it Evan's way, and Evan couldn't see it hers.

In years of alternating struggle and compromise, Nancy had seen only fleeting mirages of cooperation, visions that appeared when she got sick or withdrew, and disappeared when she got better or came forward.

After seven years of loving marriage, Nancy and Evan had finally come to a terrible impasse. Their emotional standard of living had drastically declined: they began to snap at each other, to criticize, to carp. Each felt taken advantage of: Evan, because his offering of a good arrangement was deemed unacceptable, and Nancy, because Evan wouldn't do what she deeply felt was "fair."

This struggle made its way into their sexual life—first through Nancy directly, and then through Joey. Nancy had always disdained any form of feminine wiliness or manipulation. Her family saw her as "a flaming feminist" and that was how she saw herself. As such, she felt above the underhanded ways traditional women used to get around men. She mused, "When I was a teen-ager, I vowed I would *never* use sex to get my way with a man. It is not self-respecting; it's demeaning. But when Evan refused to carry his load at home, I did, I used sex. I said, 'Look, Evan, I would not be this exhausted and asexual every night if I didn't have so much to face every morning.' " She felt reduced to an old "strategy," and her modern ideas made her ashamed of it. At the same time, she'd run out of other, modern ways.

The idea of a separation arose, and they became frightened. Nancy looked at the deteriorating marriages and fresh divorces of couples with young children around them. One unhappy husband they knew had become so uninvolved in family life (they didn't know whether his unhappiness made him uninvolved, or whether his lack of involvement had caused his wife to be unhappy) that his wife left him. In another case, Nancy felt the wife had "nagged" her husband so much that he abandoned her for another woman. In both cases, the couple was less happy after the divorce than before, and both wives took the children and struggled desperately to survive financially. Nancy took stock. She asked herself, "Why wreck a marriage over a dirty frying pan?" Is it really worth it?

UPSTAIRS-DOWNSTAIRS: A FAMILY MYTH AS "SOLUTION"

Not long after this crisis in the Holts' marriage, there was a dramatic lessening of tension over the issue of the second shift. It was as if the issue was closed. Evan had won. Nancy would do the second shift. Evan expressed vague guilt but beyond that he had nothing to say. Nancy had wearied of continually raising the topic, wearied of the lack of resolution. Now in the exhaustion of defeat, she wanted the struggle to be over too. Evan was "so good" in *other* ways, why debilitate their marriage by continual quarreling. Besides, she told me, "Women always adjust more, don't they?"

One day, when I asked Nancy to tell me who did which tasks from a long list of household chores, she interrupted me with a broad wave of her hand and said, "I do the upstairs, Evan does the downstairs." What does that mean? I asked. Matter-of-factly, she explained that the upstairs included the living room, the dining room, the kitchen, two bedrooms, and two baths. The downstairs meant the garage, a place for storage and hobbies—Evan's hobbies. She explained this as a "sharing" arrangement, without humor or irony—just as Evan did later. Both said they had agreed it was the best solution to their dispute. Evan would take care of the car, the garage, and Max, the family dog. As Nancy explained, "The dog is all Evan's problem. I don't have to deal with the dog." Nancy took care of the rest.

For purposes of accommodating the second shift, then, the Holts' garage was elevated to the full moral and practical equivalent of the rest of the house. For Nancy and Evan, "upstairs and downstairs," "inside and outside," was vaguely described like "half and half," a fair division of labor based on a natural division of their house.

The Holts presented their upstairs-downstairs agreement as a perfectly equitable solution to a problem they "once had." This belief is what we might call a "family myth," even a modest delusional system. Why did they believe it? I think they believed it because they needed to believe it, because it solved a terrible problem. It allowed Nancy to continue thinking of herself as the sort of woman whose husband didn't abuse her—a self-conception that mattered a great deal to her. And it avoided the hard truth that, in his stolid, passive way, Evan had refused to share. It avoided the truth, too, that in their showdown, Nancy was more afraid of divorce than Evan was. This outer cover to their family life, this family myth, was jointly devised. It was an attempt to agree that there was no conflict over the second shift, no tension between their versions of manhood and womanhood, and that the powerful crisis that had arisen was temporary and minor.

The wish to avoid such a conflict is natural enough. But their avoidance was tacitly supported by the surrounding culture, especially the image of the woman with the flying hair. After all, this admirable woman also proudly does the "upstairs" each day without a husband's help and without conflict.

After Nancy and Evan reached their upstairs-downstairs agreement, their confrontations ended. They were nearly forgotten. Yet, as she described their daily life months after the agreement, Nancy's resentment still seemed alive and well. For example, she said:

Evan and I eventually divided the labor so that I do the upstairs and Evan does the downstairs and the dog. So the dog is my husband's problem. But when I was getting the dog outside and getting Joey ready for childcare, and cleaning up the mess of feeding the cat, and getting the lunches together, and having my son wipe his nose on my outfit so I would have to change—then I was pissed! I felt that I was doing *everything*. All Evan was doing was getting up, having coffee, reading the paper, and saying, "Well, I have to go now," and often forgetting the lunch I'd bothered to make.

She also mentioned that she had fallen into the habit of putting Joey to bed in a certain way: he asked to be swung around by the arms, dropped on the bed, nuzzled and hugged, whispered to in his ear. Joey waited for her attention. He didn't go to sleep without it. But, increasingly, when Nancy tried it at eight or nine, the ritual didn't put Joey to sleep. On the contrary, it woke him up. It was then that Joey began to say he could only go to sleep in his parents' bed, that he began to sleep in their bed and to encroach on their sexual life.

Near the end of my visits, it struck me that Nancy was putting Joey to bed in an "exciting" way, later and later at night, in order to tell Evan something important: "You win, I'll go on doing all the work at home, but I'm angry about it and I'll make you pay." Evan had won the battle but lost the war. According to the family myth, all was well: the struggle had been resolved by the upstairs-downstairs agreement. But suppressed in one area of their marriage, this struggle lived on in another—as Joey's Problem, and as theirs.

NANCY'S "PROGRAM" TO SUSTAIN THE MYTH

There was a moment, I believe, when Nancy seemed to *decide* to give up on this one. She decided to try not to resent Evan. Whether or not other women face a moment just like this, at the very least they face the need to deal with all the feelings that naturally arise from a clash between a treasured ideal and an incompatible reality. In the age of a stalled revolution, it is a problem a great many women face.

Emotionally, Nancy's compromise from time to time slipped; she would forget and grow resentful again. Her new resolve needed maintenance. Only half aware that she was doing so, Nancy went to extraordinary lengths to maintain it. She could tell me now, a year or so after her "decision," in a matter-of-fact and noncritical way: "Evan likes to come home to a hot meal. He doesn't like to clear the table. He doesn't like to do the dishes. He likes to go watch T.V. He likes to play with his son when he feels like it and not feel like he should be with him more." She seemed resigned.

Everything was "fine." But it had taken an extraordinary amount of complex "emotion work"—the work of *trying* to feel the "right" feeling, the feeling she wanted to feel—to make and keep everything "fine." Across the nation at this particular time in history, this emotion work is often all that stands between the stalled revolution on the one hand, and broken marriages on the other.

It would have been easier for Nancy Holt to do what some other women did: indignantly cling to her goal of sharing the second shift. Or she could have cynically renounced all forms of feminism as misguided, could have cleared away any ideological supports to her indignation, so as to smooth her troubled bond with Evan. Or, like her mother, she could have sunk into quiet depression, disguised perhaps by overbusyness, drinking, overeating. She did none of these things. Instead, she did something more complicated. She became *benignly* accommodating.

How did Nancy manage to accommodate graciously? How did she really live with it? In the most general terms, she had to bring herself to *believe* the myth that the upstairs-downstairs division of housework was fair, and that it had resolved her struggle with Evan. She had to decide to accept an arrangement which in her heart of hearts she had felt was unfair. At the same time, she did not relinquish her deep beliefs about fairness.

Instead, she did something more complicated. Intuitively, Nancy seemed to *avoid* all the mental associations that reminded her of this sore point: the connections between Evan's care of the dog and her care of their child and house, between her share of family work and equality in their marriage; and between equality and love. In short, Nancy refused to consciously recognize the entire chain of associations that made her feel that something was wrong. The maintenance program she designed to avoid thinking about these things and to avoid the connections between them, was, in one way, a matter of denial. But in another way, it was a matter of intuitive genius.

First, it involved dissociating the inequity in the second shift from the inequity in their marriage, and in marriages in general. Nancy continued to care about sharing the work at home, about having an "equal marriage" and about other people having them too. For reasons that went back to her depressed "doormat" mother, and to her consequent determination to forge an independent identity as an educated, middle-class woman for whom career opportunities had opened up in the early 1980s, Nancy cared about these things. Egalitarianism as an ideology made sense of her biography, her circumstances, and the way she had forged the two. How could she *not* care? But to ensure that her concern for equality did not make her resentful in her marriage to a man remarkably resistant to change, she "rezoned" this anger-inducing territory. She made that territory much smaller: only if Evan did not take care of the dog would she be indignant. Now she wouldn't need to be upset about the double day in *general*. She could still be a feminist, still believe in fifty-fifty with housework, and still believe that working toward equality was an expression of respect and respect the basis of love. But this chain of associations was now anchored more safely to a more minor matter: how lovingly Evan groomed, fed, and walked the dog.

For Evan, also, the dog came to symbolize the entire second shift: it became a fetish. Other men, I found, had second-shift fetishes too. When I asked one man what he did to share the work of the home, he answered, "I make all the pies we eat." He didn't have to share much responsibility for the home, "pies" did it for him. Another man grilled fish. Another baked bread. In their pies, their fish, and their bread, such men converted a single act into a substitute for a multitude of chores in the second shift, a token. Evan took care of the dog.

Another way in which Nancy encapsulated her anger was to think about her work in a different way. Feeling unable to cope at home, she had with some difficulty finally arranged a half-time schedule with her boss at work. This eased her load, but it did not resolve the more elusive moral problem: within their marriage, her work and her time "mattered less" than Evan's. What Evan did with his time corresponded to what he wanted her to depend on him for, to appreciate him for; what she did with her time did not. To deal with this, she devised the idea of dividing all of her own work in the new schedule into "shifts." As she explained: "I've been resentful, yes. I was feeling mistreated, and I became a bitch to live with. Now that I've gone part-time, I figure that when I'm at the office from eight to one, and when I come home and take care of Joey and make dinner at five—all that time from eight to six is my shift. So I don't mind making dinner every night *since it's on my shift*. Before, I had to make dinner on time I considered to be *after* my shift and I resented always having to do it."

Another plank in Nancy's maintenance program was to suppress any comparison between her hours of leisure and Evan's. In this effort she had Evan's cooperation, for they both clung hard to the notion that they enjoyed an equal marriage. What they did was to deny any connection between this equal marriage and equal access to leisure. They agreed it couldn't be meaningfully claimed that Evan had more leisure than Nancy or that his fatigue mattered more, or that he enjoyed more discretion over his time, or that he lived his life more as he preferred. Such comparisons could suggest that they were both treating Evan as if he were *worth more* than Nancy, and for Nancy, from that point on, it would be a quick fall down a slippery slope to the idea that Evan did not love and honor her as much as she honored and loved him.

For Nancy, the leisure gap between Evan and herself had never seemed to her a simple, practical matter of her greater fatigue. Had it been just that, she would have felt tired but not indignant. Had it been only that, working part time for a while would have been a wonderful solution, as many other women have said, "the best of both worlds." What troubled Nancy was the matter of her worth. As she told me one day: "It's not that I mind taking care of Joey. I love doing that. I don't even mind cooking or doing laundry. It's that I feel sometimes that Evan thinks his work, his time, is worth more than mine. He'll wait for me to get the phone. It's like his time is more sacred."

As Nancy explained: "Evan and I look for different signs of love. Evan feels loved when we make love. Sexual expression is very important to him. I feel loved when he makes dinner for me or cleans up. He knows I like that, and he does it sometimes." For Nancy, feeling loved was connected to feeling her husband was being considerate of her needs, and honoring her ideal of sharing and equity. To Evan, "fairness" and respect seemed impersonal moral concepts, abstractions rudely imposed on love. He thought he expressed his respect for Nancy by listening carefully to her opinions on the elderly, on welfare, on all sorts of topics, and by consulting her on major purchases. But who did the dishes had to do with a person's role in the family, not with fairness and certainly not with love. In my interviews, a surprising number of women spoke of their fathers helping their mothers "out of love" or consideration. As one woman said, "My dad helped around a lot. He really loved my mom." But in describing their fathers, not one man I interviewed made this link between help at home and love.

SUPPRESSING THE POLITICS OF COMPARISON

In the past, Nancy had compared her responsibilities at home, her identity, and her life to Evan's, and had compared Evan to other men they knew. Now, to avoid resentment, she seemed to compare herself more to *other working mothers*—how organized, energetic, and successful she was compared to them. By this standard, she was doing great: Joey was blooming, her marriage was fine, her job was all she could expect.

Nancy also compared herself to single women who had moved further ahead in their careers, but they fit another mental category. There were two kinds of women, she thought—married and single. "A single woman could move ahead in her career but a married woman has to do a wife's work and mother's work as well." She did not make this distinction for men.

When Nancy decided to stop comparing Evan to men who helped more around the house, she had to suppress an important issue that she had often discussed with Evan: How *unusually* helpful was Evan? How unusually lucky was she? Did he do more or less than men in general? Than middle-class, educated men? What was the "going rate"?

Before she made her decision, Nancy had claimed that Bill Beaumont, who lived two doors down the street, did half the housework without being reminded. Evan gave her Bill Beaumont, but said Bill was an exception. Compared to *most men*, Evan said, he did more. This was true if "most men" meant Evan's old friends. Nancy felt "upwardly mobile" compared to the wives of those men, and she believed that they looked upon Evan as a model for their own husbands, just as she used to look up to women whose husbands did more than Evan. She also noted how much the dangerous "unionizer" she had appeared to a male friend of theirs:

One of our friends is a traditional Irish cop whose wife doesn't work. But the way they wrote that marriage, even when she had the kid and worked full time, she did everything. He couldn't understand our arrangement where my husband would help out and cook part time and do the dishes once in a while and help out with the laundry [an arrangement that didn't last]. We were *banned* from his house for a while because he told Evan, "Every time your wife comes over and talks to my wife, I get in trouble." I was considered a flaming liberal.

When the wife of Joe Collins, a neighbor on the other side, complained that Joe didn't take equal responsibility, Joe in turn would look down the invisible chain of sharing, half-sharing, and nonsharing males to someone low on his wife's list of helpful husbands and say, "At least I do a hell of a lot more than *he* does." In reply, Joe's wife would name a husband she knew who took fully half the responsibility of caring for the child and the home. Joe would answer that this man was either imaginary or independently wealthy, and then cite the example of another male friend who, though a great humorist and fisherman, did far less at home.

I began to imagine the same evening argument extending down the street of this middle-class Irish neighborhood, across the city to other cities, states, regions...wives pointing to husbands who did more, husbands pointing to men who did less. Comparisons like these—between Evan and other men, between Nancy and other women—reflect a semiconscious sense of *the going rates for a desirable attitude or behavior in an available member of the same and opposite sex.* If most of the men in their middle-class circle of friends had been given to drinking heavily, beating their wives, and having affairs, Nancy would have considered herself "lucky" to have Evan, because he didn't do those things. But most of the men they knew weren't like that either, so Nancy didn't consider Evan "above the going rate" in this way. Most of those men only halfheartedly encouraged their wives to advance at work, so Nancy felt lucky to have Evan's enthusiastic encouragement.

This idea of a "going rate" indicated the market value, so to speak, of a man's behavior or attitudes. If a man was really "rare," his wife intuitively felt grateful, or at least both of them felt she ought to. How far the whole culture, and their particular corner of it had gotten through the feminist agenda—criminalizing wife battery, disapproving of a woman's need for her husband's "permission" to work, and so on—became the cultural foundation of the judgment about how rare and desirable a man was.

The "going rate" was a tool in the marital struggle, useful in this case mainly on the male side. If Evan could convince Nancy that he did as much or more than "most men," she couldn't as seriously expect him to do more. Like most other men who didn't share, Evan felt that male "norm" was evidence on his side: men "out there" did less. Nancy was lucky he did as much as he did.

Nancy thought men "out there" did more at home but were embarrassed to say so. Given her view of "men out there," Nancy felt less lucky than seemed right to Evan, given his picture of things. Besides that, Nancy felt that sheer rarity was not the only or best measure. She felt that Evan's share of the work at home should be assessed, not by comparing it to the real inequalities in other people's lives, but by comparing it to the ideal of sharing.

Comparisons between Evan and the going rate of male helpfulness was one basis on which to appraise Evan's offerings to their marriage and the credit and gratitude due him for those offerings. The more rare, the more credit. Their ideals of manhood and womanhood formed another basis. The closer to the ideal, the more credit. And the harder it was to live up to the ideal, the more pride-swallowing it took, or the more effort shown, the more credit. Since Evan and Nancy didn't see this going rate the same way, since they differed in their ideals, and since Evan hadn't actually shown much effort in changing, Nancy had not been as grateful to Evan as he felt she should have been. Not only had she not been grateful, she'd resented him.

But now, under the new "maintenance program" to support the necessary myth of equality in her marriage, Nancy set aside the tangles in the give and take of credit. She thought now in a more "segregated" way. She compared women to women, and men to men, and based her sense of gratitude on that way of thinking. Since the going rate was unfavorable to women, Nancy felt she should feel more grateful for what Evan gave her (because it was so rare in the world) than Evan should feel for what she gave him (which was more common). Nancy did not have to feel grateful because Evan had compromised his own views on manhood; actually he had made few concessions. But she did feel she owed him gratitude for supporting her work so wholeheartedly; that was unusual.

For his part, Evan didn't talk much about feeling grateful to Nancy. He actually felt she wasn't doing enough around the house. But he said this in a curious way that avoided an Evan-Nancy comparison. He erased the distinction between Nancy and himself: his "I" disappeared into "we," leaving no "me" to compare to "you." For example, when I asked him if he felt that he did enough around the house, he laughed, surprised to be asked point-blank, and replied mildly: "No, I don't think so. No. I would have to admit that we probably could do more." Then using "we" in an apparently different way, he went on: "But I also have to say that I think we could do more in terms of the household chores than we really do. See, we let a lot more slide than we should."

Nancy made no more comparisons to Bill Beaumont, no more unfavorable comparisons to the "going rate." Without these frames of reference, the deal with Evan seemed "fair." This did not mean that Nancy ceased to care about equality between the sexes. On the contrary, she cut out magazine articles about how males rose faster in social welfare than females, and she complained about the condescending way male psychiatrists treat female social workers. She pushed her feminism "out" into the world of work, a safe distance away from the upstairs-downstairs arrangement at home.

Nancy now blamed her fatigue on "everything she had to do." When she occasionally spoke of conflict, it was conflict between her job and Joey, or between Joey and housework. Evan slid out of the equation. As Nancy spoke of him now, he had no part in the conflict.

Since Nancy and Evan no longer conceived of themselves as comparable, Nancy let it pass when Evan spoke of housework in a "male" way, as something he "would do" or "would not do," or something he did when he got around to it. Like most women, when Nancy spoke of housework, she spoke simply of what had to be done. The difference in the way she and Evan talked seemed to emphasize that their viewpoints were "naturally" different and again helped push the problem out of mind.

Many couples traded off tasks as the need arose; whoever came home first started dinner. In the past, Evan had used flexibility in the second shift to camouflage his retreat from it; he hadn't liked "rigid schedules." He had once explained to me: "We don't really keep count of who does what. Whoever gets home first is likely to start dinner. Whoever has the time deals with Joey or cleans up." He had disparaged a female neighbor who kept strict track of tasks as "uptight" and "compulsive." A couple, he had felt, ought to be "open to the flow." Dinner, he had said, could be anytime. The very notion of a leisure gap disappeared into Evan's celebration of happy, spontaneous anarchy. But now that the struggle was over, Evan didn't talk of dinner at "anytime." Dinner was at six.

Nancy's program to keep up her gracious resignation included another tactic: she would focus on the *advantages* of losing the struggle. She wasn't *stuck* with the upstairs. Now, as she talked she seemed to preside over it as her dominion. She would do the housework, but the house would feel like "hers." The new living-room couch, the kitchen cabinet, she referred to as "mine." She took up "supermom-speak" and began referring to *my* kitchen, *my* living-room curtains, and, even in Evan's presence, to *my* son. She talked of machines that helped *her*, and of the work-family conflict itself as *hers*. Why shouldn't she? She felt she'd earned that right. The living room reflected Nancy's preference for beige. The upbringing of Joey reflected Nancy's ideas about fostering creativity by giving a child controlled choice. What remained of the house was Evan's domain. As she remarked: "I never touch the garage, not ever. Evan sweeps it and straightens it and arranges it and plays with tools and figures out where the equipment goes—in fact, that's one of his hobbies. In the evening, after Joey has settled down, he goes down there and putzes around; he has a TV down there, and he figures out his fishing equipment and he just plays around. The washer and dryer are down there, but that's the only part of the garage that's my domain."

Nancy could see herself as the "winner"—the one who got her way, the one whose kitchen, living room, house, and child these really were. She could see her arrangement with Evan as *more* than fair—from a certain point of view.

As a couple, Nancy and Evan together explained their division of the second shift in ways that disguised their struggle. Now they rationalized that it was a result of their two *personalities*. For Evan, especially, there was no problem of a leisure gap; there was only the continual, fascinating interaction of two personalities. "I'm lazy," he explained. "I like to do what I want to do in my own time. Nancy isn't as lazy as I am. She's compulsive and very well organized." The comparisons of his work to hers, his fatigue to hers, his leisure time to hers—comparisons that used to point to a problem—were melted into freestanding personal characteristics, his laziness, her compulsiveness.

Nancy now agreed with Evan's assessment of her, and described herself as "an energetic person" who was amazingly "well organized." When I asked her whether she felt any conflict between work and family life, she demurred: "I work real well overnight. I pulled overnights all through undergraduate and graduate school, so I'm not too terribly uncomfortable playing with my family all evening, then putting them to bed, making coffee, and staying up all night [to write up reports on her welfare cases] and then working the next day—though I only do that when I'm down to the wire. I go into overdrive. I don't feel any conflict between the job and the child that way at all."

Evan was well organized and energetic on his job. But as Nancy talked of Evan's life at home, he neither had these virtues nor lacked them; they were irrelevant. This double standard of virtue reinforced the idea that men and women cannot be compared, being "naturally" so different.

Evan's orientation to domestic tasks, as they both described it now, had been engraved in childhood, and how could one change a whole childhood? As Nancy often reminded me, "I was brought up to do the housework. Evan wasn't." Many other men, who had also done little housework when they were boys, did not talk so fatalistically about "up-bringing," because they were doing a lot of it now. But the idea of a fate sealed so very early was oddly *useful* in Nancy's program of benign resignation. She needed it, because if the die had been cast in the dawn of life, it was inevitable that she should work the extra month a year.

This, then, was the set of mental tricks that helped Nancy resign herself to what had at one time seemed like a "bad deal." This was how she reconciled believing one thing and living with another.

HOW MANY HOLTS?

In one key way the Holts were typical of the vast majority of two-job couples: their family life had become the shock absorber for a stalled revolution whose origin lay far outside it—in economic and cultural trends that bear very differently on men and women. Nancy was reading books, newspaper articles, and watching TV programs on the changing role of women. Evan wasn't. Nancy felt benefited by these changes; Evan didn't. In her ideals and in reality, Nancy was more different from her mother than Evan was from his father, for the culture and economy were in general pressing change faster upon women like her than upon men like Evan. Nancy had gone to college; her mother hadn't. Nancy had a professional job; her mother never had. Nancy had the idea that she should be equal with her husband; her mother hadn't been much exposed to that idea in her day. Nancy felt she should share the job of earning money, and that Evan should share the work at home; her mother hadn't imagined that was possible. Evan went to college, his father (and the other boys in his family, though not the girls) had gone too. Work was important to Evan's identity as a man as it had been for his father before him. Indeed, Evan felt the same way about family roles as his father had felt in his day. The new job opportunities and the feminist movement of the 1960s and '70s had transformed Nancy but left Evan pretty much the same. And the friction created by this difference between them moved to the issue of second shift as metal to a magnet. By the end, Evan did less housework and childcare than most men married to working women—but not much less. Evan and Nancy were also typical of nearly forty percent of the marriages I studied in their clash of gender ideologies and their corresponding difference in notion about what constituted a "sacrifice" and what did not. By far the most common form of mismatch was like that between Nancy, an egalitarian, and Evan, a transitional.

But for most couples, the tensions between strategies did not move so quickly and powerfully to issues of housework and childcare. Nancy pushed harder than most women to get her husband to share the work at home, and she also lost more overwhelmingly than the few other women who fought that hard. Evan pursued his strategy of passive resistance with more quiet tenacity than most men, and he allowed himself to become far more marginal to his son's life than most other fathers. The myth of the Holts' "equal" arrangement seemed slightly more odd than other family myths that encapsulated equally powerful conflicts.

Beyond their upstairs-downstairs myth, the Holts tell us a great deal about the subtle ways a couple can encapsulate the tension caused by a struggle over the second shift without resolving the problem or divorcing. Like Nancy Holt, many women struggle to avoid, suppress, obscure, or mystify a frightening conflict over the second shift. They do not struggle like this because they started off wanting to, or because such struggle is inevitable or because women inevitably lose, but because they are forced to choose between equality and marriage. And they choose marriage. When asked about "ideal" relations between men and women in general, about what they want for their daughters, about what "ideally" they'd like in their own marriage, most working mothers "wished" their men would share the work at home.

But many "wish" it instead of "want" it. Other goals—like keeping peace at home—come first. Nancy Holt did some extraordinary behind-the-scenes emotion work to prevent her ideals from clashing with her marriage. In the end, she had confined and miniaturized her ideas of equality successfully enough to do two things she badly wanted to do: feel like a feminist, and live at peace with a man who was not. Her program had "worked." Evan won on the reality of the situation, because Nancy did the second shift. Nancy won on the cover story; they would talk about it as if they shared.

Nancy wore the upstairs-downstairs myth as an ideological cloak to protect her from the contradictions in her marriage and from the cultural and economic forces that press upon it. Nancy and Evan Holt were caught on opposite sides of the gender revolution occurring all around them. Through the 1960s, 1970s, and 1980s masses of women entered the public world of work—but went only so far up the occupational ladder. They tried for "equal" marriages, but got only so far in achieving it. They married men who liked them to work at the office but who wouldn't share the extra month a year at home. When confusion about the identity of the working woman created a cultural vacuum in the 1970s and 1980s, the image of the supermom quietly glided in. She made the "stall" seem normal and happy. But beneath the happy image of the woman with the flying hair are modern marriages like the Holts', reflecting intricate webs of tension, and the huge, hidden emotional cost to women, men, and children of having to "manage" inequality. Yet on the surface, all we might see would be Nancy Holt bounding confidently out the door at 8:30 A.M., briefcase in one hand, Joey in the other. All we might hear would be Nancy's and Evan's talk about their marriage as happy, normal, even "equal"—because equality was so important to Nancy.

31. The End of Nature

BILL MCKIBBEN

The conquest of nature is a perennial theme of American history. Facing a vast, lightly populated continent, settlers from the beginning exaggerated its emptiness, seeing themselves as alone in a "howling wilderness." Given this history, it has been hard for most people to believe that we would ever run out of space in which we could put our wastes or hide the more disagreeable effluents of our technology.

Beginning late in the 1960s a broad public recognition of the hazards of this attitude began to arise. An environmental movement questioned the matter-of-fact assumption that growth was good and recognized the need to pay attention to the environmental impact of what we did. With the exception of an eight-year effort to roll back the environmental movement under the Reagan Administration, this sensibility has influenced policy for the past generation and has become important in the thinking of tens of millions of Americans, however torn they remain about the apparent conflict between economic growth and the preservation of the environment. And in recent years, the perception of potentially world-threatening effects of technology, particularly the much discussed "greenhouse effect," have raised issues of environmentalism to a new level of concern.

Bill McKibben looks at the moral, emotional, and intellectual implications of this change in the era since 1945. Humankind has, he tells us, conquered nature. Like most conquests, the results are ambiguous at best.

Nature, we believe, takes forever. It moves with infinite slowness through the many periods of its history, whose names we can dimly recall from high-school biology—the Cambrian, the Devonian, the Triassic, the Cretaceous, the Pleistocene. At least since Darwin, nature writers have taken pains to stress the incomprehensible length of this path. "So slowly, oh, so slowly, have the great changes been brought about," John Burroughs wrote in 1912. "The Orientals try to get a hint of eternity by saying that when the Himalayas have been ground to powder by allowing a gauze veil to float against them once in a thousand years, eternity will only have just begun. Our mountains have been pulverized by a process almost as slow." We have been told that man's tenure is as a minute to the earth's day, but it is that vast day that has lodged in our minds. The age of the trilobites began six hundred million years ago. The dinosaurs lived for a hundred and fifty million years. Since even a million years is utterly unfathomable, the message is: Nothing happens quickly. Change takes unimaginable—"geologic"—time.

This idea about time is essentially misleading, for the world as we know it, the world with human beings formed into some sort of civilization, is of quite comprehensible duration. People began to collect in a rudimentary society in the north of Mesopotamia some twelve thousand years ago. Using twenty-five years as a generation, that is four hundred and eighty generations ago. Sitting here at my desk, I can think back five generations—I have photographs of four. That is, I can think back one-ninety-sixth of the way to the start of civilization. A skilled genealogist could easily get me one-fiftieth of the distance back. And I can conceive of how most of those forebears lived. From the work of archaeologists and from accounts like those in the Bible I have some sense of daily life at least as far back as the time of the Pharaohs, which is almost half the way. Three hundred and twenty generations ago, Jericho was a walled city of three thousand souls. Three hundred and twenty is a large number, but not in the way that six hundred million is a large number, not inscrutably large. And within those twelve thousand years of civilization time is not uniform. The world as we really know it dates back to the Renaissance. The world as we *really* know it dates back to the Industrial Revolution. The world as we feel comfortable in it dates back to perhaps 1945.

In other words, our sense of an unlimited future, which is drawn from that apparently bottomless well of the past, is a delusion. True, evolution, grinding on ever so slowly, has taken billions of years to create us from slime, but that does not mean that time always moves so ponderously. Over a lifetime or a decade or a year, big and impersonal and dramatic changes can take place. We have accepted the idea that continents can drift in the course of aeons, or that continents can die in a nuclear second. But normal time seems to us immune from such huge changes. It isn't, though. In the last three decades, for example, the amount of carbon dioxide in the atmosphere has increased more than ten per cent, from about three hundred and fifteen parts per million to about three hundred and fifty parts per million. In the last decade, an immense "hole" in the ozone layer has opened up above the South Pole each fall, and, according to the Worldwatch Institute, the percentage of West German forests damaged by acid rain has risen from less than ten per cent to more than fifty per cent. Last year, for perhaps the first time since that starved Pilgrim winter at Plymouth, America consumed more grain than it grew. Burroughs again: "One summer day, while I was walking along the country road on the farm where I was born, a section of the stone wall opposite me, and not more than three or four yards distant, suddenly fell down. Amid the general stillness and immobility about me, the effect was quite startling. . . . It was the sudden summing-up of half a century or more of atomic changes in the material of the wall. A grain or two of sand yielded to the pressure of long years, and gravity did the rest."

In much the same comforting way that we think of time as imponderably long, we consider the earth to be inconceivably large. Although with the advent of space flight it became fashionable to picture the planet as a small orb of life and light in a dark, cold void, that image never really took hold. To any one of us, the earth is enormous, "infinite to our senses." Or, at least, it is if we think about it in the usual horizontal dimensions. There is a huge distance between my house, in the Adirondack Mountains, and Manhattan—it's a five-hour drive through one state in one country of one continent. But from my house to Allen

Hill, near town, is a trip of five and a half miles. By bicycle it takes about twenty minutes, by car seven or eight. I've walked it in an hour and a half. If you turned that trip on its end, the twenty-minute pedal past Bateman's sandpit and the graveyard and the waterfall would take me to the height of Mt. Everest—almost precisely to the point where the air is too thin to breathe without artificial assistance. Into that tight space, and the layer of ozone above it, are crammed all that is life and all that maintains life.

This, I realize, is a far from novel observation. I repeat it only to make the case I made with regard to time. The world is not as large as we intuitively believe—space can be as short as time. For instance, the average American car driven the average American distance—ten thousand miles—in an average American year releases its own weight in carbon into the atmosphere. Imagine every car on a busy freeway pumping a ton of carbon into the atmosphere, and the sky seems less infinitely blue.

Along with our optimistic perceptions of time and space, other, relatively minor misunderstandings distort our sense of the world. Consider the American failure to convert to the metric system. Like all schoolchildren of my vintage, I spent many days listening to teachers explain litres and metres and hectares and all the other logical units of measurement, and then promptly forgot about it. All of us did, except the scientists, who always use such units. As a result, if I read that there will be a rise of 0.8 degrees Celsius in the temperature between now and the year 2000, it sounds less ominous than a rise of a degree and a half Fahrenheit. Similarly, a ninety-centimetre rise in sea level sounds less ominous than a one-yard rise—and neither of them sounds all that ominous until one stops to think that over a beach with a normal slope such a rise would bring the ocean ninety metres (that's two hundred and ninety-five feet) above its current tideline. In somewhat the same way, the logarithmic scale we use to determine the acidity or alkalinity of our soils and our waters—pH—distorts reality for anyone who doesn't use it on a daily basis. Normal rainwater has a pH of 5.6. But the acidified rain that falls on Buck Hill, behind my house, has a pH of 4.6 to 4.2, which is from ten to fourteen times as acid as normal.

Of all such quirks, though, probably the most significant is an accident of the calendar: we live too close to the year 2000. Forever we have read about the year 2000. It has become a symbol of the bright and distant future, when we will ride in air cars and talk on video phones. The year 2010 still sounds far off, almost unreachably far off, as if it were on the other side of a great body of water. But 2010 is as close as 1970—as close as the breakup of the Beatles—and the turn of the century is no farther in front of us than Ronald Reagan's election to the Presidency is behind. We live in the shadow of a number, and that makes it hard to see the future.

Our comforting sense, then, of the permanence of our natural world—our confidence that it will change gradually and imperceptibly, if at all—is the result of subtly warped perspective. Changes in our world which can affect us can happen in our lifetime—not just changes like wars but bigger and more sweeping events. Without recognizing it, we have already stepped over the threshold of such a change. I believe that we are at the end of nature.

By this I do not mean the end of the world. The rain will still fall, and the sun will still shine. When I say "nature," I mean a certain set of human ideas about the world and our place in it. But the death of these ideas begins with concrete changes in the reality around us, changes that scientists can measure. More and more frequently, these changes will clash with our perceptions, until our sense of nature as eternal and separate is finally washed away and we see all too clearly what we have done.

. . . . In 1957, two scientists at the Scripps Institution of Oceanography, in California, Roger Revelle and Hans Suess, published a paper in the journal *Tellus* on this question of the oceans. What they found may turn out to be the single most important limit in an age of limits. They found that the conventional wisdom was wrong: the upper layer of the oceans, where the air and sea meet and transact their business, would absorb less than half of the excess carbon dioxide produced by man. "A rather small change in the amount of free carbon dioxide dissolved in seawater corresponds to a relatively large change in the pressure of carbon dioxide at which the oceans and atmosphere are at equilibrium," they wrote. That is to say, most of the carbon dioxide being pumped into the air by millions of smokestacks, furnaces, and car exhausts would stay in the air, where, presumably, it would gradually warm the planet. "Human beings are now carrying out a large-scale geophysical experiment of a kind that could not have happened in the past nor be repeated in the future," they concluded, adding, with the morbid dispassion of true scientists, that this experiment, "if adequately documented, may yield a far-reaching insight into the processes of weather and climate." While there are other parts to this story—the depletion of the ozone, acid rain, genetic engineering—the story of the end of nature centers on this greenhouse experiment, with what will happen to the weather.

When we drill into an oil field, we tap into a vast reservoir of organic matter—the fossilized remains of aquatic algae. We unbury it. When we burn oil—or coal, or methane (natural gas)—we release its carbon into the atmosphere in the form of carbon dioxide. This is not pollution in the conventional sense. Carbon monoxide is pollution—an unnecessary by-product; a clean-burning engine releases less of it. But when it comes to carbon dioxide a clean-burning engine is no better than the motor in a Model T. It will emit about five and half pounds of carbon in the form of carbon dioxide for every gallon of gasoline it consumes. In the course of about a hundred years, our various engines and industries have released a very large portion of the carbon buried over the last five hundred million years. It is as if someone had scrimped and saved his entire life and then spent everything on one fantastic week's debauch. In this, if in nothing else, wrote the great biologist A. J. Lotka, "The present is an eminently atypical epoch." We are living on our capital, as we began to realize during the oil crises of the nineteen-seventies. But it is more than waste, more than a binge. We are spending that capital in such a way as to alter the atmosphere.

There has always been, at least since the start of life, a certain amount of carbon dioxide in the atmosphere, and it has always trapped a certain amount of the sun's radiation to warm the earth. If there were no atmospheric carbon dioxide, our world might resemble Mars: it would probably be so cold as to be lifeless. A little greenhouse effect is a good thing—life thrives in its warmth. The question is: How much? On Venus, the atmosphere is ninety-seven per cent carbon dioxide. As a result, it traps infrared radiation a hundred times as efficiently as the earth's atmosphere, and keeps the planet a toasty seven hundred degrees warmer than the earth. The earth's atmosphere is mostly nitrogen and oxygen; it is only about .035 per cent carbon dioxide, which is hardly more than a trace. The worries about the greenhouse effect are worries about raising that figure to .055 or .06 per cent, which is not very much. But enough, it turns out, to make everything different.

In 1957, when Revelle and Suess wrote their paper, no one even knew for certain whether carbon dioxide was increasing. The Scripps Institution hired a young researcher, Charles Keeling, and he set up monitoring stations at the South Pole and on the side of Mauna Loa, in Hawaii, eleven thousand feet above the Pacific. His data soon confirmed their hypothesis: more and more carbon dioxide was entering the atmosphere. When the first readings were taken, in 1958, the atmosphere at Mauna Loa contained about three hundred and fifteen parts per million of carbon dioxide. Subsequent readings showed that each year the amount increased, and at a steadily growing rate. Initially, the annual increase was about seven-tenths of a part per million; in recent years, the rate has doubled, to one and a half parts per million. Admittedly, one and a half parts per million sounds absurdly small. But scientists, by drilling holes in glaciers and testing the air trapped in ancient ice, have calculated that the carbon-dioxide level in the atmosphere prior to the Industrial Revolution was about two hundred and eighty parts per million, and that this was as high a level as had been recorded in the past hundred and forty thousand years. At a rate of one and a half parts per million per year, the pre-Industrial Revolution concentration of carbon dioxide would double in the next hundred and forty years. Since, as we have seen, carbon dioxide at a very low level largely determines the climate, carbon dioxide at double that very low level, small as it is in absolute terms, could have an enormous effect.

And the annual increase seems nearly certain to go higher. The essential facts are demographic and economic, not chemical. The world's population has more than tripled in this century, and is expected to double, and perhaps triple again, before reaching a plateau in the next century. Moreover, the tripled population has not contented itself with using only three times the resources. In the last hundred years, industrial production has grown fiftyfold. Four-fifths of that growth has come since 1950, almost all of it based on fossil fuels. In the next half century, a United Nations commission predicts, the planet's thirteen-trillion-dollar economy will grow five to ten times larger.

These facts are almost as stubborn as the chemistry of infrared absorption. They mean that the world will use more energy—two to three per cent more a year, by most estimates. And the largest increases may come in the use of coal—which is bad news, since coal spews more carbon dioxide into the atmosphere than any other fuel. China, which has the world's largest hard-coal reserves and recently passed the Soviet Union as the world's largest coal producer, has plans to almost double coal consumption by the year 2000. A model devised by the World Resources Institute predicts that if energy use and other contributions to carbon-dioxide levels continue to grow very quickly, the amount of atmospheric carbon dioxide will have doubled from its pre-Industrial Revolution level by about 2040; if they grow somewhat more slowly, as most estimates have it, the amount will double by about 2070. And, unfortunately, the solutions are neither obvious nor easy. Installing some kind of scrubber on a power-plant smokestack to get rid of the carbon dioxide might seem an abvious fix, except that a system that removed ninety per cent of the carbon dioxide would reduce the effective capacity of the plant by eighty per cent. One often heard suggestion is to use more nuclear power. But, because so much of our energy is consumed by automobiles and the like, even if we mustered the political will and the economic resources to quickly replace each of our non-nuclear electric plants with nuclear ones our carbon-dioxide output would fall by only about thirty per cent. The same argument would apply, at least initially, to fusion or any other clean method of producing electricity.

Burning fossil fuels is not the only method human beings have devised to increase the level of atmospheric carbon dioxide. Burning down a forest also sends clouds of carbon dioxide into the air. Trees and shrubby forests still cover forty per cent of the land on earth, but the forests have shrunk by about a fifth since pre-agricultural times, and the shrinkage is accelerating. In the Brazilian state of Pará, for instance, nearly seventy thousand square miles were deforested between 1975 and 1986; in the hundred years preceding that decade, settlers had cleared about seven thousand square miles. The Brazilian government has tried to slow the burning, but it employs fewer than nine hundred forest wardens in an area larger than Europe.

This is not news; it is well known that the rain forests are disappearing, and are taking with them a majority of the world's plant and animal species. But forget for a moment that we are losing a unique resource, a cradle of life, irreplaceable grandeur, and so forth. The dense, layered rain forest contains from three to five times as much carbon per acre as an open, dry forest—an acre of Brazil in flames equals between three and five acres of Yellowstone. Deforestation currently adds about a billion tons of carbon to the atmosphere annually, which is twenty per cent or more of the amount produced by the burning of fossil fuels. And that acre of rain forest, which has poor soil and can support crops for only a few years, soon turns to desert or to pastureland. And where there's pasture there are cows. Cows support in their stomachs huge numbers of anaerobic bacteria, which break down the cellulose that cows chew. That is why cows, unlike people, can eat grass. The bugs that digest the cellulose excrete methane, the same natural gas we use as fuel. And unburned methane, like carbon dioxide, traps infrared radiation and warms the earth. In fact, methane is twenty times as efficient as carbon dioxide at warming the planet, so even though it makes up less than two parts per million of the atmosphere it can have a significant effect. Though it may come from seemingly "natural" sources—the methanogenic bacteria—the present huge numbers of these bacteria are man's doing. Mankind owns well over a billion head of cattle, not to mention a large number of camels, horses, pigs, sheep, and goats; together, they belch about seventy-three million metric tons of methane into the air each year—a four-hundred-and-thirty-five-percent increase in the last century.

We have raised the number of termites, too. Like cows, termites harbor methanogenic bacteria, which is why they can digest wood. We tend to think of termites as house-wreckers, but in most of the world they are house-builders, erecting elaborate, rock-hard mounds twenty or thirty feet high. If a bulldozer razes a mound, worker termites can rebuild it in hours. Like most animals, they seem limited only by the supply of food. When we clear a rain forest, all of a sudden there is dead wood everywhere—food galore. As deforestation has proceeded, termite numbers have boomed; Patrick Zimmerman, of the National Center for Atmospheric Research, in Boulder, Colorado, estimates that there is more than half a ton of termites for every man, woman, and child on earth. Termites excrete phenomenal amounts of methane: a single mound may give off five litres a minute.

Researchers differ on the importance of termites as a methane source, but they agree about rice paddies. The oxygenless mud of marsh bottoms has always sheltered the methane-producing bacteria. (Methane is sometimes known as swamp gas.) But rice paddies may be even more efficient; the rice plants themselves act a little like straws, venting as much as a hundred and fifteen million tons of methane annually. And rice paddies must increase in number and size every year, to feed the world's growing population. Then, there are landfills. Twenty per cent of a typical landfill is putrescible: it rots, creating carbon dioxide and methane. At the main New York City landfill, on Staten Island, the methane is pumped from under the trash straight to the stoves of thousands of homes, but at most landfills it just seeps out.

What's more, some scientists have begun to think that these sources by themselves may not account for all the methane. For one thing, an enormous amount of methane is locked up as hydrates in the tundra and in the mud of the continental shelves. These are, in essence, methane ices; the ocean muds alone may hold ten trillion tons of methane. If the green house effect warms the oceans, if it begins to thaw the permafrost, then those ices could start to melt. Some estimates of the potential methane release from the ocean muds run as high as six hundred million tons a year—an amount that would more than double the present atmospheric concentration. This would be a nasty example of a feedback loop: warm the atmosphere and release methane; release methane and warm the atmosphere; and so on.

When all the sources of methane are combined, we have done an even more dramatic job of increasing methane than of increasing carbon dioxide. Samples of ice from Antarctic glaciers show that the concentration of methane in the atmosphere has fluctuated between 0.3 and 0.7 parts per million for the last hundred and sixty thousand years, reaching its highest levels during the earth's warmest periods. In 1987, methane composed 1.7 parts per million of the atmosphere; that is, there is now two and a half times as much methane in the atmosphere as there was at any time since the onset of the ice age preceding the most recent one. The level is now increasing at a rate of one per cent a year.

Man is also pumping smaller quantities of other greenhouse gases into the atmosphere. Nitrous oxide, the chlorofluorocarbons—which are notorious for their ability to destroy the planet's ozone layer—and several more all trap warmth with greater efficiency than carbon dioxide. Methane and the rest of these gases, even though their concentrations are small, will together account for fifty per cent of the projected greenhouse warming. They are as much of a problem as carbon dioxide. And as all these compounds warm the atmosphere it will be able to hold more water vapor—itself a potent greenhouse gas. The British Meteorological Office calculates that this extra water vapor will warm the earth two-thirds as much as the carbon dioxide alone.

Most discussion of the greenhouse gases rushes immediately to their future consequences, without pausing to let the simple fact of what has already happened sink in: the air around us—even where it's clean, and smells like spring, and is filled with birds—is significantly changed. We have substantially altered the earth's atmosphere.

That said, the question of what this new atmosphere means must arise. The direct effects are unnoticeable. Anyone who lives indoors breathes carbon dioxide at a level several times the atmospheric concentration without suffering any harm; the federal government limits industrial workers to a chronic exposure of five thousand parts per million, or almost fifteen times the current atmospheric level. A hundred years from now, a child at recess will still breathe far less carbon dioxide than a child in a classroom. This however, is only mildly good news. Changes in the atmosphere will change the weather, and *that* will change recess. The weather—the temperature, the amount of rainfall, the speed of the wind—will change. The chemistry of the atmosphere may seem an abstraction, a text written in a foreign language. But its translation into the weather of New York and Cincinnati and San Francisco will change the life of each of us.

Theories about the effects all begin with an estimate of expected warming. The wave of concern that began with Revelle and Suess's article and Keeling's Mauna Loa and South Pole data has led to the development of complex computer models of the entire globe. The models agree that when, as has been predicted, carbon dioxide (or the equivalent combination of carbon dioxide and other greenhouse gases) doubles from the pre-Industrial Revolution level, the average global temperature will increase, and that the increase will be one and a half to five and a half degrees Celsius, or three to ten degrees Fahrenheit. Perhaps the most famous of these computer models has been constructed by James Hansen and his colleagues at the National Aeronautics and Space Administration's Goddard Institute for Space Studies. Even though it remains a rough simulation of the real world, they have improved it to the point where they are willing to forecast not just the effects of a doubling of carbon dioxide but the incremental effects along the way—that is, not just the forecast for 2050 but the one for 2000.

Take Dallas, for instance. According to Hansen's calculations, the doubled level of gases would increase the annual number of days with temperatures about 100° F. from nineteen to seventy-eight. On sixty-eight days, as opposed to the current four, the nighttime temperature wouldn't fall below 80° F. A hundred and sixty-two days a year—half the year, essentially—the temperature would top 90° F. New York city would have forty-eight days a year above the ninety-degree mark, up from fifteen at present. And so on. This would clearly change the world as we know it. One of Hansen's colleagues told reporters, "It reaches a hundred and twenty degrees in Phoenix now. Will people still live there if it's a hundred and thirty degrees? A hundred and forty? (And such heat waves are possible even if the average global increase, figured over a year, is only a couple of degrees, since any average conceals huge swings.) These changes, Hansen and his colleagues said in a paper published last fall in the *Journal of Geophysical Research*, should begin to be obvious to the man in the street by the early nineteen-nineties; that is, the odds of a very hot summer will, thanks to the greenhouse effect, become better than even beginning now....

Most mornings, I hike up the hill outside my back door. Within a hundred yards, the woods swallow me up, and there is nothing to remind me of human society—no trash, no stumps, no fences, not even a real path. Looking out from the high places, you can't see road or house; it is a world apart from man. But once in a while someone will be cutting wood farther down the valley, and the snarl of a chain saw will fill the woods. It is harder these days to get caught up in the timelessness of the forest, for man is nearby. The sound of the chain saw doesn't blot out all the noises of the forest, or drive the animals away, but it does drive away the feeling that you are in another, separate, wild sphere.

Now that we have changed the most basic forces around us, the noise of that chain saw will always be in the woods. We have changed the atmosphere, and that is changing the weather. The temperature and the rainfall are no longer entirely the work of some uncivilizable force but instead are in part a product of our habits, our economies, our ways of life. Even in the most remote wilderness, where the strictest laws forbid the felling of a single tree, the sound of that saw will be clear, and a walk in the woods will be changed by its whine. The world outdoors will mean the same thing as the world indoors, the hill the same thing as the house. An idea can become extinct, just like an animal or a plant. The idea in this case is "nature"—the wild province, the world apart from man, under whose rules he was born and died. We have not ended rainfall or sunlight. The wind still blows—but not from some other sphere, some inhuman place. It is too early to tell exactly how much harder the wind will blow, how much hotter the sun will shine. That is for the future. But their *meaning* has already changed.

The argument that nature is ended is complex; profound objections to it are possible, and I will try to answer them. But to understand what is ending requires some attention to the past. Not the ancient past, not the big bang or the primal soup—the European exploration of the New World is far enough back, since it is man's *idea* of nature that is important to this discussion, and it was in response to that wild country that much of our modern notion of nature developed. North America was not unaltered by man when the Europeans arrived, but its previous occupants had treated it fairly well. Most of it was still wilderness on the eve of the Revolution, when William Bartram, one of America's first professional naturalists, set out from his native Philadelphia to tour the South. Though some of the land through which he travelled had been settled (he spent a number of nights on plantations), the settlement was sparse, and the fields of indigo and rice gave way quickly to wilderness—not the dark and forbidding wilderness of European fairy tales but a blooming, humming, fertile paradise. Every page of his diary of the journey through "North & South Carolina, Georgia, East & West Florida, the Cherokee Country, the Extensive Territories of the Muscogulges, or Creek Confederacy, and the Country of the Chactaws" shouts of the fecundity, the profligacy, of that fresh land: "I continued several miles [over] verdant swelling knolls, profusely productive of flowers and fragrant strawberries, their rich juice dyeing my horse's feet and ankles." When he stops for dinner, he picks a wild orange, and stews a fresh-caught trout in its juice over his fire.

Whatever direction he struck off in, Bartram found vigorous beauty. His diary brims over with the grand Latin binomials of a thousand plants and animals (*Kalmia latifolia,* "snowy mantled" *Philadelphus inodorus, Pinus sylvestris, Populus tremula, Rheum rhaponticum, Magnolia grandiflora*) and also with the warm common names—the bank martin, the water wagtail, the mountain cock, the chattering plover, the bumblebee. But the roll call of his adjectives is even more indicative of his mood. In the account of a single evening, he musters fruitful, fragrant, sylvan (twice), moderately warm, exceeding pleasant, charming, fine, joyful, most beautiful, pale gold, golden, russet, silver (twice), ultramarine, velvet-black, orange, prodigious, gilded, delicious, harmonious, soothing, tuneful, sprightly, elevated, cheerful (twice), high and airy, brisk and cool, clear, sweet, and healthy. And where he can't see, he imagines marvels: the fish disappearing into subterranean streams, "where, probably, they are separated from each other, by innumerable paths, or secret rocky avenues; and after encountering various obstacles, and beholding new and unthought-of scenes of pleasure and disgust, after many days absence from the surface of the world emerge again from the dreary vaults, and appear exulting in gladness, and sporting in the transparent waters of some far distant lake." But he is no Disney— this is no "Fantasia." He is a scientist recording his observations, and words like "cheerful" and "sweet" seem to be technical descriptions of the untouched world in which he wandered.

This sort of joy in the natural world was not a literary convention, a given. Much of literature regarded wilderness as ugly and crude until the Romantic movement of the late eighteenth century; Andrew Marvell, for one, referred to mountains as "ill-designed excrescences." This silliness changed into a new silliness with the Romantics. Chateaubriand's immensely popular "Atala" describes the American wilderness as full of bears "drunk with grapes, and reeling on the branches of the elm trees." But the rapturous fever took on a healthier aspect in this country. Most of the pioneers, to be sure, saw a buffalo as something to hunt, a forest as something to cut down, a flock of passenger pigeons as a call for heavy artillery (farmers would bring their hogs to feed on the carcasses raining down in the slaughter), but there were always a good many—even, or especially, among the hunters and loggers—who recognized and described the beauty and order of this early time....

The passing of nature as we have known it, like the passing of any large idea, will have its recognizable effects both immediately and over time. In 1893, when Frederick Jackson Turner announced to the American Historical Association that the frontier was closed, no one was aware that the frontier had been the defining force in American life. But in its absence this was understood. One reason we pay so little close attention to the separate natural world around us is that it has always been there and we have presumed that it always would be. As it disappears, its primal importance will become clearer, in the same way that some people think they have put their parents out of their lives, until the day comes to bury them.

Above all else, the world displays a lovely order, an order comforting in its intricacy. And the most appealing part of this harmony, perhaps, is its permanence—the sense that we are part of something with roots stretching back nearly forever and branches reaching forward just as far. Purely human life provides only a partial fulfillment of this desire for a kind of immortality. But the earth and all its processes—the sun growing plants; flesh feeding on these plants; flesh decaying to nourish more plants, to name just one cycle—give us some sense of an enduring role.

John Muir expressed this sense of immortality beautifully. Born to a stern Calvinist father, who used a belt to help him memorize the Bible, Muir eventually escaped to the woods, travelling to the Yosemite Valley of California's Sierra Nevada. The journal of his first summer there is filled with a breathless joy at the grandeur around him. Again and again in that Sierra June—"the greatest of all the months of my life"—he uses the word "immortality," and he uses it in a specific way, designed to contrast with his father's grim and selfish religion. Time ceases to have its normal meaning in those hills: "Another glorious Sierra day in which one seems to be dissolved and absorbed and sent pulsing onward we know not where. Life seems neither long nor short, and we take no more heed to save time or make haste than do the trees and stars. This is true freedom, a good practical sort of immortality." To someone in a mood like this, space is no more of a limitation than time: "We are now in the mountains and they are in us... making every nerve quiver, filling every pore and cell of us. Our flesh-and-bone tabernacle seems transparent as glass to the beauty about us, as if truly an inseparable part of it, thrilling with the air and trees, streams and rocks, in the waves of the sun—a part of all nature, neither old nor young, sick nor well, but immortal."

Some dim recognition that God and nature are interwined has led us to pay at least lip service to the idea of "stewardship" of the land. If there is a God, He probably does want us to take good care of the planet, but He may want something even more radical. The Old Testament contains in the book of Job one of the most far-reaching defenses ever written of wilderness—of nature free from the hand of man. The argument gets at the heart of what the loss of nature will mean to us. Job is, of course, a just and prosperous man brought low. He refuses to curse God, but he does demand a meeting with Him and an explanation of his misfortune. Job refuses to accept the reasoning of his orthodox friends—that he has unknowingly sinned and is therefore being punished. Their view—that the earth revolves around man, and every consequence is explained by man's actions—doesn't satisfy Job, because he knows he is innocent.

Finally, God arrives, a voice from the whirlwind. But instead of engaging in deep metaphysical discussion He talks at some length about nature, about creation. "Where were you when I laid the earth's foundation?" He asks. In an exquisite poem He lists His accomplishments, His pride in His creation always evident. Was Job there when He "put the sea behind closed doors"? Job was not; therefore, Job cannot hope to understand many mysteries, including why rain falls "on land where no one lives, to meet the needs of the lonely wastes and make grass sprout upon the ground."

"Behold now Behemoth," God roars. "He eateth grass as an ox. Lo now, his strength is in his loins. And his force is in the muscles of his belly. He moveth his tail like a cedar.... His bones are as tubes of brass. His limbs are like bars of iron.... Behold, if a river overflow he trembleth not. He is confident, though Jordan swell even to his mouth. Shall any take him when he is on the watch, or pierce through his nose with a snare?" The answer, clearly, is no: not all nature is ours to subdue.

Nature has provided a way for us to recognize God, and to talk about who He is—even, as in Job, a way for God to talk about who He is. So what will the end of nature as we have known it mean to our understanding of God and of man? For those of us who have tended to locate God in nature—who look upon spring, say, as a sign of His existence and a clue to His meaning—what does it mean that we have destroyed the old spring and replaced it with a new one, of our own devising? We as a race turn out to be stronger than we suspected—much stronger. In a sense, we turn out to be God's equal, or, at least, His rival—able to destroy creation. This idea has been building for a while. "We became less and less capable of seeing ourselves as small within creation, partly because we thought we could comprehend it statistically, but also because we were becoming creators, ourselves, of a mechanical creation by which we felt ourselves greatly magnified," the essayist Wendell Berry writes. "Why, after all, should one get excited about a mountain when one can see almost as far from the top of a building, much farther from an airplane, farther still from a space capsule?" And our nuclear weapons obviously created the possibility that we could exercise god-like powers. But the possibility is different from the fact. Though we seem to have recognized the implications of nuclear weapons and begun to back away from them, we have shown no such timidity in our wholesale alteration of nature. We are in charge now, like it or not. When God asks, as He does in Job, "Who shut in the sea with doors...and prescribed bounds for it?" and "Who can tilt the waterskins of the heavens?" we must now answer that it is us.

With this new power comes a deep sadness. I took a day's hike last fall, following the creek that runs by my door to the place where it crosses the main county road. It's a distance of maybe nine miles as the car flies, but rivers are far less efficient, and endlessly follow time-wasting, uneconomical meanders. The creek cuts some fancy figures, and so I was able to feel a bit exploratory... In a strict sense, it wasn't much of an adventure. I stopped at the store for a liverwurst sandwich at lunchtime, the path was generally downhill, the temperature stuck at an equable fifty-five degrees, and since it was the week before the hunting season opened I didn't have to sing as I walked. It isn't Yosemite, this small valley, but its beauties are absorbing, and one can say, with Muir on his mountaintop, "Up here all the world's prizes seem as nothing."

And so what if it isn't nature primeval? One of my neighbors has left several kitchen chairs along his stretch of the bank, spaced at fifty-yard intervals, for comfort in fishing. At one old homestead, a stone chimney stands at each end of a foundation now filled by a graceful birch. Near the one real waterfall, a lot of rusty pipe and collapsed concrete testifies to the mill that once stood there. But these aren't disturbing sights; they're almost comforting—reminders of the way that nature has endured and outlived and with dignity reclaimed so many schemes and disruptions of man. (A mile or so off the creek, there's a mine where a hundred and fifty years ago a visionary tried to extract pigment for paint and pack it out by mule and sledge. He rebuilt after a fire; finally, an avalanche convinced him. The path in is faint now, but his chimney, too, still stands, a small Angkor Wat of free enterprise.) Large sections of the area were once farmed; but the growing season is not much more than a hundred days in a good year, and the limits established by that higher authority were stronger than the (powerful) attempts of individual men to circumvent them, and so the farms returned to forest, with only a dump of ancient bottles or a section of stone wall as a memorial. These ruins are humbling sights, reminders of the negotiations with nature which have established the world as we know it.

Changing socks in front of the waterfall, I thought back to the spring of 1987, when a record snowfall melted in only a dozen or so warm April days. A little to the south, a swollen stream washed out a highway bridge, closing the New York Thruway for months. The creek became a river, and the waterfall, normally one of those diaphanous-veil affairs, turned into a cataract. It filled me with awe to stand there then, on the shaking ground, and think, This is what nature is capable of. But as I sat there this time, and thought about the dry summer we'd just come through, there was nothing awe-inspiring or instructive, or even lulling, in the fall of the water. It suddenly seemed less like a waterfall than like a spillway to accommodate the overflow of a reservoir. That didn't decrease its beauty, but it changed its meaning. It has begun, or will soon begin, to rain and snow when the chemicals we've injected into the atmosphere add up to rain or snow—when they make it hot enough over some tropical sea to form a cloud and send it this way. In one sense,

I will have no more control over this process then I ever did. But the waterfall seemed different, and lonelier. Instead of a world where rain had an independent and mysterious existence, I was living in a world where rain was becoming a subset of human activity: a phenomenon like smog or commerce or the noise from the skidder towing logs on the nearby road—all things over which I had no control, either. The rain bore a brand: it was a steer, not a deer. And that was where the loneliness came from. There's nothing here except us.

At the same time that I felt lonely, though, I also felt crowded— without privacy. We go to the woods in part to escape. But now there is nothing except us, and so there is no escaping other people. As I walked in the autumn woods, I saw a lot of sick trees. With the conifers, I suspected acid rain. (At least I have the luxury of only suspecting; in too many places, they know.) And so who walked with me in the woods? Well, there were the presidents of the Midwestern utilities, who kept explaining why they had to burn coal to make electricity (cheaper, fiduciary responsibility, no *proof* it kills trees), and then there were the congressmen, who couldn't bring themselves to do anything about it (personally favor, but politics the art of compromise, very busy with the war on drugs), and before long the whole human race had arrived to explain its aspirations. We like to drive, it said, air-conditioning is a necessity nowadays, let's go to the mall. Of course, the person I was flee- ing most fearfully was myself, for I drive, and I'm burning a collapsed barn behind the house next week because it is much the cheapest way to deal with it, and I live on about four hundred times the money that Thoreau conclusively proved was enough, so I've done my share to take this independent, eternal world and turn it into a science-fair project.

Our local shopping mall has a club of people who go "mall-walking" every day. They circle the shopping center en masse—Caldor to Sears to J. C. Penney, circuit after circuit, with an occasional break to shop. This seems less absurd to me now than it did at first. I like to walk in the outdoors not solely because the air is cleaner but also because outdoors we venture into a sphere larger than we are. Mall-walking involves too many other people, and too many purely human sights, ever to be more than good-natured exercise. But now, out in the wild, the sunshine on one's shoulders is a reminder that man has cracked the ozone, that, thanks to us, the atmosphere absorbs where once it released. The greenhouse effect is a more apt name than those who coined it can have imagined. The carbon dioxide and the other trace gases act like the panes of glass of a greenhouse—the analogy is accurate. But it's more than that. We have built a greenhouse—a human creation—where once there bloomed a sweet and wild garden.

32. Supreme Court Cases on Abortion

Abortion has become one of the most divisive issues in American society. Those who see it as a matter of private, individual choice or as an issue of women's rights are unequivocally in favor of the choice being in the hands of the woman. Those who see the issue strictly in terms of the right of fetuses oppose abortion in all circumstances. Others might make exceptions in cases involving rape, incest, or threats that a pregnancy might present to the life of the mother.

The Roe v. Wade *decision of 1973 attempted a compromise between the rights of women and the rights of the unborn by imposing the test of the viability of the fetus to live on its own: viability was defined as beginning twenty-four weeks after conception. The* Webster v. Reproductive Health Services *case in 1989 narrowed but did not overrule* Roe v. Wade. *It called into question the viability test, holding that a strict definition of viability was impossible in light of evolving technology, and urged the states to legislate on the matter rather than bringing it back to the court. It also upheld the right of states to refuse public facilities to women seeking an abortion, arguing that states have no obligation to guarantee all women free and equal access to abortions. This five-to-four decision provoked passionate disagreement in the court. Justice Blackmun, who wrote* Roe v. Wade, *criticized the majority in his* Webster *dissent for removing what was clear about the former case—the presumption of viability at the end of the first trimester of pregnancy—and leaving nothing definite in its place. Blackmun argued that the Missouri decision prepared the groundwork for increasingly restricted access to abortion that did, in fact, render less meaningful "the fundamental constitutional right of women to decide whether to terminate a pregnancy." Justice Scalia, the court's most vigorous opponent of* Roe v. Wade, *criticized the court's decision in* Webster *from a different perspective in his concurring brief, asserting that* Webster *"preserves a chaos."*

ROE V. WADE

MR. JUSTICE BLACKMUN delivered the opinion of the Court....

We forthwith acknowledge our awareness of the sensitive and emotional nature of the abortion controversy, of the vigorous opposing views, even among physicians, and of the deep and seemingly absolute convictions that the subject inspires. One's philosophy, one's experiences, one's exposure to the raw edges of human existence, one's religious training, one's attitudes toward life and family and their values, and the moral standards one establishes and seeks to observe, are all likely to influence and to color one's thinking and conclusions about abortion.

In addition, population growth, pollution, poverty, and racial over-tones tend to complicate and not to simplify the problem.

Our task, of course, is to resolve the issue by constitutional measurement, free of emotion and of predilection. We seek earnestly to do this, and, because we do, we have inquired into, and in this opinion place some emphasis upon, medical and medical-legal history and what that history reveals about man's attitudes toward the abortion procedure over the centuries. We bear in mind, too, Mr. Justice Holmes' admonition in his now-vindicated dissent in *Lochner v. New York*...(1905): "[The Constitution] is made for people of fundamentally differing views, and the accident of our finding certain opinions natural and familiar or novel and even shocking ought not to conclude our judgment upon the question whether statutes embodying them conflict with the Constitution of the United States."...

The principal thrust of appellant's attack on the Texas statutes is that they improperly invade a right, said to be possessed by the pregnant woman, to choose to terminate her pregnancy. Appellant would discover this right in the concept of personal "liberty" embodied in the Fourteenth Amendment's Due Process Clause; or in personal, marital, familial, and sexual privacy said to be protected by the Bill of Rights or its penumbras,...or among those rights reserved to the people by the Ninth Amendment...Before addressing this claim, we feel it desirable briefly to survey, in several aspects, the history of abortion, for such insight as that history may afford us, and then to examine the state purposes and interests behind the criminal abortion laws...

It perhaps is not generally appreciated that the restrictive criminal abortion laws in effect in a majority of States today are of relatively recent vintage. Those laws, generally proscribing abortion or its attempt at any time during pregnancy except when necessary to preserve the pregnant woman's life, are not of ancient or even of common-law origin. Instead, they derive from statutory changes effected, for the most part, in the latter half of the 19th century....

Three reasons have been advanced to explain historically the enactment of criminal abortion laws in the 19th century and to justify their continued existence.

It has been argued occasionally that these laws were the product of a Victorian social concern to discourage illicit sexual conduct. Texas, however, does not advance this justification in the present case, and it appears that no court or commentator has taken the argument seriously....

A second reason is concerned with abortion as a medical procedure. When most criminal abortion laws were first enacted, the procedure was a hazardous one for the woman....Thus, it has been argued that a State's real concern in enacting a criminal abortion law was to protect the pregnant woman, that is, to restrain her from submitting to a procedure that placed her life in serious jeopardy.

Modern medical techniques have altered this situation....

The third reason is the State's interest—some phrase it in terms of duty—in protecting prenatal life. Some of the argument for this justification rests on the theory that a new human life is present from the moment of conception. The State's interest and general obligation to protect life then extends, it is argued, to prenatal life. Only when the life of the pregnant mother herself is at stake, balanced against the life she carries within her, should the interest of the embryo or fetus not prevail. Logically, of course, a legitimate state interest in this area need not stand or fall on acceptance of the belief that life begins at conception or at some other point prior to live birth. In assessing the State's interest, recognition may be given to the less rigid claim that as long as at least *potential* life is involved, the State may assert interests beyond the protection of the pregnant woman alone....

It is with these interests, and the weight to be attached to them, that this case is concerned....

The constitution does not explicitly mention any right of privacy. In a line of decisions, however, going back perhaps as far as... 1891, the Court has recognized that a right of personal privacy, or a guarantee of certain areas or zones of privacy, does exist under the Constitution. In varying contexts, the Court or individual Justices have, indeed, found at least the roots of that right in the First Amendment,... in the Fourth and Fifth Amendments,... in the penumbras of the Bill of Rights,... in the Ninth Amendment,... or in the concept of liberty guaranteed by the first section of the Fourteenth Amendment... These decisions make it clear that only personal rights that can be deemed "fundamental" or "implicit in the concept of ordered liberty"... are included in this guarantee of personal privacy. They also make it clear that the right has some extension to activities relating to marriage,... procreation,... contraception,... family relationships,... and child rearing and education....

This right of privacy, whether it be founded in the Fourteenth Amendment's concept of personal liberty and restrictions upon state action, as we feel it is, or, as the District Court determined, in the Ninth Amendment's reservation of rights to the people, is broad enough to encompass a woman's decision whether or not to terminate her pregnancy. The detriment that the State would impose upon the pregnant woman by denying this choice altogether is apparent. Specific and direct harm medically diagnosable even in early pregnancy may be involved. Maternity, or additional offspring, may force upon the woman a distressful life and future. Psychological harm may be imminent. Mental and physical health may be taxed by child care. There is also the distress, for all concerned, associated with the unwanted child, and there is the problem of bringing a child into a family already unable, psychologically and otherwise, to care for it. In other cases, as in this one, the additional difficulties and continuing stigma of unwed motherhood may be involved. All these are factors the woman and her responsible physician necessarily will consider in consultation.

On the basis of elements such as these, appellant and some *amici* argue that the woman's right is absolute and that she is entitled to terminate her pregnancy at whatever time, in whatever way, and for whatever reason she alone chooses. With this we do not agree. Appellant's arguments that Texas either has no valid interest at all in regulating the abortion decision, or no interest strong enough to support any limitation upon the woman's sole determination, is unpersuasive. The Court's decisions recognizing a right of privacy also acknowledge that some state regulation in areas protected by that right is appropriate. As noted above, a State may properly assert important interests in safeguarding health, in maintaining medical standards, and in protecting potential life. At some point in pregnancy, these respective interests become sufficiently compelling to sustain regulation of the factors that govern the abortion decision. The privacy right involved, therefore, cannot be said to be absolute. In fact, it is not clear to us that the claim asserted by some *amici* that one has an unlimited right to do with one's body as one pleases bears a close relationship to the right of privacy previously articulated in the Court's decisions. The Court has refused to recognize an unlimited right of this kind in the past....

We, therefore, conclude that the right of personal privacy includes the abortion decision, but that this right is not unqualified and must be considered against important state interests in regulation....

A. The appellee and certain *amici* argue that the fetus is a "person" within the language and meaning of the Fourteenth Amendment. In support of this, they outline at length and in detail the well-known facts of fetal development. If this suggestion of personhood is established, the appellant's case, of course, collapses, for the fetus' right to life is then guaranteed specifically by the Amendment. The appellant conceded as much on reargument. On the other hand, the appellee conceded on reargument that no case could be cited that holds that a fetus is a person within the meaning of the Fourteenth Amendment.

The Constitution does not define "persons" in so many words.... [I]n nearly all...instances [in which the word *person* is used], the use of the word is such that it has application only postnatally. None indicates, with any assurance, that is has any possible pre-natal application.

All this, together with our observation...that throughout the major portion of the 19th century prevailing legal abortion practices were far freer than they are today, persuades us that the word "person," as used in the Fourteenth Amendment, does not include the unborn....

This conclusion, however, does not of itself fully answer the contentions raised by Texas, and we pass on to other considerations.

B. The pregnant woman cannot be isolated in her privacy. She carries an embryo and, later, a fetus, if one accepts the medical definitions of the developing young in the human uterus.... The situation therefore is inherently different from marital intimacy, or bedroom possession of obscene material, or marriage, or procreation, or education.... As we have intimated above, it is reasonable and appropriate for a State to decide that at some point in time another interest, that of health of the mother or that of potential human life, becomes significantly involved. The woman's privacy is no longer sole and any right of privacy she possesses must be measured accordingly.

Texas urges that, apart from the Fourteenth Amendment, life begins at conception and is present throughout pregnancy, and that, therefore, the State has a compelling interest in protecting that life from and after conception. We need not resolve the difficult question of when life begins. When those trained in the respective disciplines of medicine, philosophy, and theology are unable to arrive at any consensus, the judiciary, at this point in the development of man's knowledge, is not in a position to speculate as to the answer....

In view of... this, we do not agree that, by adopting one theory of life, Texas may override the rights of the pregnant woman that are at stake. We repeat, however, that the State does have an important and legitimate interest in preserving and protecting the health of the pregnant woman, whether she be a resident of the State or a nonresident who seeks medical consultation and treatment there, and that it has still *another* important and legitimate interest in protecting the potentiality of human life. These interests are separate and distinct. Each grows in substantiality as the woman approaches term and, at a point during pregnancy, each becomes "compelling."

With respect to the State's important and legitimate interest in the health of the mother, the "compelling" point, in the light of present medical knowledge, is at approximately the end of the first trimester. This is so because of the now-established medical fact... that until the end of the first trimester mortality in abortion may be less than mortality in normal childbirth. If follows that, from and after this point, a State may regulate the abortion procedure to the extent that the regulation reasonably relates to the preservation and protection of maternal health. Examples of permissible state regulation in this area are requirements as to the qualifications of the person who is to perform the abortion; as to the licensure of that person; as to the facility in which the procedure is to be performed, that is, whether it must be a hospital or may be a clinic or some other place of less-than-hospital status; as to the licensing of the facility; and the like.

This means, on the other hand, that, for the period of pregnancy prior to this "compelling" point, the attending physician, in consultation with his patient, is free to determine, without regulation by the State, that, in his medical judgment, the patient's pregnancy should be terminated. If that decision is reached, the judgment may be effectuated by an abortion free of interference by the State.

With respect to the State's important and legitimate interest in potential life, the "compelling" point is at viability. This is so because the fetus then presumably has the capability of meaningful life outside the mother's womb. State regulation protective of fetal life after viability thus has both logical and biological justifications. If the State is interested in protecting fetal life after viability, it may go so far as to proscribe abortion during that period, except when it is necessary to preserve the life or health of the mother.

Measured against these standards, Art. 1196 of the Texas Penal Code, in restricting legal abortions to those "procured or attempted by medical advice for the purpose of saving the life of the mother," sweeps too broadly. The statute makes no distinction between abortions performed early in pregnancy and those performed later, and it limits to a single reason, "saving" the mother's life, the legal justification for the procedure. The statute, therefore, cannot survive the constitutional attack made upon it here....

WEBSTER V. REPRODUCTIVE HEALTH SERVICES (1989)

Chief Justice Rehnquist announced the judgment of the Court:

Decision of this case requires us to address four sections of the Missouri Act: (a) the preamble; (b) the prohibition on the use of public facilities or employees to perform abortions; (c) the prohibition on public funding of abortion counseling; and (d) the requirement that physicians conduct viability tests prior to performing abortions....

The Act's preamble, as noted, sets forth "findings" by the Missouri legislature that "[t]he life of each human being begins at conception," and that "[u]nborn children have protectable interests in life, health, and well-being." The Act then mandates that state laws be interpreted to provide unborn children with "all the rights, privileges, and immunities available to other persons, citizens, and residents of this state," subject to the Constitution and this Court's precedents... Missouri's refusal to allow public employees to perform abortions in public hospitals leaves a pregnant woman with the same choices as if the State had chosen not to operate any public hospitals at all. The challenged provisions only restrict a woman's ability to obtain an abortion to the extent that she chooses to use a physician affiliated with a public hospital....

Having held that the State's refusal to fund abortions does not violate *Roe v. Wade,* it strains logic to reach a contrary result for the use of public facilities and employees. If the State may "make a value judgment favoring childbirth over abortion and ... implement that judgment by the allocation of public funds," surely it may do so through the allocation of other public resources, such as hospitals and medical staff.

... The viability-testing provision of the Missouri Act is concerned with promoting the State's interest in potential human life rather than in maternal health. Section 188.029 creates what is essentially a presumption of viability at 20 weeks, which the physician must rebut with tests indicating that the fetus is not viable prior to performing an abortion. It also directs the physician's determination as to viability by specifying consideration, if feasible, of gestational age, fetal weight, and lung capacity. The District court found that "the medical evidence is uncontradicted that a 20–week fetus is *not* viable," and that "$23\frac{1}{2}$ to 24 weeks gestation is the earliest point in pregnancy where a reasonable possibility of viability exists." But it also found that there may be a 4–week error in estimating gestational age, which supports testing at 20 weeks.... We think that the doubt cast upon the Missouri statute is not so much a flaw in the statute as it is a reflection of the fact that the rigid trimester analysis of the course of a pregnancy enunciated in *Roe* has resulted in ... making constitutional law in this area a virtual Procrustean bed....

Stare decisis is a cornerstone of our legal system, but it has less power in constitutional cases, where, save for constitutional amendments, this Court is the only body able to make needed changes. We have not refrained from reconsideration of a prior construction of the Constitution that has proved "unsound in principle and unworkable in practice." We think the *Roe* trimester framework falls into that category.

In the first place, the rigid *Roe* framework is hardly consistent with the notion of a Constitution cast in general terms, as ours is, and usually speaking in general principles, as ours does. The key elements of the *Roe* framework—trimesters and viability—are not found in the text of the Constitution or in any place else one would expect to find a constitutional principle. Since the bounds of the inquiry are essentially indeterminate, the result has been a web of legal rules that have become increasingly intricate, resembling a code of regulations rather than a body of constitutional doctrine. As Justice WHITE has put it, the trimester framework has left this court to serve as the country's "*ex officio* medical board with powers to approve or disapprove medical and operative practices and standards throughout the United States."

In the second place, we do not see why the State's interest in protecting potential human life should come into existence only at the point of viability, and that there should therefore be a rigid line allowing state regulation after viability but prohibiting it before viability....

The tests that [the state law] requires the physician to perform are designed to determine viability. The State here has chosen viability as the point at which its interest in potential human life must be safeguarded. It is true that the tests in question increase the expense of abortion, and regulate the discretion of the physician in determining the viability of the fetus. Since the tests will undoubtedly show in many cases that the fetus is not viable, the tests will have been performed for what were in fact second-trimester abortions. But we are satisfied that the requirement of these tests permissibly furthers the State's interest in protecting potential human life, and we therefore believe [the Missouri law] to be constitutional.

Justice O'CONNOR concurring:...

In its interpretation of Missouri's "determination of viability" provision, the plurality has proceeded in a manner unnecessary to deciding the question at hand....

Unlike the plurality, I do not understand these viability testing requirements to conflict with any of the Court's past decisions concerning state regulation of abortion. Therefore, there is no necessity to accept the State's invitation to reexamine the constitutional validity *of Roe v. Wade*. Where there is no need to decide a constitutional question, it is a venerable principle of this Court's adjudicatory processes not to do so for "[t]he Court will not 'anticipate a question of constitutional law in advance of the necessity of deciding it.' " Neither will it generally "formulate a rule of constitutional law broader than is required by the precise facts to which it is to be applied." Quite simply, "[i]t is not the habit of the court to decide questions of a constitutional nature unless absolutely necessary to a decision of the case." The court today has accepted the State's every interpretation of its abortion statute and has upheld, under our existing precedents, every provision of that statute which is properly before us. Precisely for this reason reconsideration of *Roe* falls not into any "good-cause exception" to this "fundamental rule of judicial restraint. . . . " When the constitutional invalidity of a State's abortion statute actually turns on the constitutional validity of *Roy v. Wade*, there will be time enough to reexamine *Roe*. And to do so carefully . . . .

Justice SCALIA, concurring in part and concurring in the judgment. . . .

The outcome of today's case will doubtless be heralded as a triumph of judicial statesmanship. It is not that, unless it is statesmanlike needlessly to prolong this Court's self-awarded sovereignty over a field where it has little proper business since the answers to most of the cruel questions posed are political and not juridical—a sovereignty which therefore quite properly, but to the great damage of the Court, makes it the object of the sort of organized public pressure that political institutions in a democracy ought to receive.

Justice O'CONNOR's assertion that a "fundamental rule of judicial restraint" requires us to avoid reconsidering *Roe*, cannot be taken seriously. By finessing *Roe* we do not, as she suggests, adhere to the strict and venerable rule that we should avoid "'decid[ing] questions of a constitutional nature.'" We have not disposed of this case on some statutory or procedural ground, but have decided, and could not avoid deciding, whether the Missouri statute meets the requirements of the United States Constitution. The only choice available is whether, in deciding that constitutional question, we should use *Roe v. Wade* as the benchmark, or something else. What is involved, therefore, is not the rule of avoiding constitutional issues where possible, but the quite separate principle that we will not "'formulate a rule of constitutional law broader than is required by the precise facts to which it is to be applied.'" The latter is a sound general principle, but one often departed from when good reason exists . . . .

The real question, then, is whether there are valid reasons to go beyond the most stingy possible holding today. It seems to me there are not only valid but compelling ones. Ordinarily, speaking no more broadly than is absolutely required avoids throwing settled law into confusion; doing so today preserves a chaos that is evident to anyone who can read and count. Alone sufficient to justify a broad holding is the fact that our retaining control, through *Roe*, of what I believe to be, and many of our citizens recognize to be, a political issue, continuously distorts the public perception of the role of this Court. We can now look forward to at least another Term with carts full of mail from the public, and streets full of demonstrators, urging us—their unelected and life-tenured judges who have been awarded those extraordinary, undemocratic characteristics precisely in order that we might follow the law despite the popular will—to follow the popular will. Indeed, I expect we can look forward to even more of that than before, given our indecisive decision today. And if these reasons for taking the unexceptional course of reaching a broader holding are not enough, then consider the nature of the constitutional question we avoid: In most cases, we do no harm by not speaking more broadly than the decision requires. Anyone affected by the conduct that the avoided holding would have prohibited will be able to challenge it himself, and have his day in court to make the argument.

Not so with respect to the harm that many States believed, pre-*Roe*, and many may continue to believe, is caused by largely unrestricted abortion. That will continue to occur if the States have the constitutional power to prohibit it, and would do so, but we skillfully avoid telling them so. Perhaps those abortions cannot constitutionally be proscribed. That is surely an arguable question, the question that reconsideration of *Roe v. Wade* entails. But what is not at all arguable, it seems to me, is that we should decide now and not insist that we be run into a corner before we grudgingly yield up our judgment. The only sound reason for the latter course is to prevent a change in the law—but to think that desirable begs the question to be decided....

Justice BLACKMUN...

Today, *Roe v. Wade*, and the fundamental constitutional right of women to decide whether to terminate a pregnancy, survive but are not secure. Although the Court extricates itself from this case without making a single, even incremental, change in the law of abortion, the plurality and Justice SCALIA would overrule *Roe* (the first silently, the other explicitly) and would return to the States virtually unfettered authority to control the quintessentially intimate, personal, and life-directing decision whether to carry a fetus to term. Although today, no less than yesterday, the Constitution and the decisions of this Court prohibit a State from enacting laws that inhibit women from the meaningful exercise of that right, a plurality of this Court implicitly invites every state legislature to enact more and more restrictive abortion regulations in order to provoke more and more test cases, in the hope that sometime down the line the Court will return the law of procreative freedom to the severe limitations that generally prevailed in this country before January 22, 1973. Never in my memory has a plurality announced a judgment of this Court that so foments disregard for the law and for our standing decisions.

Nor in my memory has a plurality gone about its business in such a deceptive fashion. At every level of its review, from its effort to read the real meaning out of the Missouri statute, to its intended evisceration of precedents and its deafening silence about the constitutional protections that it would jettison, the plurality obscures the portent of its analysis. With feigned restraint, the plurality announces that its analysis leaves *Roe* "undisturbed," albeit "modif[ied] and narrow[ed]." But this disclaimer is totally meaningless. The plurality opinion is filled with winks, and nods, and knowing glances to those who would do away with *Roe* explicitly, but turns a stone face to anyone in search of what the plurality conceives as the scope of a woman's right under the Due Process Clause to terminate a pregnancy free from the coercive and brooding influence of the State. The simple truth is that *Roe* would not survive the plurality's analysis, and that the plurality provides no substitute for *Roe's* protective umbrella. I fear for the future. I fear for the liberty and equality of the millions of women who have lived and come of age in the 16 years since *Roe* was decided. I fear for the integrity of, and public esteem for, this Court.

I dissent.

33. A Common Destiny: Blacks and American Society, 1989

EDITED BY GERALD DAVID JAYNES
AND ROBIN M. WILLIAMS, JR.

A Common Destiny: Blacks and American Society *summarizes a massive review of all aspects of research on the status of African Americans. The report presents a disturbing and complex picture. On the one hand, millions of African Americans have benefited from the civil rights revolution. In the course of the 1960s and 1970s somewhere between 35 and 45 percent of African American families moved into the middle class. At the same time, perhaps 30 percent of the African American community fell into ever deeper poverty. This latter trend has been particularly intense in the period after 1973, when real wages for American workers began to decline.*

Americans in the 1980s have struggled with this confusing double vision of African Americans. On the one hand, some African Americans have achieved new levels of success and acceptance. At the same time, prejudice continues on its corrosive path and African Americans constantly discover that old beliefs continue. The chilly reception of African American students in some colleges today has been especially startling to a generation that put its faith in education as the way to tolerance. Recent history suggests that we have still not discovered the need for a common national destiny.

Just five decades ago, most black Americans could not work, live, shop, eat, seek entertainment, or travel where they chose. Even a quarter century ago—100 years after the Emancipation Proclamation of 1863—most blacks were effectively denied the right to vote. A large majority of blacks lived in poverty, and very few black children had the opportunity to receive a basic education; indeed, black children were still forced to attend inferior and separate schools in jurisdictions that had not accepted the 1954 decision of the Supreme Court declaring segregated schools unconstitutional.

Today the situation is very different. In education, many blacks have received college degrees from universities that formerly excluded them. In the workplace, blacks frequently hold professional and managerial jobs in desegregated settings. In politics, most blacks now participate in elections, and blacks have been elected to all but the highest political offices. Overall, many blacks have achieved middle-class status.

Yet the great gulf that existed between black and white Americans in 1939 has only been narrowed; it has not closed. One of three blacks still live in households with incomes below the poverty line. Even more blacks live in areas where ineffective schools, high rates of dependence on public assistance, severe problems of crime and drug use, and low and declining employment prevail. Race relations, as they affect the lives of inhabitants of these areas, differ considerably from black-white relations involving middle-class blacks. Lower status blacks have less access to desegregated schools, neighborhoods, and other institutions and public facilities. Their interactions with whites frequently emphasize their subordinate status—as low-skilled employees, public agency clients, and marginally performing pupils.

The status of black Americans today can be characterized as a glass that is half full—if measured by progress since 1939—or as a glass that is half empty—if measured by the persisting disparities between black and white Americans since the early 1970s. Any assessment of the quality of life for blacks is also complicated by the contrast between blacks who have achieved middle-class status and those who have not.

The progress occurred because sustained struggles by blacks and their allies changed American law and politics, moving all governments and most private institutions from support of principles of racial inequality to support of principles of racial equality. Gradually, and often with much resistance, the behaviors and attitudes of individual whites moved in the same direction. Over the 50-year span covered by this study, the social status of American blacks has *on average* improved dramatically, both in absolute terms and relative to whites. The growth of the economy and public policies promoting racial equality led to an erosion of segregation and discrimination, making it possible for a substantial fraction of blacks to enter the mainstream of American life.

The reasons for the continuing distress of large numbers of black Americans are complex. Racial discrimination continues despite the victories of the civil rights movement. Yet, the problems faced today by blacks who are isolated from economic and social progress are less directly open to political amelioration than were the problems of legal segregation and the widely practiced overt discrimination of a few decades past. Slow overall growth of the economy during the 1970s and 1980s has been an important impediment to black progress; in the three previous decades economic prosperity and rapid growth had been a great help to most blacks. Educational institutions and government policies have not successfully responded to underlying changes in the society. Opportunities for upward mobility have been reduced for all lower status Americans, but especially for those who are black. If all racial discrimination were abolished today, the life prospects facing many poor blacks would still constitute major challenges for public policy.

This report summarizes and interprets a large body of data and research analyses concerning the position of blacks in American society since the eve of World War II. We write at a time 20 years after the Kerner Commission, following the summer riots of 1967, warned that ours was becoming a racially divided and unequal nation. We write 45 years after Gunnar Myrdal in *An American Dilemma* challenged Americans to bring their racial practices into line with their ideals. Despite clear evidence of progress against each problem, Americans face an unfinished agenda: many black Americans remain separated from the mainstream of national life under conditions of great inequality. The American dilemma has not been resolved.

The new "American dilemma" that has emerged after the civil rights era of the 1960s results from two aspirations of black Americans: equal opportunity—the removal of barriers to employment, housing, education, and political activities—and the actual attainment of equality in participation in these sectors of life.

Central to the realization of these aspirations are national policies promoting equality of opportunity for the most disadvantaged blacks (especially in areas such as employment and education) and the preservation among black people of attitudes and behaviors toward self-help and individual sacrifice that have enabled them to benefit from such opportunities. Black-white relations are important in determining the degree to which equal opportunity exists for black Americans. Whites desire equality of treatment in social institutions and in governmental policy; however, many whites are less likely to espouse or practice equality of treatment for blacks in their personal behavior. Thus, at the core of black-white relations is a dynamic tension between many whites' expectations of American institutions and their expectations of themselves. This state of relations is a significant improvement from 45 years ago when majorities of white people supported discrimination against blacks in many areas of life. But the divergence between social principle and individual practice frequently leads to white avoidance of blacks in those institutions in which equal treatment is most needed. The result is that American institutions do not provide the full equality of opportunity that Americans desire.

Foremost among the reasons for the present state of black-white relations are two continuing consequences of the nation's long and recent history of racial inequality. One is the negative attitudes held toward blacks and the other is the actual disadvantaged conditions under which many black Americans live. These two consequences reinforce each other. Thus, a legacy of discrimination and segregation continues to affect black-white relations.

In the context of American history, this continuing legacy is not surprising. Racial and ethnic differences have had crucial effects on the course of American history. In particular, black Americans' central role in several constitutional crises—their past status as slaves and the debates over slavery during the Constitutional Convention of 1787; the fighting of the Civil War; the denial of blacks' basic citizenship until the civil rights movement of the 1950s and 1960s—has frequently focused international attention on black-white relations in the United States. In view of this history, race is likely to retain much of its saliency as a feature of American society for some time.

Indeed, as the twenty-first century nears, demographic conditions will increase Americans' awareness that theirs is a multiracial society. The Bureau of the Census projects that the black population will increase from 11.7 percent of the U.S. total in 1980 to 15 percent in 2020; blacks will be nearly 1 of 5 children of school age and 1 of 6 adults of prime working age (25–54). Rising numbers of blacks will be represented both in influential occupations and positions, and among the poor, the least educated, and the jobless. At the same time, immigration trends are also increasing the numbers and proportions of Asian-Americans and Hispanics in the U.S. population. Thus, the importance of racial and ethnic minorities in general to the nation's well-being is growing.

We can summarize our main findings on the status of blacks in America in the late 1980s succinctly:

- By almost all aggregate statistical measures—incomes and living standards; health and life expectancy; educational, occupational, and residential opportunities; political and social participation—the well-being of both blacks and whites has advanced greatly over the past five decades.
- By almost all the same indicators, blacks remain substantially behind whites.

Beyond this brief picture lies a more complex set of changes that affect the *relative* status of black Americans:

- The greatest economic gains for blacks occurred in the 1940s and 1960s. Since the early 1970s, the economic status of blacks relative to whites has, on average, stagnated or deteriorated.
- The political, educational, health, and cultural statuses of blacks showed important gains from the 1940s through the 1960s. In addition, some important indicators continued to improve after the early 1970s.
- Among blacks, the experiences of various groups have differed, and status differences among those groups have increased. Some blacks have attained high-status occupations, income, education, and political positions, but a substantial minority remain in disadvantaged circumstances.

These patterns of change have been largely determined by three factors:

- Political and social activism among black Americans and their white allies led to changes in governmental policies; particularly important were sweeping improvements in the legal status of blacks.
- Resistance to social change in race relations continues in American society.
- Broad changes in overall economic conditions, especially the post-1973 slowdown in the nation's economic growth, have significantly affected social and economic opportunities for all Americans....

BLACKS AND WHITES IN A CHANGING SOCIETY

Two general developments in the status of black Americans stand out; each is reflective of a near-identical development in the population at large. First, for the period 1940–1973, real earnings of Americans improved steadily, but they stagnated and declined after 1973. Similarly, over these same periods, there was a clear record of improving average material status of blacks relative to whites followed by stagnation and decline. Second, during the post-1973 period, inequality increased among Americans as the lowest income and least skilled people were hurt most by changes in the overall economy. Similarly, there were increasing differences in material well-being and opportunities among blacks, and they have been extremely pronounced.

These developments may be understood as consequences of four interdependent events that have altered the status of blacks, relative black-white status, and race relations in the United States. These events were the urbanization and northern movement of the black population from 1940 to 1970; the civil rights movement that forced the nation to open its major institutions to black participation during the same three decades; the unprecedented high and sustained rate of national economic growth for roughly the same period; and the significant slowdown in the U.S. economy since the early 1970s.

The civil rights movement, blacks' more proximate location near centers of industrial activity, and high economic growth enabled those blacks best prepared to take advantage of new opportunities to respond with initiative and success. Increases in educational opportunities were seized by many blacks who were then able to translate better educations into higher status occupations than most blacks had ever enjoyed. Black incomes and earnings rose generally, with many individuals and families reaching middle-class and even upper middle income status. The new black middle class moved into better housing, frequently in the suburbs, and sometimes in desegregated neighborhoods. Despite much confrontation between whites and blacks as blacks abandoned traditional approaches to black-white relations, race relations eventually advanced closer to equal treatment.

At the same time, many blacks were not able to take advantage of the new conditions that developed: some were still located in areas relatively untouched by the changes; some lacked the family support networks to provide assistance; for some, better opportunities simply did not arise. Those who were left behind during the 1960s and 1970s faced and still face very different situations than poor blacks immediately before that period.

A major reason is the performance of the economy. Real weekly earnings (in constant 1984 dollars) of all American men, on average, fell from $488 in 1969 to $414 in 1984; real weekly earnings of women fell from $266 in 1969 to $230 in 1984. For the first time since the Great Depression of the 1930s, American men born in one year (e.g., 1960) may face lower lifetime real earnings than men born 10 years earlier. Among the myriad and complex responses to these economic conditions have been rising employment rates among women, but falling rates among men, while the unemployment rates of both men and women have been on an upward trend for three decades.

A generation ago, a low-skilled man had relatively abundant opportunity to obtain a blue-collar job with a wage adequate to support a family at a lower middle class level or better. Today the jobs available to such men—and women—are often below or just barely above the official poverty line for a family of four. For example, black males aged 25–34, with some high school but no diploma, earned on average $268 weekly in 1986; in 1969, black male dropouts of that age had averaged $334 weekly (in constant 1984 dollars). For white men of the same age and education, work conditions have been better, but changes over time cannot be said to have been good: in the years 1969 and 1986, mean weekly earnings were $447 and $381. Thus, among men who did not complete high school, blacks and whites had lower real earnings in 1986 than in 1969.

Obtaining a well-paying job increasingly requires a good education or a specific skill. Many young blacks and whites do not obtain such training, and the educational system in many locations is apparently not equipped to provide them. Recent reports on the state of American education sound great alarm about the future status of today's students. One in six youths dropped out of high school in 1985, and levels of scholastic achievement are disturbingly low by many measures. Young men with poor credentials, finding themselves facing low-wage job offers and high unemployment rates, frequently abandon the labor force intermittently or completely. Some choose criminal activity as an alternative to the labor market.

Greater numbers of people are today susceptible to poverty than in the recent past. With some year-to-year variation, the percentage of Americans living in poverty has been on an upward trend: from 11.2 percent in 1974 to 13.5 percent in 1986. In addition, the poor may be getting poorer in the 1980s: the average poor family has persistently had a yearly income further below the poverty line than any year since 1963.

More and more of the poor are working family heads, men and women who are employed or seeking employment but who cannot find a job that pays enough to prevent their families from sliding into or near poverty. For the more fortunate, reasonably secure from the fear of poverty, such middle-class advantages as a home in the suburbs and the ability to send their children to the best college for which they qualify are goals that were reached by their parents but may be unattainable for many of them.

Perhaps the most important consequences of the stagnating U.S. economy have been the effects on the status of children. Many members of the next generation of young adults live in conditions ill suited to prepare them to contribute to the nation's future. In 1987, 1 of 5 (20 percent) American children under age 18—white, black, Hispanic, Native American, and Asian-American—were being raised in families with incomes below official poverty standards. Among minorities the conditions were worse: for example, 45 percent of black children and 39 percent of Hispanic children were living in poverty. During the 1970s, approximately 2 of every 3 black children could expect to live in poverty for at least 1 of the first 10 years of their childhood, while an astounding 1 of 3 could expect at least 7 of those 10 years to be lived in poverty.

We cannot emphasize too much the gravity of the fact that in any given year more than two-fifths of all black children live under conditions of poverty as the 1980s draw to a close. As fertility rates decrease, the total youth population of the United States will contain a larger proportion of comparatively disadvantaged youths from minority ethnic and racial groups. This change may in turn lead to major changes in labor markets, childbearing, the armed forces, and education.

Under conditions of increasing economic hardship for the least prosperous members of society, blacks, because of their special legacy of poverty and discrimination, are afflicted sooner, more deeply, and longer. But the signs of distress that are most visible in parts of the black population are becoming more discernible within the entire population. This distress should be viewed in the context of the underlying changes within American society that affect not only black-white differences, but all disadvantaged blacks and whites who face the difficult economic conditions of the late 1980s.

DETERMINANTS OF BLACK STATUS

One major determinant of black status has been noted in the previous sections: the stagnation of the U.S. economy since 1973, which has particularly hurt lower class blacks. In this section we note two other determinants: organizational and individual resistance to change, intended and otherwise, that has erected and maintained barriers to black opportunities; and the policies of governments and private organizations aimed at improving blacks' position, which have resulted in large measure from black activism, initiative, and self-identity.

Barriers and disadvantages persist in blocking black advancement. Three such barriers to full opportunity for black Americans are residential segregation, continuance of diffuse and often indirect discrimination, and exclusion from social networks essential for full access to economic and educational opportunities. These barriers also existed for blacks who overcame them in earlier decades, but those successes were achieved in an economy that was growing rapidly and providing good wage opportunities even to low-skilled and less educated job seekers. In the 1960s, blacks seeking to help themselves also were benefited by a society more willing to expend energy and resources toward improving opportunities for the poor and minorities.

The past five decades have shown that purposeful actions and policies by governments and private institutions make a large difference in the opportunities and conditions of black Americans. Such purposeful actions and policies have been essential for past progress, and further progress is unlikely without them. Many blacks attained middle-class status because government and private programs enabled them to achieve better educations and jobs, through employment and education programs and government enforcement of equal employment opportunity.

Black initiative and identity have increasingly played primary roles in bringing about changes in government and private institutions and improvements in blacks' economic, social, and political status. This is of course evident in blacks' leadership of the civil rights movement and in their response to industrial opportunity during the great rural-to-urban migration of 1940–1970. But it is also evident in the strivings of individuals to finish high school or attain higher education; to enter a predominantly white factory, secretarial pool, or corporate law office; or to desegregate an entire institution, such as a professional sport, military combat corps, or legislative body.

Many blacks who have not succeeded live in environments in which social conditions and individual behavioral patterns are often detrimental to self-improvement. Such behaviors may be natural responses to group conditions and social forces perceived as beyond personal control. One-half of black families with children must manage their affairs with only one parent—almost always a mother. These families are overwhelmingly poor (59 percent were below the poverty line in 1987), have high rates of dependence on family assistance benefits, and live in areas with a high percentage of families in similar circumstances.

Why do such behaviors and conditions persist? There are no simple answers to this crucial question and no answers that can be validated as scientific findings. We can say, however, that the evidence does not support some popular hypotheses that purport to explain female-headed households, high birth rates to unmarried women, low labor force participation by males, or poor academic performance solely on the basis of government support programs or, more generally, on the existence of a "culture of poverty" among the black poor. Black-white cultural differences have narrowed since 1960, not widened.

Our analysis of the problem does identify a number of important contributory factors. Discrimination plays an important role in the lives of many blacks, and even in the absence of discrimination the opportunities of many blacks are limited. Black youths in poor environments probably anticipate little payoff from working for academic achievement and may underestimate their opportunities. Those in poorly staffed, dilapidated schools populated with underachieving students can easily fall into the trap of perceiving the pursuit of academic excellence as a poor investment. Inequalities in economic status to a large extent cause and interact with other status features to maintain overall black-white differences in status. Consequently, status gaps between blacks and whites will remain as long as blacks' economic status lags behind that of whites. For example, differences in black-white voting patterns result from persistent economic and social inequalities that impede electoral participation regardless of race; individual blacks now participate as much or more than whites of comparable socioeconomic status. Similarly, differences in socioeconomic status account for the entire black-white difference in high school dropout rates. In health, differences in black and white infant mortality are similarly linked to differences in economic status. In the criminal justice system, much of the differential sentencing of blacks and whites can be attributed to differences between sentences for defendants of higher and lower economic status.

Yet the status of blacks is determined by the presence of both racial stratification and class (position within the socioeconomic structure of society). Changes in black-white relations and social opportunities do not affect blacks of different status in similar ways. For example, because of higher geographic concentrations of poor households among blacks, segregated residential areas affect the quality of schools and medical care available to low-income blacks more than they affect the availability of these resources to higher income blacks or low-income whites. And we have already noted that changes in the national economy have had particularly negative effects on lower status Americans, white and black. But changes have been most detrimental to the fortunes of blacks, and opportunities were curtailed most for blacks of lowest status....

34. The United States in Relative Decline

PAUL KENNEDY

We usually see the period from the 1940s through the 1980s as the era of Cold War, of conflict between the United States and the Soviet Union, with other powers lined up on either side or remaining neutral. Paul Kennedy, in The Rise and Fall of the Great Powers, *points out that it is also the age during which the United States became the dominant force in the world, much like the British Empire in the late nineteenth and early twentieth century. And in the course of these recent years the nation has experienced "relative decline" in terms of its share of the world's economic and military strength. The Cold War has been rapidly replaced not by victory or defeat for either side but by a world of multiple powers competing with each other for wealth and security. In some sense both the United States and the Soviet Union have "lost" the Cold War—to Japan and other Pacific-rim nations, to the European Economic Community, to all those nations whose goods and resources enter our markets. In another sense the Cold War, so long as it remained cold, was not something to win or lose: it was a particular order of diplomacy among nations, one that is now passing.*

The United States remains the richest and most powerful nation on earth. Kennedy points out, however, that it suffers from "imperial overreach," laboring under global commitments made when it commanded a larger share of the world's resources. Will our essentially laissez-faire *system enable us to adjust to changing circumstances more easily than other societies? Or will our fragmentation of purpose interfere with policies needed to overcome trade and fiscal deficits and readjust our military posture? Most of all, one wonders about the resiliency of American culture as it faces unaccustomed declines in our standard of living and in our status in the world's councils and markets. Striking a new balance between defense, consumption, and investment in the future, Kennedy asserts, is the challenge that Americans face in the nineties and in the new century.*

It is worth bearing in mind the Soviet Union's difficulties when one turns to analyze the present and the future circumstances of the United States, because of two important distinctions. The first is that while it can be argued that the American share of world power has been declining *relatively* faster than Russia's over the past few decades, its problems are probably nowhere near as great as those of its Soviet rival. Moreover, its *absolute* strength (especially in industrial and technological fields) is still much larger than that of the USSR. The second is that the very unstructured, laissez-faire nature of American society (while not without its weaknesses) probably gives it a better chance of readjusting to changing circumstances than a rigid and *dirigiste* power would have. But that in turn depends upon the existence of a national leadership which can understand the larger processes at work in the world today, and is aware of both the strong and the weak points of the U.S. position as it seeks to adjust to the changing global environment.

Although the United States is at present still in a class of its own economically and perhaps even militarily, it cannot avoid confronting the two great tests which challenge the *longevity* of every major power that occupies the "number one" position in world affairs: whether, in the military/strategical realm, it can preserve a reasonable balance between the nation's perceived defense requirements and the means it possesses to maintain those commitments; and whether, as an intimately related point, it can preserve the technological and economic bases of its power from relative erosion in the face of the ever-shifting patterns of global production. This test of American abilities will be the greater because it, like Imperial Spain around 1600 or the British Empire around 1900, is the inheritor of a vast array of strategical commitments which had been made decades earlier, when the nation's political, economic, and military capacity to influence world affairs seemed so much more assured. In consequence, the United States now runs the risk, so familiar to historians of the rise and fall of previous Great Powers, of what might roughly be called "imperial overstretch": that is to say, decision-makers in Washington must face the awkward and enduring fact that the sum total of the United States' global interests and obligations is nowadays far larger than the country's power to defend them all simultaneously.

Unlike those earlier Powers that grappled with the problem of strategical overextension, the United States also confronts the possibility of nuclear annihilation—a fact which, many people feel, has changed the entire nature of international power politics. If indeed a large-scale nuclear exchange were to occur, then any consideration of the United States' "prospects" becomes so problematical as to make it pointless—even if it also is the case that the American position (because of its defensive systems, and geographical extent) is probably more favorable than, say, France's or Japan's in such a conflict. On the other hand, the history of the post-1945 arms race so far suggests that nuclear weapons, while mutually threatening to East and West, also seem to be mutually unusable—which is the chief reason why the Powers continue to increase expenditures upon their *conventional* forces. If, however, the possibility exists of the major states someday becoming involved in a nonnuclear war (whether merely regional or on a larger scale), then the similarity of strategical circumstances between the United States today and imperial Spain or Edwardian Britain in their day is clearly much more appropriate. In each case, the declining number-one power faced threats, not so much to the security of its own homeland (in the United States' case, the prospect of being conquered by an invading army is remote), but to the nation's interests abroad—interests so widespread that it would be difficult to defend them all at once, and yet almost equally difficult to abandon any of them without running further risks.

Each of those interests abroad, it is fair to remark, was undertaken by the United States for what seemed very plausible (often very pressing) reasons at the time, and in most instances the reason for the American presence has not diminished; in certain parts of the globe, U.S. interests may now appear larger to decision-makers in Washington than they were a few decades ago.

That, it can be argued, is certainly true of American obligations in the Middle East. Here is a region, from Morocco in the west to Afghanistan in the east, where the United States faces a number of conflicts and problems whose mere listing (as one observer put it) "leaves one breathless." It is an area which contains so much of the world's surplus oil supply; which seems so susceptible (at least on the map) to Soviet penetration; toward which a powerfully organized domestic lobby presses for unflinching support for an isolated but militarily efficient Israel; in which Arab states of a generally pro-western inclination (Egypt, Saudi Arabia, Jordan, the Gulf emirates) are under pressure from their own Islamic fundamentalists as well as from external threats such as Libya; and in which all the Arab states, whatever their own rivalries, oppose Israel's policy toward the Palestinians. This makes the region very important to the United States, but at the same time bewilderingly resistant to any simple policy option. It is, in addition, the region in the world which, at least in some parts of it, seems most frequently to resort to war. Finally, it contains the only territory—Afghanistan—which the Soviet Union is attempting to conquer by means of armed force. It is hardly surprising, therefore, that the Middle East has been viewed as requiring constant American attention, whether of a military or a diplomatic kind. Yet the memory of the 1979 debacle in Iran and of the ill-fated Lebanon venture of 1983, the diplomatic complexities of the antagonisms (how to assist Saudi Arabia without alarming Israel), and the unpopularity of the United States among the Arab masses all make it extremely difficult for an American government to conduct a coherent, long-term policy in the Middle East.

In Latin America, too, there are seen to be growing challenges to the United States' national interests. If a major international debt crisis is to occur anywhere in the world, dealing a heavy blow to the global credit system and especially to U.S. banks, it is likely to begin in this region. As it is, Latin America's economic problems have not only lowered the credit rating of many eminent American banking houses, but they have also contributed to a substantial decline in U.S. manufacturing exports to that region. Here, as in East Asia, the threat that the advanced, prosperous countries of the world will steadily increase tariffs against imported, low-labor-cost manufactures, and be ever less generous in their overseas-aid programs, is a cause for deep concern. All this is compounded by the fact that, economically and socially, Latin America has been changing remarkably swiftly over the past few decades; at the same time, its demographic explosion is pressing ever harder upon the available resources, and upon the older conservative governing structures, in a considerable number of states. This had led to broad-based movements for social and constitutional reforms, or even for outright "revolution"—the latter being influenced by the present radical regimes in Cuba and Nicaragua. In turn, these movements have produced a conservative backlash, with reactionary governments proclaiming the need to eradicate all signs of domestic Communism, and appealing to the United States for help to achieve that goal. These social and political fissures often compel the United States to choose between its desire to enhance democratic rights in Latin America and its wish to defeat Marxism. It also forces Washington to consider whether it can achieve its own purposes by political and economic means alone, or whether it may have to resort to military action (as in the case of Grenada).

By far the most worrying situation of all, however, lies just to the south of the United States, and makes the Polish "crisis" for the USSR seem small by comparison. There is simply no equivalent in the world for the present state of Mexican-United States relations. Mexico is on the verge of economic bankruptcy and default, its internal economic crisis forces hundreds of thousands to drift illegally to the north each year, its most profitable trade with the United States is swiftly becoming a brutally managed flow of hard drugs, and the border for all this sort of traffic is still extraordinarily permeable.

If the challenges to American interests in East Asia are farther away, that does not diminish the significance of this vast area today. The largest share of the world's population lives there; a large and increasing proportion of American trade is with countries on the "Pacific rim"; two of the world's future Great Powers, China and Japan, are located there; the Soviet Union, directly and (through Vietnam) indirectly, is also there. So are those Asian newly industrializing countries, delicate quasi-democracies which on the one hand have embraced the capitalist laissez-faire ethos with a vengeance, and on the other are undercutting American manufacturing in everything from textiles to electronics. It is in East Asia, too, that a substantial number of American military obligations exist, usually as creations of the early Cold War.

Even a mere listing of those obligations cannot fail to suggest the extraordinarily wide-ranging nature of American interests in this region. A few years ago, the U.S. Defense Department attempted a brief summary of American interests in East Asia, but its very succinctness pointed, paradoxically, to the almost limitless extent of those strategical commitments:

The importance to the United States of the security of East Asia and the Pacific is demonstrated by the bilateral treaties with Japan, Korea, and the Philippines; the Manila Pact, which adds Thailand to our treaty partners; and our treaty with Australia and New Zealand—the ANZUS Treaty. It is further enhanced by the deployment of land and air forces in Korea and Japan, and the forward deployment of the Seventh Fleet in the Western Pacific. Our foremost regional objectives, in conjunction with our regional friends and allies, are:—To maintain the security of our essential sea lanes and of the United States' interests in the region; to maintain the capability to fulfill our treaty commitments in the Pacific and East Asia; to prevent the Soviet Union, North Korea, and Vietnam from interfering in the affairs of others; to build a durable strategic relationship with the People's Republic of China; and to support the stability and independence of friendly countries.

Moreover, this carefully selected prose inevitably conceals a considerable number of extremely delicate political and strategical issues: how to build a good relationship with the PRC without abandoning Taiwan; how to "support the stability and independence of friendly countries" while trying to control the flood of their exports to the American market; how to make the Japanese assume a larger share of the defense of the western Pacific without alarming its various neighbors; how to maintain U.S. bases in, for example, the Philippines without provoking local resentments; how to reduce the American military presence in South Korea without sending the wrong "signal" to the North...

Larger still, at least as measured by military deployments, is the American stake in western Europe—the defense of which is, more than anything else, the strategic rationale of the American army and of much of the air force and the navy. According to some arcane calculations, in fact, 50 to 60 percent of American general-purpose forces are allocated to NATO, an organization in which (critics repeatedly point out) the other members contribute a significantly lower share of their GNP to defense spending even though Europe's total population and income are now larger than the USA's own. This is not the place to rehearse the various European counterarguments in the "burden-sharing" debate (such as the social cost which countries like France and West Germany pay in maintaining conscription), or to develop the point that if western Europe was "Finlandized" the USA would probably spend even more on defense than at the moment. From an American strategical perspective, the unavoidable fact is that this region has always seemed more vulnerable to Russian pressure than, say, Japan—partly because it is *not* an island, and partly because on the other side of the European land frontier the USSR has concentrated the largest proportion of its land and air forces, significantly greater than what may be reasonably needed for internal-security purposes. This still may not give Russia the military capacity to overrun western Europe, but it is not a situation in which it would be prudent to withdraw substantial U.S. ground and air forces unilaterally. Even the outside possibility that the world's largest concentration of manufacturing production *might* fall into the Soviet orbit is enough to convince the Pentagon that "the security of western Europe is particularly vital to the security of the United States."

Yet however logical the American commitment to Europe may be strategically, that fact itself is no guarantee against certain military and political complications which have led to transatlantic discord. Although the NATO alliance brings the United States and western Europe close together at one level, the EEC itself is, like Japan, a rival in economic terms, especially in the shrinking markets for agricultural products. More significantly, while *official* European policy has always been to stress the importance of being under the American "nuclear umbrella," a broad-based unease exists among the general publics at the implications of siting U.S. weapons (cruise missiles, Pershing IIs, Trident-bearing submarines—let alone neutron bombs) on European soil. But if, to return to an earlier point, both superpowers would try to avoid "going nuclear" in the event of a major clash, that still leaves considerable problems in guaranteeing the defense of western Europe by *conventional* means. In the first place, that is a very expensive proposition. Secondly, even if one accepts the evidence which is beginning to suggest that the

Warsaw Pact's land and air forces could in fact be held in check, such an argument is predicated upon a certain enhancement of NATO's current strength. From that perspective, nothing could be more upsetting than proposals to reduce or withdraw U.S. forces in Europe—however pressing that might be for economic reasons or for the purpose of buttressing American deployments elsewhere in the world. Yet carrying out a grand strategy which is both global and flexible is extremely difficult when so large a portion of the American armed forces are committed to one particular region.

In view of the above, it is not surprising that the circles most concerned about the discrepancy between American commitments and American power are the armed services themselves, simply because they would be the first to suffer if strategical weaknesses were exposed in the harsh test of war. Hence the frequent warnings by the Pentagon against being forced to carry out a global logistical juggling act, switching forces from one "hot spot" to another as new troubles emerge. If this was particularly acute in late 1983, when additional U.S. deployments in Central America, Grenada, Chad, and the Lebanon caused the former chairman of the Joint Chiefs of Staff to proclaim that the "mismatch" between American forces and strategy "is greater now than ever before," the problem had been implicit for years beforehand. Interestingly, such warnings about the American armed forces being "at full stretch" are attended by maps of "Major U.S. Military Deployment Around the World" which, to historians, look extraordinarily similar to the chain of fleet bases and garrisons possessed by that former world power, Great Britain, at the height of its strategic overstretch.

On the other hand, it is hardly likely that the United States would be called upon to defend *all* of its overseas interests simultaneously and without the aid of a significant number of allies—the NATO members in western Europe, Israel in the Middle East, and, in the Pacific, Japan, Australia, possibly China. Nor are all the regional trends becoming unfavorable to the United States in defense terms; for example, while aggression by the unpredictable North Korean regime is always possible, that would hardly be welcomed by Peking nowadays—and, in addition, South Korea itself has grown to possess over twice the population and four times the GNP of North Korea. In the same way, while the expansion of Russian forces in the Far East is alarming to Washington, that is considerably balanced off by the growing threat posed by the PRC to Russia's land and sea lines of communication with the Orient. The recent, sober admission by the U.S. defense secretary that "we can never afford to buy the capabilities sufficient to meet all of our commitments with one hundred percent confidence" is surely true; but it may be less worrying than at first appears if it is also recalled that the total of potential anti-Soviet resources in the world (United States, western Europe, Japan, PRC, Australasia) is far greater than the total of resources lined up on Russia's side.

Despite such consolations, the fundamental grand-strategical dilemma remains: the United States today has roughly the same massive array of military obligations across the globe as it had a quarter-century ago, when its shares of world GNP, manufacturing production, military spending, and armed forces personnel were so much larger than they are now. Even in 1985, forty years after its triumphs of the Second World War and over a decade after its pull-out from Vietnam, the United States had 520,000 members of its armed forces abroad (including 65,000 afloat). That total is, incidentally, substantially more than the overseas deployments in peacetime of the military and naval force of the British Empire at the height of its power. Nevertheless, in the strongly expressed opinion of the Joint Chiefs of Staff, and of many civilian experts, it is simply not enough. Despite a near-trebling of the American defense budget since the late 1970s, there has occurred a "mere 5 percent increase in the numerical size of the armed forces on active duty." As the British and French military found in their time, a nation with extensive overseas obligations will always have a more difficult "manpower problem" than a state which keeps its armed forces solely for home defense; and a politically liberal and economically laissez-faire society—aware of the unpopularity of conscription—will have a greater problem than most.

Possibly this concern about the gap between American interests and capabilities in the world would be less acute had there not been so much doubt expressed—since at least the time of the Vietnam War—about the *efficiency* of the system itself. Since those doubts have been repeatedly aired in other studies, they will only be summarized here; this is not a further essay on the hot topic of "defense reform." One major area of contention, for example, has been the degree of interservice rivalry, which is of course common to most armed forces but seems more deeply entrenched in the American system—possibly because of the relatively modest powers of the chairman of the Joint Chiefs of Staff, possibly because so much more energy appears to be devoted to procurement as opposed to strategical and operational issues. In peacetime, this might merely be dismissed as an extreme example of "bureaucratic politics"; but in actual wartime operations—say, in the emergency dispatch of the Rapid Deployment Joint Task Force, which contains elements from all four services—a lack of proper coordination could be fatal.

In the area of military procurement itself, allegations of "waste, fraud and abuse" have been commonplace. The various scandals over horrendously expensive, *under*performing weapons which have caught the public's attention in recent years have plausible explanations: the lack of proper competitive bidding and of market forces in the "military-industrial complex," and the tendency toward "gold-plated" weapon systems, not to mention the striving for large profits. It is difficult, however, to separate those deficiencies in the procurement process from what is clearly a more fundamental happening: the intensification of the impacts which new technological advances make upon the art of war. Given that it is in the high-technology field that the USSR usually appears most vulnerable—which suggests that American *quality* in weaponry can be employed to counter the superior Russian *quantity* of, say, tanks and aircraft—there is an obvious attraction in what Caspar Weinberger termed "competitive strategies" when ordering new armaments. Nevertheless, the fact that the Reagan administration in its first term spent over 75 percent more on new aircraft than the Carter regime but acquired only 9 percent more planes points to *the* appalling military-procurement problem of the late twentieth century: given the technologically driven tendency toward spending more and more money upon fewer and fewer weapon systems, would the United States and its allies really have enough sophisticated and highly expensive aircraft and tanks in reserve after the early stages of a ferociously fought conventional war? Does the U.S. Navy possess enough attack submarines, or frigates, if heavy losses were incurred in the early stages of a *third* Battle of the Atlantic? If not, the results would be grim; for it is clear that today's complex weaponry simply cannot be replaced in the short times which were achieved during the Second World War.

This dilemma is accentuated by two other elements in the complicated calculus of evolving an effective American defense policy. The first is the issue of budgetary constraints. Unless external circumstances became much more threatening, it would be a remarkable act of political persuasion to get national defense expenditures raised much above, say, 7.5 percent of GNP—the more especially since the size of the federal deficit ... points to the need to balance governmental spending as the first priority of state. But if there is a slowing-down or even a halt in the increase in defense spending, coinciding with the continuous upward spiral in weapons costs, then the problem facing the Pentagon will become much more acute.

The second factor is the sheer variety of military contingencies that a global superpower like the United States has to plan for—all of which, in their way, place differing demands upon the armed forces and the weaponry they are likely to employ. This again is not without precedent in the history of the Great Powers; the British army was frequently placed under strain by having to plan to fight on the Northwest Frontier of India *or* in Belgium. But even that challenge pales beside the task facing today's "number one." If the critical issue for the United States is preserving a nuclear deterrent against the Soviet Union, at *all* levels of escalation, then money will inevitably be poured into such weapons as the MX missile, the B-1 and "Stealth" bombers, Pershing IIs, cruise missiles, and Trident-bearing submarines. If a large-scale conventional war against the Warsaw Pact is the most probable scenario, then the funds presumably need to go in quite different directions: tactical aircraft, main battle tanks, large carriers, frigates, attack submarines, and logistical services. If it is likely that the United States and the USSR will avoid a direct clash, but that both will become more active in the Third World, then the weapons mix changes again: small arms, helicopters, light carriers, an enhanced role for the U.S. Marine Corps become the chief items on the list. Already it is clear that a large part of the controversy over "defense reform" stems from differing assumptions about the *type* of war the United States might be called upon to fight. But what if those in authority make the wrong assumption?

A further major concern about the efficiency of the system, and one voiced even by strong supporters of the campaign to "restore" American power, is whether the present decision-making structure permits a proper grand strategy to be carried out. This would not merely imply achieving a greater coherence in military policies, so that there is less argument about "maritime strategy" versus "coalition warfare," but would also involve effecting a synthesis of the United States' long-term political, economic, and strategical interests, in place of the bureaucratic infighting which seems to have characterized so much of Washington's policymaking. A much-quoted example of this is the all-too-frequent *public* dispute about how and where the United States should employ its armed forces abroad to enhance or defend its national interests—with the State Department wanting clear and firm responses made to those who threaten such interests, but the Defense Department being unwilling (especially after the Lebanon debacle) to get involved overseas except under special conditions. But there also have been, and by contrast, examples of the Pentagon's preference for taking unilateral decisions in the arms race with Russia (e.g., SDI program, abandoning SALT II) without consulting major allies, which leaves problems for the State Department. There have been uncertainties attending the role played by the National Security Council, and more especially individual national security advisers. There have been incoherencies of policy in the Middle East, partly because of the intractibility of, say, the Palestine issue, but also because the United States' strategical interest in supporting the conservative, pro-Western Arab states against Russian penetration in that area has often foundered upon the well-organized opposition of its own pro-Israel lobby. There have been interdepartmental disputes about the use of economic tools—from boycotts on trade and embargoes on technology transfer to foreign-aid grants and weapons sales and grain sales—in support of American diplomatic interests, which affect policies toward the Third World, South Africa, Russia, Poland, the EEC, and so on, and which have sometimes been uncoordinated and contradictory. No sensible person would maintain that the many foreign-policy problems afflicting the globe each possess an obvious and ready "solution"; on the other hand, the preservation of long-term American interests is certainly not helped when the decision-making system is attended by frequent disagreements within.

All this has led to questions by gloomier critics about the overall political culture in which Washington decision-makers have to operate. This is far too large and complex a matter to be explored in depth here. But it has been increasingly suggested that a country needing to reformulate its grand strategy in the light of the larger, uncontrollable changes taking place in world affairs may not be well served by an electoral system which seems to paralyze foreign-policy decision-making every two years. It may not be helped by the extraordinary pressures applied by lobbyists, political action committees, and other interest groups, all of which, by definition, are prejudiced in respect to this or that policy change; nor by an inherent "simplification" of vital but complex international and strategical issues through a mass media whose time and space for such things are limited, and whose *raison d'être* is chiefly to make money and secure audiences, and only secondarily to inform. It may also not be helped by the still-powerful "escapist" urges in the American social culture, which may be understandable in terms of the nation's "frontier" past but is a hindrance to coming to terms with today's more complex, integrated world and with *other* cultures and ideologies.

Finally, the country may not always be assisted by its division of consti-tutional and decision-making powers, deliberately created when it was geographically and strategically isolated from the rest of the world two centuries ago, and possessed a decent degree of time to come to an agreement on the few issues which actually concerned "foreign" policy, but which may be harder to operate when it has become a global su-perpower, often called upon to make swift decisions vis-à-vis countries which enjoy far fewer constraints. No single one of these presents an in-superable obstacle to the execution of a coherent, long-term American grand strategy; their cumulative and interacting effect is, however, to make it much more difficult than otherwise to carry out needed changes of policy if that seems to hurt special interests and occurs in an election year. It may therefore be here, in the cultural and domestic-political realms, that the evolution of an effective overall American policy to meet the twenty-first century will be subjected to the greatest test.

The final question about the proper relationship of "means and ends" in the defense of American global interests relates to the eco-nomic challenges bearing down upon the country, which, because they are so various, threaten to place immense strains upon decision-making in national policy. The extraordinary breadth and complexity of the American economy makes it difficult to summarize what is happening to all parts of it—especially in a period when it is sending out such contradictory signals. . . .

The first of these is the country's relative industrial decline, as mea-sured against world production, not only in older manufactures such as textiles, iron and steel, shipbuilding, and basic chemicals, but also—although it is far less easy to judge the final outcome of this level of industrial-technological combat—in global shares of robotics, aerospace, automobile, machine tools, and computers. Both of these pose immense problems: in traditional and basic manufacturing, the gap in wage scales between the United States and newly industrializing countries is proba-bly such that no "efficiency measures" will close it; but to lose out in the competition in future technologies, if that indeed should occur, would be even more disastrous. In late 1986, for example, a congressional study reported that the U.S. trade surplus in high-technology goods had plunged from $27 billion in 1980 to a mere $4 billion in 1985, and was swiftly heading into a deficit.

The second, and in many ways less expected, sector of decline is agriculture. Only a decade ago, experts in that subject were predict-ing a frightening global imbalance between feeding requirements and farming output. But such a scenario of famine and disaster stimulated two powerful responses. The first was a massive investment into Amer-ican farming from the 1970s onward, fueled by the prospect of ever-larger overseas food sales; the second was the enormous (western-world-funded) investigation into scientific means of increasing Third World crop outputs, which has been so successful as to turn growing numbers of such countries into food *exporters*, and thus competitors of the United States. These two trends are separate from, but have coincided with, the transformation of the EEC into a major producer of agricultural surpluses, because of its price-support system. In consequence, experts now refer to a "world awash in food," which in turn leads to sharp declines in agricultural prices and in American food exports—and drives many farmers out of business.

It is not surprising, therefore, that these economic problems have led to a surge in protectionist sentiment throughout many sectors of the American economy, and among businessmen, unions, farmers, and their congressmen. As with the "tariff reform" agitation in Edwardian Britain, the advocates of increased protection complain of unfair foreign practices, of "dumping" below-cost manufactures on the American market, and of enormous subsidies to foreign farmers—which, they maintain, can only be answered by U.S. administrations abandoning their laissez-faire policy on trade and instituting tough countermeasures. Many of those individual complaints (e.g., of Japan shipping below-cost silicon chips to the American market) have been valid. More broadly, however, the surge in protectionist sentiment is also a reflection of the erosion of the previously unchallenged U.S. manufacturing supremacy. Like mid-Victorian Britons, Americans after 1945 favored free trade and open competition, not just because they held that global commerce and prosperity would be boosted in the process, but also because they knew that they were most likely to benefit from the abandonment of protectionism. Forty years later, with that confidence ebbing, there is a predictable shift of opinion in favor of protecting the domestic market and the domestic producer. And, just as in that earlier British case, defenders of the existing system point out that enhanced tariffs might not only make domestic products *less* competitive internationally, but that there also could be various external repercussions—a global tariff war, blows against American exports, the undermining of the currencies of certain newly industrializing countries, and a return to the economic crisis of the 1930s.

Along with these difficulties affecting American manufacturing and agriculture there are unprecedented turbulences in the nation's finances. The uncompetitiveness of U.S. industrial products abroad and the declining sales of agricultural exports have together produced staggering deficits in visible trade—$160 billion in the twelve months to May 1986—but what is more alarming is that such a gap can no longer be covered by American earnings on "invisibles," which is the traditional recourse of a mature economy (e.g., Great Britain before 1914). On the contrary, the only way the United States can pay its way in the world is by importing ever-larger sums of capital, which has transformed it from being the world's largest creditor to the world's largest debtor nation *in the space of a few years.*

Compounding this problem—in the view of many critics, *causing* this problem—have been the budgetary policies of the U.S. government itself. Even in the 1960s, there was a tendency for Washington to rely upon deficit finance, rather than additional taxes, to pay for the increasing cost of defense and social programs. But the decisions taken by the Reagan administration in the early 1980s—i.e., large-scale increases in defense expenditures, plus considerable decreases in taxation, but *without* significant reductions in federal spending elsewhere—have produced extraordinary rises in the deficit, and consequently in the national debt, as shown in Table 1.

The continuation of such trends, alarmed voices have pointed out, would push the U.S. national debt to around $13 *trillion* by the year 2000 (fourteen times that of 1980), and the interest payments on such debt to $1.5 *trillion* (twenty-nine times that of 1980). In fact, a lowering of interest rates could bring down those estimates, but the overall trend is still very unhealthy. Even if federal deficits could be reduced to a "mere" $100 billion annually, the compounding of national debt and interest payments by the early twenty-first century will still cause quite unprecedented totals of money to be diverted in that direction. Historically, the only other example which comes to mind of a Great Power so increasing its indebtedness in *peacetime* is France in the 1780s, where the fiscal crisis contributed to the domestic political crisis.

These American trade and federal deficits are now interacting with a new phenomenon in the world economy—what is perhaps best described as the "dislocation" of international capital movements from the trade in goods and services. Because of the growing integration of the world economy, the volume of trade both in manufactures and in financial services is much larger than ever before, and together may amount to some $3 trillion a year; but that is now eclipsed by the stupendous level of capital flows pouring through the world's money markets, with the London-based Eurodollar market alone having a volume "at least 25 times that of world trade." While this trend was fueled by events in the 1970s (the move from fixed to floating exchange rates, the surplus funds flowing from OPEC countries), it has also been stimulated by the U.S. deficits, since the only way the federal government has been able to cover the yawning gap between its expenditures and its receipts has been to suck into the country tremendous amounts of liquid funds from Europe and (especially) Japan—turning the United States, as mentioned above, into the world's largest debtor country by far. It is, in fact, difficult to imagine how the American economy could have got by *without* the inflow of foreign funds in the early 1980s, even if that had the awkward consequence of sending up the exchange value of the dollar, and further hurting U.S. agricultural and manufacturing exports. But that in turn raises the troubling question about what might happen if those massive and volatile funds were pulled out of the dollar, causing its value to drop precipitously....

In the largest sense of all, therefore, the only answer to the question increasingly debated by the public of whether the United States

Table 1. U.S. Federal Deficit, Debt, and
Interest, 1980–1985
(billions of dollars)

	Deficit	Debt	Interest on Debt
1980	59.6	914.3	52.5
1983	195.4	1,381.9	87.8
1985	202.8	1,823.1	129.0

can preserve its existing position is "no"—for it simply has not been given to any one society to remain *permanently* ahead of all the others, because that would imply a freezing of the differentiated pattern of growth rates, technological advance, and military developments which has existed since time immemorial. On the other hand, this reference to historical precedents does *not* imply that the United States is destined to shrink to the relative obscurity of former leading Powers such as Spain or the Netherlands, or to disintegrate like the Roman and Austro-Hungarian empires; it is imply too large to do the former, and presumably too homogeneous to do the latter. Even the British analogy, much favored in the current political-science literature, is nót a good one if it ignores the differences in *scale*. This can be put another way: the geographical size, population, and natural resources of the British Isles would suggest that it ought to possess roughly 3 or 4 percent of the world's wealth and power, *all other things being equal;* but it is precisely because all other things are *never* equal that a peculiar set of historical and technological circumstances permitted the British Isles to expand to possess, say, 25 percent of the world's wealth and power in its prime; and since those favorable circumstances have disappeared, all that it has been doing is returning down to its more "natural" size. In the same way, it may be argued that the geographical extent, population, and natural resources of the United States suggest that it ought to possess perhaps 16 or 18 percent of the world's wealth and power, but because of historical and technical circumstances favorable to it, that share rose to 40 percent or more by 1945; and what we are witnessing at the moment is the early decades of the ebbing away from that extraordinarily high figure to a more "natural" share. That decline is being masked by the country's enormous military capabilities at present, and also by its success in "internationalizing" American capitalism and culture. Yet even when it declines to occupy its "natural" share of the world's wealth and power, a long time into the future, the United States will still be a very significant Power in a multipolar world, simply because of its size.

The task facing American statesmen over the next decades, therefore, is to recognize that broad trends are under way, and that there is a need to "manage" affairs so that the *relative* erosion of the United States' position takes place slowly and smoothly, and is not accelerated by policies which bring merely short-term advantage but longer-term disadvantage. This involves, from the president's office downward, an appreciation that technological and therefore socioeconomic change is occurring in the world faster than ever before; that the international community is much more politically and culturally diverse than has been assumed, and is defiant of simplistic remedies offered either by Washington or Moscow to its problems; that the economic and productive power balances are no longer as favorably tilted in the United States' direction as in 1945; and that, even in the military realm, there are signs of a certain redistribution of the balances, away from a bipolar to more of a multipolar system, in which the conglomeration of American economic-cum-military strength is likely to remain larger than that possessed by any one of the others individually, but will not be as disproportionate as in the decades which immediately followed the Second

World War. This, in itself, is not a bad thing if one recalls Kissinger's observations about the disadvantages of carrying out policies in what is always seen to be a bipolar world; and it may seem still less of a bad thing when it is recognized how much more Russia may be affected by the changing dynamics of world power. In all of the discussions about the erosion of American leadership, it needs to be repeated again and again that the decline referred to is relative not absolute, and is therefore perfectly natural; and that the only serious threat to the real interests of the United States can come from a failure to adjust sensibly to the newer world order.

Given the considerable array of strengths still possessed by the United States, it ought not *in theory* to be beyond the talents of successive administrations to arrange the diplomacy and strategy of this readjustment so that it can, in Walter Lippmann's classic phrase, bring "into balance ... the nation's commitments and the nation's power." Although there is no obvious, single "successor state" which can take over America's global burdens in the way that the United States assumed Britain's role in the 1940s, it is nonetheless also true that the country has fewer problems than an imperial Spain besieged by enemies on all fronts, or a Netherlands being squeezed between France and England, or a British Empire facing a bevy of challengers. The tests before the United States as it heads toward the twenty-first century are certainly daunting, perhaps especially in the economic sphere; but the nation's resources remain considerable, *if* they can be properly organized, and *if* there is a judicious recognition of both the limitations and the opportunities of American power.

Viewed from one perspective, it can hardly be said that the dilemmas facing the United States are unique. Which country in the world, one is tempted to ask, is *not* encountering problems in evolving a viable military policy, or in choosing between guns and butter and investment? From another perspective, however, the American position is a very special one. For all its economic and perhaps military decline, it remains, in Pierre Hassner's words, "the decisive actor in every type of balance and issue." Because it has so much power for good or evil, because it is the linchpin of the western alliance system and the center of the existing global economy, what it does, *or does not do*, is so much more important than what any of the other Powers decides to do.

Suggested Further Readings

I. 1945–1952

Good surveys of postwar American foreign policy include Seyom Brown, *The Faces of Power*, rev. ed. (Columbia University Press, 1983); Walter LaFeber, *America, Russia, and the Cold War, 1945-1966*, 4th ed. (Wiley, 1987); John Gaddis, *The United States and the Origins of the Cold War* (Oxford, 1972); and Gabriel and Joyce Kolko, *The Limits of Power* (Harper & Row, 1972). The book that started the "revisionist" view of the Cold War as by no means the fault exclusively of the Soviet Union is the late William Appleman Williams' *The Tragedy of American Diplomacy*, 2nd ed. (Dell, 1972). Dean Acheson defends his policies as Truman's Secretary of State in *Present at the Creation* (Norton, 1969). Alonzo Hamby's book on the Truman administration is still standard: *Beyond the New Deal* (Columbia University Press, 1973), but see the more critical Barton Bernstein, *Political Policies of the Truman Administration* (Quadrangle, 1970). Richard Polenberg's *One Nation Divisible* (Penguin, 1980) includes a description of the growth of suburbia.

II. 1952–1962

The two-volume biography of Eisenhower by Stephen E. Ambrose is standard: *Eisenhower: Soldier, General of the Army, President-Elect, 1890-1952* and *Eisenhower: the President* (1983, 1984) as is Robert Divine, *Eisenhower and the Cold War* (Oxford, 1981). On Ike's rather conservative Democratic opponent for President, see John Bartlow Martin, *Adlai E. Stevenson and the World* (Doubleday, 1976). Classics of social criticism from the era include David Reisman et al., *The Lonely Crowd* (Yale University Press, 1950); Daniel Bell, *The End of Ideology*, rev. ed. (Free Press, 1965); C. Wright Mills, *The Power Elite* (Oxford, 1956); and John Kenneth Galbraith, *The Affluent Society* (Houghton, 1958). Allen Weinstein takes aim at Alger Hiss in *Perjury* (Knopf, 1978), and Ronald Radosh and Joyce Milton find two other leftists guilty as charged in *The Rosenberg File* (Random House, 1983). Standard books on Joseph R. McCarthy include Michael Paul Rogin, *The Intellectuals and McCarthy* (MIT Press, 1967) and Robert Griffith, *The Politics of Fear: Joseph R. McCarthy and the Senate*, 2nd ed. (University of Massachusetts Press, 1970). One of many biographies of Kerouac is Dennis McNally, *Desolate Angel* (Random House, 1979). A critical view of Kennedy, among many others, is Thomas Reeves, *A Question of Character: John F. Kennedy in Image and Reality* (Viking, 1991); David Burner and Thomas R. West, while primarily concerned with the public role, give a more favorable account in *The Torch Is Passed: The Kennedy Brothers and American Liberalism* (Atheneum, 1984). The standard two-volume biography of Kennedy—the books are entitled *Jack* and *JFK*—is by Herbert Parmet (Dial, 1980, 1983). A conservative challenge to the late Michael Harrington's early study of poverty is Charles Murray, *Losing Ground* (Basic, 1984); Harrington responded in *The New American Poverty* (Penguin, 1987).

III. 1962–1968

Two comprehensive histories of the civil rights movement were published in 1989: Hugh Davis Graham, *The Civil Rights Era* (Oxford) and Robert Weisbrot's *Freedom Bound* (Norton). A more dramatically written book, covering Martin Luther King, Jr.'s life until 1963, is Taylor Branch's *Parting the Waters: America in the King Years, 1954–1963* (Simon & Schuster, 1988); an important study is Clayborne Carson, *In Struggle: SNCC and the Black Awakening of the 1960s* (Harvard University Press, 1981); see also David J. Garrow, *The FBI and Martin Luther King, Jr.* (Penguin, 1983). A statement by a then more radical figure is Eldridge Cleaver, *Soul on Ice* (McGraw-Hill, 1967). Until Robert Dallek and Robert Caro publish their presumably conflicting accounts of Johnson's presidency, a very useful book is Paul K. Conkin, *Big Daddy from the Pedernales* (Twayne, 1986); see also George E. Reddy, *The Twilight of the Presidency*, rev. ed. (New American Library, 1975). Caro's first two books in a multivolume biography are *The Path to Power* (Knopf, 1982) and *Means of Ascent* (Knopf, 1990). A good account of the year 1968 is Irwin Unger and Debi Unger, *Turning Point: 1968* (Scribner's, 1988). Quite different views from the left on the 1960s come from Todd Gitlin, *The Sixties: Years of Hope, Days of Rage* (1987) and Allen J. Matusow, *The Unraveling of America; A History of Liberalism in the 1960s* (Harper & Row, 1984); a caustic conservative counterattack is David Horowitz and Peter Collier, *Destructive Generation* (Summit, 1989). The women's movement is variously analyzed in Sara Evans, *Personal Politics* (Knopf, 1979) and Jo Freeman, *The Politics of Women's Liberation* (Longman, 1979). The New Left is interestingly treated in Wini Breines, *Community and Organization in the New Left*, 2nd ed. (Rutgers University Press, 1983).

IV. 1968–1980

A perceptive book on Richard Nixon is the revised *Nixon Agonistes* by Garry Wills (Houghton Mifflin, 1979); recent biographies include Herbert S. Parmet's *Richard Nixon and His America* (Little, Brown, 1990) and Stephen Ambrose's *Nixon: The Education of a Politician* (Simon and Schuster, 1987). On Watergate there are J. Anthony Lukas, *Nightmare: The Underside of the Nixon Years*, rev. ed. (Penguin, 1976); Philip B. Kurland, *Watergate and the Constitution* (University of Chicago Press, 1978); and John Dean, *Blind Ambition* (Simon & Schuster, 1976). A standard history of Vietnam is Stanley Karnow, *Vietnam* (Viking, 1983); perhaps the best coverage of the war in the 1960s is Geoge C. Herring, *America's Longest War: The United States and Vietnam, 1950–1975*, rev. ed. (McGraw-Hill, 1985). David Halberstam's *The Best and the Brightest* (Random House, 1972) is a hardhitting critique of American policymaking. On the influential Henry Kissinger there is Roger Morris' *Uncertain Greatness: Henry Kissinger and American Foreign Policy* (Harper & Row, 1977). On President Carter, see Betty Glad, *Jimmy Carter: From Plains to the White House* (Norton, 1980).

V. 1980–PRESENT

A major study of the Reagan administration's treatment of the environment is included in Samuel P. Hays, *Beauty, Health and Permanence; Environmental Politics in the United States, 1955-1985* (Cambridge University Press, 1985). Garry Wills's *Reagan's America: Innocents at Home* is stimulating (1987). Walter LaFeber writes from a left perspective on the United States and Latin America in *Inevitable Revolutions* (Norton, 1983). David Burner and Thomas R. West criticize conservative journalists in *Column Right* (New York University Press, 1988). George Will presents his mostly conservative arguments about the decade in *The Morning After: American Successes and Excesses, 1981–86* (Macmillan, 1987).